CALIFORNIA
NATIVE AMERICAN TRIBES

FEB 1998

EASTERN &
SOUTHEASTERN
POMO TRIBES

WITH

by
Mary Null Boulé

Illustrated by
Daniel Liddell

Merryant Publishing
Vashon, Washington

Book Number Seventeen in a series of twenty-six

This series is dedicated to Virginia Harding, whose editing expertise and friendship brought this project to fruition.

Library of Congress #92-061897

ISBN: 1-877599-40-9

Copyright © 1992, Merryant Publishing

7615 S.W. 257th St., Vashon, WA 98070.

FOREWORD

Native American people of the United States are often living their lives away from major cities and away from what we call the mainstream of life. It is, then, interesting to learn of the important part these remote tribal members play in our everyday lives.

More than 60% of our foods come from the ancient Native American's diet. Farming methods of today also can be traced back to how tribal women grew crops of corn and grain. Many of our present day ideas of democracy have been taken from tribal governments. Even some 1,500 Native American words are found in our English language today.

Fur traders bought furs from tribal hunters for small amounts of money, sold them to Europeans and Asians for a great deal of money, and became rich. Using their money to buy land and to build office buildings, some traders started business corporations which are now the base of our country's economy.

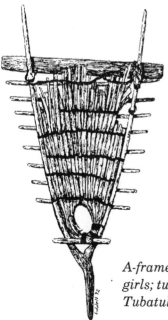

There has never been enough credit given to these early Americans who took such good care of our country when it was still in their care. The time has come to realize tribal contributions to our society today and to give Native Americans not only the credit, but the respect due them.

Mary Boulé

*A-frame cradle for
girls; tule matting.
Tubatulabal tribe.*

GENERAL INFORMATION

Out of Asia, many thousands of years ago, came Wanderers. Some historians think they were the first people to set foot on our western hemisphere. These Wanderers had walked, step by step, onto our part of the earth while hunting and gathering food. They probably never even knew they had moved from one continent to another as they made their way across a land bridge, a narrow strip of land between Siberia and what is now Russia, and the state of Alaska.

Historians do not know exactly how long ago the Wanderers might have crossed the land bridge. Some of them say 35,000 years ago. What historians do know is that these people slowly moved down onto land that we now call the United States of America. Today it would be very hard to follow their footsteps, for the land bridge has been covered with sea water since the thawing of the ice age.

Those Wanderers who made their way to California were very lucky, indeed. California was a land with good weather most of the year and was filled with plenty of plant and animal foods for them to eat.

The Wanderers who became California's Native Americans did not organize into large tribes like the rest of the North American tribes. Instead, they divided into groups, or tribelets, sometimes having as many as 250 people. A tribelet could number as few as three, to as many as thirty villages located close to each other. Some tribelets had only one chief, a leader who lived in the largest village. Many tribes had a chief for each village. Some leaders had no real power but were thought to be wise. Tribal members always listened with respect to what their chief had to say.

From 20 to 100 people could be living in one village, which usually had several houses. In most cases, these groups of people were related to each other. From five to ten people of one family lived in one house. For instance, a mother, a father, two or three children, a grandmother, or aunt or daughter-in-law might live together.

Village members together would own the land important to them for their well-being. Their land might include oak trees with precious acorns, streams and rivers, and plants which were good to eat. Streams and rivers were especially important to a tribe's quality of life. Water drew animals to it; that meant more food for the tribe to eat. Fish were a good source of food, and traveling by boat was often easier than walking long distances. Water was needed in every part of tribal life.

Village and tribelet land was carefully guarded. Each group knew exactly where the boundaries of its land were found. Boundaries were known by landmarks such as mountains or rivers, or they might also be marked by poles planted in the ground. Some boundary lines were marked by rocks, or by objects placed there by tribal members. The size of a territory had to be large enough to supply food to every person living there.

The California tribes spoke many languages. Sometimes villages close together even had a problem understanding one another. This meant that each group had to be sure of the boundaries of other tribes around them when gathering food. It would not be wise to go against the boundaries and the customs of neighbors. The Native Americans found if they respected the boundaries of their neighbors, not so many wars had to be fought. California tribes, in spite of all their differences, were not as warlike as other tribes in our country.

Not only did the California tribes speak different languages, but their members also differed in size. Some tribes were very tall, almost six feet tall. The shortest people came from the Yuki tribe which had territory in what is now Mendocino County. They measured only about 5'2" tall. All Native Americans, regardless of size, had strong, straight black hair and dark brown eyes.

TRADE

Trading between tribes was an important part of life. Inland tribes had large animal hides that coastal tribes wanted. By trading the hides to coastal groups, inland tribes would receive fish and shells, which they in turn wanted. Coastal tribes also wanted minerals and rocks mined in the mountains by inland tribes. Obsidian rock from the northern mountains was especially wanted for arrowheads. There were, as well, several minerals, mined in the inland mountains, which could be made into the colorful body paints needed for religious ceremonies.

Southern tribes particularly wanted steatite from the Gabrielino tribe. Steatite, or soapstone, was a special metal which allowed heat to spread evenly through it. This made it a good choice to be used for cooking pots and flat frying pans. It could be carved into bowls because of its softness and could be decorated by carving designs into it. Steatite came from Catalina Island in the Coastal Gabrielino territory. Gabrielinos found steatite to be a fine trading item to offer for the acorns, deerskins, or obsidian stone they needed.

When people had no items to trade but needed something, they used small strings of shells for money. The small dentalium shells, which came from the far distant Northwest coast, had great value. Strings of dentalia usually served as money in the Northern California tribes, although some dentalia was used in the Central California tribes.

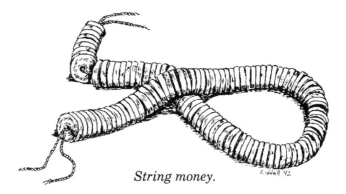

String money.

In southern California clam shells were broken and holes were bored through the center of each piece. Then the pieces were rounded and polished with sandstone and strung into strings for money. These were not thought to be as valuable as dentalia.

Strings of shell money were measured by tattoo marks on the trader's lower arm or hand.

Here is a sample of shell value:

> A house, three strings
> A fishing place, one to three strings
> Land with acorn-bearing oak trees, one to five strings

A great deal of rock and stone was traded among the tribes for making tools. Arrows had to have sharp-edged stone for tips. The best stone for arrow tips was obsidian (volcanic glass) because, when hit properly, it broke off into flakes with very sharp edges. California tribes considered obsidian to be the most valuable rock for trading.

Some tribes had craftsmen who made knives with wooden handles and obsidian blades. Often the handles were decorated with carvings. Such knives were good for trading purposes. Stone mortars and pestles, used by the women for grinding grains into flour, were good trading items.

BASKETS & POTTERY

California tribal women made beautiful baskets. The Pomo and Chumash baskets, what few are left, show us that the women of those tribes might have been some of the finest basketmakers in the world. Baskets were used for gathering and storing food, for carrying babies, and even for hauling water. In emergencies, such as flooding waters, sometimes children, women, and tribal belongings crossed the swollen rivers and streams in huge, woven baskets! Baskets were so tightly woven that not a drop of water could leak from them.

Baskets also made fine cooking pots. Very hot rocks were taken from a fire and tossed around inside baskets with a looped tree branch until food in the basket was cooked.

Most baskets were made to do a certain job, but some baskets were designed for their beauty alone and were excellent for trading. Older women of a tribe would teach young girls how to weave baskets.

Pottery was not used by many California tribes. What little there was seems to have been made by those tribes living near to the Navaho and Mohave tribes of Arizona, and it shows their style. For example, pottery of the California tribes did not have much decoration and was usually a dull red color. Designs were few and always in yellow.

Ohlone hunter wearing deerskin camouflage.

Long thin coils of clay were laid one on top the other. Then the coils were smoothed between a wooden paddle and a small stone to shape the bowl. Pottery from California Native Americans has been described as light weight and brittle (easily broken), probably because of the kind of clay soil found in California.

HUNTING & FISHING

Tribal men spent much of their time making hunting and fishing tools. Bows and arrows were built with great care, to make them shoot as accurately as possible. Carelessly made hunting weapons caused fewer animals to be killed and people then had less food to eat.

Bows made by men of Southern California tribes were made long and narrow. In the northern part of the state bows were a little shorter, thinner, and wider than those of their northern neighbors. Size and thickness of bows depended on the size trees growing in a tribe's territory. The strongest bows were wrapped with sinew, the name given to animal tendons. Sinew is strong and elastic like a rubber band.

Arrows were made in many sizes and shapes, depending on their use. For hunting larger animals, a two-piece arrow was used. The front piece of the arrow shaft was made so that it would remain in the animal,

9

even if the back part was removed or broken off. The arrow-head, or point, was wrapped to the front piece of the shaft. This kind of arrow was also used in wars.

Young boys used a simple wooden arrow with the end sharpened to a point. With this they could hunt small animals like birds and rabbits. The older men of the tribe taught boys how to make their own arrows, how to aim properly, and how to repair broken weapons.

Tribal men spent many hours making and mending fishing nets. The string used in making nets often came from the fibers of plants. These fibers were twisted to make them strong and tough, then knotted into netting. Fences, or weirs, that had one small opening for fish, were built across streams. As the fish swam through the opening they would be caught in netting or harpooned by a waiting fisherman.

Hooks, if used at all, were cut from shells. Mostly hooks could be found when the men fished in large lakes or when catching trout in high mountain areas. Hooks were attached to heavy plant fiber string.

Dip nets, made of netting attached to branches that were bent into a circle, were used to catch fish swimming near shore. Dip nets had long handles so the fishermen could reach deep into the water.

Sometimes a mild poison was placed on the surface of shallow water. This confused the fish and caused them to float to the surface of the water, where they could be scooped up by a waiting fisherman. Not enough poison was used to make humans ill.

Not all fishing was done from the shore. California tribes used two kinds of boats when fishing. Canoes, dug out of one half a log, were useful for river fishing. These were square at each end, round on the bottom, and very heavy. Some of them were well-finished, often even having a carved seat in them.

Today we think of "balsa" as a very lightweight wood, but in Spanish, the word balsa means "raft". That is why Spanish explorers called the Native American canoes, made from tule reeds, "balsa" boats.

Balsa boats were made of bundled tule reeds and were used throughout most of California. They made into safe, light-weight boats for lake and river use. Usually the balsa canoe had a long, tightly tied bundle of tule for the boat bottom and one bundle for each side of the canoe. The front of the canoe was higher than the back. Balsa boats could be steered with a pole or with a paddle, like a raft.

Men did most of the fishing, women were in charge of gathering grasses, seeds, and acorns for food. After the food was collected, it was either eaten right away or made ready for winter storage.

Except for a few southern groups, California tribes had perma-nent villages where they lived most of the year. They also had food-gathering places they returned to each year to collect acorns, salt, fish, and other foods not found near their villages.

FOOD

Many different kinds of plant food grew wild in California in the days before white people arrived. Berries and other plant foods grew in the mountains. Forests offered the local tribes everything from pine nuts to animals.

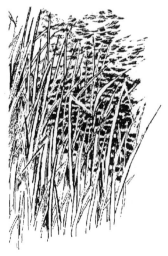

Native Americans found streams full of fish for much of the year. Inland fresh water lakes had large tule reeds growing along their shores. Tule could be eaten as food when plants were young and tender. More important,

11

however, tule was used in making fabric for clothes and for building boats and houses. Tule was probably the most useful plant the California Native Americans found growing wild in their land.

Like all deserts, the one in southern California had little water or fish, but small animals and cactus plants made good food for the local tribes. They moved from place to place harvesting whatever was ripe. Tribal members always knew when and where to find the best food in their territory.

Acorns were the main source of food for all California tribes. Acorn flour was as important to the California Native Americans as wheat is to us today. Five types of California oak trees produced acorns that could be eaten. Those from black oak and tanbark oak seem to have been the favorite kinds.

Since some acorns tasted better than others, the tastiest ones were collected first. If harvest of the favorite acorn was poor some years, then less tasty acorns had to be eaten all winter long.

So important were acorns to California Indians that most tribes built their entire year around them. Acorn harvest marked the beginning of their calendar year. Winter was counted as so many months after acorn harvest, and summer was counted by the number of months before the next acorn harvest.

Acorn harvest ceremonies usually were the biggest events of the year. Most celebrations took place in mid-October and included dancing, feasts, games of chance, and reunions with relatives. Harvest festivals lasted for many days. They were a time of joy for everyone.

The annual acorn gathering lasted two to three weeks. Young boys climbed the oak trees to shake branches; some men used long poles to knock acorns to the ground. Women loaded the nuts into large cone-shaped burden baskets and carried them to a central place where they were put in the sun to dry.

Once the acorns were dried, the women carried them back to the tribe's permanent villages. There they lined special basket-like storage granaries with strong herbs to keep insects away, then stored the acorns inside. Granaries were placed on stilts to keep animals from getting into them and were kept beside tribal houses.

Preparing acorns for each meal was also the women's job. Shells were peeled by hitting the acorns with a stone hammer on an anvil (flat) stone. Meat from the nut was then laid on a stone mortar. A mortar was usually a large stone with a slight dip on its surface. Sometimes the mortar had a bottomless basket, called a hopper, glued to its top. This kept the acorn meat from sliding off the mortar as it was beaten. The meat was then pounded with a long stone pestle. Acorn flour was scraped away from the hopper's sides with a soaproot fiber brush during this process.

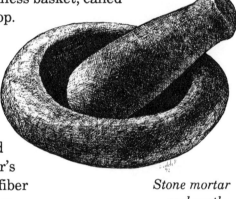

Stone mortar and pestle.

From there the flour was put into an open-worked basket and sifted. A fine flour came through the bottom of the basket, while the larger pieces were put back in the mortar for more pounding.

The most important process came after the acorn flour was sifted. Acorn flour has a very bitter-tasting tannin in it. This bitter taste was removed by a method called leaching. Many tribes leached the flour by first scooping out a hollow in sand near water. The hollow was lined with leaves to keep the flour from washing away. A great deal of hot water was poured through the flour to wash out (leach) the bitterness. Sometimes the flour was put into a basket for the leaching process, instead of using sand and leaves.

Finally the acorn flour was ready to be cooked. To make mush, heated stones were placed in the basket with the flour. A looped tree branch or two long sticks were used to toss the hot rocks around so the basket would not burn. When the mush had boiled, it could be eaten. If the flour and water mixture was baked in an earthen oven, it became a kind of bread. Early explorers wrote that it was very tasty.

Historians have estimated that one family would eat from 1500 to 2000 pounds of acorn flour a year. One reason California native Americans did not have to plant seeds and raise crops was because there were so many acorns for them to harvest each year.

Whether they ate fish or shellfish or plant food or animal meat, nature supplied more than enough food for the Native Americans who lived in California long ago. Many believed their good fortune in having fine weather and plenty to eat came from being good to their gods.

RELIGION

Tribal members had strong beliefs in the power of spirits or gods around them. Each tribe was different, but all felt the importance of never making a spirit angry with them. For that reason a celebration to thank the spirit-gods for treating them well, took place before each food gathering and before each hunting trip, and after each food harvest.

Usually spiritual powers were thought to belong to birds or animals. Most California tribespeople felt bears were very wicked and should not be eaten. But Coyote seems to have been a kind leader who helped them if they were in trouble, even though he seems to have been a bit naughty at times. Eagle was thought to be very powerful and good to native Americans. In some tribes, Eagle was almost as powerful as Sun.

Tribes placed importance on different gods, according to the tribe's needs. Rain gods were the most important spirits to desert tribes. Weather gods, who might bring less rain or warmer temperatures, were important to northern tribes. A great many groups felt there were gods for each of the winds: North, South, East and West. The four directions were usually included in their ceremonial dances and were used as part of the decorations on baskets, pots, and even tools.

Animals were not only worshipped and believed to be spirit-gods, like Deer or Antelope, but tribal members felt there was a personal animal guardian for each one of them. If a tribal member had a deer as guardian, then that person could never kill a deer or eat deer meat.

California Native Americans believed in life after death. This made them very respectful of death and very fearful of angering a dead person. Once someone died, the name of the dead person could never again be said aloud. Since it was easy to accidentally say a name aloud, the name was usually given to a new baby. Then the dead person would not become angry.

Shamans were thought to be the keepers of religious beliefs and to have the ability to talk directly to spirit-gods. It was the job of a village shaman to cure sick people, and to speak to the gods about the needs of the people. Some tribes had several kinds of shamans in one village. One shaman did curing, one scared off evil spirits, while another took care of hunters.

Not all shamans were nice, so people greatly feared their power. However, if shamans had no luck curing sick people or did not bring good luck in hunting, the people could kill them. Most shamans were men, but in a few tribes, women were doctors.

Most California tribal myths have been lost to history because they were spoken and never written down. The legends were told and retold on winter nights around the home fires. Sadly, these were forgotten after the missionaries brought Christianity to California and moved tribal members into the missions.

A few stories still remain, however. It is thought by historians that northwest California tribes were the only ones not to have a myth on how they were created. They did not feel that the world was made and prepared for human beings. Instead, their few remaining stories usually tell of mountain peaks or rivers in their own territory.

The central California tribes had creation stories of a great flood where there was only water on earth. They tell of how man was made from a bit of mud that a turtle brought up from the bottom of the water.

Many southwest tribes believed there was a time of no sky or water. They told of two clouds appearing which finally became Sky and Earth.

Throughout California, however, all tribes had myths that told of Eagle as the leader, Coyote as chief assistant, and of less powerful spirits like Falcon or Hawk.

Costumes for religious ceremonies often imitated these animals they worshipped or feared. Much time was spent in making the dance costumes as beautiful as possible. Red woodpecker feathers were so brilliant a color they were used to decorate religious headdresses, necklaces, or belts. Deerskin clothing was fringed so shell beads could be attached to each thin strip of leather.

Eagle feathers were felt to be the most sacred of religious objects. Sometimes they were made into whole robes. Usually, though, the feathers were used just for decorations. All these costumes were valuable to the people of each tribe. The

Religious feather charm.

village chief was in charge of taking care of the costumes, and there was terrible punishment for stealing them. Clothing worn everyday was not fancy like costuming for rituals.

Willow bark skirt.

CLOTHING

Central and southern California's fine weather made regular clothes not really very important to the Native Americans. The children and men went naked most of the year, but most women wore a short apron-like skirt. These skirts were usually made in two pieces, front and back aprons, with fringes cut into the bottom edges. Often the skirt was made from the inner bark of trees, shredded and gathered on a cord. Sometimes the skirt was made from tule or grass.

In northern California and in rainy or windy weather elsewhere in the state, animal-skin blankets were worn by both men and women. They were used like a cape and wrapped around the body. Sometimes the cape was put over one shoulder and under the other arm, then tied in front. All kinds of skins were used; deer, otter, wildcat, but sea-otter

17

fur was thought to be the best. If the skin was from a small animal, it was cut into strips and woven together into a fabric. At night the cape became a blanket to keep the person warm.

Because of the rainy weather in northern California, the women wore basket caps all the time. Women of the central and south tribes wore caps only when carrying heavy loads, where the forehead had to be used as support. Then a cap helped keep too much weight from being placed on the forehead.

Most California people went barefoot in their villages. For journeys into rough land, going to war, wood gathering, or in colder weather, the tribesmen in central and northwest California wore a one-piece soft shoe with no extra sole, which went high up on the leg.

Southern California tribespeople, however, wore sandals most of the time, wearing high, soled moccasins only when they traveled long distances or into the mountains. Leggings of skin were worn in snow, and moccasins were sometimes lined with grass for more comfort and warmth.

VILLAGE LIFE

Houses of the California tribes were made of materials found in their area. Usually they were round with domed roofs. Except for a few tribes, a house floor was dug into the earth a few feet. This was wise, for it made the home warmer in winter and cooler in summer. It also meant that less material was needed to make house walls.

Framework for the walls was made from bendable branches tied to support poles. Some frames of the houses were covered with earth and grass. Others were covered with large slabs of redwood or pine bark. Central California villagers made large woven mats of tule reed to cover the tops and sides of houses. In the warmer southern area, brush and smaller pieces of bark were used for house walls.

Most California Native American villages had a building called a sweathouse, where the men could be found when they were not hunting, fishing or traveling. It was a very important place for the men, who used it rather like a clubhouse. They could sweat and then scrape themselves clean with curved ribs of deer. The sweathouse was smaller than a family house. Normally it had a center pole framework with a firepit on the ground next to the pole. When the fire was lit, some smoke was allowed to escape through a hole at the top of the roof; however, most was trapped inside the building. Smoke and heat were the main reasons for having a sweathouse. Both were believed to be a way to purify tribal members' bodies. Sweathouse walls were mainly hard-packed earth. The heat produced was not a steam heat but came from a wood-fed fire.

In the center of most villages was a large house that often had no walls, just a roof held up with poles. It was here that religious dances and rituals were held, or visitors were entertained.

Dances were enjoyed and were performed with great skill. Music, usually only rhythm instruments, accompanied the dances. For some reason California Native Americans did not use drums to create rhythms for their dances. Three different kinds of rattles were used by California tribes.

One type, split-clap sticks, created rhythm for dancing. These were usually a length of cane (a hollow stick) split in half lengthwise for about two-thirds of its length. The part still uncut was tightly wound with cord so it would not split all the way. The stick was held at the tied end in one hand and hit against the palm of the other hand to make its sound.

A pebble-filled moth cocoon made rhythm for shaman duties. These could range from calling on spirits to cure

Split-stick clapper, rhythm instrument. Hupa tribe.

illnesses, to performing dances to bring rain. Probably the best sounds to beat rhythm for songs and dances came from bundles of deer hooves tied together on a stick. These rattles have a hollow, warm sound.

The only really "musical" instrument found in California was a flute made of reed that was played by blowing across the edge of one end. Melodies were not played on any of these instruments. Most North American Indians sang their songs rather than playing melodies on music instruments.

Special songs were sung for each event. There were songs for healing sick people, songs for success in hunting, war, or marriage. Women sang acorn-grinding songs and lullabies. Songs were sung in sorrow for the dead and during story-telling times. Group singing, with a leader, was the favorite kind of singing. Most songs were sung by all tribe members, but religious songs had to be sung by a special group. It was important that sacred songs not be changed through the years. If a mistake was made while singing sacred music, the singer could be punished, so only specially trained singers would sing ritual songs.

All songs were very short, some of them only 20 to 30 seconds long. They were made longer by repeating the melodies over and over, or by connecting several songs together. Songs usually told no story, just repeated words or phrases or syllables in patterns.

Song melodies used only one or two notes and harmony was never added. Perhaps that is why mission Indians, at those missions with musician priests, especially loved to sing harmony in the church choirs.

Songs and dances were good methods of passing rich tribal traditions on to the children. It was important to tribal adults that their children understand and love the tribe's heritage.

Children were truly wanted by parents in most tribes and

new parents carefully watched their tiny babies day and night, to be sure they stayed warm and dry. Usually a newborn was strapped into a cradle and tied to the mother's back so she could continue to work, yet be near the baby at all times. In some tribes, older children took care of babies of cradle age during the day to give the mother time to do all her work, while grandmothers were often in charge of caring for toddlers.

Children were taught good behavior, traditions, and tribal rules from babyhood, although some tribes were stricter than others. Most of the time parents made their children obey. Young children could be lightly punished, but in many tribes those over six or seven years old were more severely punished if they did not follow the rules.

Just as children do today, Native American youngsters had childhood traditions they followed. For instance, one tribal tradition said that when a baby tooth came out, a child waited until dusk, faced the setting sun and threw the tooth to the west. There is no mention of a generous tooth fairy, however.

Tribal parents were worried that their offspring might not be strong and brave. Some tribes felt one way to make their children stronger was by forcing them to bathe in ice cold water, even in wintertime. Every once in a while, for example, Modoc children were awakened from sleep and taken to a cold lake or stream for a freezing bath.

But if freezing baths at night were hard on young Native Americans, their days were carefree and happy. Children were allowed to play all day, and some tribes felt children did not even have to come to dinner if they didn't want to. In those tribes, children could come to their houses to eat anytime of the day.

The games boys played are not too different from those played today. Swimming, hide and seek among the tule reeds, a form of tetherball with a mud ball tied to a pole, and willow-javelin throwing kept boys busy throughout the day.

Fathers made their sons small bows and arrows, so boys spent much time trying to improve their hunting skills. They practised shooting at frogs or chipmunks. The first animal any boy killed was not touched or eaten by him. Others would carry the kill home to be cooked and eaten by villagers. This tradition taught boys always to share food.

Another hunting tool for boys was a hollowed-out willow branch. This became like a modern day beanshooter, only the Native American boys shot juniper berries instead of beans. Slingshots made good hunting weapons, as well.

Girls and boys shared many games, but girls playing with each other had contests to see who could make a basket the fastest, or they played with dolls made of tule. Together, young boys and girls played a type of ring-around-the-rosie game, climbed mountains, or built mud houses.

As children grew older, the boys followed their fathers and the girls followed their mothers as the adults did their daily work. Children were not trained in the arts of hunting or basketmaking, however, until they became teenagers.

HISTORY

Spanish missionaries, led by Fray Junipero Serra, arrived in California in 1769 to build missions along the coast of California. By 1823, fifty years later, 21 missions had been founded. Almost all of them were very successful, and the Franciscan monks who ran them were proud of how many Native Americans became Christians.

However, all was not as the monks had planned it would be. Native American people had never been around the diseases European white men brought with them. As a result, they had no immunity to such illnesses as measles, small pox, or flu. Too many mission Indians died from white men's diseases.

Historians figure there were 300,000 Native Americans living in California before the missionaries came. The missions show records of 83,000 mission Indians during mission days. By the time the Mexicans took over the missions from the Spanish in 1834, only 20,000 remained alive.

The great California Gold Rush of 1849 was probably another big reason why many of the Native Americans died during that time. White men, staking their claim to tribal lands with gold upon it, thought nothing of killing any California tribesman who tried to keep and protect his territory. Fifty-thousand tribal members died from diseases, bullets, or starvation between the gold Rush Days and 1870. By 1910, only 17,000 California Indians remained.

Although the American government tried to set aside reservations (areas reserved for Native Americans), the land given to the Indians often was not good land. Worse yet, some of the land sacred to tribes, such as burial grounds, was taken over by white people and never given back.

Sadly, mission Indians, when they became Christians, forgot the proud heritage and beliefs they had followed for thousands of years. Many wonderful myths and songs they had passed from one generation to the next, on winter nights so long ago, have been lost forever.

Today some 100,000 people can claim California Native American ancestors, but few pure-blooded tribespeople remain. Our link with the Wanderers, who came from Asia so long ago, has been forever broken.

The bullroarer made a deep, loud sound when whirled above the player's head. Tipai tribe.

Villages were usually built beside a lake, stream, or river. Balsa canoes are on the shore. Tule reeds grow along the edge of the water and are drying on poles on the right side of the picture.

Women preparing food in baskets, sit on tule mats. Tule mats are being tied to the willow pole framework of a house being built by one of the men.

POMO TRIBES
GENERAL FACTS

Historians seem to think that the name Pomo meant "at red earth hole". The reason is that Pomos mined a reddish-colored mineral, called hematite, found in the earth of their territory. Hematite was mixed with acorn flour to flavor and color bread which the Pomo women cooked. Pomos also mined and traded another red-colored mineral, magnesite, which was used to make beads. The sound "po" in the tribe's name was thought to mean either red hematite or magnesite. The "mo" sound meant 'at' in our language. Putting those meanings together explains the historians' choice of "at red earth hole".

The tribe had a huge population. Historians figure there were between 9,500 and 18,000 Pomos living on their land when white people first discovered them.

Because there were so many people scattered throughout a fairly large territory, those who study the history of humans (anthropologists) divided the branches of this large tribe according to where they lived and what language they spoke.

Below is a list of the names given to the Pomo tribelets by anthropologists:

Northwestern	Southeastern
Northeastern	Southwestern
Eastern	Southern
Central (west)	

Although they were all called Pomos, these people were not alike in any way. Of the seven different languages spoken by Pomo tribes, only a few words in all of their languages were the same. As a result, often people from neighboring villages could not even understand each other.

Some historians feel prehistoric (before any history was written about them) Pomo people lived inland, along the shores of Clear Lake. But by the time European explorers discovered them in 1579, the different tribelets had added to their land by moving westward. Pomo territory in the 1500s ran along the Pacific Coast, from just above San Francisco Bay in the south, to north of the Russian River. It stretched inland from the Pacific Ocean in the west, to the mountains east of Clear Lake.

In some places, villages were close together. In other parts of the territory, villages were farther apart. How many villages, and where they were, seemed to depend on how much food could be found in any one place.

Villages in Pomo territory were different from other tribes around them. Often little settlements clustered around one larger settlement, all of it becoming one village. If there was just one chief within this group of settlements, he lived in the largest village of the group.

Land around each group of settlements belonged to everyone who lived in the village. There were marked boundary lines for each settlement or village. Historians believe that the Pomo tribe had about 479 settlements in all, and that probably there were seventy-five main villages when European settlers arrived in the 1700s.

Anthropologists have been able to gather information about only three of the seven branches of the Pomo tribe: the West (North and Central), Eastern, and Southeastern. What facts we know are taken from notes made by anthropologists in the late 1800s. It was not until then that Americans finally became interested enough in Native American heritage to ask questions about the old way of life.

Unfortunately, by the time this research was begun, most members of the original tribe were either dead, or were so old they could not remember their early childhood. There were good reasons these old people could not remember their childhood. First, they had been very young when their parents had become mission Indians at Missions San Francisco Solano and San Rafael. Second, mission life was so completely different from tribal life, they had simply forgotten the prehistoric days.

EASTERN & SOUTHEASTERN POMO TRIBES

Southeastern Pomo people lived on small islands on East Lake and Lower Lake, two small lakes branching off from the much larger Clear Lake. Eastern Pomos built their permanent homes some distance inland from the northern end of Clear Lake, and only had food-gathering camps on the lake shore.

Clear Lake is north and east of San Francisco Bay. It is well away from the Pacific Coast, so the lake, with its fish and tules, was very important to tribelets that lived there.

It is thought there were from 1,260 to 2,205 Eastern Pomos living in this lake region before white people arrived. They lived in five main villages with wonderful names like "waterlily people" or "rock village people".

Eastern Pomos seemed to prefer living along the banks of rivers and streams which flowed into Clear Lake, rather than on the lake shores. Perhaps that was because the lake depth changed drastically every year, depending on the season.

Summers in this area were hot and dry, causing the lake water to drop as much as twenty feet some years. During the winter, rains made the lake deeper and larger. Almost every winter the lowlands around the lake flooded. In spring-time, when the snow melted, the lake became even deeper and flood lands more flooded. But by the time November arrived each year, after the long hot summer, the lake was again at its shallowest level.

Tule reed grows in flood lands.

The lake's gift to these two Pomo tribelets was two fold. First it gave them fish, which was their main food, along with acorn meal. Second, it gave them a most important plant. In the flood lands around the edges of Clear Lake grew a reed called tule.

Nearly every California tribe used tule reed in some way. Eastern and Southeastern Pomos had all the tule they could want. It was made into just about anything the Pomos needed, providing the people with houses, balsa canoes made of bundles of tule reeds, fabric for women's skirts, moccasins and leggings for men, shredded tule for beds, and diapers for babies. Even the tender new shoots and roots of the tule plants served as food.

Southeastern Pomos had fewer tribal members than the Eastern Pomos. From 390 to 1,070 tribal members were spread among three main villages, one each on Anderson

Island in East Lake, Rattlesnake Island at the tip of East Lake, and Lower Lake Island in Lower Lake. This southeastern tribelet owned the land it lived on.

Eastern Pomos who were questioned thought their land was also owned by their tribe, along with the oak trees, grass and seed places, fishing rights, and their own boat landings in Clear Lake, but no proof of ownership has ever been found. Eastern Pomos told of large poles marking the tribelet's ownership of bulb and seed fields.

Although the Eastern and Southeastern tribelets were close together in miles, they were unalike in many important ways. They spoke completely different languages, and had different religious rituals and ceremonies.

THE VILLAGES

Historian notes tell us Eastern Pomo villages were strung out along streams. Some villages were two miles long. There was usually a ceremonial house at each end of a settlement when it was stretched out so far. However, there is no information on the way Southeastern Pomo villages were laid out.

Each village had at least one round or oval ceremonial house. These were built into the ground one to two feet. Four to six large oak posts held up the roof. Heavy cottonwood or willow rafters were braced on the posts. Smaller branches were laid atop the rafters and tied with grapevines, which tightened up as they dried. The branches were then covered with dirt. Some of these ceremonial houses were as large as fifty to sixty feet across at floor level.

The villages were once described as looking like gently sloping, smoking knolls (tiny hills) because of the fires burning inside the earth-covered ceremonial houses and sweathouses.

Houses were either round, or long with rounded ends

(elliptical). House walls were made by tying tule reeds into mats, then attaching the mats to the house framework.

VILLAGE LIFE

A typical village was made up of some 235 people. They lived in about twenty houses. More than one family lived in most of the houses, but all the families were related. Usually there were at least three generations of a family living together. Each family had its own fire and own doorways. One door led to the outside and one into the common area where storage, the baking pit, and the mortar stones were located.

Usually tribelets of one tribe not only spoke different dialects (like a southern accent is to our west coast ears), but were not even very friendly to each other. All the Southeastern villages were friendly to each other. At one time, the story had been told, the three chiefs of the Southeastern tribelets' three villages were related to each other by marriage.

Families were very important to these Pomos. Stories of the family history were told at family storytimes around the fires. Each generation added its own history to those they heard year after year. Since they had no written language, the only way to keep their family history was by telling and retelling it.

The jobs people held were determined by what family they belonged to. For instance, the job of chief was inherited from a father. The chiefs of both Southeastern and Eastern Pomo tribelets were not all-powerful people who commanded villagers to obey them. Their jobs were to constantly remind villagers of Pomo rules that must be followed. This was done either by giving speeches to their people on the correct ways of living, or by setting good examples in their own lives. They could not feel they were better than others; they could not be too rich or too poor. Most of all, chiefs had to be good leaders.

Chiefs had to organize all group village activities, such as spring trapping of fish, fall gathering of acorns, and trading among other tribes for food, in case there was a shortage. If a village had too much food, then a chief arranged trade feasts with nearby villages. The scheduling of ceremonials, including the building of a ceremonial house for a feast, was also the job of a chief.

Each morning a chief awakened the village at dawn by making a speech about being good tribal members that day, then announcing the day's events. Chiefs were the masters of ceremonies for any big event like a wedding, or a funeral, or making the opening speech to welcome all visitors.

One of the most important jobs a chief had was to settle problems with other tribes and tribelets around them. Pomo people had a strong sense of territory. They would lay claim to certain hunting and food-gathering sites. Even families would mark certain oak trees with their family symbols to keep a tree as their own.

Because ownership of land and objects was so important to tribal members, trespassing on Pomo land could easily cause a war. Once in a while, Pomo warriors organize a surprise attack on the village of those who had trespassed. More often, however, both village chiefs would arrange in advance, a time and place for a battle to be fought.

At the appointed time, both sides spread out in two lines, facing each other. Arrows were shot into the air and spears were thrown at the enemy until one side was declared a winner. If a battle had no winner, the chiefs met and decided what the terms of peace would to be.

The young people of the village usually chose their own marriage partners, as long as the parents approved of the choice. When two young people were serious about marrying, the groom-to-be was invited to spend a night at the bride-to-be's house. Gifts were exchanged the next morning, with the groom's relatives bringing food, beads, rabbit skin blankets, and fine baskets to the bride's parents.

Pomo warrior in
full dress for war.
Heavy vest protects
the chest from
arrows.

The food gift was pinole and acorn soup, a symbolic meal for the newlyweds. Small beads given to the girl's family were also a symbolic gift, the small beads signifying the gift was for a young woman. The bride's family gave larger, thicker beads to the young man's family, symbols of a man's larger size.

Other symbolic gifts were exchanged between the two families but, strange as it may seem, none of the gifts were for the young couple; they were given to the parents of the couple. The young girl wore her pretty beads for only one-half an hour before they were given to her mother, who checked their value and then divided them equally between her husband's (the bride's father's) and her own families.

33

Nothing is known of Southeastern Pomo birth rituals, but the Eastern Pomos' rituals have been recorded. A child was born in the house of the new mother's parents. After the child was born, the mother's family gave the new mother a valuable bead belt and a special basket decorated with the red feathers of a woodpecker's topknot.

These gifts were given to the new father's mother when she arrived to bathe the baby. Either the mother of the new father, or his sister, came to the new mother's family house every morning and night to bathe the baby in a special basket.

If the father's family was truly pleased with the baby, a valuable necklace of magnesite beads was given to the new mother. The new mother wore it for a few days, then gave it to her mother, who divided the beads evenly between her own family and her husband's family.

Care was taken by the new father and mother to follow all the tribal rules after the baby was born. If they did not obey the rules, bad luck might come to the baby. Tribal rules said the new father must stay inside the birth home for eight days. Also, he could not hunt, fish, dance, or gamble for a month. The new mother kept herself on a special diet.

The small boys, as they grew up, stayed with their grandfathers, even sleeping with them. There were several reasons for having a boy spend his training years with his grandfather. First, the father could not take the time away from hunting and fishing to train his son. The older man had free time and had gained much experience in how to hunt and fish. He could share what he knew with the boy. He also had time to tell the tribal history and tribal laws to the young boy. Second, the boy, by sleeping with him at night, kept his grandfather warm. He could also take care of the needs of the old man. Third, a wonderful bond between boy and grandfather was built from this kind of arrangement.

Older women looked after the large family house by tending fires, minding the small children, and handling chores like basketmaking, which took a long time to complete. The younger women were grateful to have the help. Older women also trained young girls. In turn, the girls took care of their great-grandmothers and other very old village women.

Death, to the Pomos, was the worst disaster to happen to anyone. Mourning began even before a person died. Both men and women cried aloud to show their sorrow, and women would sometimes scratch their faces with their fingernails to show their sadness. There were some people who actually hit their chests in sorrow.

The body was left in the house for three or four days, while people brought gifts of robes, blankets, beads, and fine baskets. All these gifts were piled on top of the body. Relatives kept track of who gave what, so their family could return gifts of equal value when there was a death in the visitors' own families.

At the end of three or four days, the body was burned, along with the gifts given by visitors. A special area at the end of the permanent village was set aside for burning bodies. During the blaze, mourners and the village chief wailed in sorrow and continued to throw gift objects into the fire. Women of the village sang songs of mourning.

Close relatives of the dead person, both men and women, cut off their long hair. Women rubbed small pieces of clay into any short strands of hair left on their heads. Mourning lasted for one year if the villager who died was important, or if a baby had died.

Besides the funeral ceremony, there were two other major Eastern Pomo ceremonies every year. These were held in the springtime. During the ceremonial events, many dances were performed. Southeastern Pomos had three ceremonials, also held in the spring, with dancing and singing.

Two ritual dances historians have learned about are the Spear Dance and the Bear Dance. These were used in the initiation of young boys into the men's adult society. In the Bear Dance, a man would dress in a bear skin and act like a bear.

Both Eastern and Southeastern tribelets had a ceremony known as the Ghost Dance. Eastern Pomos held their ghost ceremony several months after the death of someone important, either man or woman. During the ceremony, specially trained men impersonated the villager who had died. At one point, the impersonator was laid down during the ceremony and mourning women relatives covered his body with beads.

After other rituals were performed, the people could then begin to laugh and sing and to end their time of sorrow. At the end of the ceremony a huge feast was held, signaling the time for visitors to return to their own villages.

Southeastern Pomos' ghost ceremony honored all the important foods they gathered each year. Only men could have a part in this ghost dance. The men danced to honor acorns, wild seeds, fish, and animals.

One supernatural spirit, called Kuksu, was known and worshipped in many California Native American tribes, including both Eastern and Southeastern Pomos. In some ceremonies a man dressed in black appeared. He was supposed to represent Kuksu.

Costumes for the ritual dances were beautiful. Although none have been described, it is known that brilliant bird feathers were part of the costumes, and the men wore very fancy earrings with featherwork and beading.

Probably the most eye-catching piece worn was a headpiece called "bighead" that was part of a dance costume. It was made in a pincushion design, with dogwood rods coming out of a tule bundle used as the base of the hat. The rods were decorated with white quills from bird tail feathers, probably of the bald eagle.

CLOTHING

Although some historians have written that men of the Eastern and Southeastern Pomos wore no clothes, today's tribal members have stated that men of both tribelets wore loincloths, or at least a skin apron.

Women of the tribelets wore tule skirts all year. Eastern Pomo men and women wore a short cape of shredded tule, tied at the neck. In rainy weather, the cape was pulled in at the waist with a belt. Children wore no clothes.

Men of both the Eastern and Southeastern tribelets made rabbit blankets. They served as blankets at night and were worn like capes for warmth on cool days. Both tribelets went barefooted, except when traveling in tall brush. Then they wore knee-high deerskin boots or tule moccasins with woven leggings.

TRADE

Pomo tribelets traded among themselves as well as with other tribes. The Central Pomos were the trading "middlemen" for Pomo tribelets. They traded with the Southern Pomos, then traded those Southern goods to the Northern and Eastern tribelets.

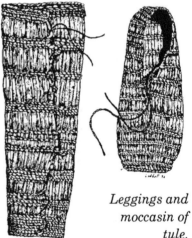

Leggings and moccasin of tule.

Southeastern Pomos traded with the Patwin and Lake Miwok tribes more than with other Pomos. Sometimes only goods were exchanged when Pomos traded, but usually string-money was used. Once a year the Southeastern Pomos traveled to Bodega Bay, in Northern Pomo territory, bringing back clam shells, one hundred pounds at a time, to make their money strings.

The shells were first broken into small pieces. Each piece was roughly shaped, a hole was drilled in it, then it was strung on plant-fiber string. After stringing these rough shell pieces, the craftsman rubbed each piece back and forth on a flat stone slab to grind the beads into smooth, even shapes. The more perfectly rounded in shape each shell bead was, the more valuable the money string.

Magnesite mines in the Southeast Pomo territory furnished a mineral that not only could be made into beautiful necklaces and bracelets, but could be used as money when strung on strings. This mineral, when baked and polished, was a pretty, reddish color. Some tribal members felt the magnesite beads to be more valuable than shell money beads. String-money was used so much by Pomos, and considered so valuable, that in the late 1800s and early 1900s, the bead-money was actually given a U.S. dollar value.

Foods, salt cakes, basket materials, shells, bows, arrows, arrowheads, obsidian blades, magnesite beads, snares, belts, robes, feathers and skins were all traded among villages.

Trading was usually done at trading sessions. When a village had articles to sell, the chief invited those of another village to visit and trading was done amidst feasting and entertainment. Pomo tribelets were known as the "great counters" of trading. Eastern Pomos worked on a base five numeral system. Southeastern Pomos used our base ten for counting. If a village had to work with very large numbers, they had a system of different-sized sticks they used to figure out totals.

FOOD

Food was so important to the Pomo tribe, that it decided every part of of their lives. The tribal year was divided into thirteen moons (months). Each moon was named for the kind of food-gathering that went on during that month.

POMO LUNAR CALENDAR

First Moon: It will be hard to go out and hunt game. (winter)

Second Moon: The fish won't come to shore

Third Moon: Fish will begin to come out.

Fourth Moon: Better weather. We can hunt and fish.

Fifth Moon: You can get clover.

Sixth: Fish will begin to run; we will move nearer the lake.

Seventh Moon: We will move back, carrying the fish.

Eighth Moon: If the moon is good we will go to Bodega Bay and get clamshells (for beads).

Ninth Moon: We will go home and even will be sent out to find good acorn crops.

Tenth Moon: We will be camping and gathering acorns.

Eleventh Moon: We will still be gathering acorns.

Twelfth Moon: We will finish the acorn gathering, move home, and get settled again.

Thirteenth Moon: We will be settled and resting, for there will be nothing to do.

From the book: *The Natural World of the California Indians. Heizer and Elsasser.*

Certain foods, like fish, acorns, grains, buckeyes, and pepperwood nuts, were stored and eaten all year long. Usually a meal was made up of dried fish and acorn mush. However, acorn meal was also made into bread. Fresh meat, fresh green leafy plants, roots, bulbs, berries, and fruits were added to the diet when they were in season.

A special treat was pinole, a favorite of both Eastern and Southeastern Pomos. Pinole was the name given to ground grain made from small grass seeds, weed seeds, or wild flower seeds. The seeds were first put through a basket sieve. Next they were cleaned with a winnower standing at a windy place and pouring seeds into another basket. The cleaned seeds were placed in a closely-woven basket with hot coals from the fire, and quickly tossed so the seeds would heat without the hot coals burning the basket. As the seeds became hot, their husks flew off, leaving the seeds with a popcorn-like taste.

After toasting, the seeds were ground in a stone mortar and sifted in a basket. This meal was put in small tightly woven baskets and served as pinole. People took pinches of the meal in their fingers to eat it. No salt had to be added, it had so much flavor.

Twined basketry hopper glued to mortar with tar.

Acorn meal was prepared as explained in the first chapter of this book. Pomo women, however, often would add clay to acorn mush. Clay helped absorb some of the bitter-tasting tannin still left in the meal, in spite of the leaching process.

Red-striped caterpillars, called army worms, only came around every six, or ten, or fifteen years, and were another favorite eating treat of Pomos. The caterpillars were thought to be a special gift from the Thunder God. The worms loved ash trees and only came in a year when there had been a great deal of fog.

These caterpillars were gathered a certain way. A trench was dug around an ash tree that was covered with them. A song, using the words, li, li, li, was sung. This was supposed to make the caterpillars shake their heads and begin to crawl down into the lower branches, or into the trench, where women could gather them in baskets. The caterpillars were drowned in cold water and roasted or boiled, then stored. Several hundred pounds of them could be gathered in a few days.

Most fish were caught in spawning seasons, when fish came to shallow water to lay eggs. Large amounts would be caught that way in a short period of time. Some fish were eaten fresh, the rest dried and stored. Pike, sucker, blackfish, carp, and bass all were eaten.

Eastern Pomos used long, cone-shaped basket traps for catching fish. These baskets were made so fish could swim into them, but could not swim out. The men also used spears and nets. Sometimes fishermen built dams made of small bushes to trap fish, so they could be scooped up in baskets.

The first fishing of the year was done in early spring (February-March), when creeks were full of water. Many kinds of fish spawned in the shallow edges of lakes, where they could be easily caught. The earliest fish were caught in the basket traps. By mid-March the water was clearer and spears could be used. Long basket traps were best when the water became warmer, and brush dams could be built.

In late March and early April, fish came closer to the lake edge, in the flooded tule swamps. It was at this time that Eastern Pomo tribelets moved to campsites on the lake's shore. Traps and nets were used during this time of year.

Little is known of the Southeastern tribelet's fishing methods, but it is thought they did more lake than stream fishing, since they lived on islands in the lake.

When Eastern Pomo hunters left their village to hunt, they carried their spears and bows on their backs, as well as

Excellent example of a balsa boat, used throughout California for fishing, made by the Pomo tribe.

their quivers, which held arrows. The quivers and skin hunting bags were made from the hides of grizzly-bear cubs.

Little is known of the kinds of bows and arrows they made, probably because fishing was their major way of getting food.

BASKETS

Women of the Pomo tribelets were thought by many people to have made the most beautiful baskets of any native tribe in the world. Not only were they so tightly woven they could carry water without having to seal them with tar, but the basket decorations and shapes were works of art.

Large twined seed-gatherer's basket to carry large load of seeds to the village.

Black and red feathers of the red-winged blackbird, red scalp feathers of the woodpecker, yellow feathers of the meadowlark and oriole, and green feathers of the mallard duck were all woven into the baskets in geometric designs. Shells and beads were also woven into the baskets. Even different colors of grass were used to form patterns.

Basket were made in many shapes, from very flat plates and trays to almost perfectly round ones. Large baskets were used for storage and for carrying heavy loads on the backs of women. Small baskets were worn low on the women's heads to protect their foreheads when they used net bands to help support the weight of heavy loads on their backs. Smaller baskets could also be used for storing beads and treasures, or for eating bowls.

Children were put in basket cradles and attached to their mothers' backs until they could walk. Traps were often made from baskets. More often than not, even baskets used every day were beautifully made and pretty to look at. Some

Pomo baskets have been saved, and can be seen in museums and at several California missions.

HISTORY

Eastern and Southeastern Pomos' land was just to the north of the most northern California Missions: Mission San Rafael and Mission San Francisco de Solano. Even though they were a distance from the missions, some tribal members did become mission Indians.

After Mexico took over the missions from Spain, in the mid-1800s, life became even more difficult than the strict mission life had been. Spain had promised one-half of the mission lands to their mission Indians. Mexican leaders did not honor that promise. Instead, as Mexican military leaders moved into the area, they claimed the land for themselves and began forcing the Native Americans to work for them in the fields and in their homes.

One story is told of how a Mexican landowner, named Vallejo, sent soldiers to a Southeastern Pomo village to bring back villagers to help Señor Vallejo harvest his crop. The Pomo men refused to go, and troops were sent to the village with orders to kill all the men of the village. The troops found the Pomo men in their sweathouse and killed them all.

One Eastern Pomo chief, Augustine, was forced to become a cowboy and herd cattle for Mexican ranchers in the 1840s. He was given meat as payment, but no money.

Unfortunately, even United States Cavalry men killed many Eastern and Southeastern Pomos as revenge for the Pomos killing two American settlers who had treated them poorly.

By 1851, there were great numbers of American settlers in Clear Lake Pomo territory. Gradually, the Pomos were forced off their land by settlers, and were hired to work on settlers' ranches and farms. Important food-gathering places of the two tribelets were now on property claimed by settlers; the

Pomos were no longer allowed to gather acorns and seeds, the old tribal food they needed to feed their families. Worse yet, grazing cattle and sheep of settlers ruined the grass and seed lands of the Native Americans.

White people's diseases hit the Pomos during the second half of the 1880s. The Pomos had never been around white people's diseases before, and they had no immunity to them. Measles, small pox, flu, and other diseases killed thousands of them at a time. Since the Pomo tribal members had always felt illness was a punishment from spirit-gods for bad behavior, they felt they must be to blame for so many deaths. They could not understand why so many fellow Pomos were dying, when the tribal rules were trying to be followed.

One community was started by an American priest for those Pomos who wished to live there. Many tribal members did move to the place, until it caught fire in 1912. The United States government then set aside reservation land with homes for those Pomos who cared to live there. Many people stayed until after World War II.

Through all the troubled times, the Eastern and Southeastern tribelets managed to keep some of their beliefs and tribal rules. In the 1970s, a few relatives of the Pomo tribelets still lived near Clear Lake in old frame government houses some of them had remodeled.

Today, Pomo tribal members shop in supermarkets but still cook the traditional tribal foods, such as acorn mush and deer meat, as special treats. Tribal language is still known by some members, but is not used as an everyday language.

Although the family incomes are still low compared to incomes of white people around them, some young Pomos have graduated from college. Best of all, the young people are beginning to revive a few of the old traditional ceremonies. The Eastern and Southeastern Pomo tribelets live on!

EAST AND SOUTHEAST POMO TRIBE OUTLINE

I. General facts
- A. Meaning of name
- B. Population of tribe before white people
- C. Branches of tribelets
- D. General territory and boundaries
    1. Village clusters or settlements
    2. Number of settlements

II. East and Southeastern Pomo tribes
- A. Eastern territory and lakes
    1. Boundaries
    2. Population
    3. Village names
    4. Climate, lakes and tule reed
- B. Southeastern territory and lake islands
    1. Population
    2. Number of villages
    3. Tribal ownership of land
- C. Villages
    1. Description of ceremonial building
    2. House description
- D. Village life
    1. Generations of relatives in one house
    2. Friendliness of Southeastern villages
    3. Chief and his jobs
    4. Marriages
        a. Picking marriage partners
        b. Marriage ceremony and customs
    5. Childbirth customs
    6. Child training by grandparents
    7. Death customs and rituals

I .History
  1. Missions and Pomo tribes
      a. Mexican take over of missions
  2. Cruelty of Mexicans
  3. Loss of land to Mexicans and Americans
  4. White man's diseases
  5. Indian reservations
J. Pomos today

GLOSSARY

AWL: a sharp, pointed tool used for making small holes in leather or wood

CEREMONY: a meeting of people to perform formal rituals for a special reason; like an awards ceremony to hand out trophies to those who earned honors

CHERT: rock which can be chipped off, or flaked, into pieces with sharp edges

COILED: a way of weaving baskets which looks like the basket is made of rope coils woven together

DIAMETER: the length of a straight line through the center of a circle

DOWN: soft, fluffy feathers

DROUGHT: a long period of time without water

DWELLING: a building where people live

FLETCHING: attaching feathers to the back end of an arrow to make the arrow travel in a straight line

GILL NET: a flat net hanging vertically in water to catch fish by their heads and gills

GRANARIES: basket-type storehouses for grains and nuts

HERITAGE: something passed down to people from their long-ago relatives

LEACHING: washing away a bitter taste by pouring water through foods like acorn meal

MORTAR: flat surface of wood or stone used for the grinding of grains or herbs with a pestle

PARCHING:	to toast or shrivel with dry heat
PESTLE:	a small stone club used to mash, pound, or grind in a mortar
PINOLE:	flour made from ground corn
INDIAN RESERVATION:	land set aside for Native Americans by the United States government
RITUAL:	a ceremony that is always performed the same way
SEINE NET:	a net which hangs vertically in the water, encircling and trapping fish when it is pulled together
SHAMAN:	tribal religious men or women who use magic to cure illness and speak to spirit-gods
SINEW:	stretchy animal tendons
STEATITE:	a soft stone (soapstone) mined on Catalina Island by the Gabrielino tribe; used for cooking pots and bowls
TABOO:	something a person is forbidden to do
TERRITORY:	land owned by someone or by a group of people
TRADITION:	the handing down of customs, rituals, and belief, by word of mouth or example, from generation to generation
TREE PITCH:	a sticky substance found on evergreen tree bark
TWINING:	a method of weaving baskets by twisting fibers, rather than coiling them around a support fiber

NATIVE AMERICAN WORDS
WE KNOW AND USE

PLANTS AND TREES
hickory
pecan
yucca
mesquite
saguaro

ANIMALS
caribou
chipmunk
cougar
jaguar
opossum
moose

STATES
Dakota – friend
Ohio – good river
Minnesota – waters that
reflect the sky
Oregon – beautiful water
Nebraska – flat water
Arizona
Texas

FOODS
avocado
hominy
maize (corn)
persimmon
tapioca
succotash

GEOGRAPHY
bayou – marshy body of
water
savannah – grassy plain
pasadena – valley

WEATHER
blizzard
Chinook (warm, dry wind)

FURNITURE
hammock

HOUSE
wigwam
wickiup
tepee
igloo

INVENTIONS
toboggan

BOATS
canoe
kayak

OTHER WORDS
caucus – group meeting
mugwump – loner politician
squaw – woman
papoose – baby

CLOTHING
moccasin
parka
mukluk – slipper
poncho

BIBLIOGRAPHY

Cressman, L. S. *Prehistory of the Far West.* Salt Lake City, Utah: University of Utah Press, 1977.

Heizer, Robert F., volume editor. *Handbook of North American Indians; California, volume 8.* Washington, D.C.: Smithsonian Institute, 1978.

Heizer, Robert F. and Elsasser, Albert B. *The Natural World of the California Indians.* Berkeley and Los Angeles, CA; London, England: University of California Press, 1980.

Heizer, Robert F. and Whipple, M.A.. *The California Indians.* Berkeley and Los Angeles, CA; London, England: University of California Press, 1971.

Heuser, Iva. *California Indians.* PO Box 352, Camino, CA 95709: Sierra Media Systems, 1977.

Macfarlen, Allen and Paulette. *Handbook of American Indian Games.* 31 E. 2nd Street, Mineola, N.Y. 11501: Dover Publications, 1985.

Murphey, Edith Van Allen. *Indian Uses of Native Plants.* 603 W. Perkins Street, Ukiah, CA 95482: Mendocino County Historical Society, © renewal, 1987.

National Geographic Society. *The World of American Indians.* Washington, DC: National Geographic Society reprint, 1989.

Tunis, Edwin. *Indians.* 2231 West 110th Street, Cleveland, OH: The World Publishing Company, 1959.

Credits:
Island Industries, Vashon Island, Washington 98070
Dona McAdam, Mac on the Hill, Seattle, Washington 98109

Acknowledgements:
Kim Walters, Library Director, and Richard Buchen,
Research Librarian, Braun Library, Southwest Museum
Special thanks

A Chronology of
Microbiology
in Historical
Context

A Chronology of Microbiology in Historical Context

Raymond W. Beck
Professor Emeritus
Department of Microbiology
University of Tennessee
Knoxville, Tennessee

ASM
PRESS

WASHINGTON, D.C.

Library of Congress Cataloging-in-Publication Data

Beck, Raymond W.
    A chronology of microbiology in historical context/Raymond W. Beck.
        p.cm.
    Includes index.
    ISBN 1-55581-193-0
    1. Microbiology—History—Chronology. I. Title

    QR21.B43 2000
    579'.09—dc21
                                                                00-025075

Cover illustrations: A photograph of the Wright brothers, Orville and Wilbur, and their airplane (courtesy of the Library of Congress) and a photogravure of a protrait of Louis Pasteur by Finnish artist Albert Edelfelt (courtesy of the American Society for Microbiology Archives; the original portrait is in the Musée d'Orsay, Paris, France).

*To my wife, Charlotte H. Beck, who
provided encouragement, enthusiasm,
and invaluable editorial assistance*

Preface

A CHRONOLOGY IS A HISTORICAL ACCOUNT that provides information that can be learned only by searching a variety of sources. The purpose of this chronology is to present events in the history of microbiology and to identify the individuals who made the events happen. A scientific chronology is based on the premises that knowing when something happened is important and that this knowledge often helps one to understand how and why a particular scientific advance occurred. In addition to this goal, *A Chronology of Microbiology* also tries to place events in a general historical context and includes advances in other scientific disciplines, such as biochemistry, cell biology, genetics, microscopy, chemistry, physics, and technology, as well as events from societal, political, and cultural history. A chronology cannot be encyclopedic, so some information must necessarily be excluded.

For many of the early events, only an approximate date is possible. The later scientific entries are based on the dates of publication of articles or books. In the 20th century, many overlapping and fundamentally related discoveries were made over short periods of time, making assignment of a particular discovery to exact dates and to specific individuals or groups of researchers difficult. In many instances, a discovery is attributed to several persons, realizing the possibility that others have been overlooked.

The choices of what to include in the chronology were made with an eye toward creating a pattern of history and should not be construed to mean that events not included are of lesser importance. The last 50 years has seen a burgeoning of knowledge in the biological sciences, making it a challenging task to trace all of the important advances. This chronology follows but a few of the more recent lines of discovery, with the realization that many other lines of discovery could have been chosen. A chronology is never finished, it will necessarily become more complete as time goes on.

A Chronology of Microbiology in Historical Context is intended to give both teachers and students of microbiology a valuable resource for teaching and learning. As a reference book, it provides ready access to information about the development of microbiology and to contextual events in other areas of science and society in general. Users of this book will be able to clarify dates of events and names of individuals responsible and, through cross-references, can learn about related discoveries in specific areas of interest.

A Chronology of Microbiology in Historical Context

ANCIENT DISEASES: *Plague or Pestilence*
An account of the reign of the emperor Shemsu, or Shememsu, in Egypt's First Dynasty reports the occurrence of a great pestilence. This may be the first recorded epidemic; the words "pestilence" and "plague" were used without exact definition in various early writings.

A. ANCIENT MEDICINE
Emperor Shen Lung writes the earliest known textbook on medicine, *The Great Herbal.*

B. CULTURE: *the Bronze Age*
The Bronze Age begins with the discovery that smelting tin ore and copper ore together makes a new, easily cast metal.

C. CULTURE: *Invention of Writing*
The Egyptians use ink to write in pictorial characters called hieroglyphics on papyrus.

ANCIENT MEDICINE
Chinese emperor Shen Nung uses herbal medicines and acupuncture.

A. ANCIENT MEDICINE
Nei Ching, an extant medical text ascribed to the Chinese emperor Huang Ti, describes observation, auscultation, palpation, and interrogation (look, listen, feel, and ask) to be used in diagnosis of illness.

B. TECHNOLOGY: *Clocks*
Water clocks appear in Egypt.

ca. 2500 B.C.	

A. CULTURE: *the Iron Age*
The Iron Age begins when it is found that smelting at very high temperatures produces a metal much harder than copper. Widespread use of iron develops slowly over the next 1,000 years.

B. CULTURE: *Writing*
Cuneiform writing, developed in Sumeria, uses about 600 signs.

ca. 2000 B.C.

TECHNOLOGY: *Glass*
In Mesopotamia, glass is accidentally made in the process of producing glazed earthenware. Although it is cut and polished, it is not molded while hot until about 1500 B.C.

ca. 1700 B.C.

MATHEMATICS: *Sumerian Mathematics / Calculation of* π
In Sumer, mathematicians calculate an approximate value for π, the ratio of the circumference of a circle to its diameter. They also develop methods for square roots, cubes, cube roots, and devise quadratic equations. (See 190, 600, 1596, 1706.)

ca. 1500 B.C.

A. ANCIENT DISEASES: *Epidemic Fevers*
The so-called Ebers papyrus, discovered by George Ebers in 1862 in a tomb in Thebes, Egypt, describes epidemic fevers and gives a description of numerous types of medication.

B. TECHNOLOGY: *Glass*
The shaping of molten glass begins.

ca. 1190 B.C.

ANCIENT DISEASES: *Plague*
Near the end of the Trojan War, the Greek army is decimated by an epidemic. That Homer's *Iliad* mentions mice or rats as well as a plague or pestilence suggests that the epidemic is bubonic plague.

ca. 1122 B.C.

ANCIENT DISEASES: *Smallpox*
A disease in China, described as causing skin pustules that increase in number, form pus, and subside, is believed to be smallpox.

ca. 1000 B.C.

FOOD BACTERIOLOGY: *Food Preservation*
Techniques for preservation of food used in China include drying, smoking, salting, and spicing. Wine, converted to vinegar, is also used for food preservation.

790–640 B.C.

ANCIENT DISEASES: *Plague*
According to accounts in *Plutarch's Lives,* translated into English in 1579, and those of Roman historian Livy (Titus Livius), plagues strike Rome in 790 B.C., 710 B.C., and 640 B.C.

585 B.C.

PHYSICS: *Magnetism and Static Electricity*
The Greek natural philosopher Thales studies the magnetic properties of both lodestone and amber, which develops an attractive force when rubbed lightly. His observations on amber may be the first report of the phenomenon of static electricity. (See 1600 A, 1660 B, 1745 B.)

ca. 460 B.C.

MEDICINE: *Hippocrates/Hippocratic School*
Hippocrates, born on the Greek island of Cos, lives from 460 to about 377 B.C. Little is known of his life other than that he traveled throughout Greece practicing medicine and teaching. A collection of more than 70 medical writings known as the "Hippocratic Corpus" is attributed to him or to others in the Hippocratic school (the school at Cos; some are from the rival school at Cnidos). Hippocrates formulates the concept that an imbalance of the four humors: blood, phlegm (nasal outflow), yellow bile, and black bile, is primarily responsible for disease. The relationship among the humors is based on the four elements of Empedocles: blood and fire (hot and dry), yellow bile and air (hot and wet), black bile and earth (cold and dry), phlegm and water (cold and wet). This concept, further developed by Galen in the second century, dominates medicine until about the 17th century. The Hippocratic oath is now believed not to have been a product of the Hippocratic school, but it continues to be a foundation of ethics in the medical profession. (See 430 B.C. B, second century.)

430 B.C.

A. ANCIENT DISEASES: *Plague of Thucydides or Plague of Athens*
Thucydides, in his *History of the Peloponnesian War,* may be the first to write that plague is contagious and that those who recover from the disease are not attacked again. Thucydides states that individuals attacked by plague go from health to sickness in an instant, with symptoms including upper respiratory distress, vomiting, pustules and ulcers, and internal intense fever. He states that birds who feed on dead animals do not attack those who die from the disease. Authorities differ widely in their interpretation of these descriptions; some believe that Thucydides was describing measles, while others favor typhus fever. At least one writer believes the condition to be ergotism. During the war between Athens and Sparta, at least one-third of the population of Athens dies of a plague.

B. CHEMISTRY: *the Four Elements*
Empedocles names the four elements: earth, water, fire, and air. Aristotle and Plato develop these ideas, which dominate concepts of the elements until the 18th century.

ca. 367–322 B.C.

BIOLOGY AND GEOCENTRIC ASTRONOMY
Aristotle begins his studies in 367 B.C. at Plato's Academy, where he remains until Plato's death in 347 B.C. His writings, along with notes prepared by his students, comprise an encyclopedic survey of almost every existing field of

ca. 367–322 B.C. *(continued)*

knowledge. His works include a description of a geocentric theory that earth is the center of the universe; a listing of 500 species of animals divided into eight classes ascending to humans but not implying evolution; an explanation of the inductive method; and clear distinction between axioms and postulates. He also describes the development of the chick embryo and the stomach of ruminant animals. His view of the different roles of arteries and veins impedes studies of the circulation of blood. In the second century, Galen's use of Aristotle's doctrines contributes strongly to their domination of scientific thought until the 16th and 17th centuries. (See second century A, second century B.)

ca. 300 B.C.

MATHEMATICS: *Euclid*

The *Elements,* prepared by the mathematician Euclid, comprises 13 books that present the geometry of the Greeks, including plane and solid geometry, the theory of incommensurables, and the theory of numbers.

ca. 280 B.C.

ANATOMY: *Function of the Heart*

Erasistratus, who is known primarily through the writings of Galen, studies the valves of the heart and correctly interprets their action in relation to the heartbeat. Even though he recognizes that the right side of the heart receives blood and pumps it to the lung, he thinks that the left side receives air from the arteries in the lung and pumps the air, or *pneuma,* to the rest of the body.

260 B.C.

MATHEMATICS AND PHYSICS: *Calculation of π, the Lever, Specific Gravity*

Archimedes calculates the value of π to be between 3 10/71 and 3 10/70 (3.1408 to 3.1428). He also computes the mathematics of the lever. Legend has it that while sitting in a bath, he discovers the "Archimedes principle" of displacement of an equal weight of water by a submerged or floating body, upon which he is said to have shouted "*Eureka!*" (I have found it!). (See 1700 B.C., 190, 600, 1596, 1706.)

ca. 250 B.C.

PHYSICS: *Mechanics and Hydrostatics*

Archimedes establishes the basic concepts of mechanics and hydrostatics.

ca. 77

A. ANCIENT DISEASES: *Rabies*

Gaius Plinius Secundus (Pliny the Elder) believes that eating the livers of mad dogs cures rabies.

B. ANCIENT BOTANY

Pedanius Dioscorides, a physician for Nero's armies, completes the first version of *De materia medica,* describing more than 600 plants, their origins, methods for preparing medicinals from them, and their uses in medicine. This book (written in Greek), along with its many revisions and versions, is one of the earliest and most famous of the beautifully illustrated "herbals" that find wide use among physicians as a type of pharmacopoeia. *De materia medica* continues to be used as late as the 17th century, but in the numerous copies made over more than a thousand years the illustrations resemble less and less the natural appearance of the plants. In 1544 Pierandrea Mattioli prepares a version with comments in Italian, and later editions in German, French, and other European languages serve to spread the work across Europe. The Italian version alone sells 30,000 copies. (See 1530 B.)

79

ANCIENT DISEASES: *Anthrax*
Shortly after the eruption of Mount Vesuvius, an epidemic, possibly anthrax, begins to cause widespread deaths among livestock in Italy. At the same time, a plague of unknown origin causes many deaths in the cities of Italy.

Second century

A. MEDICINE AND ANATOMY: *Galen*
Galen (Claudius Galenus or Galenos), a Greek physician, anatomist, and physiologist, writes extensively and polemically on both medical and philosophical subjects. His writings dominate concepts in medicine, anatomy, and physiology for about 1,500 years. Although he regards his work as extending and perfecting the concepts of Hippocrates, he is contemptuous of other physicians, both predecessors and contemporary. Galen dissects animals, and possibly humans, to obtain knowledge of both anatomy and physiology. He believes that the liver converts food to blood and that blood moves to the heart, where it is imbued with vital spirit. He believes that there are minute pores between the two ventricles of the heart. He accurately describes muscles and bones. After his death, experimentation virtually ceases for the next 1,000 years. Galen's works do not reach western Europe until about the 12th century, after being translated from the Greek to Arabic and then to Latin. Among those that have survived to modern times are *De anatomicicis administrationibus* (On anatomical procedures) and *De usu partium* (On the functions of the parts of the body).

B. PHYSICS: *Geocentric Astronomy*
Ptolemy (Claudius Ptolemaeus) flourishes in the second century. His *Almagest* includes an outline of a universe with earth at its center, the distances from earth to the sun and the moon, the sizes of the sun and moon, a catalog of stars, and the motions of the five planets. All but the latter are believed to be derived from the works of Hipparchus. His concepts of geocentric astronomy, the Ptolemaic system, perpetuate the earlier ideas of Plato and Aristotle and are dominant until Copernicus presents his heliocentric model. Ptolemy also writes *Geographica,* describing techniques for construction of maps and listing the longitudes and latitudes of many locations. (See 367–322 B.C., 1512.)

164

ANCIENT DISEASES: *Plague of Antoninus or Galen*
A plague, variously called the "plague of Antoninus" or the "plague of Galen," takes an enormous toll in Italy until about 189. Galen's description is considered the first record of a smallpox epidemic.

190

MATHEMATICS: *Calculation of π*
Liu Hu calculates π to be 3.14159. (See 1700 B.C., 600, 1596, 1706.)

250

MATHEMATICS: *Algebra*
Diophanus writes *Arithmetica,* which includes calculations in algebra.

251

ANCIENT DISEASES: *Plague in Rome*
A great epidemic sweeps through Rome and its surroundings between the years 251 and 266, killing at least two-thirds of the population. This plague devastates the region, causing farm lands to lie fallow and the entire economy to decline severely.

499

MATHEMATICS: *Calculation of π/Decimal Point*
Aryabhata, an Indian mathematician, calculates π as 3.1416, including the use of the decimal point.

ca. 500

IMMUNOLOGY: *Smallpox Immunization*
The Chinese immunize individuals against smallpox using dried scabs blown into the nostrils. This procedure evolves over the centuries to become the introduction of material into the arm. (See 1715 A, 1721 A, 1764 A.)

542

ANCIENT DISEASES: *Bubonic Plague*
At about this time, the Great Plague of Justinian, the first great epidemic that can be ascribed with some certainty to bubonic plague, strikes the Mediterranean countries, killing an estimated 100 million people over a period of about 50 years. The disease begins in Constantinople (Byzantium) and spreads east to Syria, Persia, and the Indies and westward to Africa and the continent of Europe. The contagion is attributed to changes in the atmosphere brought about by the putrefaction of animal matter.

580

ANCIENT DISEASES: *Dysentery*
Gregory, Bishop of Tours, describes an epidemic of dysentery in France. Believing that accumulation of wealth is responsible for the raging epidemic, King Chilperic, at the urging of the queen, has all of the tax lists burned.

600

MATHEMATICS: *Calculation of π*
Zu Chong-zhi and Zu Geng-shi (father and son) calculate π to be 3.1415926. (See 1700 B.C., 190, 1596, 1706.)

664

ANCIENT DISEASES: *Yellow Plague/Relapsing Fever*
A plague that some believe is bubonic plague and others think is smallpox strikes Britain. Because of the common appearance of yellowness of the skin, the disease is referred to as yellow plague, even though it is unrelated

to yellow fever. Although there is uncertainty about the type of disease, some medical historians believe it to be relapsing fever caused by a member of the genus *Borrelia*.

750

CHEMISTRY: *Calcination and Distillation*
The Arabian alchemist Jabir ibn Haiyān notes that lead increases in weight when burned in air. He also distills vinegar, obtaining a highly concentrated solution of acetic acid. Arabic science begins to appear in Europe.

857

ANCIENT DISEASES: *Ergotism*
Ergotism, first recorded in the Rhine Valley, is caused by infection of rye with the fungus *Claviceps purpurea*, which produces several types of alkaloids that contaminate bread made from the grain. Sometimes called St. Anthony's fire in humans, ergotism has symptoms that include vomiting, sensations of intense cold or heat, pain in muscles, and hallucinations.

900

A. ANCIENT DISEASES: *Botulism*
At about this time, the leader of the Byzantine Empire, Emperor Leo VI, forbids the eating of blood sausage because of its association with a fatal food poisoning now presumed to be botulism. (See 1735 A, 1820 A, 1895 C.)

B. CHEMISTRY: *Alcohol Distilled from Wine*
Arab chemists learn to distill wine to make alcohol. By the late 11th century, this technique is used in Salerno, Italy.

910

ANCIENT DISEASES: *Smallpox and Measles*
Smallpox and measles are often confused during much of the early history of medicine. In 910, Rhazes, an Arabian physician, is the first to clearly distinguish between the two diseases by descriptions of the symptoms both before and after the appearance of skin lesions.

ca. 1020

ARABIC MEDICINE
Avicenna (Abu 'Ali al-Husain ibn Abdallah ibn Sina) writes a *Canon* of medicine and perhaps *De anima*, a work on alchemy.

1070

FOOD MICROBIOLOGY: *Roquefort Cheese*
According to legend, Roquefort cheese is discovered by a shepherd who leaves a package of fresh cheese in a cave near the village of Roquefort in France. When he returns some time later, the cheese is infused with a green mold, now known as *Penicillium roqueforti*.

1095

ANCIENT DISEASES: *the First Crusade*
Pope Urban II declares the First Crusade with the purpose of winning the Holy Land from the Muslims. The ranks of the crusaders are decimated not only by deaths in battle but also by disease. Historical writers suggest various diseases, including dysentery, smallpox, bubonic plague, typhoid fever,

1095 *(continued)*

typhus fever, malaria, and scurvy. Crusades in the 12th and 13th centuries are also ravaged by disease.

1096

ANCIENT DISEASES: *Typhus Fever*
An account of what is believed to be an epidemic of typhus fever in Bohemia states that the victims had a soreness in the head but no plague glands, thus distinguishing it from bubonic plague.

ca. 1100

CHEMISTRY: *Alcohol Distillation/Brandy*
In the late 11th century, alcohol is distilled in Salerno, Italy. Italians also produce brandy.

1150

HUMAN CULTURE: *Universities*
The University of Paris is founded as universities begin to be established throughout Europe.

1163

SOCIETY AND RELIGION
The cornerstone of the Cathedral of Notre Dame is laid in Paris.

1167

CULTURE: *Universities*
Oxford University is founded.

1210

A. CHEMISTRY: *Mineral Acids*
The discovery of mineral acids results from the improvement of stills.

B. SOCIETY AND POLITICS
Genghis Khan invades northern China.

1215

SOCIETY AND POLITICS
The Magna Carta, limiting the powers of English kings, is signed by King John of England, brother of King Richard the Lion-Hearted, who leads the Third Crusade.

1217

CULTURE: *Universities*
Cambridge University is founded.

1249

OPTICAL INSTRUMENTS: *Magnifying Lenses*
Roger Bacon writes about the use of magnifying lenses to improve vision. In his *Opus majus* of 1268, he describes spectacles for farsighted persons. Spectacles come into use in Italy and in China during this century. (See 1299.)

ca. 1250

A. BOTANY: *Plant Classification*
Albertus Magnus writes *De vegetabilibus*, classifying plants into types.

B. MATHEMATICS: *Arabic Numerals and Decimals*

Returning crusaders introduce both Arabic numerals and decimals into Europe. (See 1585.)

1267

OPTICAL INSTRUMENTS: *Magnifying Lenses*

Roger Bacon refers to the use of a convergent lens as a simple magnifying device.

1299

OPTICAL INSTRUMENTS: *Spectacles*

An Italian manuscript mentions the use of the newly invented spectacles to improve vision. Spectacles may have been invented by Salvano d'Aramento degli Amati, a nobleman of Florence, who kept the method of manufacture secret. An inscription on his tombstone, dated 1317, calls him the "inventor of spectacles." Allessandro della Spina of Pisa, who dies in 1313, is credited with teaching others how to manufacture spectacles. The invention of spectacles leads to the discovery, possibly accidental, of the compound microscope and the telescope. (See 1249, 1590, 1608.)

ca. 1300

CHEMISTRY: *Sulfuric Acid*

An unknown alchemist discovers sulfuric acid.

1307

THE ARTS: *Literature*

Dante Alighieri begins writing a poem that is completed only shortly before his death in 1321, *The Divine Comedy*.

1343

ANCIENT DISEASES: *Bubonic Plague*

In a siege of Kaffa (Calla), a Crimean trading post, the Tartars are struck by bubonic plague. They place cadavers on their catapults and throw them into the city, where the inhabitants become infected. Although Kaffa is probably invaded already by the rats carrying the disease bacterium, many people flee the city, carrying the plague with them to Genoa, Venice, Constantinople, and other Mediterranean ports. (See 1348.)

1348

ANCIENT DISEASES: *Bubonic Plague*

Plague spreads across all of Europe, starting with the galleys that have left Kaffa as well as the ships out of Red Sea and Persian Gulf ports. Almost every town affected loses up to 50% of its inhabitants. Gentile da Foligno writes a detailed description of the symptoms of bubonic plague. (See 1343.)

1358

ANCIENT DISEASES: *Bubonic Plague*

Giovanni Boccaccio describes the outbreak of plague in 1348 in Florence, Italy, in his fictional book *The Decameron*. Speaking of the plague as being contagious, he warns against touching the clothes or any object that has come into contact with the sick.

1400

THE ARTS: *Literature*
Geoffrey Chaucer dies, leaving unfinished his poem *The Canterbury Tales,* 24 stories portraying medieval society.

1403

INFECTIOUS DISEASE: *Quarantine*
Bubonic plague strikes Venice. In an attempt to protect its citizens the city establishes a policy that no one can enter the city until a certain waiting period has passed. The waiting period of 40 days is the origin of the word "quarantine" (Italian *quaranta*). Although the reason for choosing the 40-day period is not known, in 1377 a station for persons suspected of having plague in Ragusa (Yugoslavia) requires a waiting period of 40 days.

1454

TECHNOLOGY: *Printing*
Johann Gutenberg invents printing from movable metal type. He publishes the Mazarin Bible in 1456.

1480

ANCIENT DISEASES: *Typhus Fever*
Typhus fever is described as being epidemic in 1480 and 1481 in Germany and France and in 1489 in Spain. The disease may be typhoid fever, since the two diseases are not differentiated until the 19th century.

1492

A. ANCIENT DISEASES: *Diphtheria*
Hartmann Schedel describes an epidemic in Nuremberg that has the characteristics of diphtheria. (See 1576, 1748 B, 1765 B.)

B. SOCIETY: *Exploration*
Christopher Columbus (Cristoforo Colombo) makes his first voyage across the Atlantic Ocean, discovering the Bahamas, Cuba, and Hispaniola (Santo Domingo).

1495

A. INFECTIOUS DISEASE: *Syphilis*
After its first appearance in 1493, syphilis becomes epidemic in Europe at the time Naples is captured by the army of Charles VIII of France. This 15th century outbreak may be the only true epidemic of syphilis to occur, later periods of the disease being regarded as endemic. It is widely held that the infection is carried to Europe by native Americans brought to Portugal by Christoper Columbus. The French call it the Neapolitan disease, the Italians call it the French or Spanish disease, and the English call it the French pox. It is also variously called Spanish, German, Polish or Turkish "pocks." Syphilis is also called "great pokkes," descriptive of the severe secondary lesions, as contrasted to "small pokkes," for the lesions of smallpox. See 1530 for origin of the name "syphilis."

B. THE ARTS: *Art*
Leonardo da Vinci paints *The Last Supper* on the wall of a refectory that stands next to the Church of Santa Maria delle Grazie in Milan, Italy.

1497

SOCIETY: *Exploration*
John Cabot (Giovanni Caboto) discovers Newfoundland and Nova Scotia, becoming the first explorer since the Vikings to reach the mainland of North America. In 1492, Christopher Columbus visited several coastal islands.

1498

INFECTIOUS DISEASE: *Syphilis*
A Summary of Medicine, by Francisco López de Villalobos, is in reality a poem, in Latin, about syphilis. There is evidence that he begins writing the poem in 1493, making him the first physician to describe the disease, which he refers to as *las buvas.* (See 1530 A.)

1500

CHEMISTRY: *Calcination/Oxidation*
Paul Ech notes a gain in weight when silver and mercury are heated. His results are published in 1613 in a set of volumes entitled *Theatrum chemicum.*

1502

SOCIETY: *Exploration*
Amerigo Vespucci (Americus Vespucius), exploring the South American coast, recognizes that Christopher Columbus is incorrect in believing that he has found Asia. He announces that he has visited a new continent, which is named America for him, in 1507, by the mapmaker Martin Waldseemüller.

1504

THE ARTS: *Art*
Michelangelo Buonarroti completes his sculpture *David.*

1507

THE ARTS: *Art*
Leonardo da Vinci finishes painting *La Gioconda* (the Mona Lisa).

1508

THE ARTS: *Art and Religion*
In Rome, Michelangelo Buonarroti begins painting the Sistine Chapel ceiling in the Vatican.

1509

SOCIETY AND POLITICS
King Henry VIII is crowned king of England.

1512

ASTRONOMY: *Heliocentric Cosmology*
Between 1510 and 1514, Nicolaus Copernicus begins a mathematical description of a sun-centered universe. His brief manuscript, *Commentariolus,* outlines his views, which refute the geocentric astronomy of Plato, Aristotle, and Ptolemy. Copernicus's complete work, *De revolutionibus orbium coelestrium,* does not appear until 1543, the year of his death. (See second century B, ca. 367–322 B.C., 1543 B, 1573, 1609.)

1513

SOCIETY: *Exploration*
Vasco Núñez de Balboa discovers the Pacific Ocean.

1518

INFECTIOUS DISEASE: *Smallpox*
Late in the year, the inhabitants of the island of Hispaniola (Santo Domingo) are infected with smallpox brought by the Spanish. In 1492, when Christopher Columbus landed here, the population was estimated at between 1 million and 5 million. An epidemic of swine fever and the atrocities committed by the Spanish have already reduced the population considerably. By early 1519, smallpox has killed about one-third of the remaining population. The disease spreads to Puerto Rico and Cuba, leaving one-third of the population dead on these islands.

1519

A. INFECTIOUS DISEASE: *Smallpox*
The smallpox epidemic in Hispaniola, Puerto Rico, and Cuba spreads to Mexico through the Yucatan Peninsula, carried by a Spanish force led by Pánfilo de Narváez, a part of the expedition of Hernando Cortés. The epidemic spreads to the north, with devastating effects, leaving more than 50% of the Aztec population dead.

B. SOCIETY: *Exploration*
Ferdinand Magellan begins the voyage that leads to the discovery of the Straits of Magellan and the entrance to the Pacific. After Magellan is killed in the Philippines in 1521, Juan Sebastian del Cano (El Cano) completes the journey around the world in 1522 in one of the five ships that began the voyage.

1526

MEDICINE: *Medical Chemistry*
The alchemist Paracelsus (Theophrastus Bombastus von Hohenheim) publicly burns the works of Galen and Avicenna to demonstrate his disdain for ancient writings. Paracelsus is known in his time for miraculous cures through his use of opium and preparations of mercury and other metallic medicines. He derives medicinal substances from plants, animals, and minerals and encourages alchemists to use distillation and extraction to obtain healing essences. He believes in the four elements of Empedocles, but he emphasizes three principles: salt, sulfur, and mercury. He is now regarded as a complex individual who was both a healer and physician, but also a magician and fraud.

1530

A. INFECTIOUS DISEASE: *Syphilis*
The name of the disease syphilis is derived from a poem entitled "Syphilis sive Morbus Gallicus," written by Girolamo Fracastoro. The poem describes the travails of the shepherd Syphylis, who suffers from the disease. The name Syphylis may have been derived from the mythological story of

Sipylus, a shepherd whom Apollo destroyed because of wrath toward Sipylus's mother Niobe, who was turned to stone on Mount Sipylus.

B. BOTANICAL ILLUSTRATION

The illustrations in Dioscorides' *De materia medica* and its imitators have become exceedingly unlike the actual appearance of plants. Plants are shown in more realistic drawings when Otto Brunfels and artist Hans Weiditz publish *Herbarum vivae eicones* (Living portraits of plants). Brunfels intends a new edition of Dioscorides' work with traditional text but also includes plants from his own region, which Weiditz paints as he sees them, showing insect damage, withered leaves, and other defects. A contemporary of Brunfels, Leonhart Fuchs, breaks further away from Dioscorides in 1542 with even more accurate drawings. (See 1542.)

1535

A. HERBAL MEDICINE

Valerius Cordus describes drugs, chemicals, and medical preparations in a pharmacopoeia called *Dispensatorium*.

B. SOCIETY AND POLITICS

Thomas More, who writes the fictional *Utopia* in 1515, and is later lord chancellor under Henry VIII, is executed by the king for refusing to swear an oath under the Act of Supremacy.

1542

MODERN BOTANY

Leonhart Fuchs publishes his book *De historia stirpium,* which breaks even further away from Dioscorides' *De materia medica* than did the work of Otto Brunfels and Hans Weiditz in 1530. Fuchs employs three artists: one who draws from nature, one who copies the drawings onto wood blocks, and one who carves the blocks for printing. Although the text still relies heavily on Dioscorides, the drawings include numerous plants from Germany and other countries, all presented with great accuracy. This volume establishes a standard that will be followed by other botanical texts. (See 77 B, 1530 B.)

1543

A. ANATOMY: *Human Anatomy*

Andreas Vesalius describes human anatomy in *De humani corporis fabrica,* with detailed drawings by Jan van Calcar.

B. ASTRONOMY: *Heliocentric Cosmology*

The complete work of Nicolaus Copernicus, *De revolutionibus orbium coelestium,* is published in the year of his death (he receives a copy while on his death bed). Copernicus has resisted making his work public because of criticism received from the theologian Martin Luther and from those who adhere to the geocentric concepts of Ptolemy. He is nonetheless persuaded by friends to allow publication, not knowing that Andreas Osiander, who supervises the printing, has written an unsigned preface which presents the work as hypothesis rather than fact. (See 367–322 B.C., second century B, 1512, 1573, 1609.)

1545

BIBLIOGRAPHY

Conrad Gesner publishes the first volume of *Bibliotheca universalis,* containing the titles of all known books in Greek, Latin, and Hebrew. He includes summaries and criticism of each. He is sometimes called the "father of bibliography." (See 1546 B.)

1546

A. INFECTIOUS DISEASE: *the Germ Theory*

Girolamo Fracastoro publishes *De contagione,* in which he proposes that infections and epidemics are caused by "seminaria," or seeds of disease. He may have regarded seminaria as living, but he also compares them to the exhalations from onions that cause tearing. He suggests three modes of transmission: direct contact, fomites (inanimate objects), and contagion at a distance (through the air). In the second book of *De contagione,* Fracastoro describes many contagions, including variola, measles, typhus fever (or typhoid fever), consumption (tuberculosis), and hydrophobia (rabies). (See 1762 A.)

B. MODERN ZOOLOGY

Conrad Gesner publishes *Historia animalium,* a description of all known animals, which is often regarded as the beginning of modern zoology. He speculates about real as well as mythical animals, such as a 300-foot-long sea serpent. His descriptions give origin, methods of capture, domestication, and use in medicine. At the time of his death he was preparing *Historia plantarum,* which was to include beautiful illustrations. These illustrations were subsequently lost but rediscovered and published in eight volumes, between 1973 and 1980.

1553

INFECTIOUS DISEASE: *Scarlet Fever*

Giovanni Filippo Ingrassia describes scarlet fever as a rash of small and large spots of a fiery red color and distinguishes it from the skin eruptions of measles. (See 1670 B.)

1558

SOCIETY AND POLITICS

Elizabeth I is crowned queen of England.

1559

ANATOMY: *Circulation of Blood*

Realdo Colombo rediscovers the lesser circulation of the blood from the heart through the lungs. His observations are among those that William Harvey uses in his studies on general circulation. In his book *De re anatomica,* Colombo describes the human embryo, the front lens of the eye, the peritoneum, and the pleura. (See 280 B.C., 1603, 1616, 1628.)

1561

ANATOMY: *Fallopian Tubes*

Fallopius (Gabriele Fallopio) publishes a treatise on the female reproductive system, in which he describes the tubes, later named the Fallopian tubes, that connect the ovaries and uterus.

1572

INFECTIOUS DISEASE: *Infections of the Skin*
Geronimo Mercuriali describes skin diseases in *De morbis cutaneis et omnibus corporis humani excrementis tractatus.*

1573

ASTRONOMY: *Supernova*
Tycho Brahe publishes *De nova stella,* describing a nova, later recognized as a supernova, that appears in 1572 in Cassiopeia. His discovery of a "new" object in the unchanging heavens establishes his reputation as a leader in astronomy. The king of Denmark provides financial assistance and the gift of an island, enabling Tycho to build an observatory equipped with the best available instruments and clocks. Tycho's concept of the planetary system was that all planets except the earth revolve around the sun and that this complex of sun and planets revolves around the earth. Johannes Kepler, Tycho's assistant in the 2 years before his death, supervises the posthumous publication of his catalog of 777 stars and observations on the sun and planets. (See 1609.)

1576

INFECTIOUS DISEASE: *Diphtheria*
Guillaume de Baillou, an early epidemiologist, describes a diphtheria epidemic in Paris. (See 1492 A, 1748 B, 1765 B.)

1579

THE ARTS: *Literature*
Thomas North translates *Lives of the Noble Grecians and Romans, Plutarch's Lives,* by the Roman biographer Plutarch, into English from an earlier French translation by Jacques Amyot.

1580

INFECTIOUS DISEASE: *Influenza*
The term *influentia coeli,* meaning celestial influence, is used to describe an epidemic that occurs in the year 1357 in Florence, Italy. The name, afterward used by other writers, becomes "influenza." (See 1732, 1781 A, 1830 A.)

1582

A. PHYSICS: *the Pendulum*
Galileo (Galileo Galilei) notices that the arcs of a swinging altar lamp in the Cathedral of Pisa seem to take the same time (as measured by his pulse rate) regardless of their length. He thus discovers the isochronism, or periodicity, of the pendulum. Late in his life he attempts to apply this principle to clocks, but it is not until 1657 that Christiaan Huygens, working with a Dutch clock maker, succeeds in building a pendulum clock. (See 1590 B, 1610.)

B. SOCIETY AND POLITICS
Pope Gregory XIII adopts a calendar designed by Christoph Clavius that corrects the Julian calendar's problem of having too many leap years, resulting in the addition of 3 days in a 400-year period. The new calendar omits

1582 *(continued)*

the leap year in years ending in hundreds unless they can be divided by 400. To correct the error of 11 days caused by the Julian calendar, Pope Gregory ordains that October 4 be followed by October 15 in the year 1582. The Gregorian calendar is immediately adopted in Catholic Europe but not adopted in Russia, Protestant England, and Protestant America. England and America make the change in 1752, Russia in 1918.

1583

BOTANY: *Plant Classification*
Andrea Cesalpino publishes *De plantis,* the first scientific classification of plants, based on the fruits and roots. He also discovers plant veins and describes seed structure and germination.

1585

MATHEMATICS: *Decimals*
Simon Stevinus publishes a booklet entitled *De thiende* (The tenth, or The tithe) illustrating the use of the decimal system. His cumbersome notation, using superscripts, is replaced with the decimal point by John Napier, inventor of logarithms. Although Stevinus's booklet leads to greater use of decimals, he is not the first to invent a decimal system, a type of decimal notation having been used in Babylon as early as 2205 B.C. Decimal systems were in use in India in the fifth and seventh centuries and in Spain in the 11th century and were introduced into England in about 1250 by Johannes de Sacrobosco (John Halifax), a mathematician who wrote an astronomy text based on Ptolemaic principles. (See 499, 1250 B.)

1586

PHYSICS: *Falling Bodies*
Simon Stevinus, by dropping objects of different weights from a height, finds that the speed of falling bodies is not proportional to their weight, as Aristotle had stated. In 1590, Galileo arrives at the same conclusion, possibly from the same type of experiment. Galileo's development of a law of falling bodies gives his work greater recognition. (See 1590 A.)

1587

THE ARTS: *Music*
Claudio Monteverdi publishes his first book of madrigals.

1588

SOCIETY AND POLITICS
The English Royal Navy defeats a large Spanish armada, with the assistance of a large storm.

1590

A. OPTICAL INSTRUMENTS: *the Microscope*
This year is often cited as the date of the invention of the microscope. Credit is usually given to Hans Jansen and his son Zacharias Jansen, who is only 2 years old in 1590, making the father-son collaboration impossible. Another claim is that the Jansens invent the telescope by about 1610, but Hans Jansen dies in 1593. By 1623 to 1624 Cornelius Drebbel in England,

Galileo in Italy, and James Metius in Holland make microscopes that are used for scientific observations. See 1608 for further information on the telescope.

B. PHYSICS: *Falling Bodies*
Galileo's studies on falling bodies, published in *De motu,* contradicts Aristotle's view that the rate of fall is related to the weight of the object. Rather, he demonstrates that all objects fall at the same rate if there is no air resistance. He is preceded in this claim by Simon Stevinus in 1586, but Galileo goes further by developing a law of falling bodies. (See 1586, 1582 A, 1610.)

C. THE ARTS: *Literature / Theater*
William Shakespeare composes the first part of *Henry VI,* a play in three parts.

1592

THE ARTS: *Theater*
Doctor Faustus, a play by Christopher Marlowe, is performed in London.

1596

MATHEMATICS: *Calculation of π*
Ludolph von Ceulen, in Cologne, calculates π to 20 decimal places, later to 35 places. (See 1700 B.C., 190, 600, 1706.)

1598

SOCIETY AND POLITICS
Boris Godunov becomes czar of Russia upon the death of Fedor I.

1600

A. PHYSICS: *Magnetism and Electricity*
William Gilbert publishes *De magnete, magneticisque corporibus, et de magno magnete tellure, physiologia nova,* reporting his experiments and observations on magnetism and electricity. He is the first to believe that the earth is a magnet and that magnetism and electricity produced by rubbing amber and certain jewels are manifestations of a single type of force. He uses the word "electrics," derived from the Greek word for amber, to describe materials that are electrified by rubbing. In 1646, Thomas Browne first uses the word "electricity." (See 550 B.C., 1660 B, 1745 B.)

B. THE ARTS: *Music*
Eurydice by Jacopo Peri, the first grand opera, is performed in Florence, Italy.

C. THE ARTS: *Literature / Theater*
William Shakespeare's *Twelfth Night* is first performed.

1603

ANATOMY: *Valves in Veins*
Hieronymus Fabricius ab Aquapendente (Girolamo Fabrici) publishes *De venarum ostiolis,* in which he illustrates the valves in the veins, having learned of them in about 1574 from Salomon Alberti, and lectures about them in 1578 or 1579. Fabricius is the teacher of William Harvey, who lectures about his discoveries of the circulation of blood in 1616 and publishes them in 1628. (See 280 B.C., 1616, 1628.)

1605

THE ARTS: *Literature*
Miguel de Cervantes writes the first part of *The History of the Valorous and Witty Knight-Errant Don Quixote.*

1606

A. CHEMISTRY: *Phlogiston*
Hapelius (Raphael Eglin) uses the term "phlogiston" to describe a quality relating to perfection or imperfection of metals when burned. Johann Becher, in 1668, and Georg Ernst Stahl, in 1697, use the word phlogiston to mean a substance released by combustion. (See 1668 C, 1697 A.)

B. THE ARTS: *Literature / Theater*
William Shakespeare writes *Macbeth.*

1607

A. INFECTIOUS DISEASE: *the Jamestown Colony*
The Jamestown colony is founded in Virginia by English explorers. More than one-half of the 105 persons who land there die during the summer of this year. In the period up to 1624, 6,454 of 7,549 colonists die. The period of 1609 to 1610 is referred to as the "starving time" of the colonists, leading some writers to believe that beriberi (a vitamin B_1 deficiency) causes many deaths. Others, who discount this claim, conclude that symptoms described are those of typhoid fever, possibly brought by a passenger on a ship from England.

B. THE ARTS: *Music*
Although Jacopo Peri's *Eurydice* is usually regarded as being the first opera, *Orfeo,* written by Claudio Monteverdi, is thought by many to be the first great opera. It is commissioned by the Duke of Mantua and performed there in this year.

1608

OPTICAL INSTRUMENTS: *the Telescope*
Although the combination of two simple lenses to make a telescope seems to have occurred at about this time, it is difficult to assign credit to any one person. There is evidence that Hans Lippershey and James Metius (Jacob Adriaanzoon) each invent a telescope in 1608. Both Lippershey and Metius submit petitions to the Dutch government for permission to manufacture such an instrument. While Lippershey's instrument is tested and at least one of them is purchased by the government, no one ever sees an instrument made by Metius. Zacharias Jansen's son, Johannes Sachariassen, contributes to the confusion by asserting in 1655 that his father, born in 1588, invented the telescope in 1590. This erroneous statement is reported in *De vero telescopii inventore,* a book by Pierre Borel that appears in 1655 to 1656. Borel's information comes from William Boreel, a childhood friend of Zacharias Jansen. There is no other evidence of Zacharias Jansen's claim that he invented the telescope. Boreel states that Adrian Metius, James Metius's brother, and Cornelius Drebbel purchased telescopes in Jansen's shop, but since the word "microscope" does not come into use until 1625,

it is possible that what they purchased was, in fact, microscopes. The word "telescope" is suggested in 1611 by a Greek poet at a banquet in Rome honoring Galileo. (See 1590.)

1609

ASTRONOMY: *Planetary Motion*
Johannes Kepler, an assistant of Tycho Brahe, publishes *Astronomica nova,* in which he shows that the planets move in ellipses, not circles. By breaking with the Ptolemaic ideas of cycles and epicycles, Kepler establishes his first and second laws of planetary motion, explained in terms of magnetic forces, being influenced by the work of William Gilbert. His third law appears in 1619 in *De harmonica mundi,* which also contains a compendium of supposed harmonies in nature. In 1627, Kepler publishes the ephemerides of the planets, based on his laws, as well as an extension of Tycho's catalog of stars, now numbering 1,005. (See 1573.)

1610

ASTRONOMY: *the Moon and Planets*
Galileo, after learning of the invention of the telescope in Holland, constructs a refracting telescope, which he uses to view celestial objects. In this year he publishes *Sidereus nuncius* (Sidereal messenger) describing many new astronomical discoveries, including mountains and plains on the moon. He assumes that the largest dark areas are seas and names them *marias.* He also observes three of Jupiter's satellites (named the Medicean Stars)—he later sees a fourth, and the vast number of stars in the Milky Way. Having noted that Venus moves around the sun, Galileo becomes a strong advocate of the Copernican heliocentric universe but is admonished by the Catholic Church for his views. He compounds his problems with the church in 1632 with his publication of *Dialogo sopra i due masimi sistemi del mondo* (Dialogue of the two principal systems of the world), in which three characters debate Aristotle's and Galileo's beliefs, with the supporter of Galileo winning the argument. He is subsequently required to appear before the Inquisition in Rome and forced to recant. Galileo spends the remainder of his life under house arrest near Florence. In 1638, his most important book, *Discorsi e dimostranzioni matematiche intorno a due nove scienze* (Discourses on the two new sciences), presents the laws of falling bodies in a vacuum, the principle of independent forces, and the theory of parabolic ballistics.

1611

LITERATURE AND RELIGION
The King James Bible is published.

1612

THE ARTS: *Art and Architecture*
Construction of the Louvre in Paris begins. It is completed in 1690.

1614

A. PHYSIOLOGY AND METABOLISM
Santorius (Santorio Santorio) studies metabolism by attempting to correlate food intake with human weight by eating and drinking while sitting in a

1614 *(continued)*

weighing chair suspended from a steelyard, in which he spends most of his time over a period of 30 years.

B. MATHEMATICS: *Logarithms*

John Napier completes and publishes a table of exponents of the number 2 that he calls "logarithms." He accomplishes multiplication and division by addition and subtraction of logarithms. (See 1617 B, 1620 A, 1621.)

1616

ANATOMY: *Circulation of Blood*

William Harvey describes some of his early experiments of heart action and circulation of blood. His first publication of this work is in 1628. (See 280 B.C., 1559, 1603.)

1617

A. CHEMISTRY: *Copper Vitriol*

Angelo Sala prepares copper vitriol from weighed amounts of copper, sulfuric acid, and water. After decomposing the copper vitriol, he finds the same proportions of components as in the original mixture.

B. MATHEMATICS: *Logarithms*

John Napier describes the use of "bones" for logarithmic calculations. (See 1614, 1620, 1622.)

1618

SOCIETY AND POLITICS

The Thirty Years' War begins in Prague when two Catholic governors are thrown from windows by Protestants—the so-called defenestration of Prague. The war devastates much of Europe until 1648.

1620

A. MATHEMATICS: *Slide Rule*

Edmund Gunter devises Gunter's scale, a forerunner of the slide rule, with logarithms along the scale that facilitate multiplying and dividing. (See 1617 B, 1622.)

B. THE SCIENTIFIC METHOD

Repudiating the ideas of deductive logic advanced by Aristotle and his followers, Francis Bacon describes the importance of inductive reasoning in scientific experimentation and in studies of nature. His book *Novum organum* is the first to discuss scientific induction as a component of the scientific method.

C. SOCIETY AND POLITICS

Pilgrims land at Plymouth, Massachusetts.

1622

MATHEMATICS: *Slide Rule*

William Oughtred converts Napier's "bones" and Gunter's scale into the slide rule. (See 1617 B, 1620 A.)

1623

A. INFECTIOUS DISEASE: *Yellow Fever*

Aleixo de Abreu writes an account of *enfermedad del gusano,* which is believed to be the first description of yellow fever.

B. BOTANY: *Plant Classification/Binomial Names*

Gaspard Bauhin uses binomial names in the classification of plants. (See 1737.)

1624

A. FERMENTATION: *Ferment*

Jean Beguin publishes a treatise on chemistry that uses the word *fermentum* to refer to the agent required to start a *fermentatio,* such as the conversion of cereal dough to bread. However, the exact meaning of the word *fermentatio* is not clear, as it has been applied to almost any natural change in both the living and nonliving. *Fermentum* becomes *ferment* in later usage.

B. SOCIETY AND POLITICS

Cardinal Richelieu dominates the French court under Louis XIII as chief minister until his death.

C. SOCIETY: *History*

Captain John Smith writes *General History of Virginia,* in which he tells the story of how an American Indian princess, Pocahontas, saves him from death.

1625

OPTICAL INSTRUMENTS: *the Microscope*

Giovanni Faber coins the word "microscope."

1626

A. PHYSIOLOGY: *Body Temperature*

Santorius measures human body temperature with a thermoscope.

B. SOCIETY AND POLITICS

Manhattan Island, later to be a part of New York City, is bought from the Canarsie chiefs of the Wappinger Confederacy by the Dutch.

1628

ANATOMY: *Circulation*

William Harvey publishes *De motu cordis,* the results of his research and conclusions on the circulation of blood. (See 280 B.C., 1559, 1603, 1616.)

1630

A. INFECTIOUS DISEASE: *Smallpox*

The Massachusetts Bay Colony established by British colonists reports its first cases of smallpox. An epidemic among the Indians ensues in 1634 with many deaths.

B. CHEMISTRY: *Calcination/Oxidation*

Having no conception of chemical combination, Jean Rey writes that the increase in weight of metals heated in air is caused by the adhesion (physical absorption) of air to the metal. Rey's work is little known and receives almost no recognition.

1634

SOCIETY: *Architecture*
Construction begins on the Taj Mahal, near Agra, India. It is completed in 1648, serving as a mosque, meeting hall, and mausoleum.

1636

CULTURE: *Universities*
Harvard College, later Harvard University, is founded in Massachusetts. It is named in 1639 after John Harvard, a principal endower of the college, an English clergyman living in Massachusetts.

1637

MATHEMATICS AND PHILOSOPHY
Several publications by René Descartes appear, including *Discours de la méthode, La dioptrique, Les météores,* and *La géométrie.* Published posthumously in 1664 are *L'Homme* and *De la formation du foetus.* In addition to *Discours,* his *Meditationes de prima philosophia* (1641) and *Principia philosophiae* (1644) lay out his philosophical doctrine of systematic doubt, his proposition *cogito ergo sum* (I think, therefore I am), and his ideas concerning dualism of mind and matter. He is the creator of analytic geometry, and the Latinized form of his name, Renatus Cartesius, gives rise to such terms as Cartesian geometry, Cartesian coordinates, and Cartesian curves. Although he makes no physiological discoveries, he influences the history of physiology with his writings by extending his concepts of the universe to include the claim that the human body is a machine that works according to physical laws. He also applies the works of Vesalius (1543) and William Harvey (1628) to his conclusions about circulation of blood, respiration, and digestion. He believes that the pineal gland is the seat of the soul.

1640

INFECTIOUS DISEASE: *Whooping Cough*
Guillaume de Baillou, in his posthumously published *Epidemiorum et ephemeridium,* provides a clear description of whooping cough. (See 1679.)

1641

A. TECHNOLOGY: *Adding Machine*
Blaise Pascal invents a machine that will add and subtract.

B. THE ARTS: *Art*
Rembrandt van Rijn paints *The Night Watch.*

1643

A. PHYSICS: *Barometer*
Evangelista Torricelli invents the barometer (published in 1663). He finds that a vacuum is created above a tube containing mercury when the tube is inverted in a dish of mercury. He notes that a 30-inch column of mercury is supported by air pressure. (See 1646 B.)

B. SOCIETY AND POLITICS
King Louis XIII of France dies, to be succeeded by his 4-year-old son, who reigns as Louis XIV until 1715. Until 1661, the government is controlled by Cardinal Giulio Mazarin.

1645

1646

TECHNOLOGY: *Air Pump*
Otto von Guericke invents the air pump (published in 1672). (See 1654.)

A. INFECTIOUS DISEASE: *Imperceptible Creatures*
Athanasius Kircher writes on many subjects, both physical and biological. His *Ars magna lucis et umbrae* includes a drawing of a magnifying glass, and in 1658 his *Scrutinium phisico-medicum pestis* discusses small, imperceptible living bodies that are sources of contagion and that can penetrate clothing, ropes, linen sheets, and anything else that has small pores. Because Kircher's writings are ambiguous, often incomprehensible, most students of his work regard them as being of little if any value.

B. PHYSICS: *Barometer*
Blaise Pascal repeats Torricelli's experiments with the mercury barometer. Using both water and red wine in a 40-foot tube, he finds that a 34-foot column of water or a 34.6-foot column of wine is supported. He therefore concludes that a fundamental force is at work. (See 1643 B.)

C. SOCIETY AND POLITICS
A civil war that began in England in 1642 ends with the defeat of King Charles I by Calvinists led by Oliver Cromwell.

1648

A. CHEMISTRY: *Evolution from Alchemy*
The complete works of Johannes Baptista van Helmont are published posthumously by his son Francis Mercurius van Helmont. van Helmont's writings mark an evolution from the teachings of alchemists like Paracelsus and lead to the beginnings of the science of chemistry. Among the many topics discussed are van Helmont's invention of the word "gas," referring to the gas from burning wood and from fermentations as "gas sylvestre," or wood gas. He differentiates gas from air, noting its production as a "wild spirit" from fermentations and chemical reactions of other types. He describes ferments that produce gas as supernatural entities. He proposes that digestion of food is a chemical process in which a series of fermentations convert food into flesh. He explains his famous experiment of 5 years' duration in which he waters a willow tree growing in an earthenware pot and attributes its gain in weight to the uptake of water. This experiment was described earlier by Cardinal P. Nicolai Cusa, but it is not clear whether or not he actually performed it, nor is it known whether or not van Helmont was aware of Cusa's idea. (See 1659 B.)

B. SOCIETY AND POLITICS
The Thirty Years' War that swept throughout Europe ends with the Peace of Westphalia.

1649

SOCIETY AND POLITICS
King Charles I of England is condemned for treason by Parliament and beheaded. Parliament abolishes the monarchy and the House of Lords and

1649 *(continued)*

declares England to be a commonwealth, with Oliver Cromwell as lord protector.

1651

SOCIETY AND POLITICS

Thomas Hobbes publishes *Leviathan,* a book on political philosophy that asserts that the monarchy must have absolute power and that the people must surrender their individual rights to the sovereign. (See 1690 B.)

1653

A. ANATOMY: *the Lymphatic System*

Olaf Rudbeck discovers the lymphatics, the system of circulatory vessels that carry lymph from the tissues back to the blood.

B. THE ARTS: *Literature*

Izaak Walton writes *The Compleat Angler.*

1654

TECHNOLOGY: *Vacuum Pump*

Otto von Guericke uses the air pump that he invented in 1645 to conduct experiments with air pressure and vacuums. He conducts a famous experiment in which two teams of eight horses fail to pull apart an evacuated metal globe formed from two separate hemispheres.

1657

A. TECHNOLOGY: *the Pendulum Clock*

Christiaan Huygens, assisted by a Dutch clock maker, constructs a pendulum clock. Although Vincenzio Galilei, son of Galileo, constructed pendulum clocks as early as 1641, Huygens' clock is the first to keep accurate time. Unfortunately, its accuracy fails on board moving ships. Huygens is acquainted with Antony van Leeuwenhoek and may have given him advice on the making of lenses for microscopes.

B. SOCIETY AND POLITICS

Holy Roman Emperor Ferdinand III dies and is succeeded by his son, who will reign as Leopold I until 1704.

1658

ANATOMY: *Red Blood Cells*

Jan Swammerdam is reported to have been the first to describe red blood cells observed microscopically in frog's blood.

1659

A. INFECTIOUS DISEASE: *Typhoid Fever*

Thomas Willis, in *De febribus,* describes the symptoms of typhoid fever.

B. FERMENTATION AND PUTREFACTION: *Mechanism*

Thomas Willis adopts Johannes van Helmont's fermentative physiology in a book that describes fermentation as an internal motion of particles. He compares fermentation and putrefaction to the separation of things into parts and mentions protection against putrefaction afforded by spices, brine, pickling, and sugar. (See 1648 A.)

1660

A. PHYSIOLOGY: *Animal Respiration*
Robert Boyle experiments with a burning candle in a bell jar enclosing a mouse and a sparrow and observes that the animals die much sooner than they do when in a jar without the burning candle. He also finds that a flame is extinguished and an animal dies in a container evacuated by means of an air pump. To explain the death of the animals, he suggests that a "vital spirit" is part of the air.

B. PHYSICS: *Static Electricity*
Otto von Guericke demonstrates that a ball of sulfur mounted on a crankshaft accumulates a sizable amount of static electricity when it is lightly rubbed while rotating. He also observes that static electricity produces light. (See 585 B.C., 1600 A, 1745 B.)

C. SOCIETY AND POLITICS
Oliver Cromwell dies in 1658, leaving the position of lord protector of the Commonwealth of England to his son Richard Cromwell. In 1660, the son of King Charles I, who was in exile on the continent, returns to England and is crowned Charles II, beginning the period of the Restoration.

D. THE ARTS: *Literature*
Samuel Pepys begins his *Diary*.

1661

A. ANATOMY: *Circulation of Blood*
Marcello Malpighi's observations of red blood cells and capillary circulation in frog's lungs completes William Harvey's description of circulation. He thinks that red blood cells are fat globules. In *De motu cordis,* Harvey mentions that he will discuss the anastomoses between the arterial and venous systems, but he does not do so. (See 1628.)

B. CHEMISTRY: *Description of Elements*
Robert Boyle writes *The Sceptical Chymist,* in which he ridicules Aristotle's "elements" of air, earth, fire, and water and Paracelsus's "principles" of sulfur, salt, and mercury. He defines a chemical element as a substance that cannot be made from other substances or changed into other substances. Although he does not give a list of substances that he considers to be elements, his definition becomes widely quoted. Boyle is referred to as the founder of modern chemistry because of his definition of chemical elements and the realization that chemistry can be studied as a science without relation to medicine or alchemy. He also introduces the experimental method into chemistry.

1662

A. CHEMISTRY: *Boyle's Gas Law*
In an appendix to a new edition of his 1660 book, *New Experiments Physico-Mechanicall,* Robert Boyle states, in what is known as Boyle's law, that the pressure and volume of a gas at constant temperature are inversely proportional. (See 1687.)

1662 *(continued)*

B. SCIENTIFIC SOCIETIES
King Charles II of England charters the Royal Society of London.

C. THE ARTS: *Architecture*
King Louis XIV of France begins building his palace at Versailles.

1664

A. PHYSIOLOGY: *Animal Respiration*
By causing air to blow continuously through the lungs of a dog, Robert Hooke shows that it is fresh air and not movement of the lungs that is essential to life.

B. SOCIETY AND POLITICS
New Amsterdam becomes New York.

1665

A. INFECTIOUS DISEASE: *Bubonic Plague*
The great plague of London kills more than 60,000 people. More than two-thirds of the population flee the city to avoid infection, but the plague is not confined to London. Nearly all of those living in some smaller villages are killed. Some attribute the fact that London is never again struck by a pandemic of plague to the Great Fire of 1666, which burns houses built closely together. The fire is confined to the Old City, however, where the plague is not as great as in other areas that are not burned.

B. BIOLOGY: *the Cell*
Robert Hooke publishes *Micrographia* with drawings of higher organisms, molds, and rusts. He introduces the term "cell" to describe the microscopic appearance of cork.

C. CHEMISTRY: *Combustion*
Robert Hooke proposes a theory of combustion in which he describes air as being composed of two substances, one required for combustion and the other inert. He also notes that plants need to breathe.

D. MATHEMATICS: *Calculus*
Isaac Newton writes about fluxions, probably the first form of differential calculus.

E. SCIENTIFIC PUBLICATION: *Royal Society of London*
The first issue of *Philosophical Transactions of the Royal Society of London,* the oldest surviving scientific journal, appears. Henry Oldenberg, secretary of the Royal Society and the person to whom Antony van Leeuwenhoek's letters are sent, manages its publication and may be considered the first journal editor. (See 1673 A.)

F. THE ARTS: *Music*
Antonio Stradivari labels his first violin.

1666

A. PHYSICS: *Spectrum of Light / Prisms*
Isaac Newton, while experimenting with a prism, discovers that white light is composed of a series of colors.

B. PHYSICS: *Gravitation*

Isaac Newton observes an apple fall from a tree and wonders why the moon does not also fall. His thoughts and calculations on these phenomena lead to a theory of gravitation, published in *Principia mathematica* in 1687.

C. SOCIETY AND POLITICS

The Great Fire destroys most of London's old city.

1667

A. INFECTIOUS DISEASE: *Smallpox*

A smallpox epidemic in Britain, in 1667 and 1668, causes at least 2,700 deaths in London alone. In 1669, Thomas Sydenham, described by some as an English Hippocrates, begins writing a description of smallpox, never to be completed, which deals largely with treatment. Even though the practice of variolization (inoculation) becomes known throughout Europe within a few years, smallpox epidemics continue for centuries. (See 1715 A, 1717, 1721 A, 1764 A.)

B. MICROSCOPY: *Binocular Microscope*

Chérubin d'Orleans designs the first binocular microscope.

C. THE ARTS: *Literature*

John Milton publishes *Paradise Lost*.

1668

A. BIOLOGY: *Spontaneous Generation of Life*

Francesco Redi performs one of the earliest controlled experiments to investigate whether or not life spontaneously arises from inanimate substances. He places meat into two dishes, leaving one open to the air and the other covered. He repeats the experiment leaving one dish open and the other covered with gauze. In both experiments, maggots appear only in the uncovered dishes. Very few people are convinced by his experiments that life cannot be spontaneously generated. (See 1748 A, 1765 A, 1858 A.)

B. CHEMISTRY: *Air and Combustion*

Johannes Mayow describes combustion and respiration as involving the "igneo-aërial" portion of air.

C. CHEMISTRY: *Combustion*

Johann Joachim Becher uses the term *terra pinguis,* meaning inflammable, to describe material released during the burning of matter. Georg Ernst Stahl later uses the term "phlogiston" in a similar context. (See 1697 A.)

1669

A. ANATOMY: *Circulation of Blood*

Richard Lower shows that the blood in the pulmonary vein is of arterial color before it reaches the heart.

B. BIOLOGY: *Life Cycles of Insects*

Jan Swammerdam publishes *Historia insectorum generalis,* in which he describes the life cycles of the mayfly, the honeybee, and other insects. After his death in 1680, his drawings of many biological observations are published, in 1737–1738, in *Biblia naturae.* He is considered the father of modern entomology.

1670

A. INFECTIOUS DISEASE: *Dysentery*
Thomas Sydenham describes a disease, probably a form of dysentery, that causes "great torment of the bowels," sometimes accompanied by fever. He states that it is usually fatal for the elderly but less so for the young.

B. INFECTIOUS DISEASE: *Measles*
Thomas Sydenham writes "Of Measles in the Year 1670," giving such an accurate description of the disease that it becomes possible for physicians to distinguish between measles and smallpox.

C. SOCIETY: *Economic Development*
The Hudson's Bay Company is founded to trade in North America.

1671

A. CHEMISTRY: *Discovery of Hydrogen*
Robert Boyle, by dissolving iron in hydrochloric or sulfuric acid, produces an inflammable gas, named hydrogen (*hidrogène*) in 1787 by Guyton de Morveau. Nicolas Lemery, in 1700, and Henry Cavendish, in 1766, obtain hydrogen by similar experiments.

B. THE ARTS: *Art*
Christopher Wren begins construction of "The Monument," commemorating the Great Fire of 1666 in London.

1673

A. OPTICAL INSTRUMENTS: *Leeuwenhoek's Microscopes*
Antony van Leeuwenhoek's first correspondence to the Royal Society of London is conveyed by Regnier de Graaf, the discoverer of Graafian follicles, to Henry Oldenberg, secretary of the Royal Society. Leeuwenhoek's letter describes his microscopic observations of mold, the sting and mouth parts of the bee, and the sting of the louse. Over the years that follow, he sends more than 200 letters describing many observations with the use of his microscopes. Leeuwenhoek makes both plano-convex and biconvex lenses for a simple microscope. Modern measurements show that his instruments achieve magnifications ranging from 30 to 200 diameters, with numerical apertures from 0.1 to 0.4. One of Leeuwenhoek's great contributions is to provide measurements of objects. He reports the sizes of grains of sand (1/30 to 1/100 of an inch), of the eye of a louse (1/250 to 1/400 of an inch), and of human red blood cells (1/3,000 of an inch). (See 1674 A, 1676, 1677, 1680, 1683 B.)

B. CHEMISTRY: *Combustion/Calcination*
Robert Boyle publishes two papers on the calcination of metals, in which he concludes that flame incorporated into the metals increases their weight. He thus retrogresses from the earlier ideas of Jean Rey. (See 1630 B.)

C. SOCIETY: *Exploration*
Jacques Marquette and Louis Joliet discover the headwaters of the Mississippi River.

1674

A. MICROSCOPY: *Protozoa, Algae, Red Blood Cells*

Antony van Leeuwenhoek describes protozoa, which he is the first to see, as "very many little animalcules." He also sees a green alga, possibly *Spirogyra,* and red blood corpuscles in human blood, noting that they cause the redness of blood. (See 1673 A, 1676, 1677, 1680, 1683 A.)

B. THE ARTS: *Literature*

Nicholas Boileau-Despréaux writes *L'Art Poétique.*

1675

A. INFECTIOUS DISEASE: *Scarlet Fever*

In describing *febris scarlatina,* Thomas Sydenham is credited with giving the disease its name as well as distinguishing it from smallpox. The name, however, may have been in common use, because Samuel Pepys writes in his *Diary* on the date of November 10, 1664, that his daughter Susan is sick with the measles, "or, at least, of a scarlett feavour." (See 1553.)

B. PHYSIOLOGY: *Animal Respiration*

Johannes Mayow places a small animal in a jar inverted over a container of water and notes that the animal consumes a portion of the air, as shown by a rise in the level of water in the jar. Also using a candle in a bell jar experiment with flies, bees, and other insects, he concludes that one of two components of air, "spiritus nitro-aereus," supports life and combustion.

1676

BACTERIOLOGY: *First Microscopic Observation of Bacteria*

Examining a preparation of pepper water with one of his microscopes, Antony van Leeuwenhoek observes some organisms that are "incredibly small" as compared with protozoa. We may assume that he sees bacteria for the first time. (See 1673 A, 1674 A, 1677, 1680, 1683 A.)

1677

MICROSCOPY: *Spermatozoa*

Antony van Leeuwenhoek is the first to observe animal spermatozoa. (See 1673 A, 1674 A, 1676, 1680, 1683 A.)

1678

FERMENTATION: *Champagne*

Dom Pérignon, in the province of Champagne, France, adds sugar to a cask of wine to start a second fermentation. The resulting wine, sparkling, or effervescent, is given the name champagne.

1679

INFECTIOUS DISEASE: *Pertussis, or Whooping Cough*

Thomas Sydenham describes the symptoms of a disease that he names pertussis, meaning severe cough. (See 1640.)

1680

A. INFECTIOUS DISEASE: *Tuberculosis*

John Bunyan refers to tuberculosis (phthisis) as the "Captain of all these men of death" in his book *The Life and Death of Mr. Badman.*

1680 *(continued)*

B. MICROSCOPY: *Yeast*

Antony van Leeuwenhoek is the first to observe yeast microscopically. (See 1673 A, 1674 A, 1676, 1677, 1683 A.)

C. FERMENTATION: *Substrate*

Johann Becher finds that sugar is necessary for fermentation.

1681

A. OPTICAL INSTRUMENTS: *the Ocular*

Christiaan Huygens devises an ocular lens for the telescope that is subsequently used for the compound microscope.

B. TECHNOLOGY: *Autoclave*

Denys Papin describes a forerunner of the autoclave when he writes of an "engine for softning bones" that he uses to obtain gelatin from animal bones.

1682

A. BIOLOGY: *Definition of Species*

John Ray publishes *Methodus plantarum nova,* in which he offers the first definition of "species" as a set of individuals whose reproduction produces new individuals similar to themselves. He applies his definition to both plants and animals. Ray is the first to divide flowering plants into monocotyledons and dicotyledons. He has a strong belief in the fixity of species but recognizes that some minor changes are possible. (See 1686.)

B. BOTANY: *Plant Anatomy and Sexuality*

Nehemiah Grew publishes, in *The Anatomy of Plants,* excellent drawings of plant structures, many of which he observes with a microscope. He describes types of tissues in plants and coins the terms "parenchyma" and "cambium." Grew also believes that flowering plants have sex organs borne in their flowers, but he does not demonstrate their presence by experimentation. He writes of pollen as the male reproductive element and ovules as the female. (See 1694.)

1683

A. BACTERIOLOGY: *Microscopic Observation of Bacteria*

Antony van Leeuwenhoek makes detailed observations and drawings of living organisms found in scrapings from teeth. It is clear from his drawings, which are later reproduced in numerous textbooks on bacteriology, that he observes bacteria. (See 1673 A, 1674 A, 1676, 1680, 1683 A.)

B. ANATOMY: *Capillary Circulation*

Antony van Leeuwenhoek's descriptions of capillary circulation are more complete than Marcello Malpighi's. (See 1661 A).

1684

MATHEMATICS: *Differential Calculus*

Gottfried Wilhelm Leibniz devises a system of differential calculus, but a controversy arises as to whether he or Isaac Newton first invented this new mathematical method. It is generally agreed that while Newton has priority of discovery, Leibniz's method is of superior facility and completeness. (See 1665 D.)

1686

BOTANY: *Plant Classification*

John Ray publishes the first volume of a three-volume work entitled *Historia generalis plantarum,* a botanical classification that describes all the plants known in Europe at this time, about 6,000 species. His natural system of classification, predating that of Carolus Linnaeus, is considered by some scientists to be his most important work. He also develops classifications of vertebrates and insects. Although he writes on many subjects, including travel and proverbs, his most widely known and reprinted work is *The Wisdom of God Manifested in the Works of the Creation* (1691). (See 1682 A, 1737.)

1687

PHYSICS: PRINCIPIA MATHEMATICA

Isaac Newton issues *Philosophiae naturalis principia mathematica,* usually known as *Principia mathematica,* in which he explains the law of gravitation and the three laws of motion and shows mathematically the relationship between pressure and volume of a gas (Boyle's law). This publication also contains the first record of his discovery of calculus. (See 1662 A.)

1690

A. MATHEMATICS: *Integral Calculus*

Jakob Bernoulli introduces the term "integral" in calculations he makes using Gottfried Leibniz's differential calculus.

B. SOCIETY AND POLITICS

John Locke publishes *Two Treatises of Civil Government,* presenting his theory of a limited monarchy under which individuals retain the right to enjoy liberty and to own property. (See 1651.)

1692

SOCIETY AND POLITICS

Witchcraft trials are held in Salem, Massachusetts.

1693

A. INFECTIOUS DISEASE: *Yellow Fever*

Based on a description written by Cotton Mather, the first outbreak of yellow fever in what is now the United States occurs in Boston, brought there from Barbados by the British fleet. The first appearance of yellow fever in the Western Hemisphere is in Barbados in 1647, possibly transported from Africa by slave trade.

B. TECHNOLOGY: *Calculating Machine*

Gottfried Leibniz invents a calculating machine that not only adds and subtracts but accomplishes multiplication by automatic addition and division by automatic repeated subtraction.

1694

BOTANY: *Sexual Reproduction in Plants*

Rudolph Jakob Camerarius publishes *De sexu plantarum epistola,* in which he describes sexual reproduction in plants. He distinguishes between types that come to be known as monoecious, dioecious, and hermaphrodite plants. (See 1682 B.)

1696

MATHEMATICS: *Integral Calculus*
Gottfried Leibniz and Jakob Bernoulli agree to use the term "calculus integralis" for the inverse of "calculus differentialis."

1697

A. FERMENTATION AND PUTREFACTION: *Process*
Georg Ernst Stahl states his belief that fermentation and putrefaction involve an internal agitation of particles (moleculae) that, when transferred to other substances, causes them to ferment or putrefy.

B. CHEMISTRY: *Phlogiston*
Georg Ernst Stahl writes that combustible materials contain phlogiston, a substance that is released upon burning. According to Stahl, both phlogiston and air are necessary to produce a flame. (See 1668 C.)

1699

A. INFECTIOUS DISEASE: *Yellow Fever*
In both Charleston, South Carolina, and Philadelphia, yellow fever causes many deaths. Over the next 45 or more years, Charleston is struck repeatedly by the disease. After a peak year in 1745, a major epidemic does not occur there again until the 1790s.

B. PHYSICS: *Gas Law*
Guillaume Amontons discovers that the volume of gases changes in direct proportion to temperature. Jacques Charles, in 1787, and Joseph Gay-Lussac, in 1802, make the same discovery, subsequently referred to as Charles's law or Gay-Lussac's law, while Amontons is forgotten.

C. PHYSICS: *Thermometer Scale*
Guillaume Amontons's observation that water always boils at the same temperature establishes a reference point for thermometer scales.

1700

THE ARTS: *Theater*
The Way of the Western World by William Congreve plays in London.

1701

CULTURE: *Universities*
Yale College is established in Connecticut as the Collegiate School. In 1718, the college is named for Elihu Yale, who provides library books and financial assistance by means of a cargo of goods from the East India Company.

1704

CHEMISTRY: *Composition of Matter*
Isaac Newton proposes that matter is composed of particles that cannot be changed into smaller parts. He states that chemical processes result from the attractions or repulsions among the particles.

1705

ASTRONOMY: *Halley's Comet*
Astronomer Edmund Halley correctly predicts that a comet, later called Halley's comet, observed in 1531, 1607, and 1682, will reappear in 1758 or 1759.

1706

MATHEMATICS: *Calculation of π*
William Jones, in *Synopsis palmariorum matheseos* (A new introduction to mathematics), is the first to use the Greek letter π for the ratio of the circumference of a circle to its diameter. (See 1700 B.C., 190, 600, 1596.)

1711

TECHNOLOGY: *the Steam Engine*
Thomas Newcomen builds the first successful steam engine.

1714

PHYSICS: *Measurement of Temperature*
Gabriel Daniel Fahrenheit invents a mercury thermometer with a temperature scale based on 0° for the temperature of a mixture of ice, water, and ammonium chloride and 96° for that of the human body. Thus, on the Fahrenheit scale, water is said to freeze at 32° and boil at 212°. (See 1741.)

1715

A. IMMUNOLOGY: *Smallpox*
Giacomo Pylarini describes how, in 1701, children in Constantinople were inoculated against smallpox by a technique that is later called variation. John Woodward, in England, receives a letter from Emmanuel Timoni mentioning the events in Constantinople. That letter is published in the *Philosophical Transactions of the Royal Society of London.* (See 1717, 1721 A, 1764 A, 1774 A.)

B. THE ARTS: *Music*
George Frederic Handel's *Water Music* is first performed.

1717

IMMUNOLOGY: *Smallpox*
Mary Wortley Montagu, wife of the British ambassador to Constantinople, writes to friends in England describing a method of smallpox inoculation called "ingrafting," in which a small amount of material from a smallpox lesion is introduced with a needle into a vein. In 1721, after Lady Montagu brings this technique to England, her son is inoculated in Turkey and then her daughter in England. In a second method developed in China and also used in England, a thread soaked in smallpox pussy material is inserted into a scratch on the arm. The various procedures for immunizing by the use of pussy material from an infected individual come to be known as "variolation" and the smallpox virus as "variola." Variolation methods are controversial since some individuals become ill and a few die. Although Lady Montagu is credited with popularizing variolation, prophylactic inoculation by various methods had been practiced for centuries in India, Persia, China, and no doubt other countries. (See 1715 A, 1721 A, 1764 A, 1774 A.)

1719

THE ARTS: *Literature*
Daniel Defoe writes *Robinson Crusoe.*

1720

A. INFECTIOUS DISEASE: *Tuberculosis*

Benjamin Martin, a physician, publishes *A New Theory of Consumptions: More Especially of a Phthisis of the Lungs,* a book that seems to have been neglected both at this time and by later writers. Martin states that consumption, or tuberculosis, may be caused by certain animalcules, or minute living creatures, that can exist in body fluids. They damage the vessels of the lung, resulting in obstruction, inflammation, ulceration, and other symptoms of the disease. His ideas predate by about 150 years the discoveries by Robert Koch, Louis Pasteur, and others in the latter part of the 19th century.

B. FERMENTATION: *Process*

At about this date, Hermann Boerhaave, who rejects the phlogiston theory, states that fermentation and putrefaction are unrelated and that fermentation can take place only in vegetable substances where they can produce either spirit (gas) or acid. He defines "ferment" as a substance that, when mixed with fermentable vegetables, causes fermentation. (See 1697 A, 1697 B.)

1721

A. IMMUNOLOGY: *Smallpox*

In Boston, at the suggestion of Cotton Mather, Zabdiel Boylston employs smallpox inoculations during an epidemic. Mather and Boylston later use statistical methods to evaluate the success of the experiment. Evidence that variolation is dangerous lies in the fact that some individuals become seriously ill and some of them die. Boylston and Mather are verbally attacked in person and in print and suffer personal assault. In London, King George I permits Hans Sloane, President of the Royal College of Physicians in London and a Secretary to the Royal Society, to conduct an experiment with smallpox variolation on condemned prisoners at Newgate Prison. This successful experiment is subsequently followed by other, similar experiments. Despite these successes, opposition to smallpox inoculation is strong, preventing its widespread use. (See 1717, 1764 A, 1774 A, 1776 A.)

B. THE ARTS: *Music*

Johann Sebastian Bach composes *The Brandenburg Concerti.*

C. THE ARTS: *Literature*

Daniel Defoe writes *Moll Flanders: the Fortunes and Misfortunes of the Famous.*

1726

A. THE ARTS: *Music*

Antonio Vivaldi composes *The Four Seasons.*

B. THE ARTS: *Literature*

Jonathan Swift publishes *Gulliver's Travels.*

1727

BOTANY: *Plant Physiology*

Stephen Hales publishes *Vegetable Statics,* covering experiments begun as early as 1705, emphasizing quantitative techniques. He studies water balance and the flow of fluids in plants, measures leaf suction and root pressure, and studies leaf growth. Hales, referred to as the "father of plant physiology," concludes that air plays a role in plant nourishment, contrary to the conclusion of Johannes van Helmont in 1648 that plant growth is attributed to the uptake of water. (See 1733.)

1728

THE ARTS: *Music*

The Beggar's Opera, with music by John Christopher Pepusch and text by John Gay, is first performed. In 1928, Kurt Weill and Bertolt Brecht adapt it to modern idiom as *The Threepenny Opera* (*Die Dreigroschenoper*).

1729

OPTICAL INSTRUMENTS: *Achromatic Lens*

Chester Moor Hall obtains achromatic lenses for the telescope by combining a concave lens made of flint glass with a convex lens made of crown glass. His invention is largely unknown and unappreciated. John Dollond is often credited with this discovery because he publicizes the lens he develops, leading to great improvement in telescopes. Achromatic lenses for the compound microscope do not appear for another century (See 1758, 1827 A.).

1732

INFECTIOUS DISEASE: *Influenza*

A pandemic of influenza, active throughout the world, begins and continues into 1733. The first infections are thought by some to be in Connecticut, while others believe that it began in Moscow. (See 1580, 1781 A, 1830 A.)

1733

PHYSIOLOGY: *Circulation of Blood and Blood Pressure*

Stephen Hales publishes *Haemastaticks,* a report of his studies on the circulation of blood and blood pressure. He is the first to measure blood pressure, accomplished by inserting glass tubes into arteries of a variety of animals, including a mare, horses, dogs, sheep, and humans. His work is the most significant investigation of circulation since that of William Harvey. (See 1628.)

1734

SOCIETY AND POLITICS

Voltaire (François-Marie Arouet) publishes *Lettres anglaises ou philosophiques* referring to the English constitution and exalting religious, social, and political freedom.

1735

A. FOOD POISONING: *Botulism*

A disease that becomes known as botulism is recognized in Germany. The name botulism, derived from *botulus,* the Latin word for sausage, comes into use at the beginning of the 19th century because of the association of the disease with eating sausage. (See 900 A, 1820 A.)

1735 *(continued)*

B. BOTANY: *Plant Classification*

Drawing from the work of John Ray in 1682 and 1686, Carolus Linnaeus (Carl von Linné) presents *Systema naturae,* his first classification of plants. His descriptions of classes of flowering plants is based on their "male" organs (the length and number of stamens). He divides the class that includes mosses and other nonflowering plants into orders on the basis of "female" organs (styles and stigmas). Linnaeus derives his terminology from Greek words connected with gender, such as *andros* (male) and *gyne* (female). At the time, many students of botany are disturbed by the sexual analogies. (See 1737, 1749 A, 1753, 1763 A, 1767 B.)

1736

INFECTIOUS DISEASE: *Scarlet Fever*

William Douglass describes the symptoms and diagnosis of scarlet fever.

1737

BOTANY: *Taxonomy*

Carolus Linnaeus writes *Genera plantarum,* describing 18,000 plant species and naming them on the basis of a binomial nomenclature derived from Gaspard Bauhin's system of 1623. In 1749 he presents a revised version of binomial nomenclature. (See 1735 B, 1749 A, 1753, 1763, 1767 B.)

1739

TECHNOLOGY: *Coal Gas*

John Clayton produces coal gas by distillation of coal and demonstrates its lighting power.

1741

PHYSICS: *Measurement of Temperature*

Anders Celsius invents the centigrade thermometer scale, with 100° as the freezing point and 0° as the boiling point of water. The scale is inverted in 1743 by Jean Pierre Christin. This thermometer is known widely as the centigrade thermometer until 1948, when an international agreement is reached to call it the Celsius thermometer or scale. (See 1714.)

1742

THE ARTS: *Music*

George Frederic Handel composes his oratorio, the *Messiah.*

1745

A. PHYSIOLOGY: *Iron in Blood*

Vicenzo Menghini discovers the presence of iron in blood, the first discovery of a trace element in living organisms.

B. PHYSICS: *Static Electricity/Leyden Jar*

Pieter van Musschenbroek and Ewald Georg von Kleist independently construct a static electricity device. They find that water contained in either glass or metal jars will develop and hold an electric charge when the jars are rubbed while rotated. Both van Musschenbroek and von Kleist discover that large charges are released when metal wires leading into the water are touched, with von Kleist refusing to work with his device any further while Musschenbroek conducts various additional experiments. Because Musschenbroek works at the University of Leyden in the Netherlands, such devices come to be known as Leyden jars. (See 585 B.C., 1600 A, 1660 B.)

1748

A. MICROBIOLOGY: *Spontaneous Generation of Life*
John Turberville Needham reports experiments conducted on the generation of "microscopical animacules" in infusions of plant or animal tissue. He is persuaded to perform the experiments by the opinion of Georges Louis Leclerc, Comte de Buffon, whose own observations lead him to conclude that mature plants are composed of identical bodies, each of which can form a new complete organism. After Needham meets Buffon and discusses these ideas with him in 1748, he sets out to determine if they are correct. In a typical experiment, Needham seals a tube containing mutton gravy with a cork to exclude the air. After the tube is heated, he later observes a variety of forms of microscopic life. He forms the conclusion that a vegetative force exists in all matter that had been a part of living plants and animals. Even though he was originally a doubter, he concludes that the microscopic creatures in the heated (or unheated) tubes develop without progenitors, leading him to become a strong proponent of spontaneous generation. (See 1668 A, 1749 B, 1765 A, 1858 A.)

B. INFECTIOUS DISEASE: *Diphtheria or Scarlet Fever*
John Fothergill publishes clinical descriptions of sore throat infections. It is not clear whether he has observed diphtheria, a combination of scarlet fever and diphtheria, or other infections. Earlier descriptions of diphtheria date from the time of Hippocrates and from the first and fifth centuries A.D. (See 1492 A, 1576.)

C. BIOLOGY: *Osmosis*
Jean Antoine Nollet discovers osmosis when he notes that water diffuses into a sugar solution across an animal membrane. (See 1881 I, 1886 H.)

1749

A. BIOLOGY: *Taxonomy*
Carolus Linnaeus expands his system of binomial nomenclature and classification of plants by establishing not only species and genera but also classes and orders. He argues that each species has a specific place in nature, in geographic location, and in the food chain. (See 1735 B, 1737, 1753, 1763 A, 1767 B.)

B. BIOLOGY: *Evolution*
Georges Louis Leclerc, Comte de Buffon, publishes the first volume of his monumental 44-volume *Histoire naturelle* (eight volumes appear after his death), discussing all of the known facts about natural science. Volume II, *Des animaux,* presents his ideas discussed with John Turberville Needham about spontaneous generation of life. Buffon's work presents the perspective of a transformationist: that many forms of life have degenerated from others that God created. He also attributes the formation of the earth,

1749 (continued)

75,000 years earlier, to a collision of a comet with the sun. His ideas are influential until the time of Charles Darwin. (See 1868 E.)

C. THE ARTS: *Literature*

Henry Fielding completes *The History of Tom Jones, a Foundling.*

1751

SOCIETY AND POLITICS

The first volume of the *Encyclopédie,* or *Dictionnaire raisonné des sciences, des arts et des métiers,* appears under the editorship of Denis Diderot. Its 28 volumes, the last being issued in 1772, include discussions of all human knowledge with articles by many well-known writers, including Jean-Jacques Rousseau and Voltaire.

1752

PHYSICS: *Electricity*

Benjamin Franklin shows that the electric spark generated by a Leyden jar is the same type of electricity as that found in lightning. During a thunderstorm he flies a kite that has a silk thread leading from a metal tip on the kite to a metal key at ground level. He finds that the electricity transmitted down the thread to the key both produces a spark and fully charges a Leyden jar. (See 1745 B.)

1753

BOTANY: *Taxonomy*

Carolus Linnaeus publishes *Species plantarum,* in which he gives a genus and species name to the 5,900 plants he has classified, thus firmly establishing a binomial system of nomenclature. His earlier efforts had resulted in long Latinate descriptive terms tedious to use and difficult to remember. (See 1735 B, 1737, 1749 A, 1763 A, 1767 B.)

1754

CHEMISTRY: *Gases*

Joseph Black completes his medical school dissertation, which is expanded and published in 1756 as *Experiments upon Magnesia Alba, Quicklime, and Some Other Alcaline Substances.* Black reports that when magnesia alba (magnesium carbonate) is heated, a gas evolves that he calls "fixed air." He discovers that when lime (calcium oxide) is left exposed to air, it turns to calcium carbonate, leading to the conclusion that some part of air is fixed air. He notes that caustic lime is converted to mild lime by fixed air and, later, that breathing converts part of air to fixed air. Fixed air is later found to be carbon dioxide. Black is the first to introduce the use of quantitative methods in chemical experiments.

1755

A. THE ARTS: *Music*

Franz Joseph Haydn composes his first quartets.

B. CULTURE: *Dictionaries*

Samuel Johnson completes *A Dictionary of the English Language.*

1757

FERMENTATION: *Carbon Dioxide*
Joseph Black uses the lime water test to demonstrate that "fixed air" (carbon dioxide) evolves from fermentation. He rediscovers Johannes van Helmont's "gas sylvestre." (See 1648 A, 1754.)

1758

OPTICAL INSTRUMENTS: *Achromatic Lenses*
John Dollond makes achromatic lenses for a telescope. Chester Moor Hall, who made similar lenses in 1729, brings legal action against Dollond, but the courts reject his claim.

1759

A. BIOLOGY: *Epigenesis/Embryology*
Casper Friedrich Wolff publishes *Theoria generationis,* in which he describes the theory of epigenesis, that the fertilized egg is a homogeneous structure from which all parts of the embryo arise de novo. (See 1828 A.)

B. SOCIETY AND POLITICS
In the Battle of the Plains of Abraham near Quebec City, British forces defeat the French, securing control of Canada for the English.

C. THE ARTS: *Literature*
  • Voltaire writes *Candide.*
  • The first two of nine volumes of *The Life and Opinions of Tristram Shandy* by Laurence Sterne are published. Sterne publishes nine volumes through 1767, but the story is never finished.

1761

A. DISEASE: *Pathology*
Giovanni Morgagni publishes *De sedibus et causis morborum per anatomen indagatis* (On the causes of diseases), an early work on pathological anatomy. His descriptions of postmortem anatomy are connected to the diseases that cause death in each case.

B. BOTANY: *Plant Hybrids*
J. G. Kölreuter begins publishing the results of his systematic studies of plant hybrids. Both Gregor Mendel and Charles Darwin know of his work when they publish their studies. (See 1859 B, 1865 B.)

1762

A. INFECTIOUS DISEASE: *Seeds of Disease*
Marcus Antonius Plenciz writes that seeds of disease may be carried in the air. These may lie dormant and then develop into numerous animalcules, some of which are invisible, as well as into beetles, flies, leeches, and the larvae of gnats. Girolamo Fracastoro proposed the concept of seeds of disease in 1546 in *De contagione.* (See 1546 A.)

B. SOCIETY AND POLITICS
Jean-Jacques Rousseau publishes *Le contrat social* expressing his view that "Man is born free yet everywhere is in chains."

1763

A. DISEASE: *Classification*

Carolus Linnaeus attempts a classification of diseases in *Genera morborum*. (See 1735 B, 1737, 1749 A, 1753, 1767 B.)

B. CULTURE: *Pottery*

Josiah Wedgwood, maternal grandfather of Charles Darwin, obtains a patent on a type of pottery that will carry his name and become widely known and collected.

1764

A. IMMUNOLOGY: *Smallpox*

Angelo Gatti publishes on inoculation against smallpox with pussy material from infected individuals, a process called variolation. He speculates that attenuating the agent that causes smallpox can make it safer to use. Gatti dies without learning of Edward Jenner's success with the cowpox virus in 1796. (See 1721 A, 1774 A, 1776 A, 1796 B.)

B. TECHNOLOGY: *Spinning Machine*

James Hargreaves's invention of the spinning jenny, patented in 1770, introduces mechanization into textile manufacturing.

1765

A. BACTERIOLOGY: *Spontaneous Generation of Life*

Lazzaro Spallanzani repeats John Turberville Needham's 1748 experiments in which meat infusions were boiled in corked glass tubes, but improves upon them by melting the tops in a flame to seal the tubes. He concludes that microorganisms do not arise spontaneously if the infusions are heated for a sufficiently long time. We now know that his success depended on protecting the infusions from contamination by microorganisms in air and some luck, in that bacterial endospores did not survive his heat treatments. Spallanzani's microscope, unlike the better instruments of Comte de Buffon and John Needham, limits his ability to see objects the size of bacteria. He suggests that food can be preserved by sealing in airtight containers. (See 1748 A, 1749 B, 1858 A, 1858 B.)

B. INFECTIOUS DISEASE: *Diphtheria*

In a monograph on the croup, Francis Home describes the clinical symptoms of diphtheria.

C. TECHNOLOGY: *Steam Engine*

James Watt greatly improves the steam engine built by Thomas Newcomen in 1711. He and Mathew Boulton, a manufacturer, begin making a new and improved steam engine in 1776. (See 1711.)

1766

A. FERMENTATION: *Gases*

Henry Cavendish publishes on "inflammable air" (hydrogen) and on several types of "fixed air" (carbon dioxide), including that produced by the action of yeast on a sugar solution and which was absorbed by aqueous sodium hydroxide. He identifies the latter gas with that derived from limestone.

B. SOCIETY AND POLITICS

Charles Mason and Jeremiah Dixon complete their survey of the boundary between Pennsylvania and Maryland. The Mason-Dixon line later separates the free states from the slave states.

A. INFECTIOUS DISEASE: *Syphilis/Gonorrhea*

John Hunter, a British physician, infects himself with both gonorrhea and syphilis, using pus from a patient with gonorrhea. In 1787, he publishes a treatise on venereal diseases in which he supports the concept that gonorrhea is an early stage of syphilis. Hunter dies in 1793 of angina pectoris, possibly a consequence of his infections. Edward Jenner, who establishes vaccination against smallpox, trains for 2 years under Hunter. Hunter is also known for his studies of comparative anatomy and embryology and for a collection of biological specimens numbering 13,600 at the time of his death. (See 1796 B.)

B. BIOLOGY: *Classification of Animalcules*

Carolus Linnaeus, in the 12th edition of *Systema naturae,* classifies animalcules as Vermes in the class Chaos with six species, the last being *Chaos infusorium.* Doubting the usefulness of microscopic observations, Linnaeus does not believe that spermatozoa exist. At the end of the Chaos, Linnaeus places a strange mixture of items: the cause of exanthema, the syphilis "virus," the agents of fermentation, spermatozoa (despite his doubts about their existence), and "the ethereal clouds suspended in the sky in the month of blossoming." (See 1735 B, 1737, 1749 A, 1753, 1763 A, 1767 B.)

INFECTIOUS DISEASE: *Cholera*

In India, a cholera epidemic in 1768 to 1769 kills as many as 60,000 in 1 year. (See 1817.)

A. TECHNOLOGY: *Spinning Frame*

Richard Arkwright patents a hydraulic spinning frame (a water frame) for the mechanical spinning of cotton warp. His invention plays a key role in England's Industrial Revolution.

B. TECHNOLOGY: *Self-Propelled Vehicle*

Nicholas Joseph Cugnot builds the first self-propelled vehicle when he attaches a steam engine to a carriage. (See 1859 F, 1885 O, 1893 F.)

A. SOCIETY: *Exploration*

James Cook finds the eastern coast of Australia and claims the land for King George III.

B. SOCIETY AND POLITICS

In what is called the Boston Massacre, British troops kill five persons in a crowd of protesters in Boston.

C. CULTURE: *Music*

Wolfgang Amadeus Mozart completes his first string quartet at the age of 14.

1771

A. CHEMISTRY: *Oxygen and Nitrogen*
Carl Wilhelm Scheele discovers that air is composed of "two fluids," calling them "fire air" (*Feuerluft,* oxygen) and "foul air" (*verdorbene Luft,* nitrogen). In 1772, Daniel Rutherford, who is often mentioned as the discoverer of nitrogen, notes that air contains a large proportion of something that extinguishes life and flame. Because of a delay at the print shop, Scheele's work is not published until 1777 after Joseph Priestley, whose experiments are done 1 to 3 years after Scheele's, independently publishes on many of the same topics. Because of the priority of Priestley's publication date, he is credited with the discovery of oxygen.

B. PLANT PHYSIOLOGY: *Oxygen Formation by Plants*
In the early 1770s, Joseph Priestley "restores" air by growing mint in air in which a candle had burned out. A candle burns, and a mouse survives in the restored air. He prepares a quantity of "air" in which a candle burns very brightly. He does not at this time recognize oxygen because he is a believer in phlogiston. He also does not note the importance of light for the growing plant and its production of oxygen. (See 1697 A and B, 1779 B, 1782.)

C. MODERN DENTISTRY
John Hunter publishes *Treatise on the Natural History of the Human Teeth,* which serves as the foundation of modern dentistry.

D. CULTURE: *Literature and Knowledge*
The first edition of *Encyclopedia Britannica* is printed.

1772

A. CHEMISTRY: *Soda Water/Carbon Dioxide*
Joseph Priestley invents soda water as a result of investigating the gases in beer vats. By finding a way to impregnate water with CO_2 from the beer fermentations, he starts an industry for making soda water.

B. CHEMISTRY: *Nitrogen*
Antoine Lavoisier gives the name "azote" to the noxious air discovered by Daniel Rutherford; he is unaware of Carl Wilhelm Scheele's earlier discovery of nitrogen in air. Although the word "azote" appears in Lavoisier's notes, it is not published until 1787. (See 1771 A.)

C. CHEMISTRY: *Combustion*
Antoine Lavoisier begins studies on combustion that lead to the overturning of the phlogiston theory. During this period, he begins his experiments on respiration. (See 1697 B, 1771 B, 1775 B.)

1773

A. BACTERIOLOGY: *First Description of Bacteria*
Otto Frederik Müller publishes what may be the first description of an organism now classified as a bacterium. In *Vermium terrestrium et fluviatilum,* his classification of Infusoria, under the Vermes, includes the genera

Monas and *Vibrio,* which contain bacterial species that he recognizes. (See 1767 B.)

B. SOCIETY AND POLITICS
The Boston Tea Party occurs when American colonists in Boston dump tea into the harbor in protest against a tax on tea.

C. THE ARTS: *Theater*
She Stoops to Conquer by Oliver Goldsmith plays in London.

1774

A. IMMUNOLOGY: *Smallpox Immunization*
The first recorded practice of using pussy material from cowpox lesions to inoculate against smallpox comes from Benjamin Jesty, a farmer and cattle breeder in Dorset, England. At the time, it is commonly believed that those who have contracted the mild disease cowpox from contact with infected cattle are subsequently immune to smallpox infection. Jesty scratches the arms of his wife and two sons with a needle and inserts pussy material from a cow's udder. All three survive a later epidemic of smallpox without incident. Jesty, who had earlier suffered a natural infection of cowpox, was immune to smallpox. (See 1721 A, 1764 A, 1776 A, 1796 B.)

B. CHEMISTRY: *Oxygen*
Joseph Priestley obtains oxygen by heating red mercuric oxide with a burning glass (magnifying glass). He reports this observation before Carl Wilhelm Scheele publishes his independent discovery of oxygen and thereby establishes priority for the discovery. (See 1771 A.)

C. CHEMISTRY: *Combustion of Metals*
Antoine Lavoisier publishes *Opuscles physiques et chimiques,* in which he reports repeating Robert Boyle's experiments (1673) on combustion of lead and tin and concludes that some portion of air is absorbed. He explains this process in 1775.

1775

A. PHYSIOLOGY: *Oxygen and Respiration*
Joseph Priestley finds that a mouse lives twice as long in the new "air" than in common air. His conclusions about these experiments are explained on the basis of the phlogiston theory. (See 1697 B, 1771 B, 1772 C, 1775 B.)

B. CHEMISTRY: *Combustion of Metals*
Antoine Lavoisier writes that combustion of metal substances causes the combination of the metal with the "purest part of air which we breath," increasing the weight of the metal. He concludes that air is composed of two components, later called oxygen and nitrogen. This work contributes strongly to his destruction of the phlogiston theory (See 1697 B, 1772 C, 1775 A, 1781 C.)

C. SOCIETY AND POLITICS
The American War of Independence begins, continuing until 1783, with the battles of Lexington, Concord, and Bunker Hill.

1776

A. IMMUNOLOGY: *Smallpox Immunization*
George Washington, commander in chief of the rebellious American Continental Army against the British, orders his entire army to be inoculated against smallpox with pussy material from infected individuals, a technique called variolation. Washington later serves as the first president of the United States. (See 1764 A, 1774 A, 1796 B.)

B. BACTERIAL PHYSIOLOGY: *Methanogenesis*
Alessandro Giuseppe Volta finds "combustible air" released from freshwater sediments in all lakes, ponds, and streams in the vicinity of Como in northern Italy. Biological methane production is later found to be caused by bacteria referred to as methanogens. Volta's combustible air is shown to be identical to the main constituent of synthetic illuminating gas, which is now called methane. (See 1906 A, 1936 B.)

C. BIOLOGY: *Human Races*
Johann Friedrich Blumenbach publishes *On the Natural Varieties of Mankind,* classifying humans into five races: Caucasian (European), Ethiopian (sub-Saharan Africans), American Indian, Malayan (Southeast Asians and Pacific Islanders), and Mongolian (East Asians).

D. SOCIETY AND POLITICS
The Continental Congress, formed by the American colonies in protest against the British, adopts the Declaration of Independence.

E. SOCIETY AND POLITICS
Economist Adam Smith publishes *The Wealth of Nations.*

F. SOCIETY: *History*
Edward Gibbon publishes the first part of his *History of the Decline and Fall of the Roman Empire.*

1777

A. PHYSIOLOGY: *Respiration*
Antoine Lavoisier notes that respiration is the slow combustion of carbon supplied by the blood and that animal heat results from the process that also forms carbonic acid.

B. THE ARTS: *Theater*
The School for Scandal by Richard Brinsley Sheridan opens in London.

1779

A. BIOLOGY: *Semen and Fertilization*
Lazzaro Spallanzani recognizes the importance of semen for fertilization of eggs.

B. PLANT PHYSIOLOGY: *Photosynthesis*
Jan Ingenhousz proves that plants produce "vital air" (oxygen) in sunlight but that without light they produce "fixed air." He also shows that plants obtain carbon from the atmosphere and not from the soil. He is thereby the first to provide evidence for the process that comes to be known as photosynthesis. (See 1782.)

1780

A. BACTERIAL FERMENTATION: *Lactic Acid*
Carl Wilhelm Scheele isolates lactic acid from soured milk. He also discovers several other compounds of biological importance: uric acid (1780), oxalic acid (1776), citric acid (1784), malic acid (1785), glycerol (1783), and casein (1780). In addition, Scheele studies several esters and aldehydes.

B. CHEMISTRY: *Oxygen*
Antoine Lavoisier introduces the term "oxygen" to replace such expressions as "dephlogisticated air" or "eminently respirable air."

C. PHYSICS: *Electricity*
Luigi Galvani observes that frog muscles twitch when in contact with two different metals, brass and iron. He attributes this effect to "animal electricity," which Alessandro Giuseppe Volta shows to be erroneous in 1800. The galvanometer, a device that detects electric current, and words such as "galvanized," meaning to stimulate or startle, are terms derived from Galvani's name. (See 1800 D.)

1781

A. INFECTIOUS DISEASE: *Influenza*
An influenza pandemic, thought to have begun in China, spreads to North America, Europe, Russia, and India. The infection rate is as high as 75% in some cities. (See 1580, 1732, 1830 A, 1847 A.)

B. CHEMISTRY: *Water Formed from Hydrogen and Oxygen*
After exploding two volumes of "inflammable air" (hydrogen) with one volume of "dephlogisticated air" (oxygen), Henry Cavendish shows that the gases are completely converted to water. He explains that "inflammable air" is a combination of phlogiston and water. Cavendish greatly improves methods for measuring volumes of gases. (See 1775 A, 1775 B, 1783 B.)

C. PHYSIOLOGY: *Cyanide*
Felice Fontana uses a distillate from the leaves of "cherry-laurel" to poison animals by ingestion or injection. The distillate is later found to contain cyanide, an inhibitor of respiration.

D. SOCIETY AND POLITICS
The states that make up the newly created United States accept the Articles of Confederation and begin to relinquish their claims to territory in the West.

1782

PLANT PHYSIOLOGY: *Photosynthesis*
Jean Senebier reports that light is needed for the restoration of air by plant growth.

1783

A. PHYSIOLOGY: *Animal Respiration*
Antoine Lavoisier and Pierre Simon de Laplace experiment on respiration in animals. They estimate heat released by measuring the quantity of ice

1783 *(continued)*

melted when a guinea pig is placed in the chamber of an ice calorimeter, devised by Laplace. By considering heat released, oxygen consumed, and carbon dioxide produced, they conclude that animal heat is produced by a process of slow combustion.

B. CHEMISTRY: *Water Formed from Hydrogen and Oxygen*
Joseph Priestley obtains water by exploding a mixture of "inflammable air" (hydrogen) and "dephlogisticated air" (oxygen). Repeating Priestley's and Henry Cavendish's experiments of 1781, Antoine Lavoisier shows that water is formed from hydrogen and oxygen. These and other experiments with calcination of metals result in acceptance of his conclusion that combustion involves the consumption of oxygen and further weakens the phlogiston theory. (See 1775 A, 1775 B, 1781 C.)

C. CHEMISTRY: *Cyanide*
Carl Wilhelm Scheele purifies cyanide.

D. TECHNOLOGY: *Balloons*
Joseph-Michel Montgolfier and Jacques-Etienne Montgolfier successfully launch an unmanned balloon that is filled with smoke and hot air. Five months later Jean Pilâtre de Rozier and Marquis François d'Arlandes make the first manned flight in a balloon, reaching a height of 500 feet and traveling about 5.5 miles. (See 1932 N.)

E. SOCIETY AND POLITICS
The American War of Independence, begun in 1775, ends with a treaty with England.

1786

A. BACTERIOLOGY: *Descriptions of Bacteria*
Otto Frederik Müller makes the first significant advance in the study of bacteria since Antonie van Leeuwenhoek's observations of 1683, when he accurately describes 150 species of bacteria according to morphology. His monograph *Animalcula infusoria fluviatilia et marina* is published 2 years after his death.

B. THE ARTS: *Music*
Wolfgang Amadeus Mozart composes the opera *Le Nozze di Figaro*.

1787

A. CHEMISTRY: *Nomenclature*
Guyton de Morveau, Antoine Lavoisier, Claude Louis Berthollet, and Antoine de Fourcroy publish *Methode de nomenclature chimique* in which chemicals are named according to their composition. Their book is a major revision of chemical nomenclature.

B. CHEMISTRY: *Charles / Gay-Lussac's Gas Law*
Jacques Alexandre César Charles discovers that a volume of a gas at constant pressure is directly proportional to its absolute temperature, a phenomenon that had been observed in 1699 by Guillaume Amontons and

again discovered in 1802 by Joseph Gay-Lussac. The principle is usually referred to as Charles's law, but sometimes as Gay-Lussac's law.

C. SOCIETY AND POLITICS
The Constitutional Convention in the newly formed United States draws up the federal Constitution.

D. THE ARTS: *Music*
Wolfgang Amadeus Mozart presents the first performance of his opera *Don Giovanni.*

1789

A. INFECTIOUS DISEASE: *Poliomyelitis*
In his book *Debility of the Lower Extremities,* Michael Underwood describes a disease having the characteristics of poliomyelitis. An Egyptian pillar from the Eighteenth Dynasty (ending 1350 B.C.) depicts a deformed man with a withered leg possibly resulting from poliomyelitis. It seems certain that the poet Walter Scott contracted a poliomyelitis infection as an infant, leaving him with a shrunken and lame right leg.

B. FERMENTATION: *Chemical Balance*
Antoine Lavoisier attempts a chemical balance of all the substances involved in fermentation, which he believes to be a purely chemical reaction.

C. PHYSIOLOGY: *Animal Respiration*
Antoine Lavoisier and Armand Séguin write a memoir (not to be read to the French Academy of Sciences until 1791 or published until 1793) stating that respiration is nothing but a slow combustion of carbon and hydrogen.

D. MODERN CHEMISTRY
Antoine Lavoisier publishes *Traité élémentaire de chimie présenté dans un ordre nouveau et d'après les découvertes modernes,* a treatise considered by some to be the beginning of chemistry as a science. This work includes an explanation of the oxygen theory of combustion, encourages the use of quantification, gives a list of the known chemical elements, explains the system of chemical nomenclature first described in 1787, and makes the first clear statement of the law of conservation of matter. (See 1787 A.)

E. SOCIETY AND POLITICS
• George Washington becomes the first president of the United States.
• The French Revolution begins with the fall of the Bastille, the royal fortress. Members of the commons, or third estate, declare that they constitute the National Assembly.

1790

A. INFECTIOUS DISEASE: *Yellow Fever*
Charleston, South Carolina, is plagued by yellow fever throughout the decade, with epidemics in 1790, 1791, 1792, 1795, 1798, and 1799.

B. CHEMISTRY: *Nitrogen*
Jean Chaptal assigns the term "nitrogen" to the gas discovered by Carl Wilhelm Scheele and Joseph Priestley to denote its association with nitric acid.

1791

A. TECHNOLOGY: *the Meter and the Gram*

A committee created by the French National Assembly recommends standards for the length of the meter and for the mass of the gram. While the metric system is adopted by law in France in 1799, and by other European countries soon after, it is not adopted by England and the United States.

B. THE ARTS: *Music*

The Magic Flute (*Die Zauberflöte*) by Wolfgang Amadeus Mozart is first presented.

1792

SOCIETY AND POLITICS

Mary Wollstonecraft publishes *Vindication of the Rights of Women,* the first complete argument for women's rights.

1793

A. INFECTIOUS DISEASE: *Yellow Fever*

At a time when Philadelphia is the temporary capital of the United States, the city is struck by an epidemic of yellow fever that kills at least 5,000 persons, about 10% of its population. Benjamin Rush, a physician and a signer of the U.S. Declaration of Independence, plays a major role in advocating preventative measures and treatments and establishing a hospital in a building referred to as Bush Hill. Rush, who creates controversy by insisting that bloodletting is the best treatment, claims cures for many persons, including himself. He also believes, with many others, that yellow fever is caused by putrid air released by decaying matter on the filthy waterfronts.

B. SOCIETY AND POLITICS

King Louis XVI of France is beheaded by the revolutionary French National Convention.

1794

BIOLOGY: *Inheritance of Acquired Characteristics*

Erasmus Darwin, grandfather of both Charles Darwin and Francis Galton, publishes *Zoonomia,* in which he proposes a "transmutation" of living forms. He describes the evolution of species over time through the survival of competing species, as well as through the inheritance of acquired characteristics.

1795

A. BACTERIAL GENUS: Myxobacterium

H. Link describes an organism he believes to be a fungus but which Ronald Thaxter shows in 1892 to be a myxobacterium.

B. SOCIETY AND POLITICS

Napoleon Bonaparte is named commander of the army of the interior for his role in saving the Tuileries Palace during the revolution of 1795.

1796

A. INFECTIOUS DISEASE: *Yellow Fever*

New Orleans experiences its first epidemic of yellow fever, with repeated epidemics occurring throughout the 19th century. Yellow fever spreads from New Orleans by way of the Mississippi and Tennessee Rivers, reaching Vicksburg; Memphis; Cairo, Illinois; St. Louis; Chattanooga; and Louisville.

B. IMMUNOLOGY: *Smallpox*

Edward Jenner, a physician practicing in Gloucestershire, England, is the first scientist to test the observation that dairymaids and other persons afflicted with the mild disease called cowpox are subsequently protected from infection by smallpox. In 1789 or 1790, Jenner inoculates his 10-month-old son with pussy material from an infected pig. Later attempts on several occasions to infect the child with smallpox suggest that the boy is immune. Jenner's own report of his first experiment, however, is the successful immunization of an 8-year-old boy, James Phipps, with material from cowpox lesions on the hands of a milkmaid. In 1798, Jenner publishes a book describing this experiment and the experiences of 16 other individuals who had become immune to smallpox after having a cowpox infection. Although Jenner did not discover or invent vaccination, his experiments prove the validity of the procedure. Benjamin Jesty and others attempted neither to study the phenomenon nor to apply their findings to individuals outside their immediate families and friends. Jenner's work begins the field of immunology. The word "vaccination" is derived from the Latin *vacca*, for cow. (See 1764 A, 1774 A, 1776 A.)

C. SOCIETY AND POLITICS

The French army under Napoleon Bonaparte invades the northern regions of Italy and defeats the Austrians. Napoleon marries Josephine de Beauharnais, whose husband was guillotined in 1794, but has the marriage annulled in 1809.

1798

A. PHYSICS: *Heat from Friction*

In experiments to determine the source of heat produced by boring cannon, Benjamin Thompson Rumford formulates a new concept of heat. He explains his vibratory theory of heat in *Experimental Inquiry Concerning the Source of Heat Excited by Friction*, establishing a relationship between work performed and heat produced.

B. BIOLOGY: *Comparative Anatomy*

Georges Cuvier, considered the father of comparative anatomy, publishes the first of his treatises comparing the anatomy of various animals. In 1817, he publishes *Le règne animal*, arranging the animal kingdom into four groups: *Mollusca, Radiata, Articulata,* and *Vertebrata*. (See 1812 B.)

C. SOCIETY AND POLITICS: *Economics and Population*

Thomas Robert Malthus publishes *Essay on the Principle of Population*, claiming that the population of the world increases exponentially while the food supply increases arithmetically and predicting a worldwide food crisis.

D. THE ARTS: *Literature*

William Wordsworth and Samuel Taylor Coleridge publish *Lyrical Ballads*, initiating the English romantic period.

1799

CHEMISTRY: *Law of Constant Composition*
Joseph Proust begins a series of experiments proving that chemical compounds always have the same proportions of their component elements. The law of constant composition becomes generally accepted by 1808.

1800

A. BACTERIOLOGY: *Sanitation of Drinking Water*
Guyton de Morveau and William Cruikshank independently use "oxymuriatic acid" (renamed chlorine in 1811 by Humphry Davy) for the sanitation of drinking water.

B. BIOLOGY: *Introduction of the Term*
Karl Burdach first uses the term "biology" to explain the morphological, physiological, and psychological attributes of humans. "Biology" becomes a widely used term through the writings of Jean-Baptiste Lamarck and Gottfried Treviranus. (See 1802 B.)

C. PHYSICS: *Infrared Radiation*
William Herschel, who discovered the planet Uranus in 1781, discovers infrared radiation.

D. PHYSICS: *Electricity*
Alessandro Giuseppe Volta, following talks with Luigi Galvani about "animal electricity," experiments with various metals and finds that electricity flows when a salt solution is used to provide contact between copper and zinc discs. He develops an "electric pile" that becomes known as a Voltaic pile. This is the first electric battery and the first device that produces a continuous flow of electricity. The unit for measuring the difference in electric potential, the volt, is named after him. (See 1780 C.)

E. SOCIETY AND POLITICS
Washington, D.C., becomes the U.S. capital.

F. THE ARTS: *Library*
The Library of Congress is founded in Washington, D.C., with an appropriation of $5,000.

G. THE ARTS: *Music*
Symphony no. 1 in C Major by Ludwig van Beethoven receives its first performance.

1801

A. PHYSICS: *Ultraviolet Radiation*
Johann Ritter discovers ultraviolet radiation.

B. PHYSICS: *Interference Patterns of Light*
Thomas Young discovers that light passing through two separate narrow slits produces an interference pattern.

C. TECHNOLOGY: *Jacquard Loom*
Joseph-Marie Jacquard develops ideas for a mechanical loom that he improves in 1805 by controlling its operation with punched cards of instruc-

tions. The punched card concept is later used by Charles Babbage in his efforts to build an analytical machine or computer. (See 1832 E.)

D. SOCIETY AND POLITICS
• An Act of Union creates the United Kingdom of Great Britain and Ireland.
• The British fleet, acting under orders of Vice Admiral Horatio Nelson, defeats the Danish fleet in the Battle of Copenhagen.

1802

A. INFECTIOUS DISEASE: *Yellow Fever*
Napoleon Bonaparte sends Charles Victor Emmanuel Leclerc and a force of 25,000 to Haiti to put down a rebellion led by Toussaint L'Ouverture. Yellow fever strikes the island, leaving about 40,000 dead, including Leclerc and nearly all of his men. This disaster is said to have led Napoleon to offer to sell all of Louisiana to the United States.

B. BIOLOGY: *Extension of Meaning of the Term*
Both Jean-Baptiste Lamarck and Gottfried Treviranus extend Karl Burdach's term "biology" to mean the study of all life. Lamarck is the first to distinguish between vertebrates and invertebrates. (See 1800 B, 1809.)

C. BOTANY: *Plant Structure*
Charles François Brisseau Mirbel states that plants are made up of continuous cellular membranous tissue and that all plants are made of cells.

D. SOCIETY AND POLITICS
The Treaty of Amiens stops hostilities between France and England.

E. CULTURE: *Universities*
The U.S. Military Academy is established to train engineers for the U.S. Army.

1803

A. CHEMISTRY: *Atomic Weights*
John Dalton revises the concept of atoms by using their weight as a distinguishing feature. He appends a table of atomic weights to a paper written about the absorption of gases by liquids. In 1808, in his book *New System of Chemical Philosophy,* he explains his ideas more fully, including his law of partial pressures, which states that in a mixture of gases each gas exerts the same pressure it would if it were the only gas present. In modern chemistry, dalton is the unit of mass of one hydrogen atom.

B. CHEMISTRY: *Electric Charge of Acids and Bases*
Jöns Berzelius and Wilhelm Hisinger, in electrolytic experiments, discover that acids and bases have opposite electrical charges.

C. SOCIETY AND POLITICS
• The Treaty of Amiens signed in 1802 is broken as Britain and France renew their war.
• Napoleon Bonaparte sells the Louisiana territory to the United States, increasing the size of the United States by about 100%.

1803 (continued)

D. THE ARTS: *Art*

Thomas Bruce, the earl of Elgin, begins shipping sculpture from Athens to the British Museum. The sculptured frieze, called the Elgin Marbles, is removed from the Parthenon, completed in 438 B.C.

1804

A. FOOD BACTERIOLOGY: *Food Preservation/Canning*

François Nicolas Appert, after several years of experimentation, opens a factory for preserving food in glass bottles using a heating process that he invents. He wins a prize from the French government in 1808. (See 1808 A, 1819 A.)

B. PLANT PHYSIOLOGY: *Photosynthesis/Nitrogen*

Nicolas Théodore de Saussure shows that plants derive their carbon from the atmosphere and not from the soil, thus repeating an observation made in 1779 by Jan Ingenhousz. de Saussure further believes that water is not the source of oxygen in photosynthesis, and that plant nitrogen is derived from the soil, not from the air.

C. CHEMISTRY: *Photooxidation*

William Wollaston discovers that guaiacum turns blue under the influence of oxygen and light.

D. GEOPHYSICS: *High-Altitude Research*

Jean-Baptiste Biot and Joseph Gay-Lussac are the first to use a balloon to do high-altitude research. They ascend about four miles and take measurements of the earth's magnetic field and of the composition of the atmosphere.

E. SOCIETY: *Exploration*

Captain Meriwether Lewis and William Clark begin their exploration of the Missouri River, searching for a water route to the Pacific Ocean. They reach the Pacific in November 1805.

F. SOCIETY AND POLITICS

• Napoleon Bonaparte is named emperor of France by the French senate and tribunal and is consecrated by Pope Pius VII.

• U.S. vice president Aaron Burr fatally wounds Alexander Hamilton in a duel.

1805

A. BIOLOGY: *Plant Geography and Guano*

Friedrich Heinrich Alexander von Humboldt publishes a report of his 5-year exploration of South America, in which he describes the varieties of plants. In 1802, he studies the large quantities of guano, the droppings of seabirds. His report leads to the export of guano to Europe, where it is used both as a fertilizer and, because of its high content of nitrates, for explosives.

B. SOCIETY AND POLITICS

In the Battle of Trafalgar, the British navy under Lord Horatio Nelson defeats a combined French and Spanish fleet. Nelson is killed in the battle, but the victory ensures English control of the seas.

C. THE ARTS: *Music*
The opera *Fidelio* by Ludwig van Beethoven is performed.

A. BIOCHEMISTRY: *First Amino Acid*
Louis-Nicolas Vauquelin gives the name "asparagine" to a substance he isolates from asparagus. Although not realized at this time, this is the first amino acid to be found.

B. CHEMISTRY: *Electrochemistry*
Humphry Davy first uses electricity to make chemical separations. In 1807, through electrical separation, he discovers potassium and sodium and, in 1808, barium, calcium, and strontium.

C. SOCIETY AND POLITICS
The French organize the Confederation of the Rhine and abolish the Holy Roman Empire.

D. CULTURE: *Dictionaries*
Noah Webster publishes *The Compendious Dictionary of the English Language,* the first of a long line of dictionaries that carry his name.

A. PHYSIOLOGY: *Tissue Respiration*
Lazzaro Spallanzani is the first to show respiration of tissues and organs. His work on respiration is published 8 years after his death.

B. CHEMISTRY: *Organic and Inorganic Compounds*
Jöns Berzelius characterizes as organic those compounds derived from either living or dead organisms or those chemically related to such compounds. All other substances are inorganic compounds.

C. TECHNOLOGY: *Steamship*
The first commercial steamship goes into operation on the Hudson River.

D. THE ARTS: *Music*
Ludwig van Beethoven's Fifth Symphony is performed.

E. THE ARTS: *Literature*
William Wordsworth publishes *Poetry in Two Volumes.*

A. FOOD BACTERIOLOGY: *Food Preservation*
Nicolas Appert, who begins bottling (canning) food in 1804, receives a prize of 12,000 francs from the French government for finding a way to preserve foods that can be carried by the armies. He reports experiments performed over two decades that show food can be successfully preserved through a heating process, which leads to modern techniques of canning. He heats foods and liquids in sealed champagne bottles, thus repeating the conditions used by Lazzaro Spallanzani in 1765 in his experiments about the spontaneous generation of life. Although not trained as a scientist, the principles he reveals are the use of sufficient heat and the exclusion of air. Appert credits earlier studies by others on the effect of heat on grape must, fruits, and meat. (See 1765 A, 1895 B.)

1808 *(continued)*

B. THE ARTS: *Literature*

Johann Wolfgang von Goethe completes part 1 of his drama *Faust*. Part 2 is completed in 1832.

1809

BIOLOGY: *Evolution*

Jean-Baptiste Lamarck clarifies his ideas of organic evolution with his publication of *Philosophie zoologique*. He proposes that evolutionary changes occur over time because of excessive use or disuse of a body part. He attributes inherited changes in animals to a physiological need to acquire new characteristics in changing environmental conditions. Lamarck's ideas are misinterpreted by critics who incorrectly state that he claimed that desire or conscious volition leads to development of new characteristics. Lamarck's use of the word *besoin* to mean "need," is mistranslated into English as "want" or "desire." (See 1812 B.)

1810

A. MICROBIOLOGY: *Fermentation*

Joseph Gay-Lussac notes that air is necessary to start a fermentation but not to continue it. He fails to understand that contamination may be caused by microorganisms from the air.

B. FOOD BACTERIOLOGY: *Food Preservation*

Nicolas Appert publishes *Le livre de tous les ménages,* subtitled *L'art de conserver, pendant plusieurs annés, toutes les substances animales et vegetales,* explaining his method for preserving food in bottles.

C. BIOCHEMISTRY: *Oxidation*

Louis Antoine Planche observes the oxidation of guaiacum by plant roots and milk. He repeats this experiment in 1820.

D. BIOCHEMISTRY: *Amino Acids*

William Wollaston isolates the amino acid cystine from a bladder stone. (See 1806 A.)

E. CHEMISTRY: *Hydrochloric Acid*

Humphry Davy proves that oxygen is not a component of hydrochloric acid, thus refuting Antoine Lavoisier's idea that all acids contain oxygen.

F. CULTURE: *Universities*

The University of Berlin is to be predominantly a research institution.

G. THE ARTS: *Literature*

Sir Walter Scott publishes his poem *The Lady of the Lake.*

1811

A. BIOCHEMISTRY: *Glucose from Starch*

Gottlieb Konstantin Kirchhoff produces glucose by boiling starch in the presence of sulfuric acid.

B. CHEMISTRY: *Avogadro's Number*

Amedeo Avogadro's suggestion that at the same temperature, pressure, and volume all gases have the same number of molecules is largely ignored until it is revived by Stanislao Cannizzaro in 1860. Josef Loschmidt first calculates Avogadro's number in 1865.

C. CHEMISTRY: *Cyanide*
Joseph Gay-Lussac studies the properties of cyanide.

D. SOCIETY AND POLITICS
At the confluence of the Tippecanoe and Wabash rivers in Indiana, General William Henry Harrison defeats the Shawnee Indians. When Harrison runs for president of the United States in 1840, with John Tyler as candidate for vice president, his campaign slogan is "Tippecanoe and Tyler Too."

E. THE ARTS: *Literature*
Jane Austen publishes her first novel, *Sense and Sensibility, a Novel by a Lady.*

1812

A. INFECTIOUS DISEASE: *Typhus Fever*
During Napoleon Bonaparte's occupation of Moscow in September and October, his army is drastically reduced by infection with typhus fever. When the French retreat from the city, they leave behind several thousand soldiers who cannot travel because of the disease. As the retreat goes through Lithuania, about 30,000 soldiers are left behind; most of them die of typhus. The pursuing Russian forces lose 62,000 to the disease. The infection spreads to civilians and reaches Germany, Switzerland, Austria, and France.

B. BIOLOGY: *Paleontology/Evolution/Catastrophism*
Georges Cuvier discovers the first fossil of a pterodactyl, a flying reptile. In his book on paleontology, recognized as the first of importance, he classifies fossils according to the Linnaean classification system. His theory that each animal arose independently and is not part of an evolutionary scheme becomes known as catastrophism because of his view that each form became extinct as the result of a global flood. Cuvier, remembered as an antievolutionist, wrote scathingly of Jean-Baptiste Lamarck's views about evolution. (See 1809.)

C. BIOLOGY: *Taxonomy*
Augustin-Pyrame de Candolle uses the word "taxonomy" for the classification of species in his encyclopedia of plants, seven volumes of which are published before his death.

D. CHEMISTRY: *Catalysis*
F. C. Vogel first describes a catalytic reaction when he shows the combination of H_2 and O_2 at room temperature in the presence of animal or plant charcoal. This is the first evidence that the formation of water from hydrogen and oxygen does not require a high temperature. (See 1837 G.)

E. TECHNOLOGY: *Camera Lucida*
William Wollaston invents the *camera lucida,* which projects an image onto a sheet of drawing paper where it can be traced. This device is used extensively to draw objects observed microscopically.

1812 (continued)

F. SOCIETY AND POLITICS

During the long battle between the British and France under Napoleon Bonaparte, the United States has engaged in neutral shipping, i.e., trading with both countries. British courts rule in a case involving the ship *Essex* that this practice must stop. The United States declares war on Britain, the War of 1812, which continues until 1814.

G. THE ARTS: *Literature*

George Gordon Byron (Lord Byron) publishes cantos 1 and 2 of his poem *Childe Harold's Pilgrimage*. Cantos 3 and 4 are published in 1818.

1813

A. CHEMISTRY: *Chemical Symbols*

Jöns Berzelius uses letters as symbols for chemical elements, a practice begun by Thomas Thompson in 1802 and 1808. Berzelius uses the first letter of the element or the first two letters, if needed, to avoid confusion.

B. SOCIETY AND POLITICS

Napoleon Bonaparte is defeated in the Battle of Leipzig (the Battle of Nations).

C. THE ARTS: *Music*

Franz Peter Schubert's Symphony no. 1 in D Major is performed.

D. THE ARTS: *Literature*

• Jane Austen publishes *Pride and Prejudice*.
• Johann Rudolf Wyss completes *The Swiss Family Robinson*, begun by his father, Johann David Wyss.

1814

A. TECHNOLOGY: *Steam Locomotive*

George Stephenson develops the first practical steam locomotive.

B. THE ARTS: *Literature and Music*

Francis Scott Key, who observes the British bombardment of Fort McHenry in Baltimore (War of 1812), writes "The Star-Spangled Banner." Shortly afterward, it is sung to the tune of "The Anacreontic Song," which John Stafford Smith wrote for the Anacreontic Society in England to honor the poetry of Anacreon. In 1931, the U.S. Congress names "The Star-Spangled Banner" the national anthem.

1815

A. BIOCHEMISTRY: *Fermentation*

Joseph Gay-Lussac checks and corrects Antoine Lavoisier's data on fermentation and writes the first version of what comes to be known as the Gay-Lussac equation for the alcoholic fermentation, now expressed as $C_6H_{12}O_6 \rightarrow 2\ CO_2 + 2\ C_2H_5OH$.

B. CHEMISTRY: *Optical Activity*

Jean-Baptiste Biot discovers optical rotation of the polarization plane of solutions of sugars and tartaric acid, as well as in turpentine and camphor. (See 1848 A.)

C. TECHNOLOGY: *Macadam Roads*

John Loudon McAdam paves roads with crushed rock. Although the practice of using asphalt or tar for paving does not come until later, such roads are called "macadam" after his name.

D. SOCIETY AND POLITICS

Napoleon Bonaparte sustains his final defeat in the Battle of Waterloo, after which he is exiled to St. Helena.

1816

A. BIOCHEMISTRY: *Sugar from Germinating Grains*

Gottlieb Konstantin Kirchhoff notes the formation of sugar in an infusion of flour from germinating grains.

B. TECHNOLOGY: *the Stethoscope*

René Laënnec invents the stethoscope.

C. THE ARTS: *Music*

Gioacchino Antonio Rossini's opera *The Barber of Seville* is performed in Rome.

1817

A. INFECTIOUS DISEASE: *Cholera Pandemic*

A pandemic of cholera spreads from India to East Africa, Asia, Japan, and the Philippines. (See 1768, 1826 A.)

B. DISEASE: *Parkinson's Disease*

James Parkinson writes *An Essay on the Shaking Palsy* describing an affliction that thereafter carries his name.

C. PLANT PHYSIOLOGY: *Chlorophyll*

Pierre Pelletier and Joseph Bienaimé Caventou isolate a substance from green plants that they name chlorophyll.

D. CHEMISTRY: *Catalysis*

Humphry Davy discovers that a heated platinum wire causes the combustion of H_2, CO, and CH_4 at temperatures lower than the ignition points of the gases.

E. THE ARTS: *Literature*

John Keats publishes his *Poems*.

1818

A. BIOCHEMISTRY: *Decomposition of Hydrogen Peroxide*

Louis Jacques Thénard discovers hydrogen peroxide and demonstrates that plant and animal tissues decompose it.

B. CHEMISTRY: *Atomic Weights*

Jöns Berzelius publishes a table of atomic weights using oxygen as 100 and includes the molecular weights of about 2,000 compounds. His relative weights are approximately those still used.

C. THE ARTS: *Literature*

• Percy Bysshe Shelley publishes his poem "Ozymandias."

• Mary Wollstonecraft Godwin Shelley, the wife of poet Percy Bysshe Shelley, writes the gothic novel *Frankenstein, or the Modern Prometheus.*

A. TECHNOLOGY: *Canning*

In canning foods, Peter Durand replaces Nicolas Appert's glass containers with steel cans. Tin linings of the metal cans are introduced in 1839 by Charles Mitchell. (See 1808 A.)

B. TECHNOLOGY: *Steamship*

The first steamship crosses the Atlantic, aided by sails through much of the journey.

C. SOCIETY AND POLITICS

At St. Peter's Fields in Manchester, England, soldiers kill 11 persons and injure hundreds. The so-called Peterloo Massacre occurs at a political meeting.

D. THE ARTS: *Literature*
- Walter Scott completes his novel *Ivanhoe.*
- Percy Bysshe Shelley writes *Prometheus Unbound.*
- John Keats completes "Ode on a Grecian Urn" and "Ode to a Nightingale."

A. FOOD POISONING: *Botulism*

Justinus Kerner, a German poet who became a physician and medical officer, describes the food poisoning disease botulism. He reports studying 230 cases of sausage poisoning; the name of the disease is derived from the Latin *botulus,* for sausage. Other names used for sausage poisoning are *Wurstvergiftung* and allantiasis. Botulism has also been called ichthyosismus because poisoning may come from dried and smoked fish. Emile-Pierre-Marie von Ermengem discovers the causative bacterium in 1895. (See 900, 1735 A, 1895 C.)

B. INFECTIOUS DISEASE: *Yellow Fever*

The city of Savannah, Georgia, with a population of 7,500, is surrounded by rice fields where the mosquito *Aedes aegypti* breeds abundantly. A destructive fire, followed by an epidemic of yellow fever, leaves about one-third of the population dead.

C. BIOCHEMISTRY: *Amino Acids*

By boiling gelatin and obtaining a substance he calls glycine, Henri Braconnot is the first to obtain an amino acid from a protein.

D. BIOCHEMISTRY: *Glucose from Wood*

Henri Braconnot boils sawdust and bark with acid and obtains glucose.

E. CHEMISTRY: *Catalysis/Platinum Black*

Edmund Davy uses platinum black to combust alcohol vapors, with the resulting formation of acetic acid.

F. THE ARTS: *Literature*

Washington Irving's collection of stories *The Sketch Book of Geoffrey Crayon, Gent* contains "Rip Van Winkle" and "The Legend of Sleepy Hollow."

G. THE ARTS: *Art*
The *Venus de Milo* is discovered in an underground chamber on the Greek Island of Melos.

1821

A. INFECTIOUS DISEASE: *Diphtheria*
Pierre Bretonneau, a physician in Tours, France, concludes that a disease that he names *diphtérite* is contagious and caused by an agent that is transmitted from person to person. The name is after the Greek *diphthera* for skin or membrane for the false membrane formed in the respiratory tract; it is later changed to *diphtérie,* or diphtheria.

B. MICROSCOPY: *Blood*
Jean Louis Prevost and, 2 years later, Jean-Baptiste Dumas promote the use of microscopes with the publication of their works on blood.

C. PHYSICS: *Electromagnetism*
Michael Faraday demonstrates that electromagnetism causes motion and lays the foundation for his invention in 1831 of an electric generator. His theory stating that the current in an electric wire produces lines of force is the first conception of an electromagnetic field. (See 1831 D, 1855 B.)

D. MATHEMATICS: *Calculus*
Augustin Louis Cauchy publishes three textbooks on mathematics that begin to put calculus into modern form.

1822

A. BACTERIAL PHYSIOLOGY: *Vinegar*
After examining the film of growth found on the surface of wine during the production of acetic acid, C. J. Persoon names it *Mycoderma mesentericum.* In 1837 Friedrich Kützing finds that the film, known as "mother of vinegar," contains microscopic organisms. In 1868, Louis Pasteur confirms that the bacteria in the film convert alcohol to acetic acid. (See 1837 C, 1868 B.)

B. PHYSICS: *Electrodynamics*
André Marie Ampère reports his experiments that lay the foundation for electrodynamics. Hans Christian Oersted observes in 1819 that magnetized needles move in electric currents, leading Ampère to other experiments that prove the magnetic effects of electric fields. In 1825 he calculates that the force between two electric wires is inversely proportional to the distance between them—the inverse square law. His name is subsequently used for the basic unit of electric current, the ampere or amp.

C. TECHNOLOGY: *Difference Engine*
Charles Babbage describes a "difference engine" that he believes will calculate tables of logarithms. Although he demonstrates a prototype, the machine is never completed. (See 1830 D, 1832 E.)

D. TECHNOLOGY: *Photography*
Joseph Nicéphore Niepce produces the first lasting photographic image on a pewter plate coated with bitumen of Judea, a type of asphalt.

E. THE ARTS: *Music*

Franz Schubert begins composing his Symphony no. 8, the so-called Unfinished Symphony, but he dies of typhus fever in 1828 before he can complete it.

1823

A. BACTERIAL SPECIES: Serratia marcescens

B. Bizio attributes an outbreak of "bloody" polenta in northern Italy to a fungus. He gives it the name *Serratia marcescens* after the Italian physicist Serafino Serrati; "marcescens" is derived from a word that means fading away. The organism is found to be a bacterium.

B. BOTANY: *Fertilization*

Giovanni Battista Amici begins a long series of studies on fertilization in plants. Over a period of 20 or more years, he notes the formation of the pollen tube, which he traces to the ovary and micropyle, showing that, in orchids, a cell present in the ovule develops into the embryo after the pollen tube reaches it. (See 1827 A.)

C. TECHNOLOGY: *Electromagnet*

William Sturgeon invents the electromagnet by placing an iron rod inside an electrical wire wound into a helix, creating a solenoid. (See 1829 A, 1831 C.)

D. SOCIETY AND POLITICS

In his annual message to Congress, U.S. president James Monroe proclaims the "Monroe Doctrine" warning European governments that the United States will oppose any attempts at colonization or other interference in the Western Hemisphere.

1825

A. BACTERIOLOGY: *Nomenclature*

Bory de St. Vincent includes a table entitled "Tableau des Ordes, des Familles et des Genres de Microscopiques" in his book *Mycologia europia,* listing several organisms now known to be bacteria. These include the genera *Spirilina* and *Vibrio*.

B. CHEMISTRY: *Benzene/Chlorine Compounds*

Michael Faraday describes and names benzene. He is also the first to find compounds that contain both chlorine and carbon.

C. CHEMISTRY: *in Germany*

Justus von Liebig opens his laboratory at the University of Giessen. In the early 19th century, German chemists begin to dominate the science of chemistry.

D. BIOCHEMISTRY: *Hematin*

Leopold Gmelin discovers hematin.

E. ZOOLOGY: *Embryology*

Karl Ernst Ritter von Baer discovers the mammalian ovum and writes that all animals that arise from the coition of male and female develop in an ovum. He states that embryos of different species at first have analogous, even indistinguishable, forms and that differentiation takes place in later development. Believing that sperm are parasites ("entozoa"), he gives them the name spermatozoa. (See 1759 A, 1677.)

F. THE ARTS: *Literature*
A portion of Samuel Pepys's *Diary,* written between 1660 and 1669, is published.

1826

A. INFECTIOUS DISEASE: *Cholera Pandemic*
A new epidemic of cholera spreads from Southeast Asia over the rest of the world. The disease reaches Poland, Germany, and Britain in 1831 and Paris in 1832. Irish immigrants bring cholera to Canada in the summer of 1832, after which it passes into the United States.

B. THE ARTS: *Literature*
James Fenimore Cooper publishes *The Last of the Mohicans.*

1827

A. MICROSCOPY: *Achromatic Objectives*
Giovanni Battista Amici, Charles Chevalier, and others develop the first achromatic objectives for the compound microscope, thus eliminating color aberrations. (See 1830 B.)

B. PHYSICS: *Brownian Movement*
Robert Brown observes the constant, irregular movement of pollen grains suspended in water. The phenomenon, which becomes known as Brownian movement or Brownian motion, is not explained mathematically until the early 20th century, when both Albert Einstein and Jean-Baptiste Perrin publish articles that deal with Brownian motion. Einstein's first important paper, in 1905, shows that by measuring the way the particles move, an inference can be made about the number of molecules per unit volume. In 1909, Perrin calculates values for Avogadro's number by using measurements of Brownian motion. Both explanations are that small particles suspended in water are bombarded by water molecules in motion because of heat.

C. CHEMISTRY: *Isomerism*
Jöns Berzelius defines chemical isomers as compounds that have the same chemical composition but different properties. He notes that cyanic acid, analyzed by Friedrich Wöhler, and fulminic acid, analyzed by Justus von Liebig, have the same composition but not the same chemical properties.

D. TECHNOLOGY: *Friction Match*
John Walker invents the friction match, called the Lucifer, which is ignited by drawing the head through sandpaper.

E. THE ARTS: *Art*
John James Audubon publishes the first of a series of volumes displaying paintings of American birds.

1827 (continued)

F. THE ARTS: *Literature*

Edgar Allan Poe's first poems appear.

G. THE ARTS: *Music*

Franz Schubert completes his song cycle *Die Winterreise.*

1828

A. ZOOLOGY: *Embryology*

Karl von Baer begins to publish his work on the development of the embryo from a single fertilized egg. He proposes that four germ layers of tissue form; later researchers regard Baer's two middle layers as a single tissue.

B. CHEMISTRY: *Urea*

Friedrich Wöhler artificially synthesizes urea by heating ammonium cynanate.

C. CHEMISTRY: *Ethyl Alcohol*

Jean-Baptiste Dumas and Polydore Boullay study the reactions of ethyl alcohol and conclude that alcohol is a hydrate of ethylene.

D. CULTURE: *Dictionaries*

Noah Webster completes *An American Dictionary of the English Language* using American rather than English spellings of many words.

1829

A. TECHNOLOGY: *Electromagnets*

Joseph Henry creates powerful electromagnets by using insulated electric wire to wrap iron bars, permitting the use of a large number of turns of wire. (See 1823 C.).

B. CULTURE: *the Braille System*

Louis Braille, blind since the age of three, invents the Braille system of finger reading, which uses raised points representing letters on the page. The system is widely accepted by about 1834.

1830

A. INFECTIOUS DISEASE: *Influenza*

An influenza pandemic beginning in this year continues until 1833. Thought to have begun in China, it becomes worldwide over the course of 3 years. (See 1781 A, 1847 A, 1889 E.)

B. MICROSCOPY: *Achromatic Lens*

Joseph Lister develops one of the achromatic lenses for microscopes, eliminating chromatic aberration. His work follows the 1827 work of Giovanni Battista Amici and Charles Chevalier. (See 1827 A.)

C. BIOCHEMISTRY: *Fermentation*

Augustin Pierre Dubrunfaut makes a clear, watery extract of malt that converts starch to sugar.

D. SCIENTIFIC SOCIETIES

Charles Babbage, in his book *Reflections on the Decline of Science in England,* discusses and identifies various types of scientific fraud. His criticism of

1831

British science leads to the formation of the British Association for the Advancement of Science. (See 1822 C, 1832 E.)

A. BIOLOGY: *Evolution*
Charles Darwin begins his voyage on the HMS *Beagle*. The trip takes him to the Galápagos Islands in 1835. (See 1859 B.)

B. CHEMISTRY: *Chloroform*
Chloroform is discovered independently by Samuel Guthrie, Justus von Liebig, and Eugène Soubeiran.

C. TECHNOLOGY: *Electrical Transformer and Generator*
Michael Faraday discovers electromagnetic induction when he builds the first type of electrical transformer. He subsequently invents a hand-operated electric generator that generates direct current. Joseph Henry independently discovers electromagnetic induction, but Faraday's report comes a few months earlier. Using the reverse concept that an electric current should produce rotary motion, Henry invents the first practical electric motor.

D. THE ARTS: *Music*
Felix Mendelssohn-Bartholdy performs his Piano Concerto no. 1 in G Minor.

1832

A. INFECTIOUS DISEASE: *Cholera*
The cholera pandemic reaches New York City, from where it spreads both west and south.

B. DISEASE: *Hodgkin's Disease*
Thomas Hodgkin discovers a cancer of the lymph nodes that is named Hodgkin's disease in 1865 by Samuel Wilks.

C. BIOLOGY: *Cell Nucleus*
Robert Brown discovers the nucleus of plant cells.

D. TECHNOLOGY: *Alternating Electrical Current*
Hippolyte Pixii invents a hand-operated electric generator that produces alternating current.

E. TECHNOLOGY: *Computer*
Charles Babbage describes a more advanced "analytical engine" than the difference engine that he proposed in 1822. Although the British government grants him funds to build the machine, the support is withdrawn by 1842, after he has spent £17,000 of government money and many thousands of pounds of his own. His concept, based on the use of punched cards that would store both numbers and the sequence of operations, is derived from the Jacquard loom. Though the machine cannot be built with the mechanical devices available, it is regarded as providing basic principles for the electronic computers that are developed more than 100 years later. (See 1801 C.)

F. THE ARTS: *Literature*
Alfred Lord Tennyson publishes "The Lady of Shalott."

A. BIOCHEMISTRY: *Diastase*
Anselme Payen and Jean François Persoz treat malt extract with alcohol and obtain a white powder that converts starch to sugar. They call this material diastase, implying the breaching of the outer layers of starch granules. Diastase is the first substance to be isolated that is later referred to as an enzyme. (See 1877 E.)

B. PHYSICS: *Electrolysis*
Michael Faraday introduces the terms "anode," "cathode," "ion," "anion," "cation," "electrolysis," and "electrolyte," which are invented for him by scholar William Whewell.

C. ETYMOLOGY: *Scientist*
William Whewell suggests that members of the British Association for the Advancement of Science call themselves "scientists" to replace the term "natural philosophers."

D. CULTURE: *Universities*
Oberlin College opens in Ohio. It becomes the first coeducational college in the United States when it admits women in 1838.

E. SOCIETY AND POLITICS
A customs union, the Zollverein, is established and includes Bavaria, Württemberg, Prussia, and Hesse-Darmstadt.

A. BIOCHEMISTRY: *Cellulose*
Anselme Payen isolates a substance from wood that he names "cellulose." He demonstrates that it can be decomposed to form glucose. (See 1820 D.)

B. TECHNOLOGY: *Photography*
William Henry Fox Talbot experiments with the light sensitivity of silver nitrate. He develops a photographic method in 1841.

C. SOCIETY AND POLITICS
Alexis Charles Henri Clérel de Tocqueville publishes *Democracy in America*. He travels for 9 months through parts of Canada and the northeastern United States, as well as through Ohio, Tennessee, and Louisiana, performing a study of penitentiary systems, but writes about the general social conditions in the country.

A. FUNGAL DISEASE: *Muscardine of Silkworms*
Agostino Maria Bassi shows that the disease muscardine (calcino) of silkworms is caused by a fungus, identified by G. Balsamo-Crivelli as a *Botrytis* species. He also demonstrates that the disease is contagious and can be controlled.

B. BIOLOGY: *Evolution*
Charles Darwin visits the Galápagos Islands and collects several types of finches, which later provide the source for his new theories on the development of separate species.

C. THE ARTS: *Music*

The opera *Lucia di Lammermoor,* by Gaetano Donizetti, is performed.

D. THE ARTS: *Literature*

Hans Christian Andersen publishes *Fairy Tales.*

1836

A. BIOCHEMISTRY: *Pepsin*

Theodor Schwann obtains pepsin from pigs' stomachs. This is the first substance to be isolated from animals that is later called an enzyme. (See 1877 E.)

B. SOCIETY AND POLITICS

A garrison of soldiers in a Franciscan mission at San Antonio called the Alamo falls to a Mexican army led by General Antonio López de Santa Anna. The entire garrison is killed, including frontiersmen James Bowie, inventor of the Bowie knife, and David (Davy) Crockett. Later this year, Texas wins its independence from Mexico in the battle at San Jacinto. The Texas forces are led by Sam Houston, a former governor of Tennessee who becomes president of the Republic of Texas, and Sidney Sherman, whose battle cry is "Remember the Alamo."

C. THE ARTS: *Literature*

Ralph Waldo Emerson's essay "Nature" is published.

1837

A. INFECTIOUS DISEASE: *Smallpox*

Native Americans living along the Missouri River are struck by smallpox, resulting in 15,000 deaths.

B. MICROBIOLOGY: *Yeast*

Theodor Schwann observes the multiplication of yeast and names it *Saccharomyces,* or sugar fungus.

C. FERMENTATION: *Yeast*

Friedrich Kützing, after making microscopic observations of yeast in alcoholic fermentations, suggests that yeast be removed from the list of chemical compounds since it is a living organism. Kützing also examines "mother of vinegar" and finds organisms smaller than yeast that he believes convert ethanol to acetic acid. His theory is confirmed in 1868 by Louis Pasteur. (See 1822 A, 1838 C, 1868 B.)

D. PROTOZOAN DISEASE: *Pébrine in Silkworms*

Agostino Maria Bassi observes the protozoa that cause the disease pébrine in silkworms.

E. BIOLOGY: *Cell Theory*

Jan Evangelista Purkinje, as a result of his studies on nerve fibers, elaborates a theory of the cell that is further expanded by Theodor Schwann and Matthias Jakob Schleiden in 1838 to 1839. In 1838, he both describes cell division and first uses the word "protoplasm" for the embryonic material in eggs. (See 1839 D, 1846 I, 1861 F.)

1837 *(continued)*

F. BIOCHEMISTRY: *Emulsin*

Friedrich Wöhler and Justus von Liebig extract emulsin from bitter almonds. In a paper reporting their results, they refer to Jöns Berzelius's ideas of catalytic power and concur with him that yeasts are not living.

G. CHEMISTRY: *Catalysis*

Jöns Berzelius develops his theory of catalysis, including ferments as catalysts and not living organisms.

H. PLANT PHYSIOLOGY: *Photosynthesis*

René Joachim Henri Dutrochet reports that plants absorb carbon dioxide only if they are green, contain chlorophyll, and are in the presence of light. He thus adds to the observations of Jan Ingenhousz in 1779 about the process that becomes known as photosynthesis. (See 1817 C.)

I. PHYSIOLOGY: *Blood Gases*

Gustav Magnus demonstrates that circulating blood contains dissolved oxygen, carbon dioxide, and nitrogen.

J. TECHNOLOGY: *Telegraphy and the Morse Code*

Samuel F. B. Morse patents a magnetic telegraph to transmit messages by means of electric wire and relays. With Alfred Vail, he develops a code of short and long impulses, dots and dashes, known as the Morse code.

K. SOCIETY AND POLITICS

Queen Victoria assumes the throne of Great Britain, which she will occupy until 1901.

L. THE ARTS: *Literature*

Charles Dickens publishes *The Posthumous Papers of the Pickwick Club* (the *Pickwick Papers*).

1838

A. BACTERIOLOGY: *Taxonomy*

Christian Gottfried Ehrenberg, a teacher of Ferdinand Cohn, publishes a report on "Infusionstierchen," or infusion animals, in which he establishes different groups among the bacteria according to shapes and sizes. He includes the generic names *Bacterium, Spirillum, Vibrio,* and *Spirochaeta.*

B. BACTERIAL PHYSIOLOGY: *Nitrogen Fixation*

Jean-Baptiste Boussingault, reporting on the results of 4 or 5 years of analyses of crop rotations and data from experiments with pots of clover and wheat, shows that leguminous plants obtain nitrogen from the air. He does not specifically mention nitrogen gas as the source of the nitrogen, and later, after severe criticism from Justus von Liebig in 1840, Boussingault states that a small quantity of ammonia in air supplies the nitrogen. He cites both von Liebig and Nicolas Théodore de Saussure, both of whom believe that ammonia is absorbed by plants. Liebig, who has done no experiments, is critical of Boussingault's analytical techniques. Saussure had performed experiments in 1804 from which he concluded that soil, not air, is the source of the nitrogen. (See 1857 B, 1886 B.)

C. FERMENTATION: *Yeast*

Based on microscopic observations of budding and growing brewer's yeast, Charles Cagniard-Latour concludes that yeast is a living organism that might cause fermentation. Pierre Turpin publishes a paper confirming the observation of Cagniard-Latour, Theodor Schwann, and Friedrich Kützing on the role of yeast in the alcoholic fermentation. (See 1837 B, 1837 C.)

D. BIOLOGY: *Cell Theory*

Matthias Jakob Schleiden investigates growing plants and concludes that all plants are composed of cells that have a nucleus. (See 1665 B, 1837 E, 1839 D, 1846 B.)

E. BIOCHEMISTRY: *Protein*

Gerardus Johannes Mulder assigns the name "protein" to substances that he believes form the basic unit of albuminous materials. His analysis reveals that the substance contains carbon, hydrogen, nitrogen, oxygen, and a few atoms of phosphorus and sulfur. The word "protein" is suggested to him by Jöns Berzelius.

F. BIOCHEMISTRY: *Hematin/Hematosin*

Louis René Lecanu isolates hematin, which he calls hematosin.

G. SOCIETY AND POLITICS

Members of the Cherokee Nation in Tennessee, Georgia, and Alabama are forced to march 800 miles to an Indian Territory in Arkansas. The "Trail of Tears" leaves approximately 4,000 dead of disease and exhaustion.

H. THE ARTS: *Literature*

Charles Dickens completes *Oliver Twist*.

1839

A. FERMENTATION: *Polemic*

A humorous article (a skit) ridiculing the conclusions of Pierre Turpin, Charles Cagniard-Latour, Theodor Schwann, and Friedrich Kützing about the role of yeast in fermentation appears in a journal edited by Friedrich Wöhler, Justus von Liebig, Jean-Baptiste Dumas, and Thomas Graham. This article may have significantly delayed the acceptance of Cagniard-Latour's conclusions about fermentation.

B. FERMENTATION: *Process*

Justus von Liebig rejects Jöns Berzelius's view, which he had accepted 2 years earlier, that fermentation is a catalytic process. Although Liebig does no new experiments, he puts forth a theory of putrefaction and fermentation as "slow combustion" caused by a state of chemical activity in which vibratory action of the sugar molecules is responsible for the formation of alcohol and carbon dioxide. He further maintains that ferment (yeast) is actually produced by the changes in fermentation.

C. FUNGAL DISEASE: *Disease of Human Skin*

In his study of favus, Johann Lucas Schönlein, following the work of Robert Remak in 1837, makes the first clear report of fungal infections of human skin. Remak is among the first to believe that all animal cells come from preexisting cells. (See 1841 A.)

1839 *(continued)*

D. BIOLOGY: *Cell Theory*

Theodor Schwann publishes *Microscopical Researches into the Similarity in the Structure and Growth of Animals and Plants,* asserting that all animals are composed of cells. Matthias Jakob Schleiden and Schwann together are credited with the formulation of the cell theory, the premise that all animal and plant life is composed of independent cells. An earlier version of the cell theory is issued by Jan Evangelista Purkinje in 1837. (See 1665 B, 1837 E, 1838 D, 1846 D.)

E. TECHNOLOGY: *Canning*

Charles Mitchell is the first to use a thin layer of tin to line steel cans, which were introduced in 1819. (See 1819 A.)

F. TECHNOLOGY: *Daguerreotype*

Louis Daguerre invents the first method for producing lasting photographic images on a silver-coated plate. His process, called the daguerreotype, is limited by the fact that it produces only a positive photographic image, which cannot be reproduced to make additional copies. (See 1834 B, 1841 B.)

G. TECHNOLOGY: *Rubber*

Upon heating a mixture of rubber and sulfur, Charles Goodyear creates a substance, named vulcanized rubber, that retains flexibility when cold and does not become sticky when hot.

H. THE ARTS: *Literature*

The Fall of the House of Usher by Edgar Allan Poe is published in *Burton's Gentleman's* magazine.

1840

A. INFECTIOUS DISEASE: *Germ Theory*

Friedrich Gustav Jacob Henle, one of Robert Koch's teachers at the University of Göttingen, includes in his book *Pathologische Untersuchungen* a chapter in which he formulates a germ theory of disease. He writes about contagion as a living entity that reproduces itself and possibly could be grown outside the body. He does not give a list of experimental steps, such as those later used by Koch that lead to the formulation of "Koch's postulates." (See 1883 B, 1876 C, 1884 D.)

B. INFECTIOUS DISEASE: *Poliomyelitis*

Jacob von Heine concludes that acute poliomyelitis is a disease of the spinal cord. His observations follow those of John Badham, who calls attention to cerebral symptoms in cases of induced paralysis in children.

C. MICROSCOPY: *Immersion Lens*

Giovanni Battista Amici makes the first practical water immersion lens for the compound microscope. (See 1874 C, 1878 H.)

D. PHYSIOLOGY: *Tissue Respiration*

It is generally recognized that respiratory combustion takes place in the capillaries of the tissues and that the "red globules" in blood carry oxygen.

E. CHEMISTRY: *Ozone*

Christian Friedrich Schönbein discovers ozone and studies its oxidative properties. He notes that it turns guaiacum blue and theorizes that ozone might be the key to all biological oxidations.

1841

A. FUNGAL DISEASE: *Medical Mycology*

David Gruby begins work on fungal infections, which marks the beginning of medical mycology. His studies over a number of years are more extensive than Johann Schönlein's observations in 1839 about fungal skin infections. (See 1839 C.)

B. TECHNOLOGY: *Photography*

William Henry Fox Talbot patents a new type of photography, the calotype method, which permits making a photographic negative image from which many copies of a positive image can be made. In time, his process replaces the daguerreotype. (See 1839 F.)

C. THE ARTS: *Literature*

• In the final installment of *The Old Curiosity Shop,* Charles Dickens describes the death of Little Nell.

• James Fenimore Cooper publishes *The Deerslayer.*

1842

A. BACTERIAL SPECIES: *Sulfur Bacteria*

V. Trevisan describes the first sulfur bacterium when he gives the name *Beggiatoa punctata* to an organism that he believes is closely related to the alga *Oscillatoria.*

B. BACTERIAL SPECIES: Sarcina

John Goodsir, an anatomist and surgeon, finds an organism that forms regular packets of spherical cells in a patient's vomit. He names it *Sarcina ventriculi* after the Latin words for bundle or packet and stomach.

C. INFECTIOUS DISEASE: *Disinfection*

Oliver Wendell Holmes shows that midwives and physicians transfer puerperal (childbed) fever from one mother to another. His suggestions that physicians should wash their hands in calcium chloride and change their clothes after conducting postmortem examinations or attending patients with puerperal fever meet with strong opposition. (See 1846 A.)

D. PHYSICS: *Law of Conservation of Energy*

Robert Mayer, a physician serving as a ship's surgeon in the tropics, notices that the venous blood of a patient is unusually red. He associates this fact with the idea that, in the hot climate, body heat is easier to maintain, and he develops an article on the difference in the specific heat of gases. Mayer, who had no mathematical training and did no experiments, asserts that forces, by which he may have meant energy, are indestructible, convertible, imponderable objects. In 1845, he states that heat is a force that may be transformed into a mechanical effect. Physicists generally acknowledge that Mayer is the first to state the law of conservation of energy. (See 1847 B, 1849 E.)

1842 (continued)

E. PHYSICS: *the Doppler Effect*

Christian Johann Doppler notices that the frequency of sound or light waves emitted by a moving source changes in relation to a stationary observer. In the so-called Doppler effect, the frequency shifts toward a higher frequency as the source approaches and to a lower frequency as it moves away.

F. THE ARTS: *Literature*

Edgar Allan Poe publishes his poem "The Raven."

1843

A. PHYSICS: *Wheatstone Bridge*

Charles Wheatstone invents the Wheatstone bridge, a method for measuring electrical resistance.

B. THE ARTS: *Literature*

Charles Dickens writes *A Christmas Carol,* creating the characters Ebenezer Scrooge, Bob Cratchit, and Tiny Tim.

C. THE ARTS: *Music*

Felix Mendelssohn–Bartholdy completes his overture to *A Midsummer Night's Dream,* which includes a wedding march widely used in Europe and the United States.

1844

A. BIOLOGY: *Evolution*

Robert Chambers publishes *Vestiges of the Natural History of Creation,* in which he discusses his concepts of evolution. He associates the development of the universe and the earth and its creatures to a fundamental law of progress. His treatment of the subject is so controversial that he publishes it anonymously because he does not wish to incur damage to his publishing business. The book is strongly criticized by both the clergy and scientists but is widely read and has 10 editions in about 10 years. Both Alfred Russel Wallace and Charles Darwin read Chambers's book, and Wallace is convinced by it that evolution causes the appearance of separate species. (See 1858 D.)

B. TECHNOLOGY: *the Telegraph*

Samuel Morse's telegraph sends a message from Baltimore to Washington, D.C.

C. SOCIETY AND POLITICS

The Young Men's Christian Association (YMCA) is founded in London to provide for the social and religious welfare of young men. (See 1855 C.)

D. THE ARTS: *Literature*

Alexandre Dumas publishes *The Three Musketeers.*

1845

A. BIOLOGY: *Protozoa*

Carol Theodor Ernst von Siebold gives the name *Protozoa* to animals whose organization is reducible to one cell.

B. BIOCHEMISTRY: *Peroxidase*
Christian Friedrich Schönbein describes the action of peroxidase, named in 1898 by Georges Linossier.

C. TECHNOLOGY: *Guncotton*
After discovering that nitrocellulose explodes, Christian Friedrich Schönbein invents guncotton.

D. CULTURE: *Universities*
The U.S. Naval Academy is founded in Annapolis, Maryland.

E. THE ARTS: *Literature*
Alexandre Dumas completes *The Count of Monte Cristo*.

1846

A. INFECTIOUS DISEASE: *Antiseptics*
Ignaz Philipp Semmelweis introduces the use of antiseptic (hypochlorite solution) in his work on prevention of the spread of puerperal fever. (See 1842 C, 1861 C.)

B. INFECTIOUS DISEASE: *Epidemiology*
Peter Ludwig Panum is sent to the Danish Faeroe Islands to investigate a measles epidemic. His report, published in 1847, though not concerned with the causative agent, becomes an important record of an epidemiological study.

C. FUNGAL DISEASE: *the Potato Blight*
The potato famine in Ireland, caused by a fungal blight (*Phytophthora infestans*), reaches its peak. One million people die by 1851. Although the famine is most severe in Ireland, where much of the population depends on potatoes for food, it is widespread across Europe and Russia.

D. MICROBIOLOGY: *Thermophiles*
M. Descloizeaux reports finding algae in thermal springs in Iceland. Some authorities speculate that other microorganisms that were reported as early as 1823 to be in thermal springs may have been chlamydobacteria. (See 1862 A, 1879 A.)

E. FERMENTATION: *Biochemistry*
Augustin Pierre Dubrunfaut finds that sucrose is cleaved before it is fermented. Later work shows the products to be glucose and fructose.

F. PHYSIOLOGY: *Animal Respiration*
In the third edition of his book *Die Organische Chemie in ihrer Anwendung auf Physiologie und Pathologie,* published in English as *Animal Chemistry,* Justus von Liebig describes the source of animal heat as being an interaction between constituents of food and oxygen distributed in the body by blood circulation.

G. BIOLOGY: *Cell Structure/Protoplasm*
Hugo von Mohl uses the word "protoplasm" to describe the granular material contained within a plant cell. He also differentiates the cell membrane, nucleus, and cellular fluid. The word protoplasm is used in 1837 by Jan Evangelista Purkinje to describe embryonic material in eggs. Its modern

1846 *(continued)*

usage gains widespread acceptance after Max Johann Sigismund Schultze includes it in his definition of a cell in 1861. (See 1837 E, 1861 F.)

H. MEDICINE: *Anesthesia*

William Thomas Morton, an American dentist, reports using ether as anesthesia for extracting teeth. The use of ether was suggested to him by the chemist Charles Jackson. Learning about ether from Morton, a British surgeon, Robert Liston, uses it while amputating a leg. Crawford Williamson Long, who actually uses ether in surgery as early as 1842, does not announce his work until after Morton's report appears, and Morton receives the recognition. However, Morton and Jackson argue over priority until Morton's death in 1868.

I. CULTURE: *Museum*

The estate of the Englishman James Smithson donates £100,000 to found the Smithsonian Institution in Washington, D.C.

1847

A. INFECTIOUS DISEASE: *Influenza*

In Britain, the "great influenza of 1847" infects about 250,000 persons, with mortality greater than that of the cholera epidemic of 1831. The disease spreads across Europe, North America, and Brazil. (See 1781 A, 1830 A, 1889 E, 1892 B.)

B. PHYSICS: *First Law of Thermodynamics*

Hermann Ludwig Helmholtz publishes "Über die Erhaltung der Kraft" ("On the Conservation of Energy"), clearly stating the principles of the first law of thermodynamics. (See 1842 D, 1849 E.)

C. MATHEMATICS: *Boolean Logic*

George Boole publishes *The Mathematical Analysis of Logic,* describing his system of symbolic logic, or algebra.

D. SOCIETY AND POLITICS

The *Manifest des Kommunismus* (*Communist Manifesto*) appears in the form of a pamphlet written by Karl Marx and Friedrich Engels, who are commissioned by the Communist League in London.

E. THE ARTS: *Literature*

- Emily Brontë publishes her novel *Wuthering Heights*.
- Charlotte Brontë publishes her novel *Jane Eyre*.

1848

A. CHEMISTRY: *Optical Activity*

Louis Pasteur makes his first important contribution to science when he announces his discovery that the differences in optical activity of sodium–ammonium tartrate and sodium–ammonium paratartrate are caused by two distinct crystalline forms. His work is based on Jean–Baptiste Biot's discovery in 1815 of the optical rotation of polarized light by certain chemicals in solution and by Eilhard Mitscherlich's discovery in 1844 of the differences in the rotation of light by the two tartrates. An important role in Pasteur's research is played by Auguste Laurent, whose concept of chemical isomorphism is instrumental in leading to the observations of different crystalline structure. (See 1815 B.)

B. PHYSICS: *Absolute Zero Temperature*
William Thomson (who becomes Lord Kelvin, baron of Largs, in 1892) shows that the temperature of absolute zero is $-273°C$ (later revised to $-273.15°C$). (See 1851 A.)

C. CHEMISTRY: *Atomic and Molecular Weights*
Stanislao Cannizzaro reformulates atomic and molecular weights on the basis of the molecular hypothesis formulated in 1811 by Amedeo Avogadro and in 1814 by André Marie Ampère.

D. SCIENTIFIC SOCIETIES
The American Association for the Advancement of Science is founded.

E. SOCIETY AND POLITICS
• An antimonarchy riot in Paris leads to the abdication of King Louis Philippe. Louis Napoleon Bonaparte, the son of Emperor Napoleon Bonaparte's youngest brother, is elected president of the Second Republic (See 1851 D, 1852 C).
• Revolutions take place throughout Europe, including Berlin, Vienna, Prague, Budapest, and the Italian states.
• The California gold rush occurs.

F. THE ARTS: *Literature*
William Makepeace Thackeray publishes *Vanity Fair: a Novel Without a Hero.*

1849

A. INFECTIOUS DISEASE: *Cholera*
John Snow presents his first observations on the transmission of the disease cholera through drinking water. The 1846 cholera pandemic in India spreads across Europe, reaching England. Snow is awarded a prize of 30,000 francs by the Institute of France for his essay on the transmission of the disease. (See 1854 C, 1856 A.)

B. BACTERIAL DISEASE: *Anthrax*
Aloys Pollender observes rod-shaped cells in the blood of cows that have died of anthrax. Pollender assumes that these are the bacteria that cause the disease but is unable to rule out the then-current idea that bacteria in diseased tissue are products of putrefaction, i.e., spontaneously generated. (See 1863 A, 1868 A, 1876 C, 1877 D, 1881 F.)

C. BIOCHEMISTRY: *Invertase*
Marcelin Berthelot obtains invertase from yeast.

D. BIOLOGY: *Histology*
Ferdinand Cohn first uses dyes such as carmine and hematoxylin to stain histological sections for microscopy. (See 1856 C, 1869 A, 1876 B.)

E. PHYSICS: *Mechanical Equivalent of Heat*
In 1839, James Prescott Joule began experiments that lead to his paper in 1849, "On the Mechanical Equivalent of Heat." In 1845, he performs an

1849 *(continued)*

experiment in which he shows that water is heated by friction when stirred with a paddle-wheel device. (See 1842 D, 1847 B.)

F. CULTURE: *Literature*

Edgar Allan Poe completes his poem "Annabel Lee" shortly before his death.

1850

A. PHYSIOLOGY: *Muscle Respiration*

Georg Liebig studies muscle respiration but overlooks Lazzaro Spallanzani's work, published in 1807.

B. PHYSICS: *Second Law of Thermodynamics*

Rudolf Emmanuel Clausius formulates an early version of the second law of thermodynamics as he begins to develop ideas in thermodynamics based on the conservation of energy (the first law of thermodynamics) and the flow of heat from warmer to cooler bodies. (See 1847 B, 1854 D.)

C. TECHNOLOGY: *Bunsen Burner*

Robert Wilhelm Bunsen invents a gas burner. He also invents a battery (1840), the grease-spot photometer (1844), the absorptiometer (1855), the filter pump (1868), and an ice calorimeter (1870).

D. THE ARTS: *Music*

Richard Wagner's opera *Lohengrin* is performed.

E. THE ARTS: *Literature*

• Alfred Lord Tennyson completes his elegy, "In Memoriam, A.H.H.," to his friend Arthur Henry Hallam, who died in 1833.
• Nathaniel Hawthorne publishes *The Scarlet Letter*.
• *David Copperfield* by Charles Dickens appears as a book after being published serially between 1849 and 1850.

1851

A. PHYSICS: *Kelvin Temperature Scale*

William Thomson (Lord Kelvin) proposes the absolute temperature scale, or Kelvin scale, based on the intervals of the Celsius thermometer, with zero set at $-273.7°C$ (later changed to $-273.15°C$), the theoretical temperature at which motion ceases in gases.

B. PHYSICS: *Foucault's Pendulum*

Jean Bernard Léon Foucault conducts a public demonstration to prove the rotation of the earth by suspending a pendulum more than 200 feet in length from the dome of the Panthéon in Paris.

C. TECHNOLOGY: *Heat Pump*

William Thomson (Lord Kelvin) demonstrates that the expansion of a gas absorbs heat that can be released in a condenser.

D. SOCIETY AND POLITICS

• A coup d'état gives Louis Napoleon Bonaparte control of the French government. (See 1852 C.)

- The first world's fair, the London Great Exhibition, opens in the Crystal Palace, an immense greenhouse-like structure built by Joseph Paxton.

E. THE ARTS: *Music*
The opera *Rigoletto* by Giuseppe Verdi is performed.

F. THE ARTS: *Literature*
- Herman Melville publishes *Moby Dick*.
- Nathaniel Hawthorne writes *The House of the Seven Gables*.

1852

A. BACTERIAL STRUCTURE: *Endospores*
Maximilian Perty publishes drawings that appear to show bacterial spores. He creates a genus called *Sporonema* and formulates a classification of bacteria as either spiral or straight and flexuous or not.

B. CHEMISTRY: *Valence*
Edward Frankland, following his studies on organometallic chemistry, formulates the theory that each type of atom can combine with a fixed number of other atoms. This concept is known as the "valence" of an atom.

C. SOCIETY AND POLITICS
Louis Napoleon Bonaparte, beginning a Second Empire in France, names himself Napoleon III. He remains in power until 1870.

D. THE ARTS: *Literature*
Harriet Beecher Stowe publishes *Uncle Tom's Cabin* in book form after previous serial publication in the *National Era*.

1853

A. BIOLOGY: *Fertilization*
George Newport, experimenting with frogs, observes microscopically the penetration of spermatozoa into ova. Although others, including Antony van Leeuwenhoek, had made similar observations with several organisms, Newport's account is reliably documented.

B. BIOCHEMISTRY: *Hemin*
By treating blood with boiling glacial acetic acid, Ludwig Teichmann obtains pure crystalline hemin.

C. PHYSICS: *the Angstrom*
Anders Jonas Ångström establishes the principles of spectroscopy when he publishes measurements of atomic spectra. In 1868 his research on the solar spectrum leads him to infer that hydrogen is present in the sun. Since 1905, his name has been used as a unit of length: 1 angstrom equals 10^{-8} centimeters.

D. TECHNOLOGY: *the Syringe*
In Britain, Alexander Wood introduces a syringe for administering morphine.

E. THE ARTS: *Music*
Giuseppe Verdi's operas *Il Trovatore* and *La Traviata* open in Rome and Venice, respectively.

A. BACTERIOLOGICAL TECHNIQUE: *Cotton Closures for Culture Tubes*
Heinrich Georg Friedrich Schröder and Theodor von Dusch introduce the use of cotton wool to close flasks and tubes in which microorganisms are grown.

B. BACTERIAL DISEASE: *Cholera Bacillus*
Filippo Facini describes the cholera bacillus and names it *Vibrio cholerae.* (See 1884 D.)

C. BACTERIAL DISEASE: *Cholera*
John Snow publishes "On the Communication of Cholera by Impure Thames Water." In 1855, his book, *On the Mode of Communication of Cholera,* provides quantitative data on the spread of the disease through water contaminated by sewage. In one of the earliest thorough epidemiological studies, he traces one outbreak in London to the Broad Street water pump (now Broadwick Street in Soho), showing it to be contaminated by raw sewage. (See 1849 A, 1856 A.)

D. PHYSICS: *Second Law of Thermodynamics/Entropy*
Rudolf Emmanuel Clausius restates the second law of thermodynamics to include a concept that he names "entropy," the increase in the amount of energy unavailable to do useful work. The second law therefore states that entropy, a measure of disorder, in the universe always increases.

E. SOCIETY AND POLITICS
Britain, France, and Turkey engage Russia in the Crimean War (which ends in 1856). In the Battle of Balaklava, James Thomas Brudenell, Lord Cardigan, leads Britain's Light Brigade in a famous cavalry charge. The cardigan sweater was named for Lord Cardigan. (See 1854 F.)

F. THE ARTS: *Literature*
 • The Battle of Balaklava in the Crimean War inspires Alfred Lord Tennyson's poem, "The Charge of the Light Brigade."
 • Henry David Thoreau publishes *Walden, or Life in the Woods.*

A. CHEMISTRY: *Agricultural Chemistry*
Justus von Liebig studies the chemical composition of fertilizers, establishing, according to some authorities, the field of agricultural chemistry.

B. PHYSICS: *Electromagnetism*
James Clerk Maxwell develops the mathematics to describe the lines of force envisioned by Michael Faraday in 1821.

C. SOCIETY AND POLITICS
The Young Women's Christian Association (YWCA) is founded in London to provide housing, food, and other assistance for young women living away from home. (See 1844 C.)

D. THE ARTS: *Literature*
 • Walt Whitman publishes his collection of poems *Leaves of Grass.*

• Henry Wadsworth Longfellow publishes his poem "The Song of Hiawatha."

• John Bartlett publishes *Familiar Quotations,* afterward known as *Bartlett's Quotations*.

• Thomas Bulfinch publishes *The Age of Fable,* generally known as *Bulfinch's Mythology*.

1856

A. TYPHOID FEVER

William Budd suggests that the infectious agent of typhoid fever passes from the infected person in feces and is contracted by other individuals through contaminated drinking water. He recommends the use of such disinfectants as chlorine water, chloride of lime, and carbolic acid to control infection. Although Budd has no experimental data to support his ideas, his book on the spread of typhoid, published in 1873, leads to a wider acceptance of his work. (See 1873 A, 1849 A, 1854 C.)

B. DISEASE: *Putrid Intoxication/Endotoxin*

Peter Ludwig Panum uses aqueous infusions of blood, brain, and decomposing feces to study "putrid intoxication." After filtering the infusions he finds that only the residue causes intoxication when injected into dogs. Because the infusions are still toxic after boiling for 11 hours, he concludes that disease and septic disease are caused by chemical agents and not by microorganisms or ferments. Panum's starting materials may have contained bacteria from which he extracts endotoxin. (See 1892 D.)

C. CHEMISTRY: *Dyes and Stains*

William Henry Perkin synthesizes the aniline dye mauve, leading to the appearance of many synthetic dyes. These dyes are subsequently used in staining biological materials and for many other applications. (See 1849 D, 1869 A, 1876 B.)

D. ANTHROPOLOGY: *Neanderthal Man*

In the Neanderthal Valley in Germany, Johann C. Fuhrott finds a fossil skull that Paul Broca proclaims is a skull from a precursor of modern humans. Although Rudolf Virchow does not agree, the Neanderthal man is gradually accepted as a legitimate subspecies of modern humans.

E. TECHNOLOGY: *Bessemer Process*

Henry Bessemer patents a process for making steel inexpensively by blasting air into molten iron and coke. The Bessemer process, which removes carbon and sulfur, employs the ideas of Robert Mushet, who failed to submit a proper patent application a few years earlier.

F. THE ARTS: *Literature*

• Gustave Flaubert's novel *Madame Bovary* is published in *La Revue de Paris,* to be reissued a year later in book form. Flaubert is prosecuted, but acquitted, for immorality.

• John Greenleaf Whittier writes the poem "Barefoot Boy."

G. THE ARTS: *Music*

The Piano Concerto in A Major by Franz Liszt is given its first performance.

A. BACTERIOLOGY: *Taxonomy*

Carl Wilhelm von Nägeli places the bacteria in the group *Schizomycetes,* the fission fungi, in the plant kingdom.

B. BACTERIAL PHYSIOLOGY: *Nitrogen Fixation*

John Bennet Lawes, Joseph Henry Gilbert, and Evan Pugh conduct crop rotation experiments at the Rothamsted Experiment Station, verifying Jean-Baptiste Boussingault's conclusion that plants take up nitrogen from the air. Their carefully controlled laboratory experiments with ignited soil fail, however, to note any difference in the growth of leguminous crops as compared with nonlegumes. It is not until 1889, after the experiments of Hermann Hellriegel and H. Wilfarth reported in 1887, that Lawes, Gilbert, and Pugh perceive that their earlier experiments excluded the possibility that bacteria could cause the formation of root nodules on the leguminous plants. Lawes is responsible for starting the Agricultural Experiment Station in Rothamsted in 1843. (See 1837 B, 1887 C, 1889 B.)

C. FERMENTATION: *Bacteria*

Louis Pasteur publishes *Mémoire sur la fermentation appelée lactique,* his first paper dealing specifically with the microbial products of fermentation, in which he shows that a bacterium causes the fermentation of sugar to form lactic acid. In 1860 he publishes on the alcoholic fermentation, having earlier presented his ideas on the germ theory of fermentation to the Science Society of Lille. Pasteur's earlier work in crystallography and with the optical isomers of amyl alcohol lay the foundation for his discovery of chemical changes caused by living organisms.

D. BIOCHEMISTRY: *Cyanide Poisoning*

Gabriel Émile Bertrand notes that, after cyanide poisoning, blood on both sides of the heart retains a red color.

E. BIOCHEMISTRY: *Glycogen*

Claude Bernard, sometimes referred to as the originator of experimental medicine, isolates and purifies a substance from liver tissue that he names glycogen.

F. PHYSIOLOGY: *Internal Environment*

Claude Bernard states his concept of the *milieu intérieur,* the constant internal environment of complex organisms. Later, Bernard discovers how the pancreas functions in the digestion of fat. (See 1859 C, 1878 D.)

G. SOCIETY AND POLITICS

The U.S. Supreme Court rules against Dred Scott, a fugitive slave, who sues for his freedom by virtue of his residence in Minnesota, a free territory. The court also rules that a black person cannot bring suit in federal courts.

A. BACTERIOLOGY: *Spontaneous Generation of Life*

In a paper presented to the Paris Academy of Sciences, Félix-Archimède Pouchet claims to have observed spontaneous generation of life after admitting air into sterilized flasks of putrifiable material. Along with his 1859 book *Hétérogénie, ou traité de la génération spontanée,* this paper is responsible, in part, for bringing Louis Pasteur into the argument over spontaneous generation. (See 1668 A, 1748 A, 1765 A, 1861 A, 1872 A, 1876 A, 1877 B.)

B. DISEASE: *Cellular Pathology*
Rudolf Virchow, in his book *Die Cellularpathologie,* adapts Matthias Jakob Schleiden's and Theodor Schwann's cell theory to cellular pathology. Disputing the notion of spontaneous generation of life, Virchow generalizes, *omnis cellula a cellula* (all cells come from other cells). He later disagrees with Louis Pasteur's and Robert Koch's germ theory of disease, arguing that disease is a consequence of cell malfunctions and is not caused by invading microorganisms. (See 1838 D, 1839 D, 1846 G, 1876 C.)

C. FERMENTATION: *Ferments*
Moritz Traube postulates that ferments should be considered well-defined chemical substances. He believes that fermentation does not depend on the activities of living cells, but on the oxidative and reductive ferments they produce. Although he studied with Justus von Liebig, he does not support Liebig's concept of vibrating molecules as explaining fermentation. Over a period of 27 years he publishes a series of papers dealing with oxidation, respiration, and fermentation.

D. BIOLOGY: *Evolution*
Alfred Russel Wallace sends Charles Darwin a paper entitled "On the Tendency of Varieties to Depart Indefinitely from the Original Type," describing his own independently derived ideas on speciation developed while on an expedition in Malaysia from 1854 to 1862. Two friends of Darwin's, botanist Joseph Dalton Hooker and geologist Charles Lyell, read Wallace's paper and an essay by Darwin to the Linnaean Society of London. Neither Wallace nor Darwin is present at this meeting, and although the presentations provoke no discussion from the attending members of the society, joint priority is established for their ideas. Darwin publishes *On the Origin of Species* in 1859. In the following years, Wallace engages in a variety of causes: spiritualism, socialism, women's rights, a campaign against vaccination for smallpox, and, following claims by astronomer Percival Lowell that intelligent life once existed on Mars, the writing of *Is Mars Habitable?* (1907), in which he argues that life can exist only on earth.

E. CHEMISTRY: *Valence of Carbon*
Friedrich Kekulé and, independently, Archibald Scott Cooper establish that the carbon atom has a valence of four and that it can combine chemically with other carbon atoms as well as with atoms or molecules of other types. Their work lays the foundation for understanding the structure of organic compounds. In 1865, Kekulé conceives of the cyclic structure of the benzene molecule.

F. THE ARTS: *Music*
In London, the Royal Opera House at Covent Garden is completed.

A. FERMENTATION: *Vitalism*

Opposing Louis Pasteur as being purely vitalistic, Marcelin Berthelot states that ferments should be identified with living organisms that produce them but are not necessary for their chemical activity.

B. BIOLOGY: *Evolution*

Charles Darwin publishes *On the Origin of Species by Means of Natural Selection,* culminating more than 20 years of study based on his travels to South America and the Galápagos Islands on the ship HMS *Beagle.* (See 1831 A, 1858.)

C. BIOCHEMISTRY: *Tissue Respiration*

Claude Bernard studies tissue respiration of liver, kidney, muscle, and brain. He and many others believe, however, that all respiration is in the blood.

D. BIOCHEMISTRY: *Lactic Acid in Muscles*

Emil Heinrich Du Bois-Reymond finds that lactic acid appears in muscles following muscular contraction or at the death of an animal.

E. TECHNOLOGY: *Refrigeration*

Ferdinand Carré builds a refrigerator that uses ammonia as coolant. The first successful refrigerator, it is used commercially, not in homes.

F. TECHNOLOGY: *Internal Combustion Engine*

Jean Etienne Lenoir builds the first useful, though inefficient, internal combustion engine using coal gas as fuel. (See 1863 E.)

G. TECHNOLOGY: *Canal*

Ferdinand de Lesseps begins construction of the Suez Canal, which he completes in 1869. (See 1880 F.)

H. THE ARTS: *Music*

Charles Gounod's opera *Faust* is performed.

I. THE ARTS: *Literature*

Charles Dickens writes *A Tale of Two Cities.*

A. FERMENTATION: *Ethyl Alcohol*

Louis Pasteur publishes *Mémoire sur la fermentation alcoölique,* introducing the use of quantitative analysis to determine the quantities of sugar consumed, and of ethyl alcohol and carbon dioxide produced by yeast during the alcoholic fermentation. His paper not only adds considerably to the argument that the alcoholic fermentation is caused by yeast, but also, for the first time, shows an increase in the mass of yeast in a culture medium that contains only sugar, ammonium salts, and trace elements, but no protein.

B. SOCIETY AND POLITICS

Florence Nightingale opens a training school for nurses at St. Thomas's hospital in London, founding modern nursing. Born in Florence, Italy, of wealthy and cultured parents, she devotes her energies from the age of 24 to nursing. After successfully reorganizing a small hospital in London in

1853, she is asked by the British secretary of war to go to Crimea to care for British soldiers in the Crimean War. Nightingale insists on sanitary measures that markedly reduce deaths from cholera, dysentery, and typhoid among the soldiers under her care. Widely recognized for her efforts there, she receives, upon her return to England, a commission to study the sanitary conditions of the army. In 1858, she publishes *Notes on the Matters Affecting the Health, Efficiency and Hospital Administration of the British Army,* the first detailed study of the housing and health of soldiers. (See 1842 C, 1846 A, 1861 C.)

C. THE ARTS: *Literature*
George Eliot publishes the novel *The Mill on the Floss.*

1861

A. BACTERIOLOGY: *Spontaneous Generation of Life*
Louis Pasteur publishes on the examination of the doctrine of spontaneous generation of life in an effort to end the controversy about the unexplained appearance of microorganisms in broths since John Turberville Needham's experiments in 1748. Pasteur performs his experiments partly in response to Félix-Archimède Pouchet's report read before the Paris Academy of Sciences in 1858 and published in 1859 in *Hétérogenie.* The academy, in an effort to settle the controversy, creates the Alhumpert Prize to be awarded to someone for experiments that "throw new light" on the question of spontaneous generation. Pasteur presents a paper describing the now-famous "swan-necked flask" experiments, in which dust-free air is freely admitted to heated flasks of nutrient medium without the subsequent development of microorganisms. The committee formed to award the prize of 2,500 francs is biased against Pouchet and awards the prize to Pasteur before Pouchet submits an entry. The actual conclusion of the controversy awaits Ferdinand Cohn's experiments in 1875 and 1876, which reveal the heat resistance of bacterial endospores. (See 1668 A, 1748 A, 1765 A, 1858 A, 1872 A, 1876 A, 1877 B.)

B. BACTERIAL PHYSIOLOGY: *Anaerobes*
Louis Pasteur describes the butyric acid fermentation and notes that the fermenting bacteria live without free oxygen. He later applies the term *anaërobies* to such bacteria, which, in 1880, Adam Prazmowski names *Clostridium.* Pasteur also notes that the presence of oxygen inhibits fermentation. Otto Warburg calls this the "Pasteur reaction" in 1926. (See 1880 A, 1926 I.)

C. INFECTIOUS DISEASE: *Antisepsis*
Ignaz Semmelweis publishes *Der Aetiologie, der Begriff und die Prophylasis des Kindbettfiebers* containing statistical data on occurrence and mortality of puerperal (childbed) fever. He requires that medical students wash their hands in chloride of lime upon leaving the autopsy room and before examining patients in the maternity ward. His results show that the disease is spread through unclean hands and instruments, but he is opposed by the director of the hospital and other physicians. Disturbed because his work goes unrecognized, he dies, insane, in 1865. However, his careful work survives

1861 *(continued)*

and is recognized as an important contribution to antiseptic medical practice. (See 1842 C, 1846 A.)

D. BIOLOGY: *Taxonomy*
John Hogg publishes an article, "On the Distinctions of a Plant and an Animal, and on a Fourth Kingdom of Nature," in which he introduces the term "protoctist" for single-celled animals. The protoctists, meaning "first beings," are later included as kingdom *Protoctista*, or *Protista*, in Herbert F. Copeland's 1961 four-kingdom system. Hogg's kingdoms are plant, animal, mineral, and regnum primogenium. (See 1866 A, 1956 A, 1969 A, 1977 A.)

E. BIOCHEMISTRY: *Muscles*
Moritz Traube lays the foundation for the biochemistry of muscle activity.

F. BIOLOGY: *Definition of a Cell*
When Max Johann Sigismund Schultze defines a cell as containing a nucleus surrounded by protoplasm, he introduces the modern meaning of the word "protoplasm."

G. CHEMISTRY: *Organic Chemistry*
Friedrich Kekulé defines organic chemistry as the study of natural and artificially produced carbon compounds.

H. TECHNOLOGY: *Refrigeration*
The first machine-chilled cold storage unit is constructed.

I. SOCIETY AND POLITICS
• The Confederate States of America are formed, and the Civil War begins in the United States (ending in 1865). Confederate forces defeat the Union army at Fort Sumter, Charleston, South Carolina, as well as at Bull Run, Manassas Junction, Virginia (the first battle of Manassas).

• Victor Emmanuel II becomes the first king of Italy, unifying all of the country except for Venetia and Rome, which join the unification in 1866 and 1870, respectively.

J. CULTURE: *Universities*
The Massachusetts Institute of Technology (MIT) is founded.

K. THE ARTS: *Literature*
Charles Dickens writes *Great Expectations*.

1862

A. MICROBIOLOGY: *Thermophiles*
Ferdinand Cohn reports that different species of algae and blue-green algae (cyanobacteria) grow at different temperatures in hot springs. (See 1846 D, 1879 A.)

B. BIOCHEMISTRY: *Hemoglobin*
Felix Hoppe (Hoppe-Seyler after 1864) discovers the absorption spectrum of hemoglobin. In 1864 he identifies oxyhemoglobin as the combined

form of hemoglobin and oxygen. Terms used earlier were hematosin, by Louis René Lecanu in 1832, and hematoglobulin by Jöns Berzelius.

C. PLANT PHYSIOLOGY: *Photosynthesis*

Julius von Sachs proves that plants synthesize starch from carbon dioxide absorbed during the process of photosynthesis. Sachs also notes that chlorophyll is contained in small structures within plant cells, later named chloroplasts.

D. SOCIETY AND POLITICS

- Otto von Bismarck becomes prime minister of Prussia. (See 1871 D.)
- Jean-Henri Dunant, after personally observing the sufferings of thousands of soldiers at Solferino in the Crimean War, publishes a description of their neglect in *Un souvenir de Solférino*. He argues for the formation of volunteer groups to aid those wounded in battle. In 1863, responding to Dunant's appeal, the International Red Cross movement is founded when delegates from 14 countries meet in Geneva, Switzerland. Dunant suffers financial setbacks in 1867 and is largely neglected until a newspaperman writes about him in 1895. After that, Dunant receives many annuities and honors, including the first Nobel Peace Prize in 1901, which he shares with Fréderic Passy, an economist who promotes international peace.

E. THE ARTS: *Literature*

Victor Hugo writes *Les misérables*.

1863

A. BACTERIAL DISEASE: *Anthrax*

Casimir Joseph Davaine reports experiments on the cause of anthrax. Aloys Pollender, Davaine, and others had observed rod-shaped bacteria in the blood of cattle dead from anthrax. Davaine successfully transmits the disease to healthy animals by inoculation with a small amount of blood from diseased animals. He refers to the bacteria as *Bacteridia*. Davaine's conclusions are not widely accepted because of the failure of similar experiments by other workers and because of claims that the *Bacteridia* are not always found in the blood of animals dead from anthrax. Robert Koch's experiments in 1876 provide substantial proof of the cause of anthrax. (See 1849 B, 1878 A, 1876 C, 1877 D, 1881 F, 1954 G.)

B. BACTERIAL DISEASE: *Cholera*

Beginning once again in India, in the Ganges, cholera spreads to ports throughout the world. For the first time, the west coast of South America is affected. By this time, public health officials recognize that cholera is spread through fecal matter in water; as a result of improved sanitation, the disease's appearance in 1873 in New York, New Orleans, and other port cities is the last outbreak of epidemic cholera in the United States.

C. BIOLOGY: *Evolution*

Thomas Henry Huxley publishes *Zoological Evidence as to Man's Place in Nature,* strongly supporting Charles Darwin's theory of evolution and stressing similarities between humans and apes.

1863 *(continued)*

D. SCIENTIFIC ORGANIZATIONS

The U.S. Congress establishes the National Academy of Sciences with the directive that it should serve to advise the government on scientific and technical matters.

E. TECHNOLOGY: *Automobile*

By attaching an internal combustion engine to a carriage, Jean Etienne Lenoir makes the first "horseless carriage" or automobile not driven by a steam engine. Lenoir's vehicle reaches speeds of about 3 miles per hour. (See 1769 B, 1885 O, 1893 F.)

F. SOCIETY AND POLITICS

Abraham Lincoln issues the Emancipation Proclamation, which led to the freedom of all slaves in states in rebellion against the United States. He also delivers his famous Gettysburg Address at the dedication of a national cemetery.

1864

A. BIOCHEMISTRY: *Hemoglobin*

George Gabriel Stokes discovers that oxyhemoglobin can be reversibly reduced with ferrous salts and other reducing agents.

B. PHYSICS: *Endothermic and Exothermic Processes*

Marcelin Berthelot, in his research that contributed to the science of thermodynamics, introduces the terms "endothermic" and "exothermic" for reactions that consume and release heat, respectively. Berthelot also introduces the device known as the bomb calorimeter for determining heats of reaction.

C. SOCIETY AND POLITICS

In Geneva, representatives of 26 nations sign a pledge to follow humanitarian rules in war regarding prisoners, wounded and sick military personnel, and civilians in war areas. The so-called Geneva Conventions are revised in 1906 and 1949.

1865

A. INFECTIOUS DISEASE: *Tuberculosis*

Jean Antoine Villemin begins inoculation experiments with tuberculous material from both humans and cows. He finds that, although the two diseases have similar causes, the course of the disease in rabbits is more rapid and widespread with bovine tuberculosis than with human tuberculosis. Although his experiments establish that tuberculosis is caused by a specific infectious agent, his report is largely ignored. In 1868, Julius Friedrich Cohnheim confirms Villemin's work, using a different experimental method. Villemin also reports to the Academy of Medicine in Paris that the disease is transmitted by inhalation of dried material from patients with tuberculosis. (See 1868 D, 1959 F.)

B. BIOLOGY: *Genetics*

Gregor Mendel's report of the results of plant hybridization experiments, begun in 1856, leads to the formulation of his laws of segregation and independent assortment of inherited characteristics. Mendel proposes that each characteristic exists as a particulate unit factor. This work is largely ignored until 1900, when it is rediscovered independently by three persons: Hugo de Vries, Erich Tschermak, and Carl Correns.

C. CHEMISTRY: *Benzene*

Friedrich Kekulé conceives of the cyclic structure of the benzene molecule. According to two versions of this story, he is said to have had this idea while in a doze either in his study or on a horse-drawn bus. Josef Loschmidt published a booklet in 1861 that contains much of the structural organic theory usually credited to Kekulé.

D. PHYSICS: *Electromagnetic Fields*

James Clerk Maxwell publishes "On the Dynamical Theory of the Electromagnetic Field," in which he presents equations relating electric and magnetic fields. He demonstrates that light is electromagnetic by calculating that the speed of electromagnetic radiation is close to the speed of light. His work is the first unification of physical phenomena, bringing together electricity, magnetism, and light.

E. SOCIETY AND POLITICS

After a Confederate defeat at Five Forks, Virginia, General Robert E. Lee surrenders to General Ulysses S. Grant at Appomattox Courthouse, ending the American Civil War. Five days later, on April 14, President Abraham Lincoln is assassinated.

F. THE ARTS: *Music*

Richard Wagner's opera *Tristan und Isolde* is performed.

G. THE ARTS: *Literature*

- Lewis Carroll publishes *Alice in Wonderland.*
- Leo Tolstoy publishes *War and Peace.*

1866

A. BIOLOGY: *Taxonomy*

Ernst Heinrich Haeckel suggests a system classifying living organisms into three kingdoms: *Plantae, Animalia,* and *Protista.* He proposes a new kingdom, *Protista,* comprising unicellular organisms and unicellular organisms that form colonies but do not have tissues. He places the single-celled forms, the bacteria and some protozoa, into a group that he calls *Monera,* because he believes them to lack a nucleus. Haeckel's ideas continue to influence classification of the bacteria and other single-celled organisms until the 1950s. Haeckel is also known as the propounder of the "biogenetic law" and the phrase "ontogeny recapitulates phylogeny," widely accepted for years but now known to be problematic. He is a believer in both evolution and abiogenesis and seeks a homogeneous and structureless substance, a living particle of albumin, capable of nourishment and reproduction. (See 1861 D, 1956 A, 1969 A, 1977 A.)

B. TECHNOLOGY: *Clinical Thermometer*

Thomas Clifford Allbut devises the clinical thermometer, in which the mercury remains at the highest temperature achieved.

1866 (continued)

C. SOCIETY AND POLITICS

The U.S. Congress passes a Civil Rights Act effectively abolishing slavery by awarding former slaves all of the rights guaranteed under the Thirteenth Amendment.

D. THE ARTS: *Literature*

Fyodor Dostoyevsky publishes *Crime and Punishment.*

1867

A. IMMUNOLOGY: *Inflammation*

Julius Friedrich Cohnheim publishes the first of his papers on experiments with frogs concerning the response of blood vessels to injury or irritation. By establishing that leukocytes pass through the capillary walls, he proves that pus is composed of degenerating blood cells. Earlier, he developed procedures for freezing tissue to prepare sections for microscopic examination, and he also devised the technique for gold staining of tissue sections.

B. ANTISEPTICS

Joseph Lister publishes on the practice of antiseptic surgery, relating how he began in 1865 using carbolic acid to reduce microbial contamination of open surgical wounds. He is influenced by the work of Louis Pasteur on the presence of microorganisms in the air and by a report of how carbolic acid reduced odor and "entozoa" in sewage in the town of Carlisle. This report, and others that follow, has significant influence on the practice of surgery. Carbolic acid, which is caustic and toxic, is later replaced in surgical practice by other antiseptics. (See 1842 C, 1861 C.)

C. PHYSICS: *Maxwell's Demon*

James Clerk Maxwell invents a hypothetical creature to illustrate the limitations of the second law of thermodynamics. His creature can open and shut a valve between two vessels, permitting fast-moving molecules to flow into one chamber while slow-moving ones move into the opposite chamber, thus increasing the temperature in one and lowering it in the other. In 1874, William Thomson (Lord Kelvin) names Maxwell's imaginary creature "Maxwell's intelligent demon," now usually shortened to "Maxwell's demon."

D. TECHNOLOGY: *Typewriter*

Christopher Latham Sholes invents the typewriter. In 1873, the Remington & Sons Fire Arms Company begins manufacture of Sholes's "qwerty" keyboard, which continues to be the standard.

E. TECHNOLOGY: *Dynamite*

Alfred Nobel patents dynamite.

F. SOCIETY AND POLITICS

• The British Parliament creates the Dominion of Canada, including the provinces of Quebec, Ontario, Nova Scotia, and New Brunswick.

• Karl Marx publishes *Das Kapital,* volume I.

G. THE ARTS: *Music*

"The Blue Danube Waltz" by Johann Strauss II is first performed.

1868

A. BACTERIOLOGY: *Taxonomy*
Casimir Joseph Davaine classifies bacteria into four groups: *Bacterium, Vibrio, Bacteridium,* and *Spirillum.* He establishes the genus *Bacteridium* for the anthrax bacterium. (See 1849 B, 1863 A, 1876 C.)

B. BACTERIAL PHYSIOLOGY: *Acetic Acid*
Louis Pasteur confirms Friedrich Kützing's observation of 1837 that bacteria convert ethyl alcohol to vinegar. Pasteur believes that a single species of bacteria, *Mycoderma aceti,* is responsible. Martinus Beijerinck assigns the name *Acetobacter aceti* in 1898. (See 1822 A, 1837 C, 1931 B.)

C. BACTERIAL PHYSIOLOGY: *Denitrification*
Jean Jacques Theophile Schloesing claims that the reduction of nitrate is responsible for the release of nitrogenous gas from urine and tobacco. He also reports that the loss of nitrogen from the soil requires anaerobic conditions and the consumption of both nitrate and organic matter. (See 1886 C.)

D. INFECTIOUS DISEASE: *Tuberculosis*
Julius Friedrich Cohnheim confirms Jean Antoine Villemin's work on the infectivity of tuberculosis by inoculating material from tuberculous lesions into the anterior ocular chambers of rabbits. He follows the course of the disease by observations through the cornea. (See 1865 A, 1959 F.)

E. BIOLOGY: *Pangenesis*
Charles Darwin, in the second volume of *The Variation of Animals and Plants under Domestication* discusses processes of inheritance and variation by proposing the "pangenesis" hypothesis, which includes the concept that tissue granules called "gemmules" make up genetic elements that are passed on to the next generation.

F. THE ARTS: *Music*
A German Requiem by Johannes Brahms is given its first performance. He also publishes his famous "Lullaby."

G. THE ARTS: *Art*
Claude Monet paints *The River.*

1869

A. BACTERIOLOGICAL TECHNIQUE: *Stains*
Hermann Hoffman is first to use a vegetable dye, carmine, to stain bacteria for microscopic observation. (See 1849 D, 1856 C, 1876 B.)

B. BACTERIAL PHYSIOLOGY: *Heat Resistance*
During his studies of the silkworm disease, Louis Pasteur notes that some bacteria have dormant stages, refractile bodies that are more resistant to heat than actively growing cells. He does not recognize these as bacterial endospores. (See 1876 C, 1877 B.).

C. INFECTIOUS DISEASE: *Silkworm Disease*
Louis Pasteur publishes the results of work begun in 1865 on the diseases of silkworms in southern France. Although he fails to identify and culture the causative microorganisms, he does save the silk industry from disaster by

1869 (*continued*)

finding at least two separate diseases and recommending ways by which dis-ease-free moth eggs can be recognized and used for breeding.

D. BIOCHEMISTRY: *Blood Gas Analysis*

Carl Friedrich Ludwig improves methods of blood gas analysis but con-cludes that respiration occurs in the blood and is regulated by oxygen sup-ply, not by tissues.

E. BIOCHEMISTRY: *Nucleic Acids*

Johann Friedrich Miescher recovers a substance containing nitrogen and phosphorus from pus cells on hospital bandages. He later finds a similar ma-terial in sperm cells from salmon. The substance is named "nuclein" be-cause of its association with the nucleus of cells. Miescher believes that nuclein serves as a source of phosphorus for other cellular synthesis and does not recognize it as an essential part of nuclear activity. Publication of his work is delayed until 1871, after it is confirmed by Felix Hoppe-Seyler, in whose laboratory he works. In the year of Miescher's discovery, Oscar Loew and Carl Wilhelm von Nägeli suggest that nuclein is simply a mix-ture of phosphate salts with protein. Nicholas Lubavin, who finds free phosphate and protein when milk is treated with boiling water, arrives at a similar conclusion. In 1889, Richard Altmann makes a preparation of nuclein containing no protein. Important discoveries about the compo-nents of nuclein are later made by another of Hoppe-Seyler's students, Albrecht Kossel. (See 1885 N.)

F. BIOLOGY: *Eugenics*

Francis Galton, grandson of Erasmus Darwin and cousin of Charles Dar-win, publishes *Hereditary Genius,* in which he expounds his ideas on breed-ing applied to human populations, or eugenics. Later, he formulates an "ancestral law of inheritance," a formula that accounts for the proportion-ally diminishing contribution of ancestors in each generation. In an 1875 letter to Charles Darwin, he essentially works out the pattern of Mendelian inheritance but never tests his ideas experimentally.

G. CHEMISTRY: *Periodic Table of Elements*

Dmitri Ivanovich Mendeleyev publishes his first periodic table of the chemical elements. Julius Lothar Meyer, in 1870, produces a table contain-ing 53 elements arranged in nine groups. Mendeleyev's table is revised in 1871 to show the periodic pattern based on families of elements having atomic weights that vary by multiples of the atomic weight of hydrogen. The periodic table is further refined in 1914 by Henry Gwyn Jeffreys Moseley, using atomic numbers.

H. SCIENTIFIC PUBLICATION: Nature

The scientific journal *Nature* is first published. Appearing in the first issue is an essay by Thomas Henry Huxley in which he quotes a number of apho-risms about nature written by Johann Wolfgang von Goethe in about 1780. Goethe wrote, "The spectacle of Nature is always new, for she is always renewing the spectators. Life is her most exquisite invention; and death is her expert contrivance to get plenty of life."

I. TECHNOLOGY: *Railroads*
A transcontinental railroad is completed in the United States with the linkage of the Union Pacific and Central Pacific Railroads in Utah.

J. TECHNOLOGY: *Canals*
The Suez Canal opens.

K. CULTURE: *Universities*
Gifton College for women is established in Britain.

1870

A. FERMENTATION: *Controversy*
Justus von Liebig publishes a lengthy critique of Louis Pasteur's claims that fermentation is caused by living microorganisms. (See 1871 B.)

B. BIOCHEMISTRY: *Fermentation*
Adolf von Baeyer suggests that cleavage of the six-carbon glucose results in the formation of two molecules of lactic acid. He also suggests that in the alcoholic fermentation, lactic acid undergoes further cleavage to yield ethyl alcohol and carbon dioxide. The lactic fermentation in muscle tissue is later called glycolysis.

C. SOCIETY AND POLITICS
The Franco-Prussian War begins; France is defeated in 1871.

D. THE ARTS: *Literature*
 • "Hitch your wagon to a star," writes Ralph Waldo Emerson in "Civilization."
 • Jules Verne publishes *Twenty Thousand Leagues Under the Sea,* a novel about a submarine under the leadership of Captain Nemo.

1871

A. BACTERIOLOGICAL TECHNIQUE: *Filter Sterilization*
Edwin Klebs suggests using unbaked clay filters to separate bacteria from liquids. One of his assistants, E. T. Tiegel, mentions the use of such filters in a paper on anthrax published the same year. (See 1884 C, 1891 A, 1931 A.)

B. FERMENTATION: *Controversy*
Louis Pasteur replies to Justus von Liebig's criticism, published in 1870, of his concepts about fermentation and challenges him to let their argument be settled by an impartial jury. Liebig, who does not reply, dies in 1873. (See 1870 A.)

C. BIOLOGY: *Evolution*
Charles Darwin publishes *The Descent of Man and Selection in Relation to Sex,* in which he discusses human evolution.

D. SOCIETY AND POLITICS
 • The Franco-Prussian war, which began in 1870, ends with the surrender of the French, who give up Alsace and part of Lorraine.

1871 *(continued)*

• All German states, except Austria, join together to form the German Empire with Wilhelm I of Prussia as emperor and Otto von Bismarck as chancellor.

E. SOCIETY: *Exploration*

When journalist Henry M. Stanley finds the explorer David Livingstone at Lake Tanganyika in Africa, he greets him with "Dr. Livingstone, I presume." Livingstone began his exploration of central and southern Africa in 1849.

F. THE ARTS: *Literature*

Lewis Carroll publishes *Through the Looking-Glass and What Alice Found There.*

G. THE ARTS: *Music*

Giuseppe Verdi's opera *Aida* is performed in Cairo. It was intended, however, for the opening of the Suez canal in 1869.

1872

A. BACTERIOLOGY: *Spontaneous Generation of Life*

Henry Charlton Bastian, a prominent British neurologist, revives the argument about spontaneous generation of life with the publication of a book entitled *The Beginnings of Life,* reporting numerous experiments in which bacterial growth appears in solutions that are boiled and cooled. In one experiment, he boils acid urine for several minutes and then neutralizes it with a potash solution prepared with distilled water he believes to be sterile, but possibly introducing contaminating bacteria. William Roberts reports the effects of acidity and alkalinity on the heat killing of bacteria in 1874, and then Ferdinand Cohn discovers the survival of heat-resistant bacterial endospores in 1877. (See 1668 A, 1748 A, 1765 A, 1858 A, 1861 A, 1876 A, 1877 B.)

B. BACTERIAL TAXONOMY: *Classification*

Ferdinand Cohn publishes the first volume of a three-volume study of bacteria entitled *Untersuchungen über Bakterien,* in which he establishes bacteriology as a separate science. He classifies bacteria in the plant kingdom because of their similarities to "Oscillarias" (known then as blue-green algae but today as cyanobacteria) and because of their mode of cell division by formation of a cross wall. His classification includes two new genera of bacteria, *Micrococcus* and *Bacillus.* He names three species of *Bacillus: Bacillus subtilis, Bacillus anthracis,* and *Bacillus ulna.* (See 1866 A, 1969 A.)

C. BACTERIOLOGICAL TECHNIQUE: *Culture Medium*

Ferdinand Cohn devises a bacteriological culture medium consisting of ammonium salts and yeast ash, to which various sugars could be added. This medium is the first to give flexibility in the choice of carbon-containing nutrients.

D. BACTERIAL ECOLOGY: *Geochemical Cycles*

Ferdinand Cohn, in *Untersuchungen über Bakterien,* first discusses the role of microorganisms in the cycling of elements in nature, now referred to as biogeochemical cycles.

E. MEDICINE: *Kaposi's Sarcoma*
Moritz K. Kaposi describes a skin disease that becomes known as Kaposi's sarcoma. This disease later is associated with acquired immune deficiency syndrome (AIDS), recognized in 1977.

F. BIOCHEMISTRY: *Hemoglobin*
Eduard Pflüger shows that blood containing hemoglobin carries oxygen to tissues. Ernst Oertmann, a colleague, does the famous "salt frog" experiment in which he demonstrates that respiration occurs in the tissues and not in blood by replacing a frog's blood with a salt solution.

G. SOCIETY
The sailing vessel *Mary Celeste* leaves New York for Genoa in November with a crew of 10. In December it is found with no one on board, but with nothing damaged. The mystery of this "ghost ship" is never solved.

H. THE ARTS: *Art*
James Whistler paints *The Artist's Mother*.

1873

A. INFECTIOUS DISEASE: *Typhoid Fever*
William Budd publishes *Typhoid Fever: Its Nature, Mode of Spreading and Prevention,* finally bringing acceptance of his ideas on the transmission of typhoid fever through contaminated water that were reported as early as 1856. This publication and those of John Snow on cholera constitute the strongest proof to this date that enteric diseases are transmitted through water. However, many physicians and hygienists continue to resist this concept. (See 1849 A, 1855 C, 1856 A.)

B. MICROSCOPY: *Substage Condenser*
Ernst Abbe designs a chromatic substage condenser for the compound microscope.

C. TECHNOLOGY: *Typewriter*
Remington & Sons Fire Arms Company attempts to market a commercial typewriter using the 1867 design of Latham Sholes.

D. THE ARTS: *Literature*
Jules Verne releases his novel *Le tour de monde en quatre-vingt jours* (Around the world in eighty days).

1874

A. BACTERIAL DISEASE: *Leprosy*
Armauer Gerhard Henrik Hansen describes *Mycobacterium leprae,* the causative agent of leprosy, now called Hansen's disease. Hansen may be the first to attribute a chronic disease to a microorganism.

B. INFECTIOUS DISEASE: *Poliomyelitis*
Adolph Kussmaul assigns the name "poliomyelitis anterior acuta" to lesions he finds in the spinal cord. The name is derived from the Greek words for gray and marrow (the gray marrow); anterior refers to the anterior horns of the spinal cord.

1874 *(continued)*

C. MICROSCOPY: *Oil Immersion*

Robert B. Tolles makes a homogeneous immersion objective lens for the compound microscope. He uses balsam oil between the lens and the coverglass.

D. CHEMISTRY: *Carbon Bonds*

Jacobus Henricus van't Hoff and, contemporaneously, Joseph-Achille Le Bel suggest that the four bonds of carbon are directed in a tetrahedral form. This concept provides an explanation of the many properties of organic compounds, including optical activity that could not be interpreted by Friedrich Kekulé's two-dimensional drawings of 1858. (See 1858 E.)

E. SOCIETY AND POLITICS

Benjamin Disraeli, who served briefly as prime minister in 1868, begins his second period as leader of a Tory government in Britain (until 1880).

F. THE ARTS: *Literature*

Thomas Hardy publishes his novel *Far from the Madding Crowd*.

G. THE ARTS: *Music*

- Giuseppe Verdi's *Requiem* is performed in Milan.
- *Die Fledermaus,* an opera by Johann Strauss II, is performed in Vienna.

1875

A. BACTERIAL TAXONOMY: *Classification*

In revising his 1872 classification of the bacteria, Ferdinand Cohn concludes that the bacteria should be included with the blue-green algae, even though they lack chlorophyll. He divides his genus *Micrococcus* into two groups, with the genus *Streptococcus* comprising the spherical bacteria that form filaments, or chains. He does not, however, assign a species to the genus, Anton Julius Friedrich Rosenbach having priority for proper use of this generic term. (See 1884 A.)

B. BACTERIOLOGICAL TECHNIQUE: *Pure Cultures*

The mycologist Joseph Schroeter grows pigmented colonies of bacteria on the cut surfaces of cooked potatoes. He also makes solid culture media from starch paste, egg albumin, bread, and meat.

C. MICROBIOLOGICAL TECHNIQUE: *Pure Cultures*

Oscar Brefeld, a mycologist, lists the rules for obtaining pure cultures of fungi: inoculate with a single spore, use a culture medium that is optimal for growth and is clear and transparent, and prevent external contamination during cultivation.

D. BIOCHEMISTRY: *Respiration*

Opposing the ozone idea of biological oxidations, Eduard Pflüger concludes that the protein in cells changes and begins to respire, to live, thus formulating a concept of a living protein (protoplasm).

E. TECHNOLOGY: *Treaty of the Meter*

The International Bureau of Weights and Measures is established in Sèvres, France, by international treaty. Prototypes are made for the meter and the kilogram.

F. SOCIETY AND POLITICS

The U.S. Congress passes a Civil Rights Act guaranteeing African Americans equal rights in public places. The state of Tennessee subsequently legislates a "Jim Crow" law making ethnic discrimination legal, but it is declared unconstitutional in 1880 by a federal circuit court. Tennessee goes on to pass another version in 1881 and is soon followed by other southern states.

G. THE ARTS: *Music*

Georges Bizet's opera *Carmen* is performed in Paris.

A. BACTERIOLOGY: *Spontaneous Generation of Life*

In 1876 and 1877 John Tyndall, a British physicist, reports a series of experiments in response to Henry Charlton Bastian's book about spontaneous generation of life. Tyndall shows that boiled hay infusions kept in open test tubes in a box containing dust-free air ("optically free") remain sterile. His experiments in which infusions are boiled for 3 minutes at 100°C are successful in achieving sterility. Later, in 1877, Tyndall experiences many failures in which bacterial growth occurs even after boiling for several hours. He eventually explains the problems as being caused by the presence of bundles of old hay in the laboratory from which heat-resistant bacteria contaminate the infusions. After performing a series of carefully conceived heating experiments, Tyndall concludes that at early periods of growth bacteria are heat labile, but in later periods they are heat stable. He develops a procedure of several cycles of heating, incubating, and reheating his culture tubes that results in sterilization even of the heat-stable phase. This technique, known as Tyndallization, becomes used as a means to achieve sterility without using steam under pressure. The heat-resistant phase is explained when Ferdinand Cohn shows in 1877 that *Bacillus* species found in hay have heat-resistant endospores. Tyndall's work is widely distributed through his lectures, pamphlets, and articles in newspapers and magazines and by the publication, in 1881, of his book *Essays on the Floating Matter of the Air in Relation to Putrefaction and Infection*. His description of heat resistance of bacteria and Cohn's work on heat resistance of spores, coupled with the earlier experiments of Louis Pasteur, strike the final blow against the doctrine of spontaneous generation of microorganisms in nutrient solutions. Tyndall's research also has far-reaching effects on aseptic procedures in medicine and surgery. (See 1668 A, 1748 A, 1765 A, 1858 A, 1861 A, 1872 A, 1877 B.)

B. BACTERIOLOGICAL TECHNIQUE: *Staining*

Carl Weigert stains bacteria with the synthetic dye methylene blue, for microscopic examination in aqueous suspension. (See 1849 D, 1869 A, 1856 C.)

C. BACTERIAL DISEASE: *Germ Theory of Disease*

Robert Koch's paper on the cause of anthrax provides the first substantial proof that a specific disease of animals is caused by a specific microorganism, thus validating the germ theory of disease. His paper is also the first specific description of bacterial endospores, with drawings of the spores of

1876 *(continued)*

Bacillus anthracis. Koch does not yet know of the heat resistance property of spores. (See 1849 B, 1863 A, 1868 A, 1877 B, 1954 G.)

D. BIOLOGY: *Fertilization*

Oscar Hertwig uses sea urchin eggs and sperm in studies of fertilization. In his publication of the first microscopic observations of fertilization he concludes that the nucleus of a single sperm is all that is required for fertilization. He also states that fertilization is not merely the fusion of two cells but the fusion of two nuclei. Although Hertwig does not actually see spermatozoa enter the egg, Hermann Fol reports observing this phenomenon in this same year. Fol also sees polyspermic fertilization that results in abnormal division of the egg.

E. BIOCHEMISTRY: *Cyanide Poisoning*

Felix Hoppe-Seyler gives the first correct explanation of cyanide poisoning when he reports that it prevents tissues from using oxygen.

F. TECHNOLOGY: *Refrigeration*

Karl von Linde produces the first practical refrigerator, using ammonia as the coolant.

G. TECHNOLOGY: *Telephone*

Alexander Graham Bell patents the telephone. Just hours after Bell files his petition, Elisha Gray submits a request for a patent on a similar device. Years of litigation follow, with the result that Bell is declared the inventor.

H. TECHNOLOGY: *Internal Combustion Engine*

Nikolaus August Otto builds the first practical four-stroke internal combustion engine. (See 1959 F.)

I. SOCIETY AND POLITICS

In a battle at Little Big Horn in Montana, Sioux Indians led by Chiefs Sitting Bull and Crazy Horse destroy a U.S. Calvary force under General George Armstrong Custer.

J. THE ARTS: *Music*

Richard Wagner's complete ring cycle, *Der Ring des Nibelungen* (the *Ring*) receives its first performance in a theater constructed especially for it in Bayreuth, Germany. Two of the four operas that constitute the *Ring, Das Rheingold* and *Die Walküre,* were performed earlier, in 1869 and 1870, respectively; but these are premiere performances of *Siegfried* and *Die Götterdämmerung.*

K. THE ARTS: *Literature*

Mark Twain (Samuel Clemens) publishes *The Adventures of Tom Sawyer.*

L. THE ARTS: *Art*

Pierre Auguste Renoir paints *Moulin de la Galette.*

1877

A. BACTERIOLOGICAL TECHNIQUE: *Staining*

Robert Koch initiates the techniques of making dried films of bacteria that are then stained. He publishes the first photomicrographs of bacteria. Koch is also the first to stain bacterial flagella, using an extract of logwood. In 1890, Friedrich Löffler develops a better method using tannic acid, ferrous sulfate, and basic fuchsin.

B. BACTERIOLOGY: *Spontaneous Generation of Life/Endospores*
Ferdinand Cohn describes the heat-resistant properties of the endospores of the hay bacillus, which he named *Bacillus subtilis* in 1872. He observes that the bacteria in unheated hay infusions have a different microscopic appearance from those present after heating. He describes small refractile bodies within the bacterial cell that he refers to as spores, and observes both the appearance of the spores during a period of growth and the conversion of a spore into a growing bacillus. He confirms that the spore phase of growth is responsible for heat resistance. This observation explains the survival of bacteria in various heating experiments carried out during the previous 200 years in the controversy about the spontaneous generation of life. The combined experiments of Louis Pasteur (1861), John Tyndall (1876), and Cohn provide the final refutation of this doctrine. (See 1668 A, 1748 A. 1765 A, 1858 A, 1861 A, 1872 A, 1876 A.)

C. BACTERIAL PHYSIOLOGY: *Nitrifying Bacteria*
Jean Jacques Theophile Schloesing and Achille Müntz show that chloroform vapors prevent the production of nitrate in sewage, thereby demonstrating that nitrate is a product of living organisms. Robert Warington repeats the experiment during the next 2 years and proceeds to demonstrate that ammonia alone serves as an initial compound for nitrification. By 1891 Warington finds that nitrification is a two-step process carried out by different bacteria. Although he does not obtain pure cultures, his descriptions are compatible with those of *Nitrosomonas* and *Nitrobacter*, which he nearly concludes are autotrophs. Because Warington's last studies are delayed in publication, Sergei Winogradsky publishes his first paper on nitrification in 1891 before Warington's paper appears. (See 1887 B, 1891 B.)

D. BACTERIAL DISEASE: *the Germ Theory and Koch's Postulates*
Edwin Klebs outlines the experimental steps necessary to prove that microorganisms cause disease. These steps later come to be known as Koch's postulates, after Robert Koch actually performs the experiments in his work on anthrax (1876) and tuberculosis (1884). (See 1876 C, 1883 B, 1884 D.)

E. BIOCHEMISTRY: *Trypsin*
Friedrich Wilhelm Kühne obtains trypsin from pancreatic tissue.

F. TECHNOLOGY: *Liquid Oxygen*
Louis-Paul Cailletet and Raoul Pierre Pictet independently produce liquid oxygen. Cailletet also successfully liquefies nitrogen, carbon monoxide, and hydrogen. (See 1898 O.)

G. TECHNOLOGY: *the Phonograph*
Thomas Alva Edison invents the phonograph.

H. THE ARTS: *Music*
Johannes Brahms's First and Second Symphonies are performed.

A. MICROBIOLOGY: *Terminology*

C. Sédillot is the first to use the word "microbe" in discussing microorganisms.

B. BACTERIOLOGICAL TECHNIQUE: *Pure Cultures*

Joseph Lister becomes the first to obtain a pure culture of a bacterium in a liquid medium when he purifies a lactic acid bacterium, *Streptococcus lactis,* by serial dilution in milk.

C. BACTERIAL SPECIES: Staphylococcus

Robert Koch describes clusters of cocci in human pus. Alexander Ogston names them *Staphylococcus* in 1881.

D. FERMENTATION: *Controversy*

After Claude Bernard dies in 1878, his friend Marcelin Berthelot and others reopen the controversy about the nature of fermentation through the posthumous publication of a paper based on Bernard's recent experiments and thoughts. Although Bernard had never openly challenged Pasteur, this publication of his laboratory notes reveals that he had opposed many of Louis Pasteur's ideas. He did not believe that ferments exert a catalytic effect and proposed that a study of the composition of yeast would reveal what substance causes the fermentation of sugar. He objected to a connection between living cells and the process of fermentation. Pasteur publishes a long critical rebuttal in 1879, in which he compares Bernard's experiments with his own and maintains that Bernard made experimental errors and misinterpretations. Pasteur also accuses Berthelot, a well-respected chemist who has his own chemical theory of fermentation, of misapplying Bernard's notes and damaging his reputation by publishing material that Bernard had kept private.

E. FERMENTATION: *Controversy*

Moritz Traube reiterates his belief, expressed 20 years earlier, that Justus von Liebig mistakenly believed that ferments are substances in a state of decomposition and that Theodor Schwann and Louis Pasteur are wrong in believing that ferments are expressions of the vital forces of lower organisms. He stresses the importance of the activation of oxygen in opposition to Felix Hoppe-Seyler's views. (See 1862 B, 1878 G).

F. INFECTIOUS DISEASE: *Yellow Fever*

The city of Memphis, Tennessee, is invaded by yellow fever brought up the Mississippi River from New Orleans. At least 5,000 people, about one-tenth of the population, die.

G. BIOCHEMISTRY: *Oxidation/Reduction*

Felix Hoppe-Seyler proposes a theory of oxidation reactions in living organisms in which the "nascent hydrogen" that is formed leads to the formation of either H_2 or H_2O and an active atom of oxygen. (See 1882 G.)

H. MICROSCOPY: *Oil Immersion*

Ernst Abbe computes the optics of a homogeneous immersion microscope objective lens, using cedar wood oil for the immersion fluid. Abbe is sometimes credited with making the first objective lens to be specifically designed for use for oil immersion, but Robert B. Tolles has priority. (See 1874 C).

I. CHEMISTRY: *Free Energy*

Josiah Willard Gibbs synthesizes the concept of free energy in his paper, "On the Equilibrium of Heterogeneous Substances." He develops an equation, $F = H - TS$, where F is the free energy, H is the heat content, S is the entropy of a chemical reaction, and T is absolute temperature. At first largely disregarded, the equation later becomes widely used, with the symbol F being changed to G in honor of Gibbs's work.

J. TECHNOLOGY: *the Microphone*

David Edward Hughes invents the microphone.

K. TECHNOLOGY: *Soap*

The Procter and Gamble Company invents Ivory soap, the floating soap, which it advertises as "99 and 44/100% pure."

L. THE ARTS: *Music*

H.M.S. Pinafore, an operetta by William S. Gilbert and Arthur Sullivan, is first performed.

M. THE ARTS: *Literature*

- Leo Tolstoy publishes *Anna Karenina.*
- Henry James writes *Daisy Miller.*

1879

A. BACTERIAL PHYSIOLOGY: *Thermophiles*

P. Miquel finds a thermophilic bacillus that grows at 70°C and higher. Although Miquel is often cited as the first to observe such bacteria, a number of other accounts indicate that thermophilic organisms, possibly chlamydobacteria, may have been observed as early as 1823. In 1927, Nobel laureate Svante Arrhenius makes the interesting speculation that the natural habitat of thermophilic bacteria is the planet Venus and that radiation pressure from the sun propels them to earth. (See 1846 D.)

B. BACTERIAL DISEASE: *the Gonococcus*

Albert Neisser discovers the organism, which he calls "gonococcus," that causes gonorrhea. In 1885, Ernst von Bumm causes infections with pure cultures of the gonococcus. In the second century, the Greek physician Galen had named the disease "gonorrhea" from the Greek words *gono* (semen) and *rhein* (to flow). The bacterium is known today as *Neisseria gonorrhoeae.* (See 1887 E.)

C. BACTERIAL DISEASE: *Psittacosis*

In Switzerland, J. Ritter reports human cases of a disease he calls pneumotyphus, meaning pneumonia with stupor. Ritter is the first to report the disease that is named psittacosis, from the Greek word for parrot, by A. Morange in 1895. The causative organism, an obligate intracellular parasitic bacterium now called *Chlamydia psittaci,* is not isolated until 1930. (See 1907 B, 1930 C, 1934 B.)

1879 *(continued)*

D. BACTERIAL DISEASE: *Plant Pathogens*

Thomas Jonathan Burrill publishes the first of a number of papers establishing that pear blight is caused by a bacterium that he calls *Micrococcus amylovorus* or *Bacillus amylovorus* (now named *Erwinia amylovora*). He also studies potato scab, peach yellows, ear rot of corn, and several other plant diseases. Because Burrill is the first to prove bacterial disease in plants, he has been referred to as the Robert Koch of plant pathology. (See 1899 B.)

E. INFECTIOUS DISEASE: *Experimental Animals for Rabies*

Pierre Victor Galtier demonstrates that rabies can be transmitted from dogs to rabbits, and then, in series, from rabbit to rabbit. Although Galtier's extensive experiments establish the use of rabbits to study rabies, it was Georg Gottfried Zinke, in 1804, who first successfully transferred rabies from an infected dog to rabbits.

F. FERMENTATION: *Controversy*

Carl Wilhelm von Nägeli dismisses the ferment theory of Moritz Traube and Felix Hoppe-Seyler, asserting that fermentation is inseparable from the substance of the living cell. (See 1858 C, 1862 B.)

G. TECHNOLOGY: *Incandescent Electric Light*

Thomas Alva Edison invents an incandescent electric light.

H. TECHNOLOGY: *the Mimeograph*

Thomas Alva Edison licenses one of his inventions to Albert Blake Dick, leading in 1888 to the production of the A. B. Dick diaphragm mimeograph machine.

I. TECHNOLOGY: *Cream Separator*

Carl Gustav Patrik de Laval invents a centrifuge for separating butterfat from milk.

J. CULTURE: *Universities*

Somerville College for women is established at Oxford University. Classes for women in Cambridge, Massachusetts, lead to the establishment of Radcliffe College.

K. THE ARTS: *Music*

William S. Gilbert's and Arthur Sullivan's operetta *Pirates of Penzance* is performed.

L. THE ARTS: *Literature*
- Fyodor Dostoyevsky publishes *The Brothers Karamazov*.
- Henrik Ibsen's play, *A Doll's House,* is performed in Copenhagen.

1880

A. BACTERIAL GENUS: Clostridium

In studies of anaerobic bacteria, Adam Prazmowski assigns the generic name *Clostridium* (from the Greek *kloster,* for spindle) to those that produce spindle-shaped endospores. (See 1861 B.)

B. BACTERIAL DISEASE: *Typhoid Bacillus*

Carl Joseph Eberth observes but does not cultivate the typhoid bacillus now known as *Salmonella typhi*. For many years microbiologists use the species name *Eberthella typhi*.

C. IMMUNOLOGY: *Chicken Cholera*

Louis Pasteur publishes a paper describing a discovery that cultures of the bacterium that causes the disease chicken cholera are attenuated by holding them for several weeks at room temperature in the laboratory. Injection of these attenuated cultures into chickens prevents infection with virulent strains of the organism. It is now believed that Émile Roux actually carried out experiments in Pasteur's laboratory in which he exposed cultures of the bacterium *Pasteurella multocida* to acid conditions, resulting in the selection of mutants with less virulence than the parent. Although Pasteur uses the word "attenuated" to mean weakened, modern usage of the term refers to selection or enrichment of mutants of lowered virulence. This use of attenuated microorganisms in vaccination is the first advance in vaccination since Edward Jenner's work in 1796. (See 1796 B, 1881 F.)

D. PROTOZOAN DISEASE: *Malaria*

Charles Louis Alphonse Laveran discovers that malaria is caused by a protozoan after noting that the characteristic dark granules found in blood of patients possess flagella and have independent movement. His observations are doubted by many scientists who believe that a bacterium causes malaria. It is not until 1884, when Ettore Marchiafava confirms that protozoans cause malaria, that Laveran's work is generally accepted. Along with Patrick Manson, Laveran suggests that the disease is transmitted by mosquitoes. In 1898, Ronald Ross proves that mosquitoes transmit malaria among birds, and Giovanni Grassi shows the cycle of human transmission. Laveran receives the Nobel Prize in physiology or medicine in 1907. (See 1883 C, 1884 I, 1885 K, 1898 J.)

E. CHEMISTRY: *Beilstein's Handbook*

Friedrich Konrad Beilstein publishes the first volume of his *Handbuch der organischen Chemie* with the intention of listing every known organic chemical. After he completes the third edition, its publication is continued by the Deutsche Chemische Gesellschaft. It continues to be a work of great value to chemists.

F. TECHNOLOGY: *Canal*

Ferdinand de Lesseps begins construction of the Panama Canal. He abandons the project in 1889 when the company supporting it goes bankrupt. The canal officially opens in 1914.

G. THE ARTS: *Art*

Auguste Rodin, in the process of working on a commission to cast a monumental work to be called *The Gates of Hell* (never completed), completes one of his greatest works, *The Thinker*.

A. BACTERIOLOGICAL TECHNIQUE: *Koch's Plate Technique*

Robert Koch publishes a paper in which he describes his methods for studying pathogenic bacteria, including his plate technique. Gelatin is added to culture medium, poured onto flat glass plates, and allowed to gel. He describes how the technique is used to isolate pure cultures of bacteria from discrete colonies growing on the surface of the solid medium. Koch also uses the plate technique for measuring the numbers of bacteria found in soil, water, food, and air. Since accurate counts are often impossible because of large numbers of colonies, dilution methods for plate counting appear in textbooks of bacteriology by about 1915. The 1881 paper, which also describes his procedures for microscopic photography, includes the first published pictures of diseased tissue containing bacteria. Koch demonstrates the plate technique at a medical congress in London in 1881 with Louis Pasteur in the audience. The plate technique is improved in 1882 by Walther Hesse and Fannie Hesse, who introduce the use of agar, and, in 1887, by Richard Julius Petri, who invents the petri dish.

B. BACTERIAL SPECIES: Staphylococcus *and* Streptococcus

Studying abscesses and other suppurative infections, Alexander Ogston differentiates *Staphylococcus* (named by him) from *Streptococcus*. He demonstrates that *Staphylococcus* is pathogenic for both guinea pigs and mice.

C. BACTERIAL SPECIES: Pneumococcus

Louis Pasteur and, independently, George Miller Sternberg inject rabbits with human saliva and subsequently isolate cultures of what are assumed to be pneumococci. The relationship of these bacteria to lobar pneumonia is not understood until experiments are begun in 1884 by Albert Fraenkel. (See 1884 G.)

D. BACTERIAL PHYSIOLOGY: *Chemotaxis*

Theodor Wilhelm Engelmann reports chemotaxis toward oxygen when he observes that bacteria under a coverslip on a microscope slide tend to accumulate at the edges or around air bubbles. The phenomenon, which he terms *Schrecksbewegung* (shock reaction), is enhanced by oxygen and inhibited by hydrogen. Engelmann also observes phototaxis in a bacterium called *Bacterium photometricum,* which is immotile in the dark and motile in light. (See 1885 C, 1893 B, 1966 B, 1969 C.)

E. BACTERIAL PHYSIOLOGY: *Denitrification*

In experiments with bacteria obtained from sewage, Ulysse Gayon and Gabriel Dupetit note the anaerobic destruction of nitrate with the production of gas. They describe this process as denitrification. (See 1868 C, 1886 C.)

F. IMMUNOLOGY: *Anthrax Vaccine*

Louis Pasteur, Charles Chamberland, and Émile Roux publish on the development of an anthrax vaccine. They describe cultivation of *Bacillus anthracis* in thin layers of growth medium at the elevated temperature of 42 to 43°C, which results in the attenuation necessary for safety of the vaccine. Pasteur believes that exposure to atmospheric oxygen is the primary cause of attenuation while the elevated temperature prevents spore formation. It is now believed that Chamberland actually prepared the vaccine used in a famous public experiment at Pouilly-le-Fort by treatment of cultures with potassium bichromate. In the Pouilly-le-Fort experiment, 48 sheep are inoculated with a virulent culture of anthrax; 24 of these animals had previously been inoculated with attenuated cultures of the anthrax bacillus. Ten cows and two goats are included in the experiment. The vaccinated animals survive, whereas those in the nonvaccinated group die. Vaccines prepared by oxygen attenuation are subsequently prepared and widely used with good success. Pasteur expands the term "vaccine" as a tribute to Edward Jenner, who originally used cowpox vaccination against smallpox. (See 1796 B, 1849 B, 1876 C, 1954 G.)

G. INFECTIOUS DISEASE: *Poliomyelitis*
An epidemic of poliomyelitis in Sweden is regarded by Karl Oscar Medin as the first true epidemic of the disease. In 1905 and 1907, his student Ivar Wickman publishes papers on poliomyelitis, referring to it as Heine-Medin disease, a name that for a few years is used instead of poliomyelitis. (See 1840 B.)

H. MICROBIOLOGY: *Sterilization*
Although Louis Pasteur and others use heat sterilization in their experiments, it is Robert Koch and his associates Gustav Wolffhügel, Georg Gaffky, and Friedrich Löffler who determine the effectiveness of both hot air sterilization and steam sterilization. Although they conclude that moist heat is more effective than dry heat, they prefer to use steam at atmospheric pressure of 100°C because of the difficulty of using steam under pressure. Other scientists later show the necessity of using steam under pressure to achieve temperatures necessary for the destruction of endospores. In 1681, Denys Papin described a steam digester, "an engine for softning bones," a forerunner of the autoclave. By 1876 the word "autoclave" has been introduced as a name for steam sterilizers with self-locking doors.

I. BOTANY: *Plant Physiology*
Wilhelm Friedrich Pfeffer publishes *Handbuch der Pflanzenphisiologie,* afterwards a standard reference on plant physiology. Among Pfeffer's important contributions are studies of the structure of vacuoles, the effect of light intensity and various other factors on photosynthesis in chloroplasts, and the use of a semipermeable membrane in the study of osmotic pressure. Jacobus Henricus van't Hoff later interprets his data and explains the process of osmosis.

J. CHEMISTRY: *Atoms*
Hermann Ludwig Helmholtz states that matter is composed of atoms and that electricity is composed of "atoms of electricity."

K. SOCIETY AND POLITICS
• U.S. president James A. Garfield is wounded on July 2 by an assassin; he dies on September 19.

1881 *(continued)*

• Clara Barton organizes the American Association of the Red Cross. (See 1862 D.)

L. CULTURE: *Universities*

In Tuskegee, Alabama, black citizens persuade Booker T. Washington to found the Tuskegee Normal and Industrial Institute.

M. THE ARTS: *Art*

Edouard Manet paints *Bar at the Folies Bergère*.

1882

A. BACTERIOLOGICAL TECHNIQUE: *Agar Culture Media*

Fannie Hesse suggests the use of agar-agar as a solidifying agent for bacteriological culture media, having learned of its use in cooking from Dutch friends from Batavia. She is the wife of Walther Hesse, who worked briefly in Robert Koch's laboratory. Agar quickly replaces gelatin as a solidifying agent in Koch's and others' laboratories because it remains solid at temperatures up to 100°C, because of its clarity, and because of its resistance to digestion by bacterial enzymes. Agar-agar, also known as Bengal isinglass and Ceylon moss, is a polysaccharide obtained from certain seaweeds.

B. BACTERIOLOGICAL TECHNIQUE: *Staining*

Paul Ehrlich improves Robert Koch's staining method for his study of the tubercle bacillus and discovers that the bacillus is acid-fast; that is, it resists decolorization with an acid alcohol after staining. Franz Ziehl and Friedrich Neelsen further modify the procedure in 1883.

C. BACTERIAL SPECIES: Pseudomonas

Carle Gessard isolates a bacterium, later known as *Pseudomonas aeruginosa,* that causes blue and green discolorations on surgical dressings.

D. BACTERIAL DISEASE: *Germ Theory of Disease / Koch's Postulates*

Robert Koch isolates *Mycobacterium tuberculosis,* the bacillus that causes tuberculosis, and publishes perhaps his best paper, establishing that a specific bacterium causes a specific disease. In this paper, and in 1884, he states concepts that become known as Koch's postulates, but which are in fact best described by Friedrich Löffler in 1883. In 1905, Koch receives the Nobel Prize in physiology or medicine for his work on tuberculosis. (See 1877 D, 1883 B.)

E. BACTERIAL DISEASE: Klebsiella pneumoniae

Carl Friedländer cultivates an organism from the lungs of a patient who has died of pneumonia. This encapsulated bacterium is known as Friedländer's pneumobacillus (or pneumoniecoccus) or as *Bacterium friedländeri.* Friedländer and Albert Fraenkel disagree as to whether or not Friedländer's bacillus or a pneumococcus isolated by Fraenkel in 1884 is responsible for lobar pneumonia. The newly introduced Gram stain technique helps resolve the controversy, since the Friedländer bacillus is gram negative while the pneumococcus is gram positive. Friedländer mentions the Gram stain briefly in an 1883 paper, a few months before Hans Christian Gram publishes his own report. Friedländer's bacillus is later recognized to be a secondary invader in cases of pneumonia. In 1885, V. Trevisan describes several new genera of bacteria, including *Klebsiella*; eventually, Friedländer's bacillus is assigned the name *Klebsiella pneumoniae*. (See 1884 G, 1884 B.)

F. INFECTIOUS DISEASE: *Tobacco Mosaic Disease*

Adolf Mayer writes that an infectious agent, which may be soluble, causes tobacco mosaic disease. Although he names the disease, he is unable to isolate the causative agent by using bacteriological techniques. Mayer concludes that the disease is caused by a bacterium whose form is not yet known, or by an unorganized ferment. His work precedes by 10 years that of Dimitri Ivanovsky (1892), who is usually credited with the discovery of the tobacco mosaic virus, and is 17 years earlier than the experiments of Martinus Beijerinck, who comes closest to recognizing that the disease is not of bacterial origin. (See 1892 D, 1899 E.)

G. BIOCHEMISTRY: *Oxidation/Reduction*

Moritz Traube proposes that both water and oxygen participate in oxidation reactions and that, as water decomposes, atomic H forms, reducing H_2O to H_2O_2. (See 1878 G.)

H. BIOLOGY: *Mitosis*

Walther Flemming publishes *Zellsubstanz, Kern und Zellteilung,* summarizing his observations of the nucleus and cell division using tissue sections stained with certain dyes. In 1879, he names the heavily stained segments in the nucleus "chromatin," noting that they form visible threads during cell division. In 1888, Wilhelm Waldeyer-Hartz names these threads "chromosomes." Flemming further describes the longitudinal division of chromosomes during cell division, a process he calls "mitosis." (See 1887 F.)

I. BIOLOGY: *Cell Division*

Eduard Adolf Strasburger, in his studies of cell division in plants, introduces the terms "nucleoplasm" and "cytoplasm" for materials inside and outside the nucleus, respectively. He uses the words "haploid" and "diploid" to describe the halving and doubling of the chromosome number during sexual reproduction. He is senior author of a textbook, *Lehrbuch der Botanik für Hochschulen,* first published in 1894 and widely used for many years.

J. MATHEMATICS: *Calculation of π*

Carl Louis Ferdinand proves that the number π is transcendental and that a circle cannot be squared.

K. SOCIETY AND POLITICS

Germany, Austria, and Italy sign the Triple Alliance, pledging to assist each other if attacked by France within the next 5 years.

L. THE ARTS: *Literature*

The fictional detective Sherlock Holmes makes his first appearance in *A Study in Scarlet* by Arthur Conan Doyle. Doyle's book *Adventures of Sherlock Holmes* is published in 1891.

M. THE ARTS: *Music*

The *1812 Overture* by Petr Ilyich Tchaikovsky is performed in Moscow with cannon explosions as sound effects.

A. BACTERIOLOGICAL TECHNIQUE: *Staining*

Friedrich Neelsen describes a modification of a technique devised by Franz Ziehl for the staining of the tubercle bacillus to differentiate it from other bacteria. The procedure, which becomes known as the Ziehl-Neelsen stain, derives from work done by Robert Koch and Paul Ehrlich in 1882.

B. BACTERIAL DISEASE: *Diphtheria/Koch's Postulates*

Edwin Klebs describes, but does not isolate, the bacterium that causes diphtheria. Friedrich Löffler cultivates and describes the same microorganism, a bacterium that becomes known as the Klebs-Löffler bacillus and is named *Corynebacterium diphtheriae* in 1896. Löffler presents, in a list of steps necessary to prove that a specific pathogen causes a specific disease, the first clear statement of Koch's postulates. Robert Koch describes his ideas in an 1884 paper on tuberculosis, but not as clearly as Löffler presents them. (See 1877 D, 1884 D, 1888 E, 1896 B.)

C. INFECTIOUS DISEASE: *Insect Transmission*

In China, Patrick Manson studies the disease elephantiasis and concludes that it is spread by mosquitoes. Elephantiasis is the first disease proved to be transmitted by insect vectors. In 1877, he suggests that malaria is transmitted by mosquitoes and later encourages Ronald Ross to consider this possibility. (See 1880 D, 1884 I, 1885 K, 1897 E, 1898 J.)

D. FERMENTATION: *Pure Cultures*

At the Carlsberg Brewery in Copenhagen, Emil Christian Hansen uses pure cultures of yeast in beer making.

E. BIOLOGY: *Genetics*

August Weismann, as a consequence of his studies with *Diptera,* proposes a germ plasm theory of inheritance. He believes that the germ line is unbroken and that the somatic cells of higher plants and animals bud off from it. Weismann develops a complex theory of heredity in which chromosomes are the elements of inheritance. His ideas are widely discussed but not totally accepted. (See 1882 H, 1889 G.).

F. BIOLOGY: *Mitosis*

Wilhelm Roux supports August Weismann's idea that germ plasm is passed from parent to progeny. He notes that the equal longitudinal division of chromosomes during mitosis must be responsible for providing each daughter cell with equal amounts of chromosomal material. He also believes that the second mitotic division fails to give equal hereditary units to daughter cells. These ideas lead to the hypothesis that the units of heredity are sorted at somatic cell divisions. (See 1883 E.)

G. PHYSIOLOGY: *Ringer Solution*

Sydney Ringer develops the Ringer solution, a saline solution containing calcium and potassium that keeps an isolated frog heart beating for a prolonged period of time.

H. BIOCHEMISTRY: *Nitrogen Determination*

John Gustav Christoffer Thorsager Kjeldahl develops a method for determining the nitrogen content of organic matter. The Kjeldahl flask used in the procedure carries his name.

I. TECHNOLOGY: *Vacuum Tube*

Thomas Alva Edison discovers the basic principle of the electronic vacuum tube, the "Edison effect," but sees no use for it.

J. SOCIETY AND POLITICS

Friedrich Wilhelm Nietzsche introduces the idea of the Superman in part one of *Also Sprach Zarathustra*.

K. THE ARTS: *Literature*

Robert Louis Stevenson publishes *Treasure Island*.

L. THE ARTS: *Music*

The Metropolitan Opera House opens in New York City with a production of *Faust* by Charles Gounod.

M. THE ARTS: *Art*

Winslow Homer paints *Inside the Bar, Tynemouth*.

1884

A. BACTERIAL SPECIES: **Streptococcus** *and* **Staphylococcus**

Anton Julius Friedrich Rosenbach makes the first valid use of the generic name *Streptococcus* when he gives the name *Streptococcus pyogenes* to a streptococcus that causes wound infections. Rosenbach also is the first to assign species names to the genus *Staphylococcus,* named by Alexander Ogston in 1881, when he describes *Staphylococcus pyogenes aureus* and *Staphylococcus pyogenes albus*. In this same paper he shortens the names to *Staphylococcus aureus* and *Staphylococcus albus*.

B. BACTERIOLOGICAL TECHNIQUE: *Gram Stain*

Hans Christian Gram introduces the Gram stain, which quickly becomes the most important method for separating bacteria into two groups: gram positive, for those that retain a primary stain after a decolorization step, and gram negative, for those that give up the stain but can be recolored with a secondary stain of contrasting color. Gram devises the staining procedure, while working in Carl Friedländer's laboratory in Berlin, in order to distinguish bacteria in stained tissue sections from nuclei and other cell structures. He notes that those bacteria that are decolorized by an alcohol treatment can be counterstained with Bismarck brown, or vesuvin. Friedländer mentions the procedure in a paper in 1883, while Gram's paper is published a few months later. In an 1886 paper Friedländer again refers to the Gram stain but does not recognize its importance. In several unpublished letters, Gram recognizes the significance of his discovery, and in 1886 several textbooks describe the method. Gram does no further work of significance in bacteriology. He becomes a clinician and in 1900 is named professor of medicine in Copenhagen. The process by which Gram differentiation takes place is not explained until 1963. (See 1929 A, 1957 A, 1963 B.)

1884 *(continued)*

C. BACTERIOLOGICAL TECHNIQUE: *Filter Sterilization*

Charles Chamberland develops an unglazed porcelain filter that retains bacteria. The "Chamberland filter" is later manufactured in various pore sizes and distributed worldwide. (See 1871 A.)

D. BACTERIAL DISEASE: *Cholera Bacillus*

While on an expedition to Egypt (1883) and India (1883 to 1884) to find the cause of cholera, Robert Koch obtains a pure culture of the causative bacterium, *Vibrio cholerae,* shortly after arriving in India. (See 1854 B.)

E. BACTERIAL DISEASE: *Typhoid Bacillus*

Georg Gaffky isolates and studies the typhoid bacillus, now named *Salmonella typhi,* which Carl Joseph Eberth first observed in 1880.

F. BACTERIAL DISEASE: *Tetanus Bacillus*

Arthur Nicolaier observes the tetanus bacillus, *Clostridium tetani,* in soil but fails to cultivate it. He produces symptoms of the disease in animals by inoculation with soil suspensions. (See 1889 D.)

G. BACTERIAL DISEASE: *Bacterial Pneumonia*

Albert Fraenkel discovers the pneumococcus, the cause of bacterial lobar pneumonia. Fraenkel and Carl Friedländer disagree as to whether or not this bacterium or Friedländer's bacillus (now named *Klebsiella pneumoniae*), isolated in 1882, is responsible for lobar pneumonia. The newly introduced Gram stain aids in settling the argument, since the Friedländer bacillus is gram negative while the pneumococcus is gram positive. Friedländer's bacillus is later recognized to be a secondary invader in cases of pneumonia. In 1884, Anton Weichselbaum gives Fraenkel's organism the name *Diplococcus pneumoniae*; it is now called *Streptococcus pneumoniae.* (See 1882 E, 1884 B.)

H. IMMUNOLOGY: *Phagocytosis*

Elie Metchnikoff gives the name "phagocytes" to certain body cells that ingest and destroy invading microorganisms and other minute foreign particles. He calls the process "phagocytosis" and coins the terms "microphages" for polymorphonuclear leukocytes and "macrophages" for fixed endothelial cells, mononuclear cells, and lymphoid masses. Although Metchnikoff develops the concept of phagocytosis, he is not the first to have considered that white blood cells play a role in immunity. Both Peter Ludwig Panum, in 1874, and George Miller Sternberg, in 1881, suggest that white blood cells consume bacteria. In 1884, the year of Metchnikoff's publication, Sternberg publishes a full account of his ideas of the role of blood cells in immunity. Metchnikoff, the chief proponent of cellular immunity, shares the 1908 Nobel Prize in physiology or medicine with Paul Ehrlich, the champion of the concept of humoral immunity. (See 1881 C, 1891 D.)

I. PROTOZOAN DISEASE: *Malaria*

Ettore Marchiafava confirms Charles Louis Alphonse Laveran's claim that malaria is caused by a protozoan. (See 1880 D, 1883 C, 1885 K, 1898 J.).

J. BIOCHEMISTRY: *Cytochrome*

Charles Alexander MacMunn finds a substance in blood that has four absorption bands that disappear when oxidized. In 1925, David Keilin names this substance "cytochrome."

K. BIOCHEMISTRY: *Hexoses/Purines*

Emil Hermann Fischer uses the reaction of phenylhydrazine with aldehydes (discovered by him in 1875) and their optical isomerism to begin a series of studies on the structure of six-carbon aldehyde sugars, or aldohexoses. He works out the structure of the 16 possible aldohexoses and portrays them in a manner that is known as the Fischer formulas. He also studies the structure of double-ring molecules important in the structure of nucleic acids, to which he assigns the name "purine" in 1898. Fischer receives the Nobel Prize in chemistry in 1902 for his work on sugars and purines. (See 1885 N.)

L. CHEMISTRY: *Kinetics*

Jacobus Henricus van't Hoff publishes the results of his work on reaction velocity and chemical equilibrium in solutions. van't Hoff receives the first Nobel Prize in chemistry in 1901.

M. TECHNOLOGY: *Automobiles*

F. H. Royce and Co. begins manufacturing motorcars in England.

N. THE ARTS: *Architecture*

The Washington Monument is completed; it is opened to the public in 1888. At 169 meters in height, it is the world's tallest structure until the erection of the Eiffel Tower in 1889 in Paris.

O. CULTURE: *Dictionaries*

The first volume of the *Oxford English Dictionary* (OED) is printed. The dictionary is not completed until 1928.

P. THE ARTS: *Literature*

Mark Twain (Samuel Clemens) publishes his novel *Huckleberry Finn.*

1885

A. BACTERIAL SPECIES: Escherichia coli *and* Enterobacter aerogenes

Theodore Escherich describes two bacteria isolated from the feces of infants and names them *Bacterium coli commune* and *Bacterium lactis aerogenes,* the latter organism causing the clotting of milk more actively than the former. In 1919, Aldo Castellani and Albert Chambers change the name of *Bacterium coli* to *Escherichia coli. Bacterium aerogenes* is now named *Enterobacter aerogenes.* Escherich also finds that some strains of *Bacterium coli* cause diarrhea in infants.

B. BACTERIAL SPECIES: Proteus

Gustave Hauser studies microorganisms he terms *Fäulnissbacterien,* or decay bacteria, and divides them into three groups: *Proteus vulgaris, Proteus mirabilis,* and *Proteus zenkeri.* The generic name *Proteus* is the name of the sea god who changes form at will. *P. zenkeri* is gram positive and is subsequently reclassified.

1885 *(continued)*

C. BACTERIAL PHYSIOLOGY: *Chemotaxis*

Wilhelm Friedrich Pfeffer reports observations similar to those made by Theodor Wilhelm Engelmann in 1881. He notes oxygen chemotaxis and also employs Engelmann's term *Schrecksbewegung*. Pfeffer finds both negative and positive chemotaxis by dipping capillary tubes containing the chemical agent into the bacterial suspension. (See 1881 D, 1893 B, 1969 C.)

D. BACTERIAL PHYSIOLOGY: *Nitrogen Fixation*

Marcelin Berthelot reports that soil fixes nitrogen directly from air. Although he suggests that bacteria might be responsible for this phenomenon, he also mentions static electricity as a possible cause; thus, some discount his distinction of discovering biological nitrogen fixation. (See 1886 B, 1888 B, 1889 B.)

E. BACTERIAL PHYSIOLOGY: *Nonlegume Symbiotic Nitrogen Fixation*

L. Hiltner grows *Alnus glutinosa* in nitrogen-free soil, both with and without the addition of nitrates. He also makes suspensions of root nodules taken from the plant and grows plants with and without addition of the suspensions. After 1 year, he concludes that either nitrate or root nodules are necessary for growth of the plant. He does not perform nitrogen determinations. (See 1886 B, 1887 C, 1902 D, 1970 B, 1978 D.)

F. INFECTIOUS DISEASE: *Serum Hepatitis*

A. Lürman publishes a description of a disease outbreak apparently transmitted to a group of shipyard workers by smallpox vaccine that contained human lymph. Lürman's account of jaundice in this outbreak is the first report of serum hepatitis. (See 1912 C, 1926 E, 1943 E.)

G. IMMUNOLOGY: *Cholera Vaccine*

Jaime Ferrán y Clua gives the first cholera vaccine to approximately 30,000 persons in Spain. Ferrán's vaccine, produced from living bacteria attenuated at room temperature, causes severe adverse reactions in many of his subjects. (See 1892 G, 1896 D.)

H. IMMUNOLOGY: *Rabies Vaccine*

Louis Pasteur develops a rabies vaccine using dried spinal cords from rabbits infected experimentally with rabies. Pasteur uses the term "virus," meaning poison, but does not know the properties of the causative microorganism. In May and June, Pasteur treats two persons who had been attacked by rabid dogs; one dies, but the other, who may not have contracted rabies, survives. In July, Pasteur uses a different sequence of injections with dried spinal cord material to treat a 9-year-old boy, Joseph Meister, who was bitten by a rabid dog. Meister survives and later becomes the gate-porter at the Pasteur Institute in Paris; he commits suicide in 1940 to avoid having to open Pasteur's crypt to German troops who invaded France in World War II. In October 1885, Pasteur successfully treats Jean-Baptiste Jupille, a 15-year-old shepherd who was badly bitten while fighting a rabid dog that was attacking some children. A statue standing outside the original building of the Pasteur Institute portrays Jupille's stand against the rabid dog. (See 1879 E.)

I. BACTERIAL DISEASE: *Antiseptics*

Paul Ehrlich suggests that some dyes might be useful in controlling bacterial infections.

J. MICROBIOLOGY: *Germfree Life*

One of Louis Pasteur's colleagues, Émile Duclaux, fails in his attempts to grow peas in completely sterile conditions. Pasteur comments on this work by stating that he had often thought of attempting to raise an animal from birth with only sterile food. But he had not attempted the experiment, partly from the belief that without bacteria, life would be impossible. He also states that a chicken egg would be a good choice for starting such an experiment. (See 1895 D, 1899 C, 1928 D.)

K. PROTOZOAN DISEASE: *Malaria*

Studying the life cycle of the malaria parasite, Camillo Golgi reports the correlation of bouts of fever with emergence of parasites from erythrocytes. (See 1880 D, 1883 C, 1898 J.)

L. ANATOMY: *Histology*

Camillo Golgi publishes a book on the histology of the nervous system. In 1873, he had developed a method of silver impregnation of nerve cells that allowed the examination of nerve fibers throughout most of their length. In disagreement with Golgi, Santiago Ramón y Cajal believes that nerve cells have no physical continuity with other nerve cells. Golgi discovers the "Golgi apparatus" (or "Golgi bodies") in 1898. Golgi shares the 1906 Nobel Prize in physiology or medicine with Ramón y Cajal.

M. PHYSIOLOGY: *Oxygen Requirements*

Paul Ehrlich publishes a book on the use of dyes to study the oxygen requirements of animals. Disregarding Moritz Traube's ideas about oxygen, he continues to discuss the living protoplasm concept.

N. BIOCHEMISTRY: *Nucleic Acids*

Albrecht Kossel, working in Felix Hoppe-Seyler's laboratory, purifies nucleic acids from the heads of spermatozoa and from nucleated avian red blood cells. In partially characterizing the structure of the nonprotein components, he finds the purines studied by Emil Hermann Fischer as well as the single-ring structures called "pyrimidines," which Adolf Pinner names in 1884. Kossel isolates two purines, adenine and guanine, and three pyrimidines, uracil, cytosine, and thymine. Although he concludes that these molecules are associated with a sugar molecule, he fails to identify the type of sugar. For these discoveries, Kossel receives the 1910 Nobel Prize in physiology or medicine. (See 1869 E, 1950 L.)

O. TECHNOLOGY: *Automobiles*

Karl Friedrich Benz builds a three-wheel automobile powered by a gasoline internal combustion engine. (See 1769 B, 1859 F, 1893 F.)

P. TECHNOLOGY: *Fingerprints*

A system for identifying fingerprints is introduced by Francis Galton. He is not the first to study the unique character of fingerprints, having been preceded by Marcello Malpighi, Jan Evangelista Purkinje, Henry Faulds, and

William Herschel. In 1886, Alphonse Bertillon develops a complex system of identification based on a combination of many physical characteristics, including fingerprints. (See 1901 P.)

Q. CULTURE: *Universities*
Stanford University, officially named Leland Stanford Junior University, is founded by Leland Stanford to honor his son, who died the previous year. The university officially opens in 1891.

R. THE ARTS: *Music*
The Mikado, an operetta by William S. Gilbert and Arthur Sullivan, is performed.

S. THE ARTS: *Literature*
William Dean Howells publishes *The Rise of Silas Lapham.*

1886

A. BACTERIAL TAXONOMY: *Classification*
Joseph Schroeter prepares the most complete system for classification of the bacteria to this date, consisting of three orders and 26 genera. The orders are *Coccobacteria* (spherical cells), *Eubacteria* (rod-shaped cells), and *Desmobacteria* (filaments).

B. BACTERIAL PHYSIOLOGY: *Symbiotic Nitrogen*
Hermann Hellriegel reports the first of his studies on nitrogen fixation by bacteria associated with the root nodules of leguminous plants. In 1888, with H. Wilfarth, he publishes an extensive report establishing that leguminous plants utilize nitrogen from the air with the active participation of bacteria and that the root nodules do not merely store protein (albuminous material) but have a causal relationship. (See 1885 D, 1885 E, 1888 B, 1889 B.)

C. BACTERIAL PHYSIOLOGY: *Denitrification*
Ulysse Gayon and Gabriel Dupetit isolate two strains of denitrifying bacteria from sewage that they name *Bacterium denitrificans* α and β. They note that the process of denitrification is not fermentation but a type of combustion of organic matter by nitrate. They recognize the release of nitrogen oxides as well as dinitrogen. By about 1895 several researchers have identified species of the genus *Pseudomonas* as denitrifiers.

D. FOOD BACTERIOLOGY: *Pasteurization*
F. Soxhlet recommends that cow's milk be boiled for 35 minutes to kill contaminating microorganisms, applying to milk purification Louis Pasteur's recommendations for preserving wine and beer. Both the holding method and flash or quick methods for pasteurization of milk follow soon after, and legal definitions of pasteurization are developed.

E. VIROLOGY: *Elementary Bodies*
John Brown Buist, whose life's work is devoted to practicing and teaching vaccination, reports a method for the fixation and staining of lymph containing vaccinia and variola viruses. He uses gentian violet to stain material from a smallpox vaccine ulcer and observes small stained granules that he

believes to be the causative agent of cowpox, the vaccination agent. What he describes as "spores of micrococci" are probably viral elementary bodies, but there is little doubt that he observes the virus since it is large enough to be seen with the oil immersion microscope. Because Buist receives little notice for his work, Enrique Paschen is credited for many years with being the first to observe the cowpox virus microscopically in 1906. (See 1882 F, 1892 E, 1899 E, 1904 D, 1906 G, 1929 F.)

F. IMMUNOLOGY: *Heat–Killed Vaccine*
Theobald Smith is the first to use a heat-killed whole-cell vaccine when he immunizes pigeons against what he believes to be the "hog-cholera bacillus." His organism proves to be unrelated to hog cholera, or swine plague disease, which is later found to be of viral etiology. Although Smith believes that he is testing the effect of bacterial chemical products (toxins), he does not remove the dead bacteria from his vaccine. As chief of the division in the department of agriculture in which Smith worked, Daniel Salmon is listed as the first author on the paper describing these experiments, while Smith is credited with performing the experiments. The generic name *Salmonella,* introduced in 1900 for this particular group of intestinal pathogens, is not widely used for some years.

G. MICROSCOPY: *Apochromatic Objectives*
In collaboration with Otto Schott and Carl Zeiss, Ernst Abbe perfects a complete series of apochromatic objective lenses for the compound microscope that form images almost free of residual color.

H. BIOLOGY: *Osmotic Pressure*
Following the earlier work of Wilhelm Friedrich Pfeffer, Jacobus Henricus van't Hoff publishes an explanation of osmotic pressure. (See 1881 I.)

I. CHEMISTRY: *Electrolytic Dissociation*
Svante Arrhenius formulates the theory of electrolytic dissociation. Arrhenius receives the Nobel Prize in chemistry in 1903 for this work. (See 1889 J, 1907 F.)

J. TECHNOLOGY: *Glass Syringe*
H. Wulfing Luer introduces the all–glass syringe.

K. SOCIETY AND POLITICS
In Chicago, a conflict between police and striking workers results in a number of deaths. The so-called Haymarket Massacre causes May 1, or May Day, to become a worldwide memorial day for revolution, now celebrated in many countries as a spring holiday.

L. THE ARTS: *Art*
The Kiss, a sensuous sculpture by Auguste Rodin intended to be a part of a larger work, *The Gates of Hell,* is completed.

M. THE ARTS: *Literature*
A novel, *The Strange Case of Dr. Jekyll and Mr. Hyde,* by Robert Louis Stevenson is published.

A. BACTERIOLOGICAL TECHNIQUE: *Petri Dish*

Richard Julius Petri, an assistant of Robert Koch, replaces the glass plates covered with a bell jar that are used for cultures made with poured melted gelatin or agar culture media with flat dishes having raised sides with an overlapping glass lid. The petri dishes, sometimes called Petri's capsules in early literature, attain universal use in microbiology. In textbooks, however, the use of glass plates and bell jars continues to be described as late as 1913.

B. BACTERIAL PHYSIOLOGY: *Chemoautotrophs*

Sergei Winogradsky publishes a study of the sulfur bacteria that includes a key to their classification. He includes such genera as *Beggiatoa* (created by V. Trevisan in 1842) and *Chromatium* (named by Maximilian Perty in 1852), later recognized to be photosynthetic. Winogradsky formulates the concept of chemoautotrophic life (chemolithotrophy) to describe organisms that obtain metabolic energy through the oxidation of inorganic substances such as ammonia and hydrogen sulfide. (See 1891 B.)

C. BACTERIAL PHYSIOLOGY: *Nonlegume Symbiotic Nitrogen Fixation*

J. Brunchorst, a student of B. Frank, studies the content of the root nodules found on nonleguminous plants such as *Alnus*. Although Frank believes the contents of the nodules on both legumes and nonlegumes are protein deposits, Brunchorst is convinced that both contain microorganisms. He assigns the name *Frankia* to the filamentous organism found in the nonlegumes in the belief that it is a fungus. (See 1885 E, 1902 D, 1970 B, 1978 D.)

D. BACTERIAL DISEASE: *Undulant Fever*

David Bruce isolates the causative agent of undulant (Malta) fever and names it *Micrococcus melitensis* for the island of Malta. In 1918, Alice Catherine Evans shows that it is not a micrococcus but a bacillus. In 1920, K. F. Meyer and E. B. Shaw coin the generic name *Brucella,* honoring David Bruce. (See 1897 D, 1914 A, 1918 B, 1920 A.)

E. BACTERIAL DISEASE: *Meningococcal Meningitis*

The causative agent of meningococcal meningitis, also known as cerebrospinal meningitis, is cultivated by Anton Weichselbaum. Ettore Marchiafava and Angelo Celli observed the bacterium, *Neisseria meningitidis,* in 1884, but did not cultivate it. The other member of this genus, *Neisseria gonorrhoeae,* is found in 1879 by Albert Neisser, after whom the genus is named. (See 1879 B.)

F. BIOLOGY: *Chromosome Number*

Edouard Joseph Louis-Marie van Beneden discovers a constant number of chromosomes in cells of a given species. He notes that during sexual reproduction, the germ cells contain half the number of chromosomes and that the full number is restored upon fusion of germ cells from the parents. The term "meiosis," derived from the Greek word meaning "to diminish," is applied to this phenomenon.

G. PHYSICS: *Photoelectric Effect*

Heinrich Rudolph Hertz discovers the photoelectric effect when he notes that ultraviolet light shining on a negative electrode increases the distance that a spark jumps.

H. PHYSICS: *Michelson–Morley Experiment*

Albert Abraham Michelson and Edward William Morley perform an experiment to determine whether light is propagated through an inert medium called ether. Their results show that the ether does not exist and provide Albert Einstein with ideas that lead him to the theory of relativity. Michelson receives the Nobel Prize in physics in 1907, the first American to be so honored.

I. THE ARTS: *Music*

Giuseppe Verdi's opera *Otello* is performed in Milan.

1888

A. BACTERIAL STRUCTURE: *Metachromatic Granules*

P. Ernst and, in 1889, Victor Babes independently observe granules in bacteria stained with methylene blue or toluidine blue. Babes calls the granules "metachromatic corpuscles," because the granules stain a reddish color and not the blue of the stain. He observes the granules in various species, but particularly in *Corynebacterium diphtheriae,* the causative agent of diphtheria, where their presence is used as a diagnostic criterion. Later studies show that an impurity in the methylene blue is responsible for the color of the granules. Noting that the granules dissolve in hot water, A. Grimme in 1902 proposes the term *Volutankugeln* for those found in *Spirillum volutans.* The name becomes "volutin" in 1904 as used by A. Meyer; "Babes-Ernst granules" is also in common usage. Although early workers believe the granules are composed of nucleic acid or nucleoprotein, they are later found to be polyphosphate. (See 1946 B, 1959 B, 1984 D.)

B. BACTERIAL PHYSIOLOGY: *Root Nodule Bacteria*

Martinus Beijerinck first isolates bacteria from the root nodules of nitrogen-fixing leguminous plants. He names the organism from the nodules of pea plants *Bacillus radicicola.* In 1879 B. Frank studies, but does not cultivate, bacteria in pea plant nodules which he names *Schinzia leguminosarum,* believing that they are related to a fungus found on the roots of alder. The alder fungus, assigned the generic name *Frankia* in 1887, is later found to be an actinomycete. In 1889, Frank recognizes his mistake and proposes a new genus, *Rhizobium,* which in combination with the species name becomes *Rhizobium leguminosarum.* (See 1886 B, 1887 C, 1901 C.)

C. BACTERIAL PHYSIOLOGY: *Bacterial Nucleus*

P. Ernst is the first to suggest that the nucleus in bacteria is a chromidial system made up of visible chromatin bodies.

D. BACTERIAL DISEASE: Salmonella *Food Infection*

A. A. Gärtner studies an outbreak of gastroenteritis in Germany, in which, out of 57 persons affected, one dies. Gärtner recovers *Bacillus (Salmonella)*

1888 *(continued)*

enteritidis from the organs of the deceased man and from the meat that he consumed. (See 1894 J, 1895 C, 1930 B.)

E. BACTERIAL DISEASE: *Diphtheria Toxin*

Émile Roux and Alexandre Émile John Yersin, working in Louis Pasteur's laboratory, show that the diphtheria bacillus produces a soluble toxin that causes symptoms of the disease in guinea pigs, rabbits, and pigeons. Friedrich Löffler, who isolated the bacterium in 1883, suggests the term "exotoxin" for the soluble toxin. (See 1890 E, 1890 B.)

F. IMMUNITY: *Antibodies*

Noting that chemicals in blood serum and body fluids kill bacteria or reduce their pathogenic effect, George Henry Falkiner Nuttall develops the theory of humoral immunity. He uses the terms "antidotes" and "antibodies," but he plays down the role of phagocytes by assigning them the role of scavenging dead bacteria killed by the antibodies.

G. SCIENTIFIC INSTITUTE: *the Pasteur Institute*

The Institut Pasteur is founded in Paris as a result of the enthusiasm created by Louis Pasteur's rabies vaccine. Its financial backing comes from private sources, including several heads of state.

H. PHYSICS: *Radio Waves*

Heinrich Rudolph Hertz, while performing experiments that confirm James Clerk Maxwell's theory that light is electromagnetic radiation, is the first to measure the long-wave radiations that come to be known as radio waves. (See 1865 D.)

I. TECHNOLOGY: *Camera*

George Eastman sells his first Kodak camera, which, though expensive, makes it possible for anyone to take photographs. The name Kodak, coined by Eastman, has no meaning.

J. SOCIETY AND POLITICS

In London, five women are murdered by a killer or killers whom the press call Jack the Ripper. Scotland Yard never solves the crimes.

K. THE ARTS: *Music*

Petr Ilyich Tchaikovsky's Symphony no. 5, the Fifth Symphony, is performed in St. Petersburg, Russia.

L. THE ARTS: *Art*

Vincent van Gogh paints *The Sunflowers*.

1889

A. BACTERIAL PHYSIOLOGY: *Indole Test*

Shibasaburo Kitasato, a student of Robert Koch, uses the nitrosoindole reaction discovered by Adolf von Baeyer in his 1870 studies of indole. The test uses sodium nitrite and sulfuric acid as reagents to detect indole production by *Bacterium coli* (*Escherichia coli*) as compared with *Bacterium typhosum* (*Salmonella typhi*), which produces no indole. In 1901, Paul Ehrlich publishes on the use of a solution of *p*-dimethylaminobenzaldehyde in ethyl alcohol to detect indole in urine. This test is applied to bacterial cultures in 1905. In 1906, A. Böhme modifies the test by adding potassium persulfate (the Ehrlich-Böhme reagent). N. Kovács makes another improvement by substituting amyl alcohol for ethyl alcohol (Kovács' reagent). (See 1936 C.)

B. BACTERIAL PHYSIOLOGY: *Nitrogen Fixation*
Wilbur O. Atwater and C. D. Woods publish the first report in the United States of nitrogen fixation by leguminous plants. Atwater's experiments with the pea plant began a few years earlier, and in 1885, prior to Hermann Hellriegel's 1886 report, he described fixation but cautioned that the experiments must be verified because of the contamination by rainwater. (See 1885 D, 1886 B, 1888 B, 1901 C.)

C. BACTERIAL PHYSIOLOGY: *β-Galactosidase*
Martinus Beijerinck develops an assay to test the fermentation of lactose by two species of the yeast *Saccharomyces*. He had noted that *Photobacterium phosphorescens* (*P. phosphoreum*) was luminescent only when glucose was present in the culture medium. He incorporates the organism into the lactose gelatin medium, onto which he inoculates the yeast and finds that light is emitted from the medium surrounding the yeast colonies. From these "luminescent plates" he concludes that an enzyme, which he calls "lactase," is secreted by the yeast. Later workers cannot successfully repeat his experiments. Emil Hermann Fischer rediscovers the enzyme in 1894 and proves that the hydrolysis of lactose is catalyzed by an enzyme.

D. BACTERIAL DISEASE: *Tetanus*
Shibasaburo Kitasato uses anaerobic methods to isolate *Clostridium tetani*, the causative agent of tetanus. (See 1884 F.)

E. VIRAL DISEASE: *Influenza*
A great influenza pandemic, called the Asiatic influenza, begins in Russia and spreads throughout Europe and the entire world. In many cities, the infection rate is 40 to 50%, with between 0.5 and 1.2% of the population dying. (See 1580, 1732, 1781 A, 1830 A, 1918 C, 1933 D.)

F. IMMUNOLOGY: *Complement/Alexine*
Hans Buchner, older brother of Eduard Buchner, continues George Henry Falkiner Nuttall's 1888 studies on bactericidal substances in blood. He also reports the lysis of red blood cells derived from another animal in the sera of immunized animals, a phenomenon later studied by Jules Bordet. Buchner gives the name "alexine" (from the Greek, "to defend") to these substances. A decade later Paul Ehrlich changes the name to "complement." (See 1895 E, 1898 I, 1899 F.)

G. BIOLOGY: *Pangenesis*
Hugo de Vries proposes a hypothesis of intracellular pangenesis. He suggests that there are many self-replicating pangens, each of which designates a single character and can be recombined in a variety of ways in progeny. (See 1868 E, 1883 E, 1883 F, 1900 K.)

1889 (continued)

H. BIOLOGY: *Fertilization*

Theodor Heinrich Boveri, in experiments with sea urchins, shows that during fertilization the egg and the spermatozoon each contribute the same number of chromosomes. His descriptions of chromosome behavior are extremely useful in the later development of genetic concepts.

I. BIOCHEMISTRY: *Nucleic Acids*

Richard Altmann, a student of Johann Friedrich Miescher, finds that nuclein can be split into a protein component and an organic acid component, to which he assigns the name "nucleic acid." (See 1869 E.)

J. CHEMISTRY: *Activation Energy*

Svante Arrhenius presents the concept of "activation energy," the energy needed to initiate a chemical reaction.

K. CULTURE: *Architecture*

The Eiffel Tower is completed, to become the world's tallest structure at 303 meters. The Paris World's Fair opens.

L. THE ARTS: *Art*

Vincent van Gogh paints *Self-Portrait with Severed Ear.*

1890

A. BACTERIAL PHYSIOLOGY: *Flagella*

Friedrich Löffler produces photographs of bacterial flagella. (See 1877 A.)

B. BACTERIAL DISEASE: *Tetanus Toxin*

By injection of filtrates of impure cultures of the tetanus bacillus into animals and finding typical symptoms of the disease, Knud Helge Faber proves that the organism produces an exotoxin. Emil Adolf Behring and Shibasaburo Kitasato also discover the toxin at about the same time (See 1891 D.)

C. IMMUNOLOGY: *Tuberculin*

Robert Koch reports the use of an extract of the tubercle bacillus, which he calls tuberculin, as a remedy for tuberculosis. In 1891 he reveals that tuberculin is a glycerin extract of both living and dead tubercle bacilli. The German government urges him to put tuberculin into widespread use, although he is not prepared to do so. Despite many claims of success by various physicians using tuberculin, it shortly becomes clear that no cures are achieved. Tuberculin, now "Old Tuberculin," is used as a diagnostic aid for tuberculosis. (See 1891 C, 1906 I, 1907 E, 1908 C.)

D. IMMUNOLOGY: *Antitoxin Against Tetanus and Diphtheria*

Emil Adolf Behring (who becomes known as Emil von Behring in 1901, the year he receives the Nobel Prize) and Shibasaburo Kitasato, working at Koch's institute in Berlin, find a serum antitoxin in the blood of animals that receive a nonlethal injection of tetanus toxin. Behring also publishes on a similar antitoxin immunity against diphtheria toxin. Together, Behring and Kitasato develop antitoxin, or serum therapy, against both tetanus and diphtheria using toxin modified by treatment with iodine trichloride in experiments with animals. Behring's and Kitasato's 1890 paper also reports the first use of serum therapy when they show that the transfer of immune serum from one animal to another confers immunity to the recipient. In 1901, Behring is the first to receive the Nobel Prize in physiology or medicine. (See 1890 E, 1893 C.)

E. IMMUNOLOGY: *Diphtheria*
Carl Fränkel, a colleague of Emil Adolf Behring and Shibasaburo Kitasato, shows that subcutaneous injections of a broth culture of heat-killed diphtheria bacilli cause immunity against living diphtheria bacilli. The day after his paper appears, Behring and Kitasato publish their paper on tetanus antitoxin (see above). A week later, Behring publishes further work on diphtheria, demonstrating various ways that immunity can be established.

F. CELL BIOLOGY: *Mitochondria*
Richard Altmann publishes a book on "elementary organisms" that he has observed in cells and equates them with bacteria. Although others regard many of his observations as being artifacts of his fixatives and staining reagents, some objects are later found to be real structures. Altmann believes that certain rodlike structures or granules carry out intracellular oxidations. In 1898, Carl Benda gives the name "mitochrondrion" to these rodlike structures.

G. BIOCHEMISTRY: *Fat Content of Milk*
Stephen Moulton Babcock develops the "Babcock test," a rapid method for determining the butterfat content of milk. This procedure makes it easier to grade milk into categories based on fat content.

H. CHEMISTRY: *Erlenmeyer Flask*
At about this time, Richard August Carl Emil Erlenmeyer, who discovered and synthesized several organic compounds and influenced the modern way of indicating double and triple bonds, invents a conical, flat-bottomed flask, the Erlenmeyer flask.

I. SOCIETY AND POLITICS
The U.S. Congress passes the Sherman Anti-Trust Act.

J. THE ARTS: *Literature*
Poems of Emily Dickinson is published posthumously.

K. THE ARTS: *Art*
Vincent van Gogh paints *Cornfield with Crows*.

1891

A. BACTERIOLOGICAL TECHNIQUE: *Filter Sterilization*
H. Nordtmeyer uses filters made of diatomaceous earth from the Berkefeld mines to purify water. "Berkefeld filters" and Chamberland filters, manufactured in various pore sizes, obtain common use among bacteriologists and virologists. (See 1871 A, 1884 C.)

B. BACTERIAL PHYSIOLOGY: *Nitrifying Bacteria*
Sergei Winogradsky isolates nitrifying bacteria by growing them in media free of organic matter and solidified with silica gel instead of agar. His discovery that carbon dioxide is the source of carbon and that energy is de-

1891 (continued)

rived from the oxidation of ammonia by *Nitrosomonas* and the oxidation of nitrite by *Nitrobacter* proves that they are autotrophs. (See 1877 C, 1887 B.)

C. IMMUNOLOGY: *Delayed Hypersensitivity*

Robert Koch discovers the phenomenon later known as delayed hypersensitivity by observing a cutaneous reaction when tuberculin is administered to guinea pigs previously infected with tuberculosis. An effect is not seen in uninfected animals. This reaction, known as the Koch reaction, is developed for diagnostic use as the tuberculin skin test. (See 1890 C, 1902 G, 1907 E, 1908 C.)

D. IMMUNOLOGY: *Antitoxins*

Paul Ehrlich shows that antibodies form against the plant toxins ricin and abrin. He writes that antibodies are responsible for immunity. Following these experiments and those of Emil Adolf Behring and Shibasaburo Kitasato in 1890 on the tetanus toxin, it is widely believed that toxins are the sole causes of infectious disease.

E. ANTHROPOLOGY: *the Java Man*

Marie Eugène Dubois discovers fossil remains in Java that he calls *Pithecanthropus erectus,* later called *Homo erectus.* The Java man is thought to be a precursor of modern humans.

F. TECHNOLOGY: *Railroads*

Construction begins on the Trans-Siberian Railway to connect Moscow with Russia's Pacific coast. The first part between Moscow and Irkutsk is opened in 1900; the railroad reaches Vladivostok in 1903 and is in full operation in 1904. At 3,200 miles, it is the world's longest railroad.

G. SOCIETY AND ECONOMICS

The American Express Company introduces the American Express Travelers Cheque. Thomas Cook & Son issued the first traveler's checks in 1874.

H. CULTURE: *Universities*

Both the University of Chicago and the California Institute of Technology are founded.

I. THE ARTS: *Literature*

- Sir Arthur Conan Doyle publishes *The Adventures of Sherlock Holmes.*
- Thomas Hardy publishes *Tess of the D'Urbervilles: A Pure Woman.*

J. THE ARTS: *Art*

Paul Gauguin paints *Two Women on the Beach* and *Woman in a Red Dress.*

1892

A. BACTERIAL DISEASE: *Gas Gangrene*

William Henry Welch and George Henry Falkiner Nuttall describe the causative agent of gas gangrene, to which they give the name *Bacillus aërogenes capsulatus.* In 1898, Adrien Veillon and A. Zuber refer to it as *Bacillus perfringens.* By 1920, the organism, widely known as Welch's bacillus, is called *Clostridium welchii,* after which *Clostridium perfringens* becomes the recognized name.

B. BACTERIAL DISEASE: Haemophilus influenzae

Following an influenza pandemic of 1889 to 1890, Richard Friedrich Johannes Pfeiffer isolates a bacterium believed to be the cause of the disease. Not until 1933 is it established that a virus causes influenza. The microorganism that Pfeiffer isolates becomes known as *Haemophilus influenzae*, a cause of meningitis in children. The organism's exact relationship to the influenza pandemic of 1889 to 1890 is not known. (See 1933 D.)

C. BACTERIAL DISEASE: *Cholera*

In August and September, 1892, the city of Hamburg, Germany, suffers a severe outbreak of cholera. Robert Koch, who has been given broad authority by the German government to deal with cholera epidemics, insists on quarantine and isolation to help control the spread of the disease. However, a well-known and respected hygienist in Hamburg, Max von Pettenkofer, strongly objects to Koch's plans. Pettenkofer believes that the cholera bacillus must first be present in groundwater, where it undergoes changes leading to miasmas that cause the disease. Koch's methods are put into effect, the epidemic subsides, and the public and the government regard Koch's concepts of the germ theory with regard to cholera to have been proved. However, Pettenkofer is not convinced. In October, he asks Koch's colleague Georg Gaffky to give him a culture of the cholera bacillus, which he promptly drinks. Pettenkofer suffers diarrhea over the next several days but recovers without further incident. He claims that this episode proves that, although the bacteria may be present in drinking water, the absence of their passage through groundwater made it impossible for him to acquire full-blown cholera.

D. BACTERIAL DISEASE: *Endotoxin*

Richard Friedrich Johannes Pfeiffer coins the term "endotoxin" for bacteria whose culture filtrates do not cause disease symptoms. He defines endotoxin as a part of the living substance of the bacterial cell that is released when cells dissolve. Among the diseases that have endotoxins as causative agents are typhoid fever, cholera, pneumonia, and cerebrospinal meningitis. (See 1856 B, 1933 B, 1954 C.)

E. INFECTIOUS DISEASE: *Tobacco Mosaic Virus*

Searching for the cause of tobacco mosaic disease, Dmitri Ivanovsky shows that the causative agent passes through candle filters that hold back bacteria. Using the term *contagium vivum fixum,* meaning a cellular infectious agent, he states that the persistence of infectivity in the filtered material is explained by the presence of resting forms, possibly spores. Not realizing that he has discovered a new type of infectious microorganism, a virus, Ivanovsky persists in considering it a bacterium. Ivanovsky is apparently unaware of Adolf Mayer's 1882 report on tobacco mosaic disease. (See 1882 F, 1899 E.)

F. IMMUNOLOGY: *Passive and Active Immunity*

Between 1892 and 1897, Paul Ehrlich publishes on theories of immunity and points out the difference between passive and active immunization. (See 1897 G.)

1892 *(continued)*

G. IMMUNOLOGY: *Cholera*

Waldemar Haffkine uses living cholera bacillus, attenuated by growth at 40°C and higher, for immunization trials in India. Although the vaccines are effective, too many side reactions occur, and vaccinations are suspended. (See 1885 G, 1896 E, 1897 F.)

H. PHYSICS: *Dewar Flask*

James Dewar invents the first thermos bottle, called the "Dewar flask," which keeps its contents either cold or hot as desired.

I. THE ARTS: *Music*

Ruggiero Leoncavallo's opera *Pagliacci* is performed in Milan.

J. THE ARTS: *Literature*

A collection of poems by Rudyard Kipling, *Barrack-Room Ballads,* including "Gunga Din" and "The Road to Mandalay," is published.

K. THE ARTS: *Art*

Henri de Toulouse-Lautrec paints *At the Moulin Rouge.*

1893

A. BACTERIAL PHYSIOLOGY: *Lactic Acid Bacteria*

Martinus Beijerinck reports that the lactic acid group of bacteria cannot decompose hydrogen peroxide, a property thought to be associated with all living cells. The fact that animal and plant tissues decompose hydrogen peroxide is well known, but the enzyme is not found until 1901, when it is named "catalase" by Oscar Loew. In 1923, M. B. McLeod and J. Gordon propose using the catalase test as a diagnostic characteristic for classifying bacteria.

B. BACTERIAL PHYSIOLOGY: *Chemotaxis*

Martinus Beijerinck demonstrates that bacteria exhibit chemotaxis toward specific concentrations of dissolved oxygen. He places bacteria in the bottom of a culture tube and overlays them with water. After a period of time they migrate into a distinct band between the bottom of the tube and the meniscus. When hydrogen replaces the air, the cells do not migrate. (See 1881 D, 1885 C, 1969 C.)

C. IMMUNOLOGY: *Tetanus Toxoid*

After treating tetanus toxin with "carbon sulphide," Paul Ehrlich finds that it retains the capability of stimulating immunity although it loses its toxicity. He suggests the name "toxoid" for the nontoxic form. Émile Roux and L. Vaillard achieve attenuation of the toxin by treatment with an iodine-potassium iodide solution. (See 1904 C, 1927 G.)

D. VIROLOGY: *Poliomyelitis*

An unusual outbreak of 26 cases of poliomyelitis in the communities outside Boston leads two local physicians to speculate that persons living in cities might be more immune than those living in suburbs. In 1894, an epidemic involving 132 individuals occurs in Rutland, Vermont, only 125 miles from Boston.

E. INFECTIOUS DISEASE: *Insect Vectors*

Theobald Smith and F. L. Kilbourne prove that the sporozoan (protozoan) disease called Texas cattle fever is spread by ticks.

F. TECHNOLOGY: *Automobiles*

Henry Ford builds his first automobile. In 1903, with a number of stockholders, he incorporates the Ford Motor Company. (See 1769 B, 1859 F, 1885 O.)

G. TECHNOLOGY: *Diesel Engine*

Rudolf Diesel develops an internal combustion engine in which the gas in the cylinder is ignited by heat developed during compression, thus eliminating the need for an electric spark. The diesel engine, being heavier than the type developed by Nikolaus August Otto, comes to be used in heavy vehicles. (See 1876 H.)

H. TECHNOLOGY: *the Zipper*

Egbert Putnam Judson invents the zipper as a fastener for clothing.

I. CULTURE: *Universities*

The Johns Hopkins Medical School and Hospital is founded in Baltimore.

J. THE ARTS: *Music*

The opera *Hansel and Gretel* by Engelbert Humperdinck is performed.

K. THE ARTS: *Art*

Edvard Munch paints *The Scream*.

1894

A. BACTERIAL STRUCTURE: *Bacterial Cell Wall*

Alfred Fischer demonstrates the presence of a bacterial cell wall. He uses plasmolysis to separate the cell membrane from the wall to reveal two separate structures. (See 1900 B, 1902 C.)

B. BACTERIAL PHYSIOLOGY: *Sulfate–Reducing Bacteria*

While investigating the accumulation of calcium sulfate in the steam boilers in a yeast factory, Martinus Beijerinck isolates a sulfate-reducing bacterium that he names *Spirillum desulfuricans*. The name is changed to *Desulfovibrio desulfuricans* in 1936 by Albert Jan Kluyver and Cornelius B. van Niel.

C. BACTERIAL DISEASE: *Plague Bacillus*

Alexandre Émile John Yersin and Shibasaburo Kitasato independently discover the bacterium that causes bubonic plague, now named *Yersinia pestis*. From Yersin's description of his work, it is clear that he successfully cultivated the bacterium and described it accurately. However, Kitasato and some of his coworkers cast doubt on Yersin's work by subsequently describing what appears to be a diplococcus and by making contradictory statements. It appears that Kitasato did observe the plague bacillus but also found a diplococcus at the same time.

D. BACTERIAL DISEASE: *Food Poisoning*

J. Denys reports that pyogenic staphylococci are responsible for illness and one death in members of a family who ate meat from a diseased cow. He

1894 *(continued)*

also finds that cultures of the bacterium cause no disease upon injection into the pleura of rabbits. (See 1888 D, 1895 C, 1914 C, 1930 B.)

E. IMMUNOLOGY: *Bacteriolysins*
Richard Friedrich Johannes Pfeiffer coins the term "bacteriolysins" for antibodies that kill cholera and typhoid bacteria regardless of the presence or absence of living phagocytic cells.

F. IMMUNOLOGY: *Diphtheria Vaccine*
Émile Roux, Alexandre Émile John Yersin, and Louis Martin begin large-scale production of diphtheria antitoxin by immunizing horses. Earlier large-scale production used sheep and goats. William Hallock Park, collaborating with Anna Wessels Williams, discovers an atypical strain of *Corynebacterium diphtheriae,* strain 8, or the Park-Williams strain, later used worldwide for the production of diphtheria toxin.

G. BIOLOGY: *Cell Membranes*
Studying the penetration of water-soluble and lipid-soluble compounds into plant root hairs, Charles E. Overton finds that lipophilic compounds penetrate more readily than hydrophilic compounds. He suggests that cell membranes behave like fatty oils and that membranes may contain cholesterol and lecithin. (See 1910 G, 1925 E, 1934, G, 1960 O, 1972 K.)

H. BIOCHEMISTRY: *Structure of Hexoses and Pentoses*
Emil Hermann Fischer works out the structures of a number of six-carbon and five-carbon sugars.

I. BIOCHEMISTRY: *Enzyme-Substrate Interaction*
After studying the action of an aqueous yeast extract on isomeric glucosides, Emil Hermann Fischer formulates his "lock-and-key" theory of enzyme and substrate interaction.

J. BIOCHEMISTRY: *Oxidizing Enzymes*
Gabriel Émile Bertrand first suggests that oxidizing enzymes contain metals. Although he thinks that the enzyme laccase contains manganese, it is later found to contain copper.

K. SOCIETY AND POLITICS
Alfred Dreyfus is court-martialed in France, accused of selling military information to Germany. He is later shown to be innocent.

L. THE ARTS: *Theater*
George Bernard Shaw's play *Arms and the Man* opens in London.

M. CULTURE: *Architecture*
London's Tower Bridge is opened.

1895

A. BACTERIAL PHYSIOLOGY: *Nitrogen Fixation*
Sergei Winogradsky is the first to isolate a bacterium capable of fixing nitrogen in culture. By repeated subculturing from soil cultures, he isolates an anaerobic sporeformer that he names *Clostridium pastorianum,* later changed to *Clostridium pasteurianum.* (See 1888 B, 1901 C, 1928 A.)

B. FOOD BACTERIOLOGY: *Food Spoilage*

Harry L. Russell reports that bacteria cause gaseous swelling and odors in canned peas. In the following year, Samuel C. Prescott and William L. Underwood report similar studies on bacterial spoilage of canned corn. Both groups of investigators recommend heating vegetables in a retort prior to sealing the cans. (See 1839 C.)

C. BACTERIAL DISEASE: *Food Poisoning / Botulism*

Emile-Pierre-Marie von Ermengem proves that botulism is caused by a toxin produced by a bacterium that he names *Bacillus botulinus,* now called *Clostridium botulinum.* When first recognized, the poisoning was thought to be associated principally with sausage or other meats. (See 900 A, 1735 A, 1820 A, 1930 B.)

D. MICROBIOLOGY: *Germfree Life*

The first successful efforts to raise animals under germfree conditions are made by George Henry Falkiner Nuttall and H. Thierfelder. They begin with a cesarean-delivered guinea pig that is kept under sterile conditions. The animal survives 8 days, leading the researchers to claim that they had refuted Louis Pasteur's claim 10 years earlier that such an experiment would fail. However, further experiments led them to reverse their stance when their experimental guineas pigs did not gain as much weight as control animals. Nuttall and Thierfelder developed many of the techniques that are followed by later investigators. (See 1885 J, 1899 C, 1928 D.)

E. IMMUNOLOGY: *Complement / Alexine*

Jules Bordet, in studies with *Vibrio cholerae,* proves that the bacteriolytic action of blood serum requires two factors, a heat-labile substance found in normal (nonimmune) blood inactivated at 55°C and the bactericidal substance present in the blood of animals immunized against a bacterium. He uses Hans Buchner's term "alexine" for the heat-labile substance found in normal blood. Paul Ehrlich changes the name of this material to "complement" in 1899. Bordet receives the 1919 Nobel Prize in physiology or medicine. (See 1898 I.)

F. BIOCHEMISTRY: *Oxidation–Reduction Reactions*

Paul Ehrlich finds that, after subcutaneous injection of a rabbit, alizarin blue and indophenol blue are taken up by different tissues. The dyes are in an oxidized or reduced state. Although Ehrlich does not think the reaction is caused by intracellular catalysts, his work leads to the discovery of indophenol oxidase. Ehrlich also notes that dimethyl-*p*-phenylenediamine and α-naphthol react to form indophenol blue. (See 1893 C, 1895 G, 1910 D.)

G. BIOCHEMISTRY: *NADI Reagent / Indophenol Oxidase*

F. Röhmann and W. Spitzer attribute the formation of indophenol blue to an enzyme in tissues. They call the mixture of α-naphthol and dimethyl-*p*-phenylenediamine the "NADI reagent," an abbreviation of the names of the two components. Some writers later erroneously attribute the discovery of the reaction to a Mr. Nadi. (See 1910 D, 1924 C, 1938 F.)

1895 *(continued)*

H. PHYSICS: *X Rays*
Wilhelm Konrad Röntgen discovers X rays.

I. PSYCHOLOGY: *Hysteria*
Sigmund Freud, with Josef Breuer, publishes *Studien über Hysterie* (Studies in hysteria).

J. TECHNOLOGY: *Motion Pictures*
Auguste and Louis Lumière obtain a patent on the "cinematographe," a machine for projection of motion pictures. The first public showing of motion pictures is in Paris.

K. THE ARTS: *Literature*
Stephen Crane writes *The Red Badge of Courage*.

L. THE ARTS: *Theater*
Oscar Wilde's play *The Importance of Being Earnest* opens in London.

1896

A. BACTERIAL DISEASE: Salmonella *Food Infection*
Emile-Pierre-Marie von Ermengem provides proof that *Salmonella enteritidis* caused the fatal food infection of a sanitary meat inspector who consumed sausage thought to have caused sickness in several individuals. The bacterium is recovered from the sausage, and after necropsy and bacteriological examination of the deceased man, it is found in liver, spleen, lung, kidney, and contents of the ileum. (See 1888 D.)

B. BACTERIAL DISEASE: *Diphtheria*
Karl Bernhard Lehmann and R. Neumann give the name *Corynebacterium diphtheriae* to the causative agent of diphtheria. (See 1883 B.)

C. IMMUNOLOGY: *Typhoid Fever*
Almroth Wright publishes a preliminary note on prophylactic immunization against typhoid fever using a killed whole-cell vaccine. He later conducts field trials with British troops in India in 1898 and in South Africa during the Boer War. Although the results appear to be satisfactory, they are not given adequate statistical verification until William Boog Leishman conducts further tests in 1904. One of Wright's students is Alexander Fleming, the discoverer of penicillin. (See 1904 F, 1922 D, 1929 B.)

D. IMMUNOLOGY: *Cholera*
Wilhelm Kolle develops a heat-killed cholera vaccine using cells grown on agar and resuspended in saline. This type of vaccine is used for many years. (See 1885 G, 1892 G.)

E. IMMUNOLOGY: *Agglutination Test*
Max Grüber discovers antibodies in blood serum that specifically agglutinate bacteria. With Herbert Edward Durham, he studies the phenomenon in test tubes and on microscope slides. Shortly afterward, Georges Fernand Isidore Widal reports that typhoid bacilli are agglutinated by sera from infected patients. For some time, the test is known as the Grüber-Widal test,

but it later comes to be known as the Widal test, which continues to be used in diagnosis of typhoid fever.

F. BIOCHEMISTRY: *Vitamins*

Christiaan Eijkman studies beriberi in the Dutch East Indies (now Indonesia), believing that it is caused by a bacterium. In the process, he accidentally discovers a disease in chickens that is caused by a dietary deficiency. His work, and that of others, shows that the required substance, now known as vitamin A, is contained in the husks of grains of rice. The idea of "essential food factors" that he suggests is later confirmed by the work of Frederick Gowland Hopkins and Casimir Funk. Funk later suggests the name "vitamine" for such essential nutrients. Eijkman and Hopkins share the Nobel Prize in physiology or medicine in 1929.

G. PHYSICS: *Radioactivity*

Antoine Henri Becquerel discovers "uranic rays" emitted by the element uranium. Studying uranic rays, Marie Curie shows that the radiation is a property of the atom, not a result of a chemical reaction. She later calls such emissions "radioactivity." (See 1898 N, 1898 N.)

H. SOCIETY: *Nobel Prizes*

Alfred Nobel dies, leaving a will that stipulates how his estate shall be used to award prizes (the Nobel Prizes) each year in five areas: physics, chemistry, physiology or medicine, literature, and peace. The first awards are made in 1901.

I. SOCIETY AND POLITICS

In the case of *Plessy v. Ferguson,* the U.S. Supreme Court upholds segregation of railroad cars in a Louisiana case and establishes the doctrine of "separate but equal" facilities for transportation, public accommodations, and education.

J. THE ARTS: *Literature*

A. E. Housman publishes a collection of poems entitled *A Shropshire Lad.*

K. THE ARTS: *Music*

Giacomo Puccini's opera *La Bohème* is performed.

L. SOCIETY: *Athletics*

The first modern Olympic Games are held in Athens, Greece, the last of the ancient games having been held in 398.

1897

A. BACTERIAL CLASSIFICATION

Walter Migula publishes volume 1 of *System der Bakterien.* Volume 2 appears in 1900. He divides the *Schizomycetes* into two classes: *Eubacteria* and *Thiobacteria,* the true bacteria and the sulfur bacteria, respectively. (See 1886 A.)

B. BACTERIAL STRUCTURE: *Nucleus*

A. Meyer introduces microchemical methods for the study of bacteria. Among his several observations using species of *Bacillus* and *Clostridium* is that the bacteria have a true nucleus. The contrary view that bacteria have no nucleus is proposed by Walter Migula and by Alfred Fischer in 1903. (See 1888 C, 1909 B, 1935 B.)

C. FERMENTATION: *Cell–Free Fermentation*

Eduard Buchner reports that a cell-free preparation of brewer's yeast, prepared by grinding yeast with quartz sand and kieselguhr (a type of diatomaceous earth) followed by filtration, causes the fermentation of various sugars to ethyl alcohol and carbon dioxide. This discovery refutes Louis Pasteur's vitalistic claim that the attribute of carrying out fermentation cannot be separated from the cells that cause it. Buchner states that the soluble ferment, which he names "zymase," is "without doubt to be regarded as a protein," a concept not resolved for about 30 years. Buchner receives the Nobel Prize in Chemistry in 1907 for this work.

D. BACTERIAL DISEASE: *Contagious Abortion in Cattle*

Bernhard Laurits Frederick Bang, known as Oluf Bang, a Danish physician and veterinarian, isolates the bacterium, which he names *Bacillus abortus,* that causes contagious abortion in cattle, also known as Bang's disease. Until the work of Alice Catherine Evans in 1918, the relationship between this bacterium and David Bruce's *Micrococcus melitensis* is not recognized. Both species are placed in the genus *Brucella* in 1920. (See 1887 D, 1914 A, 1918 B, 1920 A.)

E. PROTOZOAN DISEASE: *Malaria*

Ronald Ross discovers the malaria parasite in the *Anopheles* mosquito when he observes a fertilized oocyst in the stomach wall of mosquitoes. Ross receives the 1902 Nobel Prize in physiology or medicine for his work on malaria. (See 1880 D, 1883 C, 1885 K, 1884 I, 1898 J.)

F. IMMUNOLOGY: *Plague Vaccine*

Waldemar Haffkine, working in India, develops a vaccine using killed cells of the plague bacillus. The Plague Research Laboratory, later renamed the Haffkine Institute, is formed to produce millions of doses of the vaccine.

G. IMMUNOLOGY: *Side Chain Toxin-Antitoxin Theory*

Paul Ehrlich develops the side chain or receptor theory to explain the interaction between toxin and antitoxin. He is influenced in these ideas by Emil Hermann Fischer's lock-and-key theory of enzyme-substrate interaction. Ehrlich had earlier proposed that cells have receptors on their surface that are specific for each type of nutrient molecule. He extends this concept by proposing that antitoxin (antibody) receptors are found on the surface of cells and that combination with toxin (antigen) stimulates the overproduction of the receptors, which are released into the circulating blood.

H. IMMUNOLOGY: *Quantitation of Toxin and Antitoxin*

Emil Hermann Fischer develops methods for the quantitation of diphtheria toxin and antitoxin, thus solving the problem of testing for the potency of antisera. (See 1894 F.)

I. IMMUNOLOGY: *Precipitation Reaction*
Rudolf Kraus discovers that culture filtrates of the cholera vibrio precipitate when antiserum is added. He also demonstrates that filtrates of both the typhoid bacterium and the plague bacillus form precipitates when specific antisera are added.

J. BIOCHEMISTRY: *Oxidase*
Gabriel Émile Bertrand introduces the word "oxidase" for enzymes that catalyze oxidizing reactions.

K. BIOCHEMISTRY: *Oxidation-Reduction Reactions*
W. Spitzer discovers that indophenol oxidase (named in 1910 by Joseph Kastle) contains iron, the first observation that iron is involved in oxidation-reduction reactions.

L. PHYSICS: *the Electron*
In cathode ray experiments, J. J. Thomson proves the existence of the electron, substantiating the notion that the atom is not indivisible, as had been previously believed. The name "electron," proposed by George Johnston Stoney in 1874, is adopted for the negatively charged particles. Thomson is awarded the Nobel Prize in physics in 1906. Seven of his research assistants earn Nobel Prizes for their later work.

M. SOCIETY AND POLITICS
The Klondike gold rush begins with the discovery of gold at Bonanza Creek, Yukon, Canada.

N. THE ARTS: *Literature*
Bram Stoker publishes the novel *Dracula*.

O. THE ARTS: *Music*
John Philip Sousa and his band perform his march "The Stars and Stripes Forever."

1898

A. BACTERIAL PHYSIOLOGY: *Voges-Proskauer Test*
O. Voges and Bernhard Proskauer describe a procedure for use in distinguishing among the coli-aerogenes bacteria. They find that the addition of potash to glucose cultures causes a red color to develop in the *Aerobacter* (*Enterobacter*) *aerogenes* cultures but not in *Escherichia coli* cultures. In 1906, Arthur Harden and W. S. Walpole discover that the reaction is due to the formation of acetylmethylcarbinol (acetoin) in the cultures. The test is improved in 1931 by R. A. O'Meara, who adds creatine, and in 1936 by M. M. Barritt, who adds α-naphthol. (See 1906 B, 1910 A, 1936 C, 1937 B.)

B. BACTERIAL PHYSIOLOGY: *Durham Tubes*
Herbert Edward Durham introduces the use of small inverted glass vials in tubes of sugar fermentation media to collect gas produced by bacterial cultures. When the tubes are heated in the autoclave, air is driven from the inverted tube, which fills with the liquid medium as cooling occurs. Prior to the Durham tube, various devices, such as vials with side arms, were used for gas detection.

C. BACTERIAL DISEASE: *Bacillary Dysentery*

Kiyoshi Shiga isolates *Shigella dysenteriae,* the bacterium that causes bacillary dysentery. In 1900, Simon Flexner isolates a similar bacillus in the Philippines. However, André Chantemesse and Georges Widal may have isolated the dysentery bacillus as early as 1888. (See 1900 E, 1903 D.)

D. BACTERIAL DISEASE: *Pleuropneumonia/PPLO*

Edmond Nocard and Émile Roux, and their coworkers, begin the study of mycoplasmas, bacteria that lack rigid cell walls, when they report finding the "virus" of pleuropneumonia in cattle, the pleuropneumonia organism, or PPO. Although they cannot microscopically observe the microorganism in fluids from the lungs of infected animals, they subsequently cultivate it in collodion sacs suspended in the peritoneal cavity of rabbits and guinea pigs. Nocard and Roux note that the organism passes bacteriological filters, is pleomorphic, and is barely visible in the light microscope. Their work contributes to the misunderstandings about the properties of viruses. It is not until 1935 that other, similar organisms are found, referred to as pleuropneumonialike organisms, or PPLO. In 1929, D. G. ff. Edward and E. A. Freundt assign the name "mycoplasma." (See 1929 C, 1935 D.)

E. BACTERIAL DISEASE: *Tuberculosis*

Theobald Smith differentiates between the human and bovine types of the tubercle bacillus, pointing out the possibility of transmitting the bovine type to humans. Robert Koch contends that the bovine strain causes only a mild disease in humans and, in fact, might provide some immunity to the human type. (See 1906 I.)

F. VIROLOGY: *Bacteriophage*

Nikolae Gamaleia notes the lysis of bacteria by a substance that can be transmitted from one culture to another. Although he believes the phenomenon to be biochemical, he may have been the first to observe the action of bacterial viruses, or bacteriophages. (See 1915 C, 1917 C.)

G. VIRAL DISEASE: *Hoof-and-Mouth Disease*

Friedrich Löffler and Paul Frosch discover that the agent causing hoof-and-mouth disease of cattle passes through a bacteriological filter and cannot be seen with a microscope. This is the first animal disease to be attributed to "filterable viruses." (See 1882 F, 1892 E, 1898 H, 1899 E.)

H. INFECTIOUS DISEASE: *Myxomatosis*

Giuseppe Sanarelli searches for the causative agent of rabbit myxomatosis employing centrifugation of suspensions of infected tissue. The optically clear supernatant thus formed is capable of causing infection. He refers to the causative agent as a germ beyond visibility. (See 1882 F, 1892 E, 1898 G, 1899 E.)

I. IMMUNOLOGY: *Immune Hemolysis*

Jules Bordet, following Hans Buchner's earlier studies, finds that injecting defibrinated rabbit blood into guinea pigs causes the appearance of antibodies that cause clumping followed by rapid lysis of rabbit red blood cells.

These experiments support earlier observations of two reactants—that one (alexine or complement) is nonspecific and ineffective unless the target cells, either red blood cells or bacteria, are previously sensitized with specific antibody. (See 1889 F, 1895 E, 1901 G.)

J. PROTOZOAN DISEASE: *Insect Vector for Malaria*
Ronald Ross shows that the *Anopheles* mosquito transmits malaria to birds; he also works out the life cycle for the parasite in birds. In this same year, Giovanni Grassi completes experiments on the life cycle of malaria in humans, demonstrating that the mosquito transmits the parasite from human to human. Grassi protests the awarding of the 1902 Nobel Prize in physiology or medicine to Ross. (See 1880 D, 1883 C, 1884 I, 1885 K.)

K. BIOLOGY: *Mitochondria*
Carl Benda observes in the cytoplasm of cells small subcellular structures that he calls "mitochondria," meaning threads of cartilage, a name that is inappropriate for their structure and function. (See 1890 F, 1948 K.)

L. BIOLOGY: *Golgi Apparatus*
Camillo Golgi observes the reticular structure in the cytoplasm of cells that is later known as the Golgi apparatus or Golgi body.

M. BIOCHEMISTRY: *Peroxidase*
Georges Linossier studies and names the enzyme peroxidase.

N. PHYSICS: *Radioactive Elements*
Marie Curie, in collaboration with her husband Pierre Curie, discovers the radioactive elements thorium, polonium, and radium.

O. PHYSICS: *Liquid Hydrogen*
James Dewar, using the Joule-Thomson effect that achieves low temperatures by allowing a cooled gas under pressure to expand, cools hydrogen to $-259°C$, causing it to liquefy. Dewar demonstrates an apparatus used by Louis-Paul Cailletet in 1877.

P. PHYSICS: *Photoelectric Effect*
J. J. Thomson and Philipp Lenard demonstrate that light can cause the emission of photoelectrons from a metallic surface.

Q. SOCIETY AND POLITICS
- The Spanish-American War begins when the U.S. battleship *Maine* explodes and sinks in the harbor at Havana, Cuba.
- Hawaii, which had been declared an independent republic in 1893, is annexed by the United States. Hawaii becomes a state in 1959.

R. THE ARTS: *Literature*
- H. G. Wells writes *The War of the Worlds,* a novel about the invasion of earth by Martians. The Martians fail in this endeavor because they are "slain by the putrefactive and disease bacteria against which their systems were unprepared. . . ." (See 1938 L.)
- Henry James writes *The Turn of the Screw.*

A. BACTERIAL STRUCTURE: *Fat Globules and Glycogen*

A. Meyer uses Sudan III to stain fat globules in bacteria. In 1940, T. L. Hartman introduces the use of Sudan Black B for this purpose. Meyer also reports using an iodine solution to stain glycogen granules in a species of *Bacillus*.

B. BACTERIAL DISEASE: *Plant Disease*

Erwin Frink Smith, who proves that bacteria cause several diseases of plants, including cucurbit wilt and brown rot of potatoes, publishes a reply to published lectures by Alfred Fischer, a prominent German bacteriologist, who asserted that bacteria are unable to cause disease in plants. Smith details work done by himself, Thomas Jonathan Burrill, and others on eight different plant diseases. The paper, published in a German journal, establishes the stature of American plant physiologists among European scientists. The bacterial genus *Erwinia* is named after Smith. (See 1879 D.)

C. MICROBIOLOGY: *Germfree Life*

M. Schottleius establishes a germfree laboratory with inner rooms that are kept sterile and an anteroom in which the investigators change into sterile clothes. He successfully rears germfree chickens, but he reports that they do not survive long without intestinal bacteria. His difficulties with maintaining the chicks for long periods are laid to inadequate knowledge about nutrition at that time. By about 1913, he has limited success and changes his mind about the necessity of intestinal bacteria. (See 1885 J, 1895 D, 1928 D.)

D. INFECTIOUS DISEASE: *Yellow Fever*

Walter Reed disproves Giuseppe Sanarelli's claim that yellow fever is caused by a bacterium. Reed shows that the bacterium *Bacillus icteroides* causes the disease hog cholera. In 1900, Reed heads a commission to determine the cause of yellow fever.

E. INFECTIOUS DISEASE: *Tobacco Mosaic Virus*

Martinus Beijerinck, independently of Adolf Mayer and Dmitri Ivanovsky, shows that the tobacco mosaic disease is caused by an agent that passes through porcelain filters. He refers to it as *contagium vivum fluidum,* meaning noncellular infectious material, bringing strong criticism from Ivanovsky, who continues to believe that the disease is caused by bacteria. Of the three independent discoverers of the tobacco mosaic virus—Mayer, Ivanovsky, and Beijerinck—only Beijerinck recognizes that the agent cannot be identified with known agents of bacterial disease. (See 1882 F, 1892 E.)

F. IMMUNOLOGY: *Complement*

Paul Ehrlich introduces the term "complement" for the component in normal blood previously called "alexine" by Hans Buchner in 1889 and Jules Bordet in 1895. (See 1889 F, 1895 E.)

G. SCIENTIFIC ORGANIZATIONS: *Society of American Bacteriologists*

In December, the Society of American Bacteriologists (SAB) holds its first meeting in New Haven, Connecticut. A volunteer committee made up of Alexander Crever Abbott, Herbert W. Conn, and Edwin O. Jordan organizes the meeting and invites bacteriologists from across the country to participate. W. T. Sedgwick serves as the society's first president. In 1960, the society changes its name to the American Society for Microbiology (ASM).

H. PHYSICS: *Radioactivity/Alpha and Beta Particles*
Ernest Rutherford discovers so-called alpha and beta particles, emissions from radioactive elements. (See 1900 M.)

I. PHARMACOLOGY: *Aspirin*
The Bayer chemical firm in Germany begins the distribution of acetyl-salicylic acid under the name of aspirin, a name derived from spiraeic acid, the former name of salicylic acid. In 1893, Felix Hoffman, a chemist with the company, synthesizes the compound.

J. SOCIETY AND POLITICS
The Boer War begins in South Africa (ending in 1902) and is centered around acquisition of diamond mines by the British.

K. THE ARTS: *Music*
Jean Sibelius composes the symphony *Finlandia*.

1900

A. BACTERIAL CLASSIFICATION: *Bile Solubility of Pneumococci*
Fred Neufeld finds that, while the pneumococci are soluble in bile, the streptococci are not. The bile solubility test is used thereafter as one means to distinguish pneumococci from streptococci.

B. BACTERIAL STRUCTURE: *Plasmoptysis*
Alfred Fischer notes that in some culture media when the bacterial cell wall ruptures, the cytoplasm extrudes as a bubble. Fischer calls this phenomenon "plasmoptysis" (from the Greek *plasmo* plus *ptyein,* to spit) to distinguish it from plasmolysis, which he observed in 1894. (See 1894 A, 1902 C.)

C. BACTERIAL GENETICS: *Mutation*
Martinus Beijerinck first uses bacteria as tools for genetic research. His experiments show permanent changes in phenotypic characteristics, such as in pigment variants in *Serratia marcescens,* which he calls *Bacillus prodigiosus*. B. Bizio named this bacterium *S. marcescens* in 1823. Beijerinck concurs with Hugo de Vries that new species are produced through mutation. These experiments are reported in the same year that Gregor Mendel's work is rediscovered by Hugo de Vries, Erich Tschermak, and Carl Correns. (See 1865 B, 1900 J, 1907 A, 1934 C.)

D. BACTERIAL DISEASE: *Enteric Fever*
Hugo Schottmüller discovers the paratyphoid bacillus *Salmonella paratyphi*.

E. BACTERIAL DISEASE: *Bacillary Dysentery*
Simon Flexner, accompanying Lewellys F. Barker to the Philippines to study tropical diseases, isolates a bacterium, similar to one discovered in 1898 by Kiyoshi Shiga, that is shown to cause bacillary dysentery. The Shiga bacillus and the Flexner bacillus, which differ antigenically and in other ways, become known as *Shigella dysenteriae* and *Shigella flexneri,* respectively. (See 1898 C, 1903 D.)

1900 (continued)

F. PROTOZOAN DISEASE: *Leishmaniasis*

William Leishman discovers that trypanosomes cause kala-azar. These trypanosomes (*Leishmania*), the diseases they cause (leishmaniasis), and the Leishman stain for detection of parasites in blood all bear his name.

G. VIRAL DISEASE: *African Horse Sickness*

After examining samples of blood from horses in South Africa, John M'Fadyean finds that the causative agent of African horse sickness passes through bacteriological filters. In 1901, Arnold Theiler publishes on his extended experiments with horse sickness disease, including one that shows the agent to be filterable. M'Fadyean, however, has priority for the discovery.

H. IMMUNOLOGY: *Blood Groups*

Karl Landsteiner discovers and names three human blood groups, A, B, and O, based on agglutination of red blood cells by blood serum. He notes the importance of these groups in human blood transfusions. He discovers the AB blood group in 1902 and the MNP blood groups in 1926. (See 1926 F, 1940 N.)

I. BIOCHEMISTRY: *Adaptive Enzymes*

F. Deinert reports that yeast metabolize galactose when grown in a medium containing lactose or galactose, but not in a medium containing only glucose. He is the first to study what Henning Karström, in 1930, will refer to as adaptive enzymes. Adaptive enzymes are renamed induced enzymes in 1953. (See 1930 A.)

J. GENETICS: *Laws of Inheritance*

Gregor Mendel's paper on inherited characteristics published in 1865 has largely gone unnoticed until it is rediscovered independently by three botanists, Hugo de Vries, Erich Tschermak, and Carl Correns. Correns subsequently introduces the terms "law of segregation" and "law of independent recombination." (See 1865 B.)

K. GENETICS: *Mutation*

Hugo de Vries recognizes abrupt, discontinuous characteristics in plants that he terms "mutations," a term already in use meaning "change," and he refers to the changed plants as "mutants." Some of the changes are later shown to be caused by translocations, but others prove to be mutations. He argues that such changes, rather than the gradual changes described by Charles Darwin, account for evolution.

L. BIOCHEMISTRY: *Energy Transfer in Coupled Chemical Reactions*

Friedrich Wilhelm Ostwald introduces the concept that energy may be transferred by coupled biochemical reactions.

M. PHYSICS: *Radioactivity*

Paul Villard discovers gamma rays, a third type of emission from radioactive elements. (See 1899 H.)

N. PHYSICS: *Quantum Theory*

Max Planck proposes the quantum theory.

O. TECHNOLOGY: *Zeppelins*

Ferdinand von Zeppelin introduces the use of hydrogen-filled, rigid-framed airships widely used during World War I, known as zeppelins, which lose favor after a famous crash in 1937. In the late 1990s a newly designed type of zeppelin is successfully constructed. (See 1937 Q.)

P. SOCIETY AND POLITICS

An attack on foreigners in China, known as the Boxer Rebellion, results in the deaths of hundreds of foreigners, many of them missionaries. The term "boxer," a rough translation of the Chinese word for "band," is applied to a semiofficial military force encouraged by the empress Tzu Hsi.

Q. THE ARTS: *Music*

Giacomo Puccini's opera *Tosca* is performed.

R. THE ARTS: *Literature*

L. Frank Baum publishes *The Wizard of Oz*. (See 1939 U.)

S. THE ARTS: *Art*

Pablo Picasso produces his first well-recognized painting, *Le Moulin de la Galette*.

1901

A. BACTERIAL CLASSIFICATION: *Taxonomy*

F. D. Chester's *Manual of Determinative Bacteriology* greatly influences American bacterial taxonomists.

B. BACTERIAL CLASSIFICATION: Lactobacillus

Martinus Beijerinck publishes a survey of the rod-shaped lactic acid-producing bacteria encountered in the yeast and alcohol industries. He proposes the generic name *Lactobacillus* for these morphologically and physiologically similar organisms. (See 1893 A.)

C. BACTERIAL PHYSIOLOGY: *Nonsymbiotic Nitrogen Fixation*

Martinus Beijerinck isolates aerobic nitrogen-fixing bacteria, free-living in the soil and not associated with plant roots. He names the genus *Azotobacter* and describes two species, *Azotobacter chroococcum* and *Azotobacter agilis*. (See 1895 A, 1928 A.)

D. BACTERIAL PHYSIOLOGY: *Microbial Growth Factors*

In a water-soluble extract of yeast, E. Wildiers finds a substance that is indispensable for growth of yeast. This material, which he calls "bios," is later discovered to be a B vitamin. (See 1896 F, 1906 L, 1912 G.)

E. VIRAL DISEASE: *Fowl Plague*

Eugenio Centanni and E. Savonuzzi isolate the causative agent of fowl plague by passing it through candle filters. They try various culture media in attempts to grow this filterable virus, including an experiment with four hen's eggs in which two of the embryos are deformed. No further studies are done with eggs. It is not until 1931 that Ernest William Goodpasture, working with fowlpox virus, grows virus on the chorioallantoic membrane. By 1955, accumulating evidence suggests a close relationship between fowl plague virus and influenza virus. (See 1927 A, 1931 G, 1936 G.)

1901 (continued)

F. VIRAL DISEASE: *Yellow Fever*

Walter Reed heads a U.S. Army Yellow Fever Commission in Cuba, charged with eradicating the disease. Assisted by James Carroll, Reed discovers that the disease is caused by a filterable agent similar to that which Friedrich Löffler and Paul Frosch reported in 1898 to cause hoof-and-mouth disease of cattle. Reed's conclusion, that yellow fever is of viral etiology, is the first report of human disease caused by a virus. The commission's observation that mosquitoes transmit the disease leads to its eradication. (See 1919 D, 1936 L.)

G. IMMUNOLOGY: *Complement Fixation*

Jules Bordet and Octave Gengou demonstrate that all antigen-antibody reactions cause the attachment, or fixation, of complement to the target antigen. Their procedure is adopted in 1906 by August von Wassermann and his associates for a blood test for syphilis. (See 1895 E and 1898 I.)

H. IMMUNOLOGY: *Typhoid Vaccine*

After successfully testing a killed vaccine for typhoid fever, the U.S. Army makes typhoid vaccination compulsory. (See 1896 C, 1903 H.)

I. IMMUNOLOGY: *Autoimmunity*

Paul Ehrlich, in discussing whether or not toxic autoantibodies might be formed, uses the term "horror autotoxicus" (fear of self-poisoning). Ehrlich does not suggest that autoantibodies cannot be made, but that they are prevented from acting. His statement, largely misunderstood, somewhat impedes research on autoimmune disease. (See 1904 B, 1957 O.)

J. BIOCHEMISTRY: *Catalase*

Oscar Loew, who identifies and names the enzyme catalase, demonstrates that it is found in tissues and cells of nearly all types.

K. BIOCHEMISTRY: *Saturated Fats*

William Normann develops a hydrogenation process of unsaturated fatty acids that prevent rancidity and produces edible polyunsaturated fats. The connection between hardening of the arteries and eating polyunsaturated fats and cholesterol is made in 1913. (See 1913 D, 1953 U.)

L. SOCIETY: *Nobel Prizes*

The first Nobel laureates are named, with the awards in science going to Emil von Behring (physiology or medicine), Jacobus Henricus van't Hoff (chemistry), and Wilhelm Konrad Röntgen (physics).

M. CULTURE: *Research Institutes*

John D. Rockefeller founds the Rockefeller Institute for Medical Research. It provides laboratories for groups of collaborating investigators.

N. TECHNOLOGY: *Wireless Telegraphy*

Radio is invented when Guglielmo Marconi successfully sends a Morse code message by wireless telegraphy, or radiotelegraphy, from England to Newfoundland, using an antenna that both he and Aleksandr Stepanovich Popov invented independently in 1895. Marconi shares the 1909 Nobel

Prize in physics with Ferdinand Braun, who invented a cathode-ray oscilloscope in 1897.

O. TECHNOLOGY: *Automobiles*
The automobile manufacturer Gottlieb Daimler introduces the Mercedes motor car, named for the daughter of Emil Jellinek, an Austrian diplomat, who promises to sell 36 of the new motor cars in 1 year. In 1926, the Benz and Daimler companies merge, forming the Mercedes-Benz company. (See 1885 O.)

P. TECHNOLOGY: *Fingerprints*
Edward Richard Henry develops a system of identification based on fingerprints that is the basis for many of the modern systems. (See 1885 P.)

Q. SOCIETY AND POLITICS
U.S. president William McKinley dies of infection resulting from a gunshot wound. Shortly before McKinley is wounded, Vice President Theodore Roosevelt, who succeeds McKinley, delivers a speech on U.S. foreign policy in which he says, "Speak softly and carry a big stick."

1902

A. BACTERIAL CLASSIFICATION: Thiobacillus
A. Nathansohn isolates the first pure culture of a thiobacillus. He employs a mineral medium containing nitrate to cultivate *Thiobacillus thioparus,* an aerobic, autotrophic, sulfur-oxidizing bacterium. (See 1903 B, 1922 B.)

B. BACTERIAL CLASSIFICATION: *Pneumococci/Neufeld Quellung Reaction*
In studies with antipneumococcal sera made with different strains of the pneumococci, Fred Neufeld observes that the capsules of the bacterium "swell" (*Quellung,* in German) in the presence of type-specific serum. By so describing the phenomenon, Neufeld follows the observation made in 1896 by H. Roger, who, in treating the fungus *Oidium albicans* (now in the genus *Acrosporium*) with immune serum, notes what he refers to as a "swelling" of the cuticle. The term *Quellungsreaktion* achieves wide use after the appearance in 1933 of a paper by R. Etinger-Tulcynska in which she discusses the apparent swelling of capsules of *Diplococcus, Klebsiella,* and *Streptococcus.* It is now recognized that the capsule does not swell, or enlarge, but instead has a change in optical properties that make it more visible. The Neufeld Quellung reaction is used to classify the pneumococci according to capsular types.

C. BACTERIAL STRUCTURE: *Cell Wall and Membrane*
A. Grimme and Alfred Fischer plasmolyze bacterial cells in salt solutions and show that the cytoplasm shrinks away from a solid cell wall. They conclude that the bacteria have a cytoplasmic membrane separate from a rigid cell wall. (See 1940 A, 1941 D, 1947 A, 1951 B, 1953 D, 1958 A.)

D. BACTERIAL PHYSIOLOGY: *Actinorhizal Nitrogen Fixation*
K. Shibata studies the symbionts in the root nodules of the nonlegumes *Alnus* and *Myrica.* He concludes that the organism associated with *Alnus* is a mycobacterium, but that the symbiont in *Myrica* is an actinomycete. In

1938, R. Schaede's careful microscopic studies confirm that the root nodules of several nonlegumes contain actinomycetes. (See 1885 E, 1954 D, 1970 B, 1978 D.)

E. BACTERIAL INSECTICIDES: *Insect Pathogens*
While studying a bacterial disease of silkworms, Shigetane Ishiwata isolates an aerobic spore-forming bacterium that he refers to as "Sotto-Bacillen," meaning "sudden collapse bacillus." In the 1950s this bacterium, now called *Bacillus thuringiensis,* is used to control damage to crops caused by lepidopteran insects. (See 1915 B, 1951 F, 1953 J, 1954 H.)

F. IMMUNOLOGY: *Vaccine for Bovine Tuberculosis*
Emil von Behring uses a human strain of tubercle bacillus to prepare a "bovo-vaccine" immunization of cattle. The vaccine, used in Germany, Sweden, Russia, and America, is discontinued when it is found that the animals shed potentially infectious tubercle bacilli. This vaccine is historically important, however, because of its use of a microorganism specific for humans to make a vaccine for cattle and is the forerunner of the bacillus Calmette-Guérin (*Mycobacterium bovis* BCG) vaccine which uses a bovine strain of the tubercle bacillus to make a vaccine for humans. (See 1890 C, 1906 I.)

G. IMMUNOLOGY: *Anaphylaxis*
Paul Portier and Charles Richet discover anaphylaxis, an immediate hypersensitivity reaction that may cause death, when they make a second injection of toxin from a sea anemone into a dog that had previously received a sublethal injection of the same toxin. Richet receives the Nobel Prize in physiology or medicine in 1913 for his contributions to this area of immunology. (See 1891 C.)

H. IMMUNOLOGY: *Neutralization of Toxin*
Jan Danysz discovers that neutralization of diphtheria toxin is complete if the toxin is added in one quantity to the antiserum but is incomplete if the same amount of toxin is added in two or more increments. The Danysz phenomenon contradicts Paul Ehrlich's belief in fixed-proportion reactions between antigen and antibody. (See 1897 G.)

I. GENETICS: *Mendelian Inheritance*
William Bateson first applies Mendelian principles to animals with his work on fowl. His publication of *Mendel's Principles of Heredity: A Defence* supports Gregor Mendel's work. (See 1865 B, 1900 J, 1905 H, 1909 J.)

J. MEDICAL TECHNOLOGY: *Wright's Stain*
James Homer Wright describes a modification of a stain developed by Dmitri Leonidovich Romanowsky for study of the malarial parasite. Romanowsky stains are widely used for various types of cells and tissues, and Wright's stain becomes commonly used for staining blood smears. (See 1905 I.)

K. PHYSIOLOGY: *Blood-Gas Manometer*
Joseph Barcroft and John Scott Haldane invent a blood-gas manometer.

L. BIOCHEMISTRY: *Peptide Bond*

Emil Hermann Fischer and Franz Hofmeister independently propose that the amino acids in proteins are joined through the α-amino group of one amino acid and the α-carboxyl group of a second, forming an amide linkage. This amide linkage between two amino acids becomes known as a peptide bond.

M. TECHNOLOGY: *Facsimile Machine*

Arthur Korn constructs a device that is essentially a facsimile machine for transmitting photographs by telegraphy. In 1907, he sends a photograph from Munich to Berlin marking the beginning of its use by newspapers.

N. SOCIETY: *Education*

Cecil Rhodes dies, leaving a will stipulating the establishment of 3-year Rhodes scholarships at Oxford University.

O. THE ARTS: *Literature*
- Joseph Conrad publishes *The Heart of Darkness.*
- Beatrix Potter writes and illustrates *The Tale of Peter Rabbit.*

P. THE ARTS: *Theater*

George Bernard Shaw's play *Man and Superman* is performed in London.

1903

A. BACTERIAL CLASSIFICATION: *Hemolytic Classification of Streptococci*

Hugo Schottmüller suggests the establishment of various types of *Streptococcus* based on their ability to hemolyze red blood cells. (See 1919 A.)

B. BACTERIAL PHYSIOLOGY: *Autotroph/*Thiobacillus

As Martinus Beijerinck studies a sulfur-oxidizing bacterium, he finds that under anaerobic conditions it grows with only carbon dioxide as a source of carbon. The bacterium is given the name *Thiobacillus denitrificans.* He also names *Thiobacillus thioparus.* (See 1902 A, 1922 B.)

C. MICROBIAL PHYSIOLOGY: *Fermentation*

Eduard Buchner, Hans Buchner, and Martin Hahn find that phosphate stimulates fermentation by yeast juice.

D. BACTERIAL DISEASE: Shigella *Toxin*

Three investigators, H. Conradi, L. Rosenthal, and C. Todd, independently show that Shiga's bacillus, *Shigella dysenteriae,* produces a soluble toxin that behaves similarly to the toxins of diphtheria and tetanus. In contrast, the Flexner bacillus, *Shigella flexneri,* does not produce such a toxin.

E. BACTERIAL DISEASE: *Asymptomatic Carriers*

Mary Mallon, an asymptomatic carrier of typhoid fever, is implicated as the source of a series of typhoid outbreaks in New York City in establishments where she works as a food handler. Typhoid Mary, as she is called, is placed under detention in 1915 until her death in 1928 when she fails to respond to repeated requests to cease working in kitchens.

1903 *(continued)*

F. BACTERIAL DISEASE: *Syphilis*

Elie Metchnikoff and Émile Roux find that chimpanzees are susceptible to the "virus" of syphilis when they successfully transfer the disease from one animal to another. (See 1905 D.)

G. IMMUNOLOGY: *Flagellar and Somatic Antigens of Bacteria*

Theobald Smith and A. L. Reagh discover that antisera prepared with a *Salmonella* species referred to as the hog cholera bacillus contain two components: one that reacts with the flagella and one that reacts with non-flagellated (nonmotile) forms of the bacteria. The terms "H antigen" (for flagellar antigen) and "O antigen" (for somatic antigen) are used after 1920. (See 1920 C, 1926 A, 1941 A.)

H. IMMUNOLOGY: *Inflammation*

Nicolas Maurice Arthus observes a severe local inflammatory reaction in rabbits that receive several subcutaneous injections of nontoxic substances such as milk or horse serum. This phenomenon becomes known as the Arthus reaction. Arthus emphasizes possible hazards associated with the use of antitoxins prepared in horses; it is later learned that some pulmonary inflammations caused by repeated exposure to airborne antigens, such as fungal spores, are a form of Arthus reaction. (See 1867 A.)

I. IMMUNOLOGY: *Phagocytosis*

Almroth Wright and Stewart R. Douglas report that specific antibodies that they call "opsonins" or "bacteriotropins" reinforce the action of phagocytic leukocytes. Their discovery helps to draw the theories of cellular and humoral immunity together. (See 1884 H.)

J. IMMUNOLOGY: *Typhoid Fever*

Between 1904 and 1909 William Leishman modifies the method of preparation of Almroth Wright's typhoid vaccine and performs successful tests in India that lead to broad use of the vaccine in World War I. (See 1896 C.)

K. VIRAL DISEASE: *Rabies*

Paul Remlinger successfully passes the rabies virus through a Berkefeld filter with the largest size pores.

L. VIRAL DISEASE: *Rabies*

Adelchi Negri describes cytoplasmic inclusion structures he observes in rabies victims. Mistakenly assuming that the structures are protozoan parasites, he names them *Neurocytes hydrophobiae* in 1909 and asserts that they are the cause of rabies. These structures, since called "Negri bodies," are considered diagnostic evidence of rabies.

M. GENETICS: *Chromosomes*

Walter Stanborough Sutton and Theodor Heinrich Boveri independently propose that the behavior of chromosomes during cell division could explain Mendelian principles of segregation and independent assortment. They believe that Gregor Mendel's unit factors are the chromosomes themselves, not genes on the chromosomes. (See 1905 H.)

N. MICROSCOPY: *Ultramicroscope*

Richard Adolf Zsigmondy and Henry Siedentopf invent the ultramicroscope for use in their work on colloids. An intense light projected from the side illuminates the colloidal particles against a dark background. Zsigmondy receives the 1925 Nobel Prize in physics for this work.

O. TECHNOLOGY: *Airplanes*

Brothers Orville Wright and Wilbur Wright make the first successful airplane flight.

P. TECHNOLOGY: *Automobiles*

The Ford Motor Company incorporates and produces its first automobile, the Model A, with two cylinders and 8 horsepower.

Q. SOCIETY: *Universities and Awards*

Publisher Joseph Pulitzer endows a school of journalism at Columbia University and stipulates that part of the endowment be used for prizes for letters, drama, music, and journalism.

R. THE ARTS: *Art*

Pablo Picasso paints *The Old Guitarist*.

1904

A. MYCOLOGY: *Fungal Reproduction*

A. F. Blakeslee discovers mating types in fungi when he finds sexually incompatible strains in the fungus *Rhizopus*. Noting that sexually compatible strains are morphologically indistinguishable, he calls one "plus" and the other "minus."

B. IMMUNOLOGY: *Autoimmune Disease*

Julius Donath and Karl Landsteiner report studies on paroxysmal hemoglobinuria, a now rare disease in which large amounts of hemoglobin are discharged in urine—a condition brought on by exposure to cold. Their conclusion that the phenomenon involves both an autoantibody and complement is generally regarded as the first recognition of autoimmune disease. (See 1901 I, 1957 O.)

C. IMMUNOLOGY: *Toxoids*

Both Alexander Thomas Glenny and E. Loewenstein use formalin-treated toxins to immunize horses and other animals. Glenny prepares formalized diphtheria toxoid, while Loewenstein prepares formalized tetanus toxoid. In 1924, Gaston Léon Ramon also utilizes a formaldehyde-treated diphtheria toxin. (See 1893 C, 1927 G.)

D. VIROLOGY: *Fowlpox Virus*

Amédée Borrel observes the fowlpox virus with a light microscope, apparently unaware of John Brown Buist's observation of cowpox virus in 1887. Enrique Paschen rediscovers the cowpox virus in 1906. (See 1887 F, 1906 G.)

E. VIROLOGY: *Equine Infectious Anemia Virus*

Henri Vallée and Henri Carré prove that the agent that causes infectious anemia in horses can be filtered through bacteriological filters. This virus is

1904 *(continued)*

later classified as a lentivirus, the group in which the human immunodeficiency virus (HIV) is placed after its discovery in the 1980s.

F. BIOCHEMISTRY: *Oxidation of Fatty Acids*
Franz Knoop publishes a theory of β-oxidation of fatty acids. By attaching a phenyl residue to the terminal methyl group as an organic tracer, he determines that fatty acids are degraded through the loss of two carbon atoms at a time. Although the phenyl derivatives are not physiological compounds, these experiments introduce labeling techniques into metabolic studies.

G. BIOCHEMISTRY: *Oxidation–Reduction Reaction*
Fritz Haber publishes the first study of electrical potentials caused by an organic oxygen-reduction reaction: the quinone–hydroquinone reaction.

H. BIOCHEMISTRY: *Types of Chlorophyll*
Richard Martin Willstätter carries out a series of studies on chlorophyll between 1904 and 1916. He separates two forms, α and β, which he finds are associated with carotene and xanthophyll. Unable to understand carbon dioxide assimilation and the production of oxygen, he suggests an effect of light on a combination of chlorophyll and carbon dioxide, with the formation of a peroxide from which oxygen is released. Willstätter receives the 1915 Nobel Prize in chemistry for his studies of chlorophyll.

I. PSYCHOLOGY: *Conditioned Reflex*
Ivan Petrovich Pavlov receives the 1904 Nobel Prize in physiology or medicine for his research on the digestive system. Although his work on gastric juices is important, Pavlov is now more famous for his experiments, begun in 1907, on the conditioned reflex, showing that if a bell is rung each time a dog is given food, it will in time salivate in response to the sound of the bell alone.

J. MICROSCOPY: *Ultraviolet Microscope*
A. Köhler publishes a paper on efforts to use ultraviolet light to decrease the limit of resolution of the light microscope. (See 1942 K.)

K. TECHNOLOGY: *Railroads*
The 3,200-mile Trans-Siberian Railway, connecting Moscow and Vladivostok, becomes the world's longest rail line. (See 1891 F.)

L. TECHNOLOGY: *Automobiles*
The Detroit Automobile Company is reorganized to create the Cadillac Motor Car Company.

M. THE ARTS: *Music*
The opera *Madama Butterfly* by Giacomo Puccini is first performed in Milan.

1905

A. BACTERIAL ECOLOGY
Martinus Beijerinck, on the occasion of receiving the Leeuwenhoek medal from the Koninklijke Akademie van Wetenschappen, for the first and only time describes his approach to microbiology as being the study of microbial

ecology. Although Beijerinck's methodology had come to be used to investigate transformations of matter in the environment, he did not describe it in a publication.

B. BACTERIAL CLASSIFICATION AND PHYSIOLOGY: *Coagulase Test*
L. Loeb reports that certain species of bacteria cause the clotting of blood plasma. He notes that the pyogenic staphylococci, as compared with other bacteria tested, have a strong coagulase activity. The test is considered to be a key diagnostic characteristic for the identification of *Staphylococcus aureus*.

C. BACTERIAL PHYSIOLOGY: *Fermentation*
Franz Schardinger studies a bacterium that he names *Bacillus macerans,* isolated from the retting of flax; it is the first known acetone-producing bacterium.

D. BACTERIAL DISEASE: *Syphilis*
Fritz Schaudinn, working with the physician Eric Hoffmann, discovers a spiral bacterium in exudates from a syphilitic chancre. He names the organism *Spirocheta pallida* because of its similarity to other spirochetes. Because of its differences from other spirochetes, he later changes the name to *Treponema pallidum,* the generic name meaning "twisted thread" and the species name "pale or pallid," in reference to the difficulty of observing it microscopically. (See 1838 A.)

E. VIRAL DISEASE: *Yellow Fever*
Even though Walter Reed had established in 1901 that mosquitoes carry yellow fever, it is an epidemic in 1905, in New Orleans, that pushes public health authorities in Louisiana to take steps to control the mosquito population. The New Orleans epidemic is the last major epidemic of yellow fever in the United States.

F. VIRAL DISEASE: *Vaccinia Virus*
Adelchi Negri proves that vaccinia virus will pass through Berkefeld V filters.

G. IMMUNOLOGY: *Serum Sickness*
Clemens Peter von Pirquet and Bela Schick report their observations of serum sickness in patients injected with various animal antisera. They recognize that serum sickness is an acquired immune reaction. (See 1891 C, 1902 G.)

H. GENETICS: *Chromosomes and Genes*
William Bateson suggests that a single chromosome contains more than one genetic unit of inheritance. (See 1903 M, 1909 H.)

I. CELL BIOLOGY: *Giemsa Stain*
Gustav Giemsa describes a staining solution containing azure II-eosin, azure II, glycerin, and methanol. This solution, like Wright's stain, is a variation of the Romanowsky stain for malarial parasites. The Giemsa stain, used for staining protozoan parasites, comes into common use for staining the nucleus of animal cells and bacteria. A modification of the procedure is used by Carl Robinow in studies of the bacterial nuclear region. (See 1902 J, 1942 B.)

1906 *(continued)*

J. PHYSICS: *Photoelectric Effect*

Albert Einstein publishes a paper on the photoelectric effect, in which he uses Max Planck's idea of quanta, or discrete packets of energy. This paper is important in the development of the quantum theory and earns Einstein the 1921 Nobel Prize in physics. (See 1905 K, 1915 E.)

K. PHYSICS: *Special Relativity*

Albert Einstein publishes two other papers of seminal importance. In the first, he introduces the theory of special relativity. In the second, his concepts become expressed by the formula $E = mc^2$, where E is energy content, m is mass, and c is the speed of light. (See 1900 N, 1905 J, 1915 E.)

L. PHYSIOLOGY: *Hormones*

Ernest Henry Starling and William Maddock Bayliss coin the term "hormone" for substances secreted into the bloodstream by the thyroid, gonads, and other endocrine glands that produce effects on other organs and tissues. Starling and Bayliss had discovered secretin in 1902.

M. PSYCHOLOGY: *Intelligence Scale*

Alfred Binet and Théodore Simon establish a metrical scale of intelligence by which to determine the mental age of a child. (See 1914 J.)

N. THE ARTS: *Literature*

• E. M. Forster publishes his novel *Where Angels Fear To Tread*.
• The poet Rainer Maria Rilke publishes *Stundenbuch* (The book of hours).

O. THE ARTS: *Music*

The opera *Salomé* by Richard Strauss is performed in Dresden. After its first performance in New York's Metropolitan Opera House in 1907, financier J. P. Morgan, a major supporter of the Metropolitan, forbids further performances because of his objections to the sensuous aria and dance performed by Salomé. The opera is not performed again at the Metropolitan until 1934.

1906

A. BACTERIAL PHYSIOLOGY: *Methanogens*

N. L. Söhngen demonstrates that methane-producing bacteria can use products of cellulose-fermenting cultures as substrates: formate, acetate, butyrate, ethanol, and hydrogen and carbon dioxide. W. Omelianski claims to have isolated a cellulose-fermenting bacterium that also produces methane, but his results are not confirmed.

B. BACTERIAL PHYSIOLOGY: *2,3–Butanediol Fermentation*

Arthur Harden and W. S. Walpole discover that *Aerobacter aerogenes* produces 2,3-butanediol as a major product of the fermentation of glucose. The final fermentation broth has a nearly neutral pH. Harden also finds that a small amount of acetoin (acetylmethylcarbinol) is produced. The test for acetoin and for neutral pH becomes a means of distinguishing acid-producing gram-negative fermenters from butanediol fermenters. (See 1898 A, 1915 A.)

C. BACTERIAL DISEASE: *Pertussis*

Jules Bordet and Octave Gengou cultivate *Bordetella pertussis,* the bacterium that causes pertussis (whooping cough).

D. BACTERIAL DISEASE: *Bubonic Plague*

The British Plague Commission in Bombay establishes the role of the rat flea in the transmission of bubonic plague to humans.

E. BACTERIAL DISEASE: *Rocky Mountain Spotted Fever*

Howard Taylor Ricketts proves that Rocky Mountain spotted fever is transmitted by ticks. His death in 1910 results from infection contracted during his research on typhus fever. (See 1909 D.)

F. BACTERIAL DISEASE: *Cholera*

A new type of cholera bacillus is isolated at the El Tor quarantine station on the Gulf of Suez. The El Tor vibrio, which is unusual in forming a soluble hemolysin, appears to be limited primarily to the Celebes Islands. (See 1971 D.)

G. VIRAL DISEASE: *Cowpox Virus*

Enrique Paschen observes the cowpox virus under a light microscope, apparently unaware that John Brown Buist already made this observation in 1897. For many years Paschen receives credit for being the first to see this virus. Subsequently, many workers stained "Paschen bodies" and "Borrel bodies," named for Amédée Borrel, who made observations of the fowlpox virus in 1904. The objects observed by Buist, Borrel, Paschen, and other investigators are referred to a "viral inclusion bodies." Not until the work of Eugene Woodruff and Ernest William Goodpasture in 1929 are the inclusion bodies proved to contain many viral particles. (See 1886 E, 1904 D, 1929 F.)

H. IMMUNOLOGY: *Syphilis Serology*

August von Wassermann, Albert Neisser, Carl Bruck, and A. Schucht develop a blood test for syphilis using the complement fixation phenomenon as its basis. The test, known as the Wassermann test, establishes the use of complement fixation assays as diagnostic procedures. (See 1895 E, 1899 F, 1901 G.)

I. IMMUNOLOGY: *Tuberculosis Vaccine*

Albert Calmette and Camille Guérin begin working toward attenuating a strain of bovine tuberculosis bacillus for use as a vaccine against tuberculosis. After 13 years and 231 subcultures, at 3-week intervals, on a medium containing ox bile, they believe the vaccine to be safe for human trials. It is tested on a human child in 1921. The BCG (bacillus Calmette-Guérin) vaccine is used today to vaccinate young children in countries with a high rate of tuberculosis. (See 1880 C, 1902 F.)

J. BIOCHEMISTRY: *Hexose Diphosphate in Fermentation*

Arthur Harden and William John Young confirm that the alcoholic fermentation is stimulated by the addition of phosphate and that the phosphate forms an ester with glucose. In 1908 Young confirms that the "Harden-Young ester" is hexose diphosphate (hexose 1,6-bisphosphate). Following his many discoveries of enzymes involved in sugar fermentation, Harden receives the Nobel Prize in chemistry in 1929, which he shares with Hans von Euler-Chelpin, also a major researcher in fermentation biochemistry. (See 1914 F, 1928 F, 1933 I.)

K. BIOCHEMISTRY: *Coenzyme for Fermentation*

Arthur Harden and William Young report finding a "coferment" or "coenzyme" for the alcoholic fermentation. Both Hans Euler-Chelpin and Otto Warburg contribute to the identification of one of the components, nicotinamide adenine dinucleotide (known variously as Co-I, DPN, and NAD). The Harden-Young "coenzyme" is ultimately recognized to be a system composed of adenosine 5'-triphosphate (ATP), NAD, cocarboxylase, and magnesium. (See 1923 G.)

L. BIOCHEMISTRY: *Vitamins*

Frederick Gowland Hopkins reports that some chemicals other than proteins, carbohydrates, fats, and minerals are found in foods and are necessary to health. Hopkins and Casimir Funk are usually credited with developing the concept of vitamins, a term that Funk introduced. Hopkins and Christiaan Eijkman, who studies the cause of beriberi, share the Nobel Prize in physiology or medicine in 1929. (See 1896 F, 1901 D.)

M. BIOCHEMISTRY: *Chromatography*

Mikhail Semenovich Tsvett (or Tswett) invents chromatography when he separates chlorophyll into three components by passing an ether-alcohol extract of leaves through a column of calcium carbonate. His experiments derive from those of Friedlieb Ferdinand Runge, who, in 1834, produced separation of coal tar products by placing solutions on adsorbent paper where components migrated into colored rings. Christian Friedrich Schönbein made similar observations in about 1845, and Richard Synge and Archer Martin introduce improvements in 1941. (See 1941 M.)

N. PHYSICS: *Third Law of Thermodynamics*

Walter Hermann Nernst advances a heat theorem stating that equilibrium constants for chemical reactions can be calculated from data on heat changes. This theorem also includes the concept that absolute zero cannot be reached. For his heat theorem, sometimes called the third law of thermodynamics, Nernst receives the Nobel Prize in chemistry in 1920.

O. TECHNOLOGY: *Radio*

Lee De Forest develops an amplifier for the radio, consisting of three electrodes, that is significant in the development of radios for manufacture.

P. TECHNOLOGY: *Distress Signal*

The distress call SOS is adopted by the International Radio Telegraph Convention. After 1912 the signal (three dots, three dashes, three dots) is universally used.

Q. SOCIETY

San Francisco is struck by the strongest earthquake yet seen in America. The resulting fire destroys about two-thirds of the city, killing 2,500 persons.

R. THE ARTS: *Art*

Henri Matisse completes his painting *The Joy of Life.*

A. BACTERIAL GENETICS: *Mutation*

R. Massini isolates a strain of *Escherichia coli* that cannot ferment lactose and names it *Escherichia coli mutabile*. When cultivated on an agar medium containing dyes that color the colonies when lactose is metabolized, some colonies develop dark-red sectors in otherwise white or pink nonfermenting colonies. When the dark-red sectors are subcultured, Massini finds that they breed true for lactose fermentation. He calls the change a mutation, but R. Burri fails to find support for his conclusions and declares the change to be an adaptation. Although later workers conclude that Burri's culture is apparently not *E. coli mutabile,* Massini's work is largely discounted because of Burri's experiments. (See 1934 C, 1943 D.)

B. BACTERIAL DISEASE: *Trachoma*

Studying cases of trachoma, L. Halberstaedter and Stanilaus von Prowazek report finding inside of conjunctival cells inclusion bodies containing elementary particles that they believe are the infectious agent of trachoma. They designate the particles "Chlamydozoa," or mantle bodies, from which the generic name *Chlamydia* is derived. The name "trachoma" was first used in about A.D. 60 by Pedanius Dioscorides. (See 1930 C, 1934 B, 1957 G.)

C. BACTERIAL DISEASE: *Bubonic Plague*

The year 1907 is the peak year of a 10-year bubonic plague epidemic in India that kills at least 6 million people.

D. BACTERIAL DISEASE: *Crown Gall*

After applying Koch's postulates to the study of crown gall disease in cultivated marguerite, or Paris daisy, Erwin Frink Smith and C. O. Townsend conclude that tumor production is caused by a bacterium that they name *Bacterium tumefaciens,* now called *Agrobacterium tumefaciens*. By infecting plants with this bacterium, they produce galls on stems of tobacco, tomato, and potato and on the roots of sugar beets and peach trees. (See 1947 B, 1970, G, 1974 L, 1977 O.)

E. IMMUNOLOGY: *Tuberculosis*

Clemens Peter von Pirquet introduces a skin scratch test using Koch's Old Tuberculin as an aid in diagnosing tuberculosis. An inflammatory response at the site of the test is considered positive evidence of tuberculosis. (See 1890 C, 1891 C, 1908 C.)

F. IMMUNOLOGY: *Immunochemistry*

After observing that antigen-antibody reactions follow the chemical law of mass action, Svante Arrhenius discusses the application of the methods of physical chemistry to problems in immunology. He coins the term "immunochemistry" in a series of lectures given in 1904 and published in 1907.

G. CELL BIOLOGY: *Tissue Culture*

Ross Granville Harrison is the first to successfully grow tissues in artificial culture when he propagates nerve tissue from tadpoles in hanging drops. (See 1913 C, 1917 D, 1928 E, 1931 F, 1933 E, 1936 L.)

1907 *(continued)*

H. PROTOZOAN DISEASE: *Trypanosomiasis*

Searching for a "magic bullet," a chemical that would target disease organisms, Paul Ehrlich finds that the dye trypan red kills the trypanosome that causes sleeping sickness. Ehrlich shares the 1908 Nobel Prize in physiology or medicine with Elie Metchnikoff for his work on immunity and serum therapy.

I. BIOCHEMISTRY: *Muscle Contraction*

Walter Morley Fletcher and Frederick Gowland Hopkins establish that lactic acid appears during muscle contraction under anaerobic conditions and disappears under aerobic conditions.

J. GENETICS: *Panspermia*

Svante Arrhenius, the Nobel laureate in chemistry in 1903, uses the term "panspermia" for microorganisms that, he believes, have drifted through space to earth from some unknown source, thus seeding all life on earth. (See 1879 A.)

K. THE ARTS: *Humorous Art*

Rube Goldberg begins to publish drawings of fanciful machines designed to perform simple tasks. The drawings continue to appear until about 1966.

L. THE ARTS: *Music*

The musical Broadway musical series "The Ziegfeld Follies" begins in New York City with "The Follies of 1907." A new follies is performed almost every year until 1931.

M. THE ARTS: *Literature*

Songs of a Sourdough, a collection of first poems of Robert William Service, is published. His later work includes "The Shooting of Dan McGrew" and "The Cremation of Sam McGee."

N. THE ARTS: *Theater*

Playboy of the Western World by John Millington Synge is performed in Dublin.

O. THE ARTS: *Art*

Pablo Picasso paints *Les Demoiselles d'Avignon.*

1908

A. BACTERIAL TAXONOMY: *Classification of Cocci*

C.-E. A. Winslow and A. R. Winslow publish their study of the *Coccaceae,* dividing the spherical bacteria into parasitic and nonparasitic forms.

B. VIRAL DISEASE: *Poliomyelitis Virus*

Karl Landsteiner and Erwin Popper prove that poliomyelitis is caused by a filterable virus. They successfully infect two Old World monkeys (*Cynocephalus hamadryas* and *Macaca rhesus*) by intraperitoneal injections of a saline suspension of spinal cord material from a child that had died of the disease. Although their material is not passed through a bacteriological filter, bacterial culture tests are negative and no infection is caused by injections in mice, rabbits, and guinea pigs. Landsteiner's and Popper's experiments also establish a successful animal model for the disease. In 1909, Landsteiner and Constantin Levaditi report filtration of poliovirus through a Berkefeld V filter. (See 1909 F, 1936 F, 1949 I.)

C. IMMUNOLOGY: *Tuberculosis*
Charles Mantoux introduces the technique of injection of Old Tuberculin intradermally, between the layers of the skin. A local inflammatory reaction is regarded as positive for tuberculosis. Modifications of this test are still in use. (See 1891 C, 1907 E.)

D. BIOCHEMISTRY: *Oxidation*
Otto Heinrich Warburg publishes his first paper on biological oxidations and energetics. The study is of the use of oxygen by the developing sea urchin egg. (See 1904 G.)

E. GENETICS: *Inborn Errors of Metabolism*
Archibold Garrod, investigating the incidence and pattern of occurrence of alkaptonuria, an arthritic disease characterized by excretion of dark-colored urine, concludes that it is inherited and that a single recessive gene may be responsible. He uses the term "inborn errors of metabolism" for the malfunctioning of single gene-controlled processes, such as alkaptonuria and albinism. Because his work is not understood at the time, it has little influence on genetic concepts. Rediscovery of the single gene effect takes place in 1941 when George Beadle and Edward L. Tatum perform their experiments with the fungus *Neurospora*. (See 1941 H.)

F. CHEMISTRY: *Haber Process*
Fritz Haber develops a method for synthesis of ammonia from a direct combination of hydrogen and nitrogen gases. Ammonia is then easily converted to nitrates for use as agricultural fertilizer. His brother-in-law Carl Bosch adopts the Haber process for commercial production. The Bosch process contributes to the manufacturing of explosives for the German war effort in World War I. Haber receives the Nobel Prize in chemistry in 1918; Bosch shares the Nobel Prize in chemistry with Friedrich Bergius in 1931 for his work on chemical high-pressure methods.

G. METEOROLOGY: *Greenhouse Effect*
Svante Arrhenius describes the "greenhouse effect" that occurs when heat from the sun reflecting from the earth is absorbed by atmospheric carbon dioxide, thus trapping heat and causing a warming effect.

H. PHYSICS: *Geiger Counter*
Hans Wilhelm Geiger, a student of Ernest Rutherford, develops a device for detecting alpha particles. In 1928, working with Walther Müller, Geiger improves the device, subsequently called the Geiger-Müller counter, for the detection of beta and gamma rays.

I. TECHNOLOGY: *Automobiles*
The first Model T Ford automobile is produced in Detroit, Michigan.

J. THE ARTS: *Literature*
- E. M. Forster publishes his novel *A Room with a View*.
- Kenneth Grahame writes *The Wind in the Willows*.

A. BACTERIAL TAXONOMY: *Classification*

Segurd Orla-Jensen proposes a new system for classification of the bacteria based on what he considers to be primitive or advanced characteristics emphasizing physiological differences. Several of his new generic names replace older established terms.

B. BACTERIAL STRUCTURE: *Nucleus in Bacteria*

A. Amato argues that young cells of *Bacillus mycoides* have a single large nucleus that evolves into numerous chromidia in older cells. (See 1888 C, 1897 B, 1935 B, 1942 B.)

C. BACTERIAL STRUCTURE: *Capsule Stain*

R. Burri's use of a preparation of India ink for microscopic observation of bacterial capsules introduces a simple means for study of the shape and size of extracellular capsular material. The procedure is modified in 1911 by H. Preisz.

D. BACTERIAL DISEASE: *Rocky Mountain Spotted Fever*

Howard Ricketts suggests that a microorganism found in the blood of animals infected with Rocky Mountain spotted fever may be the causative agent. In his honor, the group of bacteria to which this organism is assigned is later named *Rickettsia*. Ricketts dies in 1910 of typhus fever, another rickettsial disease that he had investigated. (See 1916 C, 1929 E, 1951 A.)

E. BACTERIAL DISEASE: *Typhus Fever*

Charles Jules Henri Nicolle shows that typhus fever is transmitted from person to person by the body louse. Nicolle is awarded the 1928 Nobel Prize in physiology or medicine for this research, which opened the way to developing methods for preventing infection.

F. VIRAL DISEASE: *Poliomyelitis*

Simon Flexner and Paul A. Lewis, following Landsteiner's experiments in 1908, successfully filter poliovirus. After infecting monkeys by several routes—intraperitoneal, subcutaneous, intravenous, and intracerebral—they discover that the rhesus monkey used in Flexner's experiments is insusceptible to infection with polio administered orally. Flexner's conviction that the virus is strictly neurotropic works to the detriment of Carl Kling's and his colleagues' observations in 1912 of the poliovirus in the intestinal tract. (See 1908 B, 1912 B, 1936 F.)

G. IMMUNOLOGY: *Tetanus Toxin-Antitoxin*

Theobald Smith shows that a mixture of toxin and antitoxin (TAT) can be used to immunize humans against diphtheria because it reduces local reactions that are observed with the use of chemically prepared diphtheria toxoid. TAT is not put into use until 1913. (See 1913 A, 1914 E.)

H. GENETICS: *Terminology*

Wilhelm Ludwig Johannsen suggests replacing the term "Mendelian factor" with the word "gene." He also distinguishes between "genotype," the genetic material, and "phenotype," the expression of genes. William Bateson introduces the terms "genetics," "F_1" and "F_2" generations, "zygote," "homozygote," "heterozygote," and "allemorph" or "allele."

I. BIOCHEMISTRY: *Ribonucleic Acid (RNA) and Deoxyribonucleic Acid (DNA)*

Phoebus Aaron Theodor Levene and Walter Abraham Jacobs identify the sugar *d*-ribose (now D-ribose) as being a component of yeast nucleic acid. In 1929, Levene finds deoxyribose in thymus nucleic acid, thus establishing the terminology ribonucleic acid (RNA) and deoxyribonucleic acid (DNA). After 1909, he supports the idea that yeast nucleic acid is composed of a tetranucleotide composed of the four nitrogenous bases—adenine, guanine, cytosine, and uracil—whereas thymus nucleic acid contains thymine in place of uracil. The tetranucleotide concept delays the acceptance of DNA as a component of genes until Erwin Chargaff establishes the molar ratios of purine and pyrimidine bases found in nucleic acids. (See 1929 L, 1950 L, 1953 O.)

J. TECHNOLOGY: *Plastics*

Leo H. Baekeland obtains a patent on a material that he names Bakelite, the first plastic substance to be commercially manufactured.

K. SOCIETY AND POLITICS

- Robert Edwin Peary, Matthew Alexander Henson, and three other men reach the North Pole.
- The National Association for the Advancement of Colored People (NAACP) is organized with an initial membership of fewer than 60.

L. THE ARTS: *Architecture*

Architect Frank Lloyd Wright builds a unique house for Frederick G. Robie in Chicago. The Robie house's first-time features include being constructed on a slab foundation, having a garage as part of the structure, and indirect lighting.

1910

A. BACTERIAL PHYSIOLOGY: *Coliform Bacteria*

C. Revis uses the term "coliform group" in reference to the physiological properties of the gram-negative group of intestinal bacteria and their close relatives, *Bacterium coli* (*Escherichia coli*), *Bacterium typhosum* (*Salmonella typhi*), and others. This group of bacteria continues to be referred to as the "colon group" or the "colon-typhoid group" until the late 1930s. R. S. Breed and J. F. Norton reintroduce the term in 1937, and it is the title of a review article by Leland W. Parr in 1939. (See 1937 B.)

B. BACTERIAL DISEASE: *Syphilis*

Paul Ehrlich reports success with the 606th compound he tests while searching for a treatment of syphilis. This so-called magic bullet is arsphenamine, an organic arsenic-containing molecule, marketed under the names Salvarsan and 606. A more soluble form, Neosalvarsan, is introduced in 1912.

1910 (continued)

C. VIRAL DISEASE: *Fowlpox Virus*

Francesco Sanfelice reports that the fowlpox agent can be extracted by the same methods used to extract "nucleoproteid." He concludes that the agent must be caused by a "nucleoproteid" toxin.

D. BIOCHEMISTRY: *Indophenol Oxidase*

Joseph Kastle names the indophenol enzyme "indophenol oxidase." This enzyme, which Otto Warburg later calls *Atmungsferment,* is renamed cytochrome oxidase in 1938 by David Keilin. (See 1895 F, 1895 G, 1924 C, 1938 F.)

E. GENETICS: *Sex–Linked Genes*

Thomas Hunt Morgan discovers sex-linked genes in his study of the fruit fly *Drosophila.* Morgan receives the 1933 Nobel Prize in physiology or medicine for his research on genetic processes. (See 1911 G, 1915 D.)

F. BIOCHEMISTRY: *Manometry*

Thomas Gregor Brodie introduces the use of a manometer for studies on respiration. (See 1926 L.)

G. BIOCHEMISTRY: *the Langmuir Trough*

Irving Langmuir invents a flat, shallow trough to study the behavior of long-chain fatty acids and other lipids by spreading them on the surface of water contained in the trough. A movable barrier and a torsion wire device enable him to compress the film of lipid in a reproducible way. His studies contribute to concepts of lipid orientation in membranes. Langmuir receives the 1932 Nobel Prize in chemistry for his work on surface chemistry. (See 1894 G, 1925 E, 1934 G, 1960 O, 1972 K.)

H. SOCIETY AND POLITICS

Daniel Carter Beard, who wrote *Boy Pioneers and Sons of Daniel Boone,* founds the Boy Scouts of America following the establishment of the Boy Scouts of Britain 2 years earlier by Robert Stephenson Baden-Powell.

1911

A. BACTERIOLOGICAL TECHNIQUE: *Direct Microscopic Counts*

Robert S. Breed introduces a method for the direct microscopic counting of bacteria in milk that requires measurement of the size of the field of view. The Breed count method is widely adopted, and its results are compared with counts made by the standard plate count procedure. (See 1881 A.)

B. MICROBIAL PHYSIOLOGY: *Fermentation/Pyruvic Acid*

Carl Alexander Neuberg's laboratory and, independently, Otto Neubauer and Konrad Fromherz show that yeast ferment pyruvic acid and suggest that it is an intermediate in the yeast alcoholic fermentation. In 1913, Auguste Fernbach and Moise Schoen prove pyruvic acid to be an intermediate.

C. BACTERIAL DISEASE: *Tularemia*

George Walter McCoy and Charles W. Chapin discover the bacterial cause of tularemia while studying the transmission of plague by rodents. Both the species name and the name of the disease are derived from Tulare County, California, where the first isolates of the bacterium are obtained. McCoy and Chapin apply the name *Bacterium tularense* (also called *Brucella tularense* and *Pasteurella tularensis*), but it is currently called *Francisella tularensis* after Edward Francis, who carried out extensive research on the disease in the 1920s.

D. VIRAL DISEASE: *Poliomyelitis*
An official count of 3,840 cases of poliomyelitis occur in Sweden, making this the largest epidemic of the disease ever seen in one area. One investigator, W. Wernstedt, noting that localities struck by the disease in one year are likely to have few cases the next year, concludes that inapparent infection acquired during an epidemic confers immunity and is responsible for the occurrence of new cases among infants and young children. This observation, confirmed by others, leads to the use of the term "infantile paralysis."

E. VIRAL DISEASE: *Rous Sarcoma Virus*
Francis Peyton Rous's discovery that a virus causes a solid tumor, a sarcoma, in chickens is almost totally rejected by other researchers. In 1908, Bernhard Laurits Frederick (Oluf) Bang and Vilhelm Ellerman reported a viral cause of leukemia in chickens, but since leukemia was not regarded as a cancer at the time, this report did not cause a negative response. For his discovery of the Rous sarcoma virus, Rous is honored 55 years later with the 1966 Nobel Prize in physiology or medicine, which is shared with Charles B. Huggins for his work on hormone treatment of cancer.

F. IMMUNOLOGY: *Histamine*
Henry H. Dale and Patrick Laidlaw report studies on the physiological activity of β–imidazolylethylamine. This substance, later given the name histamine, was originally extracted from ergot, a fungal food-poisoning agent, but Dale and Laidlaw prepare it from histidine for these experiments. The storage of histamine in mast cells, basophils, and platelets remains unknown for 40 years. Dale had shown it to reverse the effects of epinephrine (adrenaline), and with Laidlaw, studies its anaphylactic effect and related physiological changes. For this work and for research on acetylcholine in animals, Dale shares the 1936 Nobel Prize in physiology or medicine with Otto Loewi, who pioneered research on the role of acetylcholine in transmission of nerve impulses.

G. GENETICS: *Linkage and Crossing Over*
In studies of sex-linked genes in *Drosophila,* Thomas Hunt Morgan discovers groups of genes that are inherited together in what are later called linkage groups. Morgan also notes that in some experiments, genes that are part of linkage groups do not segregate together. During meiosis, he suggests, two chromosomes cross over and exchange genes. Working in Morgan's "fly room" after 1910 are several persons who later establish outstanding research careers: two undergraduates, Alfred H. Sturtevant and Calvin B. Bridges, and one graduate student, Hermann Joseph Muller. (See 1911 H, 1931 L.)

1911 *(continued)*

H. GENETICS: *Chromosome Map*

Alfred Henry Sturtevant, while still an undergraduate working in Thomas Hunt Morgan's laboratory, using the idea that the distance of spatial separation of pairs of genes on the chromosome determines the frequency of crossing over, produces the first chromosome map of the fruit fly, *Drosophila melanogaster*. He publishes his work in 1913. (See 1911 G, 1931 L.)

I. BIOCHEMISTRY: *Glycolysis*

The term "glycolysis" was first used in the 1890s in reference to the anaerobic degradation of glucose yielding lactic acid. In 1911, Otto Fritz Meyerhof begins his research on glycolysis using calorimetric measurements of muscle contraction to determine whether the energy liberated will account for heat evolved by living animals. He also studies how the potential energy of nutrients can account for work done by cells. Over the next 3 decades he makes major contributions to understanding the pathway of glycolysis and energy metabolism. Meyerhof shares the 1922 Nobel Prize in physiology or medicine with Archibald Vivian Hill. (See 1912 D.)

J. BIOCHEMISTRY: *Oxidation/Reduction*

Alexsei Nikolaevich Bach proposes a reducing system (Redukase) that activates hydrogen. (See 1912 E, 1914 H, 1924 C.)

K. BIOCHEMISTRY: *Donnan Equilibrium*

Frederick George Donnan describes the Donnan equilibrium, a membrane equilibrium phenomenon involving the passage of ions across a semipermeable membrane.

L. PHYSICS: *Atomic Structure*

Ernest Rutherford develops a theory of atomic structure, describing the atom as having a heavy nucleus surrounded by empty space containing electrons. Niels Henrik David Bohr extends the theory in 1913. Rutherford receives the Nobel Prize in chemistry in 1908; Bohr is awarded the Nobel Prize in physics in 1922.

M. PHYSICS: *the Electron*

Robert Andrews Millikan calculates the charge on the electron. Millikan receives the 1923 Nobel Prize in physics for this work.

N. SOCIETY AND POLITICS

An expedition led by Roald Amundsen reaches the South Pole. (See 1912 I.)

O. THE ARTS: *Music*

The opera *Der Rosenkavalier* by Richard Strauss is performed.

P. THE ARTS: *Literature*

Edith Wharton's novel *Ethan Frome* is published.

Q. THE ARTS: *Art*

Marc Chagall paints *I and the Village*.

A. BACTERIAL PHYSIOLOGY: *Acetone–Butanol Fermentation*

While working in England in commercial fermentations, Chaim Azriel Weizmann isolates a bacterium that produces large amounts of acetone by fermentation of starches. He names it *Bacillus granulobacter pectinovorum,* but the name is changed to *Clostridium acetobutylicum* in 1926 by Elizabeth McCoy, E. B. Fred, W. H. Peterson, and E. G. Hastings. At the beginning of World War I, there is an increased need for acetone in the manufacture of cordite, an explosive powder that is pressed into cords after being gelatinized by acetone. In England, Canada, and the United States, Weizmann's bacterium is put into use in large-scale fermentation of maize to produce acetone. The Daniel Sieff Institute of Science in Israel, founded in 1934, is later called the Weizmann Institute. Weizmann becomes the first president of Israel in 1948.

B. VIRAL DISEASE: *Poliovirus*

Studying fatal cases of poliomyelitis in Sweden, Carl Kling, A. Petterson, and W. Wernstedt report the recovery of poliovirus from both the intestinal wall and intestinal contents. The researchers also isolate the virus from healthy family members of patients and from members of the general public. Their work is not widely accepted because of Simon Flexner's belief that the virus is strictly neurotropic. (See 1908 B, 1909 F, 1949 I, 1954 L, 1959 M.)

C. VIRAL DISEASE: *Hepatitis*

Edward Alfred Cockayne describes "epidemic catarrhal jaundice" and concludes that it and related diseases are caused by an infectious agent. He suggests that "infective hepatitis" would be a more appropriate name for the disease. (See 1885 F, 1926 E, 1943 E, 1962 Q.)

D. BIOCHEMISTRY: *Glycolysis*

Archibald Vivian Hill uses a microcalorimeter to measure the energy reactions of muscle contraction. He shows two phases of heat production, initial heat and recovery heat, which are now known to correspond to the production of lactic acid from glucose and the reverse process of gluconeogenesis. His research has a marked influence on biochemical studies carried out by other researchers. Hill shares the 1922 Nobel Prize in physiology or medicine with Otto Meyerhof. (See 1911 I.)

E. BIOCHEMISTRY: *Dehydrogenases*

Heinrich Otto Wieland publishes a number of papers between 1912 and 1922 on dehydrases, later called dehydrogenases to avoid confusion with enzymes that catalyze the removal of water from a compound. (See 1917 G, 1924 D.)

F. BIOCHEMISTRY: *Peroxidase*

Between 1912 and 1926, Richard Martin Willstätter studies horseradish peroxidase and obtains it in a highly purified form.

1912 (continued)

G. BIOCHEMISTRY: *Vitamins*

Casimir Funk introduces the term "vitamine" under the mistaken belief that the substance that cures beriberi is an amine. Jack Cecil Drummond changes the name to vitamin. In his book *Die Vitamine,* Funk suggests that beriberi, scurvy, pellagra, and probably rickets are caused by dietary deficiencies of as yet unidentified substances present in trace amounts in food. Funk and Frederick Gowland Hopkins are often credited with developing the concept of vitamins.

H. TECHNOLOGY: *the* Titanic

The steamship *S.S. Titanic,* the world's largest passenger ship, touted as being unsinkable, while on its maiden voyage strikes an iceberg and sinks. Of the 2,224 passengers, only 711 survive.

I. SOCIETY AND POLITICS

• Theodore Roosevelt, who was U.S. president from 1901 to 1909, establishes an independent political party to run for reelection against incumbent president William Howard Taft. The news media apply the name "Bull Moose Party" because he declares himself to be "fit as a bull moose." The election is won by Woodrow Wilson, who serves until 1921.

• Robert Scott and four others reach the South Pole a little over a month after the Roald Amundsen expedition. All five members of the Scott expedition die as they attempt to return to the coast. (See 1911 N.)

• In Savannah, Georgia, Juliette Gordon Low establishes the Girl Guides, renamed the Girl Scouts of America in 1913.

J. THE ARTS: *Movies*

Queen Elizabeth, made in France, is the first full-length film to be shown in the United States. Movies made this year in the United States are *Her First Biscuit* starring Mary Pickford and *The Musketeers of Pig Alley* starring Lillian Gish.

1913

A. IMMUNOLOGY: *Diphtheria*

Emil von Behring begins the use of toxin-antitoxin vaccines (TAT) to inoculate diphtheria in humans. (See 1909 G, 1914 E.)

B. IMMUNOLOGY: *the Schick Test*

Bela Schick develops a skin test to determine susceptibility to diphtheria. The Schick test involves an interdermal injection of a small amount of toxin, which combines with antitoxin to cause a localized inflammatory reaction.

C. VIROLOGY: *Tissue Culture*

Edna Steinhardt, C. Israel, and R. H. Lambert grow vaccinia virus in tissue cultures of rabbit or guinea pig corneal tissue. (See 1907 G, 1917 D, 1928 E, 1931 F, 1933 E, 1936 L.)

D. PHYSIOLOGY: *Cholesterol and Fats*

After feeding rats large amounts of animal fats and cholesterol, Nikolai Anichkov finds that they develop arteriosclerosis. (See 1901 K, 1953 U.)

E. BIOCHEMISTRY: *Fermentation Intermediates*

Carl Alexander Neuberg notes that many of the intermediates in the alcoholic fermentation and in the lactic acid fermentation in muscle are the same. (See 1926 B.)

F. BIOCHEMISTRY: *Michaelis–Menten Equation*

Leonor Michaelis and Maud Leonora Menten analyze the rate-controlling steps of enzyme reactions and formulate an equation relating enzyme concentration with substrate concentration. The Michaelis-Menten equation becomes a standard for studies of enzymatic reactions. (See 1934 L.)

G. CHEMISTRY: *Chemical Isotopes*

After showing that a radioactive element may have more than one atomic weight, Frederick Soddy proposes that atoms can be chemically identical and yet have different weights. He calls such elements "isotopes" or "isotopic elements."

H. MATHEMATICS: Principia Mathematica

Bertrand Russell and Alfred North Whitehead complete their three-volume work *Principia Mathematica,* an attempt to use logic to derive all of mathematics.

I. SOCIETY AND POLITICS

The Sixteenth Amendment to the U.S. Constitution permits Congress to levy income taxes on persons earning above $3,000 per year.

J. CULTURE: *Architecture*

The newly constructed Woolworth Building in New York City becomes the world's tallest office building at 232 meters. (See 1889 K, 1930 H, 1931 N, 1972 P.)

K. THE ARTS: *Literature*

• Marcel Proust publishes *Du côté de chez Swann* (*Swann's Way*), the first of eight novels that appear under the general title *À la recherche du temps perdu* (*Remembrance of Things Past*).
• Sax Rohmer writes *Dr. Fu Manchu.*

L. THE ARTS: *Music*

Igor Stravinsky's ballet *Le Sacre du Printemps* (*The Rite of Spring*) with choreography by Vaslav Nijinsky premiers in Paris, beginning a new period of music. However, audiences are outraged by the unusual dissonances and rhythms.

1914

A. BACTERIAL DISEASE: *Contagious Abortion*

Jacob Traum discovers the microorganism that causes contagious abortion in swine and names it *Bacillus suis.* This organism is later placed in the genus *Brucella,* which K. Meyer and E. B. Shaw name in 1920, following the work of Alice Catherine Evans in 1918. (See 1877 D, 1897 D, 1918 C, 1920 A.)

B. BACTERIAL DISEASE: *Bubonic Plague*

Arthur William Bacot and Charles James Martin discover how the rat flea is infected by the plague bacillus, *Pasteurella pestis,* and transmitted to a new host. They demonstrate the role of regurgitation of blood and plague bacillus during the flea's feeding.

C. BACTERIAL DISEASE: *Staphylococcal Food Poisoning*
M. A. Barber demonstrates that soluble toxin released by staphylococci causes food poisoning. His careful study remains largely unappreciated until the work of G. M. Dack in 1930. (See 1888 D, 1895 C, 1930 B.)

D. BACTERIAL DISEASE: *Typhus Fever*
At the beginning of World War I, typhus fever appears first in the Serbian army and then in a general epidemic. Over a 6-month period, 150,000 persons die. Nearly all of 400 doctors in Serbia contract the disease, and 126 die. The assassination of Austrian Archduke Franz Ferdinand in Bosnia precipitates a declaration of war, but Austria does not invade Serbia at this time because of the typhus epidemic.

E. IMMUNOLOGY: *Diphtheria*
William Hallock Park begins the use of toxin–antitoxin vaccines against diphtheria in New York City. This work begins the practice of routinely vaccinating children against diphtheria across the United States. (See 1909 G, 1913 A.)

F. BIOCHEMISTRY: *Fermentation/Fructose Diphosphate*
Gustav Embden's laboratory shows that the addition of the Harden–Young ester, fructose diphosphate (fructose 1,6-bisphosphate), from a soluble yeast extract to a soluble muscle extract fermentation increases the rate of lactic acid production. (See 1906 J, 1928 F, 1933 I.)

G. BIOCHEMISTRY: *Fermentation/Glucose Monophosphate*
Arthur Harden and Robert Robison detect a hexosemonophosphate in alcoholic fermentations. This compound, which becomes known as the Robison ester, is identified in 1931 by Earl Judson King and Robison as glucose monophosphate. (See 1931 K.)

H. BIOCHEMISTRY: *Iron Catalyzes Respiration*
Otto Warburg concludes that iron is a catalyst of cell respiration. (See 1924 C, 1925 G, 1928 K, 1938 F.)

I. PHYSICS: *X-Ray Spectra*
Henry Gwyn Jeffreys Moseley measures the X-ray spectra of 30 metals and shows that the spectra vary according to their position in the Mendeleyev periodic table of elements. These data lead to a revision of the periodic table with the use of atomic numbers rather than atomic weights. (See 1869 G.)

J. PSYCHOLOGY: *Intelligence Quotient*
William Stern suggests that an intelligence quotient, or IQ, of a child can be determined by dividing the mental age, as determined by the Binet and Simon tests, by the chronological age. In 1916, Lewis Madison Terman, at Stanford University, revises the Binet-Simon test to produce the widely used Stanford-Binet test. (See 1905 M.)

K. TECHNOLOGY: *Canals*

The Panama Canal, first begun in 1880, is officially opened.

L. TECHNOLOGY: *Sewage Treatment*

In Manchester, England, a plant is built that is designed to treat sewage with bacteria.

M. SOCIETY AND POLITICS

• World War I begins when archduke Franz Ferdinand and his wife are killed by a Serbian assassin in Sarajevo, Bosnia. Austria-Hungary declares war on Serbia, followed by Germany's declaration of war on Russia and France and the invasion of Belgium. Britain declares war on Germany.

• Margaret Higgins Sanger publishes *The Woman Rebel,* introducing the term "birth control." She also publishes a brochure entitled *Family Limitation,* which advocates contraception.

N. THE ARTS: *Literature*

• James Joyce publishes *Dubliners* and *A Portrait of the Artist as a Young Man.*

• Edgar Rice Burroughs publishes *Tarzan of the Apes.*

O. THE ARTS: *Theater*

The play *Pygmalion* by George Bernard Shaw opens in London. In 1956, it is transformed into a musical version as *My Fair Lady.*

1915

A. BACTERIAL PHYSIOLOGY: *Methyl Red Test*

William Mansfield Clark and H. A. Lubs report that detecting pH change by the indicator methyl red is useful in distinguishing between the coli-aerogenes group of bacteria, with *Escherichia coli* giving a positive reaction (low pH) and *Aerobacter* (*Enterobacter*) *aerogenes* giving a negative reaction. (See 1898 A, 1906 B, Parr, 1936.)

B. BACTERIAL INSECTICIDES: *Parasporal Body*

Ernst Berliner isolates the insect pathogen *Bacillus thuringiensis,* named for Thüringen, the German province that is the source of the insects examined, and notices a *Restkörper* or parasporal body inside the sporangium with the spore. Later work shows that the structure is within the sporangium but not inside the spore itself. Shigetane Ishiwata isolated this bacterium in 1902 but did not give it a scientific name. (See 1902 E, 1951 F, 1953 J, 1954 H.)

C. BACTERIOPHAGE: *Discovery*

Frederick William Twort reports that a lytic phenomenon in cultures of micrococcus may be an ultramicroscopic bacterial virus. Nevertheless, he believes the responsible agent to be a lytic enzyme that induces other bacteria in the culture to produce the same enzyme. The phenomenon is later independently discovered by Felix d'Herelle, who coins the name "bacteriophage." (See 1898 F, 1917 C, 1922 E, 1925 C.)

D. GENETICS: *Chromosomes as Agents of Inheritance*

In *The Mechanism of Mendelian Heredity,* Thomas Hunt Morgan, Calvin Bridges, Alfred Sturtevant, and Hermann Joseph Muller present their interpretation of experiments with *Drosophila* genetics as a chromosome theory.

1915 (continued)

Many geneticists continue to resist the concept that the "factors" of inheritance can be assigned to "particles of chromatin."

E. PHYSICS: *General Relativity*
Albert Einstein publishes his paper on the theory of general relativity. (See 1905 J, 1905 K.)

F. TECHNOLOGY: *Sonar*
Paul Langevin devises a piezoelectric transducer that can detect the presence and location of objects submerged under water. Called "sonar" (for sound navigation ranging), it was originally intended to be used to detect icebergs, but during World War I it came into use to detect submarines.

G. SOCIETY AND POLITICS
World War I continues with widespread fighting on both the eastern and western fronts of Germany. A torpedo launched by a German submarine sinks the passenger ship *Lusitania,* killing nearly 2,000 persons. Italy enters the war as an ally of Germany. The German army uses chlorine gas, the first use of a poisonous gas in history.

H. THE ARTS: *Literature*
W. Somerset Maugham publishes the novel *Of Human Bondage.*

I. THE ARTS: *Movies*
Filmmaker D. W. Griffith produces the controversial movie *Birth of a Nation.*

1916

A. BACTERIAL TAXONOMY: *Classification*
In the period 1916 to 1918, Robert Earle Buchanan publishes several articles on the nomenclature and classification of the bacteria. He places the bacteria in the class *Schizomycetes* and lists six orders.

B. BACTERIAL PHYSIOLOGY: *Disinfection*
W. A. Jacobs and colleagues study the bactericidal properties of hexamethylene-tetramine compounds, noting the effectiveness of the quaternary ammonium compounds in killing a wide variety of bacteria. Practical use of these compounds does not begin until after the work of Gerhard Domagk in 1935. (See 1935 C.)

C. BACTERIAL DISEASE: *Typhus Fever*
Henrique da Rocha Lima identifies the causal agent of typhus fever. He names the organism *Rickettsia prowazekii* after Howard Ricketts and Stanilaus von Prowazek, both of whom died as a result of infection contracted while studying typhus fever. (See 1909 D, 1929 E, 1951 A.)

D. IMMUNOLOGY: *Weil–Felix Reaction*
E. Weil and A. Felix discover that antibodies formed in some rickettsial infections cause the agglutination of certain strains of *Proteus* called the "X strains." Since the reactions occur only when the O antigens are exposed for combination with antibodies, the strains are later referred to as *Proteus* OX strains. (See 1903 G, 1920 C, 1921 B.)

E. VIRAL DISEASE: *Poliomyelitis*

A major epidemic of poliomyelitis in the northeastern United States causes approximately 6,000 deaths and 27,000 persons to be paralyzed, many of whom are adults. The impact of the epidemic is intensified in 1921 when Franklin Delano Roosevelt, an unsuccessful candidate for vice president that year and president from 1933 to 1945, contracts polio and is left with almost complete paralysis of both legs.

F. CHEMISTRY: *the Covalent Bond*

Gilbert Newton Lewis, in his study of the electronic theory of valence in chemical compounds, discusses the concept of the shared electron pair, or covalent bond. He explains his ideas more fully in his 1923 book *Valence and the Structure of Atoms and Molecules* and proposes the octet theory of arrangement of electrons in atoms and chemical combinations, later known as the Lewis-Langmuir theory after Irving Langmuir publicizes the concept in his talks.

G. SCIENTIFIC PUBLICATION: Journal of Bacteriology

The Society of American Bacteriologists publishes the first issue of the *Journal of Bacteriology,* edited by C.-E. A. Winslow. (See 1899 G.)

H. SOCIETY AND POLITICS

- On the German western front in World War I, a battle at the Somme River lasts about 140 days with more than 1,300,000 casualties.
- After the Mexican revolutionary Francisco "Pancho" Villa conducts raids in New Mexico, U.S. general John J. Pershing leads a force to capture him "dead or alive." Villa evades capture.

1917

A. BACTERIAL TAXONOMY: *Classification*

A committee formed by the Society of American Bacteriologists, chaired by C.-E. A. Winslow, publishes a preliminary report on "Characterization and Classification of Bacterial Types." A final report of this committee appears in 1920 and is followed in 1923 by a manual of classification, *Bergey's Manual of Determinative Bacteriology.* (See 1923 A.)

B. MICROBIAL FERMENTATION: *Citric Acid*

In 1893, C. Wehmer discovers that fungi produce citric acid. He later attempts large-scale production without success. However, in 1917, J. N. Currie finds that the mold *Aspergillus niger* produces appreciable quantities of citric acid at low pH in a growth medium containing sucrose, ammonium nitrate, and potassium phosphate. Citric acid production by extraction from fruit is now replaced by industrial production with molds.

C. BACTERIOPHAGE: *Discovery*

Félix d'Herelle, independent of Frederick Twort's observation in 1915, discovers a bacterial virus that lyses the dysentery bacillus. Giving it the name "bacteriophage," he also notes that it causes the appearance of clear zones called "plaques" in a film of bacterial growth on an agar plate. d'Herelle believes that bacteriophages are parasitic agents that, upon entering a susceptible cell, cause it to lyse, thus releasing additional bacterio-

1917 *(continued)*

phages that penetrate other cells. d'Herelle thinks that bacteriophages play a role in immunity and can be used to treat disease. (See 1898 F, 1915 C, 1922 E, 1925 C, 1929 D.)

D. VIROLOGY: *Tissue Culture*

Alexis Carrel improves on the earlier tissue culture work of Ross Harrison and of Edna Steinhardt and coworkers by using blood serum instead of lymph. Carrel also shows that viruses can be grown in tissue culture, but virologists do not immediately take advantage of this observation. (See 1907 G, 1913 C, 1928 E, 1931 F, 1933 E, 1936 L, 1948 F.)

E. IMMUNOLOGY: *Haptens and Epitopes*

Karl Landsteiner publishes early papers on the antigenicity of proteins modified by acyl and diazonium substitutions. He finds that, although the small structures cannot cause antibody formation by themselves, they can nevertheless combine with antibody made against the entire substituted protein antigen. He refers to the combining groups as "determinants" (now called epitopes) and the supporting structure as "hapten."

F. BIOLOGY: *Growth and Form of Organisms*

D'Arcy Wentworth Thompson publishes *On Growth and Form,* the first important discussion of how growth rates and sizes affect organisms.

G. BIOCHEMISTRY: *Oxidation/Reduction*

Torsten Ludwig Thunberg investigates Heinrich Wieland's concept of enzymes that oxidize certain compounds and transfer the electrons to acceptor molecules. He develops the Thunberg vacuum tube for use in his work. Over a period of years, Thunberg and Wieland develop a theory of respiration that leads to controversy with Otto Warburg. (See 1912 E, 1920 E, 1924 C.)

H. SOCIETY AND POLITICS

• The United States declares war on Germany and actively enters World War I. General John J. Pershing is named the leader of the American expeditionary force.

• The Bolsheviks seize control of the Russian government and begin calling themselves the Communist Party. The government is headed by Nikolai Lenin. (See 1923 K.)

I. THE ARTS: *Literature*

T. S. Eliot includes "The Love Song of J. Alfred Prufrock" in *Prufrock and Other Observations.*

1918

A. BACTERIAL PHYSIOLOGY: *the Growth Curve*

The first detailed analysis of the growth of bacteria in culture is published by Robert Earle Buchanan. He discusses a generalized growth curve employing a semilogarithmic plot of the logarithm of the numbers of bacteria per unit volume against time. Buchanan describes seven phases of growth: initial stationary phase, lag phase or positive growth acceleration, logarithmic phase, negative growth acceleration, maximum stationary phase, accelerated death rate, and logarithmic death phase. A detailed mathematical analysis is presented for each phase of the curve.

B. BACTERIAL PHYSIOLOGY: *Starch Hydrolysis Test*
P. W. Allen reports a method for distinguishing among bacterial species based on hydrolysis of starch contained in an agar growth medium. Addition of a solution of iodine to the cultures causes the development of the blue color of the iodine–starch reaction, whereas zones around starch-hydrolyzing colonies remain clear.

C. BACTERIAL DISEASE: *Undulant Fever and Contagious Abortion*
Alice Catherine Evans shows that the microorganisms that cause undulant (Malta) fever, contagious abortion in cattle, and contagious abortion in swine are closely related. She also notes that these bacteria are bacilli, not micrococci as David Bruce originally thought. In 1920, on the basis of Evans's work, K. Meyer and E. B. Shaw propose the generic name Brucella for these organisms. (See 1877 D, 1897 D, 1914 A, 1920 A.)

D. VIRAL DISEASE: *Influenza*
In 1918 and 1919, influenza infects an estimated 500 million persons worldwide, causing at least 25 million deaths, roughly equivalent to 1% of the world's population at this time. This pandemic, which presumably began in China, is popularly called "Spanish influenza," apparently because of its long period of activity in Spain. One of the earliest cases in the United States is reported in Kansas in March 1918. Because the influenza virus is not isolated until 1933, no examples of the virus responsible for this pandemic exist. However, this virus should be designated an H1N1 strain, according to terminology adopted in 1980 for the antigenic properties of the surface antigens hemagglutinin and neuraminidase and based on testing antibodies of persons who survived the epidemic. (See 1889 E, 1892 B, 1931 F, 1933 D, 1940 K, 1957 J.)

E. BIOLOGY: *Embryology*
Hans Spemann discovers the "organizer function" of developing embryonic tissue. He finds that organizers in the tissue, not in individual cells, influence the type of development that takes place. Spemann receives the 1935 Nobel Prize in physiology or medicine for this work.

F. FERMENTATION: *Fructose 6-Phosphate*
Carl Neuberg synthesizes fructose 6-phosphate, the "Neuberg ester." In 1932 Robert Robison shows that it is present in the alcoholic fermentation. (See 1931 K.)

G. SOCIETY AND POLITICS
In the final major battle of World War I, the Allied Forces attack along Germany's western front along the Meuse River and Argonne Forest. Germany sues for an armistice on November 4, and the agreement ending World War I is signed on November 11. The Treaty of Versailles is signed in 1919.

1918 *(continued)*

H. THE ARTS: *Literature*
• *Poems* by Gerard Manley Hopkins, who died in 1889, are collected and published by another poet, Robert Bridges.
• Vicente Blasco-Ibañez publishes the novel *The Four Horsemen of the Apocalypse.*

1919

A. BACTERIAL TAXONOMY: *Classification of Streptococci*
Following Hugo Schottmüller's earlier suggestion and experiments done with Theobald Smith, James H. Brown divides the genus *Streptococcus* into "alpha," "beta," and "gamma" types based on hemolytic reactions of colonies grown on blood agar. (See 1933 A.)

B. BACTERIAL PHYSIOLOGY: *Lactic Acid Bacteria*
Segurd Orla-Jensen publishes a monograph on the lactic acid bacteria, establishing the basic criteria for inclusion of types of bacteria in this group. In 1923, he proposes the family name *Lactobacteriaceae.* (See 1893 A.)

C. BACTERIAL DISEASE: *Infectious Abortion*
Theobald Smith and Marian S. Taylor report the results of a study of a spirillum associated with infectious abortion in cattle. Concluding that 21 of 22 strains are identical, they propose the name *Vibrio fetus.* The organism is later reclassified into the genus *Campylobacter.* (See 1963 A, 1973 F, 1980 I.)

D. VIRAL DISEASE: *Yellow Fever*
Hideyo Noguchi isolates a bacterium from the blood of a patient with yellow fever in Ecuador. He names the organism *Leptospira icteroides* and claims that it is the cause of yellow fever, challenging the earlier claim of Walter Reed and James Carroll that yellow fever is caused by a virus. In 1926, Max Theiler (who develops a yellow fever vaccine in 1936) and Andrew Sellards conclude that Noguchi's bacterium does not cause yellow fever and is identical to *Leptospira icterohaemorrhagiae,* the causative agent of Weil's disease. Noguchi is not convinced and goes to Accra, West Africa, in 1927 to study a presumed outbreak of yellow fever. He fails to recover *Leptospira* but contracts yellow fever himself and dies in 1928. In addition to Noguchi, four other researchers die of yellow fever during 1927 and 1928: William A. Young, Paul Lewis, Theodore H. Hayne, and Adrian Stokes, who, in 1927, discovers that rhesus monkeys can be infected with yellow fever. Another 27 researchers (including Max Theiler) are infected but survive. (See 1899 D, 1901 F, 1929 G, 1936 L.)

E. ETHOLOGY: *Bee Communication*
Karl von Frisch describes how bees communicate the location of a food source by performing dances on the comb. Frisch shares the 1973 Nobel Prize in physiology or medicine with Konrad Lorenz and Nikolaas Tinbergen, leaders in the field of ethology. (See 1935 N.)

F. SOCIETY AND POLITICS
The Treaty of Versailles at the end of World War I assigns total responsibility for the war. The delegates from 27 countries form the League of Na-

tions with the goals of disarmament, labor negotiations, and world health. The Soviet Union is admitted to membership in 1934, but the United States never joins. (See 1942 N.)

G. THE ARTS: *Literature*
Sherwood Anderson publishes his collection of short stories, *Winesburg, Ohio.*

1920

A. BACTERIAL DISEASE: Brucella
In honor of David Bruce, who first isolated a member of this group in 1887, Karl F. Meyer and E. B. Shaw propose the generic name *Brucella* for the bacteria that cause infectious abortion and undulant (Malta) fever. (See 1887 D, 1897 D, 1914 A, 1918 C.)

B. BACTERIAL DISEASE: *Typhus Fever*
In the 4 years at the end of World War I, 1918 to 1922, Russia has as many as 30 million cases of typhus fever, causing approximately 3 million deaths.

C. IMMUNOLOGY: *Bacterial Antigen Terminology*
E. Weil and A. Felix, who developed the Weil-Felix reaction for the diagnosis of rickettsial infections, note that motile and nonmotile types of *Proteus* exhibit different types of growth on the surface of agar media. Because the motile strains produce a thin, spreading growth that reminds Weil and Felix of the film of moisture produced by breathing on a mirror or glass plate, they refer to this type of growth as *Hauch* (the German word for breath). The nonmotile types that do not produce the film of growth are described as *ohne Hauch* (without breath). These designations are subsequently used to refer to flagellar antigens as H antigens and nonflagellar or somatic antigens as O antigens. (See 1903 G, 1916 D, 1934 D.)

D. PRION DISEASE: *Creutzfeldt–Jakob Disease*
Hans Gerhard Creutzfeldt, in 1920, and Alfons Maria Jakob, in 1921, report studies of a form of presenile dementia that becomes known as Creutzfeldt-Jakob disease. The disease is regarded as a hereditary condition until Daniel Gajdusek shows its transmissibility in 1968. Creutzfeldt-Jakob disease, now known to be caused by agents called prions, is classified as a type of spongiform encephalopathy similar to scrapie, kuru, and bovine spongiform encephalopathy. (See 1936 J, 1957 K, 1966 L, 1981 K, 1982 M, 1985 H.)

E. BIOCHEMISTRY: *Carbohydrate Oxidation Pathway*
Torsten Thunberg proposes a scheme for the sequence of intermediates in the oxidation of carbohydrates that requires linking two molecules of acetate to form succinate. His concept remains popular until it is replaced by the cycle proposed by Hans Krebs in 1937. (See 1937 J, 1937 K, 1937 L.)

F. TECHNOLOGY: *Radio*
Radio station KDKA in Pittsburgh, the first broadcasting station, announces the results of the presidential election in which Warren Harding defeats James M. Cox.

1920 *(continued)*

G. THE ARTS: *Literature*
- Sinclair Lewis publishes his novel *Main Street.*
- Edith Wharton publishes *The Age of Innocence.*

1921

A. MICROBIAL PHYSIOLOGY: *the Delft School*
When Martinus Beijerinck retires this year, it may be said that a "Delft school" of microbiology has been established. The first of a line of outstanding Dutch microbiologists, Antonie van Leeuwenhoek, was followed by Beijerinck, Albert Jan Kluyver, Cornelius B. van Niel, and Roger Y. Stanier, who is not Dutch but is a student of van Niel.

B. BACTERIAL GENETICS: *Smooth–Rough Variation*
Joseph Arthur Arkwright coins the descriptive terms "smooth" (S) and "rough" (R) for differing forms of the same species of enteric bacteria after discovering that the S types form a stable suspension in a saline solution, whereas the R types clump and settle. Cultures of S types frequently develop R-type colonies, but the R to S conversion is rare. Arkwright does not recognize the S-R variation as mutation, as is now generally known. (See 1928 C, 1931 D. 1931 D, 1944 C.)

C. BACTERIOPHAGE: *Titration*
Felix d'Herelle shows that the numbers of phage particles, the titer of phage, can be determined by counting plaques made by placing serial dilutions of phage on agar plates inoculated with susceptible bacteria. He also discovers a stepwise increase in phage titer in which there is first a latent period followed by a large increase in titer. In 1939, the one-step growth curve concept is studied in detail by Emory Ellis and Max Delbrück. (See 1939 D.)

D. IMMUNOLOGY: *Atopy/Anaphylaxis*
Carl Prausnitz and Heinz Küstner show that food allergy is a form of anaphylaxis and that the sensitivity can be passively transferred in serum from a sensitive individual to a nonsensitive individual. The term "atopy," for human hypersensitivities that are inherited, is first used in 1923 by Arthur F. Coca and Robert Anderson Cooke.

E. IMMUNOLOGY: *Tetanus*
Alexander Thomas Glenny and J. B. Buxton use tetanus toxin and antitoxin mixtures to produce active immunity. They produce large quantities of tetanus antitoxin in horses by injecting a toxin-antitoxin mixture, followed by an injection of toxin.

F. BIOCHEMISTRY: *Glutathione/Oxidation and Reduction*
Between 1921 and 1929, Frederick Gowland Hopkins discovers and crystallizes glutathione. He identifies its tripeptide composition and studies its behavior in oxidation-reduction reactions.

G. PHYSIOLOGY: *Insulin*
Frederick G. Banting, Charles Best, John J. R. MacLeod, and James Collip extract insulin from the human pancreas. They first experiment with dogs and then with humans, including Banting and Best, who receive injections.

They then begin treatment of diabetics with the hormone, which was named "insuline" in 1916 by Edward A. Sharpey-Schafer. Banting and MacLeod receive the 1923 Nobel Prize in physiology or medicine for their work on insulin. Banting shares his prize with Best while MacLeod shares his with Collip.

H. TECHNOLOGY: *Highways*
The world's first highway intended exclusively for motorized vehicles opens in Berlin. The 10-kilometer highway, the Avus Autobahn, runs from Grunewald to the suburb of Wannsee.

I. THE ARTS: *Art*
Pablo Picasso paints *Three Musicians* in the style of collage cubism.

1922

A. BACTERIOLOGICAL TECHNIQUE: *Membrane Filters*
Richard Zsigmondy and F. Buchmann obtain a patent on a membrane filter made of cellulose esters, which can remove bacteria from solutions. (See 1931 A.)

B. BACTERIAL PHYSIOLOGY: Thiobacillus thiooxidans
Selman Abraham Waksman and J. S. Joffe isolate an aerobic, sulfur-oxidizing, autotrophic bacterium that they name *Thiobacillus thiooxidans*. This bacterium is found to have the unique ability to grow and to oxidize sulfur in the range of pH 5.0 to pH 0. Waksman receives the 1952 Nobel Prize in physiology or medicine for his discovery of several antibiotics, including streptomycin. (See 1902 A.)

C. BACTERIAL PHYSIOLOGY: *Phase Variation*
F. W. Andrewes discovers that cells isolated from a single colony of *Salmonella typhimurium* have a predominant flagellar serotype. Upon subculturing of a particular serotype, he isolates a second serotype, which in turn would give rise to the first. The cultures thus alternate between two types of flagellar antigens or phases. (See 1953 L.)

D. BACTERIAL PHYSIOLOGY: *Lysozyme*
Alexander Fleming discovers that the enzyme lysozyme occurs in tears, saliva, and mucus and that it dissolves certain bacteria. Although unimportant as a defense against infection, lysozyme is later used widely in experiments in studies of the cell walls and membranes of bacteria. Fleming discovers penicillin in 1928. (See 1952 D, 1952 E, 1958 B.)

E. BACTERIOPHAGE: *Indicator Strains*
M. Lisbonne and L. Carrère find that strains of *Escherichia coli* or *Proteus* X19 produce bacteriophages that lyse *Shigella*. This is the first report of using one bacterial species to assay for bacteriophage produced by a different species. The use of the term "indicator strain" for lysogenic cultures comes into use at a later date. (See 1917 C, 1925 C.)

F. VIROLOGY: *Differential Centrifugation*
W. G. MacCallum and E. H. Oppenheimer use solutions of known specific gravity to purify vaccinia virus by centrifugation. Differential centrifugation comes into wide use after high-speed centrifuges are developed.

1922 *(continued)*

G. PLANT PHYSIOLOGY: *Quantum Requirement for Photosynthesis*

Otto Warburg uses a manometric technique to estimate the quantum requirement for photosynthesis. He concludes that four photons are needed for each molecule of oxygen produced.

H. CHEMISTRY: *Macromolecule*

Hermann Staudinger first uses the term "macromolecule" in his studies of the structure of rubber. He defines it in 1924 when he argues that large so-called polymeric molecules are not aggregates of smaller molecular weight components but are in fact large chains held together by covalent bonds, an unpopular view at that time. Unable to obtain a Svedberg ultracentrifuge, Staudinger employs viscosimetry to study proteins. In 1928 he devises the Staudinger law to express the relationship between molecular weight and viscosity. Staudinger receives the Nobel Prize in chemistry in 1953. (See 1923 J.)

I. SOCIETY AND POLITICS

Victor Emmanuel III appoints Benito Mussolini to act as premier and to form a coalition government. After World War I, Mussolini had formed the Fascist political party.

J. THE ARTS: *Literature*

- James Joyce's *Ulysses* is published in Paris.
- T. S. Eliot's poem *The Waste Land* is published.
- The *Fugitive* magazine is published in Nashville, Tennessee, with contributions from John Crowe Ransom, Allen Tate, and Robert Penn Warren.

K. THE ARTS: *Art*

Paul Klee completes his painting *Twittering Machine*.

1923

A. BACTERIAL TAXONOMY: *Classification*

A committee formed by the Society of American Bacteriologists (SAB), chaired by David H. Bergey, publishes *Bergey's Manual of Determinative Bacteriology,* which generally follows the classification suggested by a committee chaired by C.-E. A. Winslow from 1917 to 1920. The manual goes through eight editions through 1974, after which it appears in a new format beginning in 1984. (See 1984 A.)

B. BACTERIAL PHYSIOLOGY: *Catalase Test*

M. B. McLeod and J. Gordon devise a scheme for distinguishing among groups of bacteria based on the presence or absence of catalase detected by the decomposition of hydrogen peroxide. The ability to produce catalase, and thus decompose hydrogen peroxide with the appearance of bubbles of oxygen, becomes a useful test for distinguishing between aerobic and facultatively anaerobic bacteria of similar morphology and Gram stain reaction.

C. BACTERIAL PHYSIOLOGY: *Gelatin Liquefaction*

The fact that many species of bacteria produce an enzyme that hydrolyzes gelatin, known from the early days of using culture media solidified with gelatin, leads to the use of culture media solidified with agar. In 1923, M. Levine and D. C. Carpenter publish a report on the liquefaction of gelatin as measured by stab inoculation of tubes of gelatin. This form of the test, used for several decades, is commonly found in laboratory manuals for beginning students. In 1926, William C. Frazier introduces an agar medium into which gelatin is incorporated. After growth of colonies of bacteria on Frazier's gelatin agar, mercuric chloride is added to precipitate unhydrolyzed gelatin.

D. VIRAL DISEASE: *Canine Distemper Virus*
Patrick Laidlaw and George William Dunkin discover that ferrets are susceptible to canine distemper virus and are successful in preparing a vaccine by growing the virus in these animals. Laidlaw and coworkers later use ferrets to isolate influenza virus A. (See 1933 D.)

E. IMMUNOLOGY: *Pertussis*
Johannes Marius Madsen begins use of a vaccine against pertussis (whooping cough) in the Faeroe Islands. In 1933 he reports the results of vaccinations with *Bordetella pertussis* during epidemics of 1923 to 1924 and 1929. Although not conclusive proof of the efficacy of the vaccines, the results lead to trials by other investigators. (See 1933 F, 1936 K.)

F. IMMUNOLOGY: *Polysaccharide Antigens*
Michael Heidelberger and Oswald T. Avery show that the capsular polysaccharide of pneumococci, known as the soluble specific substance (SSS), is fully antigenic and capable of inducing the formation of antibody. Previous work had shown these antigens to be haptens, capable of binding antibody but unable to induce its synthesis. The notion that only proteins or glycoproteins are antigenic is overturned. (See 1929 H.)

G. BIOCHEMISTRY: *Fermentation/Coenzymes*
Hans Karl August von Euler-Chelpin and Karl Myrbäck study the Harden-Young coferment (coenzyme) and name it "cozymase." Continuing the study of the role of cozymase in dehydrogenase activity, Euler-Chelpin makes many contributions to the components of the fermentation process. Euler-Chelpin shares the 1929 Nobel Prize in chemistry with Harden for his work in this area. (See 1906 K.)

H. BIOCHEMISTRY: *Cytochrome*
David Keilin first observes the four-banded spectrum of cytochrome in his studies of the parasite *Gasterophilus*. (See 1925 G, 1938 F.)

I. CHEMISTRY: *Hydrogen Electrode*
William Mansfield Clark defines the normal hydrogen electrode as used in the study of oxygen-reduction potentials of any system.

J. TECHNOLOGY: *Ultracentrifuge*
Theodor Svedberg invents the ultracentrifuge, which permits the sedimentation of ultra-small particles, such as proteins. He develops a method for using the ultracentrifuge for determining the molecular weight of proteins. Svedberg receives the 1926 Nobel Prize in chemistry for this work.

1923 *(continued)*

K. SOCIETY AND POLITICS

Russia, the Ukraine, White Russia, and Transcaucasia form the Union of Soviet Socialist Republics (USSR), or the Soviet Union.

L. THE ARTS: *Theater*

Saint Joan by George Bernard Shaw is performed.

1924

A. BACTERIAL PHYSIOLOGY: *Succinate–Fumarate Oxidation and Reduction*

Juda Quastel and Margaret Whetham show that a resting cell suspension of *Escherichia coli* catalyzes the reversible oxidation-reduction reaction between succinate and fumarate with concomitant oxidation or reduction of methylene blue. (See 1924 D.)

B. BACTERIAL DISEASE: *Scarlet Fever*

George Frederick Dick and Gladys Rowena Dick establish the cause of scarlet fever by recovering hemolytic streptococci from nearly all cases of the disease and by causing the disease in uninfected persons by infecting them with pure cultures. The Dicks also purify the soluble erythrogenic toxin produced by the streptococci, responsible for the rash in scarlet fever, that becomes an important diagnostic tool called the Dick test.

C. BIOCHEMISTRY: *Respiratory Enzyme/* **Atmungsferment**

Otto Warburg publishes a paper in which he suggests that an iron-containing respiratory enzyme, *Atmungsferment,* is the enzyme that transfers oxygen to cells in respiration. (See 1910 D, 1925 G, 1928 K, 1938 F.)

D. BIOCHEMISTRY: *Dehydrogenase*

Alfred Fleish suggests that the dehydrogenase enzyme is an initial hydrogen acceptor in oxygen-reduction reactions. He describes the oxidation of succinic acid by succinic dehydrogenase. (See 1924 A, 1924 C.)

E. BIOCHEMISTRY: *Enzymology*

Malcolm Dixon begins his extensive studies on enzymes with experiments with xanthine oxidase.

F. BIOCHEMISTRY: *Feulgen Stain*

Robert Joschim Feulgen introduces a new staining procedure for the nucleus of cells. When DNA is treated with acid, free aldehyde groups on deoxyribose sugar are formed by removal of purine bases. The aldehyde groups react with the Schiff reagent (Hugo Schiff), a solution of fuchsin dye treated with sulfur dioxide, to form a blue color. RNA does not give this reaction.

G. BIOLOGY: *Origin of Life*

In his book *Proiskhozhdenie Zhiny,* Alexandr Ivanovich Oparin proposes that life on earth began in a primitive ocean containing a mixture of biochemicals. The "Oparin ocean scenario," as it is later called, suggests that biomolecules formed coacervates that absorbed other molecules and spontaneously divided. Oparin's ideas, and the experiments of Stanley Miller in 1953, lead biologists to believe that the first living organisms were heterotrophic, anaerobic procaryotes. (See 1953 V.)

1925

A. BACTERIAL PHYSIOLOGY: *Utilization of Citrate*

S. A. Koser devises a liquid culture medium with ammonium phosphate as the source of nitrogen that he employs to test the utilization of organic acids by bacteria. The long-term benefit is his recognition that *Aerobacter aerogenes* (now *Enterobacter aerogenes*) metabolizes citrate, whereas *Escherichia coli* does not, thus providing a tool for distinguishing these bacteria from each other. In 1926, J. S. Simmons adds agar and a pH indicator, bromthymol blue, to the Koser citrate medium, creating Simmons citrate agar. (See 1936 C.)

B. ANTIMICROBIAL AGENTS: *Bacteriocins*

André Gratia discovers that some cells in populations of *Escherichia coli* release a material that kills bacteria in the same species or closely related species. The material from *E. coli* is at first called "colicin," but after it is noted that a number of other species produce a similar substance, the general term "bacteriocin" is applied. Later work shows that bacteriocins are proteins that are specified by episomes (plasmids). (See 1954 I.)

C. BACTERIOPHAGE: *Lysogeny*

Jules Bordet and Oscar Bail independently discover the phenomenon that Bordet calls lysogeny. Bordet notes that some cultures of bacteria exhibit transmissible autolysis, which he believes to be inherited. He holds to the Lamarckian view that once the lytic agent is introduced into a culture, it becomes an acquired characteristic that is transmitted to progeny. He gives the phenomenon the name "lysogeny" but does not relate it to viruses. Bail studies strain 88 of *Escherichia coli* and proves that it is lysogenic by isolating clones that produce phage. (See 1898 F, 1915 C, 1917 C, 1922 E, 1929 D, 1936 D, 1950 I.)

D. VIRAL DISEASE: *Cowpox Virus*

Frederic Parker, Jr., and Robert N. Nye grow vaccinia virus in a cell culture made with rabbit testicle tissue. They successfully carry the virus through 11 successive cultures. (See 1913 C, 1917 D, 1936 L, 1949 I.)

E. BIOLOGY: *Membrane Structure/Lipid Bilayer*

Evert Gorter and F. Grendel conclude that the lipid in the membrane of red blood cells is in the form of a bilayer. This conclusion is reached after they determine that the surface area of the lipids extracted from the cells and spread into a monolayer in a Langmuir trough is twice that of the estimated surface area of the intact red blood cells. (See 1894 G, 1910 G, 1934 G, 1960 P, 1972 K.)

F. BIOCHEMISTRY: *Electron Transfer*

William Mansfield Clark explains that the reduction of dyes is accomplished by the transfer of an electron pair, which may or may not be accompanied by hydrogen ions.

1925 *(continued)*

G. BIOCHEMISTRY: *Cytochrome*

David Keilin publishes his first paper on cytochrome, giving credit to Charles Alexander MacMunn's observations made in 1884. (See 1884 J, 1923 H, 1929 K, 1938 F.)

H. TECHNOLOGY: *Television*

• Vladimir Zworykin invents a color television system for which he receives a patent in 1928. (See 1926 N, 1929 O, 1936 T, 1953 X.)

• The Minnesota Mining and Manufacturing Company begins to use the brand name "Scotch" for the adhesive tapes that it manufactures.

I. SOCIETY AND POLITICS

John Scopes, a science teacher in Tennessee, is the focus of a test lawsuit brought by religious fundamentalists against the teaching of evolution in public schools. The lawsuit is devised by individuals who want to bring national attention to Dayton, Tennessee, a formerly prosperous town in a state of decline. Nationwide newspaper and radio coverage is arranged, and the case is argued by former secretary of state William Jennings Bryan for the plaintiffs and Clarence Darrow and Dudley Field Malone for the defendant. After a guilty verdict, Scopes is fined $100, but the case is appealed to the Tennessee Supreme Court, which offers a divided opinion as to whether the law under which the suit is brought is constitutional. However, the Court rules that the fine exceeds that permitted by the state constitution, thus invalidating it. The Court recommends that the attorney general not retry the case, and the defense is unable to pursue the matter because by that time Scopes is no longer a state employee.

J. THE ARTS: *Literature*

• A sense of cultural change for African Americans, called the "Harlem Renaissance," gains impetus in 1925 when Alain Locke publishes *The New Negro,* an anthology of essays and art, to be followed in 1926 by Langston Hughes's collection of poems entitled *The Weary Blues.*

• Sinclair Lewis publishes his novel *Arrowsmith.*

• F. Scott Fitzgerald publishes *The Great Gatsby.*

• Virginia Woolf completes her novel *Mrs. Dalloway.*

K. THE ARTS: *Art*

Pablo Picasso completes his painting *Three Dancers.*

1926

A. BACTERIAL TAXONOMY: *Kauffmann–White Scheme for* Salmonella

Studying the flagellar and somatic antigens of members of the genus *Salmonella,* P. Bruce White recognizes the importance of the newly discovered variation. He begins the process of classification of the salmonellae based on the many different types of flagellar (H) and somatic (O) antigens. F. Kauffmann extends this work from 1935 on, and in 1941 he establishes the Kauffmann-White scheme of antigenic classification. (See 1903 F, 1916 D, 1920 C, 1941 A.)

B. MICROBIAL PHYSIOLOGY: *Fermentation*

Otto Meyerhof performs a series of experiments that essentially prove the similarities between the yeast alcoholic fermentation and muscle lactic acid fermentation. (See 1913 E.)

C. BACTERIAL DISEASE: Listeria/*Listeriosis*

Everitt George Dunne Murray, R. A. Webb, and M. B. R. Swann isolate from rabbits a bacterium that they call *Bacterium monocytogenes*. G. Hülphers first recognized and named this bacterium *Bacillus hepatis* in 1911. In 1940, J. H. H. Pirie renames it *Listeria monocytogenes*. This organism, which causes the disease called listeriosis in animals and humans, grows at low temperatures and is sometimes implicated in outbreaks of food infection.

D. VIRAL DISEASE: *Rous Sarcoma Virus*

Alexis Carrel finds that the Rous sarcoma virus will grow in a medium containing fragments of tissue. (See 1911 E, 1913 C, 1917 D, 1925 D, 1936 L, 1949 I.)

E. VIRAL DISEASE: *Serum Hepatitis*

Studying cases of hepatitis in a diabetic clinic, A. Flaum and coworkers discover that needles and syringes may be transferring the infectious agent from patient to patient. Although this report is the first to indicate how hepatitis may be transmitted, the paper receives little attention. (See 1884 F, 1912 C, 1943 E, 1962 Q.)

F. PHYSIOLOGY: *Blood Groups*

Karl Landsteiner and Philip Levine identify the MNP blood groups. For this work, and the discovery in 1900 of the ABO blood group antigens, Landsteiner is awarded the 1930 Nobel Prize in physiology or medicine. He believes, however, that he should have been recognized for his work on hapten–antibody reactions (See 1900 H, 1917 E, 1940 N.)

G. BIOCHEMISTRY: *Unity in Biochemistry*

Albert Jan Kluyver and Hendrick Jean Louis Donker publish "Unity in Biochemistry," in which they recognize that the processes of oxidation, fermentation, and biosynthesis in living organisms of diverse types follow very similar biochemical pathways. Kluyver publishes a precursor of this paper in 1924, surveying the influence of microbial activities in nature that illustrate the diversity of natural processes but that nevertheless have an underlying unity. In a 1931 paper he uses the term "comparative biochemistry," and in subsequent papers he proposes the use of microorganisms for studies of this topic.

H. BIOCHEMISTRY: *Enzyme Crystallization*

In the first crystallization of an enzyme, James Batcheller Sumner crystallizes the enzyme urease obtained from the jack bean plant (*Canavalia ensiformis*). Sumner later shows that these crystals, which have enzyme activity, are composed of protein. The particular strain of the jack bean plant used in his experiments contains a large amount of urease, while other experimenters who attempt to do similar experiments with other plants meet

1926 (continued)

with difficulties that delay acceptance of Sumner's results. Sumner receives the 1946 Nobel Prize in chemistry for his work on enzymes.

I. BIOCHEMISTRY: *Pasteur Effect*

In 1861, Louis Pasteur noted that oxygen inhibits fermentation, and in 1875 he stated that "fermentation is life without oxygen." Otto Warburg, in experiments with cancer cells, finds that ethylcarbylamine (ethyl isocyanide) permits glycolysis to occur in the presence of oxygen. He proposes a specific chemical reaction, which he refers to as the Pasteur reaction, as a link between respiration and fermentation. The term "Pasteur effect" comes to be used for the inhibition of glycolysis by oxygen. (See 1861 B, 1943 C.)

J. BIOCHEMISTRY: *Succinate-Fumarate Oxidation and Reduction*

Torsten Thunberg studies the succinate-fumarate oxidation-reduction reaction catalyzed by heart muscle, confirming the data of Juda Quastel and Margaret Whetham. (See 1924 A.)

K. BIOCHEMISTRY: *Hydrogen Transport*

Frederick Gowland Hopkins writes that hydrogen is transported in stages from primary donors to oxygen. His article does not mention David Keilin's cytochromes. (See 1925 G, 1928 K.)

L. BIOCHEMISTRY: *Manometry*

Otto Warburg introduces a new version of the manometer for use in studies of respiration. (See 1910 F.)

M. PHYSICS: *Wave Mechanics*

Erwin Schrödinger compares the behavior of the electron to a wave motion instead of to particulate matter, introducing what becomes known as "wave mechanics." Schrödinger shares the 1933 Nobel Prize in physics with Paul Dirac, who develops the concept of antimatter.

N. TECHNOLOGY

- The first all-sound motion pictures are shown.
- Using a version of the rotating disc invented by Paul Nipkov in 1886, John Logie Baird sends television images by telephone lines from London to Glasgow. He demonstrates a color television system in 1928, and for a short time in 1936 the British Broadcasting Company (BBC) permits a company started by Baird to run a television service. Baird's mechanical system gives way to electronic systems. (See 1925 H, 1929 O, 1936 T, 1953 X.)

O. THE ARTS: *Music*

Giacomo Puccini's opera *Turandot* is performed.

P. THE ARTS: *Literature*

Ernest Hemingway publishes his novel *The Sun Also Rises.*

1927

A. BACTERIAL PHYSIOLOGY: *Autotrophs*

L. G. M. Baas-Becking and G. S. Parks divide the autotrophic bacteria into five groups that oxidize, respectively, hydrogen; carbon and carbon compounds; nitrogen and nitrogen compounds; sulfur and sulfur compounds; and ferrous or manganous salts. They write balanced reactions with energy sources and electron acceptors and calculate free energy of reaction for each group. They comment that "the bacteria investigated thus far have nothing in common with Maxwell's demon." (See 1867 C.)

B. VIRAL DISEASE: *Newcastle Disease Virus*
By recognizing that Newcastle disease is distinct from fowl plague, T. M. Doyle introduces comparative study of the viruses. (See 1901 E.)

C. IMMUNOLOGY: *Tetanus Toxoid*
Gaston Léon Ramon and Christian Zoeller use tetanus toxoid to achieve active immunization in humans against tetanus. (See 1893 C, 1904 C.)

D. CELL BIOLOGY: *Mitochondria/Endosymbiosis*
Ivan E. Wallin publishes *Symbionticism and the Origin of Species,* in which he concludes that mitochondria are bacteria. His claim to having grown mitochondria outside of their host cells is never substantiated. Wallin believes that "symbionticism" (endosymbiosis) played a major role in the evolution of species. (See 1962 T, 1967 A.)

E. GENETICS: *X Rays Cause Mutation*
Hermann Joseph Muller discovers that X rays cause genetic mutations in *Drosophila,* a fruit fly. Muller receives the Nobel Prize in physiology or medicine in 1946. (See 1934 H, 1939 E.)

F. BIOCHEMISTRY: *Fermentation/Hexokinase*
Otto Meyerhof discovers an enzyme that catalyzes the conversion of glucose and phosphate to glucose-6-phosphate. The enzyme, found in yeast extract and in plasmolyzed yeast, is named hexokinase. (See 1914 G.)

G. BIOCHEMISTRY: *Creatine Phosphate*
Cyrus Hartwell Fiske and Yellapragada SubbaRow identify creatine phosphate as a compound that is hydrolyzed during muscle contraction and resynthesized during recovery. Philip Eggleton and Grace Palmer Eggleton find this same compound and give it the name "Phosphagen." (See 1929 J.)

H. BIOCHEMISTRY: *Energy Yields in Glycolysis/ATP*
Otto Meyerhof and Karl Lohmann discover that the ΔH of hydrolysis of creatine phosphate is $-14,800$ calories per mole. In 1932, they find that adenylpyrophosphate hydrolysis yields $-12,500$ calories per mole. In 1935, this compound is named adenosine 5'-triphosphate (ATP). (See 1927 G, 1929 J.)

I. BIOCHEMISTRY: *Respiratory Enzyme*
In 1927 to 1928, Otto Warburg experiments further on the iron-containing respiratory enzyme, *Atmungsferment.* (See 1924 C.)

J. PHYSICS: *Uncertainty Principle*
Werner Karl Heisenberg proposes the uncertainty principle, which states that the position and momentum of a subatomic particle cannot be determined simultaneously with absolute precision. Heisenberg receives the 1932 Nobel Prize in physics.

1927 *(continued)*

K. SOCIETY: *Exploration*
Charles Lindbergh makes the first solo airplane flight across the Atlantic.

L. THE ARTS: *Literature*
Thornton Wilder writes *The Bridge of San Luis Rey.*

1928

A. BACTERIAL PHYSIOLOGY: *Nitrogen Fixation*
K. Drewes shows that members of two genera of blue-green algae (now known to be cyanobacteria), *Anabaena* and *Nostoc,* grow without the addition of combined nitrogen to the growth medium. This is the first demonstration of nitrogen fixation by the blue-green algae. (See 1895 A, 1901 C.)

B. BACTERIAL PHYSIOLOGY: *Nitrogen Fixation*
Dean Burk and Otto Meyerhof introduce the use of manometric methods for the study of nitrogen fixation in *Azotobacter chroococcum.* They study the growth-limiting effects of nitrogen gas as well as the effects of other gases and inhibitors.

C. BACTERIAL GENETICS: *Transformation*
Frederick Griffith discovers the phenomenon of bacterial transformation when he finds that a heat-killed smooth encapsulated strain of *Diplococcus pneumoniae* (*Streptococcus pneumoniae*) transfers the ability to synthesize the capsular polysaccharide to a mutant rough strain that lacks the capsule. Because Griffith's paper is concerned with the epidemiology of pneumococcal infections, he is not interested in the basis of the transformation phenomenon. He calls the material that causes the change the "transforming principle," suggesting that it is a specific protein that permits the synthesis of the polysaccharide. Griffith dies in 1941 during World War II, 3 years before the experiments of Oswald T. Avery, Colin MacLeod, and Maclyn McCarty prove that the transforming principle is DNA. (See 1931 C, 1944 C.)

D. MICROBIOLOGY: *Germfree Life*
This year marks the beginning of experiments by two pioneers in modern studies of germfree life. James Arthur Reyniers, who begins his work in 1928, is followed in 1936 by Gösta Glimstedt. Both researchers play major roles in the development of techniques, equipment, and diets related to this type of research. Reynier's research leads to the establishment of the well-known Lobund laboratory (Laboratory of Bacteriology at the University of Notre Dame). (See 1895 D, 1899 C, 1942 A, 1949 A.)

E. VIRAL DISEASE: *Vaccinia Virus*
Hugh Bethune Maitland and Mary C. Maitland cultivate vaccinia virus in minced hen's kidney suspended in hen's serum. Detecting no growth of the hen's tissue, they refer to their experiment as "growth without tissue culture." Later workers note that the chicken cells do grow under the conditions of their experiment. (See 1917 D, 1931 F, 1933 E, 1936 L, 1948 F, 1949 I.)

F. BIOCHEMISTRY: *Fructose 1,6-Diphosphate in Fermentation*

Phoebus Levene and Albert L. Raymond show that the alcoholic fermentation intermediate, glucose diphosphate, is fructose 1,6-diphosphate (fructose 1,6-bisphosphate.) (See 1906 J, 1914 F, 1933 I.)

G. BIOCHEMISTRY: *Vitamin C*

Albert Szent-Györgyi isolates a "reducing factor" from the adrenal cortex that he calls "hexuronic acid." After it is shown to be identical to vitamin C in 1932, it is assigned the name ascorbic acid in 1933. Szent-Györgyi receives the 1937 Nobel Prize in physiology or medicine. At the same time, Norman Haworth receives the Nobel Prize in chemistry for synthesizing vitamin C. (See 1932 G, 1933 J.)

H. BIOCHEMISTRY: *Competitive Inhibitors*

Juda Quastel and W. R. Wooldridge discover competitive inhibitors of enzymes when they find that malonate inhibits the action of succinic dehydrogenase. (See 1913 E, 1934 L.)

I. SOCIETY AND POLITICS

Joseph Stalin assumes control of the Soviet Union.

J. THE ARTS: *Music*

Kurt Weill and Bertolt Brecht present *The Threepenny Opera,* adapted from *The Beggar's Opera* by John Christopher Pepusch and John Gay, first performed in 1728.

K. THE ARTS: *Literature*

D. H. Lawrence publishes *Lady Chatterley's Lover.*

1929

A. BACTERIAL STRUCTURE: *Gram Stain*

Attempting to explain the mechanism of the Gram reaction, V. Burke and M. W. Barnes conclude that differences in cell wall permeability are responsible for the more rapid decolorization of gram-negative bacteria than of gram-positive organisms. The chemistry of the bacterial cell wall is not understood at this time, and the authors have no chemical evidence to support their conclusion. Not for about 30 years is this basic concept found to be correct. (See 1884 B, 1957 A, 1963 B.)

B. ANTIBIOTICS: *Penicillin*

Alexander Fleming discovers an antibacterial substance in a culture of the mold *Penicillium notatum.* He names the substance penicillin and develops an assay to follow its production in the mold culture. Upon testing its killing effect on a few species of bacteria, he notes that it is most effective against gram-positive bacteria and least effective against gram-negative bacteria. He does no further work on penicillin, and its purification and development are later accomplished by Howard Florey and Ernst Chain. Fleming shares the Nobel Prize in physiology or medicine in 1945 with Florey and Chain. (See 1922 D, 1940 D, 1941 F.)

C. BACTERIAL DISEASE: Mycoplasma mycoides

J. Nowak gives the name *Mycoplasma peripneumoniae* to the causative organism of contagious bovine pleuropneumonia. Amédée Borrel, in 1910, had

1929 *(continued)*

used the named *Asterococcus mycoides,* but this generic name is ruled invalid because it is the name of an algal genus. In 1955, D. G. ff. Edward and E. A. Freundt prepare a classification of this group and choose the name *Mycoplasma mycoides.*

D. BACTERIOPHAGE: *Lysogeny*

Studying lysogenic *Salmonella enteriditis,* Frank Macfarlane Burnet and M. McKie conclude that a small fraction of the bacteria in a culture undergoes lysis during growth but not when the cells are resting. They also find that rough strains produce much greater amounts of phage than do smooth strains. They maintain that the activation of an inheritable constituent in the cell is necessary for the liberation of phage. (See 1925 C, 1936 D, 1950 I.)

E. VIROLOGY: *Viruses Defined*

Thomas M. Rivers publishes an article in which he reviews the facts about viruses, distinguishing them from other types of organisms. He uses the term "filterable viruses," while noting that some bacteria, vibrios, spirochetes, and protozoa are filterable. He states that the rickettsia should not be included with the viruses. Rivers discusses the long-lasting immunity conferred by viral infections, using the term "sessile antibodies," whose expression must be passed on to daughter cells. He notes that there is no evidence that viruses can respire but withholds an opinion as to whether or not they are living organisms. (See 1951 A, 1963 D, 1966 A.)

F. VIRAL DISEASE: *Fowlpox Virus Inclusion Bodies*

C. Eugene Woodruff and Ernest William Goodpasture prove that the fowlpox inclusion body contains thousands of individual viral particles, thus confirming that earlier researchers had in fact observed several different poxviruses with the light microscope. (See 1886 E, 1904 D, 1906 G.)

G. IMMUNOLOGY: *Yellow Fever*

Max Theiler successfully infects mice with yellow fever by injection into the brain. He then shows that immune serum from persons who have recovered from yellow fever neutralize the virus and protect the mice from infection. Based on these results, Wilber A. Sawyer immunizes laboratory workers with the mouse-passaged virus. Later, a similar strain of virus developed in France is used to develop the Dakar scratch vaccine, which afterward is administered to millions of persons in French West Africa. (See 1936 L.)

H. IMMUNOLOGY: *Quantitative Precipitin Reaction*

Michael Heidelberger and Forrest E. Kendall develop a method to determine the quantity of antibody combined with antigen in antigen–antibody interactions. Their procedure is to measure the amount of nitrogen in a suspension of antibody before and after the introduction of pneumococcal polysaccharide causes a precipitate to form. They later develop a colorimetric technique for use with protein-containing antigens. (See 1923 F.)

I. IMMUNOLOGY: *Delayed Hypersensitivity*

When Louis Ladislaus Dienes and E. W. Schoenheit inject egg albumin or horse serum into tuberculous foci in infected animals, they observe a delayed hypersensitivity reaction. Dienes and Schoenheit are first to show that delayed hypersensitivity of the tuberculin type is not limited to bacterial products. (See 1942 I.)

J. BIOCHEMISTRY: *Adenosine Triphosphate*

Karl Lohmann and, independently, Cyrus Fiske and Yellapragada Subba-Row, discover a compound called adenylpyrophosphate in muscle. They show that the compound can be split into adenylic acid and pyrophosphate. In 1935 Lohmann determines its structure to be adenosine $5'$-triphosphate (ATP). (See 1939 M, 1939 O, 1943 F.)

K. BIOCHEMISTRY: *Cytochrome*

David Keilin publishes a diagram demonstrating the function of cytochrome in cells. (See 1923 H, 1925 G, 1938 F.)

L. BIOCHEMISTRY: *Deoxyribonucleic Acid (DNA)*

After having isolated ribose from nucleic acid in 1909, Phoebus Levene determines that deoxyribose is a component of one type of nucleic acid. The names ribonucleic acid (RNA) and deoxyribonucleic acid (DNA) thereby become established.

M. BIOCHEMISTRY: *Hemin Structure*

Hans Fischer synthesizes hemin, proving the structure to be composed of four pyrrole rings. This structure, proposed by William Küster in 1913, was later abandoned under criticism from Fischer and others. Fischer receives the Nobel Prize in chemistry in 1930.

N. CHEMISTRY: *Stable Isotope of Nitrogen*

S. M. Naudé observes a shift in the band spectrum of nitric oxide that reveals the existence of nitrogen with a mass of 15. The naturally occurring ^{15}N is currently recovered by an exchange reaction between nitric oxide and nitric acid. (See 1935 M.)

O. TECHNOLOGY: *Television*

The National Broadcasting Company in the United States opens a television station. Two years later the Columbia Broadcasting System begins television broadcasting. (See 1925 H, 1926 N, 1936 T, 1953 X.)

P. SOCIETY AND POLITICS

The New York stock market crashes as the Dow Jones industrial average loses 30.57 points, leading to a worldwide depression.

Q. THE ARTS: *Literature*

- William Faulkner publishes *The Sound and the Fury*.
- Ernest Hemingway completes his novel *A Farewell to Arms*.
- Erich Maria Remarque publishes *All Quiet on the Western Front*.
- Thomas Wolfe writes *Look Homeward, Angel*.

R. THE ARTS: *Art*

Salvador Dali paints *The Accommodation of Desire*.

A. BACTERIAL PHYSIOLOGY: *Constitutive and Adaptive Enzymes*

Henning Karström, reporting carbohydrate metabolism in gram-negative enteric bacteria, describes constitutive enzymes as those that cells always produce independent of components of the growth medium and adaptive enzymes as those that are synthesized in response to the presence of a particular substrate. (See 1900 I, 1941 E, 1952 H.)

B. BACTERIAL DISEASE: *Staphylococcal Food Poisoning*

G. M. Dack and colleagues find that a yellow hemolytic staphylococcus is responsible for the illness of 11 individuals who had consumed sponge cake. Through the use of human volunteers, they find that culture filtrates of the staphylococci cause gastrointestinal illness within a few hours of consumption. In 1914, M. A. Barber, in a report that went largely unappreciated, found that soluble toxin released by staphylococci was responsible for a food poisoning outbreak involving milk. The role of *Staphylococcus aureus* in food poisoning begins to be accepted even though there are three earlier reports by J. Denys in 1884, R. W. G. Owen in 1906, and M. A. Barber in 1914. (See 1914 C.)

C. BACTERIAL DISEASE: *Psittacosis*

Samuel P. Bedson and G. T. Western isolate *Chlamydia psittaci,* the causative agent of psittacosis, by inoculating infectious specimens from humans and birds into parakeets. (See 1879 C, 1934 B.)

D. IMMUNOLOGY: *Instructionalist Theory of Antibody Formation*

In the early 1930s a number of investigators, including F. Breinl, F. Haurowitz, J. Alexander, and Stuart Mudd, suggest that antigens change the structure of antibodies by affecting the order of the amino acid residues in the polypeptide chains, so that they differ from the normal globulin protein found in animal blood and tissue. These ideas are known as the instructionalist theory of antibody formation. (See 1940 M, 1955 N, 1957 N.)

E. GENETICS: *Vernalization*

Trofim Denisovich Lysenko gains prominence in Russia by claiming that the growth of winter wheat can be accelerated through brief exposure to cold, a treatment called "vernalization." He maintains that a single exposure to cold confers a permanent change. In 1935 he develops a neo-Lamarckian theory by asserting that the environment alters inheritance. Because his views are accepted by the Soviet Communist Party, he continues to dominate biological research in the Soviet Union until the 1960s. (See 1809.)

F. BIOCHEMISTRY: *Iodoacetate Poisoning/Creatine Phosphate*

Einar Lundsgaard determines that muscles treated with iodoacetate can contract without the formation of lactic acid. He also shows a linear relationship between the hydrolysis of creatine phosphate and the work performed by the muscle. (See 1927 G, 1929 J.)

G. BIOCHEMISTRY: *Oxidative Phosphorylation*

Vladimir Aleksandrovich Engelhardt observes "oxidative phosphorylation," but the term is not adopted until about 1942. (See 1939 Q, 1940 J, 1941 L.)

H. TECHNOLOGY

• Charles William Beebe and Otis Barton, following Barton's design, construct a vessel for undersea exploration. Their craft, called a bathysphere, is suspended by a cable from a ship. (See 1934 P.)

• The Chrysler Building is completed in New York City. At a height of 319 meters, it is the world's tallest office building (surpassing the Woolworth Building, 1913) and the tallest structure, being higher than the Eiffel Tower (1889). It is, however, eclipsed by the Empire State Building in 1931. (See 1889 K, 1913 J, 1931 N, 1972 P, 1973 Q.)

I. THE ARTS: *Literature*

Papers from the symposium *I'll Take My Stand: the South and the Agrarian Tradition* are published, including essays by John Crowe Ransom, Donald Davidson, Allen Tate, and Robert Penn Warren.

1931

A. BACTERIOLOGICAL TECHNIQUE: *Membrane Filters*

William J. Elford develops a collodion membrane, composed of cellulose nitrate, that can be made with different pore sizes. He finds that a membrane with 140-nanometer pores holds back the influenza virus, whereas a 180-nanometer pore allows the virus to pass. Membrane filters eventually become available commercially for use in sterilizing culture media and other fluids for use in microbiology. (See 1922 A.)

B. BACTERIAL PHYSIOLOGY: *Production of Cellulose* by **Acetobacter**

H. L. A. Tarr and Harold Hibbert find that a pure culture of *Bacterium xylinum* (*Acetobacter xylinus*) produces a compound identical to cellulose when the organism is grown on hexose sugars, their anhydrides, and substances that are readily converted to hexose. In 1934, Hibbert and J. Barsha use both chemical and X-ray analysis to confirm that the membranous film on the surface of the cultures is chemically identical to cellulose. They believe that the cellulose is a component of the bacterial cell wall. (See 1822 A, 1837 C, 1868 B.)

C. BACTERIAL PHYSIOLOGY: *Smooth and Rough* **Haemophilus**

Margaret Pittman investigates variation and type specificity in strains of *Haemophilus influenzae*. Based on the appearance of colonies, she finds two types: S strains, which are smooth, large, opaque, and iridescent by transmitted light and R strains that are rough and irregular, less opaque, and not iridescent. The S strains possess capsules and produce a soluble-specific substance in culture filtrates, while the R strains lack capsules and do not produce the soluble-specific substance. The S strains are more pathogenic for animals, but spontaneous conversion from S to R occurs in artificial media. (See 1921 B, 1931 H.)

1931 *(continued)*

D. BACTERIAL GENETICS: *Transformation In Vitro*

Martin H. Dawson and Richard H. P. Sia accomplish successful transformation of pneumococcus in vitro by using heated smooth (S) cells and a rough (R)-cell culture grown in the presence of blood or serum containing anti-R antibody. (See 1928 C, 1944 C.)

E. VIRAL DISEASE: *Swine Influenza Virus*

Studying an epizootic of "hog flu," Richard Erwin Shope isolates a virus that is later found to be antigenically similar to human influenza virus A, which is discovered in 1933. (See 1933 D, 1940 K.)

F. VIROLOGY: *Virus Cultivation in Tissue Culture*

C. Hallauer reports the successful growth of fowl plague virus in cultures containing pulped chicken embryos. Noting that virus growth depends on the reproduction of the tissue cells, he suggests that a method may be found for the enumeration of virus. This work is overshadowed by Ernest William Goodpasture's success with virus cultivation in hen's eggs. (See 1917 D, 1928 E, 1933 E, 1936 L, 1948 F, 1949 I.)

G. VIROLOGY: *Virus Growth in Hen's Eggs*

Ernest William Goodpasture and Alice Miles Woodruff introduce the use of fertilized hen's eggs for the cultivation of animal viruses. They find that the fowlpox virus grows when inoculated onto the chorioallantoic membrane. (See 1901 E, 1931 F, 1936 G, 1940 J, 1946 I.)

H. IMMUNOLOGY: *Pneumococcus Capsules/Role in Phagocytosis*

René Jules Dubos and Oswald T. Avery find that an enzyme from a spore-forming anaerobic bacterium produces an enzyme that degrades the capsular polysaccharide of type III pneumococcus, but not that of other types of pneumococci. Their experiments show that this enzyme protects mice against infection with type III bacteria, and they suggest that the protective effect results from removing the capsule, thus enhancing phagocytosis of the infecting organism. (See 1921 B, 1931 C.)

I. BIOCHEMISTRY: *Bacterial and Plant Photosynthesis*

Cornelius B. van Niel shows that the photosynthesis in green plants is carried out by a process different from that of photosynthetic sulfur bacteria. His results show that plants use water as a source of electrons for the reduction (fixation) of carbon dioxide to form sugar and that gaseous oxygen is released in this process. The sulfur bacteria, on the other hand, use hydrogen sulfide as a source of the electrons for the fixation of carbon dioxide, releasing elemental sulfur. van Niel's studies revolutionize theories of photosynthesis and the methods used for experimentation. His idea about the source of oxygen in green plant photosynthesis is confirmed by Samuel Ruben, Martin David Kamen, and William Zev Hassid in 1939. (See 1939 I, 1941 I.)

J. BIOCHEMISTRY: Zwischenferment/*Glucose 6-Phosphate Dehydrogenase*

The observation of Otto Warburg and Walter Christian of an enzyme in red blood cells that oxidizes glucose 6-phosphate leads to an understanding that pathways other than glycolysis exist for the metabolism of glucose. By 1935 Warburg, Christian, and A. Griese show that the product of the reaction is 6-phosphogluconate. *Zwischenferment,* the name given the enzyme by Warburg and Christian, and later called glucose 6-phosphate dehydrogenase, is the first enzyme in a pathway known variously as the phosphogluconate pathway, the hexose monophosphate shunt, and the pentose phosphate pathway, as well as the heterolactic acid shunt and the Entner-Doudoroff pathway. (See 1950 D, 1951 E, 1952 F.)

K. BIOCHEMISTRY: *Glycolysis/Glucose Monophosphate*
Earl Judson King and Arthur Robison identify the "Robison ester" as glucose monophosphate. (See 1914 G.)

L. GENETICS: *Crossing Over*
In earlier genetic analyses by Thomas Hunt Morgan and Alfred Sturtevant, crossing over was assumed but not seen. In 1931, two papers appear that describe crossing over correlated with genetic and cytological markers. Harriet B. Creighton and Barbara McClintock observe cytological crossing over with the aid of a chromosome that has a conspicuous knob at one end. Curt Stern studies the fate of an X chromosome with a portion of a Y chromosome attached to one end. The microscopically visible markers in both experiments serve to confirm that crossing over involves the exchange of portions between chromosomes. (See 1911 G, 1911 H.)

M. PHYSICS: *the Cyclotron*
Ernest Orlando Lawrence develops the cyclotron, the first useful particle smasher. The cyclotron prepares radioactive isotopes by bombardment with nuclear particles. Lawrence receives the Nobel Prize in physics in 1939. (See 1934 M, 1934 N, 1934 O, 1939 I, 1940 B.)

N. TECHNOLOGY: *Architecture*
The Empire State Building in Manhattan is completed in New York City. At a height of 381 meters, it becomes both the world's tallest office building and the tallest structure. (See 1889 K, 1913 I, 1930 H, 1972 P, 1973 Q.)

1932

A. BACTERIAL GENETICS: *Cell-Free Transformation*
J. L. Alloway accomplishes the first cell-free transformation in *Diplococcus pneumoniae* (*Streptococcus pneumoniae*) by treating a suspension of a rough strain with an extract from a smooth strain. One method that he uses for preparing the extract yields a material that forms a thick, stringy precipitate; he does not know that it probably contains DNA. (See 1928 C, 1931 D, 1944 C.)

B. ANTIMICROBIAL AGENTS: *Sulfonamide Drugs*
Gerhard Domagk adds a sulfonamide group to an azo dye to create the drug prontosil, a forerunner of the sulfonamide drugs. J. Tréfouël and others in Daniel Bovet's laboratory show that prontosil is converted to sulfanilamide in the body, a discovery that introduces the era of the sulfa drugs. Domagk is awarded the Nobel Prize in physiology or medicine in 1937, but his acceptance is canceled by the German government. He receives

the award in 1947 but does not receive the monetary prize. (See 1940 G, 1946 E.)

C. MICROBIOLOGY: *Isolation of Coccidioides*
R. A. Stewart and K. F. Meyer develop a synthetic medium that retards the growth of most bacteria and fungi to facilitate efforts to isolate coccidioides from soil. By treating soil samples with a 30% salt solution, which coccidioides survives, they are consistently able to isolate *Coccidioides immitis* and establish that soil is a residue for this organism.

D. VIRAL DISEASE: *Shope Papillomavirus*
Richard Shope shows that the common wart of cottontail rabbits is caused by a virus. This is the first discovery of a solid tumor in animals caused by a virus since Francis Peyton Rous's 1911 description of a sarcoma virus in chickens. (See 1911 E.)

E. MICROSCOPY: *Phase Contrast*
Frits Zernike discovers the phase principle of light and subsequently publishes on the Foucault knife-edge test, which measures the accuracy of grinding mirrors for use in telescopes. This work leads him to develop the phase-contrast method of microscopy, which facilitates the examination of biological objects that have little contrast. Zernike receives the Nobel Prize in physics in 1953 for this work.

F. ELECTRON MICROSCOPY
Max Knoll and Ernst Ruska construct the first electron microscope, while E. Brüche and H. Johannson obtain the first images with the electrostatic electron microscope. Ruska shares the 1986 Nobel Prize in physics with Gerd Binnig and Heinrich Rohrer, developers of the scanning tunneling microscope. (See 1937 I, 1938 C. 1939 G, 1981 M.)

G. BIOCHEMISTRY: *ADP and ATP*
Karl Lohmann determines the chemical structure of ADP (adenosine 5′-diphosphate) and ATP (adenosine 5′-triphosphate) in 1932 and 1935, respectively. In 1934, Lohmann discusses the importance of high–energy bonds in biochemical reactions. (See 1929 J, 1941 K.)

H. BIOCHEMISTRY: *Yellow Enzyme/Flavin Mononucleotide*
Otto Warburg and Walter Christian isolate the "yellow enzyme," flavin mononucleotide or riboflavin phosphate. (See 1934 K.)

I. BIOCHEMISTRY: *Ornithine Cycle*
Hans Adolf Krebs and Kurt Henseleit report on their study of the formation of urea by the ornithine cycle. When preparing this report, Krebs does not know of the role of citrulline, but later this year, he publishes a second paper that includes citrulline in the cycle. In 1933 a paper appears, written by Krebs but under the name of a student, H. Mandersheid, presenting the circular form of the cycle as it is usually represented today.

J. BIOCHEMISTRY: *Vitamin C (Ascorbic Acid)*
Charles Glen King crystallizes an antiscurvy substance from lemon juice that is found to be identical with Albert Szent-Györgyi's hexuronic acid.

Walter Norman Haworth synthesizes and determines the structure of vitamin C in 1933 and assigns the name ascorbic acid. Haworth shares the 1937 Nobel Prize in chemistry with Paul Karrer, who is honored for his work on vitamin A. (See 1928 G, 1933 J.)

K. CHEMISTRY: *Deuterium / Isotope Labeling*
Harold Clayton Urey, working with F. G. Brickwedde and G. M. Murphy, obtains hydrogen with a mass of 2 after controlled evaporation of liquid hydrogen. This form of hydrogen, later named deuterium, is found to combine with oxygen in industrial electrolytic cells to form "heavy water." Urey becomes a pioneer in isotope labeling when he prepares various compounds containing deuterium. He also develops methods for obtaining the naturally occurring isotopes of nitrogen (^{15}N), carbon (^{13}C), and oxygen (^{18}O). Urey receives the Nobel Prize in chemistry in 1934. (See 1935 M.)

L. PHYSICS: *the Neutron*
James Chadwick's discovery of the neutron leads to the concept that the atomic nucleus is composed of positively charged protons and neutral neutrons. Chadwick receives the Nobel Prize in physics in 1935.

M. PHYSICS: *the Positron*
Carl David Anderson discovers the positron, and he also makes major contributions to the study of gamma rays, cosmic rays, and the μ meson. Anderson shares the 1936 Nobel Prize in physics with Victor Hess, who discovered cosmic rays in 1911.

N. TECHNOLOGY: *Balloon Flight to the Stratosphere*
Auguste Piccard is the first person to ascend to the stratosphere when he reaches a height of 53,153 feet in a sealed gondola attached to a balloon. Piccard turns to undersea exploration in 1948 when he constructs a bathyscaphe. (See 1783 D.)

O. SOCIETY AND POLITICS
- Franklin Delano Roosevelt is elected president of the United States.
- Mohandas Karamchand Gandhi, a Hindu nationalist leader, begins a "fast unto death" to protest the treatment of India's "untouchables." In about 1920, he began to be called Mahatma Gandhi, or Great Soul. (See 1948 P.)
- Charles Lindbergh's infant son is kidnapped and later found dead. In 1934, Bruno Hauptmann is arrested and charged with the crime. Hauptmann protests his innocence until his execution in 1936.

P. THE ARTS: *Literature*
- Erskine Caldwell's novel *Tobacco Road* is published.
- Aldous Huxley completes *Brave New World*.

1933

A. BACTERIAL TAXONOMY: *Lancefield's Classification of Streptococci*
Rebecca Lancefield differentiates among the hemolytic streptococci by means of precipitin reactions utilizing the antigenic group-specific substance carbohydrate C. She presents a serological classification of five

1933 (continued)

groups that she calls A, B, C, D, and E. The principal human pathogen, *Streptococcus pyogenes,* is in Lancefield group A. (See 1919 A, 1952 B.)

B. BACTERIAL DISEASE: *Endotoxin/Lipid A*

A. Boivin, J. Mesrobeanu, and L. Mesrobeanu, carrying out a trichloro-acetic acid extraction of gram-negative bacteria, recover a precipitate that they call fraction A. Their tests show that this fraction retains toxicity for rabbits and is not antigenic—it contains the endotoxin of these organisms. Later studies by Otto Westphal and Otto Lüderitz lead to the term lipid A for the toxic component of endotoxin. (See 1892 D, 1954 C, 1957 H, 1960 A.)

C. BACTERIOPHAGE: *Nucleic Acid*

Martin Schlesinger develops a procedure for preparing weighable amounts of the bacteriophage of *Escherichia coli* and of a phage of *Staphylococcus.* He finds a high content of phosphorus and an intense staining with the Feulgen reagent, suggesting a high content of "thymonucleic acid." (See 1935 E.)

D. VIRAL DISEASE: *Influenza Virus*

Wilson Smith, Christopher Andrewes, and Patrick Laidlaw successfully infect ferrets with human influenza virus, obtained by preparing a bacteria-free filtrate of nasal washings from human patients. This experiment proves that the causative agent of influenza is a virus, not the bacterium *Haemophilus influenzae,* as had been thought since shortly after the pandemic of 1889 to 1890. The influenza virus isolated in 1933 becomes known as influenza A after Thomas Francis isolates a different strain in 1940, which is given the name influenza B. (See 1889 E, 1892 B, 1918 D, 1931 F, 1940 K.)

E. VIROLOGY: *Roller Tube Cultivation*

George O. Gey develops a method for cultivating viruses in tissue culture tubes that are revolved horizontally to increase the oxygen supply to the cells. The method permits cultivation of large quantities of virus. (See 1928 E, 1931 F, 1936 L.)

F. IMMUNOLOGY: *Pertussis Vaccine*

Louis Wendlin Sauer reports good results from immunizing young children with phenol-treated *Bordetella pertussis.* (See 1923 E, 1936 K.)

G. CELL BIOLOGY: *Chloroplasts and Mitochondria in Plants and Algae*

A. G. Guillermond proves that photosynthetic cells contain both mitochondria and chloroplasts. (See 1937 E.)

H. BIOCHEMISTRY: *Glucose-Phosphate Isomerase*

Karl Lohmann identifies glucose-phosphate isomerase, the enzyme that catalyzes the conversion of glucose 6-phosphate to fructose 6-phosphate. (See 1918 F.)

I. BIOCHEMISTRY: *Glycolytic Intermediates*

Gustav Embden's laboratory identifies 3-phosphoglycerate and fructose diphosphate (fructose bisphosphate) as being intermediates in glycolysis. Embden found, in 1914, that fructose diphosphate stimulates fermentation. (See 1906 J, 1914 F, 1928 F.)

J. BIOCHEMISTRY: *Vitamin C (Ascorbic Acid)*

Tadeusz Reichstein and, independently, Walter Norman Haworth with Edmund Langley Hirst determine the structure and collaborate in synthesizing vitamin C. Haworth and Hirst assign the name "ascorbic acid" from the Greek meaning "no scurvy." Haworth shares the 1937 Nobel Prize in chemistry with Paul Karrer. For his work on adrenal steroids, Reichstein shares the 1950 Nobel Prize in physiology or medicine with Edward Kendall and Philip Hench, who are honored for their work with cortisone. (See 1928 G, 1932 J, 1936 R.)

K. SOCIETY AND POLITICS

Adolf Hitler is appointed chancellor of Germany and is given dictatorial powers.

L. THE ARTS: *Art*

Joan Miró completes the painting *Composition*.

1934

A. BACTERIAL PHYSIOLOGY: *Stickland Reaction*

Leonard Hubert Stickland uses washed suspensions of *Clostridium sporogenes* to study amino acid degradation. He finds that the amino acids are degraded in pairs, with certain ones (e.g., alanine, valine, and leucine) functioning as hydrogen donors and others (e.g., glycine, proline and hydroxyproline) as hydrogen acceptors. Later studies by Stickland and others reveal that many species of bacteria carry out what is later known as the "Stickland reaction."

B. BACTERIAL DISEASE: *Life Cycle of* Chlamydia

Samuel P. Bedson and J. O. W. Bland describe the life cycle of *Chlamydia psittaci*. They characterize the infectious stage as elementary bodies that are taken in by phagocytosis to become reticulate bodies; these structures then replicate by fission, ultimately releasing elementary bodies to renew the cycle. For some time these organisms are referred to as *Bedsonia*. In this same year Phillips Thygeson demonstrates the same cycle of growth in organisms causing cases of inclusion conjunctivitis. After these studies, the causative agents of both trachoma and inclusion conjunctivitis are included in the psittacosis-lymphogranuloma venereum group of atypical viruses. (See 1879 C, 1907 B, 1934 B, 1957 G.)

C. BACTERIAL GENETICS: *Mutation in Bacteria*

I. M. Lewis proves that the change from lactose negative to lactose positive in *Escherichia coli mutabile* is a mutation. He concludes that sugars and alcohols act as selective agents and do not cause variation. His conclusion about spontaneous mutation in bacteria goes unappreciated at the time, although his work predates Salvador Luria's and Max Delbrück's fluctuation test experiment by almost a decade. (See 1907 A, 1943 D.)

D. IMMUNOLOGY: *Vi Antigen in* Salmonella

A. Felix and R. M. Pitt observe that some cultures of the typhoid bacillus do not agglutinate in sera containing anti-O antibody. Because they find that this property is associated with an antigenic property that seems to

1934 *(continued)*

confer virulence, they coin the term Vi antigen. The Vi antigen is now regarded as a special class of capsular, or K, antigens. (See 1916 D, 1920 C, 1941 A.)

E. BACTERIOPHAGE: *DNA and Protein*
Martin Schlesinger, studying what is now called a T-even bacteriophage of *Escherichia coli,* uses differential centrifugation to obtain a sufficient quantity of phage for chemical analysis. He finds that it consists of approximately equal amounts of protein and DNA. However, the current idea that DNA is a tetranucleotide does not lead to a clearer understanding of the chemistry of phages. (See 1933 C.)

F. ELECTRON MICROSCOPY: *Biological Specimens*
Ladislaus László Marton is the first to report using the electron microscope for viewing biological specimens. (See 1932 F, 1937 D, 1940 A.)

G. CELL BIOLOGY: *Membrane Structure*
Hugh Davson and James Frederic Danielli begin the formulation of a concept of membrane structure. They propose that cell membranes are constructed of a lipid bilayer covered on both the inner and outer sides by a layer of protein, a "protein-lipid sandwich." The nonpolar hydrocarbon ends of the lipid bilayers face each other on the interior of the two layers, while the polar, phospholipid components are situated on the outer and inner surfaces of the membrane. They also suggest that hydrophilic proteins penetrate the bilayer at some places, serving as pores for the passage of polar compounds across the membrane. (See 1894 G, 1910 G, 1925 E, 1960 O, 1972 K.)

H. GENETICS: *Mutation/Ultraviolet Light*
Edgar Altenburg reports using ultraviolet light to cause lethal mutation in fruit flies. Although not concerned with visible mutations, he mentions seeing two changes in wing structure and one in eye color. (See 1927 E, 1939 E.)

I. BIOCHEMISTRY: *Glycolytic Intermediates*
In the years 1934 to 1936, Otto Meyerhof's laboratory identifies dihydroxyacetone phosphate, glyceraldehyde 3-phosphate, 2-phosphoglycerate, and phosphoenolpyruvate as intermediates in glycolysis.

J. BIOCHEMISTRY: *Pyruvate Kinase in Glycolysis*
Jacob Karol Parnas and coworkers identify pyruvate kinase as the enzyme that catalyzes the conversion of phosphoenolpyruvate and ADP to pyruvate and ATP. This is the first recognition that ATP is formed with energy derived from glycolysis.

K. BIOCHEMISTRY: *Flavin Mononucleotide/Warburg's Yellow Enzyme*
By separating the pigment from the protein portion of the yellow enzyme, Hugo Teodor Theorell shows the colored component to be enzymatically inactive riboflavin phosphate. For his work on oxidative enzymes, Theorell receives the 1955 Nobel Prize in physiology or medicine.

L. BIOCHEMISTRY: *Kinetics/Lineweaver-Burk Double-Reciprocal Plot*

Hans Lineweaver and Dean Burk describe a graphical method for testing and interpreting kinetic data and for determining dissociation constants for enzyme-substrate and enzyme-inhibitor reactions. The method is called a double-reciprocal plot because the reciprocal of the observed velocity of reaction is plotted against the reciprocal of the substrate concentration. Both the Michaelis-Menten constant and the theoretical maximum velocity can be interpolated from the plot. It is also easy to recognize the difference between competitive and noncompetitive inhibitors of the enzymatic reaction. (See 1913 F, 1928 H.)

M. PHYSICS: *Radioactive Carbon*

H. C. Crane and T. Lauritsen are the first to observe radioactive carbon, ^{11}C, as a product of the bombardment of boron with deuterons. Since the half-life of ^{11}C is short, about 21 minutes, biological experiments can be performed only near a cyclotron, either in Berkeley, California, or Cambridge, Massachusetts. (See 1931 M, 1934 N, 1934 O, 1939 I, 1940 B.)

N. PHYSICS: *Tritium*

Marcus Laurence Oliphant and Paul Harteck produce the radioactive isotope of hydrogen, tritium (^3H), by bombarding deuterated water (heavy water) with deuterons. (See 1931 M, 1932 K, 1934 M, 1934 O, 1939 I, 1940 B.)

O. PHYSICS: *Radioactive Phosphorus*

Frédéric Joliot-Curie (Jean-Frédéric Joliot) and Irène Joliot-Curie produce the first artificial radioactive element, ^{30}P, by the bombardment of aluminum with alpha particles. In 1935, Enrico Fermi and collaborators produce ^{32}P by irradiating phosphorus (^{31}P) with slow neutrons. Because ^{30}P has a half-life of 2.5 minutes, as compared with 14.3 days for ^{32}P, the latter compound is widely used in biological research. (See 1931 M, 1934 M, 1934 N, 1939 I, 1940 B.)

P. TECHNOLOGY

In the bathysphere that they developed in 1930, Charles William Beebe and Otis Barton reach a record depth of 3,038 feet in the ocean. (See 1930 H.)

Q. SOCIETY AND POLITICS

Adolf Hitler becomes Führer of Germany.

1935

A. BACTERIOLOGICAL TECHNIQUE: *Continuous Culture of Bacteria*

J. P. Cleary, Paul J. Beard, and C. E. Clifton report results of experiments with a modification of the continuous flow culture system devised in 1930 by L. A. Rogers and E. O. Whittier. Cleary et al. study the effects of varying concentrations of peptone and glucose and rates of aeration on the growth of *Escherichia coli*. They provide no mathematical analysis of the nutrient supply rates and growth rates. (See 1950 C, 1956 B.)

B. BACTERIAL STRUCTURE: *Bacterial Nucleus*

C. Lindegren suggests that bacteria either have a single naked gene string or a gene string encrusted with chromatin. (See 1888 C, 1897 B, 1909 B, 1942 B, 1958 E.)

1935 *(continued)*

C. BACTERIAL PHYSIOLOGY: *Disinfection*

Gerhard Domagk discovers that long-chain quaternary ammonium salts are extremely effective germicides. This work, which demonstrates the feasibility of using these compounds in medicine and in general disinfection, leads to the synthesis of a variety of such germicides. (See 1916 B.)

D. BACTERIAL PHYSIOLOGY: *L Forms of Bacteria*

Emmy Klieneberger (later Klieneberger-Nobel), studying *Streptobacillus moniliformis,* successfully cultivates cells that are described as soft, protoplasmic forms. The term L form (L is for Lister Institute) is used to designate the types of colonial growth obtained. The L forms are initially thought to be similar to pleuropneumonialike organisms (PPLO), first observed in 1898 by Edmond Nocard and Émile Roux, but the work of Louis Dienes in 1939 shows that L forms can be formed from several different species if treated with penicillin. (See 1898 D, 1939 A.)

E. BACTERIAL PHYSIOLOGY: *Heterotrophic Carbon Dioxide Utilization*

Harland G. Wood and Chester Hamlin Werkman report the first of a number of experiments on how heterotrophic bacteria utilize carbon dioxide. In carbon balance calculations from studies of the fermentation of glycerol by propionibacteria, they conclude that CO_2 is consumed. Wood and Werkman later obtain definitive evidence for fixation through the use of heavy carbon dioxide, $^{13}CO_2$, and find that the first product, oxaloacetate, is followed by the formation of malate, fumarate, succinate, and propionate. They obtain $^{13}CO_2$ from a thermal diffusion column designed by A. O. Nier. (See 1942 D.)

F. BACTERIAL DISEASE: *Q Fever*

Edward Holbrook Derrick, working in Queensland, Australia, investigates an outbreak of fever among workers in a meat plant in Brisbane. Calling the disease "Q fever," for "query" (or questionable), he subsequently isolates the causative agent from guinea pigs. The name *Rickettsia burnetii* is assigned to the organism in honor of Frank Macfarlane Burnet, but in 1948 the generic name is changed to *Coxiella* because of its differences from the rickettsiae. The genus *Coxiella* is named after Herald Rea Cox, who successfully grows rickettsia in the yolk sac of chick embryos.

G. IMMUNOLOGY: *Influenza Vaccine*

Wilson Smith employs a strain of influenza, WS, isolated from his own infection with the disease, to immunize ferrets. Animals that recover from a primary infection are found to be immune to a second challenge for a period of about 3 months. This is the first of many experiments in a search for a safe and effective vaccine for influenza. (See 1933 D.)

H. VIROLOGY: *Crystallization of the Tobacco Mosaic Virus*

Wendell Meredith Stanley uses salt fractionation techniques to crystallize the tobacco mosaic virus (TMV), the first virus to be purified in this way. His conclusion that the virus is crystalline protein is challenged in 1936 by Frederick Bawden and Norman Pirie. Stanley's methods are derived from earlier work with TMV by C. G. Vinson and A. W. Petre and from John Howard Northrop's study of the enzyme pepsin. In 1931, Vinson and Petre reported some infectivity of crystals of the virus obtained using lead acetate. Stanley shares the 1946 Nobel Prize in chemistry with Northrop and James Batcheller Sumner. (See 1936 H, 1955 G.)

I. GENETICS: *Gene Structure and Mutation*
Nicolai Timoféeff-Ressovsky, K. G. Zimmer, and Max Delbrück publish a paper on gene mutation and gene structure. The authors estimate gene size, calculated by Delbrück, as 9 micrometers (which we now know is much too large) and include a discussion that leads to the formulation of the target theory of radiation effects on genes. Delbrück also presents the concept of a "gene molecule." (See 1944 I.)

J. BIOCHEMISTRY: *Formation of 6–Phosphogluconic Acid*
Otto Warburg, Walter Christian, and A. Griese find that under aerobic conditions a yeast macerate oxidizes glucose 6-phosphate to 6-phosphogluconic acid. This reaction is later recognized as an important first step in metabolic pathways such as the Entner-Doudoroff in members of the genus *Pseudomonas* and the pentose phosphate pathway. (See 1936 O, 1950 D, 1952 F.)

K. BIOCHEMISTRY: *Phosphorylation of Hexose Derived from Glycogen*
Jakob Parnas and Thaddeus Baranowski prove that the hexose subunits derived from the enzymatic degradation of glycogen are phosphorylated in the absence of ATP. The product is later confirmed to be a mixture of glucose 6-phosphate and fructose 6-phosphate. (See 1914 G, 1918 F.)

L. BIOCHEMISTRY: *Structure of Riboflavin*
Paul Karrer synthesizes riboflavin (vitamin B_2) and proves its structure. In 1930 and afterward he works out the structure of carotene, vitamin E, and vitamin K. He also studies the chemistry of vitamin C and biotin. Karrer shares the 1937 Nobel Prize in chemistry with Norman Haworth.

M. BIOCHEMISTRY: *Isotopes in Metabolic Research*
Rudolf Schoenheimer and D. Rittenberg study the metabolic turnover of fat by feeding laboratory animals the hydrogen isotope deuterium to label fatty acids and sterol derivatives. In later studies, Schoenheimer and Rittenberg use ^{15}N to label amino acids and show that there is turnover between free amino acids and protein. (See 1904 F, 1929 M, 1932 K.)

N. ETHOLOGY: *Imprinting*
Konrad Zacharias Lorenz describes "imprinting," a phenomenon in which young birds attach to the first moving animal or inanimate object they see and regard it as a member of their own species. Lorenz shares the Nobel Prize in physiology or medicine in 1973 with Karl von Frisch and Nikolaas Tinbergen, an early ethologist. (See 1919 E.)

O. SCIENTIFIC PUBLICATION: Bacteriological News (ASM News)
A newsletter describing activities of the Society of American Bacteriologists is published. Its name is changed to *Bacteriological News* in 1957 and to *ASM*

1935 *(continued)*

News in 1963 after the society's name is changed to the American Society for Microbiology in 1960.

P. SOCIETY AND POLITICS

Under U.S. president Franklin Delano Roosevelt's "New Deal" social program, the Social Security Act is passed. Workers' incomes are taxed at 1% beginning in 1937 and rising to 3% in 1939. Qualified persons may retire at age 65 beginning in 1942.

Q. THE ARTS: *Music*

George Gershwin's opera *Porgy and Bess* is performed.

1936

A. MICROBIOLOGICAL TECHNIQUE: *Gaseous Sterilization / Ethylene Oxide*

A patent for using alkylene oxides for killing microorganisms and pests is obtained by H. Schrader and E. Bossert. G. W. Kirby and colleagues also patent the use of ethylene oxide, for use in bakeries, to control mold contamination and bacterial ropiness in bread.

B. BACTERIAL PHYSIOLOGY: *Methane Bacteria*

H. A. Barker isolates *Methanobacillus omelianskii* from sediment in the Delft canal. Barker may not be the first to obtain a methanogen in pure culture, since C. G. T. P. Schnellen reports in a 1947 thesis that he has isolated organisms he refers to as *Methanosarcina barkeri* and *Methanobacterium formicicum* at an earlier date. (See 1940 B, 1967 G.)

C. BACTERIAL PHYSIOLOGY: *IMViC Tests for Coliforms*

Leland W. Parr uses the acronym IMViC for the indole, methyl red, Voges-Proskauer, and citrate tests used to differentiate *Escherichia coli* from *Aerobacter aerogenes* (*Enterobacter*) and related bacteria. The term "coliform" does not come into widespread use until 1937. (See 1889 A, 1898 A, 1910 C, 1915 A, 1925 A, 1937 B).

D. BACTERIOPHAGE: *Lysogeny*

Eugène Wollman and Elisabeth Wollman attempt to find preformed phage in a lysogenic strain of *Bacillus megatherium* (*B. megaterium*) both by lysing the cells and by treatment with the enzyme lysozyme. Finding no intracellular phage, they explain lysogeny in terms of "infectious heredity." (See 1925 C, 1929 D, 1950 I.)

E. BACTERIOPHAGE: *Mutants*

Frank Macfarlane Burnet and D. Lush report the isolation of phage mutants in their study of bacteriophages of *Salmonella enteriditis*. (See 1945 B.)

F. VIROLOGY: *Growth of Poliomyelitis Virus in Cell Culture*

Albert Bruce Sabin and P. K. Olitsky cultivate poliomyelitis virus in human embryonic nerve tissue, obtaining proof of viral growth by injection of culture fluids into monkeys. Because of difficulty obtaining the human tissue and the necessity of using monkeys for confirmation of growth, no practical use is made of this accomplishment. The poliovirus is again successfully cultivated in 1949 by John F. Enders, Frederick C. Robbins, and Thomas H. Weller. (See 1909 F, 1912 B, 1949 I.)

G. VIROLOGY: *Growth of Influenza Virus in Eggs*
Frank Macfarlane Burnet cultivates the influenza virus in embryonated eggs. (See 1901 E, 1931 F, 1931 G, 1940 J, 1946 I.)

H. VIROLOGY: *Nucleic Acid in Tobacco Mosaic Virus*
Wendell Stanley's claim, in 1935, that crystalline tobacco mosaic virus contains only protein is challenged by Frederick C. Bawden, Norman W. Pirie, John Desmond Bernal, and Isidor Fankuchen when they report that "liquid crystalline" virus precipitates contain phosphorus and carbohydrate, identified as being contained in the ribose type of nucleic acid. Over the next several years Stanley accepts these conclusions and includes them in his description of the virus.

I. VIRAL DISEASE: *Murine Breast Cancer Virus*
John Joseph Bittner shows that mammary cancer of mice is transmitted through milk. Demonstration that a transmissible agent is present leads to recognition that the cancer has viral etiology. (See 1911 E.)

J. PRION DISEASE: *Scrapie/Spongiform Encephalopathies*
J. Cuillé and P.-L. Chelle prove that the disease scrapie is transmissible by injection of brain and spinal cord filtrates from affected animals. Scrapie, now recognized as a type of spongiform encephalopathy, is a disease of sheep known for 200 or more years. Its name is derived from a pruritus that causes infected sheep to scrape their bodies against fence posts or trees. Scrapie, kuru, bovine spongiform encephalopathy, transmissible mink encephalopathy, and chronic wasting disease in mule deer and elk may be caused by infectious protein agents called prions. (See 1920 D, 1957 K, 1966 L, 1981 K, 1982 M, 1985 H.)

K. IMMUNOLOGY: *Pertussis Vaccine*
Between 1936 and 1943, Pearl Kendrick carries out several trials of pertussis vaccines prepared by using thimerosal to inactivate freshly isolated *Bordetella pertussis* and precipitating the vaccine with alum. She emphasizes the use of nonvaccinated control groups. In light of the variable results obtained by other workers, she and G. Eldering develop a method to standardize the vaccines using units of opacity and a test of the potency of the vaccines by intracerebral challenge of mice. (See 1933 F.)

L. IMMUNOLOGY: *Yellow Fever Vaccine*
Max Theiler and associates at the Rockefeller Foundation develop a vaccine against yellow fever. They employ tissue culture techniques with a minced mixture of mouse and chick embryo to grow the virus, eventually deriving a type called 17D that is safe to use in a vaccine. The 17D strain of yellow fever virus was originally derived from a virulent virus isolated from a West African patient named Asibi (Asibi virus). Theiler subsequently grows the virus in embryonated eggs using Ernest William Goodpasture's procedures. Theiler receives the 1951 Nobel Prize in physiology or medicine. (See 1901 F, 1919 D, 1931 G.)

1936 *(continued)*

M. BIOCHEMISTRY: *Phosphofructokinase in Glycolysis*

In Jakob Parnas's laboratory, phosphofructokinase is identified as the catalyst that converts fructose 6-phosphate to fructose diphosphate (bisphosphate), requiring ATP and Mg^{2+}. (See 1914 F, 1928 F, 1933 I, 1936 N.)

N. BIOCHEMISTRY: *Aldolase in Glycolysis*

Otto Meyerhof and Karl Lohmann show that the enzyme aldolase splits fructose diphosphate (bisphosphate) to form dihydroxyacetone phosphate and glyceraldehyde 3-phosphate. (See 1928 F, 1933 I, 1936 M.)

O. BIOCHEMISTRY: *Metabolism of Phosphogluconic Acid*

Fritz Albert Lipmann and, independently, Frank Dickens study mechanisms of carbohydrate oxidation involving gluconic acid. Dickens reports that gluconic acid must be phosphorylated to be attacked by yeast enzymes. Suggesting that indophenol oxidase and cytochrome participate in the process, Dickens speculates on a mechanism for carbohydrate oxidation in vivo. Lipmann finds that phosphogluconic acid is fermented by a yeast macerate under anaerobic conditions and that CO_2 is formed. He proposes that 2-keto-6-phosphogluconate is a product. This compound later proves to be an intermediate in the Entner-Doudoroff pathway in pseudomonads. (See 1935 J, 1950 D, 1951 E, 1952 F.)

P. BIOCHEMISTRY: *Enzymatic Degradation and Synthesis of Glycogen*

Carl Ferdinand Cori and Gerty Theresa Cori demonstrate that the enzyme phosphorylase removes one glucose unit from glycogen, forming glucose 1-phosphate. In 1938, the Coris discover the interconversion reactions between glucose 1-phosphate and glucose 6-phosphate catalyzed by the enzyme phosphoglucomutase. In 1944, they demonstrate the enzymatic synthesis of glycogen in vitro. The Coris receive the 1947 Nobel Prize in physiology or medicine, shared with Bernardo Houssay for his work on pituitary hormones.

Q. BIOCHEMISTRY: *Pyridine Nucleotides*

By this date, Otto Warburg and Walter Christian have identified the pyridine nucleotides that they call diphospho-pyridine nucleotide (DPN) and triphospho-pyridine nucleotide (TPN). After 1961 these compounds become known as NAD (nicotinamide adenine dinucleotide) and NADP (nicotinamide adenine dinucleotide phosphate). (See 1938 G.)

R. PHYSIOLOGY: *Corticosteroid Compounds*

In this and following years, Edward Calvin Kendall and Philip Showalter Hench, working together, and Tadeusz Reichstein isolate and identify the corticosteroid compounds from the adrenal gland. Collectively, they study cortisone, corticosterone, 17-hydroxycorticosterone, and many other steroids. In 1948, Hench shows that cortisone is effective for treating rheumatoid arthritis. Hench, Kendall, and Reichstein share the 1950 Nobel Prize in physiology or medicine.

S. COMPUTER SCIENCE

Alan Turing publishes a paper outlining a universal calculating machine, or "Turing machine," that is a major contribution to the development of computer science.

T. TECHNOLOGY: *Television*

The first regularly scheduled television broadcasts are begun by the British Broadcasting Corporation. (See 1925 H, 1926 N, 1929 O, 1953 X.)

U. SOCIETY AND POLITICS

• The king of Great Britain, Edward VIII, abdicates the throne within a year of being crowned in order to marry a divorced commoner, Mrs. Wallis Simpson. He becomes duke of Windsor.

• The Spanish Civil War begins, continuing until 1939.

V. THE ARTS: *Literature*

Margaret Mitchell publishes her novel *Gone with the Wind*.

W. THE ARTS: *Art*

Henry Moore completes his sculpture *Two Forms*.

X. CULTURE: *Architecture*

Frank Lloyd Wright, American architect, builds a unique home called Fallingwater, in Bear Run, Pennsylvania.

1937

A. BACTERIAL STRUCTURE: D-*Glutamic Acid in Capsules*

G. Ivanovics and V. Bruckner find a D-glutamyl polypeptide in the capsule of *Bacillus anthracis,* the first report of a D-amino acid in bacteria. (See 1949 C, 1952 C.)

B. BACTERIAL PHYSIOLOGY: *Coliform Bacteria*

R. S. Breed and J. F. Norton suggest the use of the term "coliform" for lactose-fermenting bacteria identified in tests for water pollution. The term was first used by C. Revis in 1910 but not widely adopted. Leland W. Parr writes a review article entitled "Coliform Bacteria" in 1939. (See 1910 C.)

C. BACTERIAL PHYSIOLOGY: *Inhibition of Nitrogen Fixation by Hydrogen*

Perry W. Wilson and W. W. Umbreit, while studying the kinetics of nitrogen fixation in a red clover *Rhizobium trifolii* symbiosis in large bottles with specific mixtures of nitrogen and other gases, discover that nitrogen fixation is inhibited when hydrogen gas is used. Further experiments confirm that hydrogen competitively inhibits nitrogen fixation. (See 1966 C.)

D. ELECTRON MICROSCOPY: *Bacteria*

Ladislaus Marton publishes the first electron microscope photographs of bacteria. Within a few years, Stuart Mudd and his associates publish photographs made at a higher magnification and showing more detail. (See 1934 F, 1939 F, 1940 A, 1940 H, 1941 B.)

E. CELL BIOLOGY: *Procaryotic and Eucaryotic Cells*

E. Chatton proposes that the bacteria and "blue-green algae" be termed procaryotes and that all other cells be called eucaryotes. The distinction is

1937 *(continued)*

based on the absence of a true nucleus in the procaryotes. (See 1957 Q, 1962 A.)

F. VIROLOGY: *Proteins of Tobacco Mosaic Virus*
In a study following the earlier work with Frederick C. Bawden and Norman W. Pirie, John D. Bernal and Isidor Fankuchen report further crystallographic studies of tobacco mosaic virus "crystals" from infected plants. They conclude that all of the protein molecules have the same general shape and size and are composed of similar subunits.

G. IMMUNOLOGY: *Histocompatibility Complex*
Peter A. Gorer, in studies of tissue transplantation in mice, identifies antigen II as being associated with tumor rejection. Later, at the suggestion of George D. Snell, antigen II is renamed histocompatibility-2. Snell shares the 1980 Nobel Prize in physiology or medicine with Baruj Benacerraf and Jean Dausset. (See 1948 I.)

H. GENETICS: *Mutator Genes*
Milislav Demerec reports finding an unusually high frequency of spontaneous lethal mutations in some stocks of *Drosophila melanogaster* and that a recessive gene on the second chromosome is responsible. Demerec does not use the term "mutator gene," which appears in later papers. (See 1954 J.)

I. ELECTRON MICROSCOPY
James Hillier develops the first high-resolution electron microscope. His instrument has a resolving power of 100 nanometers and a magnification of 7,000-fold. (See 1932 F, 1939 G.)

J. BIOCHEMISTRY: *Citric Acid Cycle*
In their study of the biological oxidation of citrate, Carl Martius and Franz Knoop discover the sequence of biochemical reactions leading from citric acid to α-oxoglutarate. (See 1937 K, 1937 L.)

K. BIOCHEMISTRY: *Citric Acid Cycle*
Albert Szent-Györgyi proposes a pathway for the oxidation of triosephosphate that involves C_4-dicarboxylic acids. This concept is accepted by many researchers for a time instead of the cycle proposed by Hans Krebs. (See 1937 J, 1937 L.)

L. BIOCHEMISTRY: *Citric Acid Cycle*
Hans Adolf Krebs proposes the citric acid cycle after he shows the enzymatic formation of citrate from oxaloacetate and pyruvate. Krebs shares the 1953 Nobel Prize in physiology or medicine with Fritz Lipmann. (See 1937 J, 1937 K.)

M. BIOCHEMISTRY: *Electrophoresis*
In the period between 1926 and 1937, Arne Wilhelm Tiselius develops electrophoresis as a technique for separating proteins based on their migration in an electric field. He identifies serum proteins as albumin and alpha, beta, and gamma globulins. He notes that in immune rabbit serum, the gamma peak is higher than in normal serum. Tiselius receives the 1948 Nobel Prize in chemistry. (See 1938 A, 1939 H.)

N. GENETICS: *Evolution*

Theodosius Dobzhansky publishes *Genetics and the Origin of Species,* which brings together Darwinian natural selection, Mendelian genetics, mutation, and evolutionary theory. In 1970 he completes *Genetics and the Evolutionary Process.*

O. PHYSIOLOGY: *Pellagra/Nicotinic Acid*

Conrad Arnold Elvehjem proves that liver extract prevents both pellagra-like disease in baby chicks and black tongue in dogs. The following year he shows that both nicotinamide and nicotinic acid cure these diseases in animals.

P. SCIENTIFIC PUBLICATION: Bacteriological Reviews

The first issue of *Bacteriological Reviews* appears under the auspices of the Society of American Bacteriologists.

Q. TECHNOLOGY

• Chester Floyd Carlson invents xerography, a copying method by which carbon particles are transferred to local electrostatic charges on paper. It is not until 1959 that the first commercial Xerox copying machine is introduced.

• Two groups successfully build jet engines: Frank Whittle and A. A. Griffith in England and Pabst von Ohain and M. Müller in Germany. Whittle patented a jet engine in 1930. (See 1941 O.)

• The Golden Gate Bridge is completed in San Francisco, California.

• The zeppelin *Hindenburg* is destroyed by fire while trying to land in Lakehurst, New Jersey. Thirty-six of the 97 persons on board perish. The events leading to World War II and the improvement of airplanes cause the end of zeppelin manufacture. In 1997, a newly designed zeppelin built with modern materials is successfully flown.

R. SOCIETY AND POLITICS

Neville Chamberlain is named prime minister of Britain and initiates a policy of appeasement toward Germany's Adolf Hitler.

S. THE ARTS: *Art*

Pablo Picasso completes his painting *Guernica.*

1938

A. VIROLOGY: *Electrophoresis of Viruses*

Arne Wilhelm Tiselius uses electrophoretic techniques to isolate the bushy stunt virus and the cucumber mosaic virus. (See 1937 M.)

B. CELL BIOLOGY: *Microsomes/Ribosomes*

While using a high-speed centrifuge in attempts to purify the Rous sarcoma virus, Albert Claude obtains a cell fraction that is rich in RNA and contains small particles. He finds that such material can be isolated from a variety of cell types and by 1943 uses the term "microsomes" to define particles that range from 50 to 200 nanometers in diameter. In 1956, George Palade provides further studies of these particles, which become known as "ribosomes." Claude, Palade, and Christian de Duve share the 1974 Nobel Prize in physiology or medicine. (See 1955 P, 1956 Q.)

1938 (continued)

C. SCANNING ELECTRON MICROSCOPY

Manfred von Ardenne demonstrates a scanning electron microscope. (See 1932 F, 1939 G, 1970 L.)

D. BIOLOGY: *Hemoglobin in Root Nodules*

J. Pietz is the first to study the red pigment in legume root nodules, but it is H. Kubo, in 1939, who determines the absorption bands of the oxidized and reduced compound. He obtains crystals that are indistinguishable from protohemin and concludes that the red pigment is a hemoprotein analogous to hemoglobin. In 1945, David Keilin and Y. L Wang and, independently, Artturi Ilmari Virtanen confirm Kubo's conclusions. (See 1962 F.)

E. MOLECULAR BIOLOGY: *Origin of the Term*

Although many 19th century and early 20th century scientists studied molecular processes and structures and wrote of "chemical biology," the expression "molecular biology" came slowly into the scientific literature. Two persons, Warren Weaver in 1938 and William Astbury in 1947, are among the first to use the term, while many others, including André Lwoff, Jacques Monod, François Jacob, Max Delbrück, and their associates, play major roles in the beginnings of molecular biology.

F. BIOCHEMISTRY: *Cytochromes*

David Keilin with Edward Francis Hartree reports that cytochrome *a* is composed of two components: cytochrome *a* and cytochrome a_3. The a_3 component is found to be identical with the enzyme activity known as cytochrome oxidase, which is recognized as identical with Otto Warburg's *Atmungsferment* and Joseph Kastle's indophenol oxidase. (See 1910 D, 1924 C, 1938 F.)

G. BIOCHEMISTRY: *Flavin Adenine Dinucleotide*

Otto Warburg and Walter Christian obtain a purified preparation of a flavin that is later identified as flavin adenine dinucleotide (FAD). (See 1936 Q.)

H. X-RAY CRYSTALLOGRAPHY: *DNA*

William Thomas Astbury and Florence Ogilvy Bell obtain the first X-ray diffraction photographs of DNA. Their results show a regular spacing of 3.3 angstroms along a fiber axis. They comment on the significance of their data for chromosome structure and behavior and on the observation that polypeptide chains have similar spacing.

I. PHYSICS: *Nuclear Fission*

Otto Hahn discovers nuclear fission as a result of experiments performed first with the assistance of Lise Meitner and later with Fritz Strassmann. Hahn receives the 1944 Nobel Prize in physics.

J. SOCIETY AND POLITICS

The German führer, Adolf Hitler, annexes Austria, claiming that the citizens desire to be members of his Third Reich.

K. THE ARTS: *Theater*

Our Town by Thornton Wilder is first performed.

L. THE ARTS: *Radio*

A radio dramatization of H. G. Wells's novel *The War of the Worlds* is presented by actor and author Orson Welles. Widespread misunderstanding about realistic "news reports" of Martian landings in New Jersey results in panics in some areas despite repeated announcements that the program is fiction. A movie version of this story appears in 1953.

M. THE ARTS: *Art*

Henry Moore's sculpture *Recumbent Figure* is completed.

1939

A. BACTERIAL PHYSIOLOGY: *L Forms of Bacteria*

Louis Dienes proves that bacterial L forms can revert to the normal bacillary form. Penicillin, and other agents, interferes with cell wall synthesis and, in some instances, results in the formation of essentially wall-less bacteria that can nonetheless reproduce. On rare occasions, L forms regenerate cell walls. (See 1935 D.)

B. ANTIBIOTICS: *Tyrocidine and Gramicidin*

René Jules Dubos discovers a substance produced by *Bacillus brevis* that inhibits the growth of gram-positive bacteria. Substances of this type are named "antibiotics" in 1941 by Selman Waksman. Although a number of antibiotic substances, including penicillin, have been found by chance observation, this is the first antibiotic to be found through a deliberate effort. Dubos is assisted in purification experiments by Rollin D. Hotchkiss. The crude initial product, tyrothricin, is found to be a mixture of two compounds: tyrocidine and gramicidin. Both prove to be toxic for parenteral use, but gramicidin, used in topical applications, is still found today in some ointments and creams.

C. BACTERIAL INSECTICIDES

By 1939, the U.S. Department of Agriculture and other agricultural agencies develop methods to cultivate *Bacillus popilliae* and *Bacillus lentimorbus* so that preparations of their spores can be used to control the Japanese beetle. (See 1902 E, 1915 B, 1951 F, 1953 J, 1954 H.)

D. BACTERIOPHAGE: *One-Step Growth*

Emory L. Ellis and Max Delbrück publish a detailed one-step growth curve for a bacteriophage active against *Escherichia coli*. Their experimental results, showing that phage is liberated in sudden bursts, are compatible with the idea that phage liberation occurs when the cell lyses. Although Felix d'Herelle noted stepwise growth in 1921, the quantitatively detailed work of Ellis and Delbrück is the basis for much further study of bacteriophage.

E. GENETICS: *Chemical Mutagens*

Charles Thom and Robert A. Steinberg find that exposure to dyes and biological stains produce mutations in *Aspergillus niger* and other species of aspergilli. They employ aniline blue, acridine yellow, methylene blue, and methylene violet. They also report that mutations in the aspergilli are seen after growth in a medium containing sodium nitrite at pH 4.0. (See 1927 E, 1934 H.)

1939 *(continued)*

F. ELECTRON MICROSCOPY: *Viruses*

G. A. Kausche, E. Pfankuch, and Helmut Ruska publish electron microscope photographs of the tobacco mosaic virus, revealing a rod–shaped structure. Helmut Ruska is the brother of Ernst Ruska, a Nobel laureate who developed the first electron microscope in 1932. (See 1937 D, 1940 A, 1940 H.)

G. ELECTRON MICROSCOPY: *Commercial Manufacture*

An electron microscope designed by Bodo von Borries and Ernst Ruska is the first to be produced commercially, manufactured by the Siemens company.

H. IMMUNOLOGY: *Immunoglobulins*

Arne Wilhelm Tiselius and Elvin Abraham Kabat do further studies on moving boundary electrophoresis for use in separating proteins in blood serum. In 1937, Tiselius had found three types of globulin protein, named alpha, beta, and gamma. The antibodies found in the gamma peak become known as gamma globulins and later as immunoglobulins when some of the gamma proteins are found not to show antibody activity. After immunoglobulins (Igs) are found in all three peaks, a system of nomenclature develops for five classes: IgM, immunoglobulin macro; IgG, immunoglobulin gamma; IgA, a secretory antibody; IgD, a B-cell immunoregulator; and IgE, allergy-related antibody. Tiselius receives the 1948 Nobel Prize in chemistry. (See 1937 M, 1959 M, 1966 O.)

I. PLANT PHYSIOLOGY: *Radioisotopes in the Study of Photosyntheses*

In the first metabolic experiments using a radioactive isotope of carbon, produced in the cyclotron at the University of California, Berkeley, Samuel Ruben, Martin David Kamen, and William Zev Hassid study the photosynthetic uptake of $^{11}CO_2$ by barley plant leaves and by the alga *Chlorella*. They find that CO_2 is taken up in both the light and the dark, proving that the process is not light driven. In the light, radioactive sugars are produced by the barley plant. (See 1937 M, 1931 M, 1932 K, 1934 M, 1934 N, 1934 O, 1940 B.)

J. PLANT PHYSIOLOGY: *Oxygen Evolution by Chloroplasts*

Using suspensions of chloroplasts with the oxidation of hemoglobin as a sensitive detector of oxygen, Robert Hill finds that oxygen evolves only in the light in the presence of either leaf extracts or certain ferric salts. The evolution of oxygen in the presence of ferric iron or other oxidizing agents such as benzoquinone or indophenol dyes is known as the "Hill reaction."

K. PHYSIOLOGY: *Antihistamine*

Daniel Bovet discovers the first antihistamine drugs. He later develops drugs that block the action of adrenaline and noradrenaline. Bovet receives the 1957 Nobel Prize in physiology or medicine.

L. BIOCHEMISTRY: *Glycolysis*

H. Jost and H. Emde, of Gustav Embden's laboratory, propose the term "glycolysis" as a common term for both the lactic acid fermentation and alcoholic fermentation pathways.

M. BIOCHEMISTRY: *Intermediates in Glycolysis*

Jakob Parnas summarizes the work in his laboratory involving the phosphorylation of glucose 6-phosphate by ATP to yield fructose diphosphate (bisphophate) and adenosine monophosphate (AMP). (See 1929 J, 1939 O.)

N. BIOCHEMISTRY: *Intermediates in Glycolysis*

Erwin Paul Negelein and Heinz Brömel identify 1,3-diphosphoglycerate (bisphosphate) as being in the glycolytic pathway. (See 1928 F, 1933 I, 1936 M, 1936 N.)

O. BIOCHEMISTRY: *Phosphate Bond Energy in Glycolysis*

The conversion of 1,3-diphosphoglycerate (bisphospho-) and ADP to 3-phosphoglycerate and ATP is established as a mechanism to convert the energy of metabolism to phosphate bond energy. Otto Warburg, Walter Christian, Erwin Negelein, and Heinz Brömel all contribute to this work. (See 1929 J, 1939 M.)

P. BIOCHEMISTRY: *Electron Transport*

Eric Glendenning Ball constructs a diagram showing the order of the compounds in the electron transfer pathway. In 1942, he revises the sequence to include the oxidation of nicotinamide adenine dinucleotide (NAD) by flavoprotein. (See 1929 K.)

Q. BIOCHEMISTRY: *Respiratory Chain Phosphorylation*

Vladimir Belitser and Elena T. Tsybakova and, later, Severo Ochoa are the first to suggest the functioning of what is now known as respiratory chain phosphorylation. (See 1940 J, 1941 K, 1951 N.)

R. CHEMISTRY

Linus Carl Pauling publishes *The Nature of the Chemical Bond,* an influential book discussing in detail the many types of chemical bonds. In a chapter on the hydrogen bond, he mentions its probable importance in biological molecules. (See 1951 L.)

S. SOCIETY AND POLITICS

After Germany and Russia sign a nonaggression agreement, World War II begins when both countries invade Poland. England and France declare war on Germany.

T. THE ARTS: *Literature*

• James Joyce publishes *Finnegan's Wake.* The term "quark," used as a name for a type of subatomic particle, comes from this novel.
• John Steinbeck completes *The Grapes of Wrath.*

U. THE ARTS: *Movies*

• The film version of Margaret Mitchell's novel *Gone with the Wind* is released.
• The movie *The Wizard of Oz* is produced.

V. THE ARTS: *Art*

Alexander Calder's mobile sculpture *Lobster Trap and Fish Tail* is completed.

A. BACTERIAL STRUCTURE: *Electron Microscopy*

In a conference presentation of the first use of the electron microscope to study bacteria in some detail, Stuart Mudd and coworkers report the use of an electron microscope with a magnification of 50,000 diameters to show what they refer to as a "solid membrane" surrounding bacteria. Noting the shrinking of the inner cytoplasm during the fixation procedure, they refer to the outer structure of the cells without cytoplasmic content as "ghosts." They also suggest that some bacteria have tubular flagella. L. Marton published photographs of bacteria in 1937, but his interest was not primarily the study of microorganisms. (See 1937 D, 1939 F, 1940 H, 1941 B.)

B. BACTERIAL PHYSIOLOGY: *Radioisotopes in the Study of Methanogenesis*

H. A. Barker, Samuel Ruben, and Martin David Kamen employ radioactive carbon, ^{14}C, in studying the production of methane by *Methanobacterium omelianskii* and *Methanosarcina methanica*. They conclude that CO_2, acting as a hydrogen acceptor, is reduced to methane under anaerobic conditions. They produce ^{14}C by bombardment of a naturally occurring stable isotope of carbon, ^{13}C, with deuterons in a cyclotron. Not until after World War II does ^{14}C, produced in a nuclear reactor (a graphite "atomic pile") by bombardment of ^{14}N with neutrons, become widely available for research. (See 1931 M, 1934 M, 1934 N, 1934 O, 1939 I.)

C. BACTERIAL PHYSIOLOGY: *Hexosamine in Bacteria*

L. A. Epstein and Ernst Chain find an *N*-acetyl aminohexose in *Micrococcus lysodeikticus,* but they do not associate this compound with cell wall material. Methods for purifying bacterial cell wall compounds are not devised until 1951. (See 1951 B, 1953 B, 1954 B, 1956 C.)

D. ANTIBIOTICS: *Penicillin*

Howard Florey begins clinical trials with penicillin that is purified by Ernst Chain, assisted by Edward P. Abraham and Norman G. Heatley. Florey and Heatley later attempt to obtain larger quantities of penicillin for further trials. Researchers at the U.S. Department of Agriculture Northern Regional Research Laboratory find that *Penicillium chrysogenum* is a better source of penicillin than the original strain of *Penicillium notatum* isolated by Alexander Fleming in 1929. Both British and American armed forces use penicillin during World War II. Florey, Chain, and Fleming share the Nobel Prize in physiology or medicine in 1945. (See 1929 B, 1940 E, 1941 F.)

E. ANTIBIOTICS: *Penicillinase*

Edward P. Abraham and Ernst B. Chain report that crushed cells of *Bacterium coli* (*Escherichia coli*) contain a substance that destroys the growth-inhibiting properties of penicillin. Because this substance is inactivated by heat and activated papain and is not dialyzable through "cellophane" membranes, they conclude that it is an enzyme. They give the new enzyme the name "penicillinase," noting that it is not found in yeast, in *Penicillium notatum,* or in a penicillin-sensitive strain of *Staphylococcus aureus.* Penicillinase is later found to be a member of a broad class of enzymes called β-lactamases, which cleave the β-lactam ring of penicillin to form a penicilloic acid. (See 1929 B, 1940 D, 1941 F, 1944 B, 1949 G.)

F. ANTIBIOTICS: *Actinomycin*
Selman Waksman and H. Boyd Woodruff discover two antibacterial substances that they designate as actinomycin A and B, produced by a soil actinomycete. Actinomycin A proves to be highly bacteriostatic against gram-positive bacteria but less so against gram-negative bacteria, with limited use as an anticancer drug. Having first observed antibiotic production by actinomycetes in 1937, Waksman suggests the name "antibiotics" in 1941 for the antimicrobial substances produced by microorganisms. Continuing his search for antibiotics, he finds streptomycin in 1944 and neomycin in 1949. Waksman receives the Nobel Prize in physiology or medicine in 1952. (See 1944 A, 1961 T.)

G. ANTIMICROBIAL AGENTS: *Mode of Action of Sulfanilamide*
After T. C. Stamp and H. N. Green report that extracts of both streptococci and *Brucella abortus* antagonize the action of sulfanilamide, Donald D. Woods finds the same activity in yeast extract. He states that the chemical structure of the inhibitory compound appears to be related to that of sulfanilamide. Finding that *p*-aminobenzoic acid (PABA) has the same effect, Woods proposes that the mode of action of sulfanilamide is to competitively inhibit an enzyme necessary for the synthesis of PABA. (See 1932 B, 1946 E.)

H. BACTERIOPHAGE: *Electron Microscopy*
Helmut Ruska and, in a companion paper, E. Pfankuch, and G. A. Kausche publish the first electron microscope photographs of bacteriophage. They describe the phage particles as being sperm-shaped. (See 1939 F, 1942 G.)

I. BACTERIOPHAGE: *Lytic Action*
Max Delbrück characterizes two types of lysis of a strain of *Bacterium coli* (*Escherichia coli*) by a newly discovered phage. "Lysis from within" takes place when a single phage particle enters the cell and multiplies to a threshold level, at which time the cell lyses without deformation of the cell wall. "Lysis from without" is caused by adsorption of numerous phage above a threshold value, causing the cell wall to distend and be destroyed without formation of new phage particles.

J. VIROLOGY: *Cultivation and Enumeration of Viruses*
Frank Macfarlane Burnet extends Ernest William Goodpasture's techniques for growing viruses in fertilized hen's eggs. His method for titration of viral particles is to introduce dilutions of virus onto the chorioallantoic membrane of a series of eggs, followed by enumerating the pocks formed. (See 1931 G, 1936 G, 1946 I.)

K. VIRAL DISEASE: *Influenza Virus Strains B and C*
Thomas Francis isolates an influenza virus unlike that which Wilson Smith, Christopher Andrewes, and Patrick Laidlaw isolated in 1933. The 1933

1940 *(continued)*

strain becomes known as influenza A virus, the 1940 strain becomes known as influenza B virus, and a third strain, isolated in 1949 by R. M. Taylor, is named influenza C virus.

L. VIROLOGY: *Nucleic Acid in Animal Viruses*

In the 1940s several groups of researchers prove that nucleic acid is present in animal viruses. C. Hoagland et al. find DNA in vaccinia virus in 1940; A. R. Taylor et al. find RNA in equine encephalitis virus in 1941; A. R. Taylor et al. find DNA in rabbit papillomavirus in 1942; and C. A. Knight finds DNA in influenza virus in 1947.

M. IMMUNOLOGY: *Theories of Antibody Formation*

Linus Pauling modifies the "instructionalist theory" of antibody formation first formulated in the 1930s. He suggests that all antibody molecules contain the same polypeptide chains as normal globulin but differ only in the configuration of the coils in the molecule. (See 1930 D, 1955 H, 1957 N.)

N. IMMUNOLOGY: *Rh Blood Group*

Karl Landsteiner's and Alexander Wiener's discovery of the first Rh blood group antigen leads to the explanation of erythroblastosis fetalis, a hemolytic disease of newborn children. (See 1900 H, 1926 F.)

O. CHEMICAL INSECTICIDES: *Dichlorodiphenyltrichloroethane (DDT)*

Paul Herrmann Müller finds dichlorodiphenyltrichloroethane (DDT) to be an effective insecticide. It is used for the eradication of mosquitoes that carry malaria and yellow fever, the lice that carry typhus, and a variety of plant pests. During the 1960s, however, the use of DDT is discontinued because it is discovered that strains of insects resistant to DDT develop quickly and because its persistence in the food chain leads to widespread damage. Müller receives the 1948 Nobel Prize in physiology or medicine.

P. TECHNOLOGY

The Pennsylvania Turnpike opens. It is the first modern highway in the United States.

Q. SOCIETY AND POLITICS

In World War II, Norway, the Netherlands, Belgium, Luxembourg, Denmark, Romania, and France surrender to Germany. An "axis" is created by Germany, Italy, and Japan, forming a 10-year military and economic alliance.

R. THE ARTS: *Literature*

- Ernest Hemingway publishes *For Whom the Bell Tolls*.
- Carson McCullers completes her novel *The Heart Is a Lonely Hunter*.
- Richard Wright publishes the novel *Native Son*.

1941

A. BACTERIAL TAXONOMY: *Kauffmann–White Scheme for* **Salmonella**

F. Kauffmann, continuing work begun as early as 1935, including the studies of P. Bruce White, establishes a scheme of classification for the salmonellae based on their H (flagellar) and O (somatic) antigens. The Kauffmann-White scheme is subsequently used to classify the numerous variations of serological types (serovars) in the genus *Salmonella*. (See 1903 F, 1920 C, 1926 A, 1934 D.)

B. BACTERIAL STRUCTURE: *Electron Microscopy*
Following earlier studies reported in 1940, Stuart Mudd and D. B. Lackman use the electron microscope to study structural details of bacteria. Their photographs of *Bacillus* species demonstrate a cell wall and peritrichous flagella. (See 1940 A, 1940 H, 1953 E, 1958 A.)

C. BACTERIAL STRUCTURE: *Bacterial Flagella*
Adrianus Pijper presents results from 16-millimeter motion pictures of the motile typhoid bacteria. He describes how the bacterium propels itself with a long taillike spiral structure in continuous motion. He states that agglutinating antiserum causes a stiffening of the flagella, which may tangle and cause clumping. Pijper later abandons the idea that flagella are organs of locomotion. (See 1946 A, 1947 A.)

D. BACTERIAL STRUCTURE: *Differential Staining*
Georges Knaysi designs a staining procedure using potassium alum and tannic acid as mordant and carbol fuchsin as stain to color the cytoplasm, cell membrane, cell wall, and slime layer of bacteria differentially. (See 1953 D, 1958 A.)

E. BACTERIAL PHYSIOLOGY: *Diauxie/Two-Phase Growth of Bacteria*
Jacques Lucien Monod publishes his first paper on a phenomenon he calls "diauxie," a two-phase growth of bacteria when two sugars are incorporated in the growth medium. Monod concludes that as one sugar is metabolized it inhibits the utilization of the second. When the first sugar is totally consumed, a brief lag occurs during which the bacterium adapts to consumption of the second sugar. This work leads to the concept of enzyme induction and repression. (See 1900 I, 1930 A.)

F. ANTIBIOTICS: *Therapeutic Use of Penicillin*
Edward P. Abraham and the group developing penicillin report the treatment of 10 patients, with each showing some improvement in their clinical condition. They report no toxic effects of the drug and show that bacteriostatic concentrations can be maintained in the circulating blood. (See 1929 B, 1940 D, 1940 E.)

G. VIROLOGY: *Hemagglutination*
George Hirst and, independently, L. McClelland and Ronald Hare discover that influenza virus causes the clumping or agglutination of red blood cells, a phenomenon called hemagglutination.

H. MICROBIAL GENETICS: *One Gene-One Enzyme Concept*
George Beadle and Edward L. Tatum use X rays to create nutritional mutants of the fungus *Neurospora crassa*. After studying a series of such mutants, they conclude that a single gene codes for a single enzyme, thus formulating the "one gene-one enzyme" concept. At this time, when the role of DNA is not known, genes are thought to be either protein or nucleoprotein. Beadle, Tatum, and Joshua Lederberg share the 1958 Nobel Prize in physiology or medicine. (See 1927 E, 1934 H, 1939 E.)

1941 *(continued)*

I. PLANT PHYSIOLOGY: *Source of Oxygen in Photosynthesis*
Martin David Kamen, Samuel Ruben, and William Zev Hassid use H_2O and CO_2 labeled with isotopic oxygen (^{18}O) to study the fate of oxygen derived from water and from carbon dioxide during photosynthesis. They find that the molecular oxygen released is derived from water, whereas the oxygen from carbon dioxide is incorporated into organic compounds. Their experiments confirm the suggestion of Cornelius B. van Niel in 1931 that water is the source of oxygen during green plant photosynthesis.

J. BIOCHEMISTRY: *Oxidative Phosphorylation*
The review articles of Herman Moritz Kalckar and Fritz Albert Lipmann greatly influence subsequent research into the coupling of oxidation reactions to the generation of ATP (oxidative phosphorylation). In their reviews of the accomplishments of the previous decade, they emphasize the concept of enzyme-catalyzed group-transfer reactions. (See 1939 Q, 1941 K, 1951 N.)

K. BIOCHEMISTRY: *High-Energy Bonds*
Fritz Albert Lipmann proposes the concept of "high-energy group potential," using the "Lipmann squiggle" (~) to designate "high-energy bonds" as he formulates the ADP-ATP phosphate cycle. Lipmann shares the 1953 Nobel Prize in physiology or medicine with Hans Krebs. (See 1927 G, 1929 J, 1939 M, 1939 O, 1943 F, 1948 L.)

L. BIOCHEMISTRY: *Phosphorus–Oxygen Uptake Ratio*
Severo Ochoa studies the coupling between uptake of oxygen and the esterification of phosphate into ATP. In extracts from brain or heart tissue, he measures phosphorus-oxygen (P-O) ratios as high as 3 under aerobic conditions for the α–ketoglutarate-to-succinate reaction. (See 1951 N.)

M. BIOCHEMISTRY: *Chromatography*
Archer John Porter Martin and Richard Laurence Millington Synge use partition chromatography to separate amino acids and peptides. They develop both paper chromatography and column chromatography using silica gel, powdered cellulose, or potato starch. Synge and Martin share the Nobel Prize in chemistry in 1952. (See 1906 M.)

N. CHEMICAL TECHNOLOGY: *Spectrophotometer*
Arnold O. Beckman invents the spectrophotometer, an instrument that uses a quartz prism to form a spectrum of light. The instrument, which permits the analysis of chemicals based on their absorption of specific wavelengths of light, is an improvement over colorimeters, which are limited by the use of filters for the selection of wavelengths.

O. TECHNOLOGY
• Under the direction of U.S. president Franklin Delano Roosevelt, the Manhattan Project begins to develop an atomic bomb. Approximately 43,000 individuals in 37 installations in 19 states are involved, and several cities such as Oak Ridge, Tennessee, and Hanford, Washington, are cre-

ated. In July, 1945, the first nuclear bomb is exploded at a test site in New Mexico. (See 1942 M, 1945 F.)

• In England, the first airplane powered by a jet engine is flown. The engine design is based on one developed by Frank Whittle. (See 1937 Q.)

P. SOCIETY AND POLITICS

The United States enters World War II after Japan, without a declaration of war, attacks Pearl Harbor, Hawaii, sinking, capsizing, or severely damaging eight U.S. battleships on December 7. In a speech to the U.S. Congress on the next day, President Franklin Delano Roosevelt declares that December 7 is "a date which will live in infamy." Japan then declares war on both the United States and Britain.

Q. THE ARTS: *Sculpture*

Sculptor John Gutzon Borglum dies before completing the Mount Rushmore National Monument in South Dakota. His work, portraying U.S. presidents Washington, Jefferson, Lincoln, and Theodore Roosevelt, is done on a rocky mountain face. Borglum's son Lincoln does additional work on the sculpture.

1942

A. MICROBIOLOGICAL TECHNIQUE: *Axenic Life*

J. A. Baker and M. S. Ferguson report experiments in which they grow platyfish (*Xiphophorus*) free from bacteria and other microorganisms. They suggest the term "axenic" (free from strangers) to denote a living organism that is free from all other demonstrable organisms. (See 1895 D, 1899 C, 1928 D, 1949 A.)

B. BACTERIAL STRUCTURE: *Bacterial Nucleus*

Carl Robinow publishes the first of his papers on staining of the bacterial nucleus. His work becomes widely known when it appears as an addendum to René Dubos's 1945 book *The Bacterial Cell*. Robinow uses a modification of the Giemsa stain that colors both the DNA-containing material and the cell's outer structures, permitting clear visualization of the behavior of the chromatinic material during cell division. He describes division figures, using such terms as "nuclear structures," "nucleoid," and "chromosome." Although his results are widely interpreted as showing mitotic figures in bacteria, later studies with electron microscopy prove that the bacteria do not have a true nucleus and that Robinow's procedure creates artificial clumping of the cell's DNA. (See 1935 B, 1958 E, 1959 A, 1962 A, 1963 E.)

C. BACTERIAL PHYSIOLOGY: *L Forms*

Cynthia H. Pierce notes that incorporating penicillin into culture media eliminates the bacterial forms of *Streptobacillus moniliformis,* with the L forms surviving.

D. BACTERIAL PHYSIOLOGY: *Heterotrophic Carbon Dioxide Utilization*

Following their earlier report of CO_2 fixation by propionibacteria, Harland G. Wood and Chester H. Werkman with H. D. Slade and others establish carbon dioxide assimilation to be a general phenomenon among heterotrophic bacteria. Using $^{13}CO_2$, they examine species of *Aerobacter, Proteus,*

1942 *(continued)*

Streptococcus, Staphylococcus, and *Clostridium.* The label is found in malate, fumarate, and succinate, consistent with initial fixation into oxaloacetic acid. The overall reaction, CO_2 plus pyruvate yielding oxaloacetate, is called the Wood-Werkman reaction. (See 1935 E, 1945 A.)

E. BACTERIAL PHYSIOLOGY: *Intermediates in Nitrogen Fixation*
Reports that ammonia is an intermediate in nitrogen fixation date from at least 1925, but A. I. Virtanen's alternative hypothesis that hydroxylamine is the key intermediate has received much support. In studies of nitrogen fixation by *Azotobacter vinelandii,* Robert H. Burris, using ^{15}N, finds the highest amount of label in glutamine. Burris's finding, consistent with the reductive amination of glutamic acid, lends credence to the concept that ammonia is the first intermediate in nitrogen fixation. If hydroxylamine were an early intermediate, labeling would be found in aspartic acid. (See 1951 D, 1953 F.)

F. BACTERIAL PHYSIOLOGY: *Glucose Effect / Catabolite Repression*
In a study of the enzymatic activities of *Escherichia coli,* Helen M. R. Epps and Ernest F. Gale discover that the presence of glucose in the growth medium inhibits the production of amino acid deaminases. Epps and Gale use the expression "glucose effect" in discussing this phenomenon, which is later called "catabolite repression." (See 1961 D.)

G. BACTERIOPHAGE: *Electron Microscopy*
Salvador Luria and Thomas F. Anderson obtain electron microscope photographs of a bacteriophage T2 of *Escherichia coli* showing a "head" and a "tail." The first bacteriophage photographs were published in 1940 by Helmut Ruska, G. A. Kausche, and E. Pfankuch. (See 1940 H.)

H. IMMUNOLOGY: *Immunofluorescence*
Albert H. Coons, Hugh J. Creech, R. Norman Jones, and Ernst Berliner begin the use of immunofluorescence. They attach a fluorescent group, β-anthryl-carbamido, to anti-pneumococcus type III antibody and detect the distribution of the pneumococcal carbohydrate in histological sections of tissue by examining them with a fluorescence microscope. These experiments follow the earlier demonstration, by S. J. Hopkins and A. Wormall in 1933 and by Creech and Jones in 1941, that fluorescent molecules can be successfully attached to antibodies. In the 1950s, Coons's improved technique becomes commonly used.

I. IMMUNOLOGY: *Passive Cell Transfer of Hypersensitivity*
Karl Landsteiner and Merrill W. Chase report that sensitized leukocytes transfer delayed hypersensitivity. Although they do not show which cell type is involved, this paper, and a second in 1945 by Chase (Landsteiner dies in 1943) on cellular transfer of cutaneous sensitivity to tuberculin, revive interest in cellular immunology.

J. IMMUNOLOGY: *Adjuvants*
Jules Freund and Katherine McDermott formulate an adjuvant that will be widely used to increase the immune response to many types of antigens.

The preparation, later known as Freund's adjuvant, contains heat-killed tubercle bacilli in a water-in-oil emulsion.

K. MICROSCOPY: *Ultraviolet Microscopy*
E. M. Brumberg, C. R. Burch, and D. Grey develop microscope lenses for use with light in the ultraviolet range. (See 1904 J.)

L. GENETICS: *Evolution*
Julian Sorell Huxley, grandson of Thomas Henry Huxley, publishes *Evolution: the Modern Synthesis,* a key to the acceptance of the synthesis of neo-Darwinism and genetics.

M. PHYSICS: *Nuclear Chain Reaction*
A group headed by Enrico Fermi constructs an atomic pile and achieves a controlled nuclear chain reaction. This experiment is the first critical development in the Manhattan Project, created in 1941, to develop a nuclear fission bomb, or atomic bomb. In 1938, Fermi receives the Nobel Prize in physics for his discovery in 1934 that slow neutrons are more efficient than high-energy neutrons in starting nuclear reactions. (See 1941 O, 1945 F.)

N. SOCIETY AND POLITICS
• The United Nations begins when 26 countries allied against the Axis powers in World War II sign a "Declaration of United Nations" setting forth their goals in the war. In 1945 a charter for the United Nations is approved.
• In World War II, the Japanese capture Manila and take U.S. and Filipino prisoners on the Bataan peninsula in the Philippines on a "death march" to internment camps. Thousands die on the march or in the camps.

1943

A. BACTERIAL PHYSIOLOGY: *Effect of Solid Surfaces on Growth*
In a review of work performed over several years, Claude E. Zobell concludes that the attachment of bacteria to solid surfaces greatly influences their growth. Materials such as glass, plastics, porcelain, sand, and other inert materials adsorb organic nutrients from water in both the natural environment and in laboratory cultures. The attached bacteria more readily attack the adsorbed compounds than those that are in solution.

B. BACTERIAL PHYSIOLOGY: *Heat Resistance in Spores*
H. R. Curran, B. C. Brunstetter, and A. T. Myers show that bacterial endospores contain much more calcium than do vegetative cells. Other workers show a correlation between the presence of calcium and heat resistance. (See 1953 F, 1957 E, 1972 D.)

C. BACTERIAL PHYSIOLOGY: *Pasteur Effect*
Vladimir Engelhardt and V. A. Sakov perform experiments that begin to explain the inhibition of glycolysis by oxygen, the Pasteur effect. They show that the key step in glycolysis that is inhibited is the formation of fructose 1,6-bisphosphate through the inhibition of phosphofructokinase. Later work shows that the enzyme is allosterically inhibited by ATP, citrate, and Mg^{2+} and that the inhibition is relieved by ADP, cyclic AMP, and fructose 6-phosphate. (See 1861 B, 1926 I.)

1943 (continued)

D. BACTERIAL GENETICS: *Spontaneous Mutation/Fluctuation Test*

Salvador Luria and Max Delbrück publish statistical proof that bacterial mutation is a spontaneous event. Their experiments, referred to as a "fluctuation test," show that a strain of *Escherichia coli* develops resistance to lysis by a bacteriophage called T1 before exposure to contact with the phage. They calculate the mutation rate to average 2.45×10^{-8}. These experiments are sometimes referred to as the beginnings of modern bacterial genetics. Luria and Delbrück share the 1969 Nobel Prize in physiology or medicine with Alfred Hershey. (See 1907 A, 1934 C.)

E. VIRAL DISEASE: *Serum Hepatitis*

The term "serum hepatitis" is widely accepted for viral hepatitis that is chronic and transmitted by administration of convalescent serum, serum transfusion, or yellow fever vaccine. (See 1885 F, 1912 C, 1926 E, 1962 Q.)

F. BIOCHEMISTRY: *ATP in Biosynthesis*

David Nachmansohn and A. L. Machado first observe the consumption of ATP in biosynthesis. They study the formation of acetylcholine from acetate and choline in the presence of ATP. (See 1941 K.)

G. SOCIETY AND POLITICS

In World War II, after U.S. and British troops invade Sicily, Italian premier Benito Mussolini resigns. When Allied forces enter southern Italy, the new Italian government surrenders unconditionally.

H. THE ARTS: *Music*

The Richard Rodgers and Oscar Hammerstein musical *Oklahoma* is performed in a theater on Broadway in New York City.

I. THE ARTS: *Literature*

Jean-Paul Sartre publishes *Being and Nothingness*.

1944

A. ANTIBIOTICS: *Streptomycin*

Selman Waksman, with Albert Schatz and E. Bugie, discovers the antibiotic streptomycin, which is produced by the actinomycete *Streptomyces griseus*. Streptomycin is effective against gram-negative bacteria, whereas previously discovered antibiotics act primarily against gram-positive bacteria. (See 1940 F.)

B. ANTIBIOTICS: *Structure of Penicillin*

Early studies on the structure of penicillin led Edward P. Abraham, W. Baker, and Ernst Chain in 1943 to suggest that a β–lactam ring is a component of the molecule. In 1944, Robert Burns Woodward performs chemical studies that confirm the structure to be a β–lactam, but the absolute proof comes only in 1949, when Dorothy Crowfoot Hodgkin announces the results of her X-ray crystallographic analysis of the structure. (See 1949 G.)

C. BACTERIAL GENETICS: *Transforming Principle*
Oswald T. Avery, Colin MacLeod, and Maclyn McCarty, in one of the important steps toward an understanding of the biochemistry of genes, prove that the "transforming principle" of *Diplococcus pneumoniae* (*Streptococcus pneumoniae*) is DNA. The phenomenon of transformation in bacteria was discovered in 1928 by Frederick Griffith when he found that unencapsulated pneumococci gain the capacity to synthesize capsules when mixed with killed capsulated strains. Avery's group shows that DNA is the material that causes the transformation when it is transferred from the dead cells to the living cells. As crucial as these experiments are, some investigators resist the idea that DNA is responsible for genetic changes. It is not until the experiments of Alfred Hershey and Martha Chase with bacteriophage that the final proof is obtained that DNA is genetic material. Avery dies in 1955 before the scientific community fully appreciates his achievement. Although Nobel Prizes are not awarded posthumously, a publication edited by the Nobel Foundation later contains a statement of regret that Avery died before he could be recognized. (See 1928 C, 1931 D, 1953 N.)

D. BACTERIAL GENETICS: *Growth Factor Mutants*
C. H. Gray and Edward L. Tatum isolate the first mutant strains of *Escherichia coli* that require growth factors. In the next year Tatum reports on mutants having two growth factor requirements that are used by Joshua Lederberg in his initial experiments on bacterial conjugation. (See 1946 F.)

E. BACTERIOPHAGE: *the Phage Group*
Max Delbrück persuades a number of people working with bacteriophage to concentrate on a group of seven bacteriophages of *Escherichia coli*. This so-called phage treaty leads to intense work with the phages named T1, T2, T3, T4, T5, T6, and T7, which have different serological properties and for which resistant mutants of *E. coli* are known. Milislav Demerec and U. Fano publish descriptions of these phages.

F. VIRAL DISEASE: *Viral Pneumonia*
Monroe D. Eaton, Gordon Meiklejohn, and William van Herick use chick embryo tissues to cultivate virus from lung tissue or bacteriologically sterile sputum from patients with a primary atypical pneumonia. Successfully infecting cotton rats or hamsters by intranasal inoculation of the chick embryo cultures, they find that the agent in the chick embryo cultures is specifically neutralized by serum from patients who have recovered from the infection.

G. IMMUNOLOGY: *Transplantation Immunity*
Peter B. Medawar publishes a report on the results of skin autografts and skin homografts in rabbits. His conclusions, which provide convincing data on the parameters of graft rejection, were, in fact, included in an earlier book by Georg Schöne published in 1912. Medawar shares the 1960 Nobel Prize in physiology or medicine with Frank Macfarlane Burnet.

1944 *(continued)*

H. ELECTRON MICROSCOPY: *Metal Shadowing of Viruses*

Robley Cook Williams and Ralph Wyckoff develop the technique of shadowing of viruses with metallic vapors, facilitating the study of shapes of viral particles with the electron microscope. (See 1958 J.)

I. GENETICS: *What is Life?*

Erwin Schrödinger publishes *What is Life?,* in which he discusses the concept of a "gene molecule," which Max Delbrück expressed in a 1935 paper. Schrödinger suggests that chromosomes contain codes that dictate the development and functioning of an individual. The book, which gives wide exposure to Delbrück's ideas, stimulates a number of physicists, some of whom later work with Delbrück, to turn to biological investigations. Schrödinger argues that the answer to the question "What is life?" will be found in chemistry and physics. (See 1935 I.)

J. SOCIETY AND POLITICS

In January, Allied troops accomplish an assault from the sea at Anzio beach near Rome in Italy. On June 6, D-Day, a major invasion on the beaches of Normandy, France, is the beginning of the last stages of World War II, with Paris being recaptured from the Germans in August.

K. THE ARTS: *Literature*

W. Somerset Maugham publishes *The Razor's Edge.*

1945

A. BACTERIAL PHYSIOLOGY: *Heterotrophic Carbon Dioxide Fixation*

H. A. Barker and Martin David Kamen use radioactive $^{14}CO_2$ to study the distribution of the radioactive label in the formation of acetic acid by *Clostridium thermoaceticum*. In 1952, Harland G. Wood does a similar experiment with $^{13}CO_2$. Both experiments show that the label appears equally in the methyl and carboxyl atoms of acetate. (See 1935 E, 1942 D, 1955 E.)

B. BACTERIOPHAGE: *Mutants*

Salvador Luria finds bacteriophage mutants that can infect host bacteria that are resistant to infection by the parent phage. These mutant phages are called host range mutants. (See 1936 E.)

C. IMMUNOLOGY: *Pneumococcal Pneumonia*

Colin MacLeod and coworkers show that pneumococcal pneumonia can be prevented by injecting capsular polysaccharide of types I, II, V, and VII into human subjects. In a trial involving more than 17,000 subjects, they find that immunity develops within 2 weeks, but they do not determine its duration.

D. IMMUNOLOGY: *Immunological Tolerance/Chimerism in Cattle*

Ray David Owen reports that fraternal twins in cattle have the same blood type because of connection of their circulatory systems in utero. In 1948, Peter B. Medawar and Rupert E. Billingham find that skin transplants between both fraternal and identical twins are accepted. These observations contribute to theories of antibody formation: first to Niels K. Jerne's natural selection theory and then to Frank Macfarlane Burnet's clonal selection theory. (See 1955 N, 1957 N.)

E. SCIENTIFIC SOCIETIES: *General Microbiology*
The Society for General Microbiology is established in England.

F. SOCIETY AND POLITICS
- In May, Germany surrenders. to end World War II in Europe.
- In July, the world's first nuclear fission bomb, or atomic bomb, is detonated in Alamogordo, New Mexico. In August, the United States drops atomic bombs on the Japanese cities of Hiroshima and Nagasaki. (See 1941 O, 1942 M.)
- In September, Japan signs surrender papers, ending World War II.

G. THE ARTS: *Literature*
- George Orwell publishes *Animal Farm*.
- Evelyn Waugh's novel *Brideshead Revisited* is released.

H. THE ARTS: *Theater*
Tennessee Williams's play *The Glass Menagerie* is performed in New York City.

1946

A. BACTERIAL STRUCTURE: *Flagella*
Continuing his studies of motility using cinematography of motile bacteria, Adrianus Pijper concludes that motility results from a gyrating and undulating movement of the bacterial cell and not from the action of flagella. He believes that the gyrations of the cell cause surface polysaccharides to become twisted into the appearance of a tail. In 1947, using solutions of methylcellulose to slow the movement of the bacteria, he studies them in "slow motion." He concludes that the term "flagella" should be discarded in favor of "polysaccharide twirls" or "mucous twirls." (See 1941 C, 1947 A, 1948 A.)

B. BACTERIAL STRUCTURE: *Metachromatic Granules*
J. M. Wiame analyzes the metachromatic granules of yeast, concluding that they are probably composed of hexametaphosphate. (See 1888 A, 1959 B, 1984 D.)

C. BACTERIAL PHYSIOLOGY: *Nutritional Types*
André Lwoff, Cornelius B. van Niel, Francis J. Ryan, and Edward L. Tatum publish a suggested nomenclature for nutritional types of microorganisms. To describe energy sources, they use the terms "phototrophy" and "chemotrophy," with subgroups called "lithotrophs" for those that use inorganic compounds and "organotrophs" for those that use organic compounds. The term "lithotrophy" is coined by the authors. The terms "autotrophy" and "heterotrophy" refer to the organism's ability or inability to synthesize essential metabolites.

D. BACTERIAL PHYSIOLOGY: *Roll-Tube Cultivation of Anaerobes*
R. E. Hungate employs a roll-tube technique for the isolation of anaerobic, cellulolytic bacteria from the bovine rumen. The procedure, which he describes more completely in later papers, involves eliminating oxygen from

1946 *(continued)*

the culture tubes by introducing a stream of carbon dioxide through slender pipettes called Pasteur pipettes. The inoculated tubes, which contain a small quantity of cellulose agar medium, are rotated, or rolled, to distribute a thin layer of solidified medium around the inner surface. The procedure allows the tubes to be examined microscopically for such purposes as subculturing colonies of the anaerobic bacteria.

E. ANTIMICROBIAL AGENTS: *Mode of Action of Sulfonamides*

J. O. Lampen and M. J. Jones study the growth of *Streptococcus faecalis* and *Lactobacillus casei* in the presence of pteroic acid derivatives and thymine. Based on their observations that the sulfonamides have little effect on the bacteria grown in such culture media, they conclude that the mode of action of the drugs is to inhibit the synthesis of pteroylglutamic acid by way of *p*-aminobenzoic acid. (See 1932 B, 1940 G.)

F. BACTERIAL GENETICS: *Conjugation in Bacteria*

Joshua Lederberg and Edward L. Tatum report the transfer of genetic information from one bacterium to another in a process they call conjugation. They interpret their results as showing cell fusion followed by nuclear fusion, a conclusion that is found to be incorrect in later studies. The choice of *Escherichia coli* strain K-12 for these experiments is fortuitous since most wild-type strains of *E. coli* are unable to mate. Lederberg, Tatum, and George Beadle share the 1958 Nobel Prize in physiology or medicine. (See 1947 C, 1950 G, 1952 I, 1955 F.)

G. BACTERIAL GENETICS: *Prototrophs and Auxotrophs*

Francis J. Ryan and Joshua Lederberg introduce the term "prototroph" (first or minimal food) for nutritional mutants of *Neurospora* that revert to the wild-type state. This term is in contrast to "auxotroph" (increased food, used for mutants with a nutritional requirement.

H. BACTERIOPHAGE: *Recombination*

Max Delbrück and Alfred Hershey, in independent experiments, discover genetic recombination in bacteriophage.

I. VIROLOGY: *Cultivation of Viruses in Hen's Eggs*

Frank MacFarlane Burnet and W. I. B. Beveridge publish a paper describing the cultivation of viruses by inoculation into the yolk sac, amnion, chorioallantois, or embryo of fertilized hen's eggs. (See 1901 E, 1931 G, 1936 G, 1940 J.)

J. MICROBIOLOGY: *the Communicable Disease Center (Centers for Disease Control)*

The U.S. government establishes the Communicable Disease Center (CDC) in Atlanta, Georgia. An outgrowth of an agency established in 1942 to help control malaria in the U.S. armed forces, its name is changed to the Center for Disease Control in 1970, to the Centers for Disease Control in 1980, and to the Centers for Disease Control and Prevention in 1992.

K. GENETICS: *Chemical Mutagens*

C. Auerbach and J. M. Robson expose *Drosophila melanogaster* to mustard gas (dichlor-diethyl sulfide) and find up to 24% sex-linked lethal mutations.

They report seeing chromosomal inversions, large deletions, and translocations. The rate of mutation observed is less than that seen after X-irradiation but greater than with ultraviolet light treatment. In other research, J. A. Rapoport reports that formaldehyde, diethylsulfate, and diazomethane are mutagenic. (See 1927 E, 1939 E.)

L. SOCIETY AND POLITICS
The French government attempts to resume control of Vietnam, which they lost during World War II. The League of Independence of Vietnam, the Viet Minh, under the leadership of Ho Chi Minh, resists the French and war begins.

M. THE ARTS: *Literature*
- Robert Penn Warren publishes his novel *All the King's Men.*
- Eudora Welty completes her novel *Delta Wedding.*

N. THE ARTS: *Theater*
The Iceman Cometh by Eugene O'Neill opens in New York City.

1947

A. BACTERIAL STRUCTURE: *Cell Walls and Flagella*
Woutera van Iterson presents electron microscope photographs showing details of cell walls and flagella in *Pseudomonas fluorescens* and *Bacillus subtilis.* Among her observations are a distinct cell wall and the appearance of flagella as perfectly uniform threads. Some of her photographs support the idea that flagella originate in the cytoplasm and penetrate through the cell wall. She contrasts her observations with those of Adrianus Pijper. (See 1946 A, 1948 A.)

B. BACTERIAL DISEASE: *Crown Gall Disease*
Armin C. Braun is the first to suggest that DNA is the tumor-inducing principle in crown gall disease caused by *Agrobacterium tumefaciens.* Braun, working with P. R. White, had found in 1943 that crown gall can be maintained without the presence of the bacteria. Braun is then able to turn attention to a tumor-inducing principle produced by the bacteria. (See 1907 D, 1970 G, 1974 L, 1977 O.)

C. BACTERIAL GENETICS: *Linkage Map*
Joshua Lederberg publishes the first genetic linkage map of *Escherichia coli* based on analysis of unselected markers. His experiments involve crosses between two auxotrophic mutants that have different requirements for biotin and four amino acids. (See 1949 E, 1955 F.)

D. BIOCHEMISTRY: *Discovery of Coenzyme A*
Fritz Lipmann's discovery of coenzyme A, the coenzyme for acetylation, is an important addition to knowledge about the Krebs citric acid cycle. (See 1951 M.)

E. SOCIETY AND POLITICS
The European Recovery Program is authorized by the U.S. Congress. This program, suggested by U.S. secretary of state George C. Marshall and called the Marshall Plan, is intended to offer financial aid to 16 European countries.

1947 (continued)

F. TECHNOLOGY

• John Bardeen, Walter Houser Brattain, and William Bradford Shockley, at Bell Laboratories, invent the point contact transistor. Shortly afterward, Shockley's development of the junction transistor leads to the miniaturization of electronic circuits in radios, televisions, and computers. Bardeen, Brattain, and Shockley share the Nobel Prize in physics in 1956. Bardeen receives a second Nobel Prize in 1972.

• Chuck Yeager breaks the sound barrier in an experimental airplane.

• Edwin Herbert Land introduces the Land camera, which produces positive photographic prints within about 1 minute after the film is exposed. The camera uses a type of film that the Agfa firm introduced in 1928 but did not develop further at that time. The camera is known first as the Polaroid Land camera and later as the Polaroid camera.

• The first television sets for use in private homes are manufactured.

G. THE ARTS: *Drama*

Tennessee Williams's play *A Streetcar Named Desire* is performed in New York City.

1948

A. BACTERIAL STRUCTURE: *Bacterial Flagella Are Protein*

Claes Weibull reports that a chemical analysis of the flagella of *Proteus vulgaris* and *Bacillus subtilis* reveals that they are composed of protein, contrary to Adrianus Pijper's claim that they are polysaccharide twirls. In 1951, reporting on the purification of flagella by differential centrifugation, Weibull confirms that they are composed of almost pure protein and refers to them as fibrous macromolecules. (See 1941 C, 1946 A, 1947 A, 1955 C.)

B. BACTERIAL PHYSIOLOGY: *Assay for Vitamin B$_{12}$*

The fact that adding liver to diets cures patients suffering from pernicious anemia was discovered in 1926 by G. R. Minot and W. P. Murphy. Little progress was made in isolating the liver factor, partly because the only assay used human subjects with the disease. In 1948, Mary S. Shorb develops an assay using the bacterium *Lactobacillus lactis* for a factor in liver that stimulates rat growth. Edward L. Rickes and his coworkers crystallize this factor, called LLD, from liver with the aid of Shorb's assay. They choose the designation vitamin B$_{12}$ because the substance has nutritional significance and because "B$_{12}$" has not been previously used.

C. ANTIBIOTICS: *Cephalosporin*

In searching for fungi that produce antibiotics, Giuseppe Brotzu isolates *Cephalosporium acremonium* from seawater near a sewage outlet near Cagliari, Sardinia. The cultures grown on agar produce a substance that inhibits both gram-positive and gram-negative bacteria. He partially purifies the substance, crystallizes it, and injects concentrates of it into staphylococcal and streptococcal lesions, with good results. Some improvement is also seen in typhoid patients who are given the drug both intramuscularly and intravenously. Unable to pursue the development of the compound, he sends his culture to Howard Florey in England, where the group that developed penicillin carries out further studies. By 1955, G. G. F. Newton and Edward P. Abraham assign the name cephalosporin C to the compound, which is active against *Staphylococcus aureus, Salmonella typhi,* and *Escherichia coli.* By the early 1960s, when a chemical structure is worked out, it is reported that cephalosporin C has a β-lactam-dihydrothiazine ring system.

D. BACTERIAL GENETICS: *Penicillin Technique for Isolation of Mutants*

Joshua Lederberg and Norton David Zinder and, independently, Bernard D. Davis describe a technique for isolation of mutant bacteria that depends on the fact that penicillin kills only growing cells. Thus, nutritional mutants survive in a minimal growth medium containing penicillin, while prototrophs are killed.

E. BACTERIOPHAGE: *Genetic Map*

Alfred Hershey and R. Rotman develop the first genetic map of a bacteriophage. They analyze genetic recombinants obtained by dual infection of the host bacterium with host range and rapid lysis mutants.

F. VIRAL DISEASE: *Mumps Virus*

Thomas H. Weller and John F. Enders grow the mumps virus (a paramyxovirus) in tissue culture made with pieces of chick embryo. The following year they successfully cultivate the virus of poliomyelitis in tissue culture.

G. VIRAL DISEASE: *Coxsackievirus*

In performing studies of patients suffering from poliomyelitis, Gilbert Dalldorf and Grace M. Sickles discover a new virus after they inject fecal specimens intracerebrally into mice. The virus causes lesions in skeletal muscles that result in paralysis, as opposed to attacking the central nervous system as the poliovirus does. The virus is named for Coxsackie, New York, home of one of the patients from whom the virus was first recovered.

H. VIRAL DISEASE: *Animal Model for Acute Exanthems*

Frank Fenner uses the disease mousepox as a model for learning the course of infection in human exanthems such as smallpox, chickenpox, measles, and rubella. He injects the mousepox virus into the footpad of mice and follows its spread in the body from the site of entry to blood, liver and spleen, and finally to focal infections of the epidermis.

I. IMMUNOLOGY: *Histocompatibility Genes*

George D. Snell develops a number of congenic lines of mice for the purpose of studying histocompatibility genes. His work is important in determining the major histocompatibility complex.

J. IMMUNOLOGY: *Gel Diffusion Analysis*

Örjan Ouchterlony improves a test tube agar diffusion technique for antigen-antibody analysis, which Jacques Oudin developed in 1946. He places antigen and antibody into separate holes bored into a thin agar film in a petri dish and finds a line of immune precipitate where the antigen and antibody diffuse into contact. The Ouchterlony test determines the purity of antigen as well as the cross-reactivity of different antigens containing unique epitopes.

1948 *(continued)*

K. BIOCHEMISTRY: *Mitochondria and Citric Acid Cycle Enzymes*

Walter Carl Schneider and Van Rensselaer Potter find both cytochrome oxidase and succinic dehydrogenase in mitochondria and show that mitochondria oxidize some citric acid cycle intermediates. Eugene P. Kennedy and Albert Lehninger prove that mitochondria have a complete set of citric acid cycle enzymes. They also show that the glycolytic enzymes are found in the cytoplasm. (See 1890 F, 1898 K.)

L. BIOCHEMISTRY: *Synthesis of ATP*

Alexander Robertus Todd confirms the structures of ATP, ADP, and AMP by their total synthesis. Beginning in 1944, he synthesizes all of the purine and pyrimidine bases found in nucleic acids, showing how the sugar and phosphate moieties are arranged. His work proves to be important for working out the structure of DNA by James Watson and Francis Crick. Todd receives the 1957 Nobel Prize in chemistry. (See 1929 J, 1939 M, 1939 O, 1941 K, 1943 F.)

M. CHEMISTRY: *Origin of Chemical Elements*

A theory about the origin of chemical elements is published by Ralph Asher Alpher and George Gamow with Hans Albrecht Bethe, of whom they ask permission to put his name on the paper so that the concept can be called the "Alpher-Bethe-Gamow" (alpha-beta-gamma) theory. This idea is superseded by a stellar nucleosynthesis concept in 1957. Gamow later contributes to molecular biology with a concept about the genetic code. In 1939, Bethe proposed the carbon cycle for the generation of energy in stars. Bethe is awarded the 1967 Nobel Prize in physics.

N. SCIENTIFIC ORGANIZATION

The World Health Organization is established.

O. TECHNOLOGY

Auguste Piccard, who in 1932 is the first to ascend to the stratosphere in a balloon, builds an undersea exploration vessel he calls a bathyscaphe. In contrast to the bathysphere used by Charles Beebe and Otis Barton in 1934, the bathyscaphe is maneuverable. In 1960, his son, Jacques Piccard, and Don Walsh descend to a depth of 35,800 feet in a bathyscaphe named *Trieste*.

P. SOCIETY AND POLITICS

• Following the 1947 recommendations of the United Nations General Assembly, the Republic of Israel is declared in the western part of Palestine. Chaim Weizmann (who developed the acetone-butanol fermentation in 1912) is named president and David Ben-Gurion is prime minister. The countries of Transjordan, Egypt, Syria, Iraq, and Lebanon immediately attack Israel with the announced intention of driving the Israelis into the sea. (See 1912 A.)

• The Soviet forces occupying East Germany and Berlin establish a blockade, preventing highway and railroad traffic into Berlin from West

Germany. Britain and the United States begin an airlift to carry food and provisions into the city.

- Mahatma Gandhi is assassinated by a Hindu extremist. (See 1932 O.)

Q. THE ARTS: *Literature*
Norman Mailer writes *The Naked and the Dead*.

1949

A. MICROBIOLOGICAL TECHNIQUE: *Germfree Life/Gnotobiotics*
Arthur Reyniers and Philip C. Trexler develop metal isolation equipment that can withstand steam sterilization for their work with germfree animals. They propose the term "gnotobiotic," meaning "known life," to describe germfree experiments. (See 1895 C, 1928 D, 1942 A.)

B. BACTERIAL STRUCTURE: *Cell Wall Nucleotides*
James T. Park and Marvin J. Johnson report what they believe to be a new form of organically bound labile phosphate in *Staphylococcus aureus* growing in a penicillin-containing culture medium. This is the first observation of what Park later recognizes to be cell wall nucleotides. (See 1952 C, 1954 B.)

C. BACTERIAL STRUCTURE: *D–Amino Acids*
Joseph T. Holden and Esmond E. Snell find that D-alanine constitutes 1 to 2% of the dry weight of several lactic acid bacteria. When, in 1955, Snell, Norman S. Radin, and Miyoshi Ikawa discover D-alanine residues in cell wall material, they conclude that it is a component of cell wall protein. They also report the presence of glutamic acid and lysine but are unable to determine their isomeric configuration. D-Amino acids were first reported in bacteria in 1937 when a D-glutamyl polypeptide was discovered in the capsule of *Bacillus anthracis*. (See 1937 A, 1952 C.)

D. BACTERIAL STRUCTURE: *Fimbriae/Pili*
Thomas F. Anderson and, independently, A. L. Houwink report observing radial filaments on the surface of bacteria examined by electron microscopy. They note that the filaments are found both on motile and nonmotile forms and that they are easily distinguishable from flagella. A microphotograph published in 1901 by A. Hinterberger shows threadlike appendages that appear to be similar to those seen by Anderson and Houwink. Within a few years, such appendages are called "fimbriae" or "pili." (See 1955 B.)

E. BACTERIAL PHYSIOLOGY: *Photosynthetic Nitrogen Fixation*
Martin David Kamen and Howard Gest demonstrate that the photosynthetic bacterium *Rhodospirillum rubrum* can fix nitrogen. Although this is the first proof of nitrogen fixation in photosynthetic bacteria, it is now known that many species of such bacteria have this ability. (See 1928 A.)

F. MICROBIAL PHYSIOLOGY: *Photoreactivation*
In studies of ultraviolet irradiation damage to *Streptomyces griseus*, Albert Kelner finds that cold storage of irradiated conidia results in up to 100,000-fold recovery. He discovers that exposing the irradiated conidia to light greatly enhances the recovery. In other experiments with *Escherichia coli*, Kelner shows that wavelengths shorter than 5,100 angstroms cause re-

1949 *(continued)*

covery from ultraviolet light damage. These results are confirmed by Renato Dulbecco in studies with bacteriophage. Max Delbrück suggests the term "photoreactivation" for this phenomenon. (See 1953 M, 1957 F, 1960 H.)

G. ANTIBIOTICS: *Structure of Penicillin*
X-ray crystallographer Dorothy Crowfoot Hodgkin completes her study of the structure of penicillin with the aid of an electronic computer, the first to be used in determining chemical structure. Hodgkin's analysis confirms the presence of the β-lactam component of the structure, which was indicated by Robert Burns Woodward's and others' 1944 chemical studies. In 1956, Hodgkin completes 8 years of work on the structure of vitamin B_{12}, and in 1959 proves the structure of insulin. Hodgkin receives the Nobel Prize in chemistry in 1964. (See 1944 B.)

H. BACTERIOPHAGE: *Phage Replication*
In studies with T-even bacteriophage, Seymour Stanley Cohen reports that phosphorus that is incorporated into bacteriophage DNA during replication is derived from the culture medium and not from the infected host bacterium. He reports that phage protein is synthesized first, followed by synthesis of phage DNA. His work also demonstrates that host cell enzymes synthesize new phage using information provided by the infecting phage particle.

I. VIROLOGY: *Cell Culture of Poliomyelitis Virus*
John F. Enders, Frederick C. Robbins, and Thomas H. Weller use human embryonic tissue and nonneural monkey and human tissue in cell culture to cultivate all three types of the poliomyelitis virus. Enders and his coworkers find that growth of the virus causes both microscopically visible changes in the cultured cells, a cytopathic effect, and a change of pH in the culture liquid. Interest in the use of cell culture for growing viruses is reawakened by these results. Enders, Robbins, and Weller are awarded the 1954 Nobel Prize in physiology or medicine. (See 1917 D, 1936 F, 1936 L, 1948 F.)

J. BIOCHEMISTRY: *Antimicrobial Drugs and Immunosuppressants*
George Herbert Hitchings and his colleagues began in the 1940s to synthesize purine and pyrimidine derivatives that inhibit the synthesis of DNA. In 1949, Hitchings, with Elvira Falco and Peter Russell, synthesizes trimethoprim, a compound that blocks the activity of dihydrofolate reductase. Trimethoprim is administered with sulfanilamide as an effective antibacterial combination. In 1954, another of Hitchings' colleagues, Gertrude Belle Elion, synthesizes 6-mercaptopurine, recognized both as an effective antileukemic drug and as a suppressor of the immune system. 6-Mercaptopurine proves to be useful in organ transplant surgery. In 1977, Elion develops the drug acyclovir, used to treat herpes simplex virus infections as well as chickenpox and shingles. Hitchings and Elion share the 1988 Nobel Prize in

physiology or medicine with James White Black, who develops drugs for treating ulcers and for hypertension. (See 1985 G.)

K. SOCIETY AND POLITICS
• The People's Republic of China is formed with Mao Zedong as chairman of the administrative council and Zhou Enlai as premier and foreign minister.
• The Nationalist Chinese, led by Chiang Kai-shek, establish the Republic of China on the island of Taiwan (Formosa).

L. THE ARTS: *Literature*
George Orwell publishes *Nineteen Eighty-Four*.

M. THE ARTS: *Theater*
The play *Death of a Salesman* by Arthur Miller is first performed.

1950

A. BACTERIOLOGICAL TECHNIQUE: *Most Probable Number*
William G. Cochran reports a method for estimating the density of bacterial populations in liquid media by application of the theory of probability. The method involves performing serial dilution into a series of culture tubes and recording the number of tubes showing growth at each dilution. Cochran calculates the most probable number (MPN) of bacteria in the original sample as estimated from a statistical table which he originated. He cautions that certain assumptions apply: that the organisms are in random distribution in the liquid and that growth will occur whenever a culture tube contains one or more organisms. He states, "For a biologist, it is more important to be clear about these assumptions than about the details of the mathematics, which are rather intricate."

B. BACTERIAL STRUCTURE: *Flagella*
A. L. Houwink and Woutera van Iterson report that bacterial flagella originate in spherical basal granules associated with the cell membrane. (See 1947 A, 1948 A, 1988 C.)

C. BACTERIAL PHYSIOLOGY: *Continuous Culture*
Jacques Monod and, separately, Aaron Novick and Leo Szilard describe devices for maintaining a bacterial population in continuous culture at a reduced growth rate. Novick and Szilard, referring to their culture apparatus as a "chemostat," define the "generation time" as the time between two successive cell divisions. (See 1935 A, 1956 B, 1958 F.)

D. BACTERIAL PHYSIOLOGY: *Glucose Metabolism by* **Pseudomonas**
Jack J. R. Campbell and Flora C. Norris, studying the distribution of phosphorus in products of glucose metabolism by *Pseudomonas aeruginosa,* report that intermediates of the glycolytic pathway (Embden-Meyerhof-Parnas system) are absent. Having earlier found both gluconic acid and 2-keto-gluconic acid among the metabolites, they conclude that a pathway involving these compounds is functioning and suggest that it resembles reactions studied by Frank Dickens in 1936. Nathan Entner and Michael Doudoroff

1950 *(continued)*

report the complete pathway found in pseudomonads in 1952. (See 1935 J, 1936 O, 1952 F.)

E. BACTERIAL PHYSIOLOGY: *Assay of β-Galactosidase*

Joshua Lederberg introduces the use of a colorimetric enzyme assay for studying the hydrolysis of β-D-galactosides, such as the sugar lactose. After M. Seidman and Karl Paul Link synthesize *o*-nitrophenyl-β-D-galactoside (ONPG), Lederberg uses it to study the kinetics of the enzyme β-galactosidase in both intact and autolyzed cells, either adapted to growth on lactose or grown on glucose (unadapted). Hydrolysis of ONPG produces *o*-nitrophenol, a yellow compound that can be assayed colorimetrically. (See 1952 H.)

F. BACTERIAL GENETICS: *High-Frequency Conjugation*

Luca L. Cavalli-Sforza discovers the first strain of *Escherichia coli* that transfers chromosomal markers during conjugation at a frequency much higher than that reported to date. This type of organism is labeled Hfr, for high-frequency transfer. (See 1946 F, 1952 I, 1955 F.)

G. BACTERIAL GENETICS: *Genetic Markers*

Joshua Lederberg isolates a streptomycin-resistant mutant of *Escherichia coli* and introduces the use of antibiotic resistance markers into bacterial genetics. (See 1946 F.)

H. BACTERIAL GENETICS: *Test for Bacterial Conjugation*

Bernard D. Davis employs a U tube with a bacterial filter at the bottom of the U to test whether or not bacterial conjugation requires cell-to-cell contact or is a type of transformation. Mating strains inoculated into opposite arms of the U produce no recombinants when the medium is flushed back and forth, showing that cell-to-cell contact is necessary. (See 1952 K.)

I. BACTERIOPHAGE: *Lysogeny*

André Lwoff and A. Gutmann explain the phenomenon of lysogeny in *Bacillus megaterium*. They conclude that bacteriophage is perpetuated within the bacterium in a noninfectious state that they give the name "prophage," and that new phage is occasionally synthesized and released from the bacterium through lysis. Lwoff, Louis Siminovitch, and Nils Kjeldgaard find that lysogenic *B. megaterium* releases bacteriophage after exposure to ultraviolet light, a phenomenon that they call "induction of phage." Lwoff shares the 1965 Nobel Prize in physiology or medicine with François Jacob and Jacques Monod. (See 1925 C, 1929 D, 1936 D.)

J. GENETICS: *Transposable Genetic Elements*

Barbara McClintock publishes a paper describing movable genetic-controlling elements that cause pigment variation in the kernels of maize. Her conclusions about "jumping genes" are not well received by the scientific community. It is not until the mid-1970s, after similar elements have been discovered in microorganisms, that her work is appreciated. The term "transposons" for movable genes gains currency. McClintock receives the 1983 Nobel Prize in physiology or medicine. (See 1974 H.)

K. BIOLOGY: *Endoplasmic Reticulum*
Albert Claude discovers the endoplasmic reticulum.

L. MOLECULAR BIOLOGY: *DNA Structure*
Erwin Chargaff publishes data on the composition of DNA, noting that the molar ratios of purines to pyrimidines and the ratios of adenine to thymine and guanine to cytosine are approximately 1. These ratios, referred to as Chargaff's rules, are explained by James Watson's and Francis Crick's solution of the structure of DNA in 1953. The work of Chargaff and his associates finally disproves the tetranucleotide hypothesis of nucleic acid structure. (See 1938 H, 1953 O.)

M. BIOCHEMISTRY: *Photosynthetic Carbon Cycle*
In studies with $^{14}CO_2$, Melvin Calvin and his colleagues Elmer J. Badin, A. A. Benson, and J. A. Bassham identify phosphoglyceric acid as the first product showing labeled carbon in photosynthetic fixation of carbon dioxide. In 1951, they discover the key intermediates ribulose diphosphate and sedoheptulose phosphate. (See 1952 G, 1954 M, 1955 E, 1959 C.)

N. BIOCHEMISTRY: *Uridine Diphosphoglucose*
Luis F. Leloir and colleagues report finding that uridine diphosphoglucose (UDPG) functions as a coenzyme in the conversion of galactose 1-phosphate to glucose 1-phosphate. Showing the structure of UDPG, they comment on its similarity to the compound reported by Marvin Johnson and James T. Park that accumulates in bacteria grown in the presence of penicillin. Leloir receives the 1970 Nobel Prize in chemistry for his research on the biochemistry of carbohydrates. (See 1949 B, 1952 C.)

O. BIOCHEMISTRY: *Biosynthesis of Cholesterol*
Konrad Bloch and David Rittenberg use radioactive carbon ^{13}C and ^{14}C as tracers to study the biosynthetic reactions for the synthesis of cholesterol and show that all 27 carbon atoms are derived from acetate. Bloch shares the 1964 Nobel Prize in physiology or medicine with Feodor Lynen. (See 1939 I.)

P. BIOCHEMISTRY: *Amino Acid Sequence of Ribonuclease*
Stanford Moore and William Howard Stein develop a column chromatographic method for identifying and quantifying amino acids derived from the hydrolysis of protein. During 1954 to 1956, they determine the complete amino acid sequence of bovine pancreatic ribonuclease. This work complements the studies of Christian Anfinsen on the role of amino acid sequence in the tertiary structure of ribonuclease. Moore, Stein, and Anfinsen share the 1972 Nobel Prize in chemistry. (See 1953 Q.)

Q. SCIENTIFIC ORGANIZATIONS: *National Science Foundation*
The National Science Foundation is established by the U.S. Congress.

R. SOCIETY AND POLITICS
• The Korean War begins with the invasion of South Korea by North Korean troops. Following a vote by the United Nations Security Council, more than 15 countries send troops and supplies to support South Korea.

1950 (continued)

• U.S. senator Joseph McCarthy claims that the State Department employs a large number of known Communists and begins a "witch hunt" in which he accuses numerous government employees of being "card-carrying" Communists, but he is never able to substantiate his claims. McCarthy's campaign culminates in 1954 with a hearing that he holds after charging that the U.S. Army Signal Corps is operating a spy ring. The "Army-McCarthy" hearings end with a vote by the U.S. Senate condemning McCarthy for misconduct.

S. THE ARTS: *Literature*
Graham Greene publishes *The Third Man.*

T. THE ARTS: *Theater*
The play *Come Back, Little Sheba* by William Inge has its opening performance.

U. THE ARTS: *Art*
Jackson Pollock completes his picture called *One (#31, 1950).*

1951

A. BACTERIAL TAXONOMY: Rickettsia
J. D. Smith and M. G. P. Stoker report that *Rickettsia burnetii* (*Coxiella burnetii*) contains both DNA and RNA. This early study suggests that the rickettsiae are not closely related to viruses. (See 1929 E, 1953 A, 1963 D.)

B. BACTERIAL STRUCTURE: *Cell Walls*
M. R. J. Salton's and R. W. Horne's newly developed methods for the isolation and purification of bacterial cell walls lead to a clearer understanding of the chemistry and organization of these structures. (See 1951 C, 1952 C, 1952 D, 1954 B.)

C. BACTERIAL STRUCTURE: *Cell Wall Chemistry*
E. Work isolates $\alpha\epsilon$-diaminopimelic acid from the cell walls of *Corynebacterium diphtheriae* and *Mycobacterium tuberculosis.* Subsequent work by a number of investigators establishes that diaminopimelic acid occurs in peptide chains in the peptidoglycan of cell walls of many bacteria. In some bacteria, notably gram-positive cocci, lysine replaces diaminopimelic acid. (See 1952 C, 1954 B.)

D. BACTERIAL PHYSIOLOGY: *Nitrogen Fixation*
I. Zelitch and others, working with Perry W. Wilson, report that *Clostridium pasteurianum* secretes ammonia with a far greater content of ^{15}N that any other compound isolated when the bacterium is grown under nitrogen-fixing conditions. This evidence is the most specific reported thus far supporting the role of ammonia in nitrogen fixation. (See 1942 E, 1953 H.)

E. BACTERIAL PHYSIOLOGY: *Heterolactic Acid Fermentation*
R. D. DeMoss, R. D. Bard, and Irwin C. Gunsalus report finding that *Leuconostoc mesenteroides* produces lactic acid, ethanol, and carbon dioxide through the fermentation of glucose by a nonglycolytic pathway. In subsequent studies with Martin Gibbs, Gunsalus confirms the distribution of glucose carbon atoms in the products through the use of ^{14}C-labeled glucose.

They conclude that a new pathway, known as the heterolactic acid fermentation, utilizes some enzymes of the lower part of the glycolytic pathway.

F. BACTERIAL INSECTICIDES: Bacillus thuringiensis

In California, E. A. Steinhaus achieves control of the alfalfa caterpillar with sprays containing *Bacillus thuringiensis,* stimulating interest in the use of bacteria for pest control. The first use of *Bacillus thuringiensis* to control pests occurs in France just before World War II. (See 1902 E, 1915 B, 1953 J, 1954 H.)

G. BACTERIOPHAGE: *Phage Lambda*

Esther Lederberg discovers lysogeny in *Escherichia coli* strain K-12 by a bacteriophage subsequently given the name lambda (λ). Studies of this phage and its host bacterium contribute greatly to the understanding of genetic control of lysogeny.

H. BACTERIOPHAGE: *Lysogenic Conversion*

V. J. Freeman discovers that bacteriophage B of *Corynebacterium diphtheriae* is responsible for converting avirulent strains of the bacterium into virulent, toxin-producing strains. He also finds that virulent wild-type isolates of *C. diphtheriae* are lysogenic for bacteriophage B. The phenomenon of a bacterium acquiring traits through lysogenization comes to be known as lysogenic conversion.

I. VIRAL DISEASE: *Murine Leukemia Virus*

Ludwik Gross is the first to discover a murine leukemia virus occurring "spontaneously" in a strain of mouse called AKR. Gross successfully transfers the virus to newborn C3H mice, a low-leukemia strain.

J. VIRAL DISEASE: *Echoviruses*

Frederick C. Robbins, John F. Enders, Thomas H. Weller, and G. L. Florentino report the direct isolation and serologic identification of virus strains in tissue culture. They examine specimens from patients with both paralytic and nonparalytic poliomyelitis. Among the viruses isolated are some that are not neutralized by antisera to either poliovirus or coxsackievirus. In 1955, a committee of the National Foundation for Infantile Paralysis names this group of viruses the "ECHO" viruses, an acronym for enteric cytopathogenic human orphan viruses. The "orphan" terminology is used for viruses for which no disease has been recognized. (See 1963 J.)

K. MOLECULAR BIOLOGY: *Mode of Action of Antibiotics*

Fred E. Hahn and Charles L. Wisseman, Jr., report that chloromycetin, aureomycin, and terramycin inhibit "adaptive" enzyme formation in *Escherichia coli*. This is one of the first reports of antibiotic inhibition of protein synthesis. (See 1961 S, 1964 N.)

L. BIOCHEMISTRY: *Structure of Protein*

Linus Pauling and Robert Brainerd Corey find that the protein myoglobin exists as a coil containing 3.7 amino acids per turn. They name this structure the "alpha-helix," believing that another form of helix also would be found. Pauling receives the Nobel Prize in chemistry in 1954. (See 1939 R, 1950 P.)

1951 *(continued)*

M. BIOCHEMISTRY: *Acetyl Coenzyme A*

Feodor Lynen, following Fritz Lipmann's studies of coenzyme A, isolates acetyl-S-coenzyme A and studies its role in lipid metabolism. Lynen shares the 1964 Nobel Prize in physiology or medicine with Konrad Bloch. (See 1947 D.)

N. BIOCHEMISTRY: *Oxidative Phosphorylation*

Albert Lehninger finds that mitochondria oxidize reduced diphospho-pyridine nucleotide (DPNH, now called NADPH) and couple the reaction to the formation of ATP. His work shows that oxidative phosphorylation is coupled to electron transport, with oxygen as final acceptor. He reports a phosphorus-oxygen (P-O) ratio of 3. (See 1941 L.)

O. TECHNOLOGY

An experimental nuclear reactor in Idaho produces electricity. In 1955, both the states of Idaho and New York distribute electric power produced by nuclear reactors.

P. THE ARTS: *Literature*
- Herman Wouk writes his novel *The Caine Mutiny*.
- James Jones publishes the novel *From Here to Eternity*.
- J. D. Salinger's novel *The Catcher in the Rye* is published.

Q. THE ARTS: *Television*

The *I Love Lucy* television program premieres on the CBS television network.

1952

A. BACTERIAL ECOLOGY: *Isolation of Spirochetes from the Rumen*

Marvin P. Bryant finds that spirochetes, probably of the genus *Borrelia,* are normal inhabitants of the rumen in both cattle and sheep.

B. BACTERIAL STRUCTURE: *C Polysaccharide in Streptococcal Cell Walls*

Maclyn McCarty proves that the C polysaccharide, the principal cell wall carbohydrate that forms the basis of the Lancefield classification scheme for the streptococci, contains D-rhamnose and hexosamine. (See 1933 A.)

C. BACTERIAL STRUCTURE: *Cell Wall Chemistry*

After James T. Park inhibits growth of *Staphylococcus aureus* with penicillin, he isolates several different uridine 5′-pyrophosphate derivatives. Among these are uridine diphospho-muramic acid-peptide molecules containing L-alanine, D-glutamic acid, L-lysine, and two molecules of D-alanine. The discovery of the "Park nucleotides" plays an important role in deciphering the chemical structure of the cell wall and its biosynthetic pathway. (See 1949 B, 1951 B, 1951 C, 1953 B, 1954 B, 1956 C.)

D. BACTERIAL STRUCTURE: *Cell Wall Chemistry*

M. R. J. Salton finds that the enzyme lysozyme dissolves isolated cell walls of *Micrococcus lysodeikticus*. (See 1952 E, 1953 B, 1953 C.)

E. BACTERIAL STRUCTURE: *Protoplasts*

Treating a bacillus species, *Bacillus* M, with lysozyme, J. Tomcsik and S. Guex-Holzer observe the formation of spherical bodies that Claes Weibull names "protoplasts" in the next year. The fact that cell walls are lysed by lysozyme leads to an analysis of the chemical fragments thus released and subsequently to an understanding of bacterial cell wall structure. (See 1952 E, 1953 C, 1958 D.)

F. BACTERIAL PHYSIOLOGY: *Entner–Doudoroff Pathway*

Nathan Entner and Michael Doudoroff report a new pathway for oxidation of glucose in the genus *Pseudomonas*. Their studies with *Pseudomonas saccharophila* lead to the formulation of a pathway that involves 6-phosphogluconic acid, 2-keto-3-phosphogluconic acid, pyruvic acid, and 3-phosphoglyceraldehyde. (See 1935 J, 1936 O, 1950 D.)

G. BACTERIAL PHYSIOLOGY: *Photosynthesis*

Studying the light and dark metabolism of *Rhodospirillum rubrum,* J. Glover, Martin David Kamen, and H. Van Genderen conclude that during photosynthesis, the main product of carbon dioxide fixation is phosphoglyceric acid (PGA). In 1950, Melvin Calvin and coworkers reported PGA to be the product of photosynthetic CO_2 fixation by plants and algae. (See 1950 M, 1954 M, 1955 E, 1959 C.)

H. BACTERIAL PHYSIOLOGY: *Enzyme Induction*

Melvin Cohn and Jacques Monod use artificial β-galactosides to study the synthesis of β-galactosidases in bacteria. They find that certain compounds, such as thio-β-D-galactoside, lead to the synthesis of the enzyme but do not serve as substrates. They use the term "enzyme induction" instead of "adaptation" and refer to the nonmetabolized compounds as "gratuitous inducers." (See 1950 E.)

I. BACTERIAL GENETICS: *Bacterial Conjugation*

William Hayes discovers that mating in *Escherichia coli* is a unidirectional process, with some strains serving as donors of genetic factors and others as recipients. (See 1946 F, 1950 F, 1955 F.)

J. BACTERIAL GENETICS: *Replica Plating Technique*

Joshua Lederberg and Esther Lederberg introduce the technique of replica plating for the isolation of bacterial mutants without exposure to the selecting agent or condition. Colonies from a master agar plate are transferred to other plates by means of velveteen cloth held on a wooden disk. This technique essentially settles the question of whether mutations occur before or after exposure to the selecting agent.

K. BACTERIAL GENETICS: *Transduction*

Norton David Zinder and Joshua Lederberg report the discovery of a genetic transfer mechanism that they give the name "transduction." Their experiments with *Salmonella typhimurium* prove that bacteriophage P22 carries small sections of DNA from a donor bacterial cell to a recipient cell, thereby conferring a genetic trait to the recipient derived from the donor. (See 1944 C, 1946 F, 1956 H.)

1952 *(continued)*

L. BACTERIOPHAGE: *Restriction of Infection*

Salvador Luria and Mary L. Human and, independently, G. Bertani and Jean J. Weigle are among the first to study how a host bacterium restricts infection by bacteriophage that has been grown on a different host. Further study by Werner Arber in 1965 shows that host cell DNA, as well as phage DNA synthesized in a specific host, is modified by methylation, which protects it from degradation by host cell nucleases (restriction enzymes). These results are important in experiments with recombinant DNA and genetic engineering. Arber, Hamilton Othanel Smith, and Daniel Nathans share the 1978 Nobel Prize in physiology or medicine. (See 1965 Q, 1970 M, 1973 N.)

M. BACTERIOPHAGE: *Eclipse Period*

A. H. Doermann, studying T–even bacteriophage, finds a short period of time during which no newly synthesized phage particles appear after phage infection of the host cell. This period is called the "eclipse period."

N. VIROLOGY: *HeLa Cells*

George O. Gey, W. D. Coffman, and M. T. Kubicek develop the HeLa cell line from a human carcinoma for use in cultivating a wide variety of different viruses. The term "HeLa" is derived from the name of the patient from whom the carcinoma was removed.

O. VIROLOGY: *Viral Plaques*

Renato Dulbecco reports a method for the production of viral plaques in monolayers of cells in tissue culture (cell culture). His technique provides a simple method for titration of viral particles. In 1940, Frank MacFarlane Burnet introduced viral titration methods by counting pocks on the chorio-allantoic membrane of embryonated eggs. (See 1940 J.)

P. IMMUNOLOGY: *Experimental Poliomyelitis Vaccine*

Hilary Koprowski, George A. Jervis, and Thomas W. Norton report the use of a vaccine, made with live poliomyelitis virus passaged through cotton rats, that has low pathogenicity for monkeys. Administration of the vaccine by mouth results in virus growth in the intestines of test subjects; it is found to increase the antibody titer in 20 human volunteers. (See 1954 K, 1957 M.)

Q. IMMUNOLOGY: *Agammaglobulinemia*

Ogden C. Bruton reports the first study of a patient with immunological deficiency disease. He studies a young boy who is totally deficient in gamma globulins and cannot produce antibodies against bacterial infections. Bruton calls this condition agammaglobulinemia.

R. PHYSICS: *Bubble Chamber*

Donald Arthur Glaser develops the bubble chamber in which ionized particles passing through super–heated liquid leave tracks of bubbles along their trajectory. Glaser receives the Nobel Prize in physics in 1960. Luis Walter Alvarez, who develops larger versions of the bubble chamber, receives the 1968 Nobel Prize in physics.

S. TECHNOLOGY
The United States explodes a nuclear fusion bomb, or hydrogen bomb, in the Bikini Atoll in the South Pacific Ocean.

T. SOCIETY AND POLITICS
Britain's king George VI dies. His daughter assumes the throne as Elizabeth II.

U. THE ARTS: *Literature*
Ralph Ellison writes *Invisible Man.*

V. THE ARTS: *Art*
Willem de Kooning paints *Woman II.*

1953

A. BACTERIAL TAXONOMY: *Chlamydiae as Cellular Organisms*
S. A. Zahler and James W. Moulder report finding both DNA and RNA in the chlamydial organism known as feline pneumonitis virus. Although the chlamydiae have been considered to be viruses, this observation suggests they are cellular organisms. (See 1963 D, 1966 A.)

B. BACTERIAL STRUCTURE: *Cell Wall Chemistry*
After showing that bacterial cell walls are a substrate for lysozyme, M. R. J. Salton reports finding glucosamine in all cell walls examined. (See 1940 C, 1952 D, 1954 B, 1956 C.)

C. BACTERIAL STRUCTURE: *Protoplasts*
After Claes Weibull treats *Bacillus megaterium* with lysozyme to damage the cell walls, he observes spherical structures with flagella still attached that he refers to as "protoplasts." These bodies, first noted by J. Tomcsik and S. Guex-Holzer in 1952, are called "gymnoplasts" in 1954 by H. Stähelin. In 1958, a paper signed by 13 researchers in the area of bacterial anatomy recommends that the term protoplast be used to describe cells from which all cell wall components are absent. (See 1952 E, 1958 D.)

D. BACTERIAL STRUCTURE: *Staining of Cell Wall and Membrane*
C. F. Robinow and R. G. E. Murray develop a staining process, using Victoria blue, that clearly shows the presence of an intensely stained membrane underlying the cell wall. Georges Knaysi successfully stained walls and membranes in 1941, but his results were not widely accepted. (See 1941 D, 1958 A.)

E. BACTERIAL STRUCTURE: *Electron Microscopy of Bacteria*
C. B. Chapman and J. Hillier and, independently, A. Birch-Andersen, Ole Maaloe, and F. S. Sjöstrand publish electron microscope photographs of ultrathin sections of bacteria. Although the bacterial nuclear region is not clearly depicted, Chapman and Hillier conclude that there is no nuclear membrane. Birch-Andersen et al. report that the cell appears to be a spongelike structure surrounded by a membrane with a central region in which there are one or more large "vacuoles" that contain irregularly folded threads that may be the equivalent of the "nuclei" seen in stained cells. Chapman and Hillier also note "peripheral bodies" near the division septa in *Bacillus cereus,* which Philip C. Fitz-James names "mesosomes" in

1953 *(continued)*

1960. Independently, Keith Roberts Porter and J. Blum develop a microtome that makes studying thin sections of bacteria a routine matter. (See 1940 A, 1941 B, 1959 A.)

F. BACTERIAL PHYSIOLOGY: *Dipicolinic Acid and Heat Resistance in Spores*

Joan F. Powell finds that spores and spore exudates contain dipicolinic acid. Powell, H. R. Curran, R. E. Strange, and others discover that divalent calcium combines with dipicolinic acid to form complexes that seem to correlate with the development of heat resistance in spores. (See 1943 B, 1957 E, 1972 D.)

G. BACTERIAL PHYSIOLOGY: *Feedback Inhibition*

Studying the biosynthesis of tryptophan in *Escherichia coli,* Aaron Novick and Leo Szilard find that high concentrations of the amino acid block the formation of one of the intermediates in the pathway, indole 3-glycerol phosphate. They suggest that a high intracellular concentration of tryptophan inhibits the pathway of biosynthesis, whereas a low concentration permits its functioning. This type of process is later called "feedback inhibition" of enzyme activity. (See 1955 D, 1957 C, 1961 E.)

H. BACTERIAL PHYSIOLOGY: *Nitrogen Fixation*

Jack W. Newton, Perry Wilson, and Robert H. Burris prove that ammonia is a key intermediate in nitrogen fixation by *Azotobacter.* (See 1942 E, 1951 D.)

I. BACTERIAL PHYSIOLOGY: *Cell-Free Nitrogen Fixation*

Pat B. Hamilton, Wayne E. Magee, and Leonard Mortenson use a mass spectrometer, with ^{15}N as a tracer, to show that a cell-free extract of *Azotobacter vinelandii* fixes nitrogen. Results show measurable amounts of nitrogen fixation in 27% of their trials. (See 1960 C.)

J. BACTERIAL INSECTICIDES: *Parasporal Body*

Examining the parasporal body found in *Bacillus thuringiensis* by Ernst Berliner, C. L. Hannay reports that it is a crystal of protein. He notes that the crystals dissolve in alkali but does not examine them for toxicity. (See 1902 E, 1915 B, 1951 F, 1954 H.)

K. BACTERIAL GENETICS: *F Factor in Bacterial Conjugation*

William Hayes and, independently, Luca L. Cavalli-Sforza, Joshua Lederberg, and Esther Lederberg find that an "infectious agent" controls sex compatibility in conjugation by *Escherichia coli.* The Lederbergs and Cavalli-Sforza call this a "fertility factor, or F factor." Strains that possess the F factor are F$^+$, while those that lack it are F$^-$. (See 1946 F, 1950 F, 1951 I, 1956 G.)

L. BACTERIAL GENETICS: *Phase Variation in* Salmonella

Joshua Lederberg and P. R. Edwards find that phase variation in salmonellae is controlled by two separate genetic loci, H1 and H2, each of which controls the synthesis of a specific flagellar structural protein. In the individual antigenic phases, the bacteria synthesize different forms of flagellar protein. In 1956, Lederberg and Tetsuo Iino show that the control of the H1 and H2 loci resides in the H2 locus, which can exist either in the "on" or "off" states, controlling whether the H1 gene is expressed or not. They report that the state of expression can be transferred by transduction, and they compare this type of genetic modification to the movable elements that Barbara McClintock described in maize. (See 1922 C, 1950 J.)

M. BACTERIOPHAGE GENETICS: *Weigle Reactivation/Mutagenesis*
Jean J. Weigle finds that ultraviolet irradiation of *Escherichia coli* before infection with bacteriophage results in increased survival of the phage as compared with infection of nonirradiated bacteria. Increased survival is not seen if photoreactivation of the bacteria is done before infection with phage. This phenomenon is later referred to as "Weigle reactivation." Weigle also reports that the majority of the phages are mutant, and this is referred to as "Weigle mutagenesis." (See 1949 F, 1960 H, 1962 G, 1964 E.)

N. MOLECULAR BIOLOGY: *the Hershey-Chase Experiment*
Alfred Hershey and Martha Chase demonstrate that DNA is the substance of genetic material when they radioactively label bacteriophage T2 with either ^{35}S or ^{32}P, which incorporate into protein or nucleic acid, respectively. They find that only the ^{32}P-labeled DNA is carried into the infected cell that forms new phage. This experiment, which adds to the 1944 data that Oswald T. Avery, Colin MacLeod, and Maclyn McCarty obtained from their study of bacterial transformation, indicates that DNA is the substance of genes. Hershey shares the 1969 Nobel Prize in physiology or medicine with Salvador Luria and Max Delbrück. (See 1953 O, 1955 J.)

O. MOLECULAR BIOLOGY: *Structure of DNA*
James Watson and Francis Crick publish their paper describing the structure of DNA as being two chains of nucleic acid wound together in a double helix, with the nucleotide bases contained on the inside of the coil. They suggest that this structure may explain the transmission of genetic information. The proposed structure of DNA is widely accepted throughout the scientific community. Watson, Crick, and Maurice Wilkins share the 1962 Nobel Prize in physiology or medicine. Wilkins and Rosalind Franklin provide data from X-ray crystallography of DNA that are crucial to the development of the model of DNA built by Watson and Crick. Franklin dies before the Nobel Prizes are awarded for this work.

P. MOLECULAR BIOLOGY: *Biosynthesis of Feline Pneumonitis Virus*
Stanley A. Zahler and James W. Moulder study the chemical content of feline pneumonitis virus purified from infected chick embryo yolk sacs. Through the use of radioactive phosphorus, they discover that the viral nucleic acid has several times the specific activity of the other phosphorus compounds in the yolk sac. They conclude that the virus stimulates an increase in nucleic acid synthesis by tissues during a period ending several hours before the death of the embryo.

Q. MOLECULAR BIOLOGY: *Structure of Insulin*
Frederick Sanger completes the analysis of the amino acid sequence and structure of the polypeptide chains of insulin. For his work in developing

1953 *(continued)*

the chemistry of this type of analysis, Sanger receives the Nobel Prize in chemistry in 1958. He receives a second Nobel Prize in 1980. (See 1965 R, 1977 T.)

R. IMMUNOLOGY: *Immunological Tolerance*
Peter B. Medawar, with Rupert E. Billingham and Leslie Brent, shows that the introduction of foreign antigen to mice in utero results in their immunological tolerance to administration of the same antigen. These experimental results, with those of other workers, contribute to the formulation of the clonal selection theory of antibody formation proposed by Frank Macfarlane Burnet in 1957. Medawar and Burnet share the 1960 Nobel Prize in physiology or medicine.

S. IMMUNOLOGY: *Transplantation Immunity*
Nicholas Avrion Mitchison reports the passive transfer of immunity to tumor grafts by the transplantation of immune lymph nodes.

T. BIOLOGY: *Cell Cycle*
Studying the cell cycle in mammalian cells, A. Howard and S. R. Pelc show that DNA replication takes place only during the S phase and that there is a gap (G_2) between synthesis and mitosis (M) and another pause (G_1) between M and S.

U. MEDICINE: *Coronary Heart Disease*
Ancel Keys reports that persons whose diets are high in animal fat have a high incidence of coronary heart disease. (See 1901 K, 1913 D.)

V. BIOLOGY: *Origin of Life*
Based on the concepts of A. I. Oparin and J. B. S. Haldane's discussion of Oparin's work in 1929, Stanley Lloyd Miller attempts to recreate Oparin's ocean scenario for the origin of life on earth. Miller is also influenced by Harold C. Urey's articles and books on the early chemical history of the earth. Miller successfully causes the formation of some organic compounds, including amino acids, by passing electric charges through a mixture of hydrogen, methane, ammonia, and water.

W. SCIENTIFIC PUBLICATIONS: Applied Microbiology
The Society of American Bacteriologists begins publication of the journal *Applied Microbiology*.

X. TECHNOLOGY
Both the National Broadcasting Company (NBC) and the Columbia Broadcasting System (CBS) begin transmitting color television. The system used by NBC is compatible with black–and–white sets, while that of CBS is not. CBS soon begins use of the compatible system. Color television sets are not widely available until 1954. (See 1925 H, 1926 N, 1929 O, 1936 T.)

Y. SOCIETY AND POLITICS
- The Truce of Panmunjom ends the Korean War.
- Georgi Malenkov assumes the leadership of the USSR after Josef Stalin dies. Nikita Khrushchev becomes first secretary of the Communist Party.

Z. THE ARTS: *Literature*
- John Steinbeck writes *East of Eden.*
- James Baldwin publishes *Go Tell It on the Mountain.*
- Ian Fleming publishes *Casino Royale.*

AA. THE ARTS: *Theater*
- Arthur Miller's play *The Crucible* opens in New York City.
- *Waiting for Godot* by Samuel Beckett is performed in Paris.

1954

A. BACTERIAL TAXONOMY: *Atypical Mycobacteria*

M. A. Timpe and Ernest H. Runyon study acid-fast bacteria that differ from the known bovine and human tuberculosis strains isolated from human patients. Some appear to be associated with pulmonary disease, but none infect guinea pigs. Timpe and Runyon divide the organisms into three groups, two of which are virulent for mice. In 1965, Runyon refines the classification into four groups: photochromogens, scotochromogens, nonphotochromogens, and rapid growers. This scheme serves as a basis for the classification of many of the mycobacterial species other than *Mycobacterium tuberculosis.*

B. BACTERIAL STRUCTURE: *Cell Wall Chemistry*

R. E. Strange and Joan F. Powell find an amino sugar in secretions of peptides from germinating spores of three species of the genus *Bacillus.* When Strange and F. A. Dark crystallize the compound in 1956, they determine it to be 3-O-carboxyethyl-D-glucosamine (the 3-O-D-lactic acid ether of glucosamine), for which Strange proposes the common name "muramic acid." (See 1940 C, 1952 C, 1953 B, 1956 C.)

C. BACTERIAL STRUCTURE: *Lipid A / Endotoxin*

Studying the Boivin-type acid precipitates from gram-negative bacteria, Otto Westphal and Otto Lüderitz obtain a water-insoluble, chloroform-soluble fraction that they refer to as "lipid A." Westphal and Lüderitz, and others, determine that lipid A is a diglucosamine disaccharide substituted with fatty acids. By the early 1970s, lipid A is known to be the endotoxin component of the outer membrane lipopolysaccharide of gram-negative bacteria. (See 1892 D, 1933 B, 1960 A.)

D. BACTERIAL PHYSIOLOGY: *Actinorhizal Nitrogen Fixation*

A. I. Virtanen, studying the plant *Alnus,* and G. Bond, studying *Alnus, Myrica,* and other plants, demonstrate uptake of ^{15}N by actinorhizal root nodules, proving that they fix nitrogen. In 1967, W. D. P. Stewart, G. P. Fitzgerald, and R. H. Burris confirm fixation by using the acetylene reduction test. (See 1885 E, 1902 A, 1954 D, 1970 B, 1978 D.)

E. BACTERIAL PHYSIOLOGY: *Induced Enzymes*

In this year and the next, two groups of researchers, Solomon Spiegelman and colleagues, and Jacques Monod and associates, find that the enzyme β-galactosidase is synthesized primarily from amino acids in the growth medium, proving that there is no protein precursor for induced enzymes. (See 1952 H, 1953 G, 1955 D, 1957 C, 1961 E.)

F. BACTERIAL PHYSIOLOGY: *Cell-Free Photophosphorylation*

Albert Frenkel, in experiments in the light with a cell-free preparation from *Rhodospirillum rubrum,* finds that orthophosphate disappears under anaerobic conditions in the presence of catalytic amounts of adenosine polyphosphates or substrate quantities of ADP. That the product formed is ATP is demonstrated when it is added to the reaction mixture for the hexokinase-catalyzed conversion of glucose to glucose-phosphate. (See 1954 N.)

G. BACTERIAL DISEASE: *Anthrax Toxin*

Until the report this year by H. Smith and J. Keppie, no one had demonstrated a toxic factor produced by *Bacillus anthracis.* These researchers report that the plasma of guinea pigs fatally infected with the bacterium is lethal when injected into susceptible animals. The toxic agent is specifically neutralized by anthrax antiserum. (See 1968 D.)

H. BACTERIAL INSECTICIDES: *Toxicity of the Parasporal Body*

T. A. Angus discovers that pathogenesis for lepidoptoran insects shown by an organism he refers to as *Bacillus cereus* var. *sotto* (*Bacillus thuringiensis*) is caused by the protein parasporal body. He suggests that the protein is hydrolyzed by alkali in the insect larval gut, which has a normal pH of 9.5 to 10.0. (See 1902 E, 1915 F, 1951 F, 1953 J, 1967 J, 1983 J, 1986 H, 1987 B.)

I. BACTERIAL GENETICS: *Colicinogeny*

Pierre Frédéricq finds that the ability to produce colicin is readily transferred when a Col$^+$ strain of *Escherichia coli* is mixed with a Col$^-$ strain. He concludes that the Col factor behaves in a way similar to the F factor. In 1958, François Jacob and Elie Wollman include Col factors in their definition of episomes. (See 1925 B, 1967 I.)

J. BACTERIAL GENETICS: *Mutator Genes*

Henry P. Treffers, Viola Spinelli, and Nao O. Belser find an unusually high rate of mutation to resistance to streptomycin in a strain of *Escherichia coli.* They refer to the factor causing the high mutation rate as a "mutator gene." (See 1937 H.)

K. IMMUNOLOGY: *the Salk Polio Vaccine*

Jonas Edward Salk introduces a killed-virus vaccine for poliomyelitis. The vaccine includes all three types of poliovirus inactivated by formaldehyde. Large-scale experimental immunization of about 650,000 children, including approximately 200,000 who receive a harmless placebo, is carried out. Since the Salk vaccine is considered safe, widespread use begins, and by the end of 1955 more that 7 million doses are given. (See 1957 M.)

L. IMMUNOLOGY: *Measles Vaccine*

John F. Enders and Thomas C. Peebles isolate the measles virus in tissue culture. Subsequently, Milan Milovanovic and A. Mitus develop an attenuated strain by passages through human cell tissue cultures. A vaccine prepared by Samuel L. Katz in 1960 is administered to children and after 1966, following further development, is used widely.

M. BIOCHEMISTRY: *Photosynthesis*

Melvin Calvin, in collaboration with J. A. Bassham, A. A. Benson, and other researchers, reports the major conclusions from experiments that began in 1945 to determine the path of carbon in photosynthetic carbon dioxide fixation. They employ radioactive ^{14}C to discover the sequence of compounds that are synthesized leading to the formation of glucose. They present data proving that ribulose diphosphate is the primary acceptor of CO_2 and phosphoglyceric acid is the first product. Their conclusions are presented as a sequence that becomes known as the Calvin cycle, the Calvin-Benson cycle, or the Calvin-Benson-Bassham cycle. In further studies involving J. R. Quayle and R. C. Fuller, they report that extracts of *Chlorella* contain an enzyme capable of catalyzing the carboxylation of ribulose diphosphate to form phosphoglyceric acid. This enzyme, known as ribulose bisphosphate carboxylase, is found by Robert W. Dorner and colleagues to be the major protein among the leaf proteins in green plants. Calvin receives the 1957 Nobel Prize in chemistry for this work. (See 1950 M, 1952 G, 1955 E, 1959 C.)

N. BIOCHEMISTRY: *Photosynthesis by Isolated Chloroplasts*

After isolating chloroplasts from spinach leaves, Daniel Arnon reports that they carry out two photochemical processes, fixation of CO_2 and photosynthetic phosphorylation. Arnon's experiments are the first to demonstrate photophosphorylation. (See 1954 F.)

O. SOCIETY AND POLITICS

In the case of *Brown v. Board of Education* brought in Topeka, Kansas, the U.S. Supreme Court rules unanimously that segregation in public schools is unconstitutional. In a separate ruling in another case in 1958, the Court rules that schools in Little Rock, Arkansas, must follow an integration schedule, thus implementing its 1954 decision.

P. THE ARTS: *Literature*

• J. R. R. Tolkien publishes the first two volumes of *The Lord of the Rings*. The third volume appears in 1955.
• Kingsley Amis publishes *Lucky Jim*.

1955

A. MICROBIAL ECOLOGY: *Selective or Enrichment Cultures*

Cornelius B. van Niel, in a paper entitled "Natural Selection in the Microbial World," encourages the use of the "elective, selective, or enrichment technique" used by both Sergei Winogradsky and Martinus Beijerinck to study microbial ecology.

B. BACTERIAL STRUCTURE: *Fimbriae/Pili*

J. P. Duguid, I. W. Smith, G. Dempster, and P. N. Edmunds, in a report of the hemagglutinating activity of *Bacterium coli* (*Escherichia coli*), refer to the threadlike appendages seen on the bacterial cell surface as "fimbriae," meaning thread or filament. C. C. Brinton, Jr., in 1959, uses the word "pili," for hair, in a description of similar structures. In later usage, the term "pili" is usually restricted to appendages on gram-negative bacteria that

1955 *(continued)*

function in cell-to-cell gene transfer phenomena or for the attachment of some types of bacteriophage to the cell. "Fimbriae" usually refers to shorter, bristlelike appendages. (See 1949 D, 1964 F.)

C. BACTERIAL STRUCTURE: *Flagellin*
W. T. Astbury, E. Beighton, and Claes Weibull assign the name "flagellin" to the protein found in bacterial flagella. (See 1948 A.)

D. BACTERIAL PHYSIOLOGY: *Feedback Inhibition/Allosteric Inhibition*
Two groups of researchers report new observations about the phenomenon of feedback inhibition of enzyme activity. Richard Alan Yates and Arthur Beck Pardee report that cytidine triphosphate inhibits aspartic transcarbamylase, the first enzyme in the series leading to pyrimidine synthesis. Harold Erwin Umbarger reports that isoleucine inhibits threonine deaminase, thus blocking isoleucine synthesis from threonine. In 1961, noting that the inhibitor is not a steric analog of the substrate, Jacques Monod and François Jacob propose that the mechanism of end-product inhibition be called "allosteric inhibition." (See 1952 H, 1953 G, 1954 E, 1957 C, 1961 E.)

E. BACTERIAL PHYSIOLOGY: CO_2 *Fixation in Autotrophic Bacteria*
In the first report of a mechanism for carbon dioxide fixation in autotrophic bacteria, Melvin Santer and Wolf Vishniac find that *Thiobacillus thioparus* converts ribulose diphosphate and CO_2 to phosphoglyceric acid. (See 1945 A, 1950 M, 1954 M.)

F. BACTERIAL GENETICS: *Interrupted Mating in* Escherichia coli
In a study of time periods for matings between Hfr and F⁻ strains of *Escherichia coli,* Elie Wollman and François Jacob report finding the transfer of a greater number of genes at longer mating periods. They perform an interrupted mating experiment by using a high-speed blender to break apart mating pairs of cells at timed intervals. Correlating the transfer times with the genetic map for *E. coli,* they show that the times can be used to establish a map. (See 1950 F, 1952 I, 1956 F.)

G. VIROLOGY: *Crystallization of Poliovirus*
Frederick L. Schaffer and Carlton E. Schwerdt crystallize the virus of poliomyelitis. This is the first virus that infects humans or animals to be obtained in pure crystalline form. (See 1935 H.)

H. VIROLOGY: *Structure of Tobacco Mosaic Virus*
J. Ieuan Harris and C. A. Knight investigate the structure of tobacco mosaic virus by treatment with carboxypeptidase. They measure threonine released by the enzyme treatment and, from the quantitative data, conclude that the virus contains about 2,900 subunits, each with a molecular weight of approximately 17,000. Later studies confirm that the virus has 2,130 subunits with a molecular weight of 17,400. (See 1955 I, 1956 L.)

I. VIROLOGY: *Reconstitution of Tobacco Mosaic Virus*
Heinz L. Fraenkel-Conrat and Robley Cook Williams convert the tobacco mosaic virus into its component parts and then successfully reconstitute it to form an active infectious virus. They obtain the protein by ammonium

sulfate precipitation and the nucleic acid by treatment of the viral particle with a detergent, sodium dodecyl sulfate. After reconstitution, accomplished by mixing the protein solution with the nucleic acid solution, electron microscopy reveals structures characteristic of the virus. When assays for infectivity are performed on tobacco plants, typical lesions are formed. (See 1955 H, 1956 L.)

J. VIROLOGY: *Infectious RNA of Tobacco Mosaic Virus*
A. Gierer and Gerhard Felix Schramm and, independently, Heinz Fraenkel-Conrat show that the isolated ribonucleic acid from tobacco mosaic virus is infective; i.e., the RNA alone causes the disease and results in the formation of new viral particles. This discovery, coupled with Alfred Hershey's and Martha Chase's 1953 experiments with phage DNA, provides convincing evidence that nucleic acids are responsible for directing infected cells to synthesize new virions. (See 1953 N.)

K. MOLECULAR BIOLOGY: *the Cistron*
Seymour Benzer introduces the term "cistron" to describe the shortest sequence of DNA that functions as a gene. He bases the terminology on fine-structure analysis of the gene by means of genetic complementation (*cis-trans* test) of the *r*II mutants of bacteriophage T2 that cannot bring about the lysis of strains of *Escherichia coli* that carry prophage λ. The *cis-trans* terminology is introduced by J. B. S. Haldane in 1942, in an analogy from the chemical usage of the term. In 1951, E. B. Lewis describes experiments with *Drosophila* that employ techniques that will be known as the *cis-trans* test.

L. MOLECULAR BIOLOGY: *Enzymatic Synthesis of Ribonucleic Acid*
Severo Ochoa and Marianne Grunberg-Manago find an enzyme in *Azotobacter vinelandii* that catalyzes the formation of polyribonucleotides from individual nucleotides. The enzyme, polynucleotide phosphorylase, is later used by Marshall Nirenberg and Heinrich Matthaei in their 1961 experiments on the genetic code. Ochoa and Arthur Kornberg share the 1959 Nobel Prize in physiology or medicine.

M. MOLECULAR BIOLOGY: *Protein Synthesis on Ribosomes*
John W. Littlefield, Elizabeth B. Keller, Jerome Gross, and Paul C. Zamecnik find that radioactive leucine and valine are rapidly incorporated onto cytoplasmic ribonucleoprotein particles from rat liver. In 1957, when they continue these studies in a cell-free system with ribonucleoprotein particles from the Ehrlich mouse ascites tumor, they conclude that the rapid incorporation of the amino acids could represent formation of new polypeptide chains on the surface of the RNA particles. (See 1956 Q.)

N. IMMUNOLOGY: *Natural Selection Theory of Antibody Formation*
Niels K. Jerne publishes a theory of antibody formation that resembles Paul Ehrlich's side chain theory. He suggests that the specificity of immunoglobulins is constitutive. An introduced antigen selects a preexisting immunoglobulin followed by presentation of the antigen–antibody complex to macrophages, which then synthesize additional antibody molecules of that

specific type. In 1957, Jerne's theory is replaced by Frank Macfarlane Burnet's clonal selection theory. Jerne shares the 1984 Nobel Prize in physiology or medicine with César Milstein and Georges Köhler, who develop a method for producing monoclonal antibodies. (See 1897 G, 1957 N, 1974 L, 1975 N.)

O. IMMUNOLOGY: *Immunoelectrophoresis*
Pierre Grabar and Curtis A. Williams, Jr., improve the Ouchterlony double diffusion test by developing the technique of immunoelectrophoresis, permitting the analysis of complex protein mixtures. (See 1939 H, 1948 J.)

P. CELL BIOLOGY: *Lysosomes/Peroxisomes*
Christian de Duve discovers subcellular membrane-bounded structures that he names "lysosomes," which are found to contain acid hydrolases that degrade polymers. Later he also discovers "peroxisomes," membrane-bounded structures that contain enzymes that degrade fatty acids and amino acids and the enzyme catalase that degrades hydrogen peroxide. de Duve shares the 1974 Nobel Prize in physiology or medicine with Albert Claude and George Emil Palade. (See 1938 B, 1956 Q.)

Q. SCIENTIFIC ORGANIZATIONS: *American Academy of Microbiology*
The American Academy of Microbiology is established by the Society of American Bacteriologists.

R. THE ARTS: *Literature*
- Flannery O'Connor publishes "A Good Man Is Hard To Find."
- Vladimir Nabokov publishes his novel *Lolita*.

S. THE ARTS: *Theater*
- The play *Cat on a Hot Tin Roof* by Tennessee Williams opens.
- *Inherit the Wind* by Jerome Lawrence and Robert E. Lee has its first performance.

T. THE ARTS: *Art*
Mark Rothko paints *Earth and Green*.

1956

A. BIOLOGY: *Taxonomy*
Herbert F. Copeland proposes a new system of classification that departs from the traditional two kingdoms of *Plantae* and *Animalia*. He suggests four kingdoms: *Monera,* the procaryotic bacteria and blue-green algae; *Protoctista* (or *Protista*), the lower eucaryotes such as algae, protozoa, slime molds, and fungi; the *Plantae,* photosynthetic organisms ranging from bryophytes to higher plants; and *Animalia,* the multicellular animals. Copeland's four-kingdom system is replaced in 1969 by a five-kingdom system proposed by R. H. Whittaker. (See 1861 D, 1866 A, 1869 A, 1969A, 1977 A, 1990 A.)

B. BACTERIOLOGICAL TECHNIQUE: *Continuous Culture*
D. Herbert, R. Elsworth, and R. C. Telling present a thorough mathematical analysis of continuous cultures that allows quantitative prediction of the steady-state concentrations of bacteria and substrate in the culture and how

these may be expected to vary with change of medium, concentration of nutrients, and flow rate. They construct a small pilot plant, which is run successfully for periods up to 4 months for experiments with *Aerobacter cloacae*. (See 1935 A. 1950 C, 1958 F.)

C. BACTERIAL STRUCTURE: *Bacterial Cell Walls*
By this date, a number of investigators have found that the amino sugars in bacterial cell walls are *N*-acetyl glucosamine and *N*-acetyl muramic acid. M. R. J. Salton provides evidence that treating bacterial cells with lysozyme releases a disaccharide of these two compounds, assuming that the disaccharide has a β linkage. In addition, C. S. Cummings and H. Harris detect amino sugar peptides in a number of species of gram-positive bacteria. The amino sugar-peptide component of bacterial cell walls is designated by various names. In 1957, it is called simply the basal structure, followed by "mucopeptide" (1958), "glycopeptide" (1959), "glycosaminopeptide" (1964), "murein" (1964), and "peptidoglycan" (1967). "Murein" and "peptidoglycan" become the most commonly used terms. (See 1940 C, 1952 C, 1953 B, 1954 B. 1958 B.)

D. BACTERIAL PHYSIOLOGY: *β-Galactoside Permease*
Howard V. Rickenberg, Georges N. Cohen, Gerard Buttin, and Jacques Monod, after investigating the uptake of thio-β-D-galactoside, discover a stereospecific permeation system for β-galactosides in *Escherichia coli*. They apply the general name "permease" to such systems. (See 1965 I.)

E. BACTERIAL PHYSIOLOGY: *Glucose Effect*
A reversal of the glucose effect in histidase biosynthesis is discovered by Frederick C. Neidhardt and Boris Magasanik. Glucose inhibits the formation of several inducible enzymes in *Aerobacter aerogenes,* but when histidine is present in the growth medium instead of ammonium ion, the enzyme histidase is formed. They conclude that the glucose effect indicates the existence of feedback mechanisms by which the levels of intermediary metabolites control the synthesis of catabolic enzymes. (See 1942 F, 1953 G, 1955 D.)

F. BACTERIAL GENETICS: *Circular Chromosome*
After analyzing data from interrupted mating experiments, Elie Wollman, François Jacob, and William Hayes conclude that the chromosome of *Escherichia coli* is circular. (See 1955 F, 1959 A, 1963 E.)

G. BACTERIAL GENETICS: *Origin of Hfr Mating Types*
François Jacob and Elie Wollman provide evidence that Hfr mating types in *Escherichia coli* arise by mutation from F[+] strains. (See 1950 F.)

H. BACTERIAL GENETICS: *Specialized Transduction*
M. L. Morse, Joshua Lederberg, and Esther Lederberg discover that bacteriophage lambda in *Escherichia coli* K12 transfers only the genes associated with galactose metabolism. This is contrasted with the P22 transducing system in *Salmonella,* in which a number of different genes are transferred. They apply the term "specialized transduction" to lambda transduction, while the P22 type becomes known as "generalized transduction." (See 1952 K.)

1956 (continued)

I. BACTERIAL DISEASE: *Virulence Antigen of* **Pasteurella**

T. W. Burrow reports that all fully virulent strains of *Pasteurella pestis* possess an antigen that is not detectable in avirulent strains. This factor is the long-sought V antigen of this bacterium. (See 1980 J, 1980 K, 1981 F, 1984 H.)

J. VIRAL STRUCTURE: *Protein Shell*

Francis Crick and James Watson advance a hypothesis about the basic structure of small rod-shaped and spherical viruses, assuming that they possess a protein shell to protect the nucleic acid. They propose that the viral protein molecules must aggregate around the nucleic acid in a regular structure, which can be formed in a limited number of ways. They state that the number of subunits in a rod-shaped virus, such as tobacco mosaic virus, is probably unrestricted but that spherical viruses, such as bushy stunt virus, are most likely to have a number of subunits in multiples of 12. (See 1956 K, 1956 L, 1957 I, 1959 I.)

K. VIRAL STRUCTURE: *Icosahedral Structure of Viruses*

After studying the tomato bushy stunt virus, Donald L. D. Caspar provides the first evidence for a virus with icosahedral symmetry. He concludes that the number of subunits in the capsid is a multiple of 12 and most likely a multiple of 60. In 1957, a similar structure is found for turnip yellow mosaic virus by Aaron Klug, John T. Finch, and Rosalind Franklin. (See 1956 J, 1956 L, 1957 I, 1959 I.)

L. VIRAL STRUCTURE: *Tobacco Mosaic Virus*

Rosalind Franklin and Aaron Klug present evidence from X-ray diffraction studies that the tobacco mosaic virus particle is neither a smooth cylinder nor a hexagonal prism but has a rod shape with a helical groove on its surface. In other papers, Donald Caspar and Rosalind Franklin report separately on additional studies of the structure of the tobacco mosaic virus. Caspar observes that the rod-shaped virus particle is hollow, with a cylindrical hole that has a radius of about 19 angstroms. Franklin finds that the viral nucleic acid does not lie close to the particle axis and concludes that it must be embedded in the viral protein, closely related to the structural arrangement of the protein. Further studies reveal that the viral RNA has a helical configuration surrounded by the protein capsid. (See 1955 H, 1955 I, 1956 L.)

M. MOLECULAR BIOLOGY: *Messenger RNA*

Elliot Volkin and Lazarus Astrachan, in studies of T-phage infection of *Escherichia coli,* find an unusual type of RNA that follows the base composition of the infecting phage. Although they determine that it is not a precursor of the phage DNA, they are unable to assign a function to it. These observations contribute to development of the concept of messenger RNA (mRNA). (See 1961 O.)

N. MOLECULAR BIOLOGY: *Transfer RNA*

Francis Crick, in an unpublished paper, proposes that substances he calls "adaptors" must take part in positioning the amino acids into proper sequence in synthesis of a polypeptide. He later publishes a review on protein synthesis in which he mentions this concept. Later research confirms that soluble RNA (sRNA), given the name transfer RNA (tRNA), plays this role. (See 1957 P.)

O. MOLECULAR BIOLOGY: *DNA Polymerase*
Arthur Kornberg and his coworkers partially purify an enzyme from *Escherichia coli* that polymerizes triphosphate to form a DNA polymer. The enzyme is subsequently named "DNA polymerase" (later called DNA polymerase I). Kornberg and Severo Ochoa share the 1959 Nobel Prize in physiology or medicine. (See 1958 O.)

P. IMMUNOLOGY: *Bursa of Fabricius*
Bruce Glick, Timothy S. Chang, and R. George Jaap discover that the bursa of Fabricius is an immunological organ in chickens. They find that removing the bursa in very young chickens prevents the production of antibodies by the adults. By the early 1970s, evidence accumulates that bone marrow cells in humans are equivalent to the bursa-dependent cells in chickens. The cells derived from the bursa and bone marrow are later known as B cells, while those cells that are modified by the thymus are called T cells. (See 1957 N, 1961 L, 1962 S.)

Q. CELL BIOLOGY: *Ribosomes*
While studying the microsomal material obtained by ultracentrifugation, George Emile Palade describes small particles visible only in electron micrographs that are either attached to the membranes of the cytoplasmic reticulum or free in the cytoplasm. His suggestion that the particles might account for the high RNA content of the endoplasmic reticulum is subsequently proved by Palade and Philip Siekevitz and independently by Paul C. Zamecnik. In 1958, Richard B. Roberts suggests that such particles be called "ribosomes." Palade shares the 1974 Nobel Prize in physiology or medicine with Albert Claude and Christian de Duve. (See 1938 B, 1955 M, 1955 P.)

R. SOCIETY AND POLITICS
Egypt announces that it is assuming control over the Suez Canal, instigating an international crisis involving Israel, France, England, and the United Nations. Israel invades the Gaza Strip and the Sinai Peninsula, while Britain and France seize control of the Mediterranean end of the canal. A United Nations Emergency Force is assembled to assist in ending the conflict, and the invading troops withdraw.

S. THE ARTS: *Music*
The musical version of George Bernard Shaw's play *Pygmalion* appears as *My Fair Lady,* with music by Frederick Loewe and lyrics by Alan Jay Lerner.

1957

A. BACTERIAL STRUCTURE: *Gram Stain Mechanism*
F. Wensinck and J. J. Boevé find that in the first steps of Gram staining, the amount of crystal violet and iodine taken up by both gram-negative and

gram-positive bacteria is about the same. They show that the crystal violet-iodine chemical complex is easily soluble in 90% ethyl alcohol and that it is more readily extracted from gram-negative organisms than from gram-positive organisms. Since attempts by many investigators failed to prove the existence of a specific chemical in cells that bind the dye-iodine complex, Wensinck and Boevé conclude that permeability differences explain its rapid extraction from gram-negative bacteria. (See 1884 B, 1929 A, 1963 B.)

B. BACTERIAL STRUCTURE: *M Protein*
S. S. Barkulis and Margaret F. Jones report that approximately one-third of the cell wall of *Streptococcus haemolyticus* is composed of the C polysaccharide. They state that the remaining two-thirds is composed of a substance called M protein, a type-specific substance. Later studies show that the M protein is the main component of the streptococcal fimbriae. (See 1952 B.)

C. BACTERIAL PHYSIOLOGY: *Repression of Enzyme Synthesis*
Henry J. Vogel finds that arginine inhibits the synthesis of acetylornithinase, one of the enzymes in a sequence of reactions leading from glutamate to arginine. He introduces the term "enzyme repression" to describe inhibition enzyme synthesis, as opposed to "feedback inhibition," which suppresses enzyme activity. (See 1952 H, 1953 G, 1954 E, 1955 D, 1961 E.)

D. BACTERIAL PHYSIOLOGY: *Swarming in* **Proteus**
W. Howard Hughes employs cinemicrography in studies of the swarming phenomenon in *Proteus vulgaris*. He finds that the cells at the peripheries of colonies begin to form long forms, such as those he observes when the cells are exposed to penicillin. At each successive stage of swarming, the cells become more abnormal in appearance. Hughes suggests that the long forms are induced by a nonspecific volatile agent that cannot be detected when growth has been cleared from the medium. (See 1964 A, 1965 E, 1988 D.)

E. BACTERIAL PHYSIOLOGY: *Heat Resistance in Spores*
Studying synchronously grown *Clostridium roseum,* Harlyn O. Halvorson finds a correlation between the development of heat resistance and the presence of calcium-dipicolinate (Ca-DPA). In further studies, Halvorson and others find that in some sporeformers, heat resistance appears some time after Ca-DPA is synthesized, and that in some instances heat resistance is lost before Ca-DPA is released from the spore. Current opinion is that the low water content of spores is primarily responsible for heat resistance. (See 1943 B, 1953 F, 1972 D.)

F. BACTERIAL PHYSIOLOGY: *Photoreactivating Enzyme*
Claud S. Rupert, Sol H. Goodgal, and Roger M. Herriott report in vitro reactivation of irradiated transforming DNA by treatment with a soluble extract from *Escherichia coli* that is later found to be a photoreactivating enzyme. (See 1949 F, 1953 M, 1960 H, 1962 G, 1964 E.)

G. BACTERIAL DISEASE: **Chlamydia trachomatis**
F.-F. T'ang and coworkers, using embryonated hen's eggs, are the first to isolate the causative agent of trachoma, *Chlamydia trachomatis,* in culture.

They grow the chlamydiae by inoculating material from trachoma infections into the yolk sac. (See 1907 B, 1930 C, 1934 B, 1963 I, 1977 F.)

H. BACTERIAL DISEASE: *Limulus Amebocyte Test for Endotoxin*
Frederik Bang observes that the injection of a gram-negative bacterium into *Limulus polyphemus,* the horseshoe crab, results in intravascular coagulation and death. The level of amebocytes in the circulating blood is drastically reduced. Bang concludes that these effects are caused either by the living gram-negative bacterium or by endotoxin. This observation leads to the development of a highly sensitive laboratory test for the presence of endotoxin in blood serum, cerebrospinal fluid, and fluids used for injection into patients.

I. VIRAL STRUCTURE: *Polyhedral Viruses*
Aaron Klug, John T. Finch, and Rosalind Franklin perform X-ray studies on the turnip yellow mosaic virus and determine that it has a polyhedral structure. In a paper published this same year, Franklin, Klug, and Kenneth Holmes state that viruses must have helical or cubic symmetry, forming regular polyhedra. Recognizing that the virion nucleic acid has the capacity to code for only a fraction of the total protein in the viral capsid, they conclude that there must be multiple copies of identical protein subunits. Such structures necessitate identical environments for each subunit protein and limit the possible modes of assembly to platonic solids. (See 1956 J, 1956 K, 1959 I.)

J. VIRAL DISEASE: *Asian Influenza Pandemic*
An influenza pandemic originating in southwest China is found to be caused by a variant of influenza A virus termed A2, or the Asian virus. Because it differs antigenically from earlier versions of influenza A virus, prior infection with influenza A or A1 virus provides no protection against influenza A2 virus. Under terminology adopted in 1980, based on the antigenic properties of the surface proteins hemagglutinin and neuraminidase, the 1957 virus is designated H2N2.

K. PRION DISEASE: *Kuru*
Daniel Carleton Gajdusek reports the study of a degenerative and fatal disease of the cannibalistic Fore people in Papua, New Guinea. The disease, known as kuru, is at first thought to be genetically determined, but Gajdusek, following William Hadlow's suggestion that the pathology of kuru resembles that of scrapie, finds that kuru can be transmitted to chimpanzees, proving that an infectious agent is involved. Gajdusek shares the 1976 Nobel Prize in physiology or medicine with Baruch Blumberg. Kuru, scrapie, Creutzfeldt-Jakob disease, and bovine spongiform encephalopathy are grouped together as spongiform encephalopathies. After Stanley Prusiner's studies in the 1980s, the causative agent of these diseases is believed to be an infectious agent, called prions, composed only of protein. (See 1920 D, 1936 J, 1966 L, 1982 M, 1985 H.)

L. IMMUNOLOGY: *Interferon*
Alick Isaacs and Jean Lindenmann discover a substance they call "interferon," formed by fragments of chick embryo chorioallantoic membrane

exposed to heat-inactivated influenza virus. In their experiments, a protein factor is released that induces interference with virus infection in new fragments of chorioallantoic membrane. Later studies reveal that other forms of interferon act as "cytokines," substances that regulate functions of cells such as certain lymphocytes. (See 1963 P.)

M. IMMUNOLOGY: *Sabin Polio Vaccine*

Albert Bruce Sabin develops a vaccine for poliomyelitis that contains attenuated virus rather than killed virus as in the Salk vaccine. The vaccine is first tested in Mexico, Russia, and Eastern European countries, where more than 100 million individuals are vaccinated by 1960. After the vaccine is approved for use in the United States, more than 100 million persons of all ages are vaccinated by 1964. (See 1954 K.)

N. IMMUNOLOGY: *Clonal Selection Theory of Antibody Formation*

Frank Macfarlane Burnet publishes a clonal selection theory of antibody formation that replaces the natural selection theory put forward by Niels K. Jerne in 1955. Burnet proposes that in every animal there exist clones of cells that are precommitted to the synthesis of antibody molecules with a single specificity. Other key contributors to the clonal selection theory are David W. Talmage and Joshua Lederberg. Burnet shares the 1960 Nobel Prize in physiology or medicine with Peter B. Medawar. (See 1930 D, 1940 M, 1955 N, 1956 P, 1961 L, 1962 S.)

O. IMMUNOLOGY: *Autoimmune Disease*

Two sets of researchers prove that Hashimoto's chronic thyroiditis is an autoimmune disease. Ernest Witebsky and Noel R. Rose lead one group, while Deborah Doniach and Ivan M. Roitt lead the other. The disease, characterized by a lymphoid goiter, was first described in 1912 by H. Hashimoto. These two reports are among the first on autoimmune disease since about 1910. (See 1901 I, 1904 B.)

P. MOLECULAR BIOLOGY: *Transfer RNA*

Mahlon Bush Hoagland, Paul Charles Zamecnik, and Mary Louise Stephenson show that soluble RNA (sRNA) serves as a translation mediator to position amino acids in the proper sequence on the messenger RNA-ribosome complex. This form of sRNA is later given the name "transfer RNA" (tRNA) by R. Schweet. (See 1956 N.)

Q. CELL BIOLOGY: *Procaryotic and Eucaryotic Cells*

E. C. Dougherty proposes the terms "procaryotic" and "eucaryotic" to differentiate the bacteria and "blue-green algae" from all other types of cells. E. Chatton, who made the same proposal in 1937, is usually cited as the originator of this concept, but Dougherty does not refer to Chatton's paper. (See 1937 E, 1962 A.)

R. TECHNOLOGY: *Manmade Satellite*

The Soviet Union is the first country to succeed in putting a satellite into orbit around the earth. It is called *Sputnik I*.

S. TECHNOLOGY

Leon Neil Cooper, John Robert Schrieffen, and John Bardeen develop a theory of superconductivity that is known as the BCS theory. Bardeen, Cooper, and Schrieffen share the 1972 Nobel Prize in physics. It is the second Nobel Prize for Bardeen, who received the 1956 prize for his role in developing the transistor.

T. THE ARTS: *Literature*

- Boris Pasternak publishes his novel *Doctor Zhivago*.
- Jack Kerouac completes his novel *On the Road*.

U. THE ARTS: *Theater*

Endgame, a play by Samuel Beckett, is performed in London.

1958

A. BACTERIAL STRUCTURE: *Cell Wall and Membrane*

Edouard Kellenberger and Antoinette Ryter publish electron microscope photographs showing clearly that the bacterial cell wall and membrane are separate structures. The photographs of *Escherichia coli* are the first to show the outer membrane, a membranous layer lying outside the rigid cell wall. (See 1941 D, 1947 A, 1953 D, 1953 E, 1960 A.)

B. BACTERIAL STRUCTURE: *Action of Lysozyme*

W. Brumfitt, A. C. Wardlaw, and James T. Park propose that lysozyme hydrolyzes a $\beta(1-4)$ bond between *N*-acetylmuramic acid and *N*-acetylglucosamine. This reaction is confirmed in 1959 by M. R. J. Salton and Jean-Marie Ghuysen. Based on the action of lysozyme and the structure of Park nucleotides, the Park group proposes a structure of peptidoglycan consisting of alternating $\beta(1-4)$ and $\beta(1-6)$ linkages between the two amino sugars. Between 1958 and 1965, several groups of investigators studying enzymatic hydrolysis of peptidoglycan show that the linkages are all $\beta(1-4)$. (See 1952 D, 1952 E, 1953 C, 1958 D.)

C. BACTERIAL STRUCTURE: *Cell Wall Chemistry*

J. Baddiley, J. G. Buchanan, and B. Carss find polymers of glycerol phosphate and ribitol phosphate in cell walls of *Lactobacillus arabinosus* and *Bacillus subtilis*. These compounds are subsequently named teichoic (or wall) acids. (See 1961 A.)

D. BACTERIAL STRUCTURE: *Spheroplasts*

C. Hurwitz, J. M. Reiner, and J. V. Landau suggest that the term "spheroplast" be used to describe preparations of bacterial cells that have been treated to remove or inhibit cell wall synthesis but that have residual cell wall material. Spheroplast becomes the term of choice to describe gram-negative bacteria from which the peptidoglycan cell wall chemical is removed or its synthesis inhibited. (See 1952 C, 1952 E, 1953 C.)

E. BACTERIAL STRUCTURE: *Nuclear Region*

Edouard Kellenberger, Antoinette Ryter, and J. Séchaud develop procedures for fixation and embedding that permit the details of the bacterial nuclear region to be visualized, showing the fibrillar internal structure of the DNA. They conclude that there is no mitosis in bacteria, refuting earlier reported evidence of mitotic figures seen on stained preparations. Standard procedures using a plastic called Vestopal are developed for fixation and embedding. The method becomes known as the RK procedure. (See 1942 B, 1959 A, 1962 A, 1963 E.)

F. BACTERIAL PHYSIOLOGY: *Shifts in Balanced Growth*
Moselio Schaechter, Ole Maaloe, and Nils O. Kjeldgaard use a continuous culture device to study balanced or steady-state growth in *Salmonella typhimurium*. They find that neither cell size, the average number of nuclei, nor the content of RNA and DNA is affected by temperature of cultivation. Kjelgaard and Schaechter report that shifts from low growth rates to higher growth rates result in a succession of events. RNA synthesis immediately increases to the rate characteristic for the new concentration of medium components, but cell division rates and DNA synthesis continue at the same rate for appreciable times and then abruptly shift to the new rates. (See 1950 C, 1956 B.)

G. BACTERIAL GENETICS: *Episomes/Plasmids*
François Jacob and Elie Wollman propose the term "episome" for genetic elements in bacteria that can either exist autonomously in the cell or be integrated into the chromosome. They point out the similarity in properties of several such elements: temperate bacteriophage in lysogeny, fertility factors (F factors), and colicinogeny (Col factors). Extrachromosomal genetic factors, or extranuclear factors, are given various names over the years: plasmagenes, plasmons, cytogenes, and plasmids. The term "plasmid," suggested by Joshua Lederberg in 1952, replaces "episome" after William Hayes proposes in 1969 that it be used for any type of extrachromosomal element in bacteria, regardless of whether or not it integrates into the bacterial chromosome. (See 1950 I, 1953 H, 1954 I.)

H. BACTERIAL GENETICS: *Radiation–Sensitive Mutant*
Ruth Frances Hill reports the discovery of a radiation-sensitive mutant strain designated *Escherichia coli* B_s. Experiments with this mutant mark the beginning of the genetic approach to studies of DNA repair. (See 1953 M, 1957 F, 1960 H, 1962 G, 1964 E.)

I. VIRAL CULTIVATION: *Rous Sarcoma Virus*
Howard Martin Temin and H. Rubin develop an assay for Rous sarcoma virus using chick embryo cells in culture. They find that instead of killing cells and creating visible viral plaques, the virus causes transformation and multiplication of the cells, resulting in foci of infection that are visible when neutral red is added to the culture.

J. VIRAL STRUCTURE: *Double Shadowing for Electron Microscopy*
Robley Cook Williams and Kendall O. Smith introduce the technique of double shadowing with metallic vapors for an electron microscope study of the shape of the Tipula iridescent virus. By shadowing from two directions differing by 60 degrees or 180 degrees in azimuth, they can clearly discern the icosahedral shape of the viral particle. (See 1944 H.)

K. VIRAL DISEASE: *Smallpox Eradication*

The World Health Organization begins an effort to eradicate smallpox through vaccination. This initial program is limited to volunteer participation by nations where smallpox is endemic. A more extensive, global program begins in 1967. (See 1967 P, 1980 M.)

L. VIRAL DISEASE: *Burkitt's Lymphoma*

Studying a tumor of the jaw (Burkitt's lymphoma) that occurs in Ugandan children in East Africa, Denis Parsons Burkitt proposes that it is caused by a virus carried by mosquitoes. The causative agent of the tumor is isolated in 1963 by Michael Epstein and Yvonne Barr. (See 1963 L.)

M. IMMUNOLOGY: *Histocompatibility Complex*

Jean Dausset discovers a histocompatibility complex in humans similar to the one Peter Gorer found in mice. The human lymphocyte antigens are now referred to as HLA, for human histocompatibility locus A, which includes two closely linked loci numbered I and II. Dausset shares the 1980 Nobel Prize in physiology or medicine with George D. Snell and Baruj Benacerraf.

N. MOLECULAR BIOLOGY: *Semiconservative DNA Replication*

Matthew Stanley Meselson and Franklin William Stahl provide experimental proof that DNA in *Escherichia coli* is duplicated during cell division by a process termed "semiconservative replication." They use the heavy isotope of nitrogen, ^{15}N, to label the DNA in growing bacteria, followed by growth in ^{14}N, so that only previously synthesized DNA carries the heavy isotope of nitrogen. By means of density gradient centrifugation in cesium chloride, they identify three types of labeling with heavy nitrogen in double-stranded DNA: both strands are labeled, neither strand is labeled, or one strand is labeled and the other is not. They conclude that after the double-stranded DNA separates, each strand is independently copied, resulting in hybrid molecules with one strand labeled with heavy nitrogen and one strand with light nitrogen. The semiconservative mode of replication was originally suggested by James Watson and Francis Crick in 1953, shortly after they proposed the double-stranded helical structure for DNA.

O. MOLECULAR BIOLOGY: *DNA Polymerase*

Continuing the studies begun by Arthur Kornberg in 1956, I. Robert Lehman, Maurice J. Bessman, Ernest S. Simms, and Arthur Kornberg carry out further purification of DNA polymerase from *Escherichia coli*. The enzyme catalyzes the incorporation of deoxyribonucleotides from the triphosphates of deoxyguanosine, deoxycytidine, and thymidine into DNA. (See 1956 O.)

P. MOLECULAR BIOLOGY: *the Operon*

In 1958 and 1959, Arthur Pardee, François Jacob, and Jacques Monod describe a negative control mechanism of enzyme induction observed when they perform a set of experiments measuring the synthesis of β-galactosidase in *Escherichia coli*. These experiments, which collectively come to be called the PaJaMo experiment, are the first to show that enzyme synthesis is con-

1958 *(continued)*

trolled by a repressor substance that blocks synthesis. An exogenous inducer, in this case a β-galactoside, removes the repression of synthesis and the enzyme is formed. These experiments contribute to the formulation of the concept of the operon and of messenger RNA. (See 1959 N, 1959 O, 1960 M, 1965 K, 1966 F.)

Q. TECHNOLOGY

The microchip, an integrated circuit that has several electronic components on a silicon chip, is invented separately by Robert Noyce and Jack Kilby. The development of computers depends heavily on the use of integrated circuits.

R. SOCIETY AND POLITICS

The European Economic Community, also called the Common Market, is established.

S. THE ARTS: *Literature*

• Chinua Achebe publishes *Things Fall Apart*.
• Cyril Northcote Parkinson publishes *Parkinson's Law*. Among its aphorisms is "Work expands so as to fill the time available for its completion."

T. THE ARTS: *Art*

The painter Robert Rauschenberg completes his "construction" *Odalisk*.

1959

A. BACTERIAL STRUCTURE: *Electron Microscopy of Bacterial Nucleoplasm*

A. Kleinschmidt, R. K. Zahn, and D. Lang develop procedures for the gentle lysis of bacterial cells (*Micrococcus* species) and T2 bacteriophage on protein-salt solutions to reveal the structure of their DNA. The film that forms is transferred to electron microscope grids. In these preparations, DNA appears as long threads with few free ends and no branches. The authors refer to the intracellular form of DNA as "nucleoplasm." They find no structure in the bacteria that corresponds to the chromosome of eucaryotic cells. (See 1942 B, 1958 E, 1962 A, 1963 E.)

B. BACTERIAL STRUCTURE: *Metachromatic Granules*

Abe Widra grows *Aerobacter aerogenes* on corn meal agar to promote the formation of metachromatic granules. Chemical analysis shows that the granules contain polyphosphate, RNA, and protein bound to lipid. (See 1888 A, 1946 B, 1984 D.)

C. BACTERIAL PHYSIOLOGY: *Ribulose Bisphosphate Carboxylase*

R. C. Fuller and Martin Gibbs report finding ribulose bisphosphate carboxylase in the photosynthetic bacteria *Rhodospirillum, Anacystis,* and *Chromatium*. They also find the enzyme in nonphotosynthetic organisms, including *Escherichia coli, Neurospora,* and yeast. (See 1950 M, 1954 M, 1955 E.)

D. BACTERIAL PHYSIOLOGY: *Spore Formation*

Elizabeth I. Young and Philip C. Fitz-James employ bright-field, phase-contrast, and electron microscopy to study spore formation in synchronized cultures. They note two distinct chromatin bodies, one of which is near the end of the cell, as well as the formation of a transverse septum separating the end-piece chromatin from the rest of the cell. DNA synthesis ceases during the segregation process but resumes in the vegetative part of the cell as the spore continues to develop. RNA synthesis stops before the onset of sporulation.

E. ANTIBIOTICS: *Semisynthetic Penicillins*
Methicillin, the first of the semisynthetic forms of penicillin, is manufactured using 6-amino penicillanic acid as the nucleus to which acyl side chains are attached. Methicillin is found to be active against staphylococci, which produce penicillinase. In 1961, ampicillin, which is active against gram-negative bacteria, is introduced, followed in 1964 by amoxicillin, with better oral absorption properties than ampicillin.

F. BACTERIAL DISEASE: *Tuberculosis*
R. L. Riley and colleagues, using a specially designed ventilation system, expose guinea pigs to patients suffering from pulmonary tuberculosis. Over a 2-year period they find that 71 of 156 guinea pigs become infected, primarily with a single tubercle. Their data are the first to provide controlled experimental evidence for the aerial dissemination of tuberculosis. In 1865, Jean Antoine Villemin reported experiments that showed that tuberculosis is contracted by inhalation. (See 1865 A, 1868 D.)

G. BACTERIAL GENETICS: *Resistance Transfer Factors*
Two groups of researchers in Japan, Tomoichiro Akiba and colleagues and Kunitaro Ochiai with O. Sawada and colleagues, report experiments showing the transfer of multiple drug resistance from a drug-resistant strain of *Escherichia coli* to a drug-sensitive strain of *Shigella*. Both groups of researchers show that the mechanism of transfer involves neither transformation nor transduction. In a short time, several laboratories find that direct cellular contact is necessary and that the drug resistance is transferred by conjugation. Susumu Mitsuhashi proposes that the material transferred be referred to as "resistance factors," or "R factors." (See 1960 F.)

H. BACTERIOPHAGE: *φX174*
Robert L. Sinsheimer describes the purification, size, and particle weight of bacteriophage φX174, noting that it is among the smallest phage so far studied. He extracts the DNA by phenolic denaturation of the viral protein and estimates that there is one molecule per virus particle. That there is no evidence of hydrogen-bonded structure is evidence that the phage contains single-stranded DNA. (See 1962 M, 1977 T.)

I. VIRAL STRUCTURE: *Poliomyelitis Virus*
Continuing X-ray diffraction studies begun in collaboration with Rosalind Franklin, John Finch and Aaron Klug present evidence that the surface structure of the poliovirus has 60 identical protein subunits. They comment that the polyhedral structure is found in all of the small viruses studied to date, including Tipula iridescent virus, bushy stunt virus, and turnip yellow mosaic virus.

1959 *(continued)*

J. VIRAL STRUCTURE: *Capsid Protein*
André Lwoff, Thomas F. Anderson, and François Jacob are the first to use the term "capsid" as a name for the outer protein shell of viral particles. P. Wildy and D. H. Watson speak of the subunits of the capsid as "capsomeres" in 1962.

K. VIRAL STRUCTURE: *Electron Microscopy/Negative Staining*
Sydney Brenner and R. W. Horne develop a method of using a solution of phosphotungstate sprayed directly onto samples of tobacco mosaic virus and turnip yellow mosaic virus that have been prepared on grids for electron microscopy. The phosphotungstate serves as a negative stain and does not stain either the protein or the nucleic acid of the virus particles, which remain relatively electron transparent but are revealed clearly in high contrast.

L. IMMUNOLOGY: *Immunoglobulin Structure*
Rodney Robert Porter uses the protease enzyme papain to cleave immunoglobulin into three fractions, called I, II, and III. Later, fractions I and II come to be known as Fab, for "fragment antigen-binding," and fraction III as Fc, for "fragment-crystalline." Porter's work is followed by further study of immunoglobulin structure by Gerald Edelman and others. The work of Porter and Edelman leads to the formulation of the three-dimensional structure of the immunoglobulin molecule. Porter and Edelman share the 1972 Nobel Prize in physiology or medicine.

M. IMMUNOLOGY: *Immunoglobulin Classes*
Joseph F. Heremans, M. T. Heremans, and H. W. Schultze discover the secretory antibody immunoglobulin A (IgA). (See 1939 H.)

N. MOLECULAR BIOLOGY: *Repressor*
Bruce N. Ames and B. Garry propose that the enzymes involved in the synthesis of histidine are controlled by a repressor substance. Their experiments are done independently from the 1958 PaJaMo experiments of Arthur Pardee, François Jacob, and Jacques Monod and before the concept of the operon is fully developed. Later study shows that the histidine system is not controlled in the same manner as the operon but is controlled by a process called attenuation. (See 1960 M, 1963 V, 1964 K, 1974 O, 1977 P.)

O. MOLECULAR BIOLOGY: *Structural and Regulatory Genes*
François Jacob and Jacques Monod propose that two types of genes control protein synthesis: structural genes, which code for the sequence of amino acids in the protein, and regulatory genes, which control the formation of protein through the mediation of repressor substances. Their work, leading in 1960 to the concept of the operon, is done with two systems in *Escherichia coli*: phage lambda and β-galactosidase. (See 1958 P, 1959 N, 1960 M.)

P. MOLECULAR BIOLOGY: *Hyperchromicity of DNA*
Paul Doty, Julius Marmur, and N. Sueoka discover the phenomenon of hyperchromicity exhibited by DNA when it is slowly heated to separate the two strands. At a temperature that is specific for each type of DNA, a marked increase in ultraviolet absorbance is observed for DNA extracted

from a variety of microorganisms and for calf thymus DNA. The hyperchromicity is related to the percentage of guanine-cytosine base pairs. Doty and others note also that upon slow cooling, DNA absorbance decreases as the two strands "anneal."

Q. MOLECULAR BIOLOGY: *Alkaline Phosphatase*
T. S. Horiuchi and D. Mizuno discover alkaline phosphatase in *Escherichia coli* starved for phosphate. The cells degrade RNA but continue to grow and make DNA and protein. Purification of the enzyme leads to its use in various studies of the nucleic acids.

R. MOLECULAR BIOLOGY: *Hemoglobin and Myoglobin*
Max Ferdinand Perutz and, independently, John Cowdery Kendrew confirm the structure of hemoglobin and the structure of myoglobin, respectively. Perutz and Kendrew share the 1962 Nobel Prize in chemistry.

S. ANTHROPOLOGY: *Fossil Hominids*
Mary Douglas Nicol Leakey and Louis Seymour Bazett Leakey, working in the Olduvai Gorge in East Africa, find the fossil skull of a hominid that they first call *Zinjanthropus* but which is later referred to as *Australopithecus*. The following year, they find the fossil remains of *Homo habilis* (the Handy Man), dated at 1.7 million years old. In 1976, Mary Leakey finds the fossilized trail of three sets of 3.6-million-year-old footprints of individuals walking upright.

T. TECHNOLOGY
The first Xerox copying machine is made commercially available by the Haloid Xerox Company. Chester F. Carlson began the development of xerography, or dry writing, in 1937, but 23 years passed before a workable machine was developed.

U. SOCIETY AND POLITICS
Fidel Castro overthrows the Cuban government headed by Fulgencio Batista and takes the office of premier.

V. THE ARTS: *Theater*
Lorraine Hansberry's play *A Raisin in the Sun* is performed.

1960

A. BACTERIAL STRUCTURE: *Gram-Negative Outer Membrane*
W. Weidel, H. Frank, and H. H. Martin develop techniques to separate the outer membrane components from the rigid layer of the cell wall of *Escherichia coli.* They refer to the "plastic" components of the lipopolysaccharide-protein layer. By 1963, Martin develops a schematic drawing that shows the cytoplasmic membrane, a mucopeptide layer, a lipopolysaccharide layer, and a lipoprotein layer. (See 1965 C.)

B. BACTERIAL STRUCTURE: *Mesosomes/Chondrioids*
Philip C. Fitz-James uses the term "mesosomes" (middle body) for the membranous structures seen associated with the division septa and the nuclear region in gram-positive bacteria. Woutera van Iterson uses the term "chondrioids" for these structures in 1961. These membranous sacs are observed in thin sections of *Bacillus cereus* by C. B. Chapman and J. Hillier in

1960 *(continued)*

1953 and are later found in some gram–negative bacteria. Electron micros-copy also shows that mesosomes are continuous with the cytoplasmic membrane. Their exact role in the bacterial cell is still not understood, but they may function in the formation of the septum as well as for attachment of DNA during replication. (See 1963 F.)

C. BACTERIAL PHYSIOLOGY: *Cell-Free Nitrogen Fixation*

J. E. Carnahan, Leonard Mortenson, H. F. Mower, and J. E. Castle are suc-cessful in obtaining consistent, vigorous nitrogen fixation using cell-free extracts of *Clostridium pasteurianum*. In 1960, other reports of cell-free ni-trogen fixation are made for *Azotobacter* by D. J. D. Nicholas and D. J. Fischer; for *Chromatium* by Daniel Arnon and coworkers; and for *Rhodo-spirillum* by K. C. Schneider and coworkers. (See 1953 F.)

D. BACTERIAL PHYSIOLOGY: *Cyclic Adenosine Monophosphate*

Earl Wilbur Sutherland, Jr., discovers cyclic AMP (adenosine 3′,5′-monophosphate) and its role as a "second messenger" in hormone func-tion. Cyclic AMP is later found to function in a number of regulatory sys-tems, in both eucaryotes and bacteria. Sutherland is awarded the 1971 Nobel Prize in physiology or medicine. (See 1965 J, 1968 B.)

E. BACTERIAL GENETICS: *Asporogenic Mutants*

With ultraviolet radiation, Donald G. Lundgren and G. Beskid induce the formation of asporogenic mutants of *Bacillus cereus*. In a survey of a large number of culture medium nutrients, only casein hydrolysate reverses the mutational effect. In separate experiments, E. Iichinska finds that melanins accumulate in the spores of *Bacillus subtilis,* whereas the asporogenic mu-tants are poorly pigmented. The lack of the brown pigment is useful in screening for the mutants. (See 1976 H.)

F. BACTERIAL GENETICS: *Resistance Transfer Factors*

Tsutomu Watanabe and colleagues provide evidence that the resistance factor (R factor) transferring multiple drug resistance among strains of *Shigella* is carried on a plasmid (episome) that is passed by mating to other cells. Tomoichiro Akiba, Kunitaro Ochiai, Susumu Mitsuhashi, and others demonstrated in 1959 that transfer of multiple drug resistance requires cell-to-cell contact. (See 1959 G, 1967 H.)

G. BACTERIAL GENETICS: *Polar Mutations/Insertion Sequences*

Esther Lederberg studies a class of mutations in *Escherichia coli* that cause the galactose operon to lose functions. These mutations are found to be of a type called "polar," affecting the activity of gene products downstream, i.e., in the 3′ direction from the operator gene. These experiments are pre-cursors to the later discovery by other researchers that this type of mutation is caused by the insertion of DNA sequences copied from other parts of the genome. (See 1968 C, 1974 H.)

H. BACTERIAL GENETICS: *Ultraviolet Mutagenesis/Thymine Dimers*

R. Beukers and W. Berends discover that irradiating DNA with ultraviolet light produces intrastrand cyclobutane-type dimers of adjacent thymine units. The presence of such dimers causes lethal, mutagenic, and tumori-genic effects in a wide spectrum of organisms. (See 1949 F, 1953 M, 1957 F, 1962 G, 1964 E.)

I. BACTERIOPHAGE: *Male-Specific Phage*

Tim Loeb isolates a bacteriophage that specifically infects F^+ and Hfr strains of *Escherichia coli* but not F^- strains. In 1964, C. C. Brinton, Jr., and co-workers find that the male-specific phage attaches to a special type of pilus found only on male cells. (See 1964 F.)

J. VIROLOGY: *Simian Virus 40*

B. H. Sweet and M. R. Hilleman first recognize simian virus 40 (SV40) while attempting to pass virus grown in rhesus monkey or cynomolgus monkey kidneys into cultures of grivet monkey kidney. The viruses being studied can be neutralized with specific antiserum, but a new virus, SV40, is discovered that is not affected and that produces a characteristic cyto-pathic effect that leads it to be called "the vacuolating virus." (See 1962 P, 1967 N.)

K. VIRAL DISEASE: *Tumor Virus Classification*

Reporting methods for the detection of tumor viruses with the electron microscope, W. Bernhard describes three types of virus particles associated with mouse tumors and leukemias: types A, B, and C. Conditions caused by the type C leukemia virus include spontaneous lymphoid leukemia, Friend's leukemia, and Moloney's leukemia.

L. IMMUNOLOGY: *Radioimmune Assay*

Rosalyn Sussman Yalow and Solomon Berson develop the radioimmune assay (RIA). This technique permits the detection of small amounts of bio-logically active substances, such as hormones, by comparing the binding of known quantities of radioactively labeled antigen or antibody with test samples of antigen or antibody. Yalow shares the 1977 Nobel Prize in physiology or medicine with Roger Guillemin and Andrew Victor Schally, who are honored for their work on endocrine secretions.

M. MOLECULAR BIOLOGY: *the Operon*

François Jacob and Jacques Monod, with David Perrin and Carmen Sanchez, propose the concept of the "operon" to explain the regulation of protein synthesis. They suggest that in *Escherichia coli,* the regulation of synthesis of genes for the utilization of lactose is under the coordinate control of an operon, consisting of a gene for the synthesis of a repressor compound (thought to be RNA at this time but later found to be protein) that binds to an operator gene (a position on DNA adjacent to the genes for the structural proteins) and genes for the structural proteins β–galactosidase, β–galactoside permease, and a transacetylase. Regulation is based on a negative control process in which a repressor normally binds to the operator blocking synthe-sis of the structural proteins. An inducer, such as a β–galactoside, combines with the repressor molecule, preventing it from binding to the operator and thus permitting synthesis of the structural proteins. (See 1958 P, 1959 N, 1959 O.)

1960 *(continued)*

N. BIOCHEMISTRY: *Two–Light Reaction in Photosynthesis*

Robert Hill and Fay Bendall are the first to propose a "two–light" reaction in photosynthesis, based on the behavior of two different cytochromes called f and b_6. They postulate the functioning of two light-driven steps in opposition to the thermochemical gradient for electron transfer. They present a figure that is similar to the commonly drawn Z scheme to show the pathway of electrons in photosynthesis, but in their version the oxidized states are above the reduced states, the reverse of the way the scheme is now presented. (See 1961 U.)

O. CELL BIOLOGY: *Unit Membrane Concept*

J. David Robertson proposes a unitary concept of membrane structure that is similar to the proposal made by Hugh Davson and James Danielli in 1934. Robertson's "unit membrane," as it comes to be called, is a lipid bilayer with protein covering the inner and outer surfaces. His concept derives partly from electron microscope photographs of membranes stained with heavy metals. These photographs, which show the membrane as a trilaminar "railroad track" structure, are interpreted as having the metals attached to the protein layers. Later studies showing that artificial lipid bilayers containing no protein have a similar appearance when stained with osmium lead to the conclusion that membranes do not have a continuous covering of protein on their surfaces. (See 1894 G, 1910 G, 1925 E, 1934 G, 1972 K.)

P. SCIENTIFIC ORGANIZATIONS: *American Society for Microbiology*

The Society of American Bacteriologists changes its name to the American Society for Microbiology.

Q. TECHNOLOGY

Theodore Harold Maiman invents the first laser using a ruby cylinder. The name "laser" (light amplification by stimulated emission of radiation) was coined by R. Gordon Gould, who developed the concept in 1957 but was unable to gain support for a "death ray" from the U.S. Department of Defense. Charles H. Townes and Arthur Schawlow apply for a patent and publish a paper before Gould does. Schawlow shares the 1981 Nobel Prize in physics with Kai Siegbahn and Nicolaas Bloembergen.

R. SOCIETY AND POLITICS

John F. Kennedy is elected president of the United States.

S. THE ARTS: *Literature*

Harper Lee publishes *To Kill a Mockingbird*.

T. THE ARTS: *Art*

Andy Warhol paints *Soup Can*.

1961

A. BACTERIAL STRUCTURE: *Cell Wall Chemistry*

In their study of the cell wall chemistry of *Bacillus subtilis,* Ewa Janczura, H. R. Perkins, and H. J. Rogers discover four types of polymers: mucopeptide, insoluble protein, teichoic acid, and teichuronic acid. Their analysis shows that teichuronic acid consists of equimolar amounts of *N*-acetylgalactosamine and glucuronic acid. (See 1958 C.)

B. BACTERIAL STRUCTURE: *Diether Lipids in Halobacterium*
S. N. Sehgal, M. Kates, and N. E. Gibbons find that the extracted lipids from *Halobacterium cutirubrum* contain unusual phosphatides not found in other bacteria. They report that the lipids are ether-linked long-chain groups rather than ester-linked fatty acids and conclude that the lipids are diether analogs of diphosphatidyl glycerol. This is the first report of unusual cell structure in an organism that is later placed in the domain *Archaea*. (See 1963 C, 1965 D, 1975 D, 1977 C, 1977 D.)

C. BACTERIAL STRUCTURE: *Periplasm*
In studies of glucose-6-phosphatase of *Escherichia coli,* Peter Dennis Mitchell concludes that the enzyme is found in a region between the cell wall and the surface of the osmotic barrier of the plasma membrane, which he refers to as "periplasm." (See 1977 E, 1984 C, 1990 C.)

D. BACTERIAL PHYSIOLOGY: *Catabolite Repression*
Boris Magasanik assigns the name "catabolite repression," the so-called glucose effect, to the phenomenon of inhibition of synthesis of catabolic enzymes by the presence of glucose. (See 1942 F, 1956 E, 1965 J.)

E. BACTERIAL PHYSIOLOGY: *Allosteric Inhibition*
Jacques Monod and François Jacob, in a discussion of feedback inhibition of enzyme activity, note that since inhibitors are not steric analogs of the enzyme substrate, an appropriate name for the phenomenon is "allosteric inhibition." (See 1953 G, 1955 D, 1957 C.)

F. BACTERIAL PHYSIOLOGY: *Regulation of RNA Synthesis*
In studying the cessation of ribosomal RNA synthesis in cells starved for amino acids, Gunther S. Stent and Sydney Brenner use the term "stringent response" for such a control mechanism. They isolate a mutant in which this control is absent and identify a genetic locus, *relA,* the wild type being *relA*$^+$ and the relaxed mutant lacking *relA*. In *relA*$^+$ cells, they find the accumulation of two nucleotides, which they call magic spots I and II. (See 1970 F, 1975 F.)

G. BACTERIOPHAGE: *an RNA-Containing Bacteriophage*
Tim Loeb and Norton David Zinder report that the *Escherichia coli* bacteriophage f2 contains RNA only. This is the first report of an RNA-containing phage.

H. VIROLOGY: *Poliovirus Replication in Culture*
Wolfgang K. Joklik and James E. Darnell, Jr., study the adsorption and entry of ^{32}P-labeled poliovirus into HeLa cells. They find that more than 50% of the adsorbed virus releases from the cell and does not readsorb. Nearly all of the adsorbed virus is rapidly degraded inside the cell, with the radioactive label appearing in the acid-soluble fraction. In an earlier paper, Darnell and coworkers showed that viral RNA synthesis begins only about one-half hour before the appearance of mature virus and that at no time is there a large amount of free viral RNA.

1961 *(continued)*

I. VIROLOGY: *Cell Receptors for Viruses*

John J. Holland studies the nonneural tissue affinities of several enteroviruses: poliovirus, coxsackievirus, and echovirus. Finding that in vitro cell cultures develop a receptor substance that is not detectable in vivo, he concludes that the enterotropisms of these viruses are due to the affinity of viral protein for these special components of susceptible cells.

J. FUNGAL DISEASE: *Aflatoxin*

W. P. Blount first recognizes poisoning caused by toxins from fungal contamination of animal feed. His account of the death of young turkeys is followed by similar reports involving ducklings and chickens (F. D. Asplin and R. B. A. Carnaghan) and pigs (R. M. Loosmore and J. D. J. Harding). Carnaghan and his colleagues extract and purify a toxic substance from Brazilian peanut meal. They determine that the toxin, later called "aflatoxin," is produced by *Aspergillus flavus*. (See 1963 Q.)

K. IMMUNOLOGY: *Immunoglobulin Structure*

Gerald Maurice Edelman and Miroslav Dave Poulik determine that immunoglobulins are composed of two polypeptide chains with molecular weights of about 20,000 (light chains) and 50,000 (heavy chains). These data, with the enzyme cleavage data obtained by Rodney Porter, permit the structure of the immunoglobulin molecule to be formulated. Edelman and Porter share the 1972 Nobel Prize in physiology or medicine. (See 1959 L.)

L. IMMUNOLOGY: *Thymus Function*

Jacques Miller establishes the thymus gland as a major immunological organ. Along with Robert A. Good, Byron H. Waksman, and Frank Macfarlane Burnet, he shows that the thymus controls the formation of cells that function in cell-mediated immunity. The function of B cells in humoral immunity and thymus-modified cells (T cells) becomes established. (See 1956 P, 1962 S, 1968 H.)

M. CELL BIOLOGY: *Chemiosmotic Hypothesis*

Peter Dennis Mitchell proposes the chemiosmotic hypothesis for coupling electron transport to ATP synthesis during oxidative phosphorylation. He describes "chemiosmotic coupling," a term he first uses in 1958, as a process in which protons are translocated across membranes during oxidation and reduction. Hydrogen atoms pass in one direction by way of hydrogen carriers, and electrons pass in the opposite direction by electron carriers in the respiratory chain that is located in the membranes. Mitchell receives the Nobel Prize in chemistry in 1978. (See 1965 P.)

N. MOLECULAR BIOLOGY: *Nucleic Acid Hybridization*

B. D. Hall and Sol Spiegelman begin the era of nucleic acid hybridization technology with experiments in which they mix a solution of DNA from bacteriophage T2 with short sequences of radioactively labeled T2-specific RNA referred to as "probes." The hybridized probe and target DNA are separated by density gradient centrifugation. Other researchers improve the procedure by immobilizing the target nucleic acid in agar. (See 1962 W, 1963 W.)

O. MOLECULAR BIOLOGY: *Messenger RNA*

François Jacob and Jacques Monod, in a discussion of the lactose operon in *Escherichia coli,* suggest that a species of RNA that differs from transfer RNA (tRNA) carries the information from DNA to ribosomes to direct the synthesis of protein. They give the name "messenger RNA" (mRNA) to this information-carrying species of RNA. This concept is derived from the work of many investigators, including the experiments with T2 phage performed in 1956 and 1957 by Elliott Volkin and Lazarus Astrachan. Subsequently, Sydney Brenner, François Jacob, and Matthew Meselson provide direct evidence for the existence of mRNA. (See 1956 M.)

P. MOLECULAR BIOLOGY: *the Genetic Code*

Based on their experiments and those of other researchers, Francis Crick, Leslie Barnett, Sydney Brenner, and R. J. Watts-Tobin discuss the general nature of the genetic code. They suggest that the code is composed of a set of three bases that code for a single amino acid. The code, however, is degenerate in that a single amino acid can be coded by more than one set of triplet bases. In addition, the code is nonoverlapping and must be read from a fixed starting point. (See 1961 Q.)

Q. MOLECULAR BIOLOGY: *the Genetic Code*

In the first experiments leading to the deciphering of the genetic code, Marshall Nirenberg and Johann Heinrich Matthaei use synthetic polyribonucleotides as messenger RNA in the cell-free synthesis of polypeptides. Synthesis of the polyribonucleotides is made possible by Marianne Grunberg-Manago's and Severo Ochoa's 1955 discovery in bacteria of polynucleotide phosphorylase. Nirenberg's and Matthaei's use of nucleotides of random sequence makes it possible to deduce a limited number of codes for specific amino acids. (See 1961 P, 1964 L.)

R. MOLECULAR BIOLOGY: *Isolation of DNA*

Julius Marmur describes a method for the isolation of DNA from bacterial cultures. After the cells are lysed, they are treated with perchlorate, chloroform-isoamyl alcohol, and ethyl alcohol. The nucleic acid in the final aqueous phase can be "spooled off" with a glass rod.

S. MOLECULAR BIOLOGY: *Mode of Action of Chloramphenicol and Puromycin*

Daniel Nathans and Fritz Lipmann and, separately, J. Heinrich Matthaei and Marshall W. Nirenberg show that chloramphenicol and puromycin inhibit the transfer of amino acids to ribosomes in the process of polypeptide synthesis.

T. MOLECULAR BIOLOGY: *Mode of Action of Actinomycin*

E. Reich, Richard M. Franklin, Aaron J. Shatkin, and Edward L. Tatum investigate the effect of actinomycin D on growth of the DNA-containing vaccinia virus and the RNA-containing mengovirus in L cells. They report that while both RNA synthesis and the yield of the vaccinia virus is inhib-

1961 (continued)

ited, neither the synthesis of cellular DNA nor the formation of mengovirus is affected. These observations permit a distinction between RNA synthesis controlled by viral or cellular DNA from the replication of viral RNA. (See 1940 F, 1962 V.)

U. BIOCHEMISTRY: *Photochemical Systems in Photosynthesis*

L. N. M. Duysens, J. Amesz, and B. M. Kamp, in experiments with a red alga, *Porphyridium cruentum,* conclude that at least two pigment systems are functioning in photosynthesis. They determine the kinetics of cytochrome oxidation at two different wavelengths of light, 680 nanometers and 560 nanometers. In 1960, Robert Hill and Fay Bendall proposed a two–light reaction in photosynthesis. (See 1960 N.)

V. PHYSICS: *Hadrons*

Murray Gell-Mann classifies elementary particles called hadrons using a system that he calls the "eightfold way." Yuval Ne'eman works out a similar method independently. (See 1964 P.)

W. TECHNOLOGY

• The Soviet Union puts the first man in spaceflight. On April 12, Yuri Alekseyevich Gagarin is carried in a spaceship called *Vostok I* for one orbit around the earth. On August 7, Gherman S. Titov spends the first full day in space aboard the *Vostok II.*

• On May 5, Alan Shepard, Jr., makes a suborbital flight in the United States spaceship *Freedom 7.* (See 1962 X.)

X. SOCIETY AND POLITICS

• The construction of the Berlin Wall begins separating communist East Berlin from West Berlin.

• The U.S. government provides aid to a group of Cuban exiles who desire to overthrow the regime of Fidel Castro. An attempt to invade Cuba at the Bay of Pigs results in a disastrous defeat for the exiles.

• President John F. Kennedy creates the Peace Corps, intended to send young Americans to Africa, Asia, and Latin America to assist in improving agriculture, living standards, and education.

Y. THE ARTS: *Literature*

Joseph Heller publishes his novel *Catch-22.*

1962

A. BACTERIAL TAXONOMY: *Procaryotic and Eucaryotic Cells*

Roger Stanier and Cornelius B. van Niel describe their concept of the bacteria in which they follow E. Chatton's 1937 proposal that the cells of the living world be divided into two groups, procaryotes and eucaryotes. The bacteria and the "blue-green algae" (cyanobacteria) are termed procaryotic cells because they lack internal membrane structures to separate the nucleus from the cytoplasm, as well as such membrane-bounded structures as mitochondria and chloroplasts. All other cells, classified as eucaryotic cells, possess a membrane-bounded nucleus that divides by mitosis, mitochondria, and chloroplasts, if photosynthetic. Other differentiating characteristics are the chemistry of cell walls and structure of flagella. Stanier and van Niel state that nuclear division by fission takes place in bacteria but fail to note the recent observations, published by Edouard Kellenberger and Antoinette Ryter in 1958 and by A. Kleinschmidt and coworkers in 1959, about the characteristics of bacterial DNA. (See 1937 E, 1957 Q.)

B. BACTERIAL PHYSIOLOGY: Bdellovibrio

Heinz Stolp and H. Petzold report that an unusual obligate parasite of *Pseudomonas phaseolicola* causes lysis of the host bacterium. The following year, Stolp and Mortimer P. Starr assign the name *Bdellovibrio bacteriovorus* to the parasitic organism (*bdello* is Greek for leech; "bacteriovorus" refers to devouring of the host). The bdellovibrios collide with the host cell, attach to its surface, penetrate the outer membrane and cell wall, and grow in the periplasm, causing cellular lysis. (See 1961 C.)

C. BACTERIAL PHYSIOLOGY: *Cobalamin in Methionine Synthesis*

J. R. Guest and coworkers show that methyl-vitamin B_{12}, cobalamin, serves as the methyl donor in the biosynthesis of methionine by clostridia. (See 1964 C, 1984 E.)

D. BACTERIAL PHYSIOLOGY: *Ferredoxin*

Leonard Mortenson, Raymond C. Valentine, and J. E. Carnahan find an iron-containing protein that does not contain heme as a key electron-carrying component in *Clostridium pasteurianum*. This compound, which they name "ferredoxin," couples pyruvate dehydrogenase with hydrogenase in the formation of hydrogen from pyruvate. (See 1962 U, 1964 D.)

E. BACTERIAL PHYSIOLOGY: *Cytochrome-Linked Fermentation*

David C. White, Marvin P. Bryant, and D. R. Caldwell report that the strict anaerobe *Bacteroides ruminicola* contains a cytochrome similar to cytochrome *b*. Their results suggest that the bacterium performs a cytochrome-linked fermentation with electrons from glycolysis to reduce fumarate to succinate.

F. BACTERIAL PHYSIOLOGY: *Leghemoglobin*

C. A. Appleby determines that the leghemoglobin in root nodules of leguminous plants infected with rhizobia has an unusually high affinity for oxygen. He suggests that it facilitates diffusion of oxygen within the nodules. Appleby reports finding leghemoglobin both inside and outside of the peribacteroid membranes. (See 1938 D.)

G. BACTERIAL PHYSIOLOGY: *Photoreactivation*

D. L. Wulff and Claud S. Rupert report that the photoreactivating enzyme activity in a yeast extract causes the disappearance of thymine dimers in ultraviolet-damaged DNA. (See 1949 F, 1953 M, 1957 F, 1960 H, 1964 E.)

H. BACTERIAL GENETICS: *Dark Reactivation of Ultraviolet Damage*

Paul Howard-Flanders, Richard P. Boyce, Eva Simson, and Lee Theriot discover a locus on the chromosome of *Escherichia coli* that controls an enzyme for reactivating ultraviolet-damaged DNA in the absence of light. They refer to strains that are resistant to ultraviolet light as UV^R and those that are sensitive as UV^S. (This terminology is changed in 1964 to name the

1962 (continued)

genes *uvr.*) They note that the repair appears to be associated with thymine dimers. (See 1960 H, 1964 E.)

I. BACTERIOPHAGE: *Lysogeny by Phage Lambda*

Allan Campbell proposes that the DNA of bacteriophage lambda forms a circle and integrates into the chromosome of *Escherichia coli.* This idea, which is later substantiated, provides the explanation for the location of prophage within the lysogenic bacterium.

J. BACTERIOPHAGE: *RNA Phage Genome as Messenger*

Daniel Nathans, G. Notani, H. H. Schwartz, and Norton David Zinder show that the single-stranded coliphage, f2, can use its RNA genome as a messenger for protein synthesis. When f2 RNA is added to extracts from *Escherichia coli,* the f2 coat protein is synthesized.

K. VIRAL STRUCTURE: *Physical Principles for Construction of Viruses*

Donald L. D. Caspar and Aaron Klug define the physical principles for the construction of viruses. Because they recognize that icosahedral viruses have more than 60 faces, they define rules governing "quasiequivalence" for the replacement of objects with other groups of symmetrically placed structures on the surface of the virion particle. They discuss the structures of helical viruses, such as tobacco mosaic virus, and the icosahedral viruses, as well as the rules governing self-assembly of component parts of the virus.

L. VIRAL STRUCTURE: *Reovirus Double-Stranded RNA*

Peter J. Gomatos, Igor Tamm, and colleagues report that reovirus contains a type of RNA that behaves as though it is double stranded. They report that the particles are 700 to 750 angstroms in diameter, which agrees with the 1961 paper of Johng S. Rhim, Kendall O. Smith, and Joseph L. Melnick, who also stated that the reovirus has a polyhedral shape.

M. VIROLOGY: *Replicative Form of Viral Nucleic Acid*

Two reports of double-stranded replicative forms of single-stranded viruses appear. Robert L. Sinsheimer and coworkers find that the single-stranded viral DNA of the bacteriophage φX174 converts to a double-stranded form called a "replicative form." Although there is no intracellular pool of single-stranded DNA, single-stranded mature progeny virions appear in about 8 minutes. Luc Montagnier and F. K. Sanders find a similar molecule in Krebs II ascites tumor cells infected with the encephalomyocarditis virus RNA. The virion RNA of this virus is single stranded, but a double-stranded form is found in the infected cells. (See 1959 H, 1977 T.)

N. MOLECULAR VIROLOGY: *Viral RNA Polymerase*

David Baltimore and Richard M. Franklin study RNA synthesis by a virus-specific enzyme in a particulate system from L cells infected with mengovirus. The system, which incorporates all four labeled ribonucleoside triphosphates into an acid-insoluble form, is independent of DNA and distinguished from DNA-dependent enzymes by its sensitivity to manganese, its insensitivity to actinomycin, and the lack of a requirement for magnesium. (See 1963 S, 1965 M.)

O. VIROLOGY: *Production of SV40 in Sendai Virus-Fused Cells*

Several groups of workers had shown that cells transformed by simian virus 40 (SV40) would produce small amounts of virion particles when grown in the presence of cells that support SV40 replication. Large yields of SV40 are obtained when P. Gerber and, separately, Hilary Koprowski and F. Jensen take advantage of this knowledge by adding ultraviolet-inactivated Sendai virus, which causes cell fusion, to mixtures of SV40-transformed cells and cells that normally support SV40 replication. (See 1967 N.)

P. VIRAL DISEASE: *SV40 Tumors*

B. E. Eddy, G. S. Borman, G. Grubbs, and R. D. Young prove that SV40 causes tumors in 1- to 3-day-old hamsters inoculated with extracts of rhesus monkey kidney cells. After they recover the virus from the tumors, they are able to reproduce tumors upon further passage into suckling hamsters. (See 1960 J.)

Q. VIRAL DISEASE: *Hepatitis A and B*

Reporting the first of a long series of studies, Saul Krugman establishes two epidemiologically and immunologically distinct forms of hepatitis. Krugman and his colleagues designate one type MS1, which spreads by the oral route and has a short incubation period, and the other MS2, which spreads by blood and has a long incubation period. In 1973, a committee of the World Health Organization recommends calling the infectious form hepatitis A and the serum form hepatitis B, terms that F. O. MacCallum first suggested in 1947. (See 1885 F, 1912 C, 1926 E, 1943 E.)

R. VIRAL DISEASE: *Rubella Virus*

Thomas H. Weller's and F. A. Neva's isolation of the rubella virus (German measles) in tissue culture leads to the development of a vaccine.

S. IMMUNOLOGY: *Lymphocytes and the Immune Response*

James L. Gowans, D. D. McGregor, Diana M. Cowen, and C. E. Ford report that small lymphocytes can initiate reactions. Their experiments show that there are two classes of small lymphocytes: those that are immunologically committed because they, or their progenitors, have previously reacted to exposure to antigen, and those that are not committed. Gowans's work in this field shows that the small lymphocytes can function in both humoral and cellular immune phenomena and that they represent the units of selection in Frank MacFarlane Burnet's clonal selection theory. (See 1956 P, 1957 N, 1961 L, 1968 H.)

T. CELL BIOLOGY: *Chloroplasts/Endosymbiosis*

Hans Ris and Walter Plaut find that chloroplasts of *Chlamydomonas* have regions that are both Feulgen positive and acridine orange positive where fibrils can be detected by electron microscopy. Concluding that chloroplasts contain DNA, they state that the chloroplast resembles a free-living organism and that endosymbiosis must be considered a possible evolutionary step in the origin of complex cells.

U. BIOCHEMISTRY: *Function of Ferredoxin in Photosynthesis*

Kunio Tagawa and Daniel Arnon isolate from spinach chloroplasts a compound that is similar to ferredoxin. They report that it functions to accept

1962 *(continued)*

electrons released from the primary photochemical process and to transfer them to pyridine nucleotides. They also demonstrate the photoproduction of hydrogen gas by chloroplasts, showing that ferredoxin from clostridia and from other bacteria that have hydrogenases will substitute for spinach ferredoxin in the reduction of triphosphopyridine nucleotide (NADP). (See 1962 D, 1964 D.)

V. MOLECULAR BIOLOGY: *Mode of Action of Actinomycin D*

Taiki Tamaoki and Gerald Mueller find that actinomycin D inhibits DNA-controlled RNA synthesis in experiments that show the suppression of incorporation of ^{32}P in all classes of RNA in the nucleus of HeLa cells. In other experiments, Jerard Hurwitz and coworkers discover that actinomycin D and proflavin inhibit enzymatic synthesis of RNA and DNA by binding to template DNA. The inhibition, which is competitive, is reversed by increasing concentrations of DNA. (See 1961 T.)

W. MOLECULAR BIOLOGY: *Nucleic Acid Hybridization*

E. T. Bolton and Brian J. McCarthy develop a general method for the isolation of RNA that is complementary to specific regions of DNA. Their procedure, called the DNA-agar technique, is the first simple solid-phase hybridization method. Radioactively labeled DNA or RNA is added and allowed to hybridize with denatured DNA immobilized in an agar gel. The unhybridized probes are removed by washing the gel, while the hybridized probes are eluted at high temperature. (See 1961 N, 1963 W.)

X. TECHNOLOGY

• On February 20, U.S. astronaut John Glenn, in the spaceship *Friendship 7,* is the first American to reach earth orbit. (See 1961 W.)

• The first communication satellite, Telstar, is placed into earth orbit.

Y. SOCIETY AND POLITICS

• The United States establishes a military command in South Vietnam.

• The United States begins a naval and air quarantine of Cuba after it discovers that the USSR is arming Cuba with nuclear missiles. President John F. Kennedy demands that Soviet premier Nikita Khrushchev remove the missiles, which he does after the United States agrees to remove missiles from Turkey and promises not to invade Cuba.

Z. THE ARTS: *Literature*

Doris Lessing publishes *The Golden Notebook.*

AA. THE ARTS: *Theater*

Edward Albee's play *Who's Afraid of Virginia Woolf?* is performed.

1963

A. BACTERIAL TAXONOMY: *the Genus* Campylobacter

After Theobald Smith and Marian Taylor first isolated the organism they named *Vibrio fetus* in 1919, at least two other similar species have been found, *Vibrio jejuni* and *Vibrio coli.* M. Sebald and M. Véron show that these organisms are distinguished from traditional members of the genus *Vibrio* both by biochemical analysis and by determination of DNA base composition. They assign the name *Campylobacter* (curved rod) to this group. (See 1919 C, 1973 F, 1980 I.)

B. BACTERIAL STRUCTURE: *Gram Stain Mechanism*
M. R. J. Salton concludes that Gram differentiation is dependent on creation of a permeability barrier in gram-positive bacteria after treatment with high concentrations of ethyl alcohol. Salton explains that alcohol dehydration of the thick peptidoglycan layer in gram-positive bacteria creates small pores that trap the crystal violet-iodine complex, while the alcohol treatment causes greater permeability in gram-negative bacteria by extraction of outer membrane lipid. (See 1884 B, 1929 A, 1957 A.)

C. BACTERIAL STRUCTURE: *Cell Envelopes of Halophiles*
A. D. Brown and C. D. Shorey report that the cell envelopes of *Halobacterium halobium* and *Halobacterium salinarium* have the appearance of a "unit membrane." Chemical analysis of the envelopes reveals mainly protein, with no mucopeptide (peptidoglycan), a fact that Brown and K. Y. Cho confirm in 1970. (See 1961 B, 1965 D, 1975 D, 1977 C, 1977 D.)

D. BACTERIAL STRUCTURE: *Muramic Acid in Rickettsiae and Chlamydiae*
H. R. Perkins and A. C. Allison find that organisms of both the rickettsia and the psittacosis-lymphogranuloma group contain muramic acid. They state that both groups appear to have closer affinity to gram-negative bacteria than to viruses. (See 1951 A, 1963 A.)

E. BACTERIAL STRUCTURE: *Circular Chromosome*
John Cairns grows *Escherichia coli* in the presence of tritiated thymidine and, by careful lysis, releases its DNA onto an autoradiographic emulsion. After the radioactivity exposes the film, the form of the DNA is observed under a light microscope, revealing that the bacterial DNA is a circular molecule. From further studies, Cairns develops a model for the replication of the circular DNA molecule by which the chromosome develops a fork with replication moving in one direction. His diagram of the replicating circles is later referred to as θ (theta) circles. (See 1956 F, 1959 A, 1968 I, 1975 P.)

F. BACTERIAL STRUCTURE: *Membrane Attachment of Bacterial DNA*
François Jacob, Sydney Brenner, and François Cuzin propose that during replication, bacterial DNA is attached to the cell membrane in a way that results in the separation of the two strands into the two daughter cells. Jacob and Antoinette Ryter publish electron microscope photographs showing the chromosome of *Bacillus subtilis* attached to mesosomes. In 1968, Noboru Sueoka and William G. Quinn present results of both genetic and biochemical experiments with *B. subtilis,* showing that the replication origin of the chromosome is attached to the membrane. (See 1960 B.)

G. BACTERIAL GENETICS: *Bacteriophage Mu*
Austin L. Taylor reports a new temperate bacteriophage called Mu1 in *Escherichia coli*. Bacteria infected with the phage have increased mutation rates in many gene loci. He proposes that the mutations are a result of the

1963 (continued)

integration of the phage into the host cell genome at the particular loci that are affected. (See 1964 H, 1973 G.)

H. BACTERIOPHAGE: *Morphogenesis*

R. H. Epstein and colleagues study two classes of mutants of the *Escherichia coli* bacteriophage T4D. One class of mutants is temperature sensitive, forming plaques at 25°C but not at 42°C. The other class, called amber mutants, forms plaques on *E. coli* CR63 but not on *E. coli* B. The authors place the genes affected into two groups: one in which DNA synthesis is affected by the mutation and one in which phage maturation is affected. The researchers conclude that the phage particle is not formed by a crystallization of subunits, as is seen in tobacco mosaic virus, but in a more complex fashion from component parts of the head and tail structures.

I. BACTERIAL DISEASE: *Cultivation of Chlamydiae*

F. B. Gordon and coworkers use a human synovial cell line called McCoy cells to cultivate the trachoma agent from experimental simian infections. In subsequent experiments using irradiated McCoy cells, the chlamydiae are passed up to 15 times from culture to culture. (See 1957 G, 1977 F.)

J. VIROLOGY: *Picornaviruses*

A committee studying enteroviruses coins the term "picornaviruses" for small RNA-containing viruses, including polioviruses, coxsackieviruses, echoviruses, and rhinoviruses.

K. VIRAL STRUCTURE: *Polyomavirus DNA*

Renato Dulbecco and Marguerite Vogt conclude that the DNA of polyomavirus is a ring molecule composed of two complementary strands that are not cross-linked. Roger Weil and Jerome Vinograd provide similar data, and Walther Stoeckenius obtains electron microscopic evidence that the polyomavirus DNA molecules exist in both linear and cyclic forms of equal molecular weight.

L. VIRAL DISEASE: *Epstein–Barr Virus*

Michael Anthony Epstein and Yvonne Barr identify a herpes-type virus in a continuous line of Burkitt's lymphoma cells, in the first isolation of a virus associated with human cancer. Later, through the accidental infection of a technician working in another laboratory, the Epstein-Barr virus, as it is known, is found to be the cause of infectious mononucleosis.

M. IMMUNOLOGY: *Interferon Synthesis*

The fact that interferon synthesis is formed from cellular DNA and not viral nucleic acid is substantiated by the results of several experiments with actinomycin in 1963 and 1964. E. Heller, in experiments with chikungunya virus; Joyce Taylor, with Semliki Forest virus; and Robert Wagner, with chikungunya and Newcastle disease virus, report inhibition of interferon synthesis by actinomycin D, permitting viral replication. Also in 1964, Robert M. Friedman and Joseph A. Sonnabend show that *p*-fluorophenylalanine, an inhibitor of protein synthesis, prevents the formation of interferon.

N. IMMUNOLOGY: *Immune Response Genes*

Baruj Benacerraf and coworkers show that some genes in the major histocompatibility complex control immune responses to various antigens. He finds that response to a particular antigen is controlled by specific genes, which he calls immune response genes (Ir genes). Benacerraf shares the 1980 Nobel Prize in physiology or medicine with George D. Snell and Jean Dausset.

O. IMMUNOLOGY: *Idiotypes*

Three laboratories independently discover idiotypes, the antigenic determinants that characterize the specific binding site on antibodies. Leaders of the three groups are Jacques Oudin, Henry George Kunkel, and Philip George Houthem Gell.

P. IMMUNOLOGY: *Hemolytic Plaque Assay*

Niels K. Jerne and Albert A. Nordin design a simple assay for detecting individual antibody-producing cells. A mixture of potential antibody-producing cells from an animal immunized with sheep red blood cells is mixed with sheep cells in a thin film of agar, after which a solution of complement is added. Antibody-forming cells hemolyze the sheep red blood cells, forming clear plaques.

Q. FUNGAL DISEASE: *Aflatoxin*

Studying the chemical structure of aflatoxins, Gerald N. Wogan and his colleagues report that the toxins are highly substituted coumarins that have a furocoumarin configuration, like that of other, similar substances that are pharmacologically active. (See 1961 J.)

R. MOLECULAR VIROLOGY: *Poliovirus mRNA*

Seldon Penman, Klaus Scherrer, Yechiel Becker, and James E. Darnell study the relationship between messenger RNA (mRNA) and ribosomes in both normal and poliovirus-infected HeLa cells. They conclude that in infected cells the viral RNA must function as the viral mRNA, since this is the only RNA formed in appreciable amounts in infected cells treated with actinomycin.

S. MOLECULAR VIROLOGY: *RNA Polymerase*

Charles Weissmann, Lionel Simon, and Severo Ochoa report that *Escherichia coli* infected with an RNA bacteriophage, MS-2, contains an RNA-synthesizing enzyme, an "RNA synthetase," that is absent from uninfected cells. Also employing the MS-2 phage, I. Haruna and Sol Spiegelman purify a similar enzyme that they call "RNA replicase," that is, an RNA-dependent RNA polymerase. (See 1962 N, 1965 M.)

T. MOLECULAR VIROLOGY: *Lambda Exonuclease*

D. Korn and A. Weissbach discover lambda exonuclease in *Escherichia coli* lysogenized with bacteriophage lambda. A large increase in deoxyribonuclease activity is coded by the phage. In 1967, J. W. Little, I. Robert Lehman, and A. D. Kaiser purify the enzyme, important to studies with nucleic acids, and name it "lambda exonuclease" because of its preference for initiating its hydrolytic activity at the 5′ end of double-stranded DNA.

1963 *(continued)*

U. MOLECULAR BIOLOGY: *the Replicon Model*

François Jacob, Sydney Brenner, and François Cuzin propose the "replicon" model for DNA replication. A replicon is defined as a genetic element, such as a chromosome of a bacterium or a bacteriophage or the DNA of an episome, that can replicate as an entity. To account for what is known about DNA replication, the authors believe that the replicon would have a structural gene controlling the synthesis of an "initiator" and a specific element of recognition upon which the initiator would act. In today's terminology, this is called the "origin of replication."

V. MOLECULAR BIOLOGY: *Attenuation*

Bruce N. Ames and Paul E. Hartman study several classes of regulatory mutations in the histidine operon of *Escherichia coli*. By 1966, they find that many of these genes affect either the structure of the histidine transfer RNA or its ability to be charged with amino acid. In anticipation of the attenuator mechanism that is discovered later, they suggest that the regulation might be at the translation level. (See 1959 N, 1964 K, 1974 O, 1977 P.)

W. MOLECULAR BIOLOGY: *Nucleic Acid Hybridization*

A. P. Nygaard and B. D. Hall improve nucleic acid hybridization procedures when they immobilize DNA sequences on nitrocellulose paper. (See 1961 N, 1962 W.)

X. SCIENTIFIC PUBLICATION: ASM News

The name of *Bacteriological News* is changed to *ASM News*.

Y. SOCIETY AND POLITICS

U.S. president John Fitzgerald Kennedy is assassinated.

Z. THE ARTS: *Literature*

John le Carré publishes *The Spy Who Came in from the Cold*.

1964

A. BACTERIAL PHYSIOLOGY: *Swarming in* Proteus

Using time-lapse, phase-contrast microscopy, Judith F. M. Hoeniger studies swarming in *Proteus mirabilis*. She observes differentiation of short rods into elongated swarming cells and, after swarming is completed, the breakdown of swarmers into progressively shorter units. Discussing the possibility of a "swarming factor," she suggests that a metabolite binds metallic ions essential for cell division. (See 1957 D, 1965 E, 1988 D.)

B. BACTERIAL PHYSIOLOGY: *Phosphotransferase System*

Werner Kundig, Sudhamoy Ghosh, and Saul Roseman discover that phosphate bound to histidine in a protein serves as an intermediate in a phosphotransferase system in *Escherichia coli*. They find two enzymes, called I and II, that function with the histidine protein to transfer phosphate from phosphoenolpyruvate to hexose. They report that enzyme II appears to differ for different sugars.

C. BACTERIAL PHYSIOLOGY: *Cobalamin in Acetate Formation*

Noting that the work of J. R. Guest et al. had shown a role for methyl-vitamin B_{12} (cobalamin) in the biosynthesis of methionine, J. Michael Poston, K. Kuratomi, and E. R. Stadtman demonstrate that the methyl carbon of acetate is derived from $^{14}CH_3$-B_{12} during fermentation of glucose by cell-free extracts of *Clostridium thermoaceticum*. These experiments substantiate H. A. Barker's and Martin David Kamen's earlier findings that both carbon atoms of acetate are labeled when glucose is fermented in the presence of radioactively labeled carbon dioxide. (See 1945 A, 1962 C, 1984 E.)

D. BACTERIAL PHYSIOLOGY: *Nitrogen Fixation*

Leonard Mortenson proves that both ferredoxin and ATP are required for nitrogen fixation in cell-free extracts of *Clostridium pasteurianum*. He also shows that hydrogen is the source of electrons for reducing ferredoxin. (See 1962 D, 1962 U.)

E. BACTERIAL PHYSIOLOGY: *Photoreactivation*

Richard B. Setlow and W. L. Carrier use a radiation-resistant strain of *Escherichia coli* to study recovery from ultraviolet (UV) light damage to DNA. They find that thymine dimers formed in DNA are removed during the time in which the cells recover from a UV-induced delay in DNA synthesis. In a similar study, Richard P. Boyce and Paul Howard-Flanders suggest that nucleotides are inserted into the excised region of single-stranded DNA by complementary pairing with the intact strand, after which the broken phosphodiester bond is rejoined. (See 1949 F, 1953 M, 1957 F, 1960 H, 1962 G.)

F. BACTERIAL GENETICS: *the Sex Pilus*

C. C. Brinton, Jr., P. Gemski, and J. Carnahan report the discovery of a pilus on F^+ and Hfr *Escherichia coli* that is necessary for transfer of genes to F^- cells. E. M. Crawford and R. F. Gesteland report that pili of donor Hfr and F^+ strains are the site of attachment of a male-specific RNA-containing bacteriophage. Brinton and his coworkers find that the phage attach to only a few of the pili of the male strains. The term F pilus or sex pilus is used to designate such pili. (See 1960 I.)

G. MICROBIAL GENETICS: *the Holliday Junction*

Using data from studies of meiosis in several genera of fungi, Robin Holliday proposes a model for general genetic recombination. He describes and diagrams a model in which two homologous sequences of DNA pair together, followed by one strand in each duplex being nicked by endonuclease. An exchange occurs when an end of each nicked strand crosses into the other duplex, where they are joined to form a recombinant form. This process of cross-strand exchange is often called a Holliday junction.

H. BACTERIOPHAGE STRUCTURE: *Bacteriophage Mu*

C. M. To, A. Eisenstark, and H. Töreci publish electron micrographs of bacteriophage Mu that reveal its octahedral head (later found to be icosahedral) and contractile tail with two or three tail fibers. (See 1963 G, 1973 G.)

1964 *(continued)*

I. MOLECULAR VIROLOGY: *Rous Sarcoma Provirus*

Howard Martin Temin finds that inhibitors of DNA synthesis block the replication of the RNA-containing Rous sarcoma virus. He suggests that a DNA intermediate must be copied from the RNA genome of the virus. He uses the term "provirus" to describe this intermediate form. Temin summarizes experiments of the last several years that show that the virus acts as a carcinogenic agent by adding new genetic information to the cell. (See 1970 H.)

J. MOLECULAR BIOLOGY: *the Regulon*

In studies of the repressibility of the enzymes for arginine synthesis, W. K. Maas and Alvin J. Clark propose the term "regulon" for a system in which the production of all enzymes is controlled by a single repressor substance. (See 1984 F.)

K. MOLECULAR BIOLOGY: *Transcription Attenuation*

Sondra Schlesinger and Boris Magasanik make one of the first observations that transfer RNA (tRNA) functions are involved in regulating the expression of amino acid biosynthetic operons. They find that the addition of the histidine analog α-methylhistidine to cultures of *Salmonella typhimurium* results in a marked increase in the rate at which histidine biosynthetic enzymes are synthesized. Schlesinger and Magasanik determine that the analog inhibits the attachment of histidine to its corresponding tRNA. (See 1959 N, 1963 V, 1974 O, 1977 P.)

L. MOLECULAR BIOLOGY: *the Genetic Code*

Following the 1961 work of Marshall Nirenberg and Johann Matthaei, Har Gobind Khorana successfully synthesizes polyribonucleotides of known sequence so that it is possible to deduce the codes for all of the amino acids. Nirenberg reports that trinucleotides cause the binding of a single amino acid to ribosomes, thus proving that the code is three nucleotides. Sydney Brenner coins the term "codon" for the triplet of bases that specify the amino acids. Nirenberg and Khorana share the 1968 Nobel Prize in physiology or medicine with Robert Holley.

M. MOLECULAR BIOLOGY: *Colinearity of Genes and Proteins*

Charles Yanofsky, Donald R. Helinski, and colleagues demonstrate a linear correspondence between one segment of gene A and the A protein of tryptophan synthetase. Their studies, begun in 1961 with *Escherichia coli,* show that the distances between amino acid residues in the protein are representative of the values obtained by genetic recombination of the genome.

N. MOLECULAR BIOLOGY: *Mode of Action of Chloramphenicol*

D. Vazquez shows that chloramphenicol specifically prevents the binding of soluble RNA (transfer RNA) to the 50S subunit of bacterial ribosomes. Additional experiments confirm that several antibiotics—thiocymetin, streptogramin, lincomycin, celesticetin, and several macrolide antibiotics—prevent tRNA from binding. (See 1951 K, 1961 S.)

O. MOLECULAR BIOLOGY: *Mode of Action of Streptomycin*

Julian E. Davies reports that experiments with polyuracil show that streptomycin inhibits protein synthesis by binding to the 30S subunit of bacterial ribosomes.

P. PHYSICS: *the Quark*

Murray Gell-Mann uses the term "quark," borrowed from James Joyce's *Finnegans Wake,* in his classification of hadrons. Some quarks and antiquarks interact to form the various types of hadrons. Gell-Mann is awarded the 1969 Nobel Prize in physics.

Q. SCIENTIFIC ORGANIZATIONS: *American Board of Microbiology*

The American Board of Microbiology, established in 1958 by the American Academy of Microbiology, begins a program of certification for microbiologists in public health and medical fields. Its name is changed to the American Board of Medical Microbiology in 1968.

R. SOCIETY AND POLITICS

• The United States begins active participation in the war between North Vietnam and South Vietnam that began in 1959.

• In a coup, Soviet premier Nikita Khrushchev is removed from power and replaced by Aleksei Kosygin. Leonid Brezhnev becomes leader of the Communist Party.

1965

A. MOLECULAR PHYLOGENY: *Semantides*

Emile Zuckerkandl and Linus Pauling are the first to define effectively how comparing sequences of amino acid in proteins, or nucleotides in nucleic acids, can be used to define phylogenetic relationships. They refer to molecules that carry the information of genes or transcripts of such information as "semantides." Even though polypeptides are the only macromolecules whose sequence can be determined when their paper is written, the authors conclude that nucleic acids are the best choice for use in molecular phylogeny.

B. BACTERIAL ECOLOGY: *Microfossils*

Elso S. Barghoorn and Stanley A. Tyler discover microfossils, microscopic single cells resembling bacteria, in the Gunflint Chert in Canada. Carbon dating places their age at about 2,080 million years. (See 1967 B.)

C. BACTERIAL STRUCTURE: *Cell Envelope*

S. De Petris describes the several-layered structure of the cell envelope of *Escherichia coli*. According to De Petris, the structure is composed of an outer triple-layered membrane, a 50- to 55-angstrom-thick layer that can at times be resolved into globular elements, an electron transparent layer, and a triple-layered cytoplasmic membrane. (See 1960 A.)

D. BACTERIAL STRUCTURE: Halobacterium

M. Kates, L. S. Yengoyan, and P. S. Sastry continue studies of the membrane lipids in *Halobacterium cutirubrum* when they find phytanyl ether-linked isoprenoid chains rather than straight-chain hydrocarbon groups.

1965 *(continued)*

Further research shows that the structure is 2,3-di-*O*-phytanyl-*sn*-glycerol. (See 1961 B, 1963 C, 1975 D, 1977 C, 1977 D.)

E. BACTERIAL PHYSIOLOGY: *Swarming in* **Proteus**

Judith F. M. Hoeniger makes electron microscope photographs of the sequence of flagella formation by swarming cultures of *Proteus mirabilis*. Finding up to 5,000 flagella on the swarmer cells, she refers to such cells as "flagellin factories." (See 1957 D, 1964 A, 1988 D.)

F. BACTERIAL PHYSIOLOGY: *Stages of Sporulation*

Antoinette Ryter proposes that the stages of sporulation be numbered from I through VII, with I being the vegetative cell, VI the mature spore, and VII the lysis of the mother cell and release of the spore.

G. BACTERIAL PHYSIOLOGY: *Microcycle Sporogenesis*

Vladimir Vinter and Ralph A. Slepecky devise a filtration procedure that permits germinating bacterial spores to enter a new spore-forming cycle immediately without an intervening stage of vegetative growth. This phenomenon of "microcycle sporogenesis" is caused by replacing a rich growth medium with diluted medium, which prevents cell division and a return to spore formation.

H. BACTERIAL PHYSIOLOGY: *Mechanism of Penicillin Action*

James T. Park and Jack Strominger independently find that penicillin blocks synthesis of the bacterial cell wall by inhibition of an enzyme called glycopeptide transpeptidase, thereby preventing strands of peptidoglycan from becoming cross-linking.

I. BACTERIAL PHYSIOLOGY: *β–Galactoside Permease*

C. Fred Fox and Eugene P. Kennedy partially purify a component of the β-galactoside transport system of *Escherichia coli* that functions as the permease transport substance. They find that it is a protein, distinct from β-galactosidase and thioglactoside transacetylase, that does not function as an enzyme. (See 1956 D.)

J. BACTERIAL PHYSIOLOGY: *Cyclic AMP in Bacteria*

R. S. Makman and Earl W. Sutherland report that *Escherichia coli* contains the nucleotide adenosine $3',5'$-monophosphate (cyclic AMP), and the presence of glucose lowers its intracellular concentration by inhibiting both synthesis and efflux. These experiments illustrate that cyclic AMP regulates the "glucose effect." (See 1942 F, 1956 E, 1960 D, 1968 B.)

K. BACTERIAL PHYSIOLOGY: *Positive Control of Enzyme Synthesis*

Ellis Englesberg, Joseph Irr, Joseph Power, and Nancy Lee find evidence for a type of positive control of enzyme synthesis as opposed to the negative or repressor control seen in the β-galactosidase system. They find that, in *Escherichia coli,* the structural genes for the utilization of arabinose are activated by the gene product, referred to as an "activator," of an "activator gene." This molecule, which has two active sites, functions as a repressor until the presence of arabinose causes an allosteric conversion to the activator state. This process contrasts with the β-galactosidase system, where the repressor is converted into an inactive form.

L. BACTERIAL GENETICS: *Recombination–Deficient Mutants/Rec⁻*
Alvin J. Clark and Ann Dee Margulies isolate and characterize two recombination-deficient mutants, Rec⁻, that are highly sensitive to ultraviolet light. These results imply that the genetic locus, referred to as *recA,* in these mutants controls functions that control repair of photodamage to DNA. (See 1958 H.)

M. MOLECULAR VIROLOGY: *Viral RNA Polymerase*
Sol Spiegelman and colleagues report that bacteriophages MS-2 and Qβ induce the formation of two different RNA replicases in infected cells of *Escherichia coli.* The enzymes, which prefer homologous RNA, are virtually inactive on heterologous RNA. The researchers also find that the RNA produced by the replicases is fully competent to program the production of complete viral particles. (See 1962 N, 1963 S.)

N. VIRAL DISEASE: *Hepatitis B*
Baruch Samuel Blumberg, Harvey J. Alter, and S. Visnich report finding an antigen in the serum of an Australian aborigine that correlates with the presence of serum hepatitis, or hepatitis B. They use a test for the so-called "Australia antigen" to study the distribution of hepatitis B infection. Blumberg shares the 1976 Nobel Prize in physiology or medicine with Daniel Gajdusek.

O. VIRAL DISEASE: *Tumor Antigens*
Robert J. Huebner earlier described virus-specific complement-fixing antigens in adenovirus type 12 tumor extracts that react with adenovirus type 12 tumor-bearing hamster sera. Similar antigens were found by Paul H. Black and coworkers in cells transformed with simian virus 40 (SV40) and in SV40-induced tumors in hamsters. Huebner and Black, with M. David Hoggan and Wallace P. Rowe, present data substantiating that these or similar complement-fixing antigens are produced during early phases in the normal virus reproductive cycle. They believe that the antigens represent virus-induced precursor enzymes whose persistence may play a role in abnormal functioning of the tumor cells. (See 1962 P.)

P. CELL BIOLOGY: *Chemiosmotic Hypothesis*
Peter Dennis Mitchell and Jennifer Moyle publish evidence discriminating between the chemical and chemiosmotic mechanisms of electron transport phosphorylation. In 1961, Mitchell proposed chemiosmotic coupling as a mechanism by which electron transport conversion of ADP to ATP takes place. The experiments of Mitchell and Moyle, with both intact and sonically disintegrated rat liver mitochondria, demonstrate that electrons flow in one direction and protons in the opposite direction. These data contradict earlier chemical concepts of the formation and hydrolysis of high-energy complexes as intermediates leading to ATP synthesis. (See 1961 M.)

1965 (continued)

Q. MOLECULAR BIOLOGY: *Host Modification of DNA*
Werner Arber first reports a role for methionine in the modification of DNA by *Escherichia coli*. By 1968, he shows that cellular enzymes catalyze the methylation of adenine to form 6-methyl amino purine. The methylated DNA is protected from attack by cellular nucleases. This discovery of cellular modification of DNA is an important step in developing recombinant DNA techniques. (See 1970 M, 1972 M, 1973 N.)

R. MOLECULAR BIOLOGY: *Ribonucleic Acid Sequencing*
Frederick Sanger, G. G. Brownlee, and B. G. Barrell describe a two-dimensional fractionation procedure for analysis of radioactively labeled RNA. The method, which uses high-voltage ionophoresis in both directions, resolves di- and trinucleotides and most of the tetranucleotides in digests prepared with ribonuclease. They report significant differences in the 16S and 23S components of ribosomal RNA. (See 1953 Q.)

S. MOLECULAR BIOLOGY: *Base Sequence of Transfer RNA*
Robert William Holley completes 7 years of work by determining the purine and pyrimidine base sequence in alanine transfer RNA from yeast. Holley, Gobind Khorana, and Marshall Nirenberg share the 1968 Nobel Prize in physiology or medicine. (See 1961 Q, 1964 L, 1977 S, 1977 T.)

T. MOLECULAR BIOLOGY: *In Vitro Synthesis of Protein*
Robert Bruce Merrifield develops a solid-phase method for synthesizing polypeptides and proteins. By linking the amino acids to polystyrene beads, he successfully synthesizes bradykinin, a polypeptide of nine amino acid units, the two chains of insulin (21 and 30 residues), and bovine pancreatic ribonuclease (124 residues). Merrifield receives the Nobel Prize in chemistry in 1984.

U. TECHNOLOGY
The *Project Gemini* spacecraft uses fuel cells to generate electricity on board.

V. THE ARTS: *Literature*
Flannery O'Connor's *Everything That Rises Must Converge* is published posthumously.

1966

A. BACTERIAL TAXONOMY: Chlamydia
James W. Moulder discusses the relation of the chlamydiae, particularly the psittacosis group, to bacteria and viruses. L. A. Page proposes the formal name *Chlamydia,* derived from the 1907 study by L. Halberstaedter and Stanilaus von Prowazek. Based on work by several groups that demonstrated that chlamydiae contain both DNA and RNA, as well as muramic acid in their cell walls, Moulder concludes that the organisms of the psittacosis group have no relationship to the viruses, that they are more like gram-negative bacteria. (See 1907 B, 1951 A, 1963 D.)

B. BACTERIAL PHYSIOLOGY: *Chemotaxis*
Julius Adler studies chemotaxis toward oxygen of *Escherichia coli*. By using capillary tubes filled with culture medium, he finds that the bacteria migrate

into two bands. In the first, the cells metabolize aerobically, while in the second they are anaerobic. (See 1883 D, 1885 C, 1893 B, 1967 D, 1969 C, 1972 B.)

C. BACTERIAL PHYSIOLOGY: *Nitrogen Fixation*

M. J. Dilworth reports that acetylene is an inhibitor of nitrogen fixation, with either pyruvate or hydrogen as electron donor. Acetylene accepts the electrons and is reduced to ethylene. Acetylene reduction is subsequently used extensively to detect nitrogen-fixing activity. (See 1937 C.)

D. BACTERIAL PHYSIOLOGY: *Thermophiles*

Thomas D. Brock begins his studies of organisms living in the hot springs at Yellowstone National Park. He finds that 75°C is the upper limit for the growth of photosynthetic organisms, such as the cyanobacterium *Synechococcus,* but that some nonphotosynthetic bacteria exist at temperatures up to 90°C. He believes that limitations of growth at higher temperatures are related to membrane function and not to the inactivation of macromolecules. (See 1846 D, 1862 A, 1879 A, 1970 A, 1972 A.)

E. BACTERIAL PHYSIOLOGY: *Proline Uptake by Isolated Membranes*

H. R. Kaback and E. R. Stadtman find that isolated membrane preparations of a proline auxotroph of *Escherichia coli* catalyze an energy-dependent uptake of the amino acid proline. The uptake, which is oxygen dependent, is stimulated by glucose but inhibited by dinitrophenol, iodoacetamide, amytal, and phenyl hydrozone.

F. BACTERIAL PHYSIOLOGY: *Isolation of the* lac *Repressor*

Walter Gilbert and Benno Müller-Hill develop an assay for the *lac* repressor of *Escherichia coli* by measuring its binding to a radioactively labeled inducer, isopropyl-thio-galactoside, that is not metabolized. After they isolate the repressor molecule, they find that it is a protein with a molecular weight of 150,000 to 200,000.

G. ANTIBIOTICS: *Sensitivity Testing of Bacteria*

A. W. Bauer, M. M. Kirby, J. C. Sherris, and M. Turck develop a standardized single-disc procedure for testing the effectiveness of antibiotics against bacteria. Using a standard method for the preparation of inoculum and inoculation of plates, they employ a single filter paper disc impregnated with a selected concentration of antibiotic for each test. They prepare a table of 20 antibacterial agents, including sulfonamides, with measurements of zones of inhibition to be interpreted as resistant, intermediate, or sensitive to the test agent. Their procedure is commonly known as the Kirby-Bauer test.

H. BACTERIAL GENETICS: *Transposition of the* lac *Region*

Jonathan Beckwith and Ethan R. Signer develop a procedure whereby the *lac* gene of *Escherichia coli* can be transposed to specific regions of the chromosome using the transducing phage φ80 *lac.* These experiments demonstrate that the chromosome can be redesigned by moving genes from one region to another.

I. BACTERIAL GENETICS: *Genetic Nomenclature*

Milislav Demerec, Edward Adelberg, Alvin J. Clark, and Philip E. Hartman propose a uniform system of nomenclature for bacterial genetics.

1966 (continued)

Demerec and Hartman previously introduced the idea of using three-letter symbols, such as "lac" for the lactose genotype. The new proposal extends this concept by suggesting italicizing the three-letter lowercase symbols, followed by a capital letter when it is necessary to distinguish between mutant loci conferring the same general phenotype, such as *lacZ* and *lacY*. Phenotypes, which would not be italicized, would begin with a capital letter, for example, Lac⁻ would indicate an inability to use lactose. They also recommend a system of nomenclature for plasmids and episomes. The general principle proposed is adopted eventually by all *Escherichia coli* geneticists and is extended to other bacteria.

J. BACTERIAL DISEASE: *Staphylococcal Alpha-Toxin*

In studies with artificial lipid spherules (liposomes), Gerald Weissman, Grazia Sessa, and Alan W. Bernheimer show that the alpha-toxin of *Staphylococcus aureus* releases glucose, anions, and cations contained within the liposomes. They suggest that the alpha-toxin may have a similar effect on phospholipid membranes. (See 1974 J, 1981 G, 1987 D.)

K. VIRAL DISEASE: *Feline Leukemia Virus*

William Jarrett reports finding a virus in domestic cats that causes a malignant cell transformation, as well as immunosuppression similar to that later found for the human immunodeficiency virus (HIV) in 1983.

L. PRION DISEASE: *Creutzfeldt-Jakob Disease*

Daniel Gajdusek, C. J. Gibbs, Jr., and M. P. Alpers report the successful transfer of Creutzfeldt-Jakob disease to chimpanzees. The disease, first reported in 1920 and 1921 by Hans G. Creutzfeldt and Alfons M. Jakob, was formerly regarded as an inherited form of presenile dementia. Creutzfeldt-Jakob disease is now included as a type of spongiform encephalopathy similar to scrapie, kuru, and bovine spongiform encephalopathy. Gajdusek shares the 1976 Nobel Prize in physiology or medicine with Baruch Blumberg. (See 1920 D, 1957 K, 1982 M, 1985 H.)

M. IMMUNOLOGY: *T-Cell–B-Cell Interactions*

Henry N. Claman, Edward A. Chaperon, and R. Faser Triplett show that B cells form antibody by interacting with T cells. This subset of T cells becomes known as T helper (Th) cells. (See 1970 J.)

N. IMMUNOLOGY: *Lymphokines*

Barry R. Bloom and John R. David independently prove that immune lymph cells, when stimulated by the correct antigen, secrete a chemical that inhibits the migration of macrophages. They call this factor "migration inhibitory factor" (MIF). A number of other molecular mediators are later discovered by various investigators and come to be known collectively as lymphokines.

O. IMMUNOLOGY: *Immunoglobulin E*

Kimishige Ishizaka and Teruko Ishizaka discover immunoglobulin E (IgE). IgE functions in response to allergies and is involved in a mast cell cascade in inflammation. (See 1939 H.)

P. MOLECULAR BIOLOGY: *S1 Nuclease*

T. Ando finds S1 nuclease, an enzyme important in recombinant DNA experiments, in takadiastase, a dried powder made from *Aspergillus oryzae* and used to treat digestive problems. After W. D. Sutton purifies the enzyme in 1971, it is found to have a useful preference for single-stranded polynucleotides as substrate.

Q. SOCIETY AND POLITICS

The U.S. Supreme Court, in the case of *Miranda v. Arizona*, rules that any person taken into police custody has a right to counsel and to remain silent.

R. THE ARTS: *Music*

The new Metropolitan Opera House opens in Lincoln Center in New York City.

S. THE ARTS: *Literature*

* Truman Capote publishes *In Cold Blood*.
* Jacqueline Susann publishes *Valley of the Dolls*.

1967

A. EVOLUTIONARY THEORY: *Origin of Eucaryotes/Endosymbiosis*

Lynn Sagan (now Lynn Margulis) presents a theory of the origin of eucaryotic cells in which three fundamental organelles—mitochondria, photosynthetic plastids, and the basal bodies of the (9+2) flagella—were once free-living procaryotic-type cells. Through endosymbiosis they became components of a cell type that evolved into the eucaryote. She points out that a number of researchers as early as 1910 and as recently as 1962 have proposed similar ideas. (See 1927 D, 1962 T.)

B. MICROBIAL ECOLOGY: *Microfossils*

J. William Schopf and Elso S. Barghoorn find spheroidal microfossils, probably representing unicellular algalike organisms in an early Precambrian area of South Africa, called the Fig Tree Series. These organisms are dated at about 3,100 million years old. (See 1965 B.)

C. BACTERIAL STRUCTURE: Halobacterium

In this year and in 1968, Walther Stoeckenius and his colleagues, Robert Bowen and Wolf H. Kunau, report studies of the membranes found in *Halobacterium halobium*. Among their several membrane fractions is one that they refer to as the "purple membrane," whose origin and function are not known. (See 1971 B, 1980 Q, 1982 N.)

D. BACTERIAL PHYSIOLOGY: *Chemotaxis*

John B. Armstrong, Julius Adler, and Margaret M. Dahl isolate 40 mutants of *Escherichia coli* that are motile but nonchemotactic, designating the genes that regulate flagellar motion as *che*. They find that the products of the *cheY* and *cheZ* genes interact with flagellar components, the *fla* gene products. They observe an extreme counterclockwise flagellar motion in *cheY* mutants and a clockwise motion in *cheZ* mutants. (See 1966 B, 1969 C, 1985 A.)

E. BACTERIAL PHYSIOLOGY: *Minicells*

Howard I. Adler and coworkers report finding miniature cells of a mutant strain of *Escherichia coli* that either lack DNA or contain only small amounts

1967 *(continued)*

of DNA. These minicells are produced at one or both poles of otherwise normally dividing parent cells. Minicells, which do not divide after being formed, carry out some metabolic processes for a limited time.

F. BACTERIAL PHYSIOLOGY: *Nitrogen Fixation*

F. J. Bergersen and G. L. Turner separate soybean root nodules into membrane fragments, a soluble fraction, and the swollen irregularly shaped forms of the rhizobia called bacteroids. They report that all of the nitrogen-fixing and hydrogen-evolving activity is associated with bacteroids and that ammonia accumulates in the suspending medium. (See 1941 E, 1951 D, 1953 F.)

G. BACTERIAL PHYSIOLOGY: *Syntrophism*

Marvin P. Bryant and coworkers report that the methane-producing bacterium *Methanobacillus omelianskii,* isolated by H. A. Barker in 1936, is actually composed of two strains. One strain, which they designate the S strain, oxidizes ethanol to acetate with the formation of H_2; the second strain, designated *Methanobacterium* M.o.H., utilizes the released hydrogen to reduce carbon dioxide to methane. This symbiotic interaction is later termed "syntrophism." (See 1936 B, 1971 C.)

H. BACTERIAL GENETICS: *R Factors*

David H. Smith examines cultures of bacteria that were lyophilized some years earlier for the presence of antibiotic resistance factors, or R factors. The earliest positive culture is one lyophilized in 1946. It is found to carry resistance to tetracycline, streptomycin, and bluensomycin, indicating that the presence of R factors in bacteria is not a recent phenomenon. (See 1959 G, 1960 F.)

I. BACTERIAL GENETICS: *Circular Col Factor*

T. F. Roth and D. R. Helinski show that a factor that controls colicin production, a Col factor, is a circular form of DNA. (See 1925 B, 1954 I.)

J. BACTERIAL INSECTICIDES: *Nomenclature for Toxins*

A. M. Heimple proposes a nomenclature for the insecticidal toxins produced by *Bacillus thuringiensis* and similar bacteria. The toxin referred to as lecithinase C or phospholipase C is to be called alpha-toxin, the thermostable toxin is to be named beta-toxin, and the proteinaceous crystalline parasporal body is to be called delta-toxin. (See 1953 J, 1954 H, 1983 J, 1986 H, 1987 B.)

K. BACTERIAL DISEASE: *Diphtheria Toxin*

In 1962, I. Kato discovered that diphtheria toxin inhibits protein synthesis in cell-free systems derived from mammalian cells. Also in 1962, R. John Collier and A. M. Pappenheimer, Jr., had shown that the toxin inhibits the transfer of amino acids to ribosomes. In subsequent studies in a reticulocyte cell-free system, Collier finds that neither the ribosomes nor aminoacyl-transfer RNA are affected and that the toxin specifically inhibits one of the supernatant transfer factors, which he calls factor II. Factor II is now called elongation factor 2.

L. VIRAL DISEASE: *Smallpox Eradication*

Donald A. Henderson, of the Communicable Disease Center (now the Centers for Disease Control and Prevention), becomes the global director of the effort to eradicate smallpox under the auspices of the World Health Assembly of the World Health Organization. An earlier effort, begun in 1958, was limited to volunteer participation by nations in endemic areas. The announced goal of the global effort is to achieve eradication in 10 years, by December 31, 1976. After the last proven case is documented in 1977, the WHO announces in 1980 that eradication is achieved. (See 1958 K, 1980 M.)

M. VIRAL DISEASE: *Marburg Virus*

Twenty-three cases of a virus infection causing an acute febrile illness occur among workers at a pharmaceutical plant in Marburg, Germany; other cases are reported in Frankfort at a medical research institute and in Belgrade, Yugoslavia. The causative agent, called Marburg virus, causes seven deaths and six secondary infections. Marburg virus and Ebola virus are single-stranded RNA viruses classified as filoviruses. They are unique in that they are the only recognized filamentous viruses that infect mammals. (See 1969 D, 1976 H.)

N. VIRAL DISEASE: *SV40 Production in Heterokaryons*

James Watkins and Renato Dulbecco report that cells transformed by simian virus 40 (SV40) produce complete virions only when the cells are heterokaryons. Only a fraction of the heterokaryons will release newly formed virus. (See 1962 O.)

O. PRION DISEASE: *Scrapie*

An early report that the scrapie agent does not contain nucleic acid comes from Tikvah Alper and colleagues. They treat extracts from infected mouse brain with ultraviolet radiation at 254 nanometers for up to 5 hours and find no inactivation of infectivity. They note that they have no evidence of protein being associated with infectivity. (See 1936 J, 1981 K, 1982 M, 1985 I, 1985 M, 1989 F, 1989 G, 1990 H.)

P. MOLECULAR BIOLOGY: *Gamma Radiation of DNA*

William C. Summers and Waclaw Szybalski develop methods for the detection of single-strand breaks in DNA caused by gamma radiation in several species of bacteria. They detect the breaks either by cesium chloride density gradient centrifugation or by two-phase polyethylene glycol-dextran partition chromatography. They study the effect of gamma radiation on bacteriophage φ29, the infectious DNA of the phage, and transforming DNA of the host bacterium, *Bacillus subtilis*. They note that inactivation of the phage and its DNA is caused by double-strand scissions, while single-strand breaks inactivate the transforming activity.

Q. MOLECULAR BIOLOGY: *Lambda Phage Repressor*

Mark Ptashne successfully isolates the repressor molecule produced by bacteriophage λ. He confirms that the 30,000-molecular-weight protein acts as the repressor by demonstrating inhibition of host cell synthesis and

1967 *(continued)*

inhibition of production of other phage-induced proteins, and by using a mutant phage that suppresses most phage proteins other than the repressor.

R. MOLECULAR BIOLOGY: *Discovery of DNA Ligase*

DNA ligase is discovered by M. Gellert and, independently, by Bernard Weiss and Charles C. Richardson, Baldomero M. Olivera, and I. Robert Lehman. The enzyme, when purified from *Escherichia coli* infected with bacteriophage, is used in experiments to form covalent circles of lambda phage DNA. Polynucleotide ligase, named by Weiss and Richardson, catalyzes the reformation of a phosphodiester bond between nucleotides in strands of DNA, functions in normal repair processes in the cell, and finds use in genetic engineering experiments.

S. MOLECULAR VIROLOGY: *RNA Polymerase in Vaccinia Virus*

Bruce Woodson demonstrates that vaccinia virus directs messenger RNA (mRNA) synthesis under conditions that inhibit uncoating of the viral DNA. He concludes that mRNA synthesis is under direction of the parental virus and not its progeny. William E. Munyon, Enzo Paoletti, and James T. Grace, Jr., demonstrate that highly purified vaccinia virus catalyzes the synthesis of RNA from nucleotide triphosphates in vitro. The virions, therefore, contain an active RNA polymerase.

T. MOLECULAR VIROLOGY: *Poxvirus RNA Polymerase*

Joseph R. Kates and B. R. McAuslan conclude that a DNA-dependent RNA polymerase is present in poxvirus virions. They show that after viral DNA enters the cytoplasm of cells, the polymerase synthesizes an mRNA species that probably codes for early virus proteins.

U. MEDICINE AND SURGERY: *Heart Transplant*

Christiaan Neethling Barnard performs the first heart transplant on a human patient. The operation is successful, but the patient dies 18 days later from complications of pneumonia, contracted as a result of receiving drugs to prevent tissue rejection.

V. SCIENTIFIC PUBLICATION: Journal of Virology

The American Society for Microbiology begins to publish the *Journal of Virology*.

W. SOCIETY AND POLITICS

After several months of skirmishes between Israel and Syria, the Six-Day War erupts. Israel defeats both Arab and Egyptian forces and takes control of Arab Jerusalem, the Golan Heights in Syria, and the West Bank in Jordan.

X. THE ARTS: *Radio and Television*

The Corporation for Public Broadcasting is created by an act of the U.S. Congress. Within a few years, both National Public Radio (NPR) and the Public Broadcasting Service (PBS), a television company, are operating.

1968

A. BACTERIAL PHYSIOLOGY: *Cell Division in* Escherichia coli

Charles E. Helmstetter, using a membrane selection technique that he developed in 1967, works with Stephen Cooper to study rates of DNA synthesis and chromosome replication in rapidly growing *Escherichia coli*. Their procedure involves binding the cells to a Millipore membrane filter and studying the newly formed cells that are continuously eluted from the membrane. They find that although the time of initiation of a round of replication of DNA depends on the growth rate, two constants can be defined: C, the time for a replication point to traverse the genome, and D, the time between the end of a round of replication and cell division.

B. BACTERIAL PHYSIOLOGY: *Cyclic AMP*
Ira Pastan and Robert Perlman report on their investigation of the effect of cyclic AMP on the increased synthesis of several enzymes in bacteria. Among the enzymes affected are β–galactosidase, lactose permease, galacto-kinase, glycerol kinase, α–glycerol phosphate permease, L–arabinose permease, and phosphotransferase. (See 1960 D, 1965 J.)

C. BACTERIAL GENETICS: *Insertion Sequences*
In studies of mutations in the galactose operon of *Escherichia coli,* two groups of workers, Elke Jordan, Heinz Saedler, and Peter Starlinger and, independently, James A. Shapiro and Sankar Adhya, report the isolation of a set of spontaneous galactose–negative mutants of *E. coli* that they characterize as extreme polar mutations caused by the insertion of large segments of DNA into the structural genes. Density gradient analysis of lambda-transducing phages carrying various extreme polar mutations of the galactose operon are found to have higher buoyant density than phages not carrying the mutations. The size of the insertions is estimated as being between 500 and 2,000 base pairs. By 1972, researchers from these laboratories and others are referring to "insertion sequences." (See 1960 G, 1974 H.)

D. BACTERIAL DISEASE: Bacillus anthracis
Ralph E. Lincoln and his colleagues James A. Vick, Frederick Klein, and others study the physiological and neurological effects of administering both *Bacillus anthracis* and purified anthrax toxin to laboratory animals. Their results show that the terminal responses in both infection and toxemia are essentially the same. A depression of the cerebral cortical electrical activity and respiration occurs, leading to death by respiratory failure. The researchers comment that these effects are similar to those observed in clinical cases of plague, diphtheria, and tetanus. (See 1954 G.)

E. MOLECULAR VIROLOGY: *Rolling–Circle Model DNA Replication*
Following the ideas suggested by a number of researchers of copying DNA off a circle in bacteriophage replication, Walter Gilbert and David Dressler and, independently, Harvey Eisen, Luiz Pereira da Silva, and François Jacob describe similar models for replication of the DNA of bacteriophage λ. Their rolling-circle models of replication result in the formation of long concatemers of DNA, which are then cut into replicon-size pieces either by endonuclease or by a "headful" mechanism.

F. MOLECULAR VIROLOGY: *Influenza Virus RNA*
Peter Duesberg reports that influenza virus probably has five physically distinct RNA components. The RNA in the mature virion and the single-

1968 *(continued)*

and double-stranded virus-specific RNAs found in the infected cell show specific and similar heterogeneity.

G. VIRAL DISEASE: *Hong Kong Influenza Pandemic*
A variant of the Asian influenza virus, called the Hong Kong strain, emerges. The disease, which apparently began in southeast China, spreads to the United States during the fall and winter and then to western Europe. The mortality in the United States is as high as 80,000, while that in Europe is relatively low until the winter of 1969 to 1970. Using terminology adopted in 1980, the antigenic designation of this strain of virus is H3N2. (See 1973 K, 1980 O.)

H. IMMUNOLOGY: *Thymus and Lymphocytes*
Jacques Miller and G. F. Mitchell report experiments with mice from which the thymus gland is removed within 24 hours of birth (neonatal thymectomy). As adults, these animals have suppressed hypersensitivity responses and a depressed ability to form antibodies against sheep red blood cells. That these defects are corrected in the adult by injection of either thymus cells or thoracic duct lymphocytes establishes the concept that the antibody response is dependent on intact thymic function and that the lymphocytes can restore that function. (See 1956 P, 1957 N, 1961 L, 1962 S.)

I. MOLECULAR BIOLOGY: *Discontinuous Chain Growth in DNA Synthesis*
Studying DNA replication in *Escherichia coli* and *Bacillus subtilis,* Reiji Okazaki and his colleagues conclude that both strands are synthesized discontinuously in the 5' to 3' direction, resulting in the formation of small fragments that are about 10S in size. By 1970, after further experiments, the Okazaki group and, independently, V. N. Iyer and Karl G. Lark report that only one strand is synthesized discontinuously, while the other is synthesized as a single long polymer. The small fragments are subsequently referred to as "Okazaki fragments."

J. MOLECULAR BIOLOGY: *Posttranslational Processing of Polypeptides*
Donald F. Summers and Jacob V. Maizel, Jr., note that the numbers and sizes of proteins synthesized by poliovirus seem to exceed the coding capacity of the RNA genome. They suggest that some of the primary translation products are processed to form secondary products of smaller size. Two groups of researchers, John J. Holland and E. Donald Kiehn and Michael Jacobson and David Baltimore, perform experiments to substantiate this concept. Holland and Kiehn demonstrate that the messenger RNA of some small enteroviruses is translated to form very large proteins that are then specifically cleaved into smaller functional proteins. Jacobson and Baltimore use pulse-chase experiments with radioactive amino acids to show that a large polypeptide is cleaved to form the three procapsid proteins of poliovirus.

K. SOCIETY AND POLITICS
- Civil rights leader Martin Luther King, Jr., is assassinated.

• Senator Robert F. Kennedy, brother of former president John F. Kennedy, is assassinated while campaigning for the Democratic Party's nomination for the presidency.

A. BIOLOGICAL TAXONOMY: *Classification*

Robert H. Whittaker proposes a five-kingdom system of classification of living organisms: Plantae, Animalia, Fungi, Protista (protozoans and algae), and Monera (blue-green algae and bacteria). This system becomes widely accepted, replacing an earlier four-kingdom system proposed by H. F. Copeland in 1956. The Monera are later called the Procaryotae in many publications. (See 1861 D, 1866 A, 1956 A, 1977 A, 1990 A.)

B. BACTERIAL TAXONOMY: *DNA-DNA Hybridization*

Don J. Brenner, Stanley Falkow, and coworkers study the taxonomic relationships among the enterobacteria by measuring the degree of reassociation of DNA extracted from one species with that of a second species. The results of the hybridization experiments between species compare well with existing taxonomic groups.

C. BACTERIAL PHYSIOLOGY: *Chemotaxis*

Julius Adler identifies chemoreceptors in *Escherichia coli* for galactose, glucose, ribose, aspartate, and serine. The chemoreceptors detect attractant chemicals by signaling changes in concentration. The attractant chemicals, however, are neither taken up by the cells nor metabolized. (See 1885 C, 1893 B, 1966 B, 1967 D, 1972 B, 1972 C.)

D. VIRAL DISEASE: *Lassa Virus*

An American nurse working in Lassa, Nigeria, dies as a result of infection with a new viral disease that becomes known as Lassa fever. Limited to West Africa, the virus, an arenavirus, is thought to cause up to 5,000 infections each year. (See 1967 M, 1976 H.)

E. MOLECULAR BIOLOGY: *Error-Prone DNA Repair*

Sohei Kondo reports preliminary data showing that excision repair of damage to DNA results in errors in the sequence of nucleotides. These errors cause both mutation and mistakes in replication.

F. MOLECULAR VIROLOGY: *Oncogenes*

Evidence from Robert J. Huebner's and George J. Todaro's seroepidemiological studies and studies of cells in culture support the hypothesis that the genomes of cells of vertebrate species contain the information for producing C-type virus RNA. Huebner and Todaro suggest that this information, transmitted from parent to offspring, is responsible for transforming normal cells into tumor cells. They refer to these determinants of cancer as "oncogenes." (See 1976 L.)

G. MOLECULAR IMMUNOLOGY: *Amino Acid Sequence of Immunoglobulin G*

Gerald Maurice Edelman determines the sequence of amino acids in the immunoglobulin G (IgG) antibody. IgG, with 1,300 amino acids, is the longest protein sequenced at this time.

1969 *(continued)*

H. TECHNOLOGY

American astronauts Neil Alden Armstrong, Edwin Eugene Aldrin, Jr., and Michael Collins are carried to the earth's moon by the spacecraft *Apollo 11*. Armstrong and Aldrin become the first humans to walk on the moon.

I. THE ARTS: *Literature*

- Kurt Vonnegut, Jr., publishes *Slaughterhouse Five*.
- Michael Crichton publishes *The Andromeda Strain*.

1970

A. BACTERIAL ECOLOGY: Thermoplasma

Gary Darland, Thomas D. Brock, William Samsonoff, and Samuel F. Conti isolate from a coal refuse pile a thermophilic, acidophilic bacterium with no cell wall, a temperature optimum for growth of 59°C, and a pH optimum between 1 and 2. They propose the name *Thermoplasma acidophila*. (See 1966 D, 1972 A, 1982 B, 1983 A.)

B. BACTERIAL TAXONOMY: Frankia

The name *Frankia* was first used in 1887 to refer to the microsymbionts in the root nodules of nonleguminous plants such as *Alnus* and *Myrica* but was used intermittently thereafter. J. H. Becking proposes to reestablish *Frankia* as the genus for the actinomycetes now confirmed to be the endophytes of such nodules. (See 1887 C, 1902 D, 1954 D, 1978 D.)

C. BACTERIAL PHYSIOLOGY: *Autoinduction of Luminescence*

J. Woodland Hastings, Kenneth H. Nealson, and Terry Platt describe autoinduction of luminescence in *Vibrio fischeri* and *Vibrio harveyi* in broth cultures. The cultures begin to luminesce only in the late exponential or early stationary phases of growth after a chemical inducer produced by the cells attains a threshold concentration. (See 1981 B, 1982 G, 1984 G.)

D. BACTERIAL PHYSIOLOGY: *Purple Nonsulfur Bacteria*

After earlier efforts to grow purple nonsulfur bacteria under dark anaerobic conditions have failed, Robert L. Uffen and R. S. Wolfe successfully cultivate *Rhodospirillum rubrum* in the dark, using a modified Hungate technique with ethyl alcohol, acetate, or pyruvate as an energy source. Uffen and Wolfe note that H. Nakamura, in 1937, and E. F. Kohlmiller and Howard Gest, in 1951, reported that species of *Rhodospirillum* ferment organic acids under dark conditions. (See 1946 D.)

E. BACTERIAL PHYSIOLOGY: *Cometabolism*

R. S. Horvath and Martin Alexander describe how some microorganisms bring about the conversion of compounds that do not supply carbon, energy, nitrogen, or phosphorus for their use. In a process the authors call "cometabolism," substances, such as herbicides and pesticides, that are not readily metabolized are degraded in the presence of other compounds serving as an energy source.

F. BACTERIAL PHYSIOLOGY: *Stringent Response*

In studies of the stringent response of cells in which RNA synthesis ceases when starved for amino acids, M. Cashel and B. Kalbacher describe the nucleotides called magic spots I and II on chromatograms. They find magic spot I to be guanosine 5′-diphosphate-2′-diphosphate, written as ppGpp, and magic spot II to be guanosine 5′-triphosphate-2′-diphosphate, or pppGpp. These molecules serve as messengers signaling the cells to stop the synthesis of ribosomal RNA when amino acids are not available for protein synthesis. (See 1961 F, 1975 F.)

G. BACTERIAL DISEASE: *Crown Gall*
A. Petit and others working with G. Morel discover that there are two types of the bacterium *Agrobacterium tumefaciens,* which causes crown gall disease in plants. Each type induces the plant tissue to synthesize a derivative of arginine that is required for growth of the bacteria. One type of *A. tumefaciens* induces the synthesis of and requires octopine [N-α-(D-1-carboxyethyl)-L-arginine], the second induces the synthesis of and requires nopaline [N-α-(1,3-dicarboxypropyl)-L-arginine]. Gerrit Bomhoff finds that these two compounds, previously found in crown gall tissue, are synthesized under the control of plasmid DNA, later called the tumor-inducing, or Ti, plasmid, that transfers to the infected plant. (See 1907 D, 1947 B, 1974 L, 1977 O.)

H. MOLECULAR VIROLOGY: *Retroviruses*
David Baltimore and, independently, Howard Temin and Satoshi Mizutani find that some RNA-containing viruses have an enzyme that catalyzes the formation of DNA molecules from single-stranded RNA templates. Baltimore finds the enzyme, an RNA-dependent DNA polymerase, in Rauscher mouse leukemia virus and in Rous sarcoma virus, while Temin identifies the enzyme in Rous sarcoma virus. The enzyme is named "reverse transcriptase," and RNA viruses that have the enzyme are called "retroviruses." Baltimore and Temin share the 1975 Nobel Prize in physiology or medicine with Renato Dulbecco. (See 1964 I, 1980 N, 1983 L.)

I. IMMUNOLOGY: *Antibody-Combining Sites*
Comparing the sequence of amino acids in immunoglobulins, Tai Te Wu and Elvin Abraham Kabat find much variation in certain hypervariable regions. These regions are thought to be in sites that combine with antigen.

J. IMMUNOLOGY: *Suppressor T Cells*
Richard K. Gershon and K. Kondo find that T cells not only activate B cells but also serve to prevent or stop antibody formation. The suppressor T cells are given the designation T_S. (See 1966 M, 1970 K, 1973 M.)

K. IMMUNOLOGY: *T–Cell–B–Cell–Antigen Interaction*
N. Avrion Mitchison, Klaus Rajewsky, and R. B. Taylor present their hypothesis about the interaction of antigenic determinants and cells inducing the synthesis of antibodies. Their concept of how antigen functions to combine T cells and B cells leads to much further study and eventual clarification of the mechanism. (See 1966 M, 1970 J, 1973 M.)

L. MICROSCOPY: *Scanning Electron Microscope*
Albert Victor Crewe builds the first easily used scanning electron microscope. (See 1938 C.)

1970 *(continued)*

M. MOLECULAR BIOLOGY: *Restriction Enzymes*

Hamilton Othanel Smith and Kent W. Wilcox report that an enzyme, isolated from *Haemophilus influenzae,* produces site-specific breaks in unmodified DNA derived from bacteriophage T7. The enzyme is inactive on DNA from *H. influenzae* as well as on denatured DNA. This type of enzyme, called a restriction endonuclease, plays an important role in restricting, or preventing, bacteriophage infection. Host cell enzymes are protected by modification, such as the methylation reported by Werner Arber in 1965. In a companion paper, Smith and Thomas J. Kelly, Jr., identify the specific sequence of nucleotides in the recognition site for the enzyme. Subsequent studies by a number of investigators reveal that the recognition sites for the restriction endonucleases, often six base pairs in length, are palindromes, meaning that the recognition site is the same when read both forward and backward. Smith shares the 1978 Nobel Prize in physiology or medicine with Werner Arber and Daniel Nathans.

N. MOLECULAR BIOLOGY: *Polyadenylic Sequences*

Joseph Kates discovers large polyadenylic sequences in both vaccinia virus messenger RNA and in cellular polysomal RNA. In 1975, Bernard Moss, E. N. Rosenblum, and A. Gershowitz find that vaccinia virus codes for a polyadenylic polymerase that catalyzes the addition of adenylate residues to the ends of RNA molecules. The large polyadenylic sequences may confer stability to the molecule.

O. MOLECULAR BIOLOGY: *Synthesis of a Gene*

Har Gobind Khorana and colleagues use mostly chemical methods to synthesize the gene for yeast alanine transfer RNA. This is the first successful synthesis of an entire polynucleotide sequence that constitutes a functioning gene.

P. MOLECULAR BIOLOGY: *Electron Microscopy of Genes in Action*

Oscar Miller, Barbara Hamkalo, and C. A. Thomas, Jr., publish electron microscope photographs showing strands of DNA with messenger RNA (mRNA) molecules, apparently in the process of being transcribed, appearing as attached strings. Ribosomes are aligned on the newly formed mRNA molecules while they are still attached to DNA.

Q. SCIENTIFIC ORGANIZATIONS: *American Academy of Microbiology*

The American Academy of Microbiology is dissolved as a separate entity to become a part of the American Society for Microbiology.

R. SCIENTIFIC PUBLICATIONS

• The first issues of *Infection and Immunity,* published by the American Society for Microbiology, appear.

• A new publication, the *Manual of Clinical Microbiology,* is published by the American Society for Microbiology.

S. SOCIETY AND POLITICS

The Occupational Safety and Health Act becomes law, establishing an agency (the Occupational Safety and Health Administration) whose purpose is to reduce work hazards in industry.

T. THE ARTS: *Literature*
- James Dickey publishes his novel *Deliverance*. A film version appears in 1972.
- Maya Angelou publishes the first part of her autobiography, *I Know Why the Caged Bird Sings*.

1971

A. BACTERIAL STRUCTURE: *Flagella*

M. L. DePamphilis and Julius Adler and, independently, K. Dimmitt and Melvin Simon publish a series of papers describing the purification of flagella from *Escherichia coli* and *Bacillus subtilis*. Both sets of researchers employ similar procedures, in which the flagella are released by treatment of the cells with lysozyme, fractionated with ammonium sulfate, and further purified on cesium chloride gradients. DePamphilis and Adler present electron microscope photographs showing how the flagella are attached to the cell membranes. They describe structures referred to as a "hook" and a "basal body," the latter being resolved into rings that attach to the outer membrane and cell membrane in *E. coli* and to the cell membrane only in *B. subtilis*. DePamphilis and Adler illustrate these structures in diagrams that subsequently appear in microbiology textbooks. (See 1947 A, 1950 B.)

B. BACTERIAL PHYSIOLOGY: *Bacteriorhodopsin*

Dieter Österhelt and Walther Stoeckenius continue studies of the "purple membrane" that was found by Stoeckenius and colleagues in *Halobacterium halobium* in 1967. They show that the purple color is caused by the compound retinal bound to an opsinlike protein, the only protein in this membrane. In 1973, finding that the protein closely resembles the visual protein pigments of animals, they refer to it as "bacteriorhodopsin." By 1974, Österhelt, Stoeckenius, and Arlette Danon show that the retinal-bacteriorhodopsin complex generates ATP by creating a light-generated proton gradient across the membrane. This process supports slow growth of the bacterium in the absence of chemical energy sources. (See 1967 C, 1980 Q, 1982 N.)

C. BACTERIAL PHYSIOLOGY: *Coenzyme M*

B. C. McBride and Ralph S. Wolfe discover a new coenzyme in extracts from several species of the genus *Methanobacterium*. Named coenzyme M, it functions as a methyl transfer coenzyme in the formation of methane. The methanogens are later included among the *Archaebacteria* in the 1977 classification system developed by Carl R. Woese and George E. Fox. Among the unique characteristics of the methanogens are types of coenzymes not found in the *Eubacteria*. (See 1974 F.)

D. BACTERIAL DISEASE: *Cholera*

Cholera caused by the El Tor biotype, which has been limited to the Celebes Islands, is responsible for a cholera pandemic that spreads to much of Asia, the Middle East, Africa, and parts of both eastern and western Europe. (See 1906 F, 1990 E.)

E. VIROID DISEASE: *Potato Spindle Disease*

Theodor O. Diener reports a novel infectious agent that causes potato tuber spindle disease. This agent, which he calls a "viroid," is a low-molecular-weight infectious RNA containing no protein capsid or other coating. The plant diseases other than potato tuber spindle disease that are caused by viroids include citrus exocortis, chrysanthemum stunt, chrysanthemum chlorotic mottle, hop stunt, coconut palm cadang-cadang, tomato planta macho, tomato apical stunt, and tomato bunchy top. (See 1976 J, 1978 L, 1981 L.)

F. IMMUNOLOGY: *Enzyme-Linked Immunosorbent Assay*

Eva Engvall and Peterman Perlmann develop the enzyme-linked immunosorbent assay known as ELISA. In this technique, either the antibody or antigen is attached to an insoluble carrier while the opposite reagent is linked to an enzyme. The amount of enzyme-coupled antigen or antibody that is fixed to the carrier is determined by a colorimetric enzyme assay.

G. SCIENTIFIC PUBLICATION: International Journal of Systematic Bacteriology

The American Society for Microbiology assumes responsibility for publication of the *International Journal of Systematic Bacteriology*.

1972

A. BACTERIAL ECOLOGY: Sulfolobus

Thomas D. Brock, Katherine M. Brock, Robert T. Belley, and Richard L. Weiss find an unusual bacterium growing in thermal acid soils and hot springs in solfatara areas. The organism grows both heterotrophically and autotrophically, with a temperature optimum of 70 to 75°C and a pH optimum of 2 to 3. Its cell wall contains hexoseamine but not peptidoglycan. Based on its appearance as lobed spheres and its use of sulfur, it is named *Sulfolobus acidocaldarius*. In 1966, James A. Brierley found a similar organism in acid thermal waters, but he did not describe it thoroughly at that time. At present there is another species named *Sulfolobus brierleyi*.

B. BACTERIAL PHYSIOLOGY: *Chemotaxis*

Robert M. MacNab and Daniel E. Koshland, Jr., develop a temporal gradient apparatus to study how changing concentrations of chemical attractants affect bacterial motility. They find that a decrease in concentration of attractant causes a tumbling motion, whereas an increase results in coordinated movement. They suggest that the bacteria apparently detect a spatial gradient by sensing a temporal gradient as the organism moves through a liquid medium. Models for the chemotactic response include a possible memory mechanism. (See 1972 C, 1974 B, 1988 B.)

C. BACTERIAL PHYSIOLOGY: *Chemotaxis*

Howard Berg and Douglas A. Brown construct a microscope that automatically follows individual cells as they move across a microscopic field. In their terminology, the swimming motions are "runs" when the change in direction is gradual, or "twiddles" if the change is abrupt. Concluding that chemotaxis toward amino acids results from suppression of direction changes that take place spontaneously in isotropic solutions, Berg and Brown suggest that in runs the flagella operate as a bundle, while in twiddles the flagella separate into individual filaments. (See 1972 B, 1974 B.)

D. BACTERIAL PHYSIOLOGY: *Heat Resistance in Spores*
R. S. Hanson, M. V. Curry, J. V. Garner, and H. Orin Halvorson isolate mutants of *Bacillus cereus* that produce heat-resistant spores having no dipicolinic acid and low levels of calcium and magnesium. Their data indicate that calcium and dipicolinic acid are not required for thermoresistance of spores but are necessary for germination. (See 1943 B, 1953 A, 1957 E.)

E. BACTERIAL PHYSIOLOGY: *Degradative Plasmids*
In this year and in 1973, Ananda M. Chakrabarty, I. C. Gunsalus, and colleagues report that *Pseudomonas putida* and other species of pseudomonads possess plasmids carrying genes for the degradation of salicylate, octane, camphor, and naphthalene. They find that these plasmids, referred to later as "degradative plasmids," can be transferred by conjugation to other fluorescent pseudomonads. (See 1973 D, 1980 G.)

F. BACTERIAL GENETICS: *In Vitro Transformation*
Stanley N. Cohen, Annie C. Y. Chang, and Leslie Hsu report a method for transforming bacteria by treating the recipients with calcium chloride. Experiments in 1970 by M. Mandel and A. Higa showed that *Escherichia coli* treated with calcium chloride would take up phage lambda and produce viable phage. Cohen's group transforms *E. coli* with purified R-factor DNA, producing progeny that are multiply resistant to several antibiotics. (See 1944 C.)

G. BACTERIAL GENETICS: *Ames Test for Carcinogens*
Bruce N. Ames and colleagues test for potential carcinogens by determining their mutagenic effect on histidine-requiring mutants of *Salmonella typhimurium*. A test chemical, activated with rat liver homogenate, is recorded as being mutagenic if it causes back-mutation to the wild type. The authors propose that mutagenic carcinogens cause cancer by somatic mutation.

H. MOLECULAR VIROLOGY: *SV40 DNA Synthesis*
Peter Tegtmeyer isolates and characterizes three temperature-sensitive mutants of simian virus 40 (SV40). The mutations affect early functions necessary to synthesize infectious viral DNA. The product of the temperature-sensitive gene is required to initiate each round of viral DNA replication but is not required to complete cycles that have begun. (See 1960 J.)

I. VIRAL DISEASE: *Norwalk Gastroenteritis*
Albert Z. Kapikian and colleagues study an outbreak of acute infectious nonbacterial gastroenteritis in Norwalk, Ohio. By electron microscopy they find a 27-nanometer particle believed to be the causative agent of "Norwalk gastroenteritis." This type of self-limiting disease was recognized in the 1940s, but no bacterial agent was found.

J. IMMUNOLOGY: *Bone Marrow as Bursa Equivalent*
Performing in vitro experiments with human bone marrow lymphoid cells, Nabih I. Abdou and Nancy L. Abdou find a response to antiserum prepared

with pokeweed antigen. They conclude that the bone marrow cells are equivalent to bursal cells and that the pokeweed test can be used to identify bursa-dependent systems in the same way that phytohemagglutinin is used as an index for thymus-dependent systems.

K. CELL BIOLOGY: *Membrane Structure*
S. Jonathan Singer and Garth Nicolson propose a model of membrane structure in which a lipid bilayer contains proteins that are not found in a continuous layer, as Hugh Davson and James Danielli (1934) and J. D. Robertson (1960) suggested. In Singer and Nicolson's model, protein molecules are present as separate entities embedded as a mosaic in the bilayer of lipid. Because their model suggests that some proteins are free to move about within the membrane, it is described as a "fluid mosaic model" and is now generally accepted as descriptive of membrane structure. (See 1894 G, 1910 G, 1925 E, 1934 G, 1960 O.)

L. MOLECULAR BIOLOGY: *Recombinant DNA*
Janet E. Mertz and Ronald W. Davis, and separately, Joe Hedgpeth, Howard M. Goodman, and Herbert W. Boyer report that the cleavage of duplex DNA with R1 restriction endonuclease makes two single-strand staggered cleavages that generate 5'-phosphoryl and 3'-hydroxyl termini. The single-strand sections have identical, complementary sequences of four to six nucleotides. Since the generated ends of the molecule are complementary and cohesive, any two DNA molecules with R1 nuclease sites can be "recombined" to generate hybrid molecules. Mertz and Davis apply the procedure to DNA from the simian virus 40 (SV40), while Hedgpeth and colleagues employ the lambda phage of *Escherichia coli*. (See 1972 M, 1973 N.)

M. MOLECULAR BIOLOGY: *Recombinant DNA/Gene Cloning*
Paul Berg, David A. Jackson, and Robert H. Symons use restriction enzymes and DNA ligases to construct circular dimers of simian virus 40 (SV40) DNA containing genes from both lambda bacteriophage and *Escherichia coli*. They first convert SV40 DNA to a linear form and then add single-stranded homopolymers of deoxyadenosine triphosphate or deoxythymidine triphosphate to the 3'-hydroxyl ends of the DNA strands using a terminal transferase enzyme. The complementary ends are annealed with DNA polymerase and DNA ligase to form a covalently closed circular molecule. (See 1972 L, 1973 N, 1973 O, 1975 O.)

N. SCIENTIFIC PUBLICATIONS: Antimicrobial Agents and Chemotherapy
The American Society for Microbiology establishes a new journal, *Antimicrobial Agents and Chemotherapy*.

O. SOCIETY AND POLITICS
A burglary at the Democratic Party headquarters in the Watergate apartment complex in Washington, D.C., is the beginning of a series of events that lead to the resignation from office of President Richard M. Nixon.

P. THE ARTS: *Architecture*
The twin towers of the World Trade Center in New York City are completed. At a height of 417 meters, they surpass the Empire State Building. However, the Sears Tower in Chicago, built the following year, becomes the world's tallest building. (See 1889 K, 1913 I, 1930 H, 1931 N, 1973 Q.)

1973

A. BACTERIAL PHYSIOLOGY: *Chemotaxis / Chemoreceptors*
Julius Adler, Gerald L. Hazelbauer, and M. M. Dahl study the chemotaxis of *Escherichia coli* toward sugars. They identify a galactose-binding protein as the chemoreceptor for galactose and enzyme II of the phosphotransferase system as the receptor for several other sugars. (See 1966 B, 1967 D, 1969 C, 1972 B, 1972 C, 1974 B.)

B. BACTERIAL PHYSIOLOGY: *Lectins / Binding of Rhizobia to Plant Roots*
J. Hamblin and S. P. Kent find that phytohemagglutinin, a plant lectin that agglutinates red blood cells, can bind *Rhizobium phaseoli* to the roots of the bean plant *Phaseolus vulgaris*. In the next year, B. B. Bohlool and E. L. Schmidt report that lectin accounts for the specificity of *Rhizobium japonicum* for soybean plants.

C. BACTERIAL PHYSIOLOGY: *Rhizobium Symbiosis with a Nonlegume*
M. J. Trinick discovers bacteroids and rhizobia on the roots of the nonlegume *Trema aspera* (reclassified as *Parasponia rugosa*). He confirms nitrogen fixation with positive acetylene reduction tests of nodulated whole plants and detached nodules, but not with roots lacking nodules. This is the first report of a rhizobium effectively nodulating a nonlegume.

D. BACTERIAL PHYSIOLOGY: *TOL Plasmids*
Teruko Nakazawa and Takeshi Yokata and, separately, Peter A. Williams and Keith Murray report that the enzymes in *Pseudomonas putida* for the dissimilation of benzoate and methyl benzoates, or toluates, are carried on a transmissible plasmid. Williams and Murray refer to the plasmid as a "TOL plasmid." (See 1972 E, 1980 G.)

E. BACTERIAL GENETICS: *Electrophoretic Analysis of Enzymes*
Roger Milkman employs electrophoresis of extracts of *Escherichia coli* isolated from fecal specimens from various sources to estimate the genetic diversity in natural populations. His method reveals one prominent mobility class of polypeptides among several different catabolic enzymes. Milkman concludes that the neutral hypothesis of structural gene variation is incorrect and that his data support a selectionist hypothesis. (See 1980 F.)

F. BACTERIAL DISEASE: Campylobacter
Studying vibrios isolated from stool specimens, J. P. Butzler and coworkers conclude that *Campylobacter fetus* subsp. *jejuni* is an important pathogen for humans. (See 1919 C, 1963 A, 1980 I.)

G. MOLECULAR VIROLOGY: *Bacteriophage Mu*
Ellen Daniell, Ming-Ta Hsu, and others working with Norman Davidson report finding an unpaired region that forms a loop, called the G loop, in

the DNA of bacteriophage Mu. This heteroduplex structure contains about 3,000 base pairs, with 34-base-pair inverted repeats at the ends that permit the inversion of the G segment.

H. MOLECULAR VIROLOGY: *Transcriptional Map of the SV40 Genome*
George Khoury and Malcolm Martin, collaborating with a group led by Daniel Nathans, develop a transcriptional map of the simian virus 40 (SV40) genome. They find that early transcription of messenger RNA, before DNA replication, takes place on the minus strand of DNA, while late transcription is primarily from the plus strand. The pattern of transcription in cells transformed by SV40 is significantly different from that seen in lytic infection. (See 1973 I.)

I. MOLECULAR VIROLOGY: *Cleavage Map of the SV40 Genome*
Kathleen J. Danna, George H. Sack, Jr., and Daniel Nathans construct a physical map of the SV40 genome through the use of bacterial restriction endonucleases from *Haemophilus influenzae* and *Haemophilus parainfluenzae*. The map is constructed by matching overlapping segments of fragments created by the restriction enzymes. (See 1973 H.)

J. MOLECULAR VIROLOGY: *Conversion of the SV40 Genome*
Stuart P. Adler and Daniel Nathans use restriction endonucleases from several strains of *Escherichia coli* to convert the covalently closed circular SV40 DNA into a predominantly linear molecule with intact single strands. The linear molecules are converted to circular duplexes after they are denatured and permitted to renature. (See 1973 H, 1973 I.)

K. VIRAL DISEASE: *Pandemic Influenza Virus*
W. George Laver and Robert G. Webster discuss the evidence that duck and equine influenza viruses may be progenitors of the Hong Kong strain of human influenza. They find that hemagglutinin subunits from both equine and duck viruses cross-react with the Hong Kong virus in both hemagglutination-inhibition and immunodiffusion tests. Peptide maps of the heavy polypeptide chains of the hemagglutinins from the three viruses are quite different, but maps of the light chains are almost identical. The authors suggest that the three viruses may have developed from a common ancestor. (See 1968 G, 1980 O.)

L. VIRAL DISEASE: *Hepatitis A Virus*
Stephen M. Feinstone, Albert Z. Kapikian, and Robert H. Purcell use immune electron microscopy to visualize a 27-nanometer particle in the blood of every patient examined who is immunologically specific for hepatitis A disease.

M. IMMUNOLOGY: *T Cells*
R. M. Zinkernagel and P. C. Doherty perform the first experiments that directly demonstrate specifically sensitized lymphocytes in a virus-induced inflammatory extract. They grow L cells in the presence of lymphocytic choriomeningitis (LCM) virus and then expose them to cells from cerebrospinal fluid, blood, and spleen. They show the presence of cytotoxic

thymus-derived lymphocytes, referred to as T cells, which are cytotoxic against L cells infected with LCM virus but not against normal cells or cells infected with ectromelia virus. Zinkernagel and Doherty receive the Nobel Prize in physiology or medicine in 1996. (See 1968 H, 1970 J, 1970 K, 1974 M.)

N. MOLECULAR BIOLOGY: *Gene Cloning*
Stanley N. Cohen, Annie C. Y. Chang, Herbert W. Boyer, and Robert B. Helling use type II restriction endonucleases to generate fragments of DNA from two different sources. They create a hybrid plasmid that is introduced into cells of *Escherichia coli* by a transformation procedure. The cloned genes are shown to be functional and to possess genetic properties and nucleotide base sequences from both parental DNA molecules. This technique becomes known as gene cloning. (See 1972, 1972 M, 1973 O, 1975 O.)

O. MOLECULAR BIOLOGY: *Potential Hazards of Genetic Engineering*
Concerns about the potential biological hazards associated with the creation of hybrid DNA molecules lead researchers to request that federal guidelines be established for the conduct of such research. In 1973, on behalf of the attendees at a conference on nucleic acids, Maxine Singer and Dieter Söll write a letter to the National Academy of Sciences and the National Institute of Medicine. The letter, which appears in the journal *Science,* asks that a committee be established to consider this issue. In 1974, a group that identifies itself as the Committee on Recombinant DNA Molecules of the National Academy of Sciences, with Paul Berg as chairman, publishes in the journals *Nature, Science,* and the *Proceedings of the National Academy of Sciences* a request for voluntary deferment of certain types of experiments with recombinant DNA. They ask the director of the National Institutes of Health to establish an advisory committee, and they call for an international meeting to make recommendations for the regulation of experiments. In 1975, a meeting is convened at the Asilomar Conference Center in California to consider the problems of recombinant DNA research. (See 1972 L, 1972 M, 1973 N, 1975 O.)

P. SOCIETY AND POLITICS
The United States withdraws its armed forces from Vietnam.

Q. THE ARTS: *Architecture*
The Sears Tower in Chicago, at a height of 443 meters, becomes the world's tallest building. In 1997, the pinnacles of the Petronas Twin Towers in Kuala Lumpur, Malaysia, reach a height of 452 meters, but the highest usable floor is below the height of the Sears Tower. (See 1889 K, 1913 I, 1930 H, 1931 N, 1972 P.)

R. THE ARTS: *Literature*
Thomas Pynchon writes *Gravity's Rainbow.*

1974

A. BACTERIAL PHYSIOLOGY: Anabaena–Azolla *Symbiosis*
Using the acetylene reduction test, G. A. Peters and B. C. Mayne provide direct proof that the cyanobacterium *Anabaena azollae* fixes nitrogen in its

association with the aquatic fern *Azolla.* The bacteria inhabit the cavities of the aerial leaf lobe of *Azolla,* which grows in rice paddies. Upon death of the fern, nitrogen fixed by *A. azollae* is released and assimilated by the rice plants.

B. BACTERIAL PHYSIOLOGY: *Chemotaxis*
Michael Silverman and Melvin Simon and, separately, Steven H. Larsen, Julius Adler, and colleagues describe experiments that demonstrate the functioning of flagella in *Escherichia coli.* The experiments are performed with a mutant of the bacterium that cannot synthesize a flagellar filament but does produce hook and basal structures to form a "poly-hook" that is 1 to 2 micrometers in length. Antibody prepared against the poly-hook attaches or tethers the poly-hook to a glass slide where the rotation of the cell may be observed microscopically. The researchers conclude that chemical attractants cause counterclockwise rotation and repellents cause clockwise rotation. Clockwise rotation is absent in nonchemotactic mutants but present in cells that tumble. (See 1972 B, 1972 C.)

C. BACTERIAL PHYSIOLOGY: *Energy for Flagellar Movement*
Steven H. Larsen, Julius Adler, J. Jay Gargus, and Robert W. Hogg use a chemical inhibitor that uncouples oxidative phosphorylation, showing that motility ceases even when ATP is present. They also show that motility continues even when arsenic is used to inhibit ATP synthesis. They state that the source of energy for motility and chemotaxis is an intermediate in oxidative phosphorylation, not ATP directly. In a 1975 review article, Adler refers to the proton gradient described by Peter Mitchell in 1965. (See 1977 G.)

D. BACTERIAL PHYSIOLOGY: *Spore Formation*
J. Mandlestam and Sonia A. Higgs obtain synchronous replication in cultures of *Bacillus subtilis* temperature-sensitive mutants growing in a rich medium. Transfer of cells to a poor medium induces sporulation. They find that the capacity for sporulation peaks about 15 minutes after chromosome replication begins and then declines rapidly, but is restored by starting a new round of DNA replication. Their results indicate that the vegetative cell has a small window of time to commit to sporulation or to continue to divide until the next opportunity for spore formation is available.

E. BACTERIAL PHYSIOLOGY: *SOS Response to DNA Damage*
Miroslav Radman presents a hypothesis for an inducible system in *Escherichia coli* that repairs DNA damaged by ultraviolet light or other causes. His ideas were formulated a few years earlier and served as the basis for experiments that support his proposed scheme, which he calls "SOS" (the international distress signal), for the dark repair processes that result in the creation of mutants.

F. BACTERIAL PHYSIOLOGY: *Coenzyme M*
Craig D. Taylor and Ralph S. Wolfe continue studies, begun by Wolfe in 1971, on the methyl transfer coenzyme, coenzyme M, in several species of *Methanobacterium.* They report the purification, structural identification,

and chemical synthesis of three biologically active forms of the coenzyme and study its role in the formation of methane from CH_3-B_{12} by two enzymes, methyltransferase and methylreductase. (See 1971 C.)

G. BACTERIAL PHYSIOLOGY: *Ice Nucleation*
Leroy R. Maki and colleagues discover that broth suspensions of *Pseudomonas syringae* isolated from decaying alder leaves freeze at temperatures of -1.8 to $-3.8°C$, relatively warm compared with normal freezing temperatures. They believe that the formation of ice nuclei by the intact cells is responsible for causing freezing at relatively warm temperatures and comment that this bacterium may play a role in the production of ice nuclei in nature. (See 1976 C, 1985 C, 1986 C, 1986 F.)

H. BACTERIAL GENETICS: *Transposons*
R. W. Hedges and A. E. Jacob find that all plasmids transferring ampicillin resistance to other replicons show the same approximate increase in size. Concluding that the same sequence carrying the gene for ampicillin resistance must be inserted in each instance, they realize that these movable elements have a relationship to the insertion sequences (IS elements) defined earlier by Elke Jordan and James A. Shapiro. They designate those having the potential for transposition as "transposons." Later research confirms that IS elements are located at each end of such transposable genes. (See 1950 J, 1960 G, 1968 C.)

I. BACTERIAL DISEASE: *Virulence Plasmids*
Studying the transmissible plasmids of invasive strains of *Escherichia coli*, H. Williams Smith finds one plasmid that readily transfers to other strains of *E. coli* and to *Salmonella typhi*, *Salmonella typhimurium*, and *Shigella sonei*. Culture filtrates of disrupted cells carrying this plasmid, called Vir^+ strains, are toxic to chickens, mice, and rabbits. A second plasmid that appears to be identical to the colicin V plasmid is not associated with toxic activity but provides greater resistance to host defense mechanisms.

J. BACTERIAL DISEASE: *Staphylococcal Alpha-Toxin*
Paul Cassidy, Howard R. Six, and Sidney Harshman demonstrate that the alpha-toxin of *Staphylococcus aureus* disrupts artificial lipid spherules (liposomes) containing extracted lipid from erythrocytes or egg or beef lecithin. At low concentrations of toxin, glucose or glucose and hexokinase are released from the spherules, while at higher concentrations macromolecular markers are released. (See 1966 J, 1981 G, 1987 D.)

K. VIRAL DISEASE: *Non-A, Non-B Hepatitis*
In 1974 and 1975, reports from a number of investigators establish that a type of posttransfusion-associated hepatitis has no serological markers for either hepatitis A and hepatitis B virus. New terminology refers to these infections as non-A, non-B hepatitis, or NANBH. Hepatitis viruses C and E are subsequently discovered. (See 1980 P, 1989 E, 1990 G.)

L. IMMUNOLOGY: *Idiotype Networks*
Niels K. Jerne proposes the idiotype network theory, suggesting that the immune response is determined by interactions between specific idiotypes

1974 *(continued)*

on antibodies, by their counterpart anti–idiotypes, and by higher levels of anti–idiotype synthesis. Jerne shares the 1984 Nobel Prize in physiology or medicine with Georges Köhler and César Milstein. (See 1963 S.)

M. IMMUNOLOGY: *Major Histocompatibility Complex Restriction of T–Cell Toxicity*

R. M. Zinkernagel and P. C. Doherty present evidence that interaction of cytotoxic T cells with somatic cells budding the lymphocytic chorio-meningitis virus is restricted by the proteins of the major histocompatibility complex (MHC). Their experiments demonstrate that cytotoxic T cells from a virus-infected animal will kill cultured cells infected with the same virus only if both the T cells and the cultured cells express the same class of MHC proteins. (See 1973 M.)

N. MOLECULAR BIOLOGY: *Replication of Eucaryotic DNA in* Escherichia coli

Using a bacterial plasmid, pSC101, John F. Morrow and colleagues clone ribosomal RNA genes from *Xenopus laevis* into *Escherichia coli*. The plasmid, which contains both eucaryotic and procaryotic DNA, replicates in the bacterial cells. (See 1982 Q.)

O. MOLECULAR BIOLOGY: *Attenuation of Protein Synthesis*

Takashi Kasai uses the term "attenuator region" to explain the expression of the histidine operon in *Escherichia coli*. He finds that extensive deletions in the operon between the operator and the first cistron cause a two- to four-fold increase in transcription of the remaining genes. He suggests that the histidine operon is controlled by a process in which charged histidine-transfer RNA (histidine attached to its transfer RNA) recognizes an operon-specific control site, thus regulating the binding of a positive control factor to the promoter region. (See 1959 N, 1963 V, 1964 K, 1977 P.)

P. MOLECULAR BIOLOGY: *Col Factor as Cloning Vehicle*

Vickers Hershfield and colleagues use the colicinogenic factor E1 (ColE1) that exists in multiple copies in *Escherichia coli* to construct a cloning vehicle. They successfully transform *E. coli* with a plasmid formed by combining the Col factor with DNA fragments from bacteriophage carrying a tryptophane gene and a kanamycin resistance gene. (See 1973 N, 1977 Q, 1978 I.)

Q. MOLECULAR BIOLOGY: *Packaging DNA in Lambda*

Barbara Hohn and Thomas Hohn show that DNA can be packaged into DNA-free heads of bacteriophage lambda, making it feasible to use phage lambda to introduce foreign DNA into *Escherichia coli*. (See 1978 I.)

R. MOLECULAR BIOLOGY: *Structure of Chromatin*

In summarizing his studies of the structure of chromatin by X-ray diffraction analysis, Roger D. Kornberg reports that the structure is based on a repeating unit made up of two each of the four main types of histone associated with about 200 base pairs of DNA. The chromatin fibers are usually coiled or folded into a flexible, jointed chain. Upon treatment with certain nucleases, this chain is broken into separate beadlike structures called nucleosomes.

S. MEDICINE: *Computed Axial Tomography*
Computed axial tomography (CAT) scanning begins to be used for both whole-body scans and brain scans.

T. SOCIETY AND POLITICS
• Richard M. Nixon resigns as president of the United States. Vice President Gerald Ford becomes president; one month later he grants Nixon a full pardon for any federal crimes he committed or may have committed.
• Newspaper reporters Bob Woodward and Carl Bernstein publish *All the President's Men,* their account of the Watergate affair.

U. THE ARTS: *Literature*
Aleksandr Solzhenitsyn publishes *The Gulag Archipelago.*

1975

A. BACTERIAL TAXONOMY: *Identifying* **Staphylococcus** *Isolates*
Wesley E. Kloos and Karl H. Schleifer select 13 key characteristics to construct a simplified scheme for identifying staphylococci isolated from clinical specimens. Their scheme is a modified dichotomous key with 11 positions, into which they place 80% of the recognized species.

B. BACTERIAL ECOLOGY: *Direct Counts of Bacteria in Natural Waters*
Ralph J. Daley and John E. Hobbie modify a procedure, first used in 1973 by D. E. Francisco, R. A. Mah, and A. C. Rabin, for direct microscopic counts of bacteria in natural waters. The bacteria are stained with acridine orange, filtered onto a membrane, and counted microscopically with epifluorescent illumination. The modifications of the procedure, called the acridine orange direct count (AODC), include methods of preservation, types of filter membranes, and light filters.

C. BACTERIAL PHYSIOLOGY: *Magnetotactic Bacteria*
Richard Blakemore isolates bacteria from surface sediments collected from salt marshes in Cape Cod, Massachusetts, as well as from sedimentary cores from a depth of 15 meters in Buzzards Bay, Massachusetts. He finds that these motile organisms orient themselves in a magnetic field. (See 1978 E, 1979 B, 1981 A, 1988 H.)

D. BACTERIAL STRUCTURE: Halococcus *Cell Wall*
Josef Steber and Karl Heinz Schleifer report that *Halococcus morrhuae* contains no peptidoglycan in its cell wall but instead has a complex sulfated heteropolysaccharide. (See 1961 B, 1963 C, 1965 D, 1977 C, 1977 D.)

E. BACTERIAL PHYSIOLOGY: *Nitrogenase in Rhizobia*
Paul E. Bishop and colleagues report immunodiffusion tests that demonstrate the presence of the protein component of nitrogenase in cell-free extracts of *Rhizobium japonicum.* They are unable to find enzyme activity of either the molybdenum-iron or the iron protein components of the nitrogenase, but their experiments suggest that it is the bacterium, not the plant, that produces the enzyme.

1975 (continued)

F. BACTERIAL PHYSIOLOGY: *Alarmones*

John C. Stephens, Stanley W. Artz, and Bruce N. Ames find that the expression of the histidine operon in *Salmonella typhimurium* depends on the addition of guanosine 5'-diphosphate-3'-diphosphate, or ppGpp. They propose that ppGpp is an "alarmone," a general signal functioning to regulate RNA synthesis in periods of amino acid starvation. (See 1961 F, 1970 F.)

G. BACTERIAL PHYSIOLOGY: *Heat Shock Proteins*

Stephen Cooper and Therese Ruettinger isolate a temperature-sensitive mutant of *Escherichia coli* that does not synthesize a major protein at 42°C, in contrast to the parental strain and mutant strains in which nonsense suppressors of the normal allele are inserted. This is the first observation of a mutation having a pleiotropic defect, resulting in an inability to synthesize an entire set of proteins after a shift to a higher temperature. First called high temperature production proteins, they are now known as "heat shock proteins" or "heat stress proteins." (See 1978 C.)

H. BACTERIAL GENETICS: *Gene Transfer in* Rhodopseudomonas

Marc Solioz, Huei-Che Yen, and Barry Marrs report an unusual gene transfer agent in *Rhodopseudomonas capsulata* that has similarities to generalized transducing bacteriophage but without evidence of phage particles or viral activities. In further studies they obtain electron microscope photographs of small phagelike icosahedral particles with short tails. Since no phage activity is noted, the particles are referred to as "prephage." (See 1952 K, 1956 H.)

I. BACTERIAL GENETICS: *Colony Hybridization*

Michael Grunstein and David S. Hogness develop a method for screening colonies of *Escherichia coli* carrying different hybrid plasmids to find which plasmids contain a specific DNA sequence. The procedure involves forming colonies on nitrocellulose filters, lysing the bacteria in the colonies, denaturing the DNA in situ, and fixing the DNA to the filters. They hybridize radioactive RNA that defines the gene sequence of interest to the DNA on the filters and assay by autoradiography. (See 1985 D.)

J. BACTERIAL DISEASE: *Plasmid-Controlled Colonization Factor*

After studying the properties of an enterotoxigenic strain of *Escherichia coli* that colonizes the intestines of infant rabbits, Dolores G. Evans and colleagues find that this particular strain possesses specific surface antigens that promote colonization. Loss of a particular plasmid is associated with both the loss of the surface antigen and its piluslike surface structures. The researchers conclude that the plasmid controls this colonization virulence factor.

K. BACTERIAL DISEASE: *Tumor Necrosis Factor*

E. A. Carswell and colleagues find that the serum of mice infected with bacillus Calmette-Guérin (*Mycobacterium bovis* BCG) that has been treated with endotoxin contains a substance that they call tumor necrosis factor

(TNF). TNF causes necrosis of transplanted tumors in much the same way that the endotoxin does. They suggest that the TNF mediates tumor necrosis caused by endotoxin. (See 1990 I.)

L. BACTERIAL DISEASE: *Crown Gall*

In 1974 and 1975, two groups of researchers prove that the virulence of *Agrobacterium tumefaciens* requires a plasmid, later called the Ti plasmid, in the crown gall disease of plants. One group includes I. Zaenen and Van Larabeke working with Jeff Schell, and the other is composed of Bruce Watson and colleagues in Eugene W. Nester's laboratory. They show that the loss of the plasmid results in both the loss of the ability to induce crown gall and the loss of the capacity to utilize the arginine derivatives octopine and nopaline. In 1976, Gerrit Bomhoff and colleagues show that the synthesis of octopine and nopaline is controlled by plasmid genes. (See 1907 D, 1947 B, 1970 G, 1977 O.)

M. VIRAL DISEASE: *Cytomegalovirus*

In a study of renal transplant patients, Monto Ho and colleagues report a significant correlation between the development of cytomegalovirus infection and positive serology for the presence of cytomegalovirus in the donor.

N. IMMUNOLOGY: *Hybridomas/Monoclonal Antibodies*

Georges Köhler and César Milstein produce an antibody of predefined specificity when they grow a hybrid in cell culture created by fusing a B-cell myeloma cell with a plasma cell from an animal immunized with a particular antigen. The "hybridoma" produces antibody that is active only against the target antigen. Köhler and Milstein share the 1984 Nobel Prize in physiology or medicine with Niels K. Jerne.

O. MOLECULAR BIOLOGY: *Asilomar Conference on Genetic Engineering*

Following requests by scientists studying recombinant DNA molecules, a conference convened at the Asilomar Conference Center in California leads to the establishment of guidelines for carrying out experiments with recombinant DNA (genetic engineering). In 1976, the National Institutes of Health issues a set of guidelines, which have been revised several times. (See 1973 O.)

P. MOLECULAR BIOLOGY: *Bidirectional DNA Replication*

Elizabeth B. Gyurasits and R. G. Wake report that experiments with radioactive labeling of the chromosome in germinating spores of *Bacillus subtilis* prove that replication of the DNA is bidirectional. This is contrary to earlier concepts that DNA elongation was in one direction only. (See 1963 E, 1968 I.)

Q. MOLECULAR BIOLOGY: *Synthesis of Transfer RNA*

Sidney Altman reports that the biosynthesis of transfer RNA (tRNA) in *Escherichia coli* involves the transcription of the tRNA gene into a large molecule that is subsequently processed first by endonucleolytic cleavage and then by exonucleolytic cleavage. Further modifications are conversion of uracil to pseudouridine, guanine to 2-methylguanine, and adenine to isopentenyl adenine.

1975 *(continued)*

R. MOLECULAR BIOLOGY: *Messenger RNA Capping*

Cha Mer Wei and Bernard Moss, studying vaccinia virus, and, independently, Y. Furuichi, M. Morgan, S. Muthukrishnan, and Aaron J. Shatkin, working with reovirus, discover the process known as capping of messenger RNA (mRNA) when they find that the 5′ terminus of mRNA is "capped" with 7-methylguanosine. A capping enzyme, guanyl transferase, is found later. Capping is thought to promote binding of the messenger to ribosomes.

S. MOLECULAR BIOLOGY: *Southern Blot*

E. M. Southern describes a method for transferring fragments of DNA from agarose gels to cellulose acetate filters. The adsorbed DNA is then hybridized to radioactive RNA, and the hybrid molecules are detected by radioautography or fluorography. Southern analyzes fragments of DNA obtained by treatment with restriction enzymes. This widely used technique becomes known as the Southern blot procedure.

T. SCIENTIFIC PUBLICATIONS

• The *Journal of Clinical Microbiology* begins publication by the American Society for Microbiology.

• E. O. Wilson publishes *Sociobiology: the New Synthesis,* a detailed compilation and analysis of social behavior in various animals. The controversial last chapter extols the role of natural selection in human behavior.

U. SOCIETY AND POLITICS

• The Vietnam War ends when North Vietnam captures the city of Saigon.

• After a 5-year war, the Khmer Rouge takes control of the government of Cambodia and begins killing political enemies, professionals and intellectuals, and peasants.

1976

A. BACTERIAL TAXONOMY: *Use of RNA Sequencing*

After modifying the Sanger two-dimensional electrophoretic procedure, Carl Woese and coworkers successfully determine the sequence of digests of large RNA molecules 1,500 to 3,000 nucleotides in size. They also use ribonuclease T_1 to digest 16S ribosomal RNA from three related bacteria: *Bacillus pumilus, Bacillus subtilis,* and *Bacillus stearothermophilus.* Discussing the phylogenetic relatedness of the two mesophiles, Woese et al. report that the mesophiles and the thermophile have no significant differences in the primary structure of their 16S ribosomal RNA. (See 1965 R, 1977 A, 1986 A, 1990 A.)

B. BACTERIAL ECOLOGY: *Habitat of* Vibrio fischeri

E. G. Ruby and Kenneth H. Nealson report that *Photobacterium fischeri* (*Vibrio fischeri*) is found at densities of nearly 10^{10} per milliliter of the light organ fluid of a Japanese pinecone fish, *Monocentris japonica.* (See 1970 C.)

C. BACTERIAL PHYSIOLOGY: *Ice Nucleation by* Pseudomonas

When sprayed on plant leaves, corn leaf powder causes an increase in frost damage. D. C. Arny, Steven E. Lindow, and C. D. Upper isolate *Pseudomo-*

nas syringae from extracts of corn leaf powder and report an increase in frost damage when the bacterium is sprayed on leaves. They suggest that the bacteria, which cause ice nucleation, prevent the plants from reaching their normal supercooling point at which they experience frost damage. (See 1974 G, 1985 C, 1986 C, 1986 F.)

D. BACTERIAL PHYSIOLOGY: *Porins*
Taiji Nakae isolates protein aggregates from insoluble material left after *Escherichia coli* is treated with sodium dodecyl sulfate. He finds a single type of protein with a molecular weight of 36,500 that forms oligoprotein aggregates that produce diffusion channels. Nakae proposes the name "porins" for these proteins.

E. BACTERIAL GENETICS: *Sporulation Mutants*
James A. Hoch isolates mutants of *Bacillus subtilis* that are blocked at the stage 0 initiation step of sporulation. Such mutant genes are designated *spo0*. Others, which are later given such designations as *spo0A* and *spo0F,* encode proteins necessary for signal transduction and other functions necessary for transcription. (See 1960 E, 1985 A.)

F. BACTERIAL GENETICS: *Detection of Plasmid DNA*
Jane Aldrich Meyers, David Sanchez, Lynn P. Elwell, and Stanley Falkow describe a method that does not require radioisotope labeling or ultracentrifugation for the detection and characterization of plasmid DNA. They describe the detection of plasmids with molecular weights ranging from 0.6 $\times$ 10^6 to 95 $\times$ 10^6 by the use of agarose gels. (See 1981 C.)

G. BACTERIAL DISEASE: *Legionnaires' Disease*
An outbreak of a pneumonia-like disease at a convention of the American Legion in Philadelphia results in 29 deaths out of 182 cases. The source of the causative agent is not found, but epidemiologic analysis suggests that those affected contracted the disease in the lobby or in the immediate vicinity of the hotel. There is no apparent airborne or person-to-person transmission. Because the patients are nearly all attending the American Legion convention, the disease is called "Legionnaires' disease." (See 1977 L, 1978 F, 1979 H, 1980 H, 1986 I.)

H. VIRAL DISEASE: *Ebola Virus*
A highly virulent infection caused by a newly recognized virus causes hundreds of deaths in northern Zaire and southern Sudan. The virus is named Ebola virus, after a small river near the town of Yambuku in northern Zaire, where the first cases are recognized. The virus reappears in Sudan in 1979 and in Zaire in 1995. Ebola virus and Marburg virus, both filoviruses, are the only recognized filamentous viruses that infect mammals. (See 1967 M, 1969 D.)

I. VIRAL DISEASE: *Swine Flu Virus/Guillain-Barré Syndrome*
The Center for Disease Control, in an attempt to prevent an epidemic of swine influenza, recommends the manufacture and distribution of millions of doses of a specific vaccine. The epidemic fails to materialize, but the vac-

1976 *(continued)*

cine causes about 500 cases of Guillain-Barré syndrome, a type of acute febrile polyneuritis.

J. VIROID DISEASE: *Fruit Plant Infections*
Examining the viroids isolated from cucumber pale fruit disease and citrus excortis disease, Heinz L. Sänger and colleagues report that the viroids contain single-stranded, covalently closed circular RNA molecules with a high degree of self-complementarity and base pairing. In electron microscopy, they appear as collapsed circles and can be mistaken for double-stranded molecules. This is the first report of single-stranded, closed circular RNA in nature. Similar molecules are found in virions of poliovirus and encephalomyocarditis virus. (See 1971 E, 1978 L, 1981 L.)

K. IMMUNOLOGY: *Somatic Rearrangement of Immunoglobulin Genes*
Nobumichi Hozumi and Susumu Tonegawa present evidence that the genes for the variable and constant regions of immunoglobulins are joined during differentiation of B lymphocytes. Tonegawa, whose research provides details of the mechanism by which the lymphocytes produce a wide range of different antibodies, is awarded the 1987 Nobel Prize in physiology or medicine.

L. MOLECULAR BIOLOGY: *Oncogenes*
Dominique Stehelin, J. Michael Bishop, Harold E. Varmus, and Peter K. Vogt discover a gene in chickens that causes the Rous sarcoma, a malignant transformation of cells. This oncogene, the *src* gene, is found to be related to a gene found in normal chicken cells. Bishop and Varmus share the 1989 Nobel Prize in physiology or medicine for their role in this discovery.

M. SCIENTIFIC PUBLICATIONS
The journal *Applied Microbiology* is renamed *Applied and Environmental Microbiology*.

N. TECHNOLOGY
Computerized word processors begin to be used in offices. Early versions depend on a central computer.

O. THE ARTS: *Literature*
Alex Haley completes his novel *Roots*.

1977

A. BACTERIAL TAXONOMY: Archaebacteria
Based on homologies of 16S ribosomal RNA (rRNA) sequences, Carl R. Woese and George E. Fox redefine the classification of bacteria. They perform comparative cataloging of the 16S rRNA molecules by digesting them with ribonuclease T1, followed by sequence analysis of the fragments. They propose two domains, procaryotic and eucaryotic, with the procaryotic domain consisting of three urkingdoms: *Eubacteria,* for those with murein cell walls; *Archaebacteria,* for those lacking murein in their cell walls; and urcaryotes. The latter are represented by the 18S rRNA containing eucaryotic cytoplasmic organelles, namely, chloroplasts and possibly mitochondria. The *Eubacteria* include the commonly recognized bacteria, the cyanobac-

teria, and many of the mycoplasmas. At this time, the *Archaebacteria* include only the methanobacteria. (See 1976 A, 1986 A, 1990 A.)

B. BACTERIAL ECOLOGY: *Hydrothermal Vent Communities*
Robert D. Ballard and a group of investigators from several scientific institutions find clusters of mussels, clams, and vestimentiferan tubeworms of unusually large size living adjacent to hydrothermal vents of the Galápagos rift in the Pacific Ocean, 640 kilometers west of Ecuador. The researchers make dives as deep as 2,700 meters in the submersible *Alvin* to collect water samples, which are found to contain hydrogen sulfide. They assume the existence of a food chain based on sulfur-oxidizing bacteria. (See 1979 A, 1984 B.)

C. BACTERIAL STRUCTURE: Methanosarcina *Cell Walls*
Otto Kandler and Hans Hippe report that the cell wall of *Methanosarcina barkeri* lacks the components of peptidoglycan: muramic acid, glucosamine, D-glutamate, and other amino acids typical of bacterial cell walls. They find that the cell wall contains galactosamine, neutral sugars, and uronic acids and state that the material is an acid heteropolysaccharide. (See 1961 B, 1963 C, 1965 D, 1975 D, 1977 D.)

D. BACTERIAL STRUCTURE: Thermoplasma
Thomas A. Langworthy isolates C_{40} isopranol-containing glycerol ethers from *Thermoplasma acidophilum*. He finds these compounds to be fully saturated diglycerol tetraethers, in which two glycerol residues are bridged through ether linkages with two isoprenoid branched diols. (See 1961 D, 1963 C, 1965 D, 1975 D, 1977 C.)

E. BACTERIAL STRUCTURE: *Periplasm*
Jeffrey B. Stock, Barbara Rauch, and Saul Roseman estimate that the periplasm, or periplasmic space, in *Escherichia coli* and *Salmonella typhimurium* constitutes 20 to 40% of the total cell volume. Some later investigators dispute this measurement as being too small, while others consider it to be too large. (See 1961 C, 1984 C, 1990 C.)

F. BACTERIAL PHYSIOLOGY: *Cultivation of Chlamydiae*
Torvald K. Ripa and Per-Anders Mårdh improve the use of McCoy cells for cultivating chlamydiae, by adding cycloheximide to the culture medium at concentrations that depress but do not inhibit metabolism. (See 1957 G, 1963 I.)

G. BACTERIAL PHYSIOLOGY: *Energy for Flagella Movement*
M. D. Manson and colleagues use a motile strain of streptococci to show that the rotation of flagella is powered by either a transmembrane potential or a transmembrane pH gradient. They state that the proton is the only external cation required for flagella movement. (See 1974 C.)

H. BACTERIAL PHYSIOLOGY: *Chemotaxis*
Martin S. Springer, Michael F. Goy, and Julius Adler show that *Escherichia coli* must have L-methionine to respond to chemical attractants but not for maintenance of the chemotactic response. They suggest that methionine

1977 *(continued)*

donates methyl groups to a membrane protein, permitting the chemotactic response. (See 1973 A.)

I. BACTERIAL PHYSIOLOGY: *Chemotrophic Anaerobes*
Rudolf K. Thauer, Kurt Jungemann, and Karl Decker review all aspects of energy metabolism in chemotrophic anaerobic bacteria: ATP synthesis, substrate-level phosphorylation, energy conservation by electron transport phosphorylation, membrane transport, and the thermodynamic efficiency of ATP synthesis. They include two valuable tables: one detailing the free energy changes in dehydrogenation reactions, and the other presenting Gibbs free energy changes for the formation of compounds from their elements.

J. BACTERIAL PHYSIOLOGY: *Cofactor for Nitrogenase*
Vinod K. Shah and Winston Brill isolate the cofactor for the enzyme nitrogenase. Found to contain both iron and molybdenum, it is called "FeMoCo."

K. BACTERIAL PHYSIOLOGY: *Inhibition of β-Lactamase by Clavulanic Acid*
C. Reading and M. Cole report a β-lactamase inhibitor isolated from *Streptomyces clavuligerus*. The substance, which they name "clavulanic acid," inhibits the β-lactamases produced by several gram-negative species and by *Staphylococcus aureus*. By 1981, clavulanic acid is used clinically in combination with amoxicillin and other types of penicillin.

L. BACTERIAL DISEASE: *Legionnaires' Disease*
Joseph McDade, Charles C. Shepard, and others at the Center for Disease Control isolate a gram-negative, non-acid-fast bacillus from the lungs of several patients suffering from Legionnaires' disease. By employing yolk sac cultures of the bacterium as antigen in a fluorescent antibody procedure, they find that sera from many patients, as well as stored serum samples from previous epidemics, show increased antibody titer. They conclude that the disease is caused by this bacterium, named *Legionella pneumophila* in 1979 by Don J. Brenner and colleagues. (See 1976 G, 1978 F, 1979 H, 1980 H, 1986 I.)

M. BACTERIAL DISEASE: *Lyme Disease*
Alan C. Steere recognizes a nonfatal disease causing progressive neuromuscular disease in humans in the vicinity of Lyme, Connecticut. The disease, called Lyme disease, is subsequently reported in northeastern, midwestern, and western states. In 1978, both Steere and his colleagues and R. C. Wallis and coworkers prove that the tick *Ixodes dammini,* a parasite of the white-footed field mouse and deer, is the vector. (See 1982 J.)

N. BACTERIAL DISEASE: Escherichia coli *Cytotoxin*
J. Konowalchuk, J. I. Spiers, and S. Stavric describe strains of *Escherichia coli* that show cytotoxic activity against cultured Vero cells (a line of African green monkey kidney cells). They demonstrate that this toxin, which they call verotoxin, is distinct from the heat-labile enterotoxins of *E. coli*. (See 1979 I, 1982 I, 1983 E.)

O. BACTERIAL DISEASE: *Crown Gall*

Mary-Dell Chilton and colleagues in Eugene W. Nester's laboratory prove that Ti plasmid DNA from *Agrobacterium tumefaciens,* transferred into the plant tissue by the invading bacterium, causes the formation of the tumor in crown gall disease. They demonstrate the stable incorporation of plasmid DNA into the plant cells. (See 1907 D, 1947 B, 1870 G, 1974 L.)

P. MOLECULAR BIOLOGY: *Attenuation*

From about 1972 through 1977, in studies with *Escherichia coli,* Charles Yanofsky and colleagues in his laboratory obtain data clarifying the mechanism of attenuation in amino acid biosynthetic operons. They show that the leader regions of these operons contain a short peptide coding region that is rich in codons for the amino acid being synthesized. The research provides convincing evidence that specific transfer RNAs and translation are involved in transcription regulation, in which the ribosome binds to the translation initiation site for the leader peptide. (See 1959 N, 1963 V, 1964 K, 1974 O.)

Q. MOLECULAR BIOLOGY: *Cloning Vehicle/pBR322*

Francisco Bolivar and coworkers construct a new cloning vehicle, a plasmid they name pBR322, that carries resistance genes to ampicillin and tetracycline. Although it is derived from the ColE1 plasmid, it does not produce colicin. (See 1973 N, 1974 P, 1978 I.)

R. MOLECULAR BIOLOGY: *Hormone Synthesized in* **Escherichia coli**

A group led by Keiichi Itakura and Arthur D. Riggs, including Herbert W. Boyer, chemically synthesizes the gene for somatostatin, a mammalian hormone containing 14 amino acids. The gene is inserted into the plasmid pBR322, along with the gene for β-galactosidase, and introduced into *Escherichia coli* by transformation. The bacterium subsequently synthesizes somatostatin attached to the enzyme β-galactosidase, from which it is cleaved by chemical treatment. The first synthesis of a functional polypeptide product from a chemically synthesized gene, this process leads to a similar one for the synthesis of insulin. (See 1979 J.)

S. MOLECULAR BIOLOGY: *DNA Sequencing*

Allan M. Maxam and Walter Gilbert and, independently, Frederick Sanger, S. Nicklen, and A. R. Coulson develop new techniques for sequencing DNA molecules. Maxam and Gilbert use a chemical method that employs reagents that cleave DNA preferentially at each of the four nucleotides. The fragments of different lengths thus formed are resolved by electrophoresis into the different sizes of molecules. The Sanger group employs an enzymatic method with DNA polymerase, carrying out in vitro synthesis using the DNA to be sequenced as a template. Chain-terminating analogs of the normal deoxynucleoside triphosphates cause the cessation of synthesis at different points along the DNA chain. The Sanger method is now widely used for sequencing DNA. Gilbert, Sanger, and Paul Berg share the 1980 Nobel Prize in chemistry. Sanger, who was awarded the 1958 Nobel Prize in chemistry for his work on sequencing of proteins, is the first person to win two Nobel Prizes in this field. (See 1965 R.)

1977 *(continued)*

T. MOLECULAR BIOLOGY: *Sequencing of Phage DNA*

Frederick Sanger and colleagues determine the sequence of 5,375 base pairs of phage φX174, the first complete sequence of a phage genome. After the initiation and termination sites for the proteins and RNAs of nine known genes are identified, they find that two pairs of genes are coded by the same region of DNA using different reading frames. (See 1982 P.)

U. MOLECULAR BIOLOGY: *Avian Sarcoma Virus/Oncogene*

Joan Brugge and R. L. Erikson identify a 60,000-molecular-weight transformation-specific antigen in chicken cells transformed by avian sarcoma virus. They cannot, however, confirm that this antigen is a product of the *src* gene. (See 1976 L.)

V. MOLECULAR BIOLOGY: *Introns and Exons*

Studying globin genes in rabbits, Alec John Jeffreys and Richard Anthony Flavell find a 600-base-pair sequence within the gene that is noncoding. Phillip Leder finds a similar sequence in mouse globin genes. The noncoding sequences are called introns, or intervening sequences, while the sequences of coding DNA are referred to as exons. Introns are excised from the primary messenger RNA transcript before translation in protein synthesis.

W. MOLECULAR BIOLOGY: *Messenger RNA Splicing*

Two groups of researchers—one consisting of Susan M. Berget, Claire Moore, and Phillip A. Sharp, the other composed of Louise T. Chow, Richard E. Gelinas, Thomas R. Broker, and Richard J. Roberts—describe the splicing of transcribed sequences of RNA from different portions of the genome. In 1979, John Abelson describes how the entire split gene, both exons and introns, is transcribed to form a precursor molecule. The introns are removed by an RNA splicing enzyme in a complex called a "spliceosome," which contains small nuclear nucleic acids and proteins. The free ends of the exons are rejoined to form a functioning messenger RNA molecule. (See 1977 V.)

X. MOLECULAR BIOLOGY: *Structure of the Nucleosome*

John T. Finch and others working with Aaron Klug develop a technique referred to as crystallographic electron microscopy, with which they produce a low-resolution map of the structure of nucleosomes, the repeating units of chromatin. They describe the dimensions and shape of the nucleosome core and how it associates with DNA. Klug receives the 1982 Nobel Prize in chemistry for the development of this technique.

Y. BIOCHEMISTRY: *Oxidative Phosphorylation*

Celik Kaylar, Jan Rosing, and Paul D. Boyer report data that suggest two identical sites on the energy-transducing membrane of submitochondrial particles that function cooperatively during ATP synthesis or ATP hydrolysis. They propose a model in which the binding of ADP and inorganic phosphate at one site is necessary for the release of ATP from the second site. Hydrolysis of ATP is accomplished by a reversal of this sequence.

Z. MEDICINE: *Magnetic Resonance Imaging*
Magnetic resonance imaging (MRI) is tested. It is used in Britain by 1982 and approved by the U.S. Food and Drug Administration in 1984.

AA. TECHNOLOGY: *Optical Fibers*
Several companies begin testing optical fiber cables to carry voice transmissions.

BB. SOCIETY AND POLITICS
The U.S. Congress bans the manufacture of aerosol products that contain fluorocarbons because of the damage done to the atmospheric ozone layer.

1978

A. BACTERIAL PHYSIOLOGY: *Carboxydotrophic Bacteria*
In 1953, A. Kistner isolated an organism, *Hydrogenomonas carboxydovorans,* that utilizes carbon monoxide (CO). In 1976, S. Kirkconnell and George D. Hegeman isolated several strains of gram-negative bacteria using CO as the sole carbon source. They tentatively assigned their strains to the genera *Azotobacter* and *Azomonas*. In 1978, Ortwin Meyer and Hans Günter Schlegel isolate a bacterium that they believe is similar to the one that Kistner found. Assigning the name *Pseudomonas carboxydovorans,* they report that the enzymes for CO utilization are formed only during growth on CO. CO-utilizing bacteria, called "carboxydotrophic" bacteria, are thought to play a major role in maintaining relatively constant atmospheric CO levels.

B. BACTERIAL PHYSIOLOGY: *Protein Phosphorylation*
Jean Yin Wang and Daniel E. Koshland, the first to report protein kinase activity in bacteria, find at least four phosphorylated proteins in *Salmonella typhimurium* and recover serine and threonine phosphates from acid hydrolysates. They suggest that protein phosphorylation is a regulatory mechanism. (See 1979 F, 1987 A, 1988 E.)

C. BACTERIAL PHYSIOLOGY: *Heat Shock*
Two groups of researchers, Peggy Lemaux et al. and T. Yamamori et al., find that a transient increase in the rate of protein synthesis of some proteins in *Escherichia coli* occurs when they are shifted from a lower to a higher growth temperature. The new rates increase markedly after the shift but return to a steady-state level after a few minutes. The proteins involved in this response are known as "heat shock proteins," similar to proteins found in a wide variety of organisms, including humans. (See 1975 G.)

D. BACTERIAL PHYSIOLOGY: *Nitrogen Fixation/*Frankia
Dale Callaham, Peter Del Tredici, and John G. Torrey isolate an actinomycete from root nodules of the sweet fern plant, *Comptonia peregrina,* which is active in the acetylene reduction indicating nitrogen fixation. After they reinfect seedlings with the actinomycete, they reisolate the same organism. The plants grow well without an exogenous supply of nitrogen.

1978 *(continued)*

In 1970, J. H. Becking assigned the generic name *Frankia* to the endophytes of nonlegumes. (See 1885 F, 1887 C, 1902 D, 1954 D, 1970 B.)

E. BACTERIAL PHYSIOLOGY: *Magnetotactic Bacteria*

Richard Blakemore and A. J. Kalmijn prove that the cells of a magnetotactic bacterium contain intracellular iron grains, called magnetosomes, usually arranged in chains within the cell. The magnetosomes confer a permanent magnetic dipole moment to the cells, which is acted upon by the earth's magnetic field in the same way a compass needle is affected. In subsequent work, Blakemore and coworkers determine that the magnetosomes are composed of magnetic iron oxide, or magnetite, also known as lodestone. Subsequent studies by many investigators find that magnetotactic bacteria are widespread in nature and, in addition to the spirilla, have morphologies of vibroids, cocci, rods, and ovoid cells. (See 1975 C, 1979 B, 1981 A, 1988 H.)

F. BACTERIAL DISEASE: *Legionnaires' Disease*

A bacterium resembling *Legionella pneumophila,* the causative agent of Legionnaires' disease, is isolated from air conditioning vents in the hotel at which the 1976 outbreak occurred. (See 1976 G, 1977 L, 1979 H, 1980 H, 1986 I.)

G. BACTERIAL DISEASE: *Toxic Shock Syndrome*

James Todd and his colleagues report cases of seven children who exhibit "toxic shock syndrome." All of the patients have high fever, scarlitina rash, vomiting, diarrhea, desquamation of affected skin areas, and severe prolonged shock. *Staphylococcus aureus* is isolated from a variety of mucosal sites as well as from empyema and abscesses. The bacterium produces an exotoxin that is immunologically similar to the exfoliatin associated with staphylococcal phage group 1. (See 1980 L, 1982 K, 1983 H, 1984 J, 1985 E.)

H. VIRAL DISEASE: *Korean Hemorrhagic Fever/Hantavirus*

Ho Wang Lee, Pyung Woo Lee, and Karl M. Johnson identify a virus in the lungs of the striped field mouse, *Apodemus agrarius,* that causes Korean hemorrhagic fever. Using an indirect fluorescent antibody technique, they also find evidence of the virus in serum of human patients. In 1981, Lee and Lee, in collaboration with a group led by George R. French, cultivate the virus in a human cell line derived from a carcinoma of the lung. (See 1982 L, 1984 M, 1988 O.)

I. MOLECULAR BIOLOGY: *Cosmids*

John Collins and Barbara Hohn construct a hybrid plasmid using plasmid ColE1 and the cohesive end site (*cos*) of bacteriophage lambda. These types of plasmids, referred to as "cosmids," are used to clone large segments of DNA packaged in empty phage lambda heads. (See 1974 P, 1974 Q, 1977 Q.)

J. MOLECULAR BIOLOGY: *Site-Specific Mutagenesis*

Michael Smith describes a procedure for site-specific mutagenesis (site-directed mutagenesis). The technique involves synthesis of a short chain of

DNA containing a base change that differs from the natural DNA and hybridization to single-stranded DNA containing the gene being studied. The entire gene is formed by using DNA polymerase to extend the short fragment. The double-stranded molecule is then inserted into a host bacterium by transformation. Smith shares the 1993 Nobel Prize in chemistry with Kary Mullis.

K. MOLECULAR BIOLOGY: *Nucleotide Sequence of SV40*

W. Fiers and coworkers determine the 5,224-base-pair DNA sequence of simian virus 40 (SV40). From the nucleotide sequence, they are able to fix the position of the known genes and to deduce the amino acid sequences of two early proteins as well as the late proteins.

L. MOLECULAR BIOLOGY: *Nucleotide Sequence of Viroids*

Hans J. Gross and coworkers find that the potato tuber disease viroid is a covalently closed ring of 359 ribonucleotides. Because of intramolecular base-pairing and other structural features, the molecule forms a rodlike secondary structure. They are the first to report the complete molecular structure for a eucaryotic pathogen. (See 1971 E, 1976 J, 1981 L.)

M. SCIENTIFIC PUBLICATIONS

Bacteriological Reviews, first published in 1937, changes its name to *Microbiological Reviews.* In 1997, the name changes again to *Microbiology and Molecular Biology Reviews.*

N. SOCIETY AND POLITICS

• Pope Paul VI dies, and his successor, John Paul I, dies shortly after assuming the pontificate. The first non-Italian pope since 1523, Karol Wojtyla, is elected and becomes Pope John Paul II.

• Treaties that will turn over the operation of the Panama Canal from the United States to Panama on 31 December 1999 are signed.

1979

A. MICROBIAL ECOLOGY: *Deep-Sea Bacteria*

Two groups of researchers, one led by Holger W. Jannasch and Carl O. Wirsen and a second led by John B. Corliss, reinvestigate the hydrothermal vent communities of invertebrates found in 1977. They discover concentrations of sulfur-oxidizing bacteria in the waters of hydrothermal vents at temperatures up to 300°C and at depths of up to 3,000 meters. Jannasch and Wirsen collect water from thermal vents at eastern Pacific sea floor spreading centers. When examined microscopically by epifluorescence, the water appears to be milky-blue caused by bacteria. Direct cell counts on filters averaged 5×10^5 to 5×10^6 per milliliter. Making dives in the submersible *Alvin,* Corliss finds concentrations of sulfur-oxidizing and heterotrophic bacteria of up to 10^9 per milliliter in the thermal vents in the Galápagos rift. He also observes large communities of clams, mussels, limpets, and tube worms, as Robert Ballard reported 2 years earlier. Studies of these communities have led to the conclusion that significant bacterial chemosynthesis takes place in the deep-sea thermal vents. The rich content of H_2S in the water supports the growth of the sulfur-oxidizing bacteria,

1979 *(continued)*

which in turn form the base of a food chain for specifically adapted inverte-brates. Other bacteria found in the vent plumes include those that oxidize methane, hydrogen, iron, and manganese. (See 1977 B, 1984 B.)

B. BACTERIAL PHYSIOLOGY: *Magnetotactic Bacteria*

Richard P. Blakemore, D. Maratea, and Ralph S. Wolfe apply a magnetic field to sediments collected from a freshwater swamp and successfully iso-late a magnetic spirillum. The bacterium is grown in a chemically defined medium containing ferric quinate as a source of iron and succinate as a source of carbon. (See 1975 C, 1978 E, 1981 A, 1988 H.)

C. BACTERIAL ECOLOGY: Synechococcus

John B. Waterbury and colleagues report the widespread occurrence of a small marine cyanobacterium that they assign to the genus *Synechococcus*. The bacterium is found in concentrations of up to 10^5 per milliliter in the euphotic zone in various oceans. One strain studied in some detail by Robert R. L. Guillard ranges in size from about 0.9 to 1.3 by 1.8 to 2.2 micrometers. No attempt is made to grow the organisms in culture. (See 1988 A.)

D. BACTERIAL PHYSIOLOGY: *Syntrophism*

Michael J. McInerney, Marvin P. Bryant, and Norbert Pfennig isolate a new species of syntrophic bacterium by coculture with either a hydrogen-utilizing methanogen or a hydrogen-utilizing desulfovibrio. The organism, an anaerobic, gram-negative, helical rod, which they name *Syntrophomonas wolfei,* degrades both odd-numbered and even-numbered fatty acids, but with different end products. (See 1967 G.)

E. BACTERIAL PHYSIOLOGY: *Bioluminescence*

E. Peter Greenberg, J. Woodland Hastings, and Shimon Ulitzur suggest that autoinduction is not restricted to luminous bacteria. They report that a number of nonluminous marine bacteria secrete a substance that induces the luciferase system in *Beneckea harveyi*.

F. BACTERIAL PHYSIOLOGY: *Enzyme Regulation by Phosphorylation*

Marit Garnak and Henry C. Reeves report that the phosphorylation of isocitrate dehydrogenase results in loss of enzyme activity. This is the first report that identifies the endogenous substrate of a protein kinase and the concomitant regulation of its activity. (See 1978 B, 1987 A.)

G. BACTERIAL PHYSIOLOGY: *Plasmid-Encoded Proteins*

Aziz Sancar, Adelle M. Hack, and W. Dean Rupp develop a simple method for the identification of plasmid-encoded proteins. By using a strain of *Escherichia coli* that terminates DNA synthesis, but not plasmid DNA replication, after ultraviolet (UV) irradiation, they can detect pro-teins made under the direction of the plasmid.

H. BACTERIAL DISEASE: *Legionnaires' Disease*

George K. Morris and colleagues and, independently, C. B. Fliermans and coworkers isolate the bacterium that causes Legionnaires' disease from environmental sources. Following an outbreak of the disease in 1978, the Morris group isolates the bacterium from air-conditioning cooling towers, nearby creek water, and mud from the creek. The Fliermans group reports that more than 90% of 200 samples of water from 23 lakes in Georgia and South Carolina are positive. This is the first reported isolation of *Legionella pneumophila* or related serotypes from habitats not associated with outbreaks of the disease. (See 1976 G, 1977 L, 1978 F, 1980 H, 1986 I.)

I. BACTERIAL DISEASE: *Cytotoxic* Escherichia coli/*Verotoxin*

W. G. Wade, B. T. Thom, and M. Evans report experiments with 252 strains of *Escherichia coli* obtained from stool specimens of children with diarrhea. They test for the presence of heat-labile toxins by using Vero cells in culture. All of the strains cause a characteristic morphological response, with three strains showing a cytotoxic effect. (See 1977 N, 1982 I, 1983 E.)

J. MOLECULAR BIOLOGY: *Synthesis of Insulin by* Escherichia coli

Following the successful synthesis of the hormone somatostatin in 1977, a group including David V. Goeddel, Keiichi Itakura, and Arthur D. Riggs synthesizes the genes A and B for human insulin and inserts them separately into the plasmid pBR322 containing the promoter, operator, and part of the code for the bacterial enzyme β-galactosidase. Genes A and B are transformed separately in *Escherichia coli,* which synthesizes a fused protein containing both insulin and a portion of β-galactosidase protein. The insulin proteins, cleaved from the bacterial protein and joined with disulfide bonds, form a functional molecule. In 1982 the U.S. Food and Drug Administration approves marketing of the synthesized insulin under the name Humalin, which is approved for sale in the United Kingdom at the same time.

K. MOLECULAR BIOLOGY: *Sequencing of 16S Ribosomal RNA*

Two groups, Jürgen Brosius et al. and Philippe Carbon et al., determine the sequence of 16S ribosomal RNA (rRNA) from *Escherichia coli.* The Brosius group first sequences the 16S rRNA gene and from it infers the sequence of the rRNA, while the Carbon group employs rapid gel methods to determine the complete sequence.

L. TECHNOLOGY

In the first major incident involving a nuclear power plant in the United States, an accident at the Three Mile Island generating station near Harrisburg, Pennsylvania, creates concern that the reactor may explode. Despite some damage caused by cooling water, the reactor does not shut down.

M. SOCIETY AND POLITICS

Egypt and Israel sign a peace treaty ending a long-standing state of war. Both Egyptian president Anwar el-Sadat and Israeli prime minister Menachem Begin give credit to the role played by U.S. president Jimmy Carter in negotiating the treaty.

N. THE ARTS: *Literature*

William Styron publishes *Sophie's Choice.*

A. BACTERIAL ECOLOGY: *Bacterioplankton*

Jed A. Fuhrman and Farooq Azam estimate the rate of heterotrophic bacterioplankton production in waters collected in Antarctica, British Columbia, and California. After measuring populations in filtered samples and the incorporation of thymidine into bacterial DNA, they conclude that the important secondary production that occurs in bacterioplankton makes them a vital component of the food web.

B. BACTERIAL ECOLOGY: *Isolation of Bacterial DNA from Soil*

Using a modification of procedures devised by Julius Marmur in 1961, Vigdis Lid Torsvik successfully isolates bacterial DNA from soil. He notes that the isolated DNA represents the genetic information from nearly all of the bacteria present in the soil sample, in proportion to the relative abundance of each type of bacterium.

C. BACTERIAL PHYSIOLOGY: *Alternative Nitrogenase*

Working with strains of *Azotobacter vinelandii* that cannot fix nitrogen (Nif$^-$), Paul E. Bishop, Donna Marie L. Jarlenski, and Diane R. Heterington isolate strains that are Nif$^+$ but lack both the α and β subunits of dinitrogenase. They find that mutants carry the same Nif$^-$ mutation as the parents but produce a form of dinitrogenase not inhibited by tungsten, which is known to competitively inhibit FeMoCo, the prosthetic group of nitrogenase. The researchers conclude that an alternative nitrogen-fixing system is expressed under conditions of molybdenum starvation. (See 1986 E, 1988 G.)

D. BACTERIAL PHYSIOLOGY: *Alternative Pathway for CO$_2$ Fixation*

Georg Fuchs and Erhard Stupperich find a new pathway for CO$_2$ fixation in methanogens. They study autotrophic CO$_2$ fixation in *Methanobacterium thermoautotrophicum* either by long-term labeling of the organism with acetate uniformly labeled with ^{14}CO$_2$ or with pyruvate labeled in carbon atom 3. The acetate label appears in compounds derived from acetyl coenzyme A (acetyl-CoA), pyruvate, oxaloacetate, α-ketoglutarate, hexosemonophosphates, and pentose phosphates. The pyruvate label appears only in compounds derived directly from pyruvate. The data indicate that pyruvate is synthesized by reductive carboxylation of acetyl CoA and that hexose and pentose phosphates are synthesized from CO$_2$ by way of acetyl CoA and pyruvate. (See 1982 C.)

E. BACTERIAL PHYSIOLOGY: *Sugar Expulsion Process*

Jonathan Reizer and Charles Panos describe the regulation of the intracellular concentration of a methyl-β-thiogalactoside-phosphate in *Streptococcus pyogenes*. After observing a vectorial process that expels the compound in the presence of lactose or 2-deoxy-D-glucose, they suggest that the process may function to select a preferred sugar transported by the phosphotransferase system, thus regulating intracellular sugar phosphate accumulation. (See 1983 D.)

F. BACTERIAL GENETICS: *Electrophoretic Analysis of Enzymes*

Robert K. Selander and Bruce R. Levin perform a survey of the electrophoretic variation among 20 enzymes from clones of *Escherichia coli* selected from natural populations, including some cultures supplied by Roger Milkman from his 1973 experiments. Selander and Levin find a genetic diversity about twice that reported by Milkman but note that the number of genotypes is limited. They conclude that the rates of genetic recombination in natural populations of *E. coli* are low. (See 1973 E.)

G. BACTERIAL GENETICS: *Patentability of Bacteria*
The U.S. Supreme Court issues a decision that permits living organisms to be patented. The U.S. Patent and Trademark Office asks the court to review a patent application, filed in 1971, by Ananda Chakrabarty and the General Electric Company to patent a bacterium that can degrade crude oil. The Court's decision results in the awarding of a patent, in 1981, for a strain of *Pseudomonas* created by conjugation that can degrade camphor, octane, salicylate, and naphthalene. (See 1972 E, 1973 D.)

H. BACTERIAL DISEASE: *Legionnaires' Disease*
After inoculating amoeba and *Legionella pneumophila* together on agar plates, Timothy J. Rowbotham reports that not only do the amoeba ingest the bacterium, but also *L. pneumophila* is pathogenic for amoeba of the genera *Acanthamoeba* and *Naegleria*. He suggests that human infection may result from inhaling either infected amoeba or the vesicles containing the bacteria. (See 1976 G, 1977 L, 1978 F, 1979 H, 1986 I.)

I. BACTERIAL DISEASE: Campylobacter
Noting that the epidemiology of *Campylobacter fetus* infections have not been studied systematically, J. L. Penner and J. N. Hennessy use heat-stable antigens, extracted from 114 isolates, to establish 23 different serotypes by means of a passive hemagglutination technique. (See 1919 C, 1963 A, 1973 F.)

J. BACTERIAL DISEASE: *Plague*
Philip B. Carter, Robert J. Zahorchak, and Robert R. Brubaker report that the virulence of *Yersinia enterocolitica* for mice is related to the production of plague V and W antigens. These antigens are identical to those found in both *Yersinia pestis* and *Yersinia pseudotuberculosis*. (See 1956 I, 1980 K, 1981 F, 1984 H.)

K. BACTERIAL DISEASE: *Plasmid–Mediated Invasiveness*
Don L. Zink and colleagues are the first to report plasmid-mediated invasion of tissue by an enteric bacterium. In a study of *Yersinia enterocolitica*, they find that all invasive strains contain a plasmid with a molecular weight of 41×10^6. Loss of the plasmid from a strain is accompanied by a loss of invasiveness. They also report that the chromosomal genes code for the heat-stable toxin produced by this bacterium. (See 1956 I, 1980 J, 1981 F, 1984 H.)

L. BACTERIAL DISEASE: *Toxic Shock Syndrome*
Following the 1978 reports of toxic shock syndrome, a sizable number of similar infections involving *Staphylococcus aureus* are reported to the Centers for Disease Control. The majority of the patients are women who are apparently infected during their menstrual periods. After Kathryn N. Shanks and coworkers study association of the use of tampons with the toxic shock

syndrome, their data show that, while most of the infected women use tampons, the correlation of tampon use and infection is much lower than the incidence of tampon use in the general population. The researchers suggest that new types of materials introduced recently into tampons may favor establishing *S. aureus* in the vagina. (See 1978 J, 1982 K, 1983 H, 1984 J, 1985 E, 1987 E, 1989 D.)

M. VIRAL DISEASE: *Smallpox Eradication*
The World Health Assembly issues a resolution declaring that smallpox has been eradicated. This achievement results from a worldwide vaccination program begun in 1967 by the World Health Organization. The last proven case of smallpox occurred in Somalia in 1977. (See 1958 K, 1967 L.)

N. VIRAL DISEASE: *Human T-Cell Leukemia Virus (HTLV)*
Working in the laboratory of Robert Charles Gallo, Bernard Poiesz, F. W. Ruscetti, J. S. Reitz, F. W. Mier, and others isolate a retrovirus from a patient with leukemia. The first human retrovirus to be found, it is given the name human T-cell leukemia virus (HTLV), but the name is subsequently changed to human T-cell lymphoma virus and then to HTLV-1 after a second, similar virus is discovered. When the disease human acquired immunodeficiency syndrome is recognized, some researchers believe that it is caused by an HTLV type of virus. (See 1970 H, 1981 J, 1983 L, 1984 K, 1984 L, 1985 F.)

O. VIRAL DISEASE: *Nomenclature for Influenza Viruses*
The World Health Organization adopts a system of nomenclature for influenza viruses based on two types of glycoprotein spikes found on the viral envelope. Hemagglutinin spikes are designated "H," while neuraminidase spikes are designated "N." Since both hemagglutinin and neuraminidase contain a number of different antigenic determinants, viruses from various sources having similar antigens are placed in the same group. The viruses that cause epidemics or pandemics are known to have hemagglutinin type H1, H2, or H3 and neuraminidase type N1 or N2. The influenza virus that caused the 1918 to 1919 pandemic is believed to have been of the subtype H1N1 (although no isolates of the virus now exist). A 1977 virus is also H1N1, while those isolated between 1957 and 1968 are typed H2N2. In 1968 an H3N2 influenza virus was found.

P. VIRAL DISEASE: *Delta Agent*
In 1977, Mario Rizzetto and coworkers find an antigen, called the "delta agent," in the liver of human subjects with chronic hepatitis B surface antigen hepatitis. In 1980, Rizzetto and colleagues extend the previous investigation with a study of chimpanzees experimentally infected with hepatitis B virus. A small RNA that is associated with the delta antigen is found in the serum of the infected chimpanzees. This RNA genome is smaller than the genomes of known RNA viruses but larger than viroids that cause infection in higher plants. The researchers speculate that the RNA is the genetic material of the delta agent. Further research reveals that because the

delta agent requires hepatitis B virus as a helper to supply envelope proteins, it can only infect those persons infected with hepatitis B virus.

Q. MOLECULAR BIOLOGY: *Crystallization of Bacteriorhodopsin*
Hartmut Michel and Dieter Österhelt, by combining the membrane protein of the purple membranes of *Halobacterium halobium* with amphoteric molecules, succeed in obtaining crystals. However, the crystals are not highly enough organized to obtain X-ray diffraction patterns. (See 1967 C, 1971 B, 1982 N.)

R. MOLECULAR BIOLOGY: *Human Polymorphic DNA Locus/DNA Fingerprinting*
Arlene R. Wyman and Ray White discover a locus in the human genome containing a high level of DNA sequence polymorphism. Their observations of at least eight variants at the locus lead the authors to comment that a marker system using such information can be applied to family genetic linkage studies. Their discovery leads to the later development of the technique known as "DNA fingerprinting." (See 1985 K.)

S. METEORITE EXTINCTION OF LIFE
Luis Walter Alvarez and his son Walter Alvarez propose that a meteorite that struck the earth 70 million years ago led to the extinction of dinosaurs and much plant life.

T. SOCIETY AND POLITICS
In a disagreement over the Shatt al Arab waterway, Iraq invades Iran, beginning a war that lasts until 1990.

U. THE ARTS: *Literature*
Umberto Eco publishes *The Name of the Rose*.

1981

A. BACTERIAL PHYSIOLOGY: Aquaspirillum magnetotacticum
D. Maratea and Richard P. Blakemore examine the properties of the magnetic aquatic spirillum that they isolated in 1979. Based on its properties of being microaerophilic and chemoheterotrophic, they assign it the species name *Aquaspirillum magnetotacticum*. (See 1975 C, 1978 E, 1979 B, 1988 H.)

B. BACTERIAL PHYSIOLOGY: *Bioluminescence*
Anatole Eberhard and coworkers identify the autoinducer of bioluminescence in *Photobacterium fischeri* (*Vibrio fischeri*) as *N*-(3-oxohexnoyl)-3-aminohydro-2(3H)-furanone, also called *N*-(β-ketocaproyl) homoserine lactone. This compound is tested against other members of the genus and found to be active only with *P. fischeri*. (See 1970 C, 1982 G, 1984 G.)

C. BACTERIAL PHYSIOLOGY: *Detection and Isolation of Plasmids*
C. I. Kado and S.-T. Liu describe a procedure for the detection and isolation of plasmids ranging in size from 2.6 to 350 megadaltons. The procedure involves treating bacterial cells at elevated temperature with alkaline sodium dodecyl sulfate to release the plasmid circular DNA, while degrading chromosomal DNA. (See 1976 F.)

1981 *(continued)*

D. BACTERIAL GENETICS: *Nitrogen Fixation*

Two groups of investigators, Zsofia Banfalvi and colleagues and Charles Rosenberg and coworkers, find that *Rhizobium meliloti* contains large indigenous plasmids that carry the genes for both nodulation, *nod,* and nitrogen fixation, *nif.* (See 1982 E.)

E. BACTERIAL INSECTICIDES: Bacillus thuringiensis *Toxin Gene*

H. Ernest Schnepf and Helen R. Whiteley transfer the toxin gene of *Bacillus thuringiensis* into *Escherichia coli* by constructing a recombinant plasmid consisting of the vector pBR322 and DNA from the plasmid of the bacterium. *E. coli* subsequently produces a protein antigen detected by the use of antibodies against the crystal protein of *B. thuringiensis*. Protein extracts of the transformed *E. coli* are toxic to the larvae of *Manduca sexta,* the tobacco hornworm. (See 1967 J, 1982 F, 1986 B, 1987 C, 1989 A.)

F. BACTERIAL DISEASE: *Virulence Plasmids in* Yersinia

Daniel Portnoy and Stanley Falkow and, independently, D. M. Ferber and R. R. Brubaker study the plasmids of *Yersinia* species. Comparing the virulence-associated plasmids found in *Yersinia pestis* and *Yersinia enterocolitica,* Portnoy and Falkow find a 55% DNA sequence homology distributed over 80% of the genomes. Some strains of *Y. pestis* grown on calcium-free medium have either large deletions in the plasmid or an insertion that may have been caused by an insertion element. Ferber and Brubaker, who also examine *Y. pestis,* report that those strains of the organism that are calcium dependent contain plasmids of 6 and 45 megadaltons and also produce the bacteriocin pesticin. (See 1954 I, 1980 J, 1980 K, 1984 H.)

G. BACTERIAL DISEASE: *Staphylococcal Alpha-Toxin*

Sucharit Bhakdi, Roswitha Füssle, and Jørgen Tranum-Jensen report that the native alpha-toxin of *Staphylococcus aureus* is secreted as a hydrophilic peptide and that ring-shaped or cylindrical hexamers of the monomers form when deoxycholate is present. The hexamers prove to be identical to the toxin complex that forms on and in target cell membranes. The researchers suggest that the toxin forms transmembrane pores. (See 1966 J, 1974 J, 1987 D.)

H. VIRAL DISEASE: *Acquired Immunodeficiency Syndrome*

In June, the Centers for Disease Control (CDC) in Atlanta, Georgia, publishes its first report of cases of pneumocystis pneumonia caused by *Pneumocystis carinii* in young homosexual men in both New York City and Los Angeles. Physicians, led by Michael Gottlieb in Los Angeles and Henry Masur in New York City, report finding *P. carinii* and *Candida* infections in previously healthy homosexual young men. The patients tested display a marked reduction in T-cell lymphocyte populations. At the same time, unusual occurrences of Kaposi's sarcoma are noted among homosexual men in both New York and California. Of particular concern is that many of these patients die, and others show no signs of recovery. The CDC suggests a connection between opportunistic infections and a cellular-immune dysfunction related to a common exposure. Early opinions of physicians are that the basic disease is caused by cytomegalovirus combined with drug therapy, which leads to development of Kaposi's sarcoma and then to serious opportunistic infections. By 1982, the disease is being called acquired immune deficiency syndrome; the name later becomes acquired immunodeficiency syndrome, or AIDS. (See 1872 E, 1983 I, 1983 L, 1984 K.)

I. VIRAL DISEASE: *Hepatocellular Carcinoma*
Studying more than 22,000 Chinese men in Taiwan, R. Palmer Beasley and colleagues find that the incidence of primary hepatocellular carcinoma (PHC) is considerably higher among those who carry the hepatitis B virus surface antigen than among those who are noncarriers. Their results support the hypothesis that hepatitis B virus has a primary role in the etiology of PHC. (See 1965 N.)

J. PRION DISEASE: *Scrapie-Associated Fibrils*
Patricia A. Merz, Robert A. Somerville, and Henryk M. Wisniewski identify unusual fibrils in scrapie-infected brain tissue that are absent from normal brain. They refer to the fibers as "scrapie-associated fibrils," or SAF. (See 1936 J, 1968 L, 1981 K, 1982 M, 1983 M.)

K. PRION DISEASE: *Scrapie*
Stanley B. Prusiner and his research group present five lines of evidence that the causative agent of scrapie contains hydrophobic protein. Using preparations of the scrapie agent more highly purified than those used earlier, they discover that both proteinase K and diethylpyrocarbonate result in inactivation of infectious properties. (See 1920 D, 1936 J, 1957 K, 1967 O, 1982 M, 1985 J, 1989 F, 1989 G, 1990 H.)

L. VIROID DISEASE: *Absence of Genes for Polypeptides*
James Haseloff and Robert H. Symons report that chrysanthemum stunt viroid contains 356 ribonucleotides. Comparison of their data with those obtained for potato stunt viroid suggests that neither the positive strand nor the putative negative strand contains sequences that code for functional polypeptide products. (See 1971 E, 1976 J, 1978 L.)

M. MOLECULAR BIOLOGY: *Ribozymes*
While studying the excision of introns and splicing of exons in a precursor ribosomal RNA from a species of *Tetrahymena,* Paula J. Grabowski, Arthur J. Zaug, and Thomas R. Cech observe that both excision and splicing occur in a control experiment that contains no nuclear enzymes. They cannot rule out that a tightly bound protein is the catalyst but suggest that the RNA itself has enzyme activity. Further experiments by Cech's group and by Sidney Altman confirm enzymatic activity in some forms of RNA called "ribozymes." (See 1982 O, 1983 N.)

N. MICROSCOPY: *Scanning Tunneling Microscope*
Gerd Karl Binnig and Heinrich Rohrer complete the development of the scanning tunneling microscope. Binnig and Rohrer share the 1986 Nobel Prize in physics with Ernst Ruska, who invented an electron microscope in 1932. (See 1932 F, 1938 C.)

1981 (continued)

O. SCIENTIFIC PUBLICATION: Molecular and Cellular Biology
The American Society for Microbiology begins publishing a new journal, *Molecular and Cellular Biology*.

P. THE ARTS: *Literature*
Maya Angelou publishes *The Heart of a Woman*.

1982

A. BACTERIAL TAXONOMY: *Genus* **Bradyrhizobium**
The symbiotic nitrogen bacterium *Rhizobium japonicum* has properties that clearly separate it from other members of the genus. D. C. Jordan transfers this species to a new genus, *Bradyrhizobium* (from the Greek *bradys,* meaning "slow"), which is characterized by slow growth, having a generation time of more than 8 hours.

B. BACTERIAL ECOLOGY: *Thermophilic, Lithotrophic Methanogen*
Harald Huber, Karl O. Stetter, and coworkers isolate a novel thermophilic lithotrophic methanogen from geothermally heated sea sediments. Combining data from the composition of its envelope and its guanine–cytosine content with DNA-RNA hybridization studies, the researchers determine that a new species has been found and name it *Methanococcus thermolithotrophicus*. Although thermophilic methanogens have been described previously, this is the first lithotrophic species to be found. (See 1983 A.)

C. BACTERIAL PHYSIOLOGY: *Carbohydrate Synthesis from Acetyl Coenzyme A*
Kathrin Jansen, Georg Fuchs, and Erhard Stupperich continue the study, begun in 1980, of autotrophic carbohydrate synthesis in *Methanobacterium thermoautotrophicum*. They propose a pathway of carbohydrate synthesis from acetyl coenzyme A, by way of pyruvate, phosphoenolpyruvate, and phosphoglycerate, resulting in the formation of fructose 1,6-bisphosphate and glucose 6-phosphate. (See 1980 D.)

D. BACTERIAL PHYSIOLOGY: *Synthesis of Acetyl Coenzyme A from CO*
Sho-Ih Hu, Harold L. Drake, and Harland G. Wood find a new pathway for the synthesis of acetyl coenzyme A (acetyl-CoA). They purify enzymes from *Clostridium thermoaceticum* which catalyze the synthesis of acetyl-CoA from carbon monoxide and methyltetrahydrofolate and coenzyme A. The methyl group of acetyl-CoA is derived from methyltetrahydrofolate, and the carboxyl-thioester group is derived from carbon monoxide. In 1983, when Steve W. Ragsdale and colleagues purify the carbon monoxide dehydrogenase from *C. thermoaceticum,* they show that it is a nickel-containing iron-sulfur protein. (See 1985 B.)

E. BACTERIAL GENETICS: *Self-Transmissible Plasmid for* **Rhizobium**
Although the plasmids that code for nodulation and nitrogen fixation in several species of rhizobia are transmissible, the megaplasmid of *Rhizobium meliloti* is not. Adam Kondorosi and colleagues create a self-transmissible plasmid for this species and successfully insert it into other rhizobia and into

Agrobacterium sp. The transduced bacteria cause small ineffective nodules on the host plant, *Medicago sativa.* (See 1981 D.)

F. BACTERIAL INSECTICIDES: Bacillus thuringiensis *Delta-Toxin Genes*

José M. Gonzalez, H. T. Dulmage, Barbara J. Brown, and Bruce C. Carlton show that the genes for the delta-toxin of *Bacillus thuringiensis* are carried on a plasmid. After demonstrating that strains cured of individual plasmids no longer make the toxin, they find high-frequency transfer of plasmids carrying the genes between strains of the bacterium. (See 1967 J, 1981 E, 1986 B, 1987 C, 1989 A.)

G. BACTERIAL GENETICS: *Cloning of Luciferase Genes*

Robert Belas and colleagues, working with Michael Silverman, use a derivative of Tn*5* to clone the luciferase genes from a mutant *Vibrio harveyi* strain that is deficient in light production. After the genes *luxA* and *luxB* are transferred into *Escherichia coli,* light production is activated by removal of the transposon and addition of aldehyde to the culture medium. (See 1984 G.)

H. BACTERIAL DISEASE: *Enteropathogenic* Escherichia coli

The Centers for Disease Control investigates two outbreaks of an unusual gastrointestinal illness affecting at least 47 persons in Oregon and Michigan. Although no previously recognized bacteria are isolated from stool cultures, the investigators find a rare serotype of *Escherichia coli,* O157:H7, which is also isolated from one beef patty served at a restaurant where some of the illnesses apparently originated. The only previous isolation of this serotype, in 1975, came from a single case of hemorrhagic colitis. The data strongly suggest that this strain is responsible for the more recent outbreaks. In subsequent years, *E. coli* O157:H7 is implicated in a number of episodes of gastrointestinal disease involving sizable numbers of individuals and resulting in a number of deaths. (See 1982 I, 1983 E.)

I. BACTERIAL DISEASE: *Shiga-Like Toxin Production by* Escherichia coli

Alison D. O'Brien and colleagues find that some strains of *Escherichia coli* from diarrheal illness produce a toxin that is similar to *Shigella dysenteriae* type 1 toxin. Their report cites a number of serotypes of *E. coli,* but not type O157:H7, which is not known at the time of their investigation. (See 1977 N, 1979 I, 1983 E.)

J. BACTERIAL DISEASE: *Lyme Disease*

Willy Burgdorfer and coworkers isolate a treponema-like spirochete from *Ixodes dammini,* the field mouse tick that carries Lyme disease. Examination of sera from patients with the disease proves positive for antibodies against the spirochete. The causative organism is named *Borrelia burgdorferi.* (See 1977 M.)

K. BACTERIAL DISEASE: *Toxic Shock Syndrome*

A. L. Reingold and colleagues report a study of the occurrence of toxic shock syndrome associated with infections by *Staphylococcus aureus.* While earlier reports implied a strong association of the syndrome with menstruat-

1982 (continued)

ing women, these researchers find cases in a wide range of clinical settings and various infected sites, including focal cutaneous and subcutaneous lesions, surgical wound infections, postpartum infections, abscesses, and primary bacteremia. The toxic shock syndrome can occur in both sexes of any age group or race.

L. VIRAL DISEASE: *Korean Hemorrhagic Fever/Hantavirus*

Ho Wang Lee, Luck Ju Baek, and Karl M. Johnson report that the causative agent of Korean hemorrhagic fever resides principally in the striped field mouse, *Apodemus agrarius*. In Seoul, Korea, and nearby cities they also find the virus in *Rattus norvegicus* and *Rattus rattus*. The virus is named Hantaan virus after the Han River that runs through Seoul. (See 1978 H, 1984 M, 1988 O.)

M. PRION DISEASE: *Spongiform Encephalopathies*

Stanley Prusiner coins the term "prions" for proteinaceous infectious particles of the agent that causes scrapie. With David C. Bolton and Michael P. McKinley, Prusiner isolates a protein of 27,000 to 30,000 daltons that is resistant to digestion by proteinase K. The protein is referred to as PrP 27–30. Prusiner's work, and that of others, shows that the agent contains protein but no detectable nucleic acid. Prions are believed by some to cause a number of diseases classified as spongiform encephalopathies in addition to scrapie: kuru, Creutzfeldt-Jakob disease, bovine spongiform encephalopathy, transmissible mink encephalopathy, and chronic wasting disease in mule deer and elk. For his discovery and investigations of prions, Prusiner receives the 1997 Nobel Prize in physiology or medicine. (See 1920 D, 1936 J, 1957 K, 1966 L, 1967 O, 1981 J, 1981 K, 1982 M, 1985 H.)

N. MOLECULAR BIOLOGY: *Structure of Photosynthetic Reaction Center*

After crystallizing the membrane protein from the purple membrane of *Halobacterium halobium,* Hartmut Michel successfully crystallizes the membrane protein complex in the nonsulfur purple photosynthetic bacterium *Rhodopseudomonas viridis*. Assisted by Wolfram Bode, he obtains X-ray diffraction patterns. He and Johann Deisenhofer, Otto Epp, Kunio Miki, and Robert Huber continue to study the structure of this photosynthetic reaction center, leading to papers in 1984 and 1985 that report the folding pattern of the four-subunit protein and the details of the positions of the electron-carrying cofactors: quinones, iron, and bacteriopheophytin. They subsequently determine the electron transfer process in the reaction center. The 1988 Nobel Prize in chemistry is awarded to Michel, Huber, and Deisenhofer. (See 1967 C, 1971 B, 1980 Q.)

O. MOLECULAR BIOLOGY: *Ribozymes*

Kelly Kruger and other associates of Thomas R. Cech confirm that a species of ribosomal RNA from *Tetrahymena* carries out both excision of an intervening sequence and subsequent splicing without the participation of protein enzymes. Following these experiments, they coin the expression "ribozyme" for this type of RNA. Cech and Sidney Altman, who independently discovers ribozymes, receive the 1989 Nobel Prize in chemistry. (See 1981 M, 1983 N.)

P. MOLECULAR BIOLOGY: *Sequencing of Phage DNA*
Frederick Sanger and colleagues are the first to use a strategy based on sequencing of random sections of DNA to complete the sequence in a bacteriophage. They use cloned restriction enzyme fragments to sequence the 48,502 base pairs of phage lambda. (See 1977 T, 1979 K.)

Q. MOLECULAR BIOLOGY: *Cloning Full–Length Complementary DNA*
Seeking to obviate the problems associated with cloning full-length complementary DNA (cDNA) sequences, Hiroto Okayama and Paul Berg develop procedures by which full-length rabbit α-globin and β-globin are successfully cloned. They attribute the success of their procedure to having the plasmid DNA vector serve as the primer for both the first- and second-strand cDNA synthesis, omitting nuclease from any of the steps, and selective cloning of the cDNA copies. (See 1974 N.)

R. MOLECULAR BIOLOGY: *Gene Transfer by Electroporation*
E. Neumann and coworkers insert the herpes simplex virus thymidine kinase (TK) gene into suspensions of mouse L cells using a process they call "electroporation." Stable transformed cells are created when a mixture of plasmid DNA containing the TK gene and L cells is subjected to a brief 8-kilovolt/centimeter electric pulse. The researchers postulate that the electric pulse creates pores in the cell membrane that anneal after the current is removed.

S. SOCIETY AND POLITICS
In April, Argentina occupies the Falkland Islands, a British protectorate. In June, after less than 3 months of fighting, British troops force a surrender of the Argentine forces, ending the Falklands war.

T. THE ARTS: *Literature*
Alice Walker publishes her novel *The Color Purple*.

1983

A. BACTERIAL TAXONOMY: Archaebacteria
Wolfram Zillig and colleagues name two new genera of *Archaebacteria*: *Thermofilum* and *Thermococcus*. Both are characterized by lacking muramic acid in their cell walls and by having phytanol and saturated polyisoprenoid alcohols in their membranes. *Thermofilum,* which forms long, stiff filaments, was isolated from solfataras in Iceland using anaerobic enrichment techniques at 88°C. *Thermococcus* was isolated from solfataric marine water holes at Vulcano, Italy. This spherical bacterium grows at 88°C utilizing sulfur respiration. Another new genus, *Pyrodictium,* is found in a submarine solfataric region near Vulcano Island, Italy, by Karl O. Stetter, Helmut König, and Erko Stackebrandt. This disc-shaped bacterium has an optimum temperature for growth at 105°C and forms an unusual network of fibers. *Pyrodictium* is a hydrogen-sulfur autotroph that forms the iron-sulfur mineral pyrite. It contains no muramic acid, and its membrane contains isopranyl ether lipids, characteristic of the archaebacteria.

1983 *(continued)*

B. BACTERIAL PHYSIOLOGY: *Metabolism of Thermophilic Archaebacteria*

F. Fischer, Wolfram Zillig, Karl O. Stetter, and G. Schreiber study the metabolism of *Thermoproteus* and *Thermodiscus,* which grow at temperatures above 85°C, and *Pyrodictium,* which grows at 105°C. They report that these bacteria, which obtain energy from the oxidation of sulfur, producing hydrogen sulfide, and can use carbon dioxide as the only source of carbon, represent a new type of chemolithoautotrophic metabolism.

C. BACTERIAL PHYSIOLOGY: *Effects of Aerobic and Anaerobic Growth*

Martin W. Smith and Frederick C. Neidhardt, in experiments with *Escherichia coli,* find important differences in the polypeptides synthesized under aerobic conditions and those synthesized under anaerobic conditions of growth. Of approximately 170 individual polypeptides examined, 18 reach their highest levels during anaerobic growth, including four of the glycolytic enzymes. Under aerobic conditions, 19 polypeptides are at their highest levels, including the pyruvate dehydrogenase complex, some of the tricarboxylic acid cycle enzymes, and superoxide dismutase.

D. BACTERIAL PHYSIOLOGY: *Inducer Expulsion*

Michael J. Reizer, Milton H. Saier, Jr., and colleagues show that *Streptococcus pyogenes* accumulates thiomethyl-β-D-galactoside as the phosphate ester through the action of the phosphotransferase system. In the presence of glucose, the free galactoside is rapidly expelled from the cell by a process they refer to as "inducer expulsion." They provide evidence that the process comprises two separate reactions: intracellular dephosphorylation and the subsequent efflux of the free sugar. (See 1980 E.)

E. BACTERIAL DISEASE: *Shiga–Like Toxin of* Escherichia coli

W. M. Johnson, H. Lior, and G. S. Benzanson study an outbreak of hemorrhagic colitis caused by *Escherichia coli* O157:H7, similar to that reported by the Centers for Disease Control in 1982. Johnson's group finds that O157:H7 produces verocytotoxin similar to that reported by W. G. Wade's group in 1979. In other experiments, Alison D. O'Brien and colleagues find the production of a Shiga-like toxin by strains of *E. coli* O157:H7 similar to the toxin they reported in 1982 in other strains of *E. coli.* O'Brien prefers the term Shiga-like toxin to the term verotoxin because the former more precisely describes the properties of the O157:H7 toxin. (See 1977 N, 1979 I, 1982 I.)

F. BACTERIAL DISEASE: *Bacteriophage Carries* Escherichia coli *Verotoxin Genes*

S. M. Scotland and others report that the genes for verotoxin production (Shiga-like toxin) by *Escherichia coli* strain 19 are carried on a bacteriophage. Their experiments show that the genes are not carried by plasmids, and they successfully transfer the bacteriophage to *E. coli* K12, which becomes toxin positive. (See 1977 N, 1979 I, 1982 I, 1983 E.)

G. BACTERIAL DISEASE: *Peptic Ulcer*

J. Robin Warren and Barry Marshall describe a bacterium found in gastric biopsy specimens. Warren finds small curved and S-shaped bacilli closely associated with surface epithelium, which are difficult to observe but stain well with a silver-staining procedure. Culturing the bacteria by techniques for isolating *Campylobacter* species, Marshall notes that they have short spirals and possess up to five sheathed flagella arising from one pole. Warren and Marshall suggest that this bacterium may play a role in peptic ulcer and gastric cancer, a view that becomes substantiated after a number of years, particularly from the success achieved by treating the ulcers with antibiotics. The bacterium, originally named *Campylobacter pylori,* is later called *Helicobacter pylori.*

H. BACTERIAL DISEASE: *Toxic Shock Syndrome*

Patrick M. Schlievert and Debra A. Blomster investigate factors affecting the in vitro production of the staphylococcal exotoxin type C associated with toxic shock syndrome. They find that toxin production is more likely to be produced by incubation at 37°C than at 30°C and that more toxin is produced aerobically than anaerobically at both pH 7 and pH 8. Toxin formation is suppressed by a 3% concentration of glucose. (See 1978 G, 1980 L, 1982 K, 1984 J, 1985 E.)

I. BACTERIAL DISEASE: *Cat Scratch Disease-Like Infection in AIDS*

Douglas J. Wear and associates are among the first to recognize that a bacterium causes cat scratch disease after examining the lymph nodes of patients with the disease. Using the Warthin-Starry silver impregnation stain, they observe bacteria with a gram-negative appearance in the walls of capillaries in the folicular hyperplasia and within abscesses. Using convalescent-phase serum from recovered patients, the researchers perform an immunoperoxidase stain that confirms their conclusions that bacteria cause cat scratch disease. A second group of researchers led by Mark H. Stoler finds a similar bacterium in a Kaposi's sarcoma–like lesion on an AIDS patient. (See 1988 K, 1988 L, 1990 D.)

J. BACTERIAL INSECTICIDES: Bacillus thuringiensis *Delta–Toxin*

A. Tojo and K. Aizawa show that larval gut proteases cleave amino acids from both the C terminus and the N terminus of the delta-toxin of *Bacillus thuringiensis,* leaving a core that retains the toxic activity. In 1986, Muhammad Z. Haider, Barbara H. Knowles and David J. Ellar demonstrate that solubilizing the crystal delta-toxin under reducing conditions, activating it with trypsin, and treating it with larval gut proteases from susceptible insects results in a toxic preparation. (See 1967 J, 1981 E, 1986 H, 1987 B, 1988 I, 1989 A.)

K. BACTERIAL DISEASE: *Invasion by* Neisseria

Zell A. McGee and colleagues report using human fallopian tube organ culture to study the invasion of mucosal tissue by *Neisseria gonorrhoeae.* They describe several steps in the invasion process: attachment to microvilli of nonciliated cells, phagocytosis of the gonococci, transport of phagocytic

1983 *(continued)*

vacuoles containing gonococci to the base of the cell, and exocytosis of gonococci with phagocytic vacuoles into subepithelial tissue. (See 1988 J.)

L. VIRAL DISEASE: *Human Immunodeficiency Virus (HIV)/AIDS*

A research group headed by Luc Montagnier and including Françoise Barré-Sinoussi, Jean-Claude Chermann, and several others report isolation of the virus that causes AIDS. Determining that this virus is distinct from the human T-cell leukemia virus (HTLV), Montagnier and his associates refer to their isolate as lymphadenopathy-associated virus (LAV). At the same time, a group led by Robert Charles Gallo finds a virus in AIDS patients that they name HTLV-III (human T-cell lymphoma virus III). After subsequent investigations determine that Montagnier's LAV and Gallo's HTLV-III are identical, it is believed that cultures in Gallo's laboratory were contaminated with a culture of virus sent from Montagnier's laboratory. In 1986, an international committee on viral taxonomy recommends using the term human immunodeficiency virus (HIV) for the virus that causes AIDS, the human acquired immunodeficiency syndrome. (See 1970 H, 1980 N, 1981 H, 1984 K, 1984 L, 1985 G.)

M. PRION DISEASE: *Scrapie–Associated Fibrils*

Patricia A. Merz and colleagues report that scrapie-associated fibrils (SAF) are found in the brains of rodents experimentally infected with Creutzfeldt-Jakob disease as well as in the brains of some cases of human Creutzfeldt-Jakob disease. In separate experiments, H. Diringer and coworkers report similar results with scrapie-infected hamster brains. These fibrils, first found in brain tissue of scrapie-infected mice, are thought either to be the cause of these diseases or to represent a pathological response to them. (See 1920 D, 1936 J, 1957 K, 1967 O, 1981 K, 1982 M, 1983 M.)

N. MOLECULAR BIOLOGY: *Ribozymes*

Cecelia Guerrier-Takada and other associates of Sidney Altman discover that the RNA portion of ribonuclease P purified from *Bacillus subtilis* and *Escherichia coli* possesses enzyme activity, while the protein portion of the enzyme has no catalytic effect. This work confirms the 1981 and 1982 observations of Thomas Cech and colleagues that enzymatic activity is found in a form of ribosomal RNA called ribozymes. Altman and Cech share the 1989 Nobel Prize in chemistry. (See 1981 M, 1982 O.)

1984

A. BACTERIOLOGY: *Taxonomy*

Bergey's Manual of Systematic Bacteriology, the first edition of a new version of *Bergey's Manual of Determinative Bacteriology,* is published. The new manual has a broader scope than previous editions.

B. BACTERIAL ECOLOGY: *Phylogeny of Hydrothermal Vent Bacteria*

David A. Stahl, David J. Lane, Gary J. Olsen, and Norman R. Pace compare the nucleotide sequences in 5S ribosomal RNA extracted from bacterial symbionts associated with two hydrothermal vent animals: a tube worm and a clam. The bacteria, sulfur-based chemoautotrophs that support the growth of the invertebrates, are found to be closely related to and affiliated with the same phylogenetic grouping as *Escherichia coli* and *Pseudomonas aeruginosa*. (See 1977 B, 1979 A.)

C. BACTERIAL STRUCTURE: *Periplasmic Gel*
After studying the cell envelope of gram-negative bacteria, both by scanning and transmission electron microscopy using different embedding techniques, Jan A. Hobot and coworkers conclude that the space between the outer membrane and the plasma membrane may be filled with peptidoglycan in the form of a gel. (See 1961 C, 1977 E, 1990 C.)

D. BACTERIAL STRUCTURE: *Metachromatic Granules*
John A. Webster and colleagues examine the metachromatic granules of *Spirillum itersonii, Corynebacterium diphtheriae,* and *Micrococcus luteus* by electron microprobe X-ray analysis. They find that the granules contain only polyphosphate and divalent cations. (See 1888 A, 1946 B, 1959 B.)

E. BACTERIAL PHYSIOLOGY: *Cobalamin Synthesis*
Randall M. Jeter, Baldomera M. Olivera, and John S. Roth find that *Salmonella typhimurium* synthesizes cobalamin (vitamin B_{12}) only under anaerobic conditions, even though the enzymes can be detected in aerobically grown cultures. They suggest that synthesis is not seen aerobically because cobalamin is required as a cofactor only under anaerobic conditions. (See 1945 A, 1962 C, 1964 C.)

F. BACTERIAL PHYSIOLOGY: *Global Regulation*
Susan Gottesman defines a "global regulon" as a system in which more than one operon represents genes in more than one metabolic pathway. Systems that are globally regulated include SOS regulation, heat shock response, and catabolite repression. (See 1964 J.)

G. BACTERIAL GENETICS: *Cloning of Luciferase Genes*
Thomas O. Baldwin and coworkers clone both the α and β subunits of the luciferase of *Vibrio harveyi* into *Escherichia coli* using the plasmid pBR322. They report that a promoter contained in the plasmid is responsible for bright luminescence when *n*-decanal is added. Since *E. coli* supplies reduced flavin mononucleotide, luminescence takes place without an energy transfer system. (See 1982 G.)

H. BACTERIAL DISEASE: *Virulence Plasmids in* Yersinia
Daniel Portnoy and colleagues report finding a common virulence plasmid in *Yersinia pestis, Yersinia pseudotuberculosis,* and *Yersinia enterocolitica*. The plasmid mediates Ca^{2+} dependence and encodes some outer membrane proteins. Portnoy, Stanley Falkow, and others previously reported that calcium dependency is not only associated with virulence but is essential for it. (See 1956 I, 1980 J, 1980 K, 1981 F.)

I. BACTERIAL DISEASE: *Phage Conversion of Shiga-Like Toxins*
Alison D. O'Brien discovers that two different bacteriophages isolated from high toxigenic strains of *Escherichia coli* O157:H7 causing hemorrhagic colitis convert *E. coli* K12 to produce high-titer Shiga-like toxin. Discovery of a phage of almost identical characteristics from a strain that causes infantile

1984 *(continued)*

diarrhea, *E. coli* O26, leads to the conclusion that a family of Shiga toxin-converting phages may exist. (See 1983 F.)

J. BACTERIAL DISEASE: *Toxic Shock Syndrome*

Gorm Wagner and coworkers report that during the 90-minute period after insertion of tampons, the intravaginal oxygen tension rises to a level similar to that of atmospheric oxygen. They suggest that the increased oxygen level may encourage *Staphylococcus aureus* to grow and produce the toxin that causes toxic shock syndrome. (See 1978 G, 1980 L, 1982 K, 1983 H, 1985 E.)

K. VIRAL DISEASE: *AIDS/Sexual Transmission*

David D. Ho and coworkers report the isolation of the virus HTLV-III from both semen and blood of a healthy homosexual man whose serum contains antibodies against the virus. This finding establishes both the sexual transmission of AIDS and the existence of healthy asymptomatic carriers. (See 1981 H, 1983 L, 1984 L, 1985 F, 1985 G.)

L. VIRAL DISEASE: *AIDS/CD4 (T4) Receptor*

Several groups of researchers confirm that a subset of T lymphocytes that carry the CD4 antigen (also called the T4 antigen) serve as essential targets of the AIDS virus. Contributors to this research include Mika Popovic and colleagues in Robert Gallo's laboratory, A. G. Dalgleish and coworkers, and D. Klatzmann and other associates of Luc Montagnier. (See 1983 L, 1984 K, 1985 F, 1985 G, 1987 F, 1988 M.)

M. VIRAL DISEASE: *Hantavirus*

J. W. LeDuc, G. A. Smith, and K. M. Johnson report finding hantaviruslike viruses in domestic rats captured in the United States.

N. TECHNOLOGY: *CD-ROM*

A new type of sound recording device, a compact disc with read-only memory, the CD-ROM, is introduced.

1985

A. BACTERIAL PHYSIOLOGY: *Regulation of Chemotaxis and Sporulation*

After Ann Stock, Daniel E. Koshland, and Jeff Stock purify the chemotaxis protein CheY of *Salmonella typhimurium,* they discover that its complete amino acid sequence of 129 residues is homologous to that of another chemotaxis protein, CheB, as well as to the N-terminal region of the *Bacillus subtilis* Spo0A protein, a transcription factor necessary for the initiation of sporulation. The researchers suggest a possible homology between the chemotaxis system and the systems that regulate gene expression in response to environmental stimuli. (See 1967 D, 1987 A, 1988 E, 1988 F.)

B. BACTERIAL PHYSIOLOGY: *Carbon Monoxide Dehydrogenase*

Harland G. Wood and his associates, Harold L. Drake and Sho-Ih Hu, first suggested in 1982 that carbon monoxide dehydrogenase is a key intermediate in the synthesis of acetic acid by acetogenic bacteria. In 1985, Steve W.

Ragsdale and Wood present a scheme for the biosynthesis of acetate that places carbon monoxide dehydrogenase as the central enzyme of the pathway leading from H_2 and CO_2 or CO through acetyl coenzyme A. (See 1982 D.)

C. BACTERIAL GENETICS: *Ice Nucleation Genes*
Cindy Orser and colleagues clone and characterize the DNA segments carrying the *ice* genes responsible for the ice nucleation properties of *Pseudomonas syringae* and *Erwinia herbicola*. Ice nucleation activity is transferred to *Escherichia coli* by means of a cosmid vector. (See 1974 G, 1976 C, 1986 C, 1986 F.)

D. BACTERIAL GENETICS: *DNA–DNA Colony Hybridization*
Gary S. Sayler and colleagues develop a colony hybridization technique for detecting specific gene sequences in environmental samples. They use labeled DNA to find colonies containing a toluene catabolic plasmid in colonies of *Escherichia coli*. Colony hybridization techniques, similar to one developed in 1975 by Michael Grunstein and David S. Hogness, have been used to detect specific organisms in foods. (See 1975 I, 1988 B.)

E. BACTERIAL DISEASE: *Toxic Shock Syndrome*
In 1984, Patrick M. Schlievert and Julia A. Kelly studied the possible association of the use of tampons and the occurrence of toxic shock syndrome. They reported that while regular tampons had little effect on growth but inhibited toxin production by *Staphylococcus aureus,* high-absorbency tampons had variable effects on growth while generally inhibiting toxin production. In 1985, Schlievert reports that high-absorbency tampons bind sufficient magnesium to inhibit toxin production.

F. VIRAL DISEASE: *AIDS/Neurologic Disease*
David D. Ho and colleagues isolate HTLV-III from patients suffering from neurologic disease related to AIDS. Their recovery of the virus from cerebrospinal fluid and brain tissue suggests that HTLV-III is neurotropic and may be the cause of chronic meningitis and dementia. (See 1983 L, 1984 K, 1984 L, 1985 G, 1987 F, 1988 M.)

G. VIRAL DISEASE: *AZT and AIDS*
Hiroaki Mitsuya and a group of investigators, including Robert Gallo, Dani Bolognesi, and Sam Broder, describe how 3′-azido-3′-deoxythymidine (also called azidothymidine, zidovudine, or AZT) inhibits the cytopathic effect of HTLV-III/LAV. They find that AZT competitively inhibits the viral reverse transcriptase. This first report of an antiviral agent that inhibits HIV in vitro is a chemotherapeutic breakthrough for the treatment of AIDS. AZT was synthesized in 1978 by Tai-Shun Lin and William H. Prusoff. (See 1983 L, 1984 K, 1984 L, 1985 F, 1987 F, 1988 M.)

H. PRION DISEASE: *Bovine Spongiform Encephalopathy*
Cattle in Britain are diagnosed with a type of spongiform encephalopathy disease resembling scrapie that may have been transmitted to cattle by using scrapie-infected sheep carcasses in cattle feed. The possible relationship of Creutzfeldt-Jakob disease in humans and the possibility that the disease can

1985 *(continued)*

be transmitted to humans who eat beef is a source of concern. The news media coin the term "mad cow disease," adding to the anxiety about the spread of infection. Another widespread outbreak in cattle in Britain occurs in 1995 and 1996. (See 1920 D, 1936 J, 1957 K, 1966 L, 1982 M.)

I. PRION DISEASE: *Scrapie Prion Messenger RNA*
Bruce Chesebro and colleagues synthesize an oligonucleotide probe that represents the messenger RNA (mRNA) sequence corresponding to the amino acid sequence of prion protein PrP 27–30. Using this probe, they identify a complementary DNA (cDNA) clone from scrapie-infected mouse brain. The cDNA clone is hybridized to mRNA from both scrapie-infected brain tissue and noninfected tissue, suggesting that PrP 27–30 is a normal component of brain tissue. In a similar set of experiments, B. Oesch, Stanley Prusiner, and C. Weissman clone a PrP 27–30-specific cDNA from scrapie-infected hamster brain. The hamster clone proves to have 84% base homology with the cDNA sequence cloned from mice. (See 1967 O, 1981 J, 1981 K, 1982 M, 1983 M, 1989 F, 1989 G, 1990 H.)

J. MOLECULAR BIOLOGY: *Zinc Fingers*
J. Miller, A. D. McLachlan, and Aaron Klug find that transcription factor IIIA in *Xenopus* oocytes contains short sequences of amino acids folded around a zinc atom to form separate domains that are repeated in tandem. "Zinc fingers" serve to bind the protein closely to DNA and activate the transcription of eucaryotic ribosomal RNA. Other types of zinc-containing structures that interact with DNA are discovered by other researchers.

K. MOLECULAR BIOLOGY: *DNA Fingerprinting*
Based on their observations of a large number of dispersed tandem-repetitive "minisatellite" regions in human DNA, Alec J. Jeffreys, Victoria Wilson, and Swee Lay Thein suggest that a DNA probe based on a 16-base-pair core sequence of such regions can be used as an individual-specific "DNA fingerprint." Techniques based on this concept come to be widely used in paternity testing and forensic science, as well in broader studies in both plant and animal genetics.

L. TECHNOLOGY: *Optical Fiber*
An optical fiber that carries simultaneously 300,000 telephone conversations and 200 high-resolution television channels is made.

1986

A. BACTERIAL TAXONOMY: *Phylogeny Based on Analysis of Ribosomal RNA*
Norman R. Pace, David A. Stahl, David J. Lane, and Gary J. Olsen publish a review of the techniques of ribosomal RNA (rRNA) analysis that are used to analyze relatedness of natural bacterial populations. They discuss the use of data obtained from the analysis of both 5S rRNA and 16S rRNA for phylogenetic measurements and as molecular chronometers for evolutionary relationships. (See 1976 A, 1977 A, 1990 A.)

B. BACTERIAL ECOLOGY: *Survival of Pathogens in Marine Environments*

D. J. Grimes and colleagues working with Rita Colwell find that many gram-negative enteric pathogenic bacteria may enter into a state of dormancy in marine environments. These organisms remain viable and potentially virulent but are nonculturable by standard methods.

C. BACTERIAL ECOLOGY: *Environmental Release of Ice Nucleation Bacteria*

Steven E. Lindow and colleagues create Ice⁻ strains that lack the capacity to function in ice nucleation by deleting genes from *Pseudomonas syringae* and *Pseudomonas fluorescens*. They propose carrying out field trials to determine if plants sprayed with the Ice⁻ bacteria will be protected from frost damage. (See 1974 G, 1976 C, 1985 C, 1986 F.)

D. BACTERIAL PHYSIOLOGY: *Two-Component Regulatory Systems*

B. Tracy Nixon, Clive W. Ronson, and Frederick M. Ausubel study the response to environmental stimuli involving nitrogen assimilatory genes *ntrB* and *ntrC* in a *Bradyrhizobium* species. According to their proposal, these genes comprise a two-component regulatory system that transduces information about environmental stimuli to either transcriptional activating proteins or proteins that modulate maturation of outer membrane proteins or flagellar motion.

E. BACTERIAL PHYSIOLOGY: *Vanadium–Containing Alternative Nitrogenase*

Robert L. Robson and John R. Postgate report that an alternative nitrogenase system occurs in a strain of *Azotobacter chroococcum* that has the structural genes for conventional nitrogenase deleted. In this form of nitrogenase, one component of the two-component system contains vanadium rather than the molybdenum found in the conventional nitrogenase. A similar vanadium-containing nitrogenase is found in *Azobacter vinelandii* by Brian J. Hales and colleagues. (See 1980 C, 1988 G.)

F. BACTERIAL GENETICS: *Ice Nucleation Genes*

Gareth Warren, Loren Corotto, and Paul Wolber perform comparative DNA sequence analysis on the ice nucleation genes of *Pseudomonas syringae* and *Pseudomonas fluorescens*. They report that the two genes, having a number of different amino acid codons, have randomized the third bases in homologous sequences. The *P. syringae* gene is internally repetitive, suggesting that a protein with repetitive structure may be involved in the ice nucleation phenomenon. (See 1974 G, 1976 C, 1985 C, 1986 C.)

G. BACTERIAL INSECTICIDES: *Delta–Toxin Gene Transfer to Root-Colonizing Bacteria*

Mark G. Obukowicz and coworkers clone the delta-toxin gene of *Bacillus thuringiensis* into a transposon, creating a Tn5tox element that is transposed from a vector plasmid into corn root-colonizing strains of *Pseudomonas fluorescens* and *Agrobacterium radiobacter*. The bacteria are shown to express the

1986 *(continued)*

tox gene both by Western blot analysis and by toxicity against the tobacco hornworm, *Manduca sexta*. (See 1967 J, 1981 E, 1982 F, 1986 G, 1987 C, 1989 A.)

H. BACTERIAL INSECTICIDES: *Delta-Toxin of* Bacillus thuringiensis

In experiments with a cell line from the tobacco hornworm, *Manduca sexta,* Leigh H. English and Lewis C. Cantley show that the delta-toxin of *Bacillus thuringiensis* is a potent inhibitor of a membrane-bound vanadate-sensitive adenosine triphosphatase, a potassium *p*-nitrophenylphosphatase activity catalyzed by a sodium pump, and ion transport. (See 1983 J, 1987 B, 1988 I.)

I. BACTERIAL DISEASE: *Legionnaires' Disease*

Earlier reports by Timothy Rowbotham (1980), C. M. Anand and colleagues (1983), and Barry S. Fields and coworkers (1984) showed that *Legionella pneumophila* grows intracellularly in amoeba and ciliated protozoa. In 1986, James M. Barbaree and his group report the isolation of amoeba and ciliates containing *L. pneumophila* from air-conditioning cooling water towers, confirming the idea that protozoa are reservoirs for survival of the legionella in such environments. (See 1976 G, 1977 L, 1978 F, 1979 H, 1980 H.)

J. BACTERIAL DISEASE: *Meningitis*

An epidemic of meningitis that started in the northern part of Norway in 1974 has spread to the rest of the country and to parts of Europe, South Africa, Chile, Cuba, and Florida. Using multilocus enzyme electrophoresis, Dominique A. Caugant and colleagues identify a group of 22 closely related clones of *Neisseria meningitidis* as being responsible for the many outbreaks of meningitis. They report that although serogroup A is usually the type that causes epidemics, the majority of the strains found in their study are in serogroup B, with a few in serogroup C. (See 1989 C, 1990 F.)

K. VIRAL DISEASE: *Transgenic Plants Are Resistant to Tobacco Mosaic Virus*

Patricia Powell Abel, Roger N. Beachy, Robert T. Fraley, and coworkers show that plants can be transformed genetically for resistance to viral diseases. They introduce into tobacco cells a chimeric gene containing cloned complementary DNA of the coat protein gene of the tobacco mosaic virus (TMV) by combining the coat protein gene with the Ti plasmid of *Agrobacterium tumefaciens* from which the tumor-inducing genes are removed. Regenerated plants from the transformed cells express TMV messenger RNA and coat protein as a nuclear trait. Up to 60% of the seedlings from the self-fertilized transgenic plants that express the TMV coat protein are resistant to infection with TMV.

L. VIRAL DISEASE: *Delta Agent*

Kang Sheng Wang and colleagues and, independently, A. Kos and colleagues employ biochemical and electron microscopic data to show that the hepatitis delta agent contains a covalently closed circular, single-stranded RNA genome. This is the first animal virion to be shown to contain circular RNA. Wang et al. report that the genome contains 1,678 nucleotides and an open reading frame encoding an antigen that binds specifically to antisera from patients with chronic hepatitis delta-viral infections. (See 1980 P.)

M. TECHNOLOGY: *Nuclear Power Plant*

A nuclear power plant at Chernobyl near Kiev in the USSR explodes, releasing clouds of radioactive fallout that reach across Europe. A number of plant workers and firefighters die from radiation illness within a few weeks, and it is predicted that many thousands will suffer from the exposure in the coming years.

1987

A. BACTERIAL PHYSIOLOGY: *Chemotaxis/Protein Phosphorylation*

After purifying the proteins involved in signal transduction in chemotaxis, J. Fred Hess, Kenji Oosawa, Philip Matsumura, and Melvin I. Simon show that the product of the *cheA* gene is rapidly autophosphorylated. Dephosphorylation takes place in the presence of the CheY and CheZ proteins. Phosphorylation of CheA by ATP is thought to play a major role in chemotaxis. (See 1978 B, 1979 F, 1985 A, 1988 B, 1988 E, 1989 F.)

B. BACTERIAL INSECTICIDES: *Delta-Toxin of* **Bacillus thuringiensis**

Barbara H. Knowles and David J. Ellar propose that the delta-toxin of *Bacillus thuringiensis* binds to the plasma membrane of midgut epithelial cells of susceptible insects either by inserting into the membrane or by perturbing the membrane and creating small pores. The formation of the pores leads to an equilibration of ions across the membrane, resulting in a net inflow of ions accompanied by an influx of water, causing cell swelling and lysis. (See 1967 J, 1983 J, 1986 H, 1988 I.)

C. BACTERIAL INSECTICIDES: *Transgenic Plants*

Three groups of investigators, one led by Mark Vaeck, one led by David A. Fischhoff, and the other including Kenneth A. Barton, Helen R. Whiteley, and Ning-Sung Yang, insert a modified toxin gene from *Bacillus thuringiensis* into cells of either tobacco or tomato plants (Barton et al.) using a transformation system based on the Ti plasmid of *Agrobacterium tumefaciens*. After regeneration, the recombinant plants are resistant to attack by lepidopteran larvae. (See 1981 E, 1982 F, 1986 G.)

D. BACTERIAL DISEASE: *Staphylococcal Alpha-Toxin*

Hajime Ikigai and Taiji Nakae previously showed that when the alpha-toxin of *Staphylococcus aureus* interacts with cell membranes, the fluorescence of tryptophan residues increases with the degree of hexamer formation by the toxin. In studies with liposomes, they find that the secreted monomeric form of the toxin does not form hexamers until it interacts with membranes. (See 1966 J, 1974 J, 1981 G.)

E. BACTERIAL DISEASE: *Streptococcal Toxic Shock*

Lawrence A. Cone and colleagues report that toxin-producing group A streptococci cause toxic shock syndrome in patients with streptococcal cellulitis. (See 1989 D.)

F. VIRAL DISEASE: *HIV Binding Protein for CD4 Cells*

After finding that an envelope glycoprotein of the human immunodeficiency virus (HIV) binds to the CD4 antigen on T lymphocytes, L. A.

1987 *(continued)*

Lasky and colleagues show that a recombinant form of glycoprotein 120 (gp120) binds with high affinity to a recombinant CD4 antigen. (See 1983 L, 1984 K, 1985 G, 1988 M.)

G. VIRAL DISEASE: *Vaccinia Virus Termination Factor*

Stewart Shuman, Steven S. Broyles, and Bernard Moss purify a DNA-dependent RNA polymerase from cores of vaccinia virus. They resolve the in vitro transcription system into two components: a fraction with RNA polymerase activity that transcribes beyond the known in vivo 3′ terminus and a fraction that restores efficient termination when returned to the polymerase fraction. Although the termination factor copurifies with a messenger RNA-capping enzyme, it does not appear to require a 5′ cap for its activity.

H. VIRAL DISEASE: *Measles*

Ronald M. Davis and colleagues report on an outbreak of measles that occurred in 1985 on an Indian reservation in Montana. Despite a high rate of immunization, the epidemic spreads through 12 successive rounds of infection, suggesting that the transmission of measles may persist in some settings even when measles-eliminating strategies have been implemented.

I. MOLECULAR BIOLOGY: *Polymerase Chain Reaction*

Kary Mullis and Fred A. Faloona describe a polymerase chain reaction (PCR) that exponentially amplifies a nucleic acid sequence in vitro. The technique uses a desired sequence of DNA, two oligonucleotides that are complementary to different strands of the sequence to be amplified, and the four deoxynucleoside triphosphates. After polymerization is catalyzed by DNA polymerase, the reaction products are denatured by heat, and additional polymerase is added. Repeating the procedure through many cycles yields numerous copies of the desired sequence. The procedure is first mentioned, but not described, in a paper by Randall K. Saiki et al. in 1985. In 1988, the technique is greatly improved by use of a heat-stable DNA polymerase derived from a thermophilic bacterium, *Thermus aquaticus*. Mullis shares the 1993 Nobel Prize in chemistry with Michael Smith, who develops site-specific mutagenesis.

J. MOLECULAR BIOLOGY: *Transformation of Mammalian Cells*

Claudia Chen and Hiroto Okayama report that high-efficiency transformation (10 to 50%) of cultured mammalian cells may be achieved by causing the gradual precipitation of a plasmid DNA-calcium phosphate mixture onto the cells.

K. SOCIETY AND POLITICS

The Dow Jones industrial average on the New York Stock Exchange falls 508 points on "Black Monday," causing worldwide losses in stock exchanges.

L. THE ARTS: *Literature*

The novel *Beloved* by Toni Morrison is published.

A. BACTERIAL ECOLOGY: *Picoplankton/*Prochlorococcus

Using shipboard flow cytometry, Sallie W. Chisolm and coworkers discover abundant concentrations of a picoplankton in the deep euphotic zone of ocean waters. While the organism passes through a 0.8-nanometer filter, it is mostly held back by a 0.6-nanometer filter. The cells fluoresce red and contain a divinyl chlorophyll *a*-like pigment. DNA sequence data obtained in 1992 reveal that these bacteria, named *Prochlorococcus marinus,* are more closely related to cyanobacteria than to *Prochlorothrix* and *Prochloron.* Brian Palenik successfully cultures them, but not axenically, using trace-metal clean techniques. They will grow on inorganic nitrogen and phosphorus sources, but urea is usually used as a nitrogen source. Because of its abundance in the euphotic zone of tropical and temperate waters, *P. marinus* is believed to be the most abundant photosynthetic organism in the oceans, perhaps on earth. (See 1979 C.)

B. BACTERIAL TAXONOMY: *Nucleic Acid Probes for Identification*

Stephen J. Giovannoni, Edward F. DeLong, Gary J. Olsen, and Norman R. Pace design oligodeoxynucleotide sequences to use as probes for binding to 16S ribosomal RNA (rRNA) that is attached to nylon membranes. The rRNA molecules, obtained from archaebacteria, eubacteria, and eucaryotes, can be identified through the specific binding of the appropriate probe. The technique is also applied successfully to intact bacterial cells. (See 1985 D.)

C. BACTERIAL STRUCTURE: *Bacterial Flagella*

Robert M. Macnab's review of the flagellar and motility genes in *Salmonella typhimurium* includes an illustration of the details of flagella and basal body structure and the known genes for each.

D. BACTERIAL PHYSIOLOGY: *Swarmer Cell Differentiation*

From studies of swarmer cell differentiation in *Vibrio parahaemolyticus,* Linda McCarter, Marcia Hilmen, and Michael Silverman conclude that the flagellum is a dynamometer that senses restriction of flagella movement and activates the genes that induce the formation of swarmer cells. (See 1957 D, 1964 A, 1965 E.)

E. BACTERIAL PHYSIOLOGY: *Chemotaxis/Protein Phosphorylation*

After studying the phosphorylation of protein products of the *che* genes in both in vitro and in vivo experiments, J. Fred Hess, Kenji Oosawa, Nachum Kaplan, and Melvin I. Simon conclude that the phosphorylation of three of these proteins, CheA, CheB, and CheY, is necessary for signal transduction in the chemotactic response. They suggest that CheA has three functional domains: one that interacts with CheB and CheY, one that regulates phosphorylation, and one that receives signals that regulate CheA activity. They conclude that signal transduction in bacterial chemotaxis involves the transfer of phosphate through a cascade of phosphorylated proteins. (See 1978 B, 1979 F, 1985 A, 1987 A, 1988 F.)

F. BACTERIAL PHYSIOLOGY: *Cross Talk Between Signal Transduction Systems*

Alexander J. Ninfa and colleagues demonstrate that NR_{II}, a protein kinase that regulates transcription of genes for nitrogen regulation, and CheA, a protein that regulates chemotaxis, have cross-specificities. Since each can phosphorylate a protein in the other system, these data suggest that a common phosphotransfer mechanism operates in the two systems. (See 1985 A, 1987 A, 1988 E.)

G. BACTERIAL PHYSIOLOGY: *Alternative Nitrogenase*

John R. Chisnell, R. Pemakumar, and Paul E. Bishop isolate a third type of nitrogenase from *Azotobacter vinelandii*. The enzyme, expressed only in molybdenum-deficient systems, lacks significant amounts of molybdenum, vanadium, and tungsten but contains a small amount of zinc. Both molybdenum and vanadium repress its synthesis. (See 1980 C, 1986 E.)

H. BACTERIAL PHYSIOLOGY: *Magnetosome Membrane*

Yuri A. Gorby, Terry J. Beveridge, and Richard P. Blakemore use a large magnet to purify magnetosomes from cells of a magnetotactic bacterium that was disrupted with a French pressure cell. The chain of magnetosomes is surrounded by a lipid membrane not unlike that of other cell membranes, although it contains two unique proteins that may play a role in magnetite production. (See 1975 C, 1978 E, 1979 B, 1981 A.)

I. BACTERIAL INSECTICIDES: *Binding Sites for Delta-Toxin of* Bacillus thuringiensis

Christina Hofmann and colleagues find that the delta-toxin of *Bacillus thuringiensis* binds specifically to brush border membrane vesicles of the larval midgut of the cabbage butterfly *Pieris brassicae*. They also report that a delta-toxin that kills both the tobacco hornworm (*Manduca sexta*) and the cabbage butterfly binds to brush border membranes of both insects, but a toxin that kills the cabbage butterfly but not the hornworm would bind only to *Pieris* membranes. (See 1983 J, 1986 H, 1987 B.)

J. BACTERIAL DISEASE: *Model for* Neisseria *Infection*

Jay H. Shaw and Stanley Falkow report that a human adenocarcinoma endometrial cell line supports invasion by gonococci. Gentamycin is used to kill those bacteria that are not taken up by the cells. After invasion, the cells are treated with ethylenediaminetetraacetate (EDTA) to release internalized bacteria for enumeration by plate counting. When microfilament formation by the cells is inhibited, no invasion occurs. The authors also note that piliation of the bacteria apparently has no role in invasiveness. This model will permit further studies of gonococcal invasion in vitro. (See 1983 K.)

K. BACTERIAL DISEASE: *Cat Scratch Disease Bacterium*

Charles K. English and his associates report the isolation of a bacterium from the lymph nodes of patients with cat scratch disease. They also find small pleomorphic forms that they believe are wall-defective variants of the bacterium. In 1991, Don J. Brenner and colleagues assign the name *Afipia felis* to this bacterium, which is gram negative and motile by a single flagellum. The generic name is derived from the Armed Forces Institute of Pathology, where the organism was first isolated. In 1990, other researchers report identifying a second bacterium that causes cat scratch disease. (See 1983 I, 1988 L, 1990 D.)

L. BACTERIAL DISEASE: *Bacillary Angiomatosis in AIDS Patients*
Philip E. LeBoit and colleagues report cases of bacillary angiomatosis, a new opportunistic infection in patients with AIDS. The patients have skin lesions that resemble Kaposi's sarcoma but are found by electron microscopy to contain bacillary forms similar to gram–negative rods. Immunoperoxidase staining using antisera against cultured cat scratch disease bacteria shows a positive reaction. The infections regress after antibiotic therapy. Bacillary angiomatosis and cat scratch disease are later found to be caused by the same bacterium. (See 1983 I, 1988 K, 1990 D.)

M. VIRAL DISEASE: *HIV Binding Protein for CD4 Cells*
A. Nygren and coworkers show that two cleaved fragments of an HIV glycoprotein, gp120, bind specifically to CD4 cells. (See 1983 L, 1984 K, 1987 F.)

N. VIRAL DISEASE: *Western Equine Encephalitis*
Chang S. Hahn and coworkers compare the nucleotide sequence of western equine encephalitis (WEE) virus with other alphaviruses. Their results show clearly that this virus is a recombinant, probably between an eastern equine encephalitis (EEE) virus and a Sindbis-like virus. WEE virus has antigenic specificity similar to that of Sindbis virus as well as the encephalogenic properties of EEE virus.

O. VIRAL DISEASE: *Leakey Virus / Hantavirus*
Luck Ju Baek and colleagues isolate a new serotype of a hantalike virus from wild rodents, *Mus musculus,* near Leakey, Texas. "Leakey virus" causes hemorrhagic fever with renal syndrome.

P. GENETICS: *Human Genome Project*
The National Institutes of Health appoints James Watson director of the human genome research program. The goals of this program include mapping and sequencing the human genome.

Q. SCIENTIFIC PUBLICATION: Clinical Microbiology Reviews
The first issue of *Clinical Microbiology Reviews* is published by the American Society for Microbiology.

R. THE ARTS: *Literature*
• Salman Rushdie publishes *Satanic Verses,* which Muslims believe contains blasphemy. In 1989, Iran's Ayatollah Khomeini offers a reward of $3 million to anyone who will kill him. The British government breaks diplomatic relationships with Iran and protects Rushdie.

• Bonnie Anderson and Judith Zinsser publish a survey of women's world history in *A History of Their Own.*

A. BACTERIAL INSECTICIDES: *Classification of Delta-Toxin*

Herman Höfte and Helen R. Whiteley propose a nomenclature and classification of the delta-toxin crystal proteins and their genes of *Bacillus thuringiensis* based on the deduction of their structure from DNA sequences and on their host range. The genes are designated *cry,* for crystal protein, and placed in four groups, I, II, III, and IV, with a total of 13 genes that specify a group of related insecticidal proteins. (See 1981 E, 1982 F, 1986 G, 1987 C.)

B. BACTERIAL DISEASE: *Virulence of* Salmonella

Patricia I. Fields, Eduardo A. Groisman, and Fred Heffron isolate mutants of *Salmonella typhimurium* that are unable to survive in mouse peritoneal macrophages. The mutants are susceptible to the effects of defensins, low-molecular-weight peptides with antimicrobial activity produced by leukocytes. The researchers report that the bacterial *phoP* gene, which is involved in the formation of a nonspecific phosphatase, is responsible for the resistance of nonmutant forms to some antimicrobial mechanisms of the host. The gene may have regulatory function in the expression of virulence factors.

C. BACTERIAL DISEASE: *Meningitis*

Patrick S. Moore and coworkers study epidemic meningitis in sub-Saharan Africa, where epidemics of the disease occur every 8 to 12 years. They report that electrophoretic enzyme typing shows that a single serogroup A complex designated III-1 is responsible for recent outbreaks in Chad, Nepal, Saudi Arabia, and Ethiopia. More than 40,000 cases in Ethiopia are caused by an organism that reacts to antibodies raised against the III-1 clone. (See 1986 J, 1990 F.)

D. BACTERIAL DISEASE: *Streptococcal Toxic Shock*

In the period between 1986 and 1988, Dennis L. Stevens and colleagues study 20 patients with group A streptococcal infections characterized by severe local tissue destruction as well as life-threatening systemic toxicity caused by a scarlet fever-like toxin. Six of the patients die. (See 1987 E.)

E. VIRAL DISEASE: *Hepatitis C*

Qui-Lim Choo and others working with Michael Houghton recover virus by centrifugation of plasma from a chimpanzee that has a high titer of non-A, non-B hepatitis (NANBH). After extraction of the viral nucleic acid, they construct a complementary DNA library using bacteriophage λdt11. A clone that they call hepatitis C virus is isolated after the library is screened with serum from a patient diagnosed with NANBH. (See 1990 G.)

F. PRION DISEASE: *Nucleic Acid Associated with Prion Protein*

T. K. Sklaviadis, Laura Manuelidis, and Elias E. Manuelidis report using velocity sedimentation and isopycnic sucrose gradients to prepare the infectious agent of Creutzfeldt-Jakob disease in experimentally infected rodents.

They find that the size of the agent is greater than that of a monomeric protein and that its density is similar to that of nucleic acid-protein complexes. Sklaviadis and associates also separate most of the protein from an infectious fraction containing nucleic acid. They suggest that the Creutzfeldt-Jakob disease prion is viruslike in size and density. (See 1967 O, 1981 J, 1981 K, 1982 M, 1985 I, 1989 G, 1990 H.)

G. PRION DISEASE: *Mitochondrial Involvement in Scrapie Infection*

Judd M. Aiken, Judy L. Williamson, and R. F. Marsh construct complementary DNA libraries from both the brain membrane and cytoskeletal preparations of scrapie-infected hamster brain. Because four clones that hybridize preferentially to cytoskeletal preparations also have significant similarities to mouse mitochondrial DNA, they suggest a role for mitochondria in the scrapie infection. (See 1967 O, 1981 J, 1981 K, 1982 M, 1985 I, 1989 F, 1990 H.)

H. PHYSICS: *Cold Fusion*

Stanley Pons and Martin Fleischmann report that they have achieved "cold fusion," the fusion of atomic nuclei at room temperature. Other researchers are unable to confirm their results.

I. SOCIETY AND POLITICS

The tanker *Exxon Valdez* runs aground in Prince William Sound in Alaska, spilling oil that spreads over more than 100 square miles and killing wildlife in the ocean and on the shoreline.

J. CULTURE: *Dictionary*

The second edition of the *Oxford English Dictionary* is published. The first edition was published in 1884.

1990

A. BACTERIAL TAXONOMY: Eucarya, Bacteria, *and* Archaea

Carl R. Woese, Otto Kandler, and Mark L. Wheelis propose a new system of classification of living organisms based on the comparison of the nucleotide sequences of ribosomal RNA from a wide selection of eubacteria, archaebacteria, and eucaryotic organisms. They designate three principal groups, called taxons: *Eucarya, Bacteria,* and *Archaea.* A major distinguishing characteristic is the composition of cell membranes. The *Eucarya* have glycerol fatty acid diesters, the *Bacteria* have diacyl glycerol diesters, and the *Archaea* have membranes that contain isoprenoid glycerol diethers or diglycerol tetraethers. Woese et al. abandon the use of the term *Archaebacteria* because it incorrectly suggests a specific relationship between the *Archaea* and the *Bacteria.* The *Archaea* are subdivided into two kingdoms, the *Euryarchaeota* (euryotes) and the *Crenarchaeota* (crenotes). The *Euryarchaeota* include the methanogens, extreme halophiles, sulfate reducers, and two groups of thermophiles. The *Crenarchaeota,* all of which are thermophiles, include organisms called thermoacidophiles, sulfur-dependent archaebacteria, eocytes, and extreme thermophiles. (See 1861 D, 1866 A, 1956 A, 1969 A, 1976 A, 1977 A, 1986 A.)

1990 *(continued)*

B. BACTERIAL ECOLOGY: *Bacteriophage–Bacteria Interaction in Marine Systems*

Using hollow-fiber ultracentrifugation, Lita M. Proctor and Jed A. Fuhrman concentrate 40 to 80 liters of prefiltered sea water for examination by electron microscopy. With negative staining they observe a wide array of virions with counts as high as 10^9 per liter that resemble bacteriophages. Counts of both heterotrophic bacteria and cyanobacteria of up to 10^9 per liter are performed by means of epifluorescence or autofluorescence for phototrophs. Their data suggest that bacteriophage infection causes significant mortality among marine procaryotes.

C. BACTERIAL STRUCTURE: *Periplasm*

Based on calculations of the amount of space occupied by enzymes and electron carriers known to be found in the periplasm, John E. van Wielink and Johannis A. Duine estimate that the periplasmic space is much wider than what is often assumed. Earlier reports had suggested that the periplasm occupies 20 to 40% of the cell volume, with widths ranging from 7 to 33 nanometers. These investigators conclude that the width of the space may be as much as 50 nanometers, which would equal about 30% of the average cell volume. (See 1961 C, 1977 E, 1984 C.)

D. BACTERIAL DISEASE: *Bacillary Angiomatosis and Cat Scratch Disease*

David Relman and coworkers, examining tissues of three unrelated patients with bacillary angiomatosis, find that a unique 16S RNA gene sequence is associated with a causative bacterium. This bacterium is distinct from the bacterium *Afipia felis* that Charles English found in 1988 to be associated with cat scratch disease. On the basis of their observations, Relman et al. conclude that the disease is caused by a previously uncharacterized rickettsialike organism similar to *Rickettsia quintana,* which causes trench fever. *R. quintana,* which was renamed *Rochalimaea quintana* in 1984, is renamed *Bartonella quintana* in 1993. Leonard N. Slater and his associates isolate a bacterium from several patients: two with AIDS, another with a septicemia after a bone marrow transplant, and two immunocompetent patients with febrile illnesses. The organism that Slater's group studies may be differentiated from *Rochalimaea* (*Bartonella*) *quintana* on the basis of restriction endonuclease digests of DNA and by electrophoresis of cell membrane preparations. In 1992, R. L. Regnery and coworkers propose the name *Rochalimaea henselae* for this bacterium, but it becomes *Bartonella henselae* in 1993 when Don Brenner and colleagues combine the genera *Rochalimaea* and *Bartonella.* (See 1983 I, 1988 K, 1988 L.)

E. BACTERIAL DISEASE: *Cholera Epidemic*

An epidemic of cholera begins in Peru, probably in the harbor at Lima, where it is believed that bacteria in contaminated bilge water from a ship from eastern Asia infects fish and shellfish. The outbreak, caused by the El Tor biotype of *Vibrio cholerae,* results in at least 366,000 cases with nearly 4,000 deaths by the end of 1991. The epidemic is spread to a more limited extent to other countries by air travel of infected individuals and by fruits and vegetables exported from South America. (See 1906 F, 1971 D.)

F. BACTERIAL DISEASE: *Meningitis*

To investigate possible coincident infections that may predispose individuals for meningococcal disease, Patrick S. Moore and colleagues perform a matched case-control study of patients in Chad. The patients with meningococcal infection are found more likely than the control subjects to have other respiratory infections. Viruses detected include adenovirus, parainfluenza virus, respiratory syncytial virus, and rhinovirus, and *Mycoplasma* infections are also detected. The researchers suggest that the coincident infections may help explain the epidemiological characteristics of group A meningococcal meningitis. (See 1986 J, 1989 C.)

G. VIRAL DISEASE: *Hepatitis E*

Gregory R. Reyes and coworkers successfully isolate a complementary DNA clone that represents a portion of the genome of enterically transmitted non-A, non-B hepatitis virus. They suggest the name hepatitis E virus. (See 1989 E.)

H. PRION DISEASE: *Mitochondrial Involvement with the Scrapie Agent*

Judd M. Aiken, Judy L. Williamson, Lynne M. Borchardt, and R. F. Marsh find that scrapie-infected brain preparations contain the so-called D loop of the mitochrondrial DNA. This observation further strengthens the results of earlier studies indicating that the scrapie protein, PrP, is associated with nucleic acid. (See 1967 O, 1981 K, 1982 M, 1989 F, 1989 G.)

I. IMMUNOLOGY: *Lipopolysaccharide Binding Protein*

Ralf R. Schumann and colleagues find a trace protein in plasma that binds to the lipid A moiety of the lipopolysaccharide of gram-negative bacteria. This protein, referred to as lipopolysaccharide binding protein (LBP), may control host responses to lipopolysaccharide by forming complexes that bind to monocytes and macrophages, resulting in the secretion of tumor necrosis factor. (See 1975 K.)

J. SOCIETY AND POLITICS

- Iraq and Iran agree to end their war, which began in 1980, with Iraq accepting all of Iran's terms to terminate the fighting.
- In a conflict that is known as the Gulf War, Iraq invades Kuwait, causing the United Nations to impose sanctions and create an embargo on oil sales. The United States and the Soviet Union agree to a united stand against military aggression in the Gulf region.

Index of Names

Abbe, Ernst, 1873 B, 1878 H, 1886 G
Abbott, Alexander Crever, 1899 G
Abdou, Nabih I., 1972 J
Abdou, Nancy L., 1972 J
Abel, Patricia Powell, 1986 K
Abelson, John, 1977 W
Abraham, Edward P., 1940 D, 1940 E, 1941 F, 1944 B, 1948 C
Achebe, Chinua, 1958 S
Adelberg, Edward, 1966 I
Adhya, Sankar, 1968 C
Adler, Howard I., 1967 E
Adler, Julius, 1966 B, 1967 D, 1969 C, 1971 A, 1973 A, 1974 B, 1974 C, 1977 H
Adler, Stuart P., 1973 J
Adriaanzoon, Jacob, 1608
Aiken, Judd M., 1989 G, 1990 H
Aizawa, K., 1983 J
Akiba, Tomoichiro, 1959 G, 1960 F
Albee, Edward, 1962 AA
Alberti, Salomon, 1603
Aldrin, Edwin Eugene, Jr., 1969 H
Alexander, J., 1930 D
Alexander, Martin, 1970 E
Alighieri, Dante, 1307
Allbut, Thomas Clifford, 1866 B
Allen, P. W., 1918 B
Allison, A. C., 1963 D
Alloway, J. L., 1932 A
Alper, Tikvah, 1967 O
Alpers, M. P., 1966 L

Alpher, Ralph Asher, 1948 M
Altenburg, Edgar, 1934 H
Alter, Harvey J., 1965 N
Altman, Sidney, 1975 Q, 1981 M, 1982 O, 1983 N
Altmann, Richard, 1869 E, 1889 I, 1890 F
Alvarez, Luis Walter, 1952 R, 1980 S
Alvarez, Walter, 1980 S
Amati, Salvano d'Aramento degli, 1299
Amato, A., 1909 B
Ames, Bruce N., 1959 N, 1963 V, 1972 G, 1975 F
Amesz, J., 1961 U
Amici, Giovanni Battista, 1823 B, 1827 A, 1830 B, 1840 C
Amis, Kingsley, 1954 P
Amontons, Guillaume, 1699 A, 1699 C, 1787 B
Ampère, André Marie, 1822 B, 1848 C
Amundsen, Roald, 1911 N, 1912 I
Amyot, Jacques, 1579
Anand, C. M., 1986 I
Andersen, Hans Christian, 1835 D
Anderson, Bonnie, 1988 R
Anderson, Carl David, 1932 M
Anderson, Sherwood, 1919 G
Anderson, Thomas F., 1942 G, 1949 D, 1959 J
Ando, T., 1966 P
Andrewes, Christopher Howard, 1933 D, 1940 K

Andrewes, F. W., 1922 C
Anfinsen, Christian, 1950 P
Angelou, Maya, 1970 T, 1981 P
Ångstrom, Anders Jonas, 1853 C
Angus, T. A., 1954 H
Anichkov, Nikolai, 1913 D
Appert, Nicolas, 1804 A, 1808 A, 1810 B, 1819 A
Appleby, C. A., 1962 F
Arber, Werner, 1952 L, 1965 Q, 1970 M
Archimedes, 260 B.C., ca. 250 B.C.
Aristotle, ca. 430 B.C. B, ca. 367 B.C. B, second century B, 1512, 1586, 1590 B, 1620 B, 1661 B
Arkwright, Joseph Arthur, 1921 B
Arkwright, Richard, 1769 A
Armstrong, John B., 1967 D
Armstrong, Neil Alden, 1969 H
Arnon, Daniel Israel, 1954 N, 1960 C, 1962 U
Arny, D. C., 1976 C
Arrhenius, Svante August, 1879 A, 1886 I, 1889 J, 1907 F, 1907 J, 1908 G
Arthus, Nicolas Maurice, 1903 H
Artz, Stanley W., 1975 F
Aryabhata, 499
Asplin, F. D., 1961 J
Astbury, William Thomas, 1938 E, 1938 H, 1955 C
Astrachan, Lazarus, 1956 M, 1961 O

Atwater, Wilbur O., 1889 B
Audubon, John James, 1827 E
Auerbach, C., 1946 K
Austen, Jane, 1811 E, 1813 D
Ausubel, Frederick M., 1986 D
Avery, Oswald T., 1923 F, 1928 C, 1931 H, 1944 C, 1953 N
Avicenna, ca. 1020, 1526
Avogadro, Lorenzo Romano Amedeo Carlo, 1811 B, 1848 C
Azam, Farooq, 1980 A

Baas-Becking, L. G. M., 1927 A
Babbage, Charles, 1801 C, 1822 C, 1830 D, 1832 E
Babcock, Stephen Moulton, 1890 G
Babes, Victor, 1888 A
Bach, Alexsei Nikolaevich, 1911 J
Bach, Johann Sebastian, 1721 B
Bacon, Francis, 1620 B
Bacon, Roger, 1249, 1267
Bacot, Arthur William, 1914 B
Baddiley, J., 1958 C
Baden-Powell, Robert Stephenson, 1910 H
Badham, John, 1840 B
Badin, Elmer J., 1950 M
Baek, Luck Ju, 1982 L, 1988 O
Baekeland, Leo H., 1909 J
Bail, Oscar, 1925 C
Baird, John Logie, 1926 N
Baker, J. A., 1942 A
Baker, W., 1944 B
Balboa, Vasco Núñez de, 1513
Baldwin, James, 1953 Z
Baldwin, Thomas O., 1984 G
Ball, Eric Glendenning, 1939 P
Ballard, Robert D., 1977 B, 1979 A
Balsamo-Crivelli, G., 1835 A
Baltimore, David, 1962 N, 1968 J, 1970 H
Banfalvi, Zsofia, 1981 D
Bang, Bernhard Laurits Frederick (Oluf), 1897 D, 1911 E
Bang, Frederik, 1957 H
Banting, Frederick G., 1921 G
Baranowski, Thaddeus, 1935 K
Barbaree, James, M., 1986 I
Barber, M. A., 1914 C, 1930 B
Barcroft, Joseph, 1902 K
Bard, R. D., 1951 E
Bardeen, John, 1947 F, 1957 S
Barghoorn, Elso Sterrenberg, 1965 B, 1967 B

Barker, H. A., 1936 B, 1940 B, 1945 A, 1964 C, 1967 G
Barker, Lewellys F., 1900 E
Barkulis, S. S., 1957 B
Barnard, Christiaan Neethling, 1967 U
Barnes, M. W., 1929 A
Barnett, Leslie, 1961 P
Barr, Yvonne, 1958 L, 1963 L
Barrell, B. G., 1965 R
Barré-Sinoussi, Françoise, 1983 L
Barritt, M. M., 1898 A
Barsha, J., 1931 B
Bartlett, John, 1855 D
Barton, Clara, 1881 K
Barton, Kenneth A., 1987 C
Barton, Otis, 1930 H, 1934 P, 1948 O
Bassham, J. A., 1950 M, 1954 M
Bassi, Agostino Maria, 1835 A, 1837 D
Bastian, Henry Charlton, 1872 A, 1876 A
Bateson, William, 1902 I, 1905 H, 1909 H
Batista, Fulgencio, 1959 U
Bauer, A. W., 1966 G
Bauhin, Gaspard, 1623 B, 1737
Baum, Lyman Frank, 1900 R
Bawden, Frederick C., 1935 H, 1936 H, 1937 F
Bayliss, William Maddock, 1905 L
Beachy, Roger N., 1986 K
Beadle, George Wells, 1908 E, 1941 H, 1946 F
Beard, Daniel Carter, 1910 H
Beard, Paul J., 1935 A
Beasley, R. Palmer, 1981 I
Becher, Johann Joachim, 1606 A, 1668 C, 1680 C
Becker, Yechiel, 1963 R
Beckett, Samuel, 1953 AA, 1957 U
Becking, J. H., 1970 B, 1978 D
Beckman, Arnold O., 1941 N
Beckwith, Jonathan, 1966 H
Becquerel, Antoine Henri, 1896 G
Bedson, Samuel P., 1930 C, 1934 B
Beebe, Charles William, 1930 H, 1934 P, 1948 O
Beethoven, Ludwig van, 1800 G, 1805 C, 1807 D
Begin, Menachem, 1979 M
Beguin, Jean, 1624 A
Behring, Emil Adolf, 1890 B, 1890 D, 1890 E, 1891 D, 1901 L, 1902 F, 1913 A

Beighton, E., 1955 C
Beijerinck, Martinus Willem, 1868 B, 1882 F, 1888 B, 1889 C, 1893 A, 1893 B, 1894 B, 1899 E, 1900 C, 1901 B, 1901 C, 1903 B, 1905 A, 1921 A, 1955 A
Beilstein, Friedrich Konrad, 1880 E
Belas, Robert, 1982 G
Belitser, Vladimir Aleksandrovich, 1939 Q
Bell, Alexander Graham, 1876 G
Bell, Florence Ogilvy, 1938 H
Belley, Robert T., 1972 A
Belser, Nao O., 1954 J
Benacerraf, Baruj, 1937 G, 1958 M, 1963 N
Benda, Carl, 1890 F, 1898 K
Bendall, Fay, 1960 N, 1961 U
Ben-Gurion, David, 1948 P
Benson, A. A., 1950 M, 1954 M
Benz, Karl Friedrich, 1885 O
Benzanson, G. S., 1983 E
Benzer, Seymour, 1955 K
Berends, W., 1960 H
Berg, Howard, 1972 C
Berg, Paul, 1972 M, 1973 O, 1977 S, 1982 Q
Bergersen, F. J., 1967 F
Berget, Susan M., 1977 W
Bergey, David H., 1923 A
Bergius, Friedrich, 1908 F
Berliner, Ernst, 1915 B, 1942 H, 1953 J
Bernal, John Desmond, 1936, 1937 F
Bernard, Claude, 1857 E, 1857 F, 1859 C, 1878 D
Bernhard, W., 1960 K
Bernheimer, Alan W., 1966 J
Bernoulli, Jakob, 1690 A, 1696
Bernstein, Carl, 1974 T
Berson, Solomon, 1960 L
Bertani, G., 1952 L
Berthelot, Marcelin, 1849 C, 1859 A, 1864 B, 1878 D, 1885 D
Berthollet, Claude Louis, 1787 A
Bertillon, Alphonse, 1885 P
Bertrand, Gabriel Émile, 1857 D, 1894 J, 1897 J
Berzelius, Jöns Jakob, 1803 B, 1807 B, 1813 A, 1818 B, 1827 C, 1837 F, 1837 G, 1838 E, 1839 B, 1862 B
Beskid, G., 1960 E
Bessemer, Henry, 1856 E

Bessman, Maurice J., 1958 O
Best, Charles, 1921 G
Bethe, Hans Albrecht, 1948 M
Beukers, R., 1960 H
Beveridge, Terry J., 1988 H
Beveridge, W. I. B., 1946 I
Bhakdi, Sucharit, 1981 G
Billingham, Rupert E., 1945 D, 1953 R
Binet, Alfred, 1905 M
Binnig, Gerd Karl, 1932 F, 1981 N
Biot, Jean-Baptiste, 1804 D, 1815 B, 1848 A
Birch-Andersen, A., 1953 E
Bishop, J. Michael, 1976 L
Bishop, Paul E., 1975 E, 1980 C, 1988 G
Bittner, John Joseph, 1936 I
Bizet, Georges, 1875 G
Bizio, B., 1823 A, 1900 C
Black, James White, 1949 J
Black, Joseph, 1754, 1757
Black, Paul H., 1965 O
Blair, Eric Arthur, *see* Orwell, George
Blakemore, Richard P., 1975 C, 1978 E, 1979 B, 1981 A, 1988 H
Blakeslee, A. F., 1904 A
Bland, J. O. W., 1934 B
Blasco-Ibañez, Vicente, 1918 H
Bloch, Konrad Emil, 1950 O, 1951 M
Bloembergen, Nicolaas, 1960 Q
Blomster, Debra A., 1983 H
Bloom, Barry R., 1966 N
Blount, W. P., 1961 J
Blum, J., 1953 E
Blumberg, Baruch Samuel, 1957 K, 1965 N, 1966 L
Blumenbach, Johann Friedrich, 1776 C
Boccaccio, Giovanni, 1358
Bode, Wolfram, 1982 N
Boevé, J. J., 1957 A
Bohlool, B. B., 1973 B
Böhme, A., 1889 A
Bohr, Niels Henrik David, 1911 L
Boileau-Despréaux, Nicholas, 1674 B
Boivin, A., 1933 B
Bolivar, Francisco, 1977 Q
Bolognesi, Dani, 1985 G
Bolton, David C., 1982 M
Bolton, E. T., 1962 W

Bomhoff, Gerrit, 1970 G, 1975 L
Bonaparte, Louis Napoleon, 1848 E, 1851 D, 1852 C
Bonaparte, Napoleon, 1795 B, 1796 C, 1802 A, 1803 C, 1804 F, 1812 A, 1812 F, 1813 B, 1815 D, 1848 E
Bond, G., 1954 D
Boole, George, 1847 C
Borchardt, Lynne M., 1990 H
Bordet, Jules Jean Baptiste Vincent, 1889 F, 1895 E, 1898 I, 1899 F, 1901 G, 1906 C, 1925 C
Boreel, William, 1608
Borel, Pierre, 1608
Borglum, John Gutzon, 1941 Q
Borglum, Lincoln, 1941 Q
Borman, G. S., 1962 P
Borrel, Amédée, 1904 D, 1906 G, 1929 C
Bosch, Carl, 1908 F
Bossert, E., 1936 A
Boullay, Polydore, 1828 C
Boulton, Mathew, 1765 C
Boussingault, Jean Baptiste, 1838 B, 1857 B
Boveri, Theodor Heinrich, 1889 H, 1903 M
Bovet, Daniel, 1932 B, 1939 K
Bowen, Robert, 1967 C
Bowie, James, 1836 B
Boyce, Richard P., 1962 H, 1964 E
Boyer, Herbert W., 1972 L, 1973 N, 1977 R
Boyer, Paul D., 1977 Y
Boyle, Robert, 1660 A, 1661 B, 1662 A, 1671 A, 1673 B, 1774 C
Boylston, Zabdiel, 1721 A
Braconnot, Henri, 1820 C, 1820 D
Brahe, Tycho, 1573, 1609
Brahms, Johannes, 1868 F, 1877 H
Braille, Louis, 1829 B
Brattain, Walter Houser, 1947 F
Braun, Armin C., 1947 B
Braun, Karl Ferdinand, 1901 N
Brecht, Bertolt, 1728, 1928 J
Breed, R. S., 1910 A, 1911 A, 1937 B
Brefeld, Oscar, 1875 C
Breinl, F., 1930 D
Brenner, Don J., 1969 B, 1977 L, 1988 K, 1990 D
Brenner, Sydney, 1959 K, 1961 F, 1961 O, 1961 P, 1963 F, 1963 U, 1964 L

Brent, Leslie, 1953 R
Bretonneau, Pierre, 1821 A
Brezhnev, Leonid Ilyich, 1964 R
Brickwedde, F. G., 1932 K
Bridges, Calvin B., 1911 G, 1915 D
Bridges, Robert, 1918 H
Brierley, James A., 1972 A
Brill, Winston, 1977 J
Brinton, C. C., Jr., 1955 B, 1960 I, 1964 F
Broca, Paul, 1856 D
Brock, Katherine M., 1972 A
Brock, Thomas D., 1966 D, 1970 A, 1972 A
Broder, Sam, 1985 G
Brodie, Thomas Gregor, 1910 F
Broker, Thomas R., 1977 W
Brömel, Heinz, 1939 N, 1939 O
Brontë, Charlotte, 1847 E
Brontë, Emily, 1847 E
Brosius, Jürgen, 1979 K
Brotzu, Giuseppe, 1948 C
Brown, A. D., 1963 C
Brown, Barbara J., 1982 F
Brown, Douglas A., 1972 C
Brown, James H., 1919 A
Brown, Robert, 1827 B, 1832 C
Browne, Thomas, 1600 A
Brownlee, G. G., 1965 R
Broyles, Steven S., 1987 G
Brubaker, Robert R., 1980 J, 1981 F
Bruce, David, 1887 D, 1897 D, 1918 C, 1920 A
Bruce, Thomas, 1803 D
Brüche, E., 1932 F
Bruck, Carl, 1906 H
Bruckner, V., 1937 A
Brudenell, James Thomas (Lord Cardigan), 1854 E
Brugge, Joan, 1977 U
Brumberg, E. M., 1942 K
Brumfitt, W., 1958 B
Brunchorst, J., 1887 C
Brunfels, Otto, 1530 B, 1542
Brunstetter, B. C., 1943 B
Bruton, Ogden C., 1952 Q
Bryan, William Jennings, 1925 I
Bryant, Marvin P., 1952 A, 1962 E, 1967 G, 1979 D
Buchanan, J. G., 1958 C
Buchanan, Robert Earle, 1916 A, 1918 A
Buchmann, F., 1922 A

Buchner, Eduard, 1889 F, 1897 C, 1903 C

Buchner, Hans, 1889 F, 1895 E, 1898 I, 1899 F, 1903 C

Budd, William, 1856 A, 1873 A

Bugie, E., 1944 A

Buist, John Brown, 1886 E, 1904 D, 1906 G

Bulfinch, Thomas, 1855 D

Bunsen, Robert Wilhelm, 1850 C

Bunyan, John, 1680 A

Buonarroti, Michelangelo, 1504, 1508

Burch, C. R., 1942 K

Burdach, Karl, 1800 B, 1802 B

Burgdorfer, Willy, 1982 J

Burk, Dean, 1928 B, 1934 L

Burke, V., 1929 A

Burkitt, Denis Parsons, 1958 L

Burnet, Frank Macfarlane, 1929 D, 1935 F, 1936 E, 1936 G, 1940 J, 1944 G, 1945 D, 1946 I, 1952 O, 1953 R, 1955 N, 1957 N, 1961 L, 1962 S

Burr, Aaron, 1804 F

Burri, R., 1907 A, 1909 C

Burrill, Thomas Jonathan, 1879 D, 1899 B

Burris, Robert H., 1942 E, 1953 H, 1954 D

Burroughs, Edgar Rice, 1914 N

Burrow, T. W., 1956 I

Buttin, Gerard, 1956 D

Butzler, J. P., 1973 F

Buxton J. B., 1921 E

Byron, George Gordon (Lord Byron), 1812 G

Cabot, John, 1497

Cagniard-Latour, Charles, 1838 C, 1839 A

Cailletet, Louis-Paul, 1877 F, 1898 O

Cairns, John, 1963 E

Calder, Alexander, 1939 V

Caldwell, D. R., 1962 E

Caldwell, Erskine, 1932 P

Callaham, Dale, 1978 D

Calmette, Albert, 1906 I

Calvin, Melvin, 1950 M, 1952 G, 1954 M

Camerarius, Rudolph Jakob, 1694

Campbell, Allan, 1962 I

Campbell, Jack J. R., 1950 D

Cannizzaro, Stanislao, 1811 B, 1848 C

Cantley, Lewis C., 1986 H

Capote, Truman, 1966 S

Carbon, Philippe, 1979 K

Carlson, Chester Floyd, 1937 Q, 1959 T

Carlton, Bruce C., 1982 F

Carnaghan, R. B. A., 1961 J

Carnahan, J. E., 1960 C, 1962 D, 1964 F

Carpenter, D. C., 1923 C

Carré, Ferdinand, 1859 E

Carré, Henri, 1904 E

Carrel, Alexis, 1917 D, 1926 D

Carrère, L., 1922 E

Carrier, W. L., 1964 E

Carroll, James, 1901 F, 1919 D

Carroll, Lewis, 1865 G, 1871 F

Carss, B., 1958 C

Carswell, E. A., 1975 K

Carter, Jimmy, 1979 M

Carter, Philip B., 1980 J

Cashel, M., 1970 F

Caspar, Donald L. D., 1956 K, 1956 L, 1962 K

Cassidy, Paul, 1974 J

Castellani, Aldo, 1885 A

Castle, J. E., 1960 C

Castro, Fidel, 1959 U, 1961 X

Cauchy, Augustine Louis, 1821 D

Caugant, Dominique A., 1986 J

Cavalli-Sforza, Luca L., 1950 F, 1953 K

Cavendish, Henry, 1671 A, 1766 A, 1781 B, 1783 B

Caventou, Joseph Bienaimé, 1817 C

Cech, Thomas R., 1981 M, 1982 O, 1983 N

Celli, Angelo, 1887 E

Celsius, Anders, 1741

Centanni, Eugenio, 1901 E

Cervantes, Miguel de, 1605

Cesalpino, Andrea, 1583

Chadwick, James, 1932 L

Chagall, Marc, 1911 Q

Chain, Ernst Boris, 1929 B, 1940 C, 1940 D, 1940 E, 1944 B

Chakrabarty, Ananda M., 1972 E, 1980 G

Chamberlain, Neville, 1937 R

Chamberland, Charles, 1881 F, 1884 C

Chambers, Albert, 1885 A

Chambers, Robert, 1844 A

Chang, Annie C. Y., 1972 F, 1973 N

Chang, Timothy S., 1956 P

Chantemesse, André, 1898 C

Chaperon, Edward A., 1966 M

Chapin, Charles W., 1911 C

Chapman, C. B., 1953 E, 1960 B

Chaptal, Jean, 1790 B

Chargaff, Erwin, 1909 I, 1950 L

Charles I (king of England), 1646 C, 1649, 1660 C

Charles II (king of England), 1660 C, 1662 B

Charles VIII (king of France), 1495 A

Charles, Jacques Alexandre César, 1699 B, 1787 B

Chase, Martha, 1944 C, 1953 N, 1955 J

Chase, Merrill W., 1942 I

Chatton, E., 1937 E, 1957 Q, 1962 A

Chaucer, Geoffrey, 1400

Chelle, P.-L., 1936 J

Chen, Claudia, 1987 J

Chermann, Jean-Claude, 1983 L

Chesebro, Bruce, 1985 I

Chester, F. D., 1901 A

Chevalier, Charles, 1827 A

Chiang Kai-shek, 1949 K

Chilperic (king of France), 580

Chilton, Mary-Dell, 1977 O

Chisnell, John R., 1988 G

Chisolm, Sallie W., 1988 A

Cho, K. Y., 1963 C

Choo, Qui-Lim, 1989 E

Chow, Louise T., 1977 W

Christian, Walter, 1931 J, 1932 H, 1935 J, 1936 Q, 1938 G, 1939 O

Christin, Jean Pierre, 1741

Claman, Henry N., 1966 M

Clark, Alvin J., 1964 J, 1965 L, 1966 I

Clark, William, 1804 E

Clark, William Mansfield, 1915 A, 1923 I, 1925 F

Claude, Albert, 1938 B, 1950 K, 1955 P, 1956 Q

Clausius, Rudolf Emmanuel, 1850 B, 1854 D

Clavius, Christoph, 1582 B

Clayton, John, 1739

Cleary, J. P., 1935 A

Clemens, Samuel, *see* Twain, Mark

Clifton, C. E., 1935 A

Della Spina, Allessandro, 1299
DeLong, Edward F., 1988 B
Demerec, Milislav, 1937 H,
 1944 E, 1966 I
de Morveau, Guyton, 1671 A,
 1787 A, 1800 A
DeMoss, R. D., 1951 E
Dempster, G., 1955 B
de Narváez, Pánfilo, 1519 A
Denys, J., 1894 D, 1930 B
DePamphilis, M. L., 1971 A
De Petris, S., 1965 C
de Rozier, Jean Pilâtre, 1783 D
Derrick, Edward Holbrook, 1935 F
de Sacrobosco, Johannes, 1585
de Santa Anna, Antonio López,
 1836 B
de Saussure, Nicolas Théodore,
 1804 B, 1838 B
Descartes, René, 1637
Descloizeaux, M., 1846 D
de St. Vincent, Bory, 1825 A
de Tocqueville, Alexis Charles
 Henri Clérel, 1834 C
de Villalobos, Francisco López,
 1498
de Vries, Hugo, 1865 B, 1889 G,
 1900 C, 1900 J, 1900 K
Dewar, James, 1892 H, 1898 O
d'Herelle, Félix, 1915 C, 1917 C,
 1921 C, 1939 D
Dick, Albert Blake, 1879 H
Dick, George Frederick, 1924 B
Dick, Gladys Rowena, 1924 B
Dickens, Charles, 1837 L, 1838 H,
 1841 C, 1843 B, 1850 E,
 1859 I, 1861 K
Dickens, Frank, 1936 O, 1950 D
Dickenson, Emily, 1890 J
Dickey, James, 1970 T
Diderot, Denis, 1751
Diener, Theodor O., 1971 E
Dienes, Louis Ladislaus, 1929 I,
 1935 D, 1939 A
Diesel, Rudolf, 1893 G
Dilworth, M. J., 1966 C
Dimmitt, K., 1971 A
Diophanus, 250
Dioscorides, Pedanius, ca. 77 B,
 1530 B, 1542, 1907 B
Dirac, Paul, 1926 M
Diringer, H., 1983 M
Disraeli, Benjamin, 1874 E
Dixon, Jeremiah, 1766 B
Dixon, Malcolm, 1924 E
Dobzhansky, Theodosius, 1937 N

Doermann, A. H., 1952 M
Doherty, P. C., 1973 M, 1974 M
Dollond, John, 1729, 1758
Domagk, Gerhard, 1916 B,
 1932 B, 1935 C
Donath, Julius, 1904 B
Doniach, Deborah, 1957 O
Donizetti, Gaetano, 1835 C
Donker, Hendrick Jean Louis,
 1926 G
Donnan, Frederick George, 1911 K
Doppler, Christian Johann, 1842 E
d'Orleans, Chérubin, 1667 B
Dorner, Robert W., 1954 M
Dostoyevsky, Fyodor, 1866 D,
 1879 L
Doty, Paul, 1959 P
Doudoroff, Michael, 1950 D,
 1952 F
Dougherty, E. C., 1957 Q
Douglas, Stewart R., 1903 I
Douglass, William, 1736
Doyle, Arthur Conan, 1882 L,
 1891 I
Doyle, T. M., 1927 B
Drake, Harold L., 1982 D, 1985 B
Drebbel, Cornelius, 1590 A, 1608
Dressler, David, 1968 E
Drewes, K., 1928 A
Dreyfus, Alfred, 1894 K
Drummond, Jack Cecil, 1912 G
Dubois, Marie Eugène, 1891 E
Du Bois-Reymond, Emil Heinrich,
 1859 D
Dubos, René Jules, 1931 H,
 1939 B, 1942 B
Dubrunfaut, Augustin Pierre,
 1830 C, 1846 E
Duclaux, Émile, 1885 J
Duesberg, Peter, 1968 F
Duguid, J. P., 1955 B
Duine, Johannis A., 1990 C
Dulbecco, Renato, 1949 F,
 1952 O, 1963 K, 1967 N,
 1970 H
Dulmage, H. T., 1982 F
Dumas, Alexandre, 1844 D,
 1845 E
Dumas, Jean-Baptiste André,
 1821 B, 1828 C, 1839 A
Dunant, Jean-Henri, 1862 D
Dunkin, George William, 1923 D
Dupetit, Gabriel, 1881 E, 1886 C
Durand, Peter, 1819 A
Durham, Herbert Edward, 1896 E,
 1898 B

Dutrochet, René Joachim Henri,
 1837 H
Duysens, L. N. M., 1961 U

Eastman, George, 1888 I
Eaton, Monroe D., 1944 F
Eberhard, Anatole, 1981 B
Ebers, George, 1500 B.C.
Eberth, Carl Joseph, 1880 B,
 1884 E
Ech, Paul, 1500
Eco, Umberto, 1980 U
Eddy, B. E., 1962 P
Edelman, Gerald Maurice, 1959 L,
 1961 K, 1969 G
Edison, Thomas Alva, 1877 G,
 1879 G, 1879 H, 1883 I
Edmunds, P. N., 1955 B
Edward VIII (king of England),
 1936 U
Edward, D. G. ff., 1898 D, 1929 C
Edwards, P. R., 1953 L
Eggleton, Grace Palmer, 1927 G
Eggleton, Philip, 1927 G
Ehrenberg, Christian Gottfried,
 1838 A
Ehrlich, Paul, 1882 B, 1883 A,
 1884 H, 1885 I, 1885 M,
 1889 A, 1889 F, 1891 D, 1892 F,
 1893 C, 1895 E, 1895 F, 1897 G,
 1899 F, 1901 I, 1902 H, 1907 H,
 1910 B, 1955 N
Eijkman, Christiaan, 1896 F,
 1906 L
Einstein, Albert, 1827 B, 1887 H,
 1905 J, 1905 K, 1915 E
Eisen, Harvey, 1968 E
Eisenstark, A., 1964 H
Eldering, G., 1936 K
Elford, William J., 1931 A
Elion, Gertrude Belle, 1949 J
Eliot, George, 1860 C
Eliot, T. S., 1917 I, 1922 J
Elizabeth I (queen of England),
 1558
Elizabeth II (queen of England),
 1952 T
Ellar, David J., 1983 J, 1987 B
Ellerman, Vilhelm, 1911 E
Ellis, Emory L., 1921 C, 1939 D
Ellison, Ralph, 1952 U
Elsworth, R., 1956 B
Elvehjem, Conrad Arnold, 1937 O
Elwell, Lynn P., 1976 F
Embden, Gustav, 1914 F, 1933 I,
 1939 L

Emde, H., 1939 L

Emerson, Ralph Waldo, 1836 C, 1870 D

Empedocles, ca. 460 B.C., ca. 430 B.C. B, 1526

Enders, John Franklin, 1936 F, 1948 F, 1949 I, 1951 J, 1954 L

Engelhardt, Vladimir Aleksandrovich, 1930 G, 1943 C

Engelmann, Theodore Wilhelm, 1881 D, 1885 C

Engels, Friedrich, 1847 D

Englesberg, Ellis, 1965 K

English, Charles K., 1988 K, 1990 D

English, Leigh H., 1986 H

Engvall, Eva, 1971 F

Entner, Nathan, 1950 D, 1952 F

Epp, Otto, 1982 N

Epps, Helen M. R., 1942 F

Epstein, L. A., 1940 C

Epstein, Michael Anthony, 1958 L, 1963 L

Epstein, R. H., 1963 H

Erasistratus, ca. 280 B.C.

Erikson, R. L., 1977 U

Erlenmeyer, Emil, 1890 H

Ernst, P., 1888 A, 1888 C

Escherich, Theodore, 1885 A

Etinger-Tulcynska, R., 1902 B

Euclid, ca. 300 B.C.

Evans, Alice Catherine, 1887 D, 1897 D, 1914 A, 1918 C

Evans, Dolores G., 1975 J

Evans, M., 1979 I

Faber, Giovanni, 1625

Faber, Knud Helge, 1890 B

Fabricius ab Aquapendente, Hieronymus, 1603

Facini, Filippo, 1854 B

Fahrenheit, Gabriel Daniel, 1714

Falco, Elvira, 1949 J

Falkow, Stanley, 1969 B, 1976 F, 1981 F, 1984 H, 1988 J

Fallopius, 1561

Faloona, Fred A., 1987 I

Fankuchen, Isidor, 1936 H, 1937 F

Fano, U., 1944 E

Faraday, Michael, 1821 C, 1825 B, 1831 C, 1833 B, 1855 B

Faulds, Henry, 1885 P

Faulkner, William, 1929 Q

Fedor I (czar of Russia), 1598

Feinstone, Stephen M., 1973 L

Felix, A., 1916 D, 1920 C, 1934 D

Fenner, Frank, 1948 H

Ferber, D. M., 1981 F

Ferdinand III (Holy Roman Emperor), 1657 B

Ferdinand, Archduke Franz, 1914 D, 1914 M

Ferdinand, Carl Louis, 1882 J

Ferguson, M. S., 1942 A

Fermi, Enrico, 1934 O, 1942 M

Fernbach, Auguste, 1911 B

Ferrán y Clua, Jaime, 1885 G

Feulgen, Robert Joschim, 1924 F

Fielding, Henry, 1749 C

Fields, Barry S., 1986 I

Fields, Patricia, 1989 B

Fiers, W., 1978 K

Finch, John T., 1956 K, 1957 I, 1959 I, 1977 X

Fischer, Alfred, 1894 A, 1897 B, 1899 B, 1900 B, 1902 C

Fischer, D. J., 1960 C

Fischer, Emil Hermann, 1884 K, 1885 N, 1889 C, 1894 H, 1894 I, 1897 G, 1897 H, 1902 L

Fischer, F., 1983 B

Fischer, Hans, 1929 M

Fischhoff, David A., 1987 C

Fiske, Cyrus Hartwell, 1927 G, 1929 J

Fitzgerald, F. Scott, 1925 J

Fitzgerald, G. P., 1954 D

Fitz-James, Philip C., 1953 E, 1959 D, 1960 B

Flaubert, Gustave, 1856 F

Flaum, A., 1926 E

Flavell, Richard Anthony, 1977 V

Fleischmann, Martin, 1989 H

Fleish, Alfred, 1924 D

Fleming, Alexander, 1896 C, 1922 D, 1929 B, 1940 D

Fleming, Ian, 1953 Z

Flemming, Walther, 1882 H

Fletcher, Walter Morley, 1907 I

Flexner, Simon, 1898 C, 1900 E, 1909 F, 1912 B

Fliermans, C. B., 1979 H

Florentino, G. L., 1951 J

Florey, Howard Walter, 1929 B, 1940 D, 1948 C

Fol, Hermann, 1876 D

Fontana, Felice, 1781 C

Ford, C. E., 1962 S

Ford, Gerald R., Jr., 1974 T

Ford, Henry, 1893 F

Forster, E. M., 1905 N, 1908 J, 1924 H

Fothergill, John, 1748 B

Foucault, Jean Bernard Léon, 1851 B

Fox, C. Fred, 1965 I

Fox, George E., 1971 C, 1977 A

Fracastoro, Girolamo, 1530 A, 1546 A, 1762 A

Fraenkel, Albert, 1881 C, 1882 E, 1884 G

Fraenkel-Conrat, Heinz L., 1955 I, 1955 J

Fraley, Robert T., 1986 K

Francis, Edward, 1911 C

Francis, Thomas, Jr., 1933 D, 1940 K

Francisco, D. E., 1975 B

Frank, B., 1887 C, 1888 B

Frank, H., 1960 A

Fränkel, Carl, 1890 E

Frankland, Edward, 1852 B

Franklin, Benjamin, 1752

Franklin, Richard M., 1961 T, 1962 N

Franklin, Rosalind, 1953 O, 1956 K, 1956 L, 1957 I, 1959 I

Frazier, William C., 1923 C

Fred, E. B., 1912 A

Frédéricq, Pierre, 1954 I

Freeman, V. J., 1951 H

French, George R., 1978 H

Frenkel, Albert, 1954 F

Freud, Sigmund, 1895 I

Freund, Jules, 1942 J

Freundt, E. A., 1898 D, 1929 C

Friedländer, Carl, 1882 E, 1884 B, 1884 G

Friedman, Robert M., 1963 M

Fromherz, Konrad, 1911 B

Frosch, Paul, 1898 G, 1901 F

Fuchs, Georg, 1980 D, 1982 C

Fuchs, Leonhart, 1530 B, 1542

Fuhrman, Jed A., 1980 A, 1990 B

Fuhrott, Johann C., 1856 D

Fuller, R. C., 1954 M, 1959 C

Funk, Casimir, 1896 F, 1906 L, 1912 G

Furuichi, Y., 1975 R

Füssle, Roswitha, 1981 G

Gaffky, Georg Theodore August, 1881 H, 1884 E, 1892 C

Gagarin, Yuri Alekseyevich, 1961 W

Gajdusek, Daniel Carleton, 1920 D, 1957 K, 1965 N, 1966 L

Gale, Ernest F., 1942 F

Galen, ca. 460 B.C., ca. 367 B.C., ca. 280 B.C., second century A, 164, 1526, 1879 B

Galilei, Vincenzio, 1657 A

Galileo, 1582 A, 1586, 1590 A, 1590 B, 1608, 1610, 1657 A

Gallo, Robert Charles, 1980 N, 1983 L, 1984 L, 1985 G

Galtier, Pierre Victor, 1879 E

Galton, Francis, 1794, 1869 F, 1885 P

Galvani, Luigi, 1780 C, 1800 D

Gamaleia, Nikolae, 1898 F

Gamow, George, 1948 M

Gandhi, Mohandas Karamchand, 1932 O, 1948 P

Garfield, James A., 1881 K

Gargus, J. Jay, 1974 C

Garnak, Marit, 1979 F

Garner, J. V., 1972 D

Garrod, Archibold, 1908 E

Garry, B., 1959 N

Gärtner, A. A., 1888 D

Gatti, Angelo, 1764 A

Gauguin, Paul, 1891 J

Gay, John, 1728

Gay-Lussac, Joseph, 1699 B, 1787 B, 1804 D, 1810 A, 1811 C, 1815 A

Gayon, Ulysse, 1881 E, 1886 C

Geiger, Hans Wilhelm, 1908 H

Gelinas, Richard E., 1977 W

Gell, Philip George Houthem, 1963 O

Gellert, M., 1967 R

Gell-Mann, Murray, 1961 V, 1964 P

Gemski, P., 1964 F

Genderen, H. Van, 1952 G

Genghis Khan, 1210 B

Gengou, Octave, 1901 G, 1906 C

George I (king of England), 1721 A

George VI (king of England), 1952 T

Gerber, P., 1962 O

Gershon, Richard K., 1970 J

Gershowitz, A., 1970 N

Gershwin, George, 1935 Q

Gesner, Conrad, 1545, 1546 B

Gessard, Carle, 1882 C

Gest, Howard, 1949 E, 1970 D

Gesteland, R. F., 1964 F

Gey, George O., 1933 E, 1952 N

Ghosh, Sudhamoy, 1964 B

Ghuysen, Jean-Marie, 1958 B

Gibbon, Edward, 1776 F

Gibbons, N. E., 1961 B

Gibbs, C. J., Jr., 1966 L

Gibbs, Josiah Willard, 1878 I

Gibbs, Martin, 1951 E, 1959 C

Giemsa, Gustav, 1905 I

Gierer, A., 1955 J

Gilbert, Joseph Henry, 1857 B

Gilbert, Walter, 1966 F, 1968 E, 1977 S

Gilbert, William, 1600 A, 1609

Gilbert, William Schwenck, 1878 L, 1879 K, 1885 R

Giovannoni, Stephen J., 1988 B

Gish, Lillian, 1912 J

Glaser, Donald Arthur, 1952 R

Glenn, John, 1962 X

Glenny, Alexander Thomas, 1904 C, 1921 E

Glick, Bruce, 1956 P

Glimstedt, Gösta, 1928 D

Glover, J., 1952 G

Gmelin, Leopold, 1825 D

Godunov, Boris, 1598

Goeddel, David V., 1979 J

Goethe, Johann Wolfgang von, 1808 B, 1869 H

Goldberg, Rube, 1907 K

Goldsmith, Oliver, 1773 C

Golgi, Camillo, 1885 K, 1885 L, 1898 L

Gomatos, Peter J., 1962 L

Gonzalez, José M., 1982 F

Good, Robert A., 1961 L

Goodgal, Sol H., 1957 F

Goodman, Howard M., 1972 L

Goodpasture, Ernest William, 1901 E, 1906 G, 1929 F, 1931 F, 1931 G, 1936 L, 1940 J

Goodsir, John, 1842 B

Goodyear, Charles, 1839 G

Gorby, Yuri A., 1988 H

Gordon, F. B., 1963 I

Gordon, J., 1893 A, 1923 B

Gorer, Peter A., 1937 G, 1958 M

Gorter, Evert, 1925 E

Gottesman, Susan, 1984 F

Gottlieb, Michael, 1981 H

Gould, R. Gordon, 1960 Q

Gounod, Charles, 1859 H, 1883 L

Gowans, James L., 1962 S

Goy, Michael F., 1977 H

Grabar, Pierre, 1955 O

Grabowski, Paula J., 1981 M

Grace, James T., Jr., 1967 S

Graham, Thomas, 1839 A

Grahame, Kenneth, 1908 J

Gram, Hans Christian, 1882 E, 1884 B

Grant, Ulysses S., 1865 E

Grassi, Giovanni, 1880 D, 1898 J

Gratia, André, 1925 B

Gray, C. H., 1944 D

Gray, Elisha, 1876 G

Green, H. N., 1940 G

Greenberg, E. Peter, 1979 E

Greene, Grahame, 1950 S

Gregory (bishop of Tours), 580

Gregory XIII (Pope), 1582 B

Grendel, F., 1925 E

Grew, Nehemiah, 1682 B

Grey, D., 1942 K

Griese, A., 1931 J

Griffith, A. A., 1937 Q

Griffith, D. W., 1915 I

Griffith, Frederick, 1928 C, 1944 C

Grimes, D. J., 1986 B

Grimme, A., 1888 A, 1902 C

Groisman, Eduardo A., 1989 B

Gross, Hans J., 1978 L

Gross, Jerome, 1955 M

Gross, Ludwik, 1951 I

Grubbs, G., 1962 P

Grüber, Max, 1896 E

Gruby, David, 1841 A

Grunberg-Manago, Marianne, 1955 L, 1961 Q

Grunstein, Michael, 1975 I, 1985 D

Guérin, Camille, 1906 I

Guerrier-Takada, Cecelia, 1983 N

Guest, J. R., 1962 C, 1964 C

Guex-Holzer, S., 1952 E, 1953 C

Guillard, Robert R. L., 1979 C

Guillemin, Roger, 1960 L

Guillermond, A. G., 1933 G

Gunsalus, Irwin Clyde, 1951 E, 1972 E

Gunter, Edmund, 1620 A

Gutenberg, Johann, 1454

Guthrie, Samuel, 1831 B

Gutmann, A., 1950 I

Gyurasits, Elizabeth B., 1975 P

Haber, Fritz, 1904 G, 1908 F

Hack, Adelle M., 1979 G

Hadlow, William, 1957 K

Haeckel, Ernst Heinrich, 1866 A

Haffkine, Waldemar, 1892 G, 1897 F

Hahn, Chang S., 1988 N
Hahn, Fred E., 1951 K
Hahn, Martin, 1903 C
Hahn, Otto, 1938 I
Haider, Muhammad Z., 1983 J
Haiyān, Jabir ibn, 750
Halberstaedter, L., 1907 B, 1966 A
Haldane, J. B. S., 1953 V, 1955 K
Haldane, John Scott, 1902 K
Hales, Brian J., 1986 E
Hales, Stephen, 1727, 1733
Haley, Alex, 1976 O
Hall, B. D., 1961 N, 1963 W
Hall, Chester Moor, 1729, 1758
Hallauer, C., 1931 F
Halley, Edmund, 1705
Halvorson, Harlyn O., 1957 E
Halvorson, H. Orin, 1972 D
Hamblin, J., 1973 B
Hamilton, Alexander, 1804 F
Hamilton, Pat B., 1953 I
Hamkalo, Barbara, 1970 P
Hammerstein, Oscar, 1943 H
Handel, George Frederic, 1715 B,
    1742
Hannay, C. L., 1953 J
Hansberry, Lorraine, 1959 V
Hansen, Armauer Gerhard Henrik,
    1874 A
Hansen, Emil Christian, 1883 D
Hanson, R. S., 1972 D
Hapelius, 1606 A
Harden, Arthur, 1898 A, 1906 B,
    1906 J, 1906 K, 1914 G
Harding, J. D. J., 1961 J
Harding, Warren, 1920 F
Hardy, Thomas, 1874 F, 1891 I
Hare, Ronald, 1941 G
Hargreaves, James, 1764 B
Harris, H., 1956 C
Harris, J. Ieuan, 1955 H
Harrison, Ross Granville, 1907 G,
    1917 D
Harrison, William Henry, 1811 D
Harshman, Sidney, 1974 J
Harteck, Paul, 1934 N
Hartman, Paul E., 1963 V
Hartman, Philip E., 1966 I
Hartman, T. L., 1899 A
Hartree, Edward Francis, 1938 F
Haruna, I., 1963 S
Harvard, John, 1636
Harvey, William, 1559, 1603,
    1616, 1628, 1637, 1661 A, 1733
Haseloff, James, 1981 L

Hashimoto, H., 1957 O
Hassid, William Zev, 1931 I,
    1939 I, 1941 I
Hastings, E. G., 1912 A
Hastings, J. Woodland, 1970 C,
    1979 E
Hauptmann, Bruno, 1932 O
Haurowitz, F., 1930 D
Hauser, Gustave, 1885 B
Haworth, Walter Norman,
    1928 G, 1932 J, 1933 J, 1935 L
Hawthorne, Nathaniel, 1850 E,
    1851 F
Haydn, Franz Joseph, 1755 A
Hayes, William, 1952 I, 1953 K,
    1956 F, 1958 G
Hayne, Theodore H., 1919 D
Hazelbauer, Gerald L., 1973 A
Heatley, Norman G., 1940 D
Hedges, R. W., 1974 H
Hedgpeth, Joe, 1972 L
Heffron, Fred, 1989 B
Hegeman, George D., 1978 A
Heidelberger, Michael, 1923 F,
    1929 H
Heimple, A. M., 1967 J
Heisenberg, Werner Karl, 1927 J
Helinski, Donald R., 1964 M,
    1967 I
Heller, E., 1963 M
Heller, Joseph, 1961 Y
Helling, Robert B., 1973 N
Hellriegel, Hermann, 1857 B,
    1886 B, 1889 B
Helmholtz, Hermann Ludwig,
    1847 B, 1881 J
Helmstetter, Charles E., 1968 A
Hemingway, Ernest, 1926 P,
    1929 Q, 1940 R
Hench, Philip Showalter, 1933 J,
    1936 R
Henderson, Donald A., 1967 L
Henle, Friedrich Gustav Jacob,
    1840 A
Hennessy, J. N., 1980 I
Henry VIII (king of England),
    1509, 1535 B
Henry, Edward Richard, 1901 P
Henry, Joseph, 1829 A, 1831 C
Henseleit, Kurt, 1932 I
Henson, Matthew Alexander,
    1909 K
Herbert, D., 1956 B
Heremans, Joseph F., 1959 M
Heremans, M. T., 1959 M
Herriott, Roger M., 1957 F

Herschel, William, 1800 C, 1885 P
Hershey, Alfred Day, 1943 D,
    1944 C, 1946 H, 1948 E,
    1953 N, 1955 J
Hershfield, Vickers, 1974 P
Hertwig, Oscar, 1876 D
Hertz, Heinrich Rudolph, 1887 G,
    1888 H
Hess, J. Fred, 1987 A, 1988 E
Hess, Victor, 1932 M
Hesse, Fannie Eilshemius, 1881 A,
    1882 A
Hesse, Walther, 1881 A, 1882 A
Heterington, Diane R., 1980 C
Hibbert, Harold, 1931 B
Higa, A., 1972 F
Higgs, Sonia A., 1974 D
Hill, Archibald Vivian, 1911 I,
    1912 D
Hill, Robert, 1939 J, 1960 N,
    1961 U
Hill, Ruth Frances, 1958 H
Hilleman, M. R., 1960 J
Hillier, James, 1937 I, 1953 E,
    1960 B
Hilmen, Marcia, 1988 D
Hiltner, L., 1885 E
Hinterberger, A., 1949 D
Hipparchus, second century B
Hippe, Hans, 1977 C
Hippocrates, ca. 460 B.C.
Hirst, Edmund Langley, 1933 J
Hirst, George, 1941 G
Hisinger, Wilhelm, 1803 B
Hitchings, George Herbert, 1949 J
Hitler, Adolf, 1933 K, 1934 Q,
    1937 R, 1938 J
Ho, David D., 1984 K, 1985 F
Ho, Monto, 1975 M
Ho Chi Minh, 1946 L
Hoagland, C., 1940 L
Hoagland, Mahlon Bush, 1957 P
Hobbes, Thomas, 1651
Hobbie, John E., 1975 B
Hobot, Jan A., 1984 C
Hoch, James A., 1976 E
Hodgkin, Dorothy Crowfoot,
    1944 B, 1949 G
Hodgkin, Thomas, 1832 B
Hoeniger, Judith F. M., 1964 A,
    1965 E
Hoffman, Felix, 1899 I
Hoffman, Hermann, 1869 A
Hoffmann, Eric, 1905 D
Hofmann, Christina, 1988 I

Hofmeister, Franz, 1902 L
Höfte, Herman, 1989 A
Hogg, John, 1861 D
Hogg, Robert W., 1974 C
Hoggan, M. David, 1965 O
Hogness, David S., 1975 I, 1985 D
Hohn, Barbara, 1974 Q, 1978 I
Hohn, Thomas, 1974 Q
Holden, Joseph T., 1949 C
Holland, John J., 1961 I, 1968 J
Holley, Robert William, 1964 L,
    1965 S
Holliday, Robin, 1964 G
Holmes, Kenneth, 1957 I
Holmes, Oliver Wendell, 1842 C
Home, Francis, 1765 B
Homer, ca. 1190 B.C.
Homer, Winslow, 1883 M
Hooke, Robert, 1664 A, 1665 B,
    1665 C
Hooker, Joseph Dalton, 1858 D
Hopkins, Frederick Gowland,
    1896 F, 1906 L, 1907 I, 1912 G,
    1921 F, 1926 K
Hopkins, Gerard Manley, 1918 H
Hopkins, S. J., 1942 H
Hoppe-Seyler, Felix, 1862 B,
    1869 E, 1876 E, 1878 E,
    1878 G, 1879 F, 1885 N
Horiuchi, T. S., 1959 Q
Horne, R. W., 1951 B, 1959 K
Horvath, R. S., 1970 E
Hotchkiss, Rollin D., 1939 B
Houghton, Michael, 1989 E
Houseman, A. E., 1896 J
Houssay, Bernardo, 1936 P
Houston, Sam, 1836 B
Houwink, A. L., 1949 D, 1950 B
Howard, A., 1953 T
Howard-Flanders, Paul, 1962 H,
    1964 E
Howells, William Dean, 1885 S
Hozumi, Nobumichi, 1976 K
Hsu, Leslie, 1972 F
Hsu, Ming-Ta, 1973 G
Hu, Liu, 190
Hu, Sho-Ih, 1982 D, 1985 B
Huang Ti (emperor of China), ca.
    2595 B.C. A
Huber, Harald, 1982 B
Huber, Robert, 1982 N
Huebner, Robert J., 1965 O,
    1969 F
Huggins, Charles B., 1911 E
Hughes, David Edward, 1878 J

Hughes, Langston, 1925 J
Hughes, W. Howard, 1957 D
Hugo, Victor, 1862 E
Hülphers, G., 1926 C
Human, Mary L., 1952 L
Humperdinck, Englebert, 1893 J
Hungate, R. E., 1946 D
Hunter, John, 1767 A, 1771 C
Hurwitz, C., 1958 D
Hurwitz, Jerard, 1962 V
Huxley, Aldous, 1932 P
Huxley, Julian Sorell, 1942 L,
Huxley, Thomas Henry, 1863 C,
    1869 H, 1942 L
Huygens, Christiaan, 1582 A,
    1657 A, 1681 A

Ibsen, Henrik, 1879 L
Iichinska, E., 1960 E
Iino, Tetsuo, 1953 L
Ikawa, Miyoshi, 1949 C
Ikigai, Hajime, 1987 D
Inge, William, 1950 T
Ingenhousz, Jan, 1779 B, 1804 B,
    1837 H
Ingrassia, Giovanni Filippo, 1553
Irr, Joseph, 1965 K
Irving, Washington, 1820 F
Isaacs, Alick, 1957 L
Ishiwata, Shigetane, 1902 E, 1915 B
Ishizaka, Kimishige, 1966 O
Ishizaka, Teruko, 1966 O
Israel, C., 1913 C
Itakura, Keiichi, 1977 R, 1979 J
Ivanovics, G., 1937 A
Ivanovsky, Dmitri Iosifovich,
    1882 F, 1892 E, 1899 E
Iyer, V. N., 1968 I

Jaap, R. George, 1956 P
Jack the Ripper, 1888 J
Jackson, Charles, 1846 H
Jackson, David A., 1972 M
Jacob, A. E., 1974 H
Jacob, François, 1938 E, 1950 I,
    1954 I, 1955 D, 1955 F, 1956 F,
    1956 G, 1958 G, 1958 P,
    1959 J, 1959 N, 1959 O,
    1960 M, 1961 E, 1961 O,
    1963 F, 1963 U, 1968 E
Jacobs, W. A., 1916 B
Jacobs, Walter Abraham, 1909 I
Jacobson, Michael, 1968 J
Jacquard, Joseph-Marie, 1801 C
Jakob, Alfons Maria, 1920 D,
    1966 L

James, Henry, 1878 M, 1898 R
Janczura, Ewa, 1961 A
Jannasch, Holger W., 1979 A
Jansen, Hans, 1590 A
Jansen, Kathrin, 1982 C
Jansen, Zacharias, 1590 A, 1608
Jarlenski, Donna Marie L., 1980 C
Jarrett, William, 1966 K
Jeffreys, Alec John, 1977 V,
    1985 K
Jellinek, Emil, 1901 O
Jenner, Edward, 1767 A, 1796 B,
    1880 C, 1881 F
Jensen, F., 1962 O
Jerne, Niels K., 1945 D, 1955 N,
    1957 N, 1963 P, 1974 L,
    1975 N
Jervis, George A., 1952 P
Jesty, Benjamin, 1774 A, 1796 B
Jeter, Randall M., 1984 E
Joffe, J. S., 1922 B
Johannsen, Wilhelm Ludwig,
    1909 H
Johannson, H., 1932 F
John (king of England), 1215
John Paul I (Pope), 1978 N
John Paul II (Pope), 1978 N
Johnson, Karl M., 1978 H, 1982 L,
    1984 M
Johnson, Marvin J., 1949 B,
    1950 N
Johnson, Samuel, 1755 B
Johnson, W. M., 1983 E
Joklik, Wolfgang K., 1961 H
Joliet, Louis, 1673 C
Joliot-Curie, Frédéric, 1934 O
Joliot-Curie, Irène, 1934 O
Jones, James, 1951 P
Jones, M. J., 1946 E
Jones, Margaret F., 1957 B
Jones, R. Norman, 1942 H
Jones, William, 1706
Jordan, D. C., 1982 A
Jordan, Edwin O., 1899 G
Jordan, Elke, 1968 C, 1974 H
Jost, H., 1939 L
Joule, James Prescott, 1849 E
Joyce, James, 1914 N, 1922 J,
    1939 T, 1964 P
Judson, Egbert Putnam, 1893 H
Jungemann, Kurt, 1977 I
Jupille, Jean-Baptiste, 1885 H

Kaback, H. R., 1966 E
Kabat, Elvin Abraham, 1939 H,
    1970 I

Land, Edwin Herbert, 1947 F
Landau, J. V., 1958 D
Landsteiner, Karl, 1900 H, 1904 B, 1908 B, 1909 F, 1917 E, 1926 F, 1940 N, 1942 I
Lane, David J., 1984 B, 1986 A
Lang, D., 1959 A
Langevin, Paul, 1915 F
Langmuir, Irving, 1910 G, 1916 F
Langworthy, Thomas A., 1977 D
Larabeke, Van, 1975 L
Lark, Karl G., 1968 I
Larsen, Steven H., 1974 B, 1974 C
Lasky, L., 1987 F
Laurent, Auguste, 1848 A
Lauritsen, T., 1934 M
Laver, W. George, 1973 K
Laveran, Charles Louis Alphonse, 1880 D, 1884 I
Lavoisier, Antoine, 1772 B, 1772 C, 1774 C, 1775 B, 1777 A, 1780 B, 1783 A, 1783 B, 1787 A, 1789 B, 1789 C, 1789 D, 1810 E, 1815 A
Lawes, John Bennet, 1857 B
Lawrence, D. H., 1928 K
Lawrence, Ernest Orlando, 1931 M
Lawrence, Jerome, 1955 S
Leakey, Louis Seymour Bazett, 1959 S
Leakey, Mary Douglas Nicol, 1959 S
Le Bel, Joseph-Achille, 1874 D
LeBoit, Philip E., 1988 L
Lecanu, Louis René, 1838 F, 1862 B
le Carré, John, 1963 Z
Leclerc, Charles Victor Emmanuel, 1802 A
Leclerc, Georges Louis, *see* de Buffon, Comte
Leder, Phillip, 1977 V
Lederberg, Esther M., 1951 G, 1952 J, 1953 K, 1956 H, 1960 G
Lederberg, Joshua, 1941 H, 1944 D, 1946 F, 1946 G, 1947 C, 1948 D, 1950 E, 1950 G, 1952 J, 1952 K, 1953 K, 1953 L, 1956 H, 1957 N, 1958 G
LeDuc, J. W., 1984 M
Lee, Harper, 1960 S
Lee, Ho Wang, 1978 H, 1982 L
Lee, Nancy, 1965 K

Lee, Pyung Woo, 1978 H
Lee, Robert E., 1865 E, 1955 S
Leeuwenhoek, Antony van, 1657 A, 1665 E, 1673 A, 1674 A, 1676, 1677, 1680 B, 1683 A, 1683 B, 1786 A, 1853 A, 1921 A
Lehman, I. Robert, 1958 O, 1963 T, 1967 R
Lehmann, Karl Bernhard, 1896 B
Lehninger, Albert Lester, 1948 K, 1951 N
Leibniz, Gottfried Wilhelm, 1684, 1690 A, 1693 B, 1696
Leishman, William Boog, 1896 C, 1900 F, 1903 J
Leloir, Luis F., 1950 N
Lemaux, Peggy, 1978 C
Lemery, Nicolas, 1671 A
Lenard, Philipp, 1898 P
Lenin, Nikolai (Vladimir Ilyich Ulyanov), 1917 H
Lenoir, Jean Etienne, 1859 F, 1863 E
Leo VI (emperor of the Byzantine Empire), 900
Leoncavallo, Ruggiero, 1892 I
Leopold I (Holy Roman Emperor), 1657 B
Lerner, Alan Jay, 1956 S
Lessing, Doris, 1962 Z
Levaditi, Constantin, 1908 B
Levene, Phoebus Aaron Theodor, 1909 I, 1928 F, 1929 L
Levin, Bruce R., 1980 F
Levine, M., 1923 C
Levine, Philip, 1926 F
Lewis, E. B., 1955 K
Lewis, Gilbert Newton, 1916 F
Lewis, I. M., 1934 C
Lewis, Meriwether, 1804 E
Lewis, Paul A., 1909 F, 1919 D
Lewis, Sinclair, 1920 G, 1925 J
Liebig, Georg, 1850 A
Lin, Tai-Shun, 1985 G
Lincoln, Abraham, 1863 F, 1865 E
Lincoln, Ralph E., 1968 D
Lindbergh, Charles, 1927 K, 1932 O
Lindegren, C., 1935 B
Lindenmann, Jean, 1957 L
Lindow, Steven E., 1976 C, 1986 C
Lineweaver, Hans, 1934 L
Link, H., 1795 A
Link, Karl Paul, 1950 E

Linnaeus, Carolus, 1686, 1735 B, 1737, 1749 A, 1753, 1763 A, 1767 B
Linossier, Georges, 1845 B, 1898 M
Lior, H., 1983 E
Lipmann, Fritz Albert, 1936 O, 1937 L, 1941 J, 1941 K, 1947 D, 1951 M, 1961 S
Lippershey, Hans, 1608
Lisbonne, M., 1922 E
Lister, Joseph Jackson, 1830 B, 1867 B, 1878 B
Liston, Robert, 1846 H
Liszt, Franz, 1856 G
Little, J. W., 1963 T
Littlefield, John W., 1955 M
Liu, S.-T., 1981 C
Livingstone, David, 1871 E
Livy, 790 B.C.
Locke, Alain, 1925 J
Locke, John, 1690 B
Loeb, L., 1905 B
Loeb, Tim, 1960 I, 1961 G
Loew, Oscar, 1869 E, 1893 A, 1901 J
Loewe, Frederick, 1956 S
Loewenstein, E., 1904 C
Loewi, Otto, 1911 F
Löffler, Friedrich August Johannes, 1877 A, 1881 H, 1882 D, 1883 B, 1888 E, 1890 A, 1898 G, 1901 F
Lohmann, Karl, 1927 H, 1929 J, 1932 G, 1933 H, 1936 N
Long, Crawford Williamson, 1846 H
Longfellow, Henry Wadsworth, 1855 D
Loosmore, R. M., 1961 J
Lorenz, Konrad Zacharias, 1919 E, 1935 N
Loschmidt, Johann Josef, 1811 B, 1865 C
Louis XIII (king of France), 1624 B
Louis XIV (king of France), 1643 B, 1662 C
Louis XVI (king of France), 1793 B
Louis Philippe (king of France), 1848 E
L'Ouverture, Toussaint, 1802 A
Low, Juliette Gordon, 1912 I
Lowell, Percival, 1858 D
Lower, Richard, 1669 A

Meyer, Julius Lothar, 1869 G
Meyer, Karl F., 1887 D, 1914 A, 1918 C, 1920 A, 1932 C
Meyer, Ortwin, 1978 A
Meyerhof, Otto Fritz, 1911 I, 1912 D, 1926 B, 1927 F, 1927 H, 1928 B, 1934 I, 1936 N
Meyers, Jane Aldrich, 1976 F
M'Fadyean, John, 1900 G
Michaelis, Leonor, 1913 F
Michel, Hartmut, 1980 Q, 1982 N
Michelangelo, 1504, 1508
Michelson, Albert Abraham, 1887 H
Mier, F. W., 1980 N
Miescher, Johann Friedrich, 1869 E, 1889 I
Migula, Walter, 1897 A, 1897 B
Miki, Kunio, 1982 N
Milkman, Roger, 1973 E, 1980 F
Miller, Arthur, 1949 M, 1953 AA
Miller, J., 1985 J
Miller, Jacques Francis Albert Pierre, 1961 L, 1968 H
Miller, Oscar, 1970 P
Miller, Stanley Lloyd, 1924 G, 1953 V
Millikan, Robert Andrews, 1911 M
Milovanovic, Milan, 1954 L
Milstein, César, 1955 N, 1974 L, 1975 N
Milton, John, 1667 C
Minot, G. R., 1948 B
Miquel, P., 1879 A
Mirbel, Charles François Brisseau, 1802 C
Miró, Joan, 1933 L
Mitchell, Charles, 1819 A, 1839 E
Mitchell, G. F., 1968 H
Mitchell, Margaret, 1936 V, 1939 U
Mitchell, Peter Dennis, 1961 C, 1961 M, 1965 P, 1974 C
Mitchison, Nicholas Avrion, 1953 S, 1970 K
Mitscherlich, Eilhard, 1848 A
Mitsuhashi, Susumu, 1959 G, 1960 F
Mitsuya, Hiroaki, 1985 G
Mitus, A., 1954 L
Mizuno, D., 1959 Q
Mizutani, Satoshi, 1970 H
Monet, Claude, 1868 G
Monod, Jacques Lucien, 1938 E, 1941 E, 1950 C, 1950 I, 1952 H,

1954 E, 1955 D, 1956 D, 1958 P, 1959 N, 1959 O, 1960 M, 1961 O, 1961 E
Monroe, James, 1823 D
Montagnier, Luc, 1962 M, 1983 L, 1984 L
Montagu, Mary Wortley, 1717
Monteverdi, Claudio, 1587, 1607 B
Montgolfier, Jacques-Etienne, 1783 D
Montgolfier, Joseph-Michel, 1783 D
Moore, Claire, 1977 W
Moore, Henry, 1936 W, 1938 M
Moore, Patrick S., 1989 C, 1990 F
Moore, Stanford, 1950 P
Morange, A., 1879 C
More, Thomas, 1535 B
Morel, G., 1970 G
Morgagni, Giovanni, 1761 A
Morgan, J. P., 1905 O
Morgan, M., 1975 R
Morgan, Thomas Hunt, 1910 E, 1911 G, 1911 H, 1915 D, 1931 L
Morley, Edward William, 1887 H
Morris, George, 1979 H
Morrison, Toni, 1987 L
Morrow, John F., 1974 N
Morse, M. L., 1956 H
Morse, Samuel F. B., 1837 J, 1844 B
Mortenson, Leonard, 1953 I, 1960 C, 1962 D, 1964 D
Morton, William Thomas, 1846 H
Moseley, Henry Gwyn Jeffreys, 1869 G, 1914 I
Moss, Bernard, 1970 N, 1975 R, 1987 G
Moulder, James W., 1953 A, 1953 P, 1966 A
Mower, H. F., 1960 C
Moyle, Jennifer, 1965 P
Mozart, Wolfgang Amadeus, 1770 C, 1786 B, 1787 D, 1791 B
Mudd, Stuart, 1930 D, 1937 D, 1940 A, 1941 B
Mueller, Gerald, 1962 V
Mulder, Gerardus Johannes, 1838 E
Muller, Hermann Joseph, 1911 G, 1915 D, 1927 E
Müller, M., 1937 Q
Müller, Otto Frederik, 1773 A, 1786 A
Müller, Paul Herrmann, 1940 O

Müller, Walther, 1908 H
Müller-Hill, Benno, 1966 F
Mullis, Kary, 1978 J, 1987 I
Munch, Edvard, 1893 K
Müntz, Achille, 1877 C
Munyon, William E., 1967 S
Murphy, G. M., 1932 K
Murphy, W. P., 1948 B
Murray, Everitt George Dunne, 1926 C
Murray, Keith, 1973 D
Murray, R. G. E., 1953 D
Mushet, Robert, 1856 E
Mussolini, Benito, 1922 I, 1943 G
Muthukrishnan, S., 1975 R
Myers, A. T., 1943 B
Myrbäck, Karl, 1923 G

Nabokov, Vladimir, 1955 R
Nachmansohn, David, 1943 F
Nakae, Taiji, 1976 D, 1987 D
Nakamura, H., 1970 D
Nakazawa, Teruko, 1973 D
Napier, John, 1585, 1614 B, 1617 B
Nathans, Daniel, 1952 L, 1961 S, 1962 J, 1970 M, 1973 I, 1973 H, 1973 J
Nathansohn, A., 1902 A
Naudé, S. M., 1929 N
Nealson, Kenneth H., 1970 C, 1976 B
Needham, John Turberville, 1748 A, 1749 B, 1765 A, 1861 A
Neelsen, Friedrich, 1882 B, 1883 A
Ne'eman, Yuval, 1961 V
Negelein, Erwin Paul, 1939 N, 1939 O
Negri, Adelchi, 1903 L, 1905 F
Neidhardt, Frederick C., 1956 E, 1983 C
Neisser, Albert Ludwig Siegmund, 1879 B, 1887 E, 1906 H
Nelson, Horatio, 1801 E, 1805 B
Nernst, Walter Hermann, 1906 N
Nester, Eugene W., 1975 L, 1977 O
Neubauer, Otto, 1911 B
Neuberg, Carl Alexander, 1911 B, 1913 E, 1918 F
Neufeld, Fred, 1900 A, 1902 B
Neumann, E., 1982 R
Neumann, R., 1896 B
Neva, F. A., 1962 R
Newcomen, Thomas, 1711, 1765 C

Perutz, Max Ferdinand, 1959 R
Peters, G. A., 1974 A
Peterson, W. H., 1912 A
Petit, A., 1970 G
Petre, A. W., 1935 H
Petri, Richard Julius, 1881 A,
1887 A
Petterson, A., 1912 B
Petzold, H., 1962 B
Pfankuch, E., 1939 F, 1940 H,
1942 G
Pfeffer, Wilhelm Friedrich, 1881 I,
1885 C, 1886 H
Pfeiffer, Richard Friedrich
Johannes, 1892 B, 1892 D,
1894 E
Pfennig, Norbert, 1979 D
Pflüger, Eduard, 1872 F, 1875 D
Phipps, James, 1796 B
Picasso, Pablo, 1900 S, 1903 R,
1907 O, 1921 I, 1925 K, 1937 S
Piccard, Auguste, 1932 N, 1948 O
Piccard, Jacques, 1948 O
Pickford, Mary, 1912 J
Pictet, Raoul Pierre, 1877 F
Pierce, Cynthia H., 1942 C
Pietz, J., 1938 D
Pijper, Adrianus, 1941 C, 1946 A,
1947 A, 1948 A
Pinner, Adolf, 1885 N
Pirie, J. H. H., 1926 C
Pirie, Norman W., 1935 H,
1936 H, 1937 F
Pitt, R. M., 1934 D
Pittman, Margaret, 1931 C
Pixii, Hippolyte, 1832 D
Planche, Louis Antoine, 1810 C
Planck, Max, 1900 N, 1905 J
Plato, ca. 430 B.C. B, 367 B.C.,
second century B.C. B, 1512
Platt, Terry, 1970 C
Plaut, Walter, 1962 T
Plenciz, Marcus Antonius, 1762 A
Pliny the Elder, ca. 77 A
Plutarch, 790 B.C., 1579
Poe, Edgar Allan, 1827 F, 1839 H,
1842 F, 1849 F
Poiesz, Bernard, 1980 N
Pollender, Aloys, 1849 B, 1863 A
Pollock, Jackson, 1950 U
Pons, Stanley, 1989 H
Popov, Aleksandr Stepanovich,
1901 N
Popovic, Mika, 1984 L
Popper, Erwin, 1908 B
Porter, Keith Roberts, 1953 E

Porter, Rodney Robert, 1959 L,
1961 K
Portier, Paul, 1902 G
Portnoy, Daniel, 1981 F, 1984 H
Postgate, John R., 1986 E
Poston, J. Michael, 1964 C
Potter, Beatrix, 1902 O
Potter, Van Rensselaer, 1948 K
Pouchet, Félix-Archimède, 1858 A,
1861 A
Poulik, Miroslave Dave, 1961 K
Powell, Joan F., 1953 F, 1954 B
Power, Joseph, 1965 K
Prausnitz, Carl, 1921 D
Prazmowski, Adam, 1861 B,
1880 A
Preisz, H., 1909 C
Prescott, Samuel C., 1895 B
Prevost, Jean Louis, 1821 B
Priestley, Joseph, 1771 A, 1771 B,
1772 A, 1774 B, 1775 A,
1783 B, 1790 B
Proctor, Lita M., 1990 B
Proskauer, Bernhard, 1898 A
Proust, Joseph, 1799
Proust, Marcel, 1913 K
Prusiner, Stanley B., 1957 K,
1981 K, 1982 M, 1985 I
Prusoff, William H., 1985 G
Ptashne, Mark, 1967 Q
Ptolemy, second century B, 1512,
1543 B
Puccini, Giacomo, 1896 K,
1900 Q, 1904 M, 1926 O
Pugh, Evan, 1857 B
Pulitzer, Joseph, 1903 Q
Purcell, Robert H., 1973 L
Purkinje, Jan Evangelista, 1837 E,
1839 D, 1846 G, 1885 P
Pylarini, Giacomo, 1715 A
Pynchon, Thomas, 1973 R

Quastel, Juda Hirsch, 1924 A,
1926 J, 1928 H
Quayle, J. R., 1954 M
Quinn, William G., 1963 F

Rabin, A. C., 1975 B
Radin, Norman S., 1949 C
Radman, Miroslav, 1974 E
Ragsdale, Steve W., 1982 D,
1985 B
Rajewsky, Klaus, 1970 K
Ramon, Gaston Léon, 1904 C,
1927 C
Ramón y Cajal, Santiago, 1885 L

Ransom, John Crowe, 1922 J,
1930 I
Rapoport, J. A., 1946 K
Rauch, Barbara, 1977 E
Rauschenberg, Robert, 1958 T
Ray, John, 1682 A, 1686, 1735 B
Raymond, Albert L., 1928 F
Reading, C., 1977 K
Reagh, A. L., 1903 G
Redi, Francesco, 1668 A
Reed, Walter, 1899 D, 1901 F,
1905 E, 1919 D
Reeves, Henry C., 1979 F
Regnery, R. L., 1990 D
Reich, E., 1961 T
Reichstein, Tadeusz, 1933 J,
1936 R
Reiner, J. M., 1958 D
Reingold, A. L., 1982 K
Reitz, J. S., 1980 N
Reizer, Jonathan, 1980 E
Reizer, Michael J., 1983 D
Relman, David, A, 1990 D
Remak, Robert, 1839 C
Remarque, Erich Maria, 1929 Q
Rembrandt van Rijn, 1641 B
Remlinger, Paul, 1903 K
Renoir, Pierre Auguste, 1876 L
Revis, C., 1910 A, 1937 B
Rey, Jean, 1630 B, 1673 B
Reyes, Gregory R., 1990 G
Reyniers, James Arthur, 1928 D,
1949 A
Rhazes, 910
Rhim, Johng S., 1962 L
Rhodes, Cecil, 1902 N
Richard the Lion-Hearted (king of
England), 1215
Richardson, Charles C., 1967 R
Richelieu, Cardinal, 1624 B
Richet, Charles, 1902 G
Rickenberg, Howard V., 1956 D
Rickes, Edward L., 1948 B
Ricketts, Howard Taylor, 1906 E,
1909 D, 1916 C
Riggs, Arthur D., 1977 R, 1979 J
Riley, R. L., 1959 F
Rilke, Rainer Maria, 1905 N
Ringer, Sydney, 1883 G
Ripa, Torvald K., 1977 F
Ris, Hans, 1962 T
Rittenberg, David, 1935 M,
1950 O
Ritter, J., 1879 C
Ritter, Johann, 1801 A

Schoen, Moise, 1911 B
Schoenheimer, Rudolf, 1935 M
Schoenheit, E. W., 1929 I
Schönbein, Christian Friedrich,
    1840 E, 1845 B, 1845 C,
    1906 M
Schöne, Georg, 1944 G
Schönlein, Johann Lucas, 1839 C,
    1841 A
Schopf, J. William, 1967 B
Schott, Otto, 1886 G
Schottleius, M., 1899 C
Schottmüller, Hugo, 1900 D,
    1903 A, 1919 A
Schrader, H., 1936 A
Schramm, Gerhard Felix, 1955 J
Schreiber, G., 1983 B
Schrieffen, John Robert, 1957 S
Schröder, Heinrich Georg
    Friedrich, 1854 A
Schrödinger, Erwin, 1926 M, 1940,
    1944 I
Schroeter, Joseph, 1875 B, 1886 A
Schubert, Franz Peter, 1813 C,
    1822 E, 1827 G
Schucht, A., 1906 H
Schultze, H. W., 1959 M
Schultze, Max Johann Sigismund,
    1846 G, 1861 F
Schumann, Ralf R., 1990 I
Schwann, Theodor, 1836 A,
    1837 B, 1837 E, 1838 C,
    1839 A, 1839 D, 1858 B,
    1878 E
Schwartz, H. H., 1962 J
Schweet, R., 1957 P
Schwerdt, Carlton E., 1955 G
Scopes, John, 1925 I
Scotland, S. M., 1983 F
Scott, Dred, 1857 G
Scott, Robert, 1912 I
Scott, Walter, 1789 A, 1810 G,
    1819 D
Sebald, M., 1963 A
Séchaud, J., 1958 E
Sedgwick, W. T., 1899 G
Sédillot, C., 1878 A
Séguin, Armand, 1789 C
Sehgal, S. N., 1961 B
Seidman, M., 1950 E
Selander, Robert K., 1980 F
Sellards, Andrew, 1919 D
Semmelweis, Ignaz Philipp,
    1846 A, 1861 C
Senebier, Jean, 1782
Serrati, Serafino, 1823 A

Service, Robert William, 1907 M
Sessa, Grazia, 1966 J
Setlow, R. B., 1964 E
Shah, Vinod K., 1977 J
Shakespeare, William, 1590 C,
    1600 C, 1606 B
Shanks, Kathryn N., 1980 L
Shapiro, James A., 1968 C,
    1968 H, 1974 H
Sharp, Phillip A., 1977 W
Sharpey-Schafer, Edward A.,
    1921 G
Shatkin, Aaron J., 1961 T, 1975 R
Shaw, E. B., 1887 D, 1914 A,
    1918 C, 1920 A
Shaw, George Bernard, 1894 L,
    1902 P, 1914 O, 1923 L, 1956 S
Shaw, Jay H., 1988 J
Shelley, Mary Wollstonecraft
    Godwin, 1792, 1818 C
Shelley, Percy Bysshe, 1818 C,
    1819 D
Shemsu (emperor of China), ca.
    3180 B.C.
Shen Lung (emperor of China), ca.
    3000 B.C. A
Shen Nung (emperor of China), ca.
    2750 B.C.
Shepard, Alan, Jr., 1961 W
Shepard, Charles C., 1977 L
Sheridan, Richard Brinsley, 1777 B
Sherman, Sidney, 1836 B
Sherris, J. C., 1966 G
Shibata, K., 1902 D
Shiga, Kiyoshi, 1898 C, 1900 E
Shockley, William Bradford,
    1947 F
Sholes, Christopher Latham,
    1867 D, 1873 C
Shope, Richard Erwin, 1931 E,
    1932 D
Shorb, Mary S., 1948 B
Shorey, C. D., 1963 C
Shuman, Stewart, 1987 G
Sia, Richard H. P., 1931 D
Sibelius, Jean, 1899 K
Sickles, Grace M., 1948 G
Siedentopf, Henry, 1903 N
Siegbahn, Kai, 1960 Q
Siekevitz, Philip, 1956 Q
Signer, Ethan R., 1966 H
Silverman, Michael, 1974 B,
    1982 G, 1988 D
Siminovitch, Louis, 1950 I
Simmons, J. S., 1925 A
Simms, Ernest S., 1958 O

Simon, Lionel, 1963 S
Simon, Melvin I., 1971 A, 1974 B,
    1987 A, 1988 E
Simon, Théodore, 1905 M
Simpson, Mrs. Wallis, 1936 U
Simson, Eva, 1962 H
Singer, Maxine, 1973 O
Singer, S. Jonathan, 1972 K
Sinsheimer, Robert L., 1959 H,
    1962 M
Sitting Bull (Chief), 1876 I
Six, Howard R., 1974 J
Sjöstrand, F. S., 1953 E
Sklaviadis, T. K., 1989 F
Slade, H. D., 1942 D
Slater, Leonard N., 1990 D
Slepecky, Ralph A., 1965 G
Sloane, Hans, 1721 A
Smith, Adam, 1776 E
Smith, David H., 1967 H
Smith, Erwin Frink, 1899 B,
    1907 D
Smith, G. A., 1984 M
Smith, H., 1954 G
Smith, H. Williams, 1974 I
Smith, Hamilton Othanel, 1952 L,
    1970 M
Smith, I. W., 1955 B
Smith, J. D., 1951 A
Smith, John, 1624 C
Smith, John Stafford, 1814 B
Smith, Kendall O., 1958 J, 1962 L
Smith, Martin W., 1983 C
Smith, Michael, 1978 J, 1987 I
Smith, Theobald, 1886 F, 1893 E,
    1898 E, 1903 G, 1909 G,
    1919 A, 1919 C, 1963 A
Smith, Wilson, 1933 D, 1935 G,
    1940 K
Smithson, James, 1846 I
Snell, Esmond E., 1949 C
Snell, George Davis, 1937 G,
    1948 I, 1958 M, 1963 N
Snow, John, 1849 A, 1854 C,
    1873 A
Soddy, Frederick, 1913 G
Söhngen, N. L., 1906 A
Solioz, Marc, 1975 H
Söll, Dieter, 1973 O
Solzhenitsyn, Aleksandr, 1974 U
Somerville, Robert A., 1981 J
Sonnabend, Joseph A., 1963 M
Sousa, John Philip, 1897 O
Southern, E. M., 1975 S

Soxhlet, F., 1886 D

Spallanzani, Lazzaro, 1765 A, 1779 A, 1807 A, 1808 A, 1850 A

Spemann, Hans, 1918 E

Spiegelman, Solomon, 1954 E, 1961 N, 1963 S, 1965 M

Spiers, J. I., 1977 N

Spinelli, Viola, 1954 J

Spitzer, W., 1895 G, 1897 K

Springer, Martin S., 1977 H

Stackebrandt, Erko, 1983 A

Stadtman, E. R., 1964 C, 1966 E

Stähelin, H., 1953 C

Stahl, David A., 1984 B, 1986 A

Stahl, Franklin William, 1958 N

Stahl, Georg Ernst, 1606 A, 1668 C, 1697 A, 1697 B

Stalin, Joseph, 1928 I, 1953 Y

Stamp, T. C., 1940 G

Stanford, Leland, 1885 Q

Stanier, Roger Y., 1921 A, 1962 A

Stanley, Henry M., 1871 E

Stanley, Wendell Meredith, 1935 H, 1936 H

Starling, Ernest Henry, 1905 L

Starlinger, Peter, 1968 C

Starr, Mortimer P., 1962 B

Staudinger, Hermann, 1922 H

Stavric, S., 1977 N

Steber, Josef, 1975 D

Steere, Alan C., 1977 M

Stehelin, Dominique, 1976 L

Stein, William Howard, 1950 P

Steinbeck, John Ernst, 1939 T, 1953 Z

Steinberg, Robert A., 1939 E

Steinhardt, Edna, 1913 C, 1917 D

Steinhaus, E. A., 1951 F

Stent, Gunther S., 1961 F

Stephens, John C., 1975 F

Stephenson, George, 1814 A

Stephenson, Mary Louise, 1957 P

Stern, Curt, 1931 L

Stern, William, 1914 J

Sternberg, George Miller, 1881 C, 1884 H

Sterne, Laurence, 1759 C

Stetter, Karl O., 1982 B, 1983 A, 1983 B

Stevens, Dennis L., 1989 D

Stevenson, Robert Louis, 1883 K, 1886 M

Stevinus, Simon, 1585, 1586, 1590 B

Stewart, R. A., 1932 C

Stewart, W. D. P., 1954 D

Stickland, Leonard Hubert, 1934 A

Stock, Ann, 1985 A

Stock, Jeffrey, 1977 E, 1985 A

Stoeckenius, Walther, 1963 K, 1967 C, 1971 B

Stoker, Bram, 1897 N

Stoker, M. G. P., 1951 A

Stokes, Adrian, 1919 D

Stokes, George Gabriel, 1864 A

Stoler, Mark H., 1983 I

Stolp, Heinz, 1962 B

Stoney, George Johnston, 1897 L

Stowe, Harriet Beecher, 1852 D

Stradivari, Antonio, 1665 F

Strange, R. E., 1953 F, 1954 B

Strasburger, Eduard Adolf, 1882 I

Strassmann, Fritz, 1938 I

Strauss, Johann, II, 1867 G, 1874 G

Strauss, Richard, 1905 O, 1911 O

Stravinsky, Igor Fyodorovich, 1913 L

Strominger, Jack, 1965 H

Stupperich, Erhard, 1980 D, 1982 C

Sturgeon, William, 1823 C

Sturtevant, Alfred Henry, 1911 G, 1911 H, 1915 D, 1931 L

Styron, William, 1979 N

SubbaRow, Yellapragada, 1927 G, 1929 J

Sueoka, Noboru, 1959 P, 1963 F

Sullivan, Arthur, 1878 L, 1879 K, 1885 R

Summers, Donald F., 1968 J

Summers, William C., 1967 P

Sumner, James Batcheller, 1926 H, 1935 H

Susanne, Jaqueline, 1966 S

Sutherland, Earl Wilbur, Jr., 1960 D, 1965 J

Sutton, W. D., 1966 P

Sutton, Walter Stanborough, 1903 M

Svedberg, Theodor, 1923 J

Swammerdam, Jan, 1658, 1669 B

Swann, M. B. R., 1926 C

Sweet, B. H., 1960 J

Swift, Jonathan, 1726 B

Sydenham, Thomas, 1667 A, 1670 A, 1670 B, 1675 A, 1679

Symons, Robert H., 1972 M, 1981 L

Synge, John Millington, 1907 N

Synge, Richard Laurence Millington, 1906 M, 1941 M

Szent-Györgyi, Albert, 1928 G, 1932 J, 1937 K

Szilard, Leo, 1950 C, 1953 G

Szybalski, Waclaw, 1967 P

Taft, William Howard, 1912 I

Tagawa, Kunio, 1962 U

Talbot, William Henry Fox, 1834 B, 1841 B

Talmage, David W., 1957 N

Tamaoki, Taiki, 1962 V

Tamm, Igor, 1962 L

T'ang, F.-F., 1957 G

Tarr, H. L. A., 1931 B

Tate, Allen, 1922 J, 1930 I

Tatum, Edward L., 1908 E, 1941 H, 1944 D, 1946 C, 1946 F, 1961 T

Taylor, A. R., 1940 L

Taylor, Austin L., 1963 G

Taylor, Craig D., 1974 F

Taylor, Joyce, 1963 M

Taylor, Marian S., 1919 C, 1963 A

Taylor, R. B., 1970 K

Taylor, R. M., 1940 K

Tchaikovsky, Petr Ilyich, 1882 M, 1888 K

Tegtmeyer, Peter, 1972 H

Teichmann, Ludwig, 1853 B

Telling, R. C., 1956 B

Temin, Howard Martin, 1958 I, 1964 I, 1970 H

Tennyson, Alfred Lord, 1832 F, 1850 E, 1854 F

Terman, Lewis Madison, 1914 J

Thackeray, William Makepeace, 1848 F

Thales, 585 B.C.

Thauer, Rudolf K., 1977 I

Thaxter, Ronald, 1795 A

Theiler, Arnold, 1900 G

Theiler, Max, 1919 D, 1929 G, 1936 L

Thein, Swee Lay, 1985 K

Thénard, Louis Jacques, 1818 A

Theorell, Hugo Teodor, 1934 K

Theriot, Lee, 1962 H

Thierfelder, H., 1895 D

Thom, B. T., 1979 I

Thom, Charles, 1939 E

Thomas, C. A., Jr., 1970 P

Thompson, D'Arcy Wentworth, 1917 F

Thompson, Thomas, 1813 A

Subject Index

Alamo, 1836 B
alarmone, 1975 F
albinism, 1908 E
albuminous materials, 1838 E, 1886 B
alcohol distillation, 900 B, ca. 1100
alcoholic fermentation, 1815 A, 1837 C, 1838 C,
	1857 C, 1860 A, 1870 B, 1906 J, 1906 K,
	1911 B, 1913 E, 1914 G, 1918 F, 1926 B,
	1928 F, 1939 L
aldohexoses, 1884 K
aldolase, 1936 N
alexine, 1889 F, 1895 E, 1898 I, 1899 F
algae, 1674 A, 1846 D, 1862 A
algebra, 250, 1847 C
Alhumpert Prize, 1861 A
Alice in Wonderland (Lewis Carroll), 1865 G
alizarin blue, 1895 F
alkaline phosphatase, 1959 Q
alkaptonuria, 1908 E
alkylene oxides, sterilization with, 1936 A
All Quiet on the Western Front (Erich Maria
	Remarque), 1929 Q
All the King's Men (Robert Penn Warren), 1946 M
All the President's Men (Bob Woodward and Carl
	Bernstein), 1974 T
allantiasis, 1820 A
allele, 1909 H
allelomorph, 1909 H
allosteric inhibition, 1943 C, 1955 D, 1961 E
Almagest (Ptolemy), second century B
Alnus, 1885 E, 1887 C, 1902 D, 1954 D, 1970 B
alpha particles, 1899 H, 1934 O
alpha-helix, in proteins, 1951 L
Alpher-Bethe-Gamow theory of origin of chemical
	elements, 1948 M
Also Sprach Zarathustra (Friedrich Wilhelm Nietzsche),
	1883 J
alternating current, 1832 D
amber, magnetic properties, 585 B.C., 1600 A
America, naming of, 1502
American Academy of Microbiology, 1955 Q, 1970 Q
American Association for the Advancement of
	Science, 1848 D
American Board of Medical Microbiology, 1964 Q
American Board of Microbiology, 1964 Q
An American Dictionary of the English Language (Noah
	Webster), 1828 D
American Society for Microbiology (ASM), 1899 G,
	1960 P, 1970 Q
	publications, 1916 G, 1935 O, 1937 P, 1953 W,
		1963 X, 1967 V, 1970 R, 1971 G, 1972 N,
		1975 T, 1976 M, 1978 M, 1981 O, 1988 Q
American War of Independence, 1775 C, 1783 E
Ames test, 1972 G
amino acid, 1806 A, 1810 D, 1820 C, 1902 L
	D-amino acids, 1937 A, 1949 C
	degradation, 1934 A
	starvation for, 1961 F, 1970 F, 1975 F
amino acid deaminases, 1942 F
6-amino penicillanic acid, 1959 E
ammonia, chemical synthesis, 1908 F

amoxicillin, 1959 E, 1977 K
AMP, 1939 M, 1948 L
ampere, 1822 B
ampicillin, 1959 E
amplifier, radio, 1906 O
Anabaena, 1928 A
Anabaena-Azolla symbiosis, 1974 A
"The Anacreontic Song," 1814 B
anaerobes, 1861 B
	chemotrophic, 1977 I
	roll-tube cultivation, 1946 D
anaerobic methods, 1889 D
anaërobies, 1861 B
analytic geometry, 1637
analytical engine, 1832 E
anaphylaxis, 1902 G, 1911 F, 1921 D
anatomy
	comparative, 1767 A, 1798 B
	human, 1543 A
	pathological, 1761 A
Ancestral Law of Inheritance, 1869 F
Andromeda Strain (Michael Crichton), 1969 I
anesthesia, 1846 H
angstrom, 1853 C
aniline dye, 1856 C
Animal Chemistry (Justus von Liebig), 1846 F
animal electricity, 1780 C, 1800 D
Animal Farm (George Orwell), 1945 G
animal heat, 1777 A, 1783 A, 1846 F
animal kingdom, 1798 B
Animalcula infusoria fluviatilia et marina (Otto Frederik
	Müller), 1786 A
animalcules, 1674 A, 1720 A, 1762 A, 1767 B
Animalia (kingdom), 1866 A, 1956 A, 1969 A
anion, origin of term, 1833 B
Anna Karenina (Leo Tolstoy), 1878 M
"Annabel Lee" (Edgar Allan Poe), 1849 F
anode, origin of term, 1833 B
Anopheles mosquito, 1897 E, 1898 J
anthrax, 79, 1849 B, 1863 A, 1868 A, 1871 A,
	1876 C, 1877 D
	toxin, 1954 G, 1968 D
	vaccine, 1881 F
antibiotic inhibition of protein synthesis, 1951 K
antibiotic resistance, 1950 G, 1967 H
antibiotic sensitivity testing, 1966 G
antibodies, 1888 F, 1891 D, 1939 H
	antibody-combining sites, 1970 I
	clonal selection theory, 1945 D, 1953 R, 1955 N,
		1957 N, 1962 S
	instructionalist theory, 1930 D, 1940 M
	monoclonal, 1955 N, 1975 N
	natural selection theory, 1945 D, 1955 N, 1957 N
	secretory, 1959 M
antigen
	bacterial somatic, 1903 G
	flagellar, 1903 G
	polysaccharide, 1923 F
	virulence, 1956 I
antihistamines, 1939 K
antimatter, 1926 M

Bacillus ulna, 1872 B
bacteria
  conjugation, 1946 F, 1950 F, 1950 H, 1952 I,
    1953 K
  descriptions, 1773 A, 1786 A
  first seen, 1676, 1683 A
  lysis, 1898 F
  transformation, 1928 C, 1931 D, 1932 A, 1944 C,
    1972 F
Bacteria (taxon), 1990 A
The Bacterial Cell (René Dubos), 1942 B
bacterial insecticides, 1902 E, 1915 B, 1939 C,
    1951 F, 1953 J, 1954 H, 1967 J, 1981 E,
    1982 F, 1983 J, 1986 G, 1986 H, 1987 B,
    1987 C, 1988 I, 1989 A
bacterial nuclear region, 1958 E
bacterial viruses, 1898 F, 1915 C, 1917 C
bactericidal substances, 1889 F, 1895 E
Bacteridia, 1863 A
Bacteridium, 1868 A
bacteriocin, 1925 B
bacteriolysins, 1894 E
bacteriophage, 1898 F, 1915 C, 1917 C, 1922 E,
    1925 C, 1929 D, 1933 C, 1936 D, 1939 D,
    1940 H, 1944 E
  B, toxin production, 1951 H
  DNA and protein, 1934 E
  DNA sequencing, 1982 P
  eclipse period of synthesis, 1952 M
  f2, 1961 G, 1962 J
  genetic map, 1948 E
  induction, 1950 I
  infection, restriction of, 1952 L
  lambda, 1951 G, 1956 H, 1959 O, 1962 I,
    1963 T, 1967 Q, 1974 Q, 1982 P
  lysis, 1940 I
  male-specific, 1960 I, 1964 F
  morphogenesis, 1963 H
  MS-2, 1963 S, 1965 M
  Mu, 1963 G, 1964 H, 1973 G
  mutants, 1936 E, 1945 B, 1953 M
  nucleic acid, 1933 C
  one-step growth curve, 1939 D
  P22, 1952 K, 1956 H
  φX174, 1959 H, 1962 M, 1977 T
  Qβ, 1965 M
  recombination, 1946 H
  replication, 1949 H, 1968 E
  RNA-containing, 1961 G, 1962 J, 1964 F
  structure, 1942 G
  T phages, 1942 G, 1943 D, 1944 E, 1949 H,
    1956 M
  titer, 1921 C
bacteriophage-bacteria interactions, marine systems,
    1990 B
bacterioplankton, 1980 A
bacteriorhodopsin, 1971 B, 1980 Q
bacteriotropins, 1903 I
Bacterium, 1838 A, 1868 A
Bacterium coli, 1889 A, 1910 A, 1940 E
Bacterium coli commune, 1885 A

Bacterium denitrificans, 1886 C
Bacterium friedländeri, 1882 E
Bacterium lactis aerogenes, 1885 A
Bacterium monocytogenes, 1926 C
Bacterium photometricum, 1881 D
Bacterium tularense, 1911 C
Bacterium tumefaciens, 1907 D
Bacterium typhosum, 1889 A, 1910 A
Bacterium xylinum, 1931 B
Bacteroides ruminicola, 1962 E
Bakelite, 1909 J
balanced growth, 1958 F
balloon flights, 1783 D, 1932 N
Bang's disease, 1897 D
Bar at the Folies Bergère (Edouard Manet), 1881 M
The Barber of Seville (Gioacchino Antonio Rossini),
    1816 C
"Barefoot Boy" (John Greenleaf Whittier), 1856 F
barium, 1806 B
barometer, 1643 A, 1646 B
Barrack-Room Ballads (Rudyard Kipling), 1892 J
Bartlett's Quotations (John Bartlett), 1855 D
Bartonella, 1990 D
Bastille, 1789 E
Bataan death march, 1942 N
bathyscaphe, 1932 N, 1948 O
bathysphere, 1930 H, 1934 P
battery, 1800 D, 1850 C
battles
  Balaklava, 1854 E, 1854 F
  Copenhagen, 1801 D
  Leipzig, 1813 B
  Manassas, 1861 I
  Nations, 1813 B
  Plains of Abraham, 1759 B
  Somme, 1916 H
  Trafalgar, 1805 B
  Waterloo, 1815 D
Bay of Pigs, 1961 X
Bayer chemical firm, 1899 I
BCG vaccine, 1902 F, 1906 I
BCS theory of superconductivity, 1957 S
Bdellovibrio bacteriovorus, 1962 B
Beagle (ship), 1831 A, 1859 B
Bedsonia, 1934 X
bees, communication, 1919 E
The Beggar's Opera (John Christopher Pepusch and
    John Gay), 1728
Beggiatoa, 1842 A, 1887 B
The Beginning of Life (Henry Charlton Bastian),
    1872 A, 1876 A
Beilstein's handbook, 1880 E
Being and Nothingness (Jean-Paul Sartre), 1943 I
Beloved (Toni Morrison), 1987 L
Bengal isinglass, 1882 A
benzene, 1825 B, 1858 E, 1865 C
Bergey's Manual of Determinative Bacteriology (David
    Bergey), 1917 A, 1923 A
Bergey's Manual of Systematic Bacteriology, 1984 A
beriberi, 1607 A, 1896 F, 1912 G
Berkefeld filters, 1891 A

Berlin Wall, 1961 X
Bessemer process, 1856 E
beta particles, 1899 H
beta-galactosidase, 1889 C, 1950 E, 1952 H, 1954 E,
    1958 P, 1959 O, 1960 M
  assay, 1950 E
  permease, 1956 D, 1960 M, 1965 I
beta-D-galactosides, 1950 E
beta-imidazolylethylamine (histamine), 1911 F
beta-lactam, 1944 B, 1949 G
beta-lactamase, 1940 E, 1977 K
Biblia Naturae (Jan Swammerdam), 1669 B
bibliography, 1545
Bibliotheca Universalis (Conrad Gesner), 1545
bile solubility, pneumococci, 1900 A
Binet-Simon test, 1914 J
binomial nomenclature, 1623 B, 1737, 1749 A, 1753
biogenetic law, 1866 A
biogeochemical cycles, 1872 D
biological oxidations, 1840 E, 1875 D, 1908 D, 1937 J
biology, first uses of term, 1800 B, 1802 B
bioluminescence, 1889 C, 1970 C, 1979 E, 1981 B,
    1984 G
bios (growth factor), 1901 D
biosynthesis, ATP requirement, 1943 F
biotin, 1935 L
Birth of a Nation (D. W. Griffith), 1915 I
Bismarck brown, 1884 B
bitumen of Judea, 1822 D
"Black Monday," stock market crash, 1987 L
blockade of Berlin, 1948 P
blood
  circulation, 1559, 1616, 1628, 1637, 1661 A,
      1669 A, 1683 B, 1733
  iron content, 1745 A
  "red globules" carrying oxygen, 1840 D
  serum, bacteriolytic and bactericidal action,
      1895 E, 1896 E
blood agar, hemolytic reactions, 1919 A
blood gas(es), 1837 I, 1869 D
blood group antigens, 1926 F
blood groups, 1900 H
blood pressure, 1733
blood-gas manometer, 1902 K
"bloody" polenta, 1823 A
"The Blue Danube Waltz" (Johann Strauss II),
    1867 G
blue-green algae, 1862 A, 1872 B, 1875 A, 1928 A,
    1937 E, 1956 A, 1957 Q, 1962 A, 1969 A
body louse, vector for typhus fever, 1909 E
Boer War, 1896 C, 1899 J
boiling temperature, water, 1699 C, 1714, 1741
Bolsheviks, 1917 H
bomb, nuclear fusion or hydrogen, 1952 S
bomb calorimeter, 1864 B
bone marrow, as bursa equivalent, 1972 J
bone marrow cells, 1956 P
Boolean logic, 1847 C
Bordetella pertussis, 1906 C, 1923 E, 1933 F, 1936 K
Borrel bodies, 1906 G
Borrelia, 664, 1952 A

Borrelia burgdorferi, 1982 J
Bosch process, 1908 D
Boston Massacre, 1770 B
Boston Tea Party, 1773 B
botanical illustration, ca. 77 B, 1530 B, 1542
Botrytis, in silkworm disease, 1835 A
botulism, 900 A, 1735 A, 1820 A, 1895 C
bovine pancreatic ribonuclease, 1950 P, 1965 T
bovine pleuropneumonia, 1929 C
bovine spongiform encephalopathy, 1920 D, 1936 J,
    1957 K, 1966 L, 1982 M, 1985 H
bovine tuberculosis, 1865 A, 1902 F, 1906 I
bovo-vaccine, 1902 F
Boxer Rebellion, 1900 P
Boy Pioneers and Sons of Daniel Boone (Daniel Carter
    Beard), 1910 H
Boy Scouts of America, 1910 H
Boy Scouts of Britain, 1910 H
Boyle's law, 1662 A, 1687
bradykinin, 1965 T
Bradyrhizobium, 1982 A, 1986 D
Braille system, 1829 B
Brandenburg Concerti (Johann Sebastian Bach), 1721 B
Brave New World (Aldous Huxley), 1932 P
Brideshead Revisited (Evelyn Waugh), 1945 G
The Bridge of San Luis Rey (Thornton Wilder), 1927 L
British Association for the Advancement of Science,
    1830 D
British Plague Commission, 1906 D
Broad Street water pump, 1854 C
Bronze Age, ca. 3000 B.C. B
The Brothers Karamazov (Fyodor Dostoyevsky),
    1879 L
Brown v. Board of Education, 1954 O
Brownian movement, 1827 B
Brucella, 1887 D, 1914 A, 1918 C, 1920 A, 1940 G
Brucella tularense, 1911 C
bubble chamber for ionized particles, 1952 R
bubonic plague, ca. 1190 B.C., 542, 664, 1095, 1343,
    1348, 1358, 1403, 1665 A, 1894 C, 1906 D,
    1907 C, 1914 B
Bulfinch's Mythology (Thomas Bulfinch), 1855 D
Bull Moose Party, 1912 I
Bull Run, 1861 I
Bunsen burner, 1850 C
Burkitt's lymphoma, 1958 L, 1963 L
bursa of Fabricius, 1956 P
bushy stunt virus, 1938 A, 1956 J, 1956 K, 1959 I
2,3-butanediol, 1906 B
butterfat content, milk, 1890 G
butyric acid fermentation, 1861 B

C

C polysaccharide, streptococcal cell walls, 1952 B,
    1957 B
The Caine Mutiny (Herman Wouk), 1951 P
calcination, 750, 1500, 1630 B, 1673 B, 1783 B
calcium
  discovery, 1806 B
  in heat resistance in spores, 1943 B, 1953 F,
      1957 E, 1972 D

calculating machine, 1693 B, 1936 F

calculus
  differential, 1665 D, 1684, 1687, 1690 A, 1696
  integral, 1690 A, 1696
  modern notation, 1821 D

California Institute of Technology, 1891 H

calorimetric measurement, muscle contraction, 1911 I

calotype photography, 1841 B

Calvin-Benson-Bassham cycle, 1954 M

cambium, 1682 B

Cambodia, 1975 U

Cambridge University, 1217

camera lucida, 1812 E

cAMP, *see* cyclic AMP

Campylobacter, 1919 C, 1963 A, 1973 F, 1980 I

Campylobacter pylori, 1983 G

Canada, 1867 F

Canavalia ensiformis, 1926 H

cancer, lymph nodes, 1832 B

Candida, infection in AIDS, 1981 H

Candide (Voltaire), 1759 C

canine distemper virus, 1923 D

canned foods, bacterial spoilage, 1895 B

canning, 1804 A, 1808 A, 1819 A, 1839 E

Canon (Avicenna), ca. 1020

The Canterbury Tales (Geoffrey Chaucer), 1400

capillary circulation, 1661 A, 1683 B

capsid, 1959 J

capsomeres, 1959 J

capsular polysaccharide, 1923 F, 1928 C, 1931 H, 1945 C

capsules, bacterial, 1909 C
  D-amino acids in, 1937 A
  Haemophilus, 1931 C
  pneumococci, 1923 F, 1928 C, 1931 H, 1944 C

"Captain of all these men of death," from *The Life and Death of Mr. Badman* (John Bunyan), 1680 A

carbohydrate synthesis, 1982 C

carbolic acid, 1867 B

carbon bonds, 1874 D

carbon dioxide
  adsorbed by plants, 1779 B, 1804 B, 1837 H, 1862 C
  in blood, 1837 I
  discovery, 1754
  fixation, 1891 B, 1954 M, 1955 E, 1980 D
  heterotrophic utilization, 1935 E, 1942 D, 1945 A
  produced by fermentation, 1757, 1766 A, 1772 A, 1839 B, 1860 A, 1870 B, 1897 C
  produced by respiration, 1777 A, 1783 A

carbon isotopes, 1932 K, 1934 M, 1935 E, 1940 B, 1942 D

carbon monoxide, 1978 A, 1982 D

carbon monoxide dehydrogenase, 1985 B

carbon sulfide, 1893 C

carboxydotrophic bacteria, 1978 A

carcinogens, Ames test, 1972 G

carcinoma, primary hepatocellular, 1981 I

Carmen (Georges Bizet), 1875 G

carmine stain, 1849 D, 1869 A

carotene, 1904 H, 1935 L

Cartesian coordinates, 1637

Cartesian curves, 1637

Cartesian geometry, 1637

casein, 1780 A

Casino Royale (Ian Fleming), 1953 Z

Cat on a Hot Tin Roof (Tennessee Williams), 1955 S

cat scratch disease, 1983 I, 1988 K, 1988 L, 1990 D

catabolite repression, 1942 F, 1961 D, 1984 F

catalase, 1893 A, 1901 J, 1923 B

catalysis
  chemical, 1812 D, 1817 D, 1820 E
  enzymatic, 1878 D, 1889 C, 1893 A, 1894 I, 1895 G, 1897 J
  theory of, 1837 G

catastrophism, 1812 B

The Catcher in the Rye (J. D. Salinger), 1951 P

Catch-22 (Joseph Heller), 1961 Y

cathode, origin of term, 1833 B

cation, origin of term, 1833 B

CD4 lymphocytes, 1984 L, 1987 F, 1988 M

CD-ROM, 1984 N

cell
  definition, 1861 F
  origin of term, 1665 B
  plant, 1802 C

cell cycle, mammalian, 1953 T

cell division, 1837 E, 1882 H, 1882 I, 1903 M, 1968 A

cell envelope, bacterial, 1963 C, 1965 C, 1984 C

cell membrane, 1846 G, 1894 G
  bacterial, 1894 A, 1940 A, 1941 D, 1950 B, 1953 D, 1954 C, 1958 A, 1960 A, 1963 F, 1965 C, 1965 D, 1966 E, 1967 C, 1971 A, 1971 B
  structure, 1894 G, 1925 E, 1934 G, 1960 O, 1972 K

cell receptors for viruses, 1961 I

cell respiration, 1914 H

cell theory, 1837 E, 1838 D, 1839 D, 1846 G, 1858 B

cell wall nucleotides, 1949 B

cell walls, bacterial, 1900 B, 1902 C, 1922 D, 1929 A, 1931 B, 1939 A, 1940 C, 1941 B, 1941 D, 1947 A, 1949 B, 1949 C, 1951 B, 1951 C, 1952 B, 1952 C, 1952 D, 1952 E, 1953 B, 1953 C, 1953 D, 1954 B, 1956 C, 1957 B, 1958 A, 1958 C, 1960 A, 1961 A, 1965 H, 1972 A, 1975 D, 1977 C
  acid heteropolysaccharide, 1977 C
  amino sugar-peptide component, 1956 C
  C polysaccharide, 1952 B
  diaminopimelic acid, 1951 C
  glucosamine, 1953 B
  Halococcus, 1975 D
  lysine, 1951 C
  muramic acid, 1952 C, 1954 B, 1956 C, 1958 B, 1963 D, 1966 A

murein, 1956 C
N-acetyl glucosamine, 1956 C
peptidoglycan, 1956 C
stain, 1953 D
structure, 1952 B, 1952 C, 1952 D
sulfated heteropolysaccharide, 1975 D
cell-free preparation, yeast, 1897 C
cell-free transformation, 1932 A
cell-mediated immunity, 1961 L
cellular and humoral immunity, theories of, 1903 I
cellular pathology, 1858 B
cellulose, 1834 A, 1906 A, 1931 B
Centers for Disease Control, 1946 J, 1967 L, 1976 I,
    1977 L, 1980 L, 1981 H, 1982 H, 1983 E
centigrade scale, 1741
centrifugation, differential, 1922 F
cephalosporin, 1948 C
Cephalosporium acremonium, 1948 C
Ceylon moss, 1882 A
Chamberland filter, 1884 C, 1891 A
champagne, 1678
Chaos infusorium, 1767 B
"Characterization and Classification of Bacterial
    Types" (C.-E. A. Winslow), 1917 A
Chargaff's rules, 1950 L
"Charge of the Light Brigade" (Alfred Lord
    Tennyson), 1854 F
Charles's law, 1699 B, 1787 B
chemical element
    definition, 1661 B
    listing of, 1789 D
    origin, 1948 M
    periodic table, 1869 G
chemical isomers, 1827 C
chemical nomenclature, 1787 A, 1789 D
chemical separations, 1806 B
chemical symbols, 1813 A
chemiosmotic hypothesis, 1961 M, 1965 P
chemistry, origin as a science, 1789 D
chemoautotrophy, 1887 B, 1946 C
chemolithotrophy, 1887 B, 1946 C
chemostat, 1950 C
chemotaxis, 1881 D, 1885 C, 1893 B, 1966 B,
    1967 D, 1969 C, 1972 B, 1972 C, 1973 A,
    1974 B, 1974 C, 1977 H, 1985 A, 1987 A,
    1988 E
    chemoreceptors, 1969 C, 1973 A
    methionine requirement, 1977 H
    microscope, automatic tracking, 1972 C
    protein phosphorylation, 1987 A, 1988 E
    proteins, 1985 A
    regulation, 1985 A
    runs and twiddles, 1972 C
    source of energy, 1974 C
    temporal gradient apparatus, 1972 B
chemotrophic anaerobes, 1977 I
chemotrophy, 1946 C
Chernobyl (nuclear power plant), 1986 M
Cherokee Nation, 1838 G
cherry-laurel, 1781 C
chicken cholera, 1880 C

childbed (puerperal) fever, 1842 C, 1846 A,
    1861 C
Childe Harold's Pilgrimage (Lord Byron), 1812 G
chimerism in cattle, 1945 D
Chlamydia, 1907 B, 1963 D, 1963 I
    cellular structure, 1953 A
    classification, 1966 A
    cultivation, 1963 I, 1977 F
    muramic acid, 1963 D
Chlamydia psittaci, 1879 C, 1930 C, 1934 B
Chlamydia trachomatis, 1957 G
chlamydobacteria, 1846 D
Chlamydozoa, 1907 B
chloramphenicol, 1961 S, 1964 N
chlorine, 1800 A
chlorine gas, use in war, 1915 G
chloroform, 1831 B
chlorophyll, 1817 C, 1837 H, 1904 H
chloroplasts
    discovery, 1862 C
    DNA content, 1962 T
    as endosymbionts, 1962 T
    photosynthesis, 1881 I, 1939 J, 1954 N
    in plants and algae, 1933 G
cholera, 1768, 1817 A, 1826 A, 1832 A, 1849 A,
    1854 B, 1854 C, 1863 B, 1873 A, 1884 D,
    1885 G, 1892 C, 1894 E, 1895 E, 1896 D,
    1897 I, 1906 F, 1971 D, 1990 E
cholera bacillus, *see Vibrio cholerae*
cholera vaccine, 1885 G, 1896 D
cholesterol, 1894 G, 1901 K, 1913 D, 1950 O
chondrioids, 1960 B
chorioallantoic membrane, virus cultivation, 1931 G,
    1946 I, 1952 O
A Christmas Carol (Charles Dickens), 1843 B
chromatin, 1882 H, 1974 R
Chromatium, 1887 B, 1960 C
chromatography, 1906 M, 1941 M
chromosomes, 1882 H, 1903 M
    bacterial, 1942 B, 1956 F, 1963 E
    integration of phage, 1962 I
    map, 1911 H
    number, 1887 F
    unit of inheritance, 1905 H, 1915 D
chronic wasting disease, 1936 J, 1982 M
chrysanthemum chlorotic mottle, 1971 E
chrysanthemum stunt, 1971 E
Chrysler Building, 1930 H
cinematographe, 1895 J
circulation of blood, *see* blood circulation
cis-trans test, 1955 K
cistron, 1955 K
citrate, utilization, 1925 A, 1936 C
citric acid, 1780 A, 1917 B
citric acid cycle, 1937 J, 1937 K, 1937 L, 1947 D,
    1948 K
citrulline, 1932 I
citrus exocortis, 1971 E
Civil Rights Act, 1866 C, 1875 F
Civil War, U.S., 1861 I, 1865 E
"Civilization" (Ralph Waldo Emerson), 1870 D

classification
    animalcules, 1767 B
    animals, ca. 367 B.C.
    bacteria, 1773 A, 1825 A, 1838 A, 1852 A,
        1866 A, 1872 B, 1875 A, 1887 B, 1897 A,
        1900 A, 1901 A, 1901 B, 1902 A, 1902 B,
        1903 A, 1905 B, 1908 A, 1909 A, 1916 A,
        1917 A, 1919 A, 1923 A, 1926 A, 1933 A,
        1941 A, 1954 A, 1956 A, 1969 A, 1977 A,
        1986 A, 1990 A
    biological, 1866 A, 1956 A, 1969 A, 1990 A
    diseases, 1763 A
    fossils, 1812 B
    plants, ca. 1250 A, 1583, 1623 B, 1686, 1735 B,
        1749 A, 1812 C
Claviceps purpurea, 857
clavulanic acid, 1977 K
clocks, water, ca. 2595 B.C. B
clonal selection theory of antibody formation,
    1945 D, 1955 N, 1962 S
cloning, full-length cDNA, 1982 Q
cloning vehicle, pBR322, 1977 Q
Clostridium
    discovery, 1861 B
    naming of, 1880 A
Clostridium acetobutylicum, 1912 A
Clostridium botulinum, 1895 C
Clostridium pasteurianum, 1895 A, 1951 D, 1960 C,
    1962 D, 1964 D
Clostridium perfringens, 1892 A
Clostridium roseum, 1957 E
Clostridium sporogenes, 1934 A
Clostridium tetani, 1884 F, 1889 D
Clostridium thermoaceticum, 1945 A, 1964 C, 1982 D
Clostridium welchii, 1892 A
coagulase test, 1905 B
coal gas, 1739, 1859 F
cobalamin, 1962 C, 1964 C, 1984 E
cocarboxylase, 1906 K
Coccaceae, 1908 A
Coccidioides, 1932 C
Coccobacteria, 1886 A
coconut palm cadang-cadang, 1971 E
codon, 1964 L
coenzymes
    A, 1947 D, 1951 M
    fermentation, 1906 K, 1923 G
    M, 1971 C, 1974 F
    uridine diphospho-glucose, 1950 N
Col factors, 1954 I, 1958 G, 1967 I, 1974 P
cold fusion, 1989 H
cold storage unit, 1861 H
coli-aerogenes bacteria, 1898 A
colicins, 1925 B, 1954 I, 1967 I
coliform bacteria, 1910 A, 1936 C, 1937 B
"Coliform Bacteria" (Leland W. Parr), 1937 B
colinearity of genes and proteins, 1964 M
college, coeducational, 1833 D
colon-typhoid group, 1910 A
colony hybridization, 1975 I
The Color Purple (Alice Walker), 1982 T

combustion, 1665 C, 1668 B, 1668 C, 1673 B,
    1772 C, 1774 C, 1775 B, 1783 B, 1789 C,
    1789 D
Come Back, Little Sheba (William Inge), 1950 T
cometabolism, 1970 E
Common Market, 1958 R
Communicable Disease Center, *see* Centers for
    Disease Control
communication satellite, 1962 X
The Communist Manifesto (Karl Marx and Friedrich
    Engels), 1847 D
Communist Party, 1917 H
compact disc, sound recording, 1984 N
comparative anatomy, 1798 B
comparative biochemistry, 1926 G
The Compendious Dictionary of the English Language
    (Noah Webster), 1806 D
competitive inhibitors, of enzymes, 1928 H
The Compleat Angler (Izaak Walton), 1653 B
complement, 1889 F, 1895 E, 1898 I, 1899 F
complement fixation, 1901 G, 1906 H
Composition (Joan Miró), 1933 L
computed axial tomography (CAT), 1974 S
computers, 1801 C, 1832 E, 1936 S, 1958 Q,
    1976 N
conditioned reflex, 1904 I
Confederate States of America, 1861 I
Confederation of the Rhine, 1806 C
conjugation, bacterial, 1946 F, 1950 F, 1950 H,
    1952 I, 1953 K
Constitution, U.S., 1787 C
constitutive enzymes, 1930 A
consumption, *see* tuberculosis
contagious abortion, 1897 D, 1914 A, 1918 C
contagium vivum fixum, 1892 E
contagium vivum fluidum, 1899 E
Continental Congress, 1776 D
continuous culture, bacteria, 1935 A, 1950 C, 1956 B
convergent lens, 1267
copper ore, smelting, ca. 3000 B.C. B
copper vitriol, 1617 A
cordite, 1912 A
Cornfield with Crows (Vincent van Gogh), 1890 K
coronary heart disease, 1953 U
corticosteroids, 1936 R
cortisone, 1936 R
Corynebacterium diphtheriae, 1883 B, 1888 A, 1894 F,
    1896 B, 1951 H
cosmic rays, 1932 M
cosmids, 1978 I
cotton wool, as flask closure, 1854 A
The Count of Monte Cristo (Alexandre Dumas), 1845 E
coupled biochemical reactions, 1900 L
covalent bond, 1916 F
Covent Garden, 1858 F
cowpox, 1774 A, 1796 B
cowpox virus, 1904 D, 1906 G, 1925 D
Coxiella, 1935 F
coxsackievirus, 1948 G
cozymase, 1923 G
cream separator, 1879 I

creatine phosphate, 1927 G, 1930 F
"The Cremation of Sam McGee" (Robert William Service), 1907 M
Crenarchaeota (crenotes), 1990 A
Creutzfeldt-Jakob disease, 1920 D, 1957 K, 1966 L, 1982 M, 1983 M, 1989 F
Crime and Punishment (Fyodor Dostoyevsky), 1866 D
Crimean War, 1853 E, 1854 F, 1860 B, 1862 D
crossing over, 1911 G, 1931 L
croup, 1765 B
crown gall, 1907 D, 1947 B, 1970 G, 1975 L, 1977 O
The Crucible (Arthur Miller), 1953 AA
Crusade, First, 1095
Crystal Palace, 1851 D
Cuba-U.S. missile crisis, 1962 Y
cubes and cube roots, ca. 1700 B.C.
cucumber mosaic virus, 1938 A
cucurbit wilt, 1899 B
culture media, 1872 C, 1875 B, 1882 A
cuneiform writing, ca. 2500 B.C. B
cyanide, 1781 C, 1783 C, 1811 C, 1857 D, 1876 E
cyanobacteria, 1872 B, 1966 D, 1979 C, 1988 A
cyclic AMP, 1943 C, 1960 D, 1965 J, 1968 B
cyclotron, 1931 M
Cynocephalus hamadryas, 1908 B
cystine, 1810 D
cytidine triphosphate, 1955 D
cytochrome, 1884 J, 1923 H, 1925 G, 1929 K
cytochrome *a*, 1938 F
cytochrome oxidase, 1910 D, 1938 F, 1948 K
cytochrome-linked fermentation, 1962 E
cytogenes, 1958 G
cytokines, 1957 L
cytomegalovirus, 1975 M, 1981 H
cytoplasm, 1882 I
cytosine, 1885 N
cytotoxin, *Escherichia coli*, 1977 N, 1979 I

D

daguerreotype, 1839 F, 1841 B
Daisy Miller (Henry James), 1878 M
Dakar scratch vaccine, 1929 G
Dalton's law, 1803 A
Daniel Sieff Institute of Science, 1912 A
Danysz phenomenon, 1902 H
dark reactivation of ultraviolet damage, 1962 H
Das Kapital (Karl Marx), 1867 F
Das Rheingold (Richard Wagner), 1876 J
David (Michelangelo), 1504
David Copperfield (Charles Dickens), 1850 E
D-Day, World War II, 1944 J
DDT, 1940 O
De anatomicis administrationibus (Galen), second century A
De anima (Avicenna), ca. 1020
De contagione (Girolamo Fracastoro), 1546 A, 1762 A
De harmonica mundi (Johannes Kepler), 1609
De historia stirpium (Leonhart Fuchs), 1542
De humani corporis fabrica (Andreas Vesalius), 1543 A
De la formation du foetus (René Descartes), 1637

De magnete, magneticisque corporibus, et de magno magnete tellure, physiologia nova (William Gilbert), 1600 A
De materia medica (Dioscorides), ca. 77 B, 1530 B, 1542
De morbis cutaneis et omnibus corporis humani excrementis tractatus (Geronimo Mercuriali), 1572
De motu (Galileo), 1590 B
De motu cordis (William Harvey), 1628
De nova stella (Tycho Brahe), 1573
De plantis (Andrea Cesalpino), 1583
De re anatomica (Realdo Colombo), 1559
De revolutionibus orbium coelestium (Nicolaus Copernicus), 1543 B
De sedibus et causis morborum per anatomen indagatis (Giovanni Morgagni), 1761 A
De sexu plantarum epistola (Rudolph Jakob Camerarius), 1694
De thiende (Simon Stevinus), 1585
De usu partium (Galen), second century A
De vegetabilibus (Albertus Magnus), ca. 1250 A
De venarum ostiolis (Hieronymus Fabricius ab Aquapendente), 1603
De vero telescopii inventore (Pierre Borel), 1608
Death of a Salesman (Arthur Miller), 1949 M
Debility of the Lower Extremities (Michael Underwood), 1789 A
The Decameron (Giovanni Boccaccio), 1358
decimal point, 499
decimals, ca. 1250 B, 1585
Declaration of Independence, 1776 D
deep-sea bacteria, hydrothermal vents, 1979 A
The Deerslayer (James Fenimore Cooper), 1841 C
dehydrases, 1912 E
dehydrogenases, 1912 E, 1924 D
Delft School, 1921 A
Deliverance (James Dickey), 1970 T
delta agent, 1980 P, 1986 L
Delta Wedding (Eudora Welty), 1946 M
delta-toxin, *Bacillus thuringiensis*, 1967 J, 1981 E, 1982 F, 1983 J, 1986 G, 1986 H, 1987 B, 1987 C, 1988 I, 1989 A
  genes, 1981 E, 1982 F, 1986 G, 1987 C, 1989 A
  mode of action, 1983 J, 1986 H, 1987 B, 1987 C, 1988 I
denitrification, 1868 C, 1881 E, 1886 C
dentistry, 1771 C
deoxyribonucleic acid (DNA), 1909 I, 1929 L, 1938 H, 1944 C, 1950 L, 1953 O
  chlamydiae, 1953 A
  chloroplast, 1962 T
  circular, 1963 E
  colony hybridization, 1985 D
  double helix, 1953 O
  electron microscopy, 1959 A, 1970 P
  fingerprinting, 1980 R, 1985 K
  gamma radiation damage, 1967 P
  hybridization, agar technique, 1962 W
  hyperchromicity, 1959 P
  introns and exons, 1977 V
  isolation, 1961 R, 1980 B

genes, 1967 D, 1988 C
hook, 1971 A, 1974 B
motion pictures, 1941 C
mucous twirls, 1946 A
peritrichous, 1941 B
polysaccharide twirls, 1946 A
protein, 1948 A
purification, 1971 A
rotation, 1974 B
flagellin, 1955 C
flagellin factories, 1965 E
flavin adenine dinucleotide (FAD), 1938 G
flavin mononucleotide, 1932 H, 1934 K
fleas, transmission of bubonic plague, 1906 D
Flexner bacillus, 1900 E, 1903 D
fluctuation test, 1943 D
fluorocarbons, 1977 BB
fluxions, 1665 D
food
    preservation, ca. 1000 B.C., 1765 A, 1804 A,
        1808 A, 1810 B
    spoilage, 1895 B
food allergy, 1921 D
food infection, 1888 D, 1896 A, 1926 C
food poisoning, 900, 1735 A, 1820 A, 1894 D,
    1895 C, 1914 C, 1930 B
foot-and-mouth disease, *see* hoof-and-mouth disease
For Whom the Bell Tolls (Ernest Hemingway), 1940 R
Fore people, New Guinea, 1957 K
fossil, pterodactyl, 1812 B
Foucault knife-edge test, 1932 E
Foucault's pendulum, 1851 B
The Four Horsemen of the Apocalypse (Vicente Blasco-
    Ibañez), 1918 H
The Four Seasons (Antonio Vivaldi), 1726 A
four-kingdom classification, 1956 A
fowl plague, 1901 E, 1927 B
fowlpox inclusion body, 1929 F
fowlpox virus, 1901 E, 1904 D, 1910 C, 1931 F
Francisella tularensis, 1911 C
Franco-Prussian War, 1870 C, 1871 D
Frankenstein, or the Modern Prometheus (Mary
    Wollstonecraft Godwin Shelley), 1818 C
Frankia, 1887 C, 1888 B, 1970 B, 1978 D
free energy, 1878 I, 1927 A, 1977 I
Freedom 7, 1961 W
French pox, 1495 A
French Revolution, 1789 E
Freund's adjuvant, 1942 J
friction, heat production, 1798 A
friction match, 1827 D
Friedländer's bacillus, 1882 E, 1884 G
Friendship 7, 1962 X
From Here to Eternity (James Jones), 1951 P
fructose-1,6-bisphosphate, 1914 F, 1928 F, 1933 I,
    1936 M, 1936 N, 1939 M, 1943 C
fructose-6-phosphate, 1918 F, 1933 H, 1935 K,
    1936 M
fruit fly, *see Drosophila*
fuel cells, 1965 U
The Fugitive (magazine), 1922 J

fungal infections
    blight of potatoes, 1846 C
    human skin, 1839 C, 1841 A
Fungi (kingdom), 1969 A

G

Galápagos Islands, 1831 A, 1835 B, 1859 B
galvanometer, 1780 C
gamma radiation of DNA, 1967 P
gamma rays, 1900 M
gas, 1671 A, 1754, 1781 B
    fermentation, 1766 A, 1772 A
    laws, 1662 A, 1687, 1699 B, 1787 B
    origin of term, 1648 A
    sylvestre, 1648 A, 1757
gas burner, 1850 C
gas gangrene, 1892 A
Gasterophilus, 1923 H
gastroenteritis, nonbacterial, 1972 I
The Gates of Hell (Auguste Rodin), 1880 G, 1886 L
Gay-Lussac equation, 1815 A
Gay-Lussac's law, 1699 B, 1787 B
Geiger counter, 1908 H
gel diffusion analysis, 1948 J
gelatin liquefaction, 1923 C
Gemini, Project (spacecraft), 1965 U
gemmules, 1868 E
Genera morborum (Carolus Linnaeus), 1763 A
Genera plantarum (Carolus Linnaeus), 1737
General History of Virginia (John Smith), 1624 C
general relativity, 1915 E
generalized transduction, 1956 H
generation time, bacterial, 1950 C
genes
    agents of inheritance, 1915 D
    chemotaxis, 1967 D
    cloning, 1972 L, 1972 M, 1973 N, 1979 J
    definition, 1909 H
    flagellar motion, 1967 D
    molecule, 1935 I, 1944 I
    mutation, 1935 I
    regulatory, 1959 O
    structural, 1959 O
    structure, theory of, 1935 I
    toxin production, 1951 H, 1981 E
    transfer agent, *Rhodopseudomonas capsulata*, 1975 H
genetic code, 1961 P, 1961 Q, 1964 L
genetic engineering, 1952 L, 1973 O, 1975 O,
    1977 R, 1979 J
genetic loci, H1 and H2, 1953 L
genetic map, 1947 C
    bacteriophage, 1948 E
    Escherichia coli, 1955 F
genetics
    nomenclature, 1966 I
    recombination, 1964 G
    terminology, 1909 H
    transfer mechanism, 1952 K
Genetics and the Evolutionary Process (Theodosius
    Dobzhansky), 1937 N
Geneva Conventions, 1864 C

genotype, 1909 H
geocentric astronomy, ca. 367 B.C., second century B, 1512, 1543 B
Geographica (Ptolemy), second century B
geometry, ca. 300 B.C., 1637
germ layers, 1828 A
germ plasm theory of inheritance, 1883 E, 1883 F
germ theory
    of disease, 1546 A, 1840 A, 1858 B, 1876 C
    of fermentation, 1857 C
German Empire, 1871 D
German measles, 1962 R
A German Requiem (Johannes Brahms), 1868 F
germfree life, 1885 J, 1895 D, 1899 C, 1928 D, 1949 A
Gettysburg Address, 1863 F
Giemsa stain, 1905 I, 1942 B
Gifton College, 1869 K
Girl Scouts of America, 1912 I
glass, ca. 2000 B.C., 1500 B.C. B
The Glass Menagerie (Tennessee Williams), 1945 H
global regulon, 1984 F
globulins, electrophoresis, 1937 M
gluconeogenesis, 1912 D
gluconic acid, 1936 O, 1950 D
glucosamine, in cell walls, 1953 B
glucose
    effect, 1942 F, 1956 E, 1961 D, 1965 J
    from starch, 1811 A
    from wood, 1820 D
glucose diphosphate, 1928 F
glucose monophosphate, 1914 G, 1931 K
glucose-6-phosphate, 1933 H, 1935 J, 1935 K
glucose-6-phosphate dehydrogenase, 1931 J
glucose-phosphate isomerase, 1933 H
D-glutamyl polypeptide, capsular, 1937 A
glutathione, 1921 F
glyceraldehyde-3-phosphate, 1934 I, 1936 N
glycerol, 1780 A
glycogen, 1857 E, 1899 A, 1936 P
glycolysis, 1911 I, 1912 D, 1927 H, 1933 I, 1934 I, 1934 J, 1936 M, 1936 N, 1939 L, 1939 M, 1939 N, 1939 O, 1943 C
glycopeptide, 1956 C
glycopeptide transpeptidase, 1965 H
glycosaminopeptide, 1956 C
gnotobiotics, 1949 A
Go Tell It on the Mountain (James Baldwin), 1953 Z
gold rushes, 1848 E, 1897 M
The Golden Notebook (Doris Lessing), 1962 Z
Golgi body, 1885 L, 1898 L
Gone with the Wind (Margaret Mitchell), 1936 V, 1939 U
gonorrhea, 1767 A, 1879 B
"A Good Man Is Hard To Find" (Flannery O'Connor), 1955 R
gram, defined, 1791 A
Gram stain, 1882 E, 1884 B, 1884 G, 1929 A, 1957 A, 1963 B
gramicidin, 1939 B
The Grapes of Wrath (John Steinbeck), 1939 T
gratuitous inducers, 1952 H

gravitation, 1666 B, 1687
Gravity's Rainbow (Thomas Pynchon), 1973 R
grease-spot photometer, 1850 C
Great Expectations (Charles Dickens), 1861 K
The Great Gatsby (F. Scott Fitzgerald), 1925 J
The Great Herbal (Emperor Shen Lung), ca. 3000 B.C. A
great pokkes, 1495 A
greenhouse effect, 1908 G
Gregorian calendar, 1582 B
growth factor, 1901 D
Grüber-Widal test, 1896 E
guaiacum, 1804 C, 1810 C, 1840 E
guanine, 1885 N
guano, 1805 A
Guernica (Pablo Picasso), 1937 S
Guillain-Barré syndrome, 1976 I
The Gulag Archipelago (Aleksandr Solzhenitsyn), 1974 U
Gulf War, 1990 J
Gulliver's Travels (Jonathan Swift), 1726 B
guncotton, 1845 C
"Gunga Din" (Rudyard Kipling), 1892 J
Gunter's scale, 1620 A, 1622
gymnoplasts, 1953 C

H

H antigen, 1903 G, 1920 C
Haber process, 1908 F
hadrons, 1961 V, 1964 P
Haemastaticks (Stephen Hales), 1733
Haemophilus influenzae, 1892 B, 1931 C, 1933 D, 1970 M
Haffkine Institute, 1897 F
Halley's comet, 1705
Halobacterium cutirubrum, 1961 B, 1965 D
Halobacterium halobium, 1963 C, 1967 C, 1971 B, 1980 Q
Halobacterium salinarium, 1963 C
Halococcus, 1975 D
halophiles, 1963 C
Handbuch der organischen Chemie (Friedrich Konrad Beilstein), 1880 E
Handbuch der Pflanzenphisiologie (Wilhelm Friedrich Pfeffer), 1881 I
Hansel and Gretel (Englebert Humperdinck), 1893 J
Hansen's disease, 1874 A
hantavirus, 1978 H, 1982 L, 1984 M, 1988 O
haploid, 1882 I
hapten, 1917 E
Harden-Young coenzyme, 1906 K, 1923 G
Harden-Young ester, 1906 J
"Harlem Renaissance," 1925 J
Harvard University, 1636
Hashimoto's chronic thyroiditis, 1957 O
Hawaii, annexation by U.S., 1898 Q
hay bacillus, 1877 B
hay infusions, 1876 A, 1877 B
Haymarket Massacre, 1886 K
heart, function, ca. 280 B.C.
The Heart Is a Lonely Hunter (Carson McCullers), 1940 R

The Heart of a Woman (Maya Angelou), 1981 P
The Heart of Darkness (Joseph Conrad), 1902 O
heart transplant, 1967 U
heat shock proteins, 1975 G, 1978 C
heat theorem, 1906 N
heavy water, 1932 K, 1934 N
Heine-Medin disease, 1881 G
HeLa cells, 1952 N
Helicobacter pylori, 1983 G
heliocentric cosmology, second century B, 1512,
    1543 B, 1610
hemagglutination, 1941 G
hematin, 1825 D, 1838 F
hematosin, 1838 F, 1862 B
hematoxylin, 1849 D
hemin, 1853 B, 1929 M
hemoglobin
    absorption spectrum, 1862 B
    oxidation-reduction, 1864 A
    oxygen transport, 1872 F
    root nodules, 1938 D
    structure, 1959 R
hemolysis, immune, 1898 I
hemolytic classification of streptococci, 1903 A
hemolytic plaque assay, 1963 P
Henry VI (William Shakespeare), 1590 C
hepatitis
    A, 1962 Q, 1973 L
    B, 1962 Q, 1965 N, 1981 I
    C, 1989 E
    delta, 1980 P, 1986 L
    E, 1990 G
    infectious, 1912 C
    non-A, non-B, 1974 K, 1989 E
    serum, 1885 F, 1926 E, 1943 E
Her First Biscuit (motion picture), 1912 J
herbal medicine, ca. 3000 B.C., ca. 2750 B.C.,
    ca. 77 B, 1535 A
Herbarum Vivae Eicones (Otto Brunfels and Hans
    Weiditz), 1530 B
Hereditary Genius (Francis Galton), 1869 F
hermaphrodite, 1694
Hershey-Chase experiment, 1953 N
Hétérogénie, ou traité de la génération spontanée (Félix-
    Archimède Pouchet), 1858 A
heterolactic acid fermentation, 1951 E
heterolactic acid shunt, 1931 J
heteropolysaccharide, cell wall, 1975 D, 1977 C
heterozygote, 1909 H
hexamethylene-tetramine compounds, 1916 B
hexokinase, 1927 F
hexose monophosphate, 1914 G
hexose monophosphate shunt, 1931 J
hexose 1,6-bisphosphate, 1906 J
hexoses, structure, 1894 H
hexuronic acid, 1928 G, 1932 J
Hfr mating types, 1956 G
Hfr strain, 1950 F, 1960 I, 1964 F
hieroglyphics, ca. 3000 B.C. C
high-energy bonds, 1932 G, 1941 K
high-energy group potential, 1941 K

high-frequency transfer, genetic markers, 1950 F
highways, 1921 H, 1940 P
Hill reaction, 1939 J
Hindenburg (zeppelin), 1937 Q
Hippocratic oath, ca. 460 B.C.
Hippocratic school, ca. 460 B.C.
Hiroshima, atomic bomb in World War II, 1945 F
Hispaniola (Santo Domingo), 1492 B, 1518
histamine, 1911 F
histidase, 1956 E
histidine, synthesis, 1959 N
histidine operon, 1974 O
histocompatibility complex, 1937 G, 1948 I, 1958 M,
    1963 N
Histoire naturelle (Georges Louis Leclerc), 1749 B
histology, 1849 D, 1885 L
Historia animalium (Conrad Gesner), 1546 B
Historia insectorum generalis (Jan Swammerdam), 1669 B
Historia plantarum (Conrad Gesner), 1546 B
The History of the Decline and Fall of the Roman Empire
    (Edward Gibbon), 1776 F
History of the Peloponnesian War (Thucydides), 430
    B.C. A
History of the Valorous and Witty Knight-Errant Don
    Quixote (Miguel de Cervantes), 1605
A History of Their Own (Bonnie Anderson and Judith
    Zinsser), 1988 R
The History of Tom Jones, a Foundling (Henry
    Fielding), 1749 C
HIV, see human immunodeficiency virus
H.M.S. Pinafore (W. S. Gilbert and Arthur Sullivan),
    1878 L
Hodgkin's disease, 1832 B
hog cholera, 1886 F, 1899 D
hog flu, 1931 E
Holliday junction, 1964 G
Holy Roman Empire, 1806 C
hominids, prehistoric, 1891 E, 1959 S
homografts, 1944 G
homozygote, 1909 H
Hong Kong influenza pandemic, 1968 G
hoof-and-mouth disease, 1898 G, 1901 F
hop stunt disease, 1971 E
hormones, 1905 L
horror autotoxicus, 1901 I
horseradish peroxidase, 1912 F
host range mutants, bacteriophage, 1945 B
hot air sterilization, 1881 H
The House of the Seven Gables (Nathaniel Hawthorne),
    1851 F
HTLV-1, 1980 N
HTLV-III, 1983 L, 1985 F
Huckleberry Finn (Mark Twain), 1884 P
Hudson's Bay Company, 1670 C
Humalin, 1979 J
human(s)
    body temperature, 1626 A
    exanthems, 1948 H
    genome research program, 1988 P
    races, 1776 C
    retrovirus, 1980 N

Infusionstierchen, 1838 A
Infusoria, 1773 A
ingrafting, smallpox, 1717
Inherit the Wind (Jerome Lawrence and Robert E. Lee), 1955 S
ink, ca. 3000 B.C. C
inorganic compounds, defined, 1807 B
insect life cycles, 1669 B
insecticide
    bacterial, *see* bacterial insecticides
    chemical, 1940 O
insertion sequences, 1960 G, 1968 C, 1974 H
Inside the Bar, Tynemouth (Winslow Homer), 1883 M
Institut Pasteur, 1885 H, 1888 G
instructionalist theory of antibody formation, 1930 D, 1940 M
insulin, 1921 G, 1953 Q, 1965 T, 1979 J
intelligence quotient (IQ), 1914 J
intelligence scale, metrical, 1905 M
interferon, 1957 L, 1963 M
internal combustion engine, 1859 F, 1863 E, 1876 H, 1885 O, 1893 G
International Bureau of Weights and Measures, 1875 E
interrupted mating, 1955 F, 1956 F
introns, 1977 V, 1977 W
invertase, 1849 C
invertebrates, 1802 B
Invisible Man (Ralph Ellison), 1952 U
iodoacetate poisoning, 1930 F
ion, origin of term, 1833 B
Iran-Iraq War, 1980 T, 1990 J
iron
    blood, 1745 A
    catalyst of respiration, 1914 H
Iron Age, ca. 2500 B.C. A
Is Mars Habitable? (Alfred Russel Wallace), 1858 D
isochronism, 1582 A
isotope(s), chemical, 1913 G
isotope labeling, 1932 K
Israel, 1948 P
Ivanhoe (Walter Scott), 1819 D
Ivory soap, 1878 K
Ixodes dammini, 1977 M, 1982 J

J
jack bean plant, 1926 H
Jacquard loom, 1801 C, 1832 E
Jamestown colony, 1607 A
Jane Eyre (Charlotte Brontë), 1847 E
Japanese beetle, 1939 C
jet engine, 1937 Q, 1941 O
Johns Hopkins Medical School and Hospital, 1893 I
The Joy of Life (Henri Matisse), 1906 R
Julian calendar, 1582 B
jumping genes, 1950 J
Justinian, plague of, 542

K
kala-azar, 1900 F
Kaposi's sarcoma, 1872 E, 1981 H, 1983 I, 1988 L

Kastle's indophenol oxidase, 1910 D, 1938 F
Kauffmann–White scheme, 1926 A, 1941 A
Kelvin scale, 1851 A
2-keto-gluconic acid, 1950 D
2-keto-6-phosphogluconate, 1936 O
2-keto-3-phosphogluconic acid, 1952 F
Khmer Rouge, 1975 U
kieselguhr, 1897 C
kinetics, chemical, 1884 L
King James Bible, 1611
King of Italy (first), 1861 I
Kirby-Bauer test, 1966 G
The Kiss (Auguste Rodin), 1886 L
Kjeldahl nitrogen analysis, 1883 H
Klebsiella, 1882 E, 1902 B
Klebsiella pneumoniae, 1882 E, 1884 G
Klebs–Löffler bacillus, 1883 B
Klondike gold rush, 1897 M
Koch's plate technique, 1881 A
Koch's postulates, 1840 A, 1877 D, 1882 D, 1883 B
Korean hemorrhagic fever, 1978 H, 1982 L
Korean War, 1950 R, 1953 Y
Koser citrate medium, 1925 A
Kovács' reagent, 1889 A
Krebs citric acid cycle, *see* citric acid cycle
kuru, 1920 D, 1936 J, 1957 K, 1966 L, 1982 M

L
L forms, 1935 D, 1939 A, 1942 C
La Bohème (Giacomo Puccini), 1896 K
La Dioptrique (René Descartes), 1637
La Géométrie (René Descartes), 1637
La Traviata (Giuseppe Verdi), 1853 E
labeling techniques, chemical, 1904 F
lac region, transposition, 1966 H
lac repressor, 1966 F
laccase, 1894 J
lactic acid
    fermentation, 1780 A, 1857 C, 1870 B, 1913 E, 1914 F, 1926 B, 1939 L
    muscle, 1859 D, 1907 I, 1912 D
lactic acid bacteria, 1878 B, 1893 A, 1901 B, 1919 B
Lactobacillus, 1901 B
Lactobacillus arabinosus, 1958 C
Lactobacillus lactis, 1948 B
Lactobacteriaceae, 1919 B
Lady Chatterley's Lover (D. H. Lawrence), 1928 K
The Lady of the Lake (Walter Scott), 1810 G
Lancefield's classification, streptococci, 1933 A, 1952 B
Langmuir trough, 1910 G
L'Art Poétique (Nicholas Boileau-Despréaux), 1674 B
laser, 1960 Q
Lassa virus, 1969 D
The Last of the Mohicans (James Fenimore Cooper), 1826 B
The Last Supper (Leonardo da Vinci), 1495 B
laws
    conservation of energy, 1842 D
    conservation of matter, 1789 D
    constant composition, 1799

Methodus plantarum nova (John Ray), 1682 A
methyl red test, 1915 A, 1936 C
methyl transfer coenzyme, 1971 C
methylene blue, reduction of, 1924 A
methylreductase, 1974 F
methyltransferase, 1974 F
metric system, 1791 A
Metropolitan Opera House, 1883 L, 1905 O, 1966 R
MHC restriction of T-cell toxicity, 1974 M
Michaelis-Menten equation, 1913 F, 1934 L
Michelson-Morley experiment, 1887 H
microcalorimeter, 1912 D
microchip, 1958 Q
Micrococcus, 1872 B, 1875 A
Micrococcus amylovorus, 1879 D
Micrococcus lysodeikticus, 1940 C, 1952 D
Micrococcus melitensis, 1887 D, 1897 D
microcycle sporogenesis, 1965 G
microfossils, 1965 B, 1967 B
Micrographia (Robert Hooke), 1665 B
microphages, 1884 H
microphone, 1878 J
microscope
    binocular, 1667 B
    coining of term, 1625
    invention, 1590 A
    Leeuwenhoek's, 1673 A
microscopic photography, 1881 A
Microscopical Researches into the Similarity in the Structure and Growth of Animals and Plants (Theodor Schwann), 1839 D
microscopy
    achromatic lenses, *see* lenses, achromatic
    apochromatic lenses, *see* lenses, apochromatic
    electron, *see* electron microscopy
    epifluorescence, 1975 B
    examination of blood, 1821 B
    freezing of tissue sections, 1867 A
    gold staining of tissue sections, 1867 A
    homogeneous immersion objective lens, 1874 C, 1878 H
    phase-contrast, 1932 E
    substage condenser, 1873 B
    ultraviolet, 1904 J, 1942 K
microsomes, 1938 B
microtome, 1953 E
A Midsummer Night's Dream (Felix Mendelssohn-Bartholdy), 1843 C
migration inhibitory factor (MIF), 1966 N
The Mikado (W. S. Gilbert and Arthur Sullivan), 1885 R
milieu intérieur, 1857 F
Military Academy, U.S., 1802 E
milk, fat content, 1890 G
The Mill on the Floss (George Eliot), 1860 C
mimeograph machine, 1879 H
mineral acids, 1210 A
minicells, *Escherichia coli*, 1967 E
Miranda v. Arizona, 1966 Q
mitochondria, 1890 F, 1898 K, 1927 D, 1933 G, 1948 K, 1951 N

mitosis, 1882 H, 1883 F, 1953 T
    in bacteria, 1942 B, 1958 E
Moby Dick (Herman Melville), 1851 F
molecular biology, origin of term, 1938 E
molecular phylogeny, 1965 A
molecular weights, 1848 C
Moll Flanders (Daniel Defoe), 1721 C
Mollusca, 1798 B
Mona Lisa (Leonardo da Vinci), 1507
Monas, 1773 A
Monera (kingdom), 1956 A, 1969 A
monoclonal antibodies, 1955 N, 1975 N
monocotyledons, 1682 A
monoecious plants, 1694
Monroe Doctrine, 1823 D
"The Monument" (Christopher Wren), 1671 B
moon landing, 1969 H
Morse code, 1837 J
most probable number (MPN), 1950 A
mother of vinegar, 1822 A, 1837 C
motility, bacterial, 1946 A, 1974 C
motion pictures, 1895 J, 1926 N
Moulin de la Galette (August Renoir), 1876 L
Mount Rushmore National Monument, 1941 Q
mousepox, 1948 H
Mrs. Dalloway (Virginia Woolf), 1925 J
mucopeptide, 1956 C
multiple drug resistance, 1959 G
mumps virus, 1948 F
muramic acid, *see* cell walls, bacterial
murein, 1956 C
murine breast cancer virus, 1936 I
murine leukemia virus, 1951 I
muscardine (calcino), silkworm disease, 1835 A
muscle
    biochemistry, 1861 E
    calorimetric measurement, 1911 I
    contraction, 1859 D, 1907 I
    energy reactions, 1912 D
    fermentation, 1870 B
    respiration, 1850 A
The Musketeers of Pig Alley (motion picture), 1912 J
mustard gas, 1946 K
mutagenesis, site-specific, 1978 J
mutagens
    chemical, 1939 E, 1946 K
    dyes and biological stains, 1939 E
    ultraviolet light, 1934 H, 1949 F, 1953 M, 1960 H, 1965 L, 1974 E
    X rays, 1927 E
mutants
    amber, 1963 H
    asporogenic, 1960 E, 1976 E
    bacteriophage host range, 1945 B
    growth factor, 1944 D
    isolation, penicillin technique, 1948 D
    nutritional, 1941 H
    radiation-sensitive, 1958 H
    recombination-deficient, 1965 L
    sporulation, 1976 E
    temperature-sensitive, 1963 H

Norwalk gastroenteritis, 1972 I
Nostoc, 1928 A
Notes on the Matters Affecting the Health, Efficiency and Hospital Administration of the British Army (Florence Nightingale), 1860 B
Novum organum (Francis Bacon), 1620 B
nuclear chain reaction, 1942 M
nuclear fission, 1938 I
nuclear power plant, 1979 L, 1986 M
nuclear reactor, electricity produced by, 1951 O
nucleic acid, 1869 E, 1885 N, 1889 I
   hybridization, 1961 N, 1962 W, 1963 W
   probes, 1961 N, 1988 B
nuclein, 1869 E, 1889 I
nucleoid, 1942 B
nucleoplasm, 1882 I, 1959 A
nucleoproteid toxin, 1910 C
nucleosomes, 1974 R, 1977 X
nucleus
   bacterial, 1888 C, 1897 B, 1909 B, 1935 B, 1942 B
   cell, 1832 C, 1838 D, 1846 G, 1861 F, 1866 A, 1876 D, 1882 H, 1882 I
nursing, 1860 B

O

O antigen, 1903 G, 1920 C
Oberlin College, 1833 D
Occupational Safety and Health Act, 1970 S
octet theory, electrons, 1916 F
octopine, 1970 G, 1975 L
Odalisk (Robert Rauschenberg), 1958 T
Ode on a Grecian Urn (John Keats), 1819 D
Of Human Bondage (W. Somerset Maugham), 1915 H
"Of Measles in the Year 1670" (Thomas Sydenham), 1670 B
Oidium albicans, 1902 B
Okazaki fragments, 1968 I
The Old Curiosity Shop (Charles Dickens), 1841 C
The Old Guitarist (Pablo Picasso), 1903 R
Old Tuberculin, 1890 C, 1907 E, 1908 C
Old World monkeys, 1908 B
Olduvai Gorge, 1959 S
Oliver Twist (Charles Dickens), 1838 H
Olympic Games, 1896 L
"omnis cellula a cellula," from *Die Cellularpathologie* (Rudolf Virchow), 1858 B
On Growth and Form (D'Arcy Wentworth Thompson), 1917 F
On the Causes of Diseases (Giovanni Morgagni), 1761 A
"On the Communication of Cholera by Impure Thames Water" (John Snow), 1854 C
"On the Distinctions of a Plant and an Animal, and on a Fourth Kingdom of Nature" (John Hogg), 1861 D
"On the Dynamical Theory of the Electromagnetic Field" (James Clerk Maxwell), 1865 D
"On the Equilibrium of Heterogeneous Substances" (Josiah Willard Gibbs), 1878 I

On the Mode of Communication of Cholera (John Snow), 1854 C
On the Natural Varieties of Mankind (Johann Friedrich Blumenbach), 1776 C
On the Origin of Species by Means of Natural Selection (Charles Darwin), 1858 D, 1859 B
On the Road (Jack Kerouac), 1957 T
"On the Tendency of Varieties to Depart Indefinitely from the Original Type" (Alfred Russel Wallace), 1858 D
oncogenes, 1969 F, 1976 L, 1977 U
One (#31, 1950) (Jackson Pollock), 1950 U
one gene–one enzyme hypothesis, 1941 H
one-step growth curve, 1939 D
o-nitrophenyl-β-D-galactopyranoside (ONPG), 1950 E
"ontogeny recapitulates phylogeny," 1866 A
Oparin ocean scenario, 1924 G, 1953 V
operator gene, 1960 M
operon, 1958 P, 1959 O, 1960 M
opsonins, 1903 I
optical activity, 1815 B, 1848 A
optical fiber cables, 1977 AA, 1985 L
optical isomerism, 1884 K
optical rotation, 1815 B
Opus majus (Roger Bacon), 1249
Opuscles physiques et chimiques (Antoine Lavoisier), 1774 C
Orfeo (Claudio Monteverdi), 1607 B
organic chemistry, defined, 1861 G
organic compounds, 1807 B, 1858 E
organizer function, embryonic tissue, 1918 E
organotrophs, 1946 C
origin of life, 1924 G, 1953 V
ornithine cycle, 1932 I
Oscillarias, 1872 B
Oscillatoria, 1842 A
osmosis, 1748 C
osmotic pressure, 1881 I, 1886 H
Otello (Giuseppe Verdi), 1887 I
Ouchterlony test, 1948 J, 1955 O
Our Town (Thornton Wilder), 1938 K
outer membrane, bacterial, 1958 A, 1960 A
oxalic acid, 1780 I
Oxford English Dictionary (*OED*), 1884 O, 1989 J
Oxford University, 1167
oxidase, 1897 J
oxidation
   guaiacum, 1810 C
   succinic acid, 1924 A, 1924 D
oxidation-reduction, 1878 G, 1897 K, 1911 J, 1917 G, 1921 F, 1924 A, 1924 D
oxidative phosphorylation, 1930 G, 1941 J, 1951 N, 1965 P, 1977 Y
oxidizing enzymes, metal content, 1894 J
oxygen, 1771 A, 1774 B, 1775 B, 1780 B
   isotope, 1932 K
   liquid, 1877 F
   production by plants, 1771 B, 1779 B
oxyhemoglobin, 1862 B, 1864 A
oxymuriatic acid, 1800 A

ozone, in biological oxidations, 1840 E, 1875 D
ozone layer, 1977 BB
Ozymandias (Percy Bysshe Shelley), 1818 C

P

PABA, *see p*-aminobenzoic acid
Pagliacci (Ruggiero Leoncavallo), 1892 I
PaJaMo experiment, 1958 P
palindromes, 1970 M
p-aminobenzoic acid (PABA), 1940 G, 1946 E
Panama Canal, 1880 F, 1914 K, 1978 N
pancreas, 1857 F
pangenesis, 1868 E, 1889 G
pangens, 1889 G
panspermia, 1907 J
papyrus, ca. 3000 B.C. C
Paradise Lost (John Milton), 1667 C
parasporal body, 1915 B, 1953 J, 1954 H, 1967 J
paratyphoid bacillus, 1900 D
parenchyma, 1682 B
Paris World's Fair, 1889 K
Park nucleotides, 1952 C
Parkinson's disease, 1817 B
Parkinson's Law (Cyril Northcote Parkinson), 1958 S
Park-Williams strain, *Corynebacterium diphtheriae*, 1894 F
paroxysmal hemoglobinuria, 1904 B
Paschen bodies, 1906 G
Passage to India (E. M. Forster), 1924 H
Pasteur effect, 1926 I, 1943 C
Pasteur Institute, 1885 H, 1888 G
Pasteur reaction, 1926 I
Pasteurella multocida, 1880 C
Pasteurella pestis, 1914 B, 1956 I
Pasteurella tularensis, 1911 C
pasteurization of milk, 1886 D
patentability of bacteria, 1980 G
pathogenic bacteria, marine environments, 1986 B
Pathologische Untersuchungen (Jacob Henle), 1840 A
Peace Corps, 1961 X
Peace of Westphalia, 1648 B
peach yellows disease, 1879 D
pear blight disease, 1879 D
Pearl Harbor, 1941 P
pébrine (silkworm disease), 1837 D
pellagra, 1912 G, 1937 O
pendulum, periodicity, 1582 A
pendulum clock, 1657 A
penicillin, 1929 B, 1935 D, 1939 A, 1940 D, 1940 E, 1948 D, 1952 C
    mechanism of action, 1965 H
    semisynthetic, 1959 E
    structure, 1944 B, 1949 G
    therapeutic use, 1941 F
penicillinase, 1940 E
Penicillium chrysogenum, 1940 D
Penicillium notatum, 1929 B, 1940 D
Penicillium roqueforti, 1070
Pennsylvania Turnpike, 1940 P
pentose(s), structure, 1894 H

pentose phosphate pathway, 1931 J, 1935 J
People's Republic of China, 1949 K
pepsin, 1836 A
peptic ulcer, 1983 G
peptide bond, 1902 L
peptidoglycan, 1956 C
periodic table, 1869 G, 1914 I
periplasm, 1961 C, 1977 E, 1984 C, 1990 C
permease, 1956 D, 1965 I
peroxidase, 1845 B, 1898 M
peroxisomes, 1955 P
pertussis, 1679, 1906 C, 1923 E, 1933 F, 1936 K
pertussis vaccine, 1923 E, 1933 F, 1936 K
pesticin, 1981 F
pestilence, ca. 3180 B.C., ca. 1190 B.C.
Peterloo Massacre, 1819 C
petri dish, 1881 A, 1887 A
Petri's capsules, 1887 A
Petronas Twin Towers, 1973 Q
phage group, 1944 E
phagocytes, 1884 H, 1888 F
phagocytic leukocytes, 1903 I
phagocytosis, 1884 H, 1903 I, 1931 H
pharmacopeia, ca. 77 B, 1535 A
phase variation, *Salmonella*, 1922 C, 1953 L
phenotype, 1909 H
Philosophiae naturalis principia mathematica (Isaac Newton), 1687
Philosophical Transactions of the Royal Society of London, 1665 E
Philosophie zoologique (Jean-Baptiste Lamarck), 1809
phlogiston, 1606 A, 1668 C, 1697 B, 1720 B, 1771 B, 1772 C, 1775 A, 1775 B, 1781 B, 1783 B
phonograph, 1877 G
phosphagen, 1927 G
phosphate, requirement for fermentation, 1903 C, 1906 J
phosphoenolpyruvate, 1934 I, 1934 J, 1964 B
phosphofructokinase, 1936 M, 1943 C
phosphoglucomutase, 1936 P
phosphogluconate pathway, 1931 J
phosphogluconic acid, 1935 J, 1936 O
phosphoglycerate, 1933 I, 1934 I, 1939 N, 1952 G
phosphorus isotopes, radioactive, 1934 O
phosphorus-oxygen ratio, 1941 L, 1951 N
phosphorylase, 1936 P
phosphorylation
    of hexose, 1935 K
    respiratory chain, 1939 Q
phosphotransferase system, 1964 B, 1980 E
Photobacterium fischeri, 1976 B, 1981 B
photocopier, 1937 Q, 1959 T
photoelectric effect, 1887 G, 1898 P, 1905 J
photography, 1822 D, 1834 B, 1839 F, 1841 B, 1888 I, 1947 F
photomicrographs of bacteria, 1877 A
photooxidation, 1804 C
photophosphorylation, cell-free, 1954 F
photoreactivation, 1949 F, 1957 F, 1962 G, 1964 E

photosynthesis, 1779 B, 1782, 1804 B, 1837 H,
    1862 C, 1881 I, 1931 I, 1954 M, 1954 N
  carbon cycle, 1950 M, 1954 M
  carbon dioxide fixation, 1954 M
  ferredoxin in, 1962 U
  Hill reaction, 1939 J
  isolated chloroplasts, 1954 N
  oxygen evolution, 1939 J
  pigment systems, 1961 U
  quantum requirement, 1922 G
  source of oxygen, 1931 I, 1941 I
  two–light reaction, 1960 N, 1961 U
  uptake of $^{11}CO_2$, 1939 I
photosynthetic bacteria, 1949 E, 1952 G, 1959 C
photosynthetic phosphorylation, 1954 N
phototaxis, 1881 D
phototrophy, 1946 C
phylogeny
  molecular, 1965 A
  ribosomal RNA homologies, 1986 A
physical map, simian virus 40 genome, 1973 I
phytanyl ether, *Halobacterium* membrane, 1965 D
phytohemagglutinin, 1973 B
Phytophthora infestans, 1846 C
pi (π), ca. 1700 B.C., ca. 260 B.C., 190, 499, 600,
  1596, 1706, 1882 J
Piano Concerto in A Major (Franz Liszt), 1856 G
Piano Concerto no. 1 in G Minor (Felix
  Mendelssohn-Bartholdy), 1831 D
picoplankton, 1988 A
picornaviruses, 1963 J
Pilgrims, 1620 C
pili, 1949 D, 1955 B, 1960 I, 1964 F
The Pirates of Penzance (W. S. Gilbert and Arthur
  Sullivan), 1879 K
plague, ca. 3180 B.C., 1190 B.C., 790 B.C., 79, 251,
  1095, 1897 F; *see also* bubonic plague
  of Antoninus (smallpox), 164
  of Athens, 430 B.C. A
  of Galen (smallpox), 164
  of Thucydides (measles or typhus), 430 B.C. A
  V and W antigens, 1980 J
  yellow plague, 664
plague research laboratory, 1897 F
planetary motion, 1609
Plantae (kingdom), 1866 A, 1956 A, 1969 A
plants
  anatomy and sexuality, 1682 B
  carbon dioxide uptake, 1837 H
  carbon from the atmosphere, 1779 B, 1804 B
  classification, ca. 1250 A, 1583, 1623 B, 1686,
    1735 B, 1749 A, 1812 C
  encyclopedia, 1812 C
  fertilization, 1823 B
  geography, 1805 A
  hybrids, 1761 B, 1865 B
  nitrogen source, 1804 B
  physiology, 1727, 1881 I
  sexual reproduction, 1694
  structure, 1802 C
  water balance, 1727

plaques, bacteriophage, 1917 C
plasmagenes, 1958 G
plasmids
  cloning of genes by, 1973 N
  controlled colonization factor, 1975 J
  degradative, 1972 E
  detection and isolation, 1976 F, 1981 C
  invasiveness mediated by, 1980 K
  origin of term, 1958 G
  proteins encoded by, 1979 G
  resistance factors, 1960 F
  TOL, 1973 D
  tumor-inducing (Ti), 1970 G, 1975 L, 1977 O,
    1986 K, 1987 C
  virulence, 1974 I, 1981 F
plasmolysis, 1894 A
plasmons, 1958 G
plasmoptysis, 1900 B
plastics, 1909 J
plate count, dilution methods, 1881 A
Playboy of the Western World (John Millington Synge),
  1907 N
Plessy v. Ferguson, 1896 I
pleuropneumonia organisms, 1898 D
pleuropneumonialike organisms, 1898 D
Plutarch's Lives, 790 B.C., 1579
Plymouth, Massachusetts, 1620 C
pneuma, ca. 280 B.C.
pneumococcal pneumonia, 1945 C
pneumococci, 1881 C, 1882 E, 1884 G, 1902 B,
  1931 D
  bile solubility, 1900 A
  capsules, 1902 B, 1923 F, 1931 D
  distinguished from streptococci, 1900 A
Pneumocystis carinii, pneumonia, 1981 H
pneumotyphus, 1879 C
Pocahontas, 1624 C
Poems (Gerard Manley Hopkins), 1918 H
Poems (John Keats), 1817 E
Poems of Emily Dickinson, 1890 J
Poetry in Two Volumes (William Wordsworth),
  1807 E
poliomyelitis, 1789 A, 1840 B, 1874 B, 1881 G,
  1893 D, 1909 F, 1911 D, 1916 E, 1952 P,
  1954 K, 1957 M
  vaccine, 1952 P, 1954 K, 1957 M
poliovirus, 1908 B, 1912 B, 1936 F, 1949 I, 1959 I,
  1961 H
  crystallization, 1955 G
  filtration, 1908 B
  mRNA, 1963 R
  polyhedral structure, 1959 I
pollen, 1682 B
pollen tube, 1823 B
polonium, 1898 N
polyadenylic sequences, mRNA, 1970 N
polymerase chain reaction, 1987 I
polymorphonuclear leukocytes, 1884 H
polyomavirus, 1963 K
polypeptide synthesis, aerobic versus anaerobic,
  1983 C

polysaccharide antigens, 1923 F
Porgy and Bess (George Gershwin), 1935 Q
porins, 1976 D
A Portrait of the Artist as a Young Man (James Joyce), 1914 N
positron, 1932 M
posttranslational processing, polypeptides, 1968 J
potato famine, 1846 C
potato scab disease, 1879 D
potato tuber spindle disease, 1971 E
poxvirus RNA polymerase, 1967 T
precipitation reaction, antisera, 1897 I
precipitin reaction, quantitative, 1929 H
prephage, 1975 H
preservation of food, ca. 1000 B.C., 1804 A, 1808 A, 1810 B
Pride and Prejudice (Jane Austen), 1813 D
Prince William Sound, Alaska, 1989 I
Principia mathematica (Isaac Newton), 1666 B, 1687
Principia Mathematica (Bertrand Russell and Alfred North Whitehead), 1913 H
Principia philosophiae (René Descartes), 1637
printing, 1454
prions, 1920 D, 1936 J, 1957 K, 1966 L, 1967 O, 1981 J, 1981 K, 1982 M, 1983 M, 1985 H, 1985 I, 1989 F, 1989 G, 1990 H
prisms, 1666 A
Procaryotae (kingdom), 1969 A
procaryotes, 1937 E, 1956 A, 1957 Q, 1962 A
procaryotic domain, 1977 A
Prochlorococcus marinus, 1988 A
proflavin, 1962 V
Proiskhozhdenie Zhiny (Alexandr Ivanovich Oparin), 1924 G
Prometheus Unbound (Percy Bysshe Shelley), 1819 D
prontosil, 1932 B
prophage, 1950 I, 1962 I
protein
    alpha-helix, 1951 L
    heat shock, 1975 G, 1978 C
    origin of term, 1838 E
    phosphorylation, 1978 B
    structure, 1951 L
    synthesis, 1951 K, 1955 M, 1961 S, 1965 T, 1968 J
protein kinase, 1978 B, 1979 F
proteinaceous infectious particles, 1982 M
Proteus, 1885 B, 1916 D, 1920 C
Protista (kingdom), 1861 D, 1866 A, 1956 A, 1969 A
protoctist, 1861 D
Protoctista, 1956 A
protoplasm, 1837 E, 1846 G, 1861 F
protoplasts, 1952 E, 1953 C
prototroph, 1946 G
protozoa, 1674 A, 1676, 1837 D, 1845 A, 1880 D, 1884 I, 1885 K, 1893 E
protozoan disease, 1880 D, 1884 I, 1885 K, 1893 E
provirus, 1964 I
Prufrock and Other Observations (T. S. Eliot), 1917 I
Pseudomonas, 1882 C, 1886 C
Pseudomonas aeruginosa, 1882 C, 1950 D

Pseudomonas carboxydovorans, 1978 A
Pseudomonas fluorescens, 1986 C
Pseudomonas phaseolicola, 1962 B
Pseudomonas putida, 1972 E, 1973 D
Pseudomonas saccharophila, 1952 F
Pseudomonas syringae, 1974 G, 1976 C, 1985 C, 1986 C
psittacosis, 1879 C, 1930 C
psittacosis group, 1966 A
psittacosis-lymphogranuloma group, 1934 B, 1963 D
pteroylglutamic acid, 1946 E
Ptolemaic system, second century B, 1609
Public Broadcasting Service, 1967 X
puerperal fever, 1842 C, 1846 A, 1861 C
Pulitzer Prize, 1903 Q
pure culture, 1875 B, 1875 C, 1878 B, 1881 A, 1883 D
purines, 1884 K, 1885 N, 1948 L, 1950 L
puromycin, 1961 S
purple membrane, 1967 C, 1971 B, 1980 Q, 1982 N
purple nonsulfur bacteria, 1970 D
putrefaction, 1659 B, 1697 A, 1720 B, 1839 B
putrid intoxication, 1856 B
Pygmalion (George Bernard Shaw), 1914 O, 1956 S
pyridine nucleotides, 1936 Q
pyrimidines, 1885 N, 1948 L, 1950 L
Pyrodictium, 1983 A, 1983 B
pyruvate, 1911 B, 1934 I, 1934 J

Q

Q fever, 1935 F
quadratic equations, ca. 1700 B.C.
quantification, in chemistry, 1754, 1789 D
quantitative analysis, alcoholic fermentation, 1860 A
quantum theory, 1900 N, 1905 J
quarantine, 1403
quark, 1939 T, 1964 P
quasiequivalence, rules for virus construction, 1962 K
quaternary ammonium compounds, 1916 B, 1935 C
Queen Elizabeth (movie), 1912 J
quinone-hydroquinone oxidation-reduction, 1904 G

R

R factors, 1959 G, 1967 H
*r*II mutants, bacteriophage T2, 1955 K
rabbit papillomavirus, 1940 L
rabies, ca. 77 A, 1546 A, 1879 E, 1885 H, 1903 K, 1903 L
Radcliffe College, 1879 J
Radiata, 1798 B
radiation
    electromagnetic, 1865 D, 1888 H
    infrared, 1800 C
    radioactive, 1896 G
    ultraviolet, 1801 A
radio, 1901 N, 1906 O, 1938 L
radio waves, 1888 H
radioactive elements, 1896 G, 1898 N, 1899 H, 1900 M, 1931 M, 1934 O, 1939 I, 1940 B
    artificial, 1934 O
radioimmune assay, 1960 L

radiotelegraphy, 1901 N
radium, 1898 N
railroad, transcontinental, 1869 I
A Raisin in the Sun (Lorraine Hansberry), 1959 V
rat flea, vector for plague bacillus, 1914 B
Rauscher mouse leukemia virus, 1970 H
"The Raven" (Edgar Allan Poe), 1842 F
The Razor's Edge (W. Somerset Maugham), 1944 K
recombinant DNA, 1952 L, 1972 L, 1972 M,
    1975 O
recombination-deficient mutants, 1965 L
Recumbent Figure (Henry Moore), 1938 M
The Red Badge of Courage (Stephen Crane), 1895 K
red blood cells, 1658, 1661 A, 1673 A, 1674 A,
    1889 F
Red Cross, 1862 D, 1881 K
reducing system, 1911 J
Reflections on the Decline of Science in England (Charles
    Babbage), 1830 D
refrigerator, 1859 E, 1876 F
Regnum Primogenium, 1861 D
regulatory genes, 1959 O
regulatory systems, two-component, 1986 D
regulon, 1964 J
relapsing fever, 664
reovirus, 1962 L, 1975 R
replica plating technique, 1952 J
replicative form, viral nucleic acid, 1962 M
replicon model, 1963 U
repressor, 1958 P, 1959 N
repressor substance, 1959 N, 1959 O, 1960 M
Requiem (Giuseppe Verdi), 1874 G
resistance transfer factors, 1959 G, 1960 F
respiration
    animal and air (oxygen), 1660 A, 1664 A, 1668 B,
        1675 B, 1775 A, 1783 A, 1846 F
    as combustion, 1777 A, 1783 A, 1789 C, 1846 F
    inhibition by cyanide, 1781 C
    studies, 1910 F
    theory, 1917 G
    tissue, 1807 A, 1840 F, 1850 A, 1859 C, 1869 D,
        1875 D
respiratory chain phosphorylation, 1939 Q
respiratory enzyme, 1924 C, 1927 I
Restkörper, 1915 B
Restoration, in England, 1660 C
restriction endonucleases, 1970 M, 1972 L, 1972 M,
    1973 I, 1973 J, 1973 N
restriction of bacteriophage infection, 1952 L
retroviruses, 1970 H, 1980 N
reverse transcriptase, 1970 H, 1985 G
Rh blood group antigen, 1940 N
rhesus monkey, 1909 F
rheumatoid arthritis, 1936 R
rhizobial symbiosis, nonlegume, 1973 C
Rhizobium, 1888 B
    bacteroids, 1967 F
    nitrogenase, 1975 E
Rhizobium japonicum, 1973 B, 1982 A
Rhizobium leguminosarum, 1888 B
Rhizobium meliloti, 1981 D, 1982 E

Rhizobium phaseoli, 1973 B
Rhizopus, 1904 A
Rhodes scholarships, 1902 N
Rhodopseudomonas capsulata, 1975 H
Rhodopseudomonas viridis, 1982 N
Rhodospirillum, 1960 C
Rhodospirillum rubrum, 1949 E, 1952 G, 1970 D
riboflavin, 1935 L
riboflavin phosphate, 1932 H, 1934 K
ribonuclease, 1950 P, 1965 T
ribonucleic acid (RNA), 1909 I, 1929 L
    double-stranded, 1962 L
    enzymatic synthesis, 1955 L
    sequencing, 1965 R, 1976 A
    single-stranded, circular, 1976 J
    synthesis, 1961 F, 1970 O
D-ribose, 1909 I
ribosomal RNA
    as a molecular chronometer, 1986 A
    sequencing, 1979 K
    use in bacterial phylogeny, 1976 A, 1977 A,
        1986 A, 1988 B, 1990 A
ribosomes, 1938 B, 1955 M, 1956 Q
ribozymes, 1981 M, 1982 O, 1983 N
ribulose bisphosphate carboxylase, 1954 M, 1959 C
ribulose diphosphate, 1950 M, 1954 M
ricin, 1891 D
rickets, 1912 G
Rickettsia, 1909 D
Rickettsia burnetii, 1935 F, 1951 A
Rickettsia prowazekii, 1916 C
Rickettsia quintana, 1990 D
Rigoletto (Giuseppe Verdi), 1851 E
Ringer solution, 1883 G
"Rip Van Winkle" (Washington Irving), 1820 F
The Rise of Silas Latham (William Dean Howells),
    1885 S
The River (Claude Monet), 1868 G
RK (Ryter-Kellenberger) procedure, 1958 E
RNA, *see* ribonucleic acid
RNA polymerase, viral, 1962 N, 1963 S, 1965 M,
    1967 S, 1967 T
RNA replicase, 1963 S, 1965 M
RNA synthetase, 1963 S
RNA-dependent DNA polymerase, 1970 H
"The Road to Mandalay" (Rudyard Kipling), 1892 J
Robie house (Frank Lloyd Wright), 1909 L
Robinson Crusoe (Daniel Defoe), 1719
Robison ester, 1914 G, 1931 K
Rochalimaea, 1990 D
Rockefeller Institute for Medical Research, 1901 M
Rocky Mountain spotted fever, 1906 E, 1909 D
roller tube cultivation of viruses, 1933 E
rolling-circle replication, 1968 E
Romanowsky stains, 1902 J, 1905 I
A Room with a View (E. M. Forster), 1908 J
root nodules
    bacteria, 1857 B, 1886 B, 1888 B, 1967 F
    hemoglobin, 1938 D
    nonleguminous plants, 1885 E, 1887 C
Roots (Alex Haley), 1976 O

Roquefort cheese, 1070
Rothamsted Experiment Station, 1857 B
Rous sarcoma virus, 1911 E, 1926 D, 1958 I, 1964 I,
    1970 H, 1976 L
Royal Opera House, 1858 F
Royal Society of London, 1662 B, 1665 E, 1673 A,
    1715 A
Rube Goldberg cartoons, 1907 K
rubella virus, 1962 R

S

S1 nuclease, 1966 P
Saccharomyces, 1837 B
Saint Joan (George Bernard Shaw), 1923 L
Salem, Massachusetts, 1692
Salmonella, 1886 F, 1926 A, 1941 A
Salmonella enteriditis, 1888 D, 1896 A, 1929 D,
    1936 E
Salmonella paratyphi, 1900 D
Salmonella typhi, 1880 B, 1884 E, 1889 A, 1910 A
Salmonella typhimurium, 1922 C, 1972 G, 1989 B
Salomé (Richard Strauss), 1905 O
salt frog experiment, 1872 G
salting of food, ca. 1000 B.C.
Salvarsan, 1910 B
Sarcina ventriculi, 1842 B
Satanic Verses (Salman Rushdie), 1988 R
satellite
    communication, 1962 X
    earth orbit, 1957 R
scanning electron microscope, 1938 C, 1970 L
scanning tunneling microscope, 1981 N
scarlet fever, 1553, 1675 A, 1736, 1748 B, 1924 B
The Scarlet Letter (Nathaniel Hawthorne), 1850 E
The Sceptical Chymist (Robert Boyle), 1661 B
Schick test, 1913 B
Schiff reagent, 1924 F
Schinzia leguminosarum, 1888 B
schizomycetes, 1857 A, 1897 A, 1916 A
The School for Scandal (Richard Brinsley Sheridan),
    1777 B
Schrecksbewegung, 1881 D, 1885 C
scientific fraud, 1830 D
scientific induction, 1620 B
scientific method, 1620 B
scientist, origin of term, 1833 C
Scopes trial, 1925 I
Scotch tape, 1925 H
scrapie, 1920 D, 1936 J, 1957 K, 1966 L, 1967 O,
    1981 J, 1981 K, 1982 M, 1983 M, 1985 I,
    1989 G, 1990 H
scrapie-associated fibrils, 1981 J, 1983 M
The Scream (Edvard Munch), 1893 K
Scrutinium phisico-medicum pestis (Athanasius Kircher),
    1646 A
scurvy, 1095, 1912 G
sea urchin eggs, metabolism in, 1876 D, 1889 H,
    1908 D
secretin, 1905 L
sedoheptulose phosphate, 1950 M
seeds of disease, 1546 A, 1762 A

segregation (racial), 1875 F, 1896 I, 1954 O
segregation and independent assortment, 1865 B,
    1903 M
selective cultures, 1955 A
Self-Portrait with Severed Ear (Vincent van Gogh),
    1889 L
semantides, 1965 A
semen, fertilization, 1779 A
semiconservative replication, 1958 N
seminaria, 1546 A
Sense and Sensibility, a Novel by a Lady (Jane Austen),
    1811 E
serovars, 1941 A
Serratia marcescens, 1823 A, 1900 C
serum sickness, 1905 G
serum therapy, 1890 D
sewage treatment, 1914 L
sex pilus, 1964 F
sex-linked genes, 1910 E, 1911 G
Shawnee Indians, 1811 D
She Stoops to Conquer (Oliver Goldsmith), 1773 C
Sherman Anti-Trust Act, 1890 I
Shiga bacillus, 1900 E, 1903 D
Shiga-like toxin, 1982 I, 1983 E, 1983 F, 1984 I
Shigella dysenteriae, 1898 C, 1900 E, 1903 D
Shigella flexneri, 1900 E, 1903 D
Shigella toxin, 1903 D
shock reaction, in chemotaxis, 1881 D
"The Shooting of Dan McGrew" (Robert William
    Service), 1907 M
Shope papillomavirus, 1932 D
A Shropshire Lad (A. E. Housman), 1896 J
side chain theory, toxin and antitoxin interaction,
    1897 G, 1955 N
Siegfried (Richard Wagner), 1876 J
signal transduction systems
    chemotaxis, 1987 A, 1988 E
    cross talk, 1988 F
silkworm disease, 1835 A, 1837 D, 1869 B
simian virus 40
    discovery, vacuolating, 1960 J
    DNA nucleotide sequence, 1978 K
    DNA synthesis, 1972 H
    genome, interconversion of circular and linear,
        1973 J
    genome maps, 1973 H, 1973 I
    growth in heterokaryons, 1962 O, 1967 N
    temperature-sensitive mutants, 1972 H
    tumors, 1962 P, 1965 O
Simmons citrate agar, 1925 A
Sioux Indians, 1876 I
Sistine Chapel, 1508
site-specific mutagenesis, 1978 J
606 (Salvarsan), 1910 B
Six-Day War, 1967 W
Sixteenth Amendment, U.S. Constitution, 1913 I
Sketch Book of Geoffrey Crayon, Gent (Washington
    Irving), 1820 F
Slaughterhouse-Five (Kurt Vonnegut, Jr.), 1969 I
slavery, abolition, 1866 C
sleeping sickness, 1907 H

slide rule, 1620 A, 1622
slime layer, staining of, 1941 D
small pokkes, 1495 A
smallpox, ca. 1122 B.C., 164, ca. 500, 664, 910,
    1495 A, 1518, 1519 A, 1630 A, 1667 A,
    1670 B, 1675 A, 1715 A, 1717, 1721 A,
    1764 A, 1774 A, 1776 A, 1796 B, 1837 A,
    1881 F
    eradication, 1958 K, 1967 L, 1980 M
    immunization, ca. 500
    vaccination, 1774 A, 1776 A, 1796 B, 1885 F
    variolation, 1715 A, 1717, 1721 A, 1764 A,
        1776 A
Smithsonian Institution, 1846 I
smoked food, ca. 1000 B.C.
smooth-rough variation, 1921 B
Social Security Act, 1935 P
Society for General Microbiology, 1945 E
Society of American Bacteriologists, 1899 G, 1916 G,
    1917 A, 1923 A, 1935 O, 1937 P, 1953 W,
    1955 Q, 1960 P
Sociobiology: the New Synthesis (E. O. Wilson), 1975 T
soda water, 1772 A
soluble RNA (sRNA), 1957 P
soluble-specific substance, 1923 F
somatic antigens, 1903 G
somatostatin, synthesized by *Escherichia coli*, 1977 R
Somerville College, 1879 J
sonar, 1915 F
"Song of Hiawatha" (Henry Wadsworth Longfellow),
    1855 D
Songs of a Sourdough (Robert William Service),
    1907 M
Sophie's Choice (William Styron), 1979 N
SOS distress call, 1906 P
SOS response, 1974 E
Sotto-Bacillen, 1902 E
The Sound and the Fury (William Faulkner), 1929 Q
sound barrier, 1947 F
Soup Can (Andy Warhol), 1960 T
South Pole, exploration, 1911 N, 1912 I
Southern blot, 1975 S
Soviet Union, *see* Union of Soviet Socialist Republics
spaceflight, 1961 W, 1962 X
    moon landing, 1969 H
Spanish Armada, 1588
Spanish Civil War, 1936 U
Spanish disease, 1495 A
Spanish influenza, 1918 D
Spanish-American War, 1898 Q
Sparta, 430 B.C. A
special relativity, 1905 K
specialized transduction, 1956 H
species, definition, 1682 A, 1749 A, 1753
Species plantarum (Carolus Linnaeus), 1753
spectacles, 1249, 1299
spectrophotometer, 1941 N
spectroscopy, 1853 C
spermatozoa, 1677, 1767 B, 1825 E, 1853 A, 1876 D
spheroplast, 1958 D
spices, food preservation, ca. 1000 B.C.

spinning, hydraulic frame, 1769 A
spinning jenny, 1764 B
spiraeic acid, 1899 I
Spirilina, 1825 A
Spirillum, 1838 A, 1868 A
Spirillum desulfuricans, 1894 B
Spirillum volutans, 1888 A
spiritus nitro-aereus, 1675 B
Spirochaeta, 1838 A
Spirocheta pallida, 1905 D
spirochetes, rumen, 1952 A
Spirogyra, 1674 A
spliceosome, 1977 W
spongiform encephalopathy, 1936 J, 1957 K, 1982 M,
    1985 H
spontaneous generation, 1668 A, 1748 A, 1749 B,
    1765 A, 1808 A, 1858 A, 1858 B, 1861 A,
    1872 A, 1876 A, 1877 B
spores
    formation, 1959 D, 1974 D
    heat resistance and dipicolinic acid, 1953 F,
        1957 E, 1972 D
    melanin accumulation, 1960 E
Sporonema, 1852 A
sporulation, 1965 F, 1965 G, 1974 D, 1976 E,
    1985 A
Sputnik I, 1957 R
The Spy Who Came in from the Cold (John le Carré),
    1963 Z
square roots, ca. 1700 B.C.
src gene, 1976 L
St. Anthony's fire, 857
St. Peter's Fields, 1819 C
staining
    bacteria, 1869 A, 1876 B, 1877 A, 1882 B,
        1884 B
    differential, 1882 B, 1883 A, 1884 B, 1941 D
    Gram stain, 1882 E, 1884 B, 1884 G, 1929 A,
        1957 A, 1963 B
    histological sections, 1849 D
    tubercle bacillus, 1882 B, 1883 A
Stanford University, 1885 Q
Stanford-Binet test, 1914 J
Staphylococcus, 1878 C, 1881 B, 1884 A, 1975 A
Staphylococcus albus, 1884 A
Staphylococcus aureus, 1884 A, 1905 B, 1930 B
    alpha-toxin, 1966 J, 1974 J, 1981 G, 1987 D
    food poisoning, 1894 D, 1914 C, 1930 B
    pyogenic, 1905 B
Staphylococcus pyogenes albus, 1884 A
Staphylococcus pyogenes aureus, 1884 A
starch, plant synthesis, 1862 C
starch hydrolysis test, 1918 B
"Stars and Stripes Forever" (John Philip Sousa),
    1897 O
"The Star-Spangled Banner," 1814 B
static electricity, 585 B.C., 1660 B, 1745 B
Staudinger law, 1922 H
steady-state growth, 1958 F
steam engine, 1711, 1765 C, 1769 B
steamship, 1807 C, 1819 B

telegraph, 1837 J, 1844 B, 1901 N
telephone, 1876 G
telescope, 1608, 1610, 1681 A, 1729, 1758
television, 1925 H, 1926 N, 1929 O, 1936 T,
    1947 F, 1951 Q, 1953 X, 1967 X
Telstar, 1962 X
temperature measurement, 1714, 1741
Tess of the D'Urbervilles: A Pure Woman (Thomas
    Hardy), 1891 I
tetanus
    antitoxin, 1890 D, 1909 G, 1921 E
    bacillus, 1884 F, 1889 D
    toxin, 1890 B
    toxoid, 1893 C, 1927 C
tetranucleotide, 1909 I, 1934 E, 1950 L
Texas cattle fever, 1893 E
textbook on medicine, ca. 3000 B.C. A
Theatrum chemicum (Paul Ech), 1500
Theoria generationis (Kasper Friedrich Wolff), 1759 A
Thermococcus, 1983 A
thermodynamics, 1847 B, 1850 B, 1854 D, 1864 B,
    1867 C, 1906 N
Thermofilum, 1983 A
thermometer, clinical, 1866 B
thermometer scales, 1699 C, 1714, 1741, 1851 A
thermophiles, 1846 D, 1862 A, 1879 A, 1966 D,
    1970 A, 1972 A, 1982 B, 1983 B
Thermoplasma, 1970 A, 1977 D
thermos bottle, 1892 H
thermoscope, 1626 A
Thermus aquaticus, 1987 I
theta circles, replication of DNA, 1963 E
Things Fall Apart (Chinua Achebe), 1958 S
The Thinker (Auguste Rodin), 1880 G
Thiobacillus, 1902 A
Thiobacillus denitrificans, 1903 B
Thiobacillus thiooxidans, 1922 B
Thiobacillus thioparus, 1902 A, 1903 B
Thiobacteria, 1897 A
The Third Man (Graham Greene), 1950 S
Third Reich, 1938 J
Thirty Years' War, 1618, 1648 B
Thomas Cook & Son, 1891 G
Three Dancers (Pablo Picasso), 1925 K
Three Mile Island nuclear power plant, 1979 L
Three Musicians (Pablo Picasso), 1921 I
The Three Musketeers (Alexandre Dumas), 1844 D
Threepenny Opera (Kurt Weill and Bertolt Brecht),
    1928 J
threonine deaminase, 1955 D
Through the Looking-Glass and What Alice Found There
    (Lewis Carroll), 1871 F
thymectomy, neonatal, 1968 H
thymine, 1885 N
thymine dimers, 1960 H, 1962 G, 1962 H, 1964 E
thymonucleic acid, 1933 C
thymus gland, 1961 L, 1968 H
thymus nucleic acid, 1909 I
Ti plasmid, 1970 G, 1975 L, 1977 O, 1986 K,
    1987 C
ticks, vectors of disease, 1893 E

tin cans, 1839 E
tin ore, smelting, ca. 3000 B.C. B
Tipula iridescent virus, 1958 J
tissue culture, 1907 G, 1913 C, 1917 D, 1936 F
    virus cultivation, 1926 D, 1928 E, 1931 F, 1936 F,
        1944 F, 1949 I
tissue respiration, 1807 A
tissue transplantation, 1937 G
Titanic (steamship), 1912 H
To Kill a Mockingbird (Harper Lee), 1960 S
tobacco mosaic virus, 1882 F, 1892 E, 1899 E,
    1935 H, 1936 H, 1937 F, 1939 F, 1955 H,
    1955 I, 1955 J, 1956 L, 1959 K, 1986 K
Tobacco Road (Erskine Caldwell), 1932 P
Tom Sawyer (Mark Twain), 1876 K
Tosca (Giacomo Puccini), 1900 Q
Tower Bridge, 1894 M
toxic shock syndrome, 1978 G, 1980 L, 1982 K,
    1983 H, 1984 J, 1985 E
    streptococcal, 1987 E, 1989 D
    tampons and, 1980 L, 1984 J, 1985 E
toxin
    abrin, 1891 D
    botulism, 1895 C
    diphtheria, 1888 E, 1894 F
    ricin, 1891 D
    tetanus, 1890 B, 1891 D, 1893 C
toxin–antitoxin vaccines (TAT), 1909 G, 1913 A,
    1914 E
toxoid
    diphtheria, 1904 C, 1914 E
    tetanus, 1893 C, 1904 C, 1927 C
trachoma, 1907 B, 1934 B, 1957 G, 1963 I
Trail of Tears, 1838 G
*Traité élémentaire de chimie présenté dans un ordre nouveau
    et d'après les découvertes modernes* (Antoine
    Lavoisier), 1789 D
transacetylase, 1960 M
transcontinental railroad, 1869 I
transcriptional map, SV40 genome, 1973 H
transduction, 1952 K, 1956 H
transfer RNA (tRNA), 1956 N, 1957 P, 1965 S
    biosynthesis, 1975 Q
    in vitro synthesis, 1970 O
    nucleotide sequence, 1965 S
transformation, bacterial, *see* bacteria, transformation
transformation, in vitro, 1931 D, 1972 F
transformation-specific antigen, 1977 U
transforming principle, 1928 C, 1944 C
transgenic plants, 1986 K, 1987 C
transistor, 1947 F
transmissible mink encephalopathy, 1936 J, 1982 M
transmutation, 1794
transplantation immunity, 1944 G, 1953 S
transposable elements, 1950 J
transposons, 1950 J, 1974 H
Trans-Siberian Railway, 1891 F, 1904 K
travelers' checks, 1891 G
Treasure Island (Robert Louis Stevenson), 1883 K
A Treatise on the Natural History of the Human Teeth
    (John Hunter), 1771 C

Woman II (Willem de Kooning), 1952 V
Woman in a Red Dress (Paul Gauguin), 1891 J
The Woman Rebel (Margaret Higgins Sanger), 1914 M
Wood-Werkman reaction, 1942 D
Woolworth Building, 1913 J, 1930 H
word processors, 1976 N
World Health Assembly, 1980 M
World Health Organization, 1948 N, 1958 K,
    1962 Q, 1967 L, 1980 M
World Trade Center, 1972 P
World War I, 1914 M, 1915 G, 1916 H, 1917 H,
    1918 G, 1919 F
World War II, 1939 S, 1940 Q, 1941 P, 1942 N,
    1943 G, 1944 J, 1945 F
Wright's stain, 1902 J
Wurstvergiftung, 1820 A
Wuthering Heights (Emily Brontë), 1847 E

X

X rays, 1895 H
   crystallography, 1938 H
   diffraction, polio virus, 1959 I
   mutations caused by, 1927 E
   spectra, 1914 I
xanthine oxidase, 1924 E
xerography, 1937 Q, 1959 T

Y

Yale College, 1701
yeast
   alcoholic fermentation, 1766 A, 1838 C, 1839 A,
      1839 B, 1860 A, 1878 D, 1883 D, 1889 C,
      1897 C, 1911 B

microscopic observations, 1680 B, 1837 C
   multiplication, 1837 B
yellow enzyme, 1932 H, 1934 K
yellow fever, 1623 A, 1693 A, 1699 A, 1790 A,
    1793 A, 1796 A, 1802 A, 1820 B, 1878 F,
    1899 D, 1901 F, 1905 E, 1919 D, 1929 G,
    1936 L
Yellow Fever Commission, 1901 F
yellow plague, 664
Yersinia, virulence plasmids, 1981 F, 1984 H
Yersinia enterocolitica, 1980 J, 1980 K, 1984 H
Yersinia pestis, 1894 C, 1981 F, 1984 H
Yersinia pseudotuberculosis, 1984 H
Young Men's Christian Association (YMCA),
    1844 C
Young Women's Christian Association (YWCA),
    1855 C

Z

Zellsubstanz, Kern und Zellteilung (Walther Flemming),
    1882 H
zeppelins, 1900 O, 1937 Q
"The Ziegfeld Follies," 1907 L
Ziehl-Neelsen stain, 1883 A
zinc fingers, 1985 J
Zollverein, 1833 E
Zoological Evidence as to Man's Place in Nature (Thomas
    Henry Huxley), 1863 C
zoology, 1546 B
Zoonomia (Erasmus Darwin), 1794
Zwischenferment, 1931 J
zygote, 1909 H
zymase, 1897 C